Prov

and the Côte d'Azur

Anwer Bati and John Ardagh

Prentice Hall Travel

New York • London • Toronto • Sydney • Tokyo • Singapore

THE AMERICAN EXPRESS ® TRAVEL GUIDES

Published in the United States by
Prentice Hall General Reference
15 Columbus Circle
New York, NY 10023

PRENTICE HALL is a registered
trademark and colophon is a
trademark of Prentice-Hall, Inc.

Edited, designed and produced by
Castle House Press, Llantrisant
Mid Glamorgan CF7 8EU
Wales

© American Express Publishing
Corporation Inc. 1994

Contact Library of Congress for full
CIP data.

ISBN 0-671-86829-2

The editors thank Neil Hanson and
Alex Taylor of Lovell Johns, David
Haslam, Anna Holmes, Alison Franks,
Muriel and Alf Jackson and Sylvia
Hughes-Williams for their help and
co-operation during the preparation
of this edition. Thanks are also due to
the staff of the French Government
Tourist Office in London.

This guidebook is a revised, updated
and expanded adaptation of *The
American Express Pocket Guide to the
South of France* by John Ardagh (1983,
2nd edition 1987). Some illustrations
were first used in *The Mitchell Beazley
pocket guide to Architecture* by Patrick
Nuttgens (1980).

FOR THE SERIES:
Series Editor:
  David Townsend Jones
Map Editor: David Haslam
Indexer: Hilary Bird
Gazetteer: Anna Holmes
Cover design: Roger Walton Studio

FOR THIS EDITION:
Edited on desktop by:
  Eileen Townsend Jones
Art editors: Castle House Press
Illustrators: Jeremy Ford
  (David Lewis Artists),
  Illustrated Arts, Rodney Paull,
  Sylvia Hughes-Williams
Cover photo:
  Explorer/G. Thouvenin

FOR MITCHELL BEAZLEY:
Art Director: Andrew Sutterby
Production: Katy Sawyer
Publisher: Sarah Bennison

PRODUCTION CREDITS:
Maps by Lovell Johns,
  Oxford, England
Typeset in Garamond and
  News Gothic
Desktop layout in Corel
  Ventura Publisher
Reproduction by M & E
  Reproductions, Great Baddow,
  Essex, England
Linotronic output by
  Tradespools Limited, Frome,
  England

Contents

Culture, history and background
by John Ardagh

Planning your visit
by Anwer Bati and John Ardagh

The daily necessities
by Anwer Bati and John Ardagh

Provence and the Côte d'Azur
in three chapters by Anwer Bati and John Ardagh:

1. Western Provence

2. Western Côte d'Azur and the central hinterland

3. Eastern Côte d'Azur and Nice's hinterland

Practical information
by Anwer Bati

Words and phrases

Maps

• The authors and publishers are grateful to the following for their kind permission to reprint extracts from the titles named below: Charles Scribner's Sons (US) and The Bodley Head (UK), for three quotations from *Tender is the Night* (1939) by F. Scott Fitzgerald; Curtis Brown Ltd (US/UK) for two quotations from *Aspects of Provence* (1952) by James Pope-Hennessy; Victor Gollancz for a quotation from *Picasso* (1958) by Sir Roland Penrose; and Viking Penguin Inc. (US) and Faber and Faber Ltd (UK) for a quotation from *Monsieur or the Prince of Darkness* (1974) by Lawrence Durrell.

How to use this book

Few guidelines are needed to understand how this book works:

- For the general organization of the book, see CONTENTS on the pages preceding this one.
- Chapters are arranged alphabetically, with headwords appearing in **CAPITALS.**
- These headwords are followed by location and practical information printed in *italics*.
- Map references to the color maps at the back of the book are given in the italic text below each headword. They are also given with the INDEX entries.
- Subject headers, similar to those used in telephone directories, are printed in CAPITALS in the top corner of each page.
- If you cannot find what you need, check in the comprehensive and exhaustively cross-referenced INDEX at the back of the book.

CROSS-REFERENCES
These are printed in SMALL CAPITALS, referring you to other sections or alphabetical entries in the book. Care has been taken to ensure that such cross-references are self-explanatory. Often, page references are also given, although their excessive use would be intrusive and ugly.

FLOORS
We use the European convention for the naming of floors in this book: "ground floor" means the floor at ground level (called by Americans the "first floor").

AUTHOR'S ACKNOWLEDGMENTS
Anwer Bati would like to thank the following for all their help in organizing research trips to Provence: Marc Humphries at the French Government Tourist Office in London, Tink Denis of the CDT Var, Sandrine Carsalade of the CRT Riviera-Côte d'Azur, Valerie Coutant of the CDT Vaucluse, Keith Tottem of the Monaco Tourist and Convention Centre, Mireille Rebaudo-Martini of the SBM, Anik Breed and Bernard McCoy of Air France, Erika Schule-Grosso of Relais et Châteaux, Elizabeth Martin of Leading Hotels, Gillian Green of Air France Holidays, Kim Tylee of British Midland, Sue Lowry of Columbus Communications, Frederic Prades in St-Rémy-de-Provence, Martha Walger in Avignon, Fabienne Pons in Aix-en-Provence and Jacqueline Neujean in Arles.

Also, for their research help and tireless driving: Richard Roberts, Clare Morgan and Sophie McPherson. And for her support and assistance: Lorraine Belloni.

Key to symbols

☎	Telephone	≋	Swimming pool	
Fx	Fax	🐚	Good beach nearby/	
★	Recommended sight		private beach	
☆	Worth a visit	⚲	Tennis	
✿	Good value (in its class)	✓	Golf	
i	Tourist information	🐎	Riding	
⇌	Parking	🐟	Fishing	
🏛	Building of architectural interest	⬍	Elevator	
†	Church	⬜	TV in each room	
🔟	Free entrance	📞	Telephone in each	
🔄	Entrance fee payable		room	
■	Entrance expensive	🐾	Dogs not allowed	
✗	Guided tour	⚕	Gym/fitness facilities	
■	Cafeteria	⬠	Sauna	
≪	Good view	☼	Solarium	
✗	Photography forbidden	♣	Conference facilities	
✿	Special interest for children	⬛	Business center	
⚑	Hotel	⅄	Bar	
▬	Simple hotel	▣	Mini-bar	
🏨	Luxury hotel	⎓	Restaurant	
AE	American Express	▬	Simple restaurant	
◉	Diners Club	⬭	Luxury restaurant	
◉	MasterCard/Eurocard	⌐	A la carte available	
VISA	Visa/Carte Bleue	▬	Set (fixed-price) menu	
♿	Facilities for disabled		available	
	people	⇒	Good wines	
▤	Air conditioning	♩	Nightlife	
▤	Meal obligatory	⇔	Open-air dancing	
▬	Pension available	◉	Disco dancing	
▣	Secure garage	♫	Live music	
▱	Quiet hotel	✵	Dancing	
✿	Garden	✦	Casino/gambling	

PRICE CATEGORIES

▭	Cheap	▥	Expensive
▥	Inexpensive	▥	Very expensive
▥	Moderately priced		

Our price categories for **hotels** are explained on page 46. Those for **restaurants** are explained on page 50.

About the authors

Londoner **Anwer Bati** is a freelance author, journalist and television producer and director. He writes on a wide variety of subjects including cinema, books, the media, food, travel, design, style and psychology. His work for many leading British newspapers includes *The Times, Sunday Times, Guardian, Daily Mail, Daily Express, Today, Evening Standard* and *Sunday Telegraph,* and he has been widely published in British magazines. Overseas, he has written for *The Australian* and *Toronto Star* newpapers. He is the author of two books, *The Shattered Dream* (about the British economy, 1981) and *The Cigar Companion* (a guide to handmade cigars, published in the UK and US, 1993). In British television, he has worked on documentaries for the BBC, London Weekend Television, Channel 4 and TV-am. He has also written comedy, documentary and other scripts.

John Ardagh, who wrote *The American Express Pocket Guide to the South of France* (1983), upon which this book is based, is a writer, journalist and lecturer and noted authority on France and Germany. He is the author of several important studies of contemporary French and German life, including *France Today* (revised edition 1993), *Rural France* (1983), *Writers' France* (1989) and *Germany and the Germans* (revised edition 1991). His study of modern Ireland will be published in 1994, and he is currently working on *The Oxford Book of France.* He has also worked on the staff of *The Times* and *Observer,* and is currently continental editor of *The Good Hotel Guide.* He sees himself as a European and is passionately devoted to the ideal of a united Europe. He lives with his German wife Katinka and their three adored Burmese cats in Kensington, London.

A message from the editors

Time and change are the implacable enemies of travel authors and editors, and you, the readers, are our allies in keeping them in check. The moment we publish, some museum or hotel somewhere will change its name, or move, or even close down. Some restaurants deploy menu notices like the following genuine authenticated example: "These items may or may not be available at all times, and sometimes not at all and other times all the time." And telephone authorities the world over share a passion for changing their numbers like you and I change shirts.

We want you to write to tell us what's wrong (and right!) in the book: what's changed, closed, improved or gotten worse. Time prevents our responding to most such letters, but they are all truly welcomed and contribute greatly to the preparation of the next edition.

British readers should write to me c/o **American Express Travel Guides**, Mitchell Beazley, Reed Books, Michelin House, 81 Fulham Road, London SW3 6RB. American readers should write to me c/o **American Express Travel Guides**, Prentice Hall Travel, 15 Columbus Circle, New York, NY 10023.

David Townsend Jones, Series Editor, American Express Travel Guides

Provence
and the Côte d'Azur

Heartland, hinterland and playground

This guide includes the whole of the modern French *région* of Provence/Alpes/Côte d'Azur. As its name implies, it has three elements. There is the historic heartland of Provence, on the plain around Avignon, Aix and Marseille. There is the wild and hilly hinterland, stretching up to the high Alps along the Italian border. And there is the strip of coast around Nice and Cannes, a highly urbanized tourist playground, which the English named the Riviera and the French now call the Côte d'Azur. This book also strays into Languedoc, to take in the Nîmes area west of the Rhône, which although not today part of Provence is strongly Provençal in character and tradition.

Provence is a magic name with a magic appeal. Recently, for several years, two books topped all the British non-fiction best-seller lists: *A Year in Provence* and *Toujours Provence,* both by Peter Mayle, an Englishman who settled in the Lubéron hills near Avignon and wittily described his life there. Their phenomenal success was due in part to the charms of Mr Mayle's writing, but also to their titles and subject-matter — to the cult of Provence that has today seized the imagination of a part of the middle-classes of northern Europe. To buy a little red-roofed farmstead amid the vineyards, to sit in the October sun drinking local wine while London or Hamburg drizzles, to stroll to the café for a gossipy *pastis* with the Pagnolesque villagers, to hear the cicada and scent the wild thyme, to eat fabulous fish soups and garlicky mountain lamb — this is the dream of many a jaded northerner, even if few actually try to achieve it, and even if the reality, entwined with traffic-jams, bureaucracy and suspicious neighbors, might well fall short of the ideal.

For the visitor, Provence does indeed offer an unrivaled mix of sensuous and intellectual delights. Art and landscape, wine and sunshine, ancient history and modern sophistication, fuse into an alchemy that makes a heady impact on mind and senses alike. No other part of the world, surely, provides so dazzling a density and variety of interest in one relatively small area.

For 2,500 years Provence has been a meeting place of civilizations. Each has left a strong imprint, so that almost every bend in the road reveals something different and surprising, be it medieval abbey or museum of modern art. The only unsurprising factor is that vast crowds are drawn to this paradise: the art is to learn how to dodge them, as far as you can.

Upon the lovely landscape, history lies in dense layers. Ancient Celto-Ligurian tribes, Greek and Roman colonizers, early Christians, destructive barbarians, all came here in their turn. It is the land where the Roman legions passed, leaving behind them the finest array of Roman monuments outside Italy, including the Pont du Gard and the great arenas of Arles and Nîmes. It is the land where the troubadours sang in the gaunt castle of Les Baux, and where the Popes ruled in their palace at Avignon; the land, too, where the crowned heads of Europe came to gamble at Monte Carlo in the Belle Époque — now as much a part of history as Romans or troubadours — and where Picasso painted in the castle at Antibes. Today, Provence is more than ever a land of contrasts: oil refineries and nuclear centers in the Rhône valley; remote medieval hill-villages; Cannes and Nice with their glittering promenades and luxury apartment blocks; the naturist beaches of St-Tropez; the racist slogans of the Front National.

Unlike all the rest of France save nearby Languedoc, Provence is truly Mediterranean. Drive down from the north, over the mountains or via the Rhône valley, and you cross that mysterious cultural frontier that separates Europe's north from its south. Suddenly the sun beats stronger, the light is clearer, the air drier. Hills terraced with vine and olive roll to blue horizons; the air carries the scent of pines, or maybe a hint of thyme or lavender; the stone houses all have red-tiled roofs; lone cypresses stand by old barns. In village squares, under shady plane trees, old men play *boules,* or drink *pastis* with black olives; and out in the fields, the special white light of Provence dazzles and reflects on the chalky hillsides, just as Cézanne and Van Gogh saw it. Even in winter the air is usually clear and bright — but Provence is then whipped periodically by its icy north wind, the Mistral.

The scenery is extremely diverse. The entire coast from Marseille to Italy is one of Europe's most beautiful, a succession of rocky headlands and wooded coves, strung with umbrella pines and sometimes with palms, cacti and bright flowers. Near the coast, hilly forests of pine, oak and cork alternate with lush valleys, which in spring are carpeted with flowers, including fragrant mimosa. Hills rise behind, steeply in places, notably along the eastern part of the Côte d'Azur from Nice to Menton. Most of this coast today is heavily urbanized, a succession of resorts and camp sites. Yet nothing in Provence is more striking than the contrast between this crowded coast and the silent hinterland, unspoiled and serene, that begins just inland. Behind Nice are ancient hilltop villages, and beyond these rise the snowy Alps, good for skiing and climbing.

Provence's central hinterland is a succession of limestone plateaux stretching west from the Alps to Mont Ventoux ("windy mount"). Here are pine forests, gorges, rolling hills where sheep are put to grass, and an exhilarating sense of freedom and space. To the west, the broad Rhône valley leads down to the plain between the Rhône delta and Avignon. This is very fertile country, covered with vineyards and orchards, although the plains are broken by several ranges of barren limestone hills.

MODERN CHANGE: HAS PROVENCE BEEN SPOILED?

Provence in the past four decades has been swept forward by a tide of modernization and growing prosperity — even if, as elsewhere, this has leveled off in recent years. The economy and society have changed considerably. Improvements in farming have led to a huge rural exodus: less than 10 percent of people today work on the land, against over 35 percent in 1945. The overall population has been growing too, due to the sunny south's appeal to migrants from Paris and elsewhere. After 1962 it was also swelled by the return to France from Algeria of nearly a million French colonists, of whom about a third settled in Provence.

Today, despite the strength of its peasant roots, Provence is above all a sophisticated urban society. And this is not true just of the chic resorts of the coast: old towns such as Aix and Avignon are highly sophisticated too. For better or for worse, towns have mushroomed with the addition of large new suburbs. They have huge hypermarkets, and on the edge of Aix and Marseille are big new student campuses. The level of car ownership is one of Europe's highest — and all too apparently so.

Back in the 1950s, a resort such as Cassis, near Marseille, was still just a quiet fishing village, much as Dufy and Matisse had painted it a few decades earlier. There were as yet few tourists or cars. Most quayside hotels had no private bathrooms, but they lavishly served superb Proven-çal food at low prices — and no one had yet heard of *nouvelle cuisine*. Today, large blocks of vacation apartments have been built on the hill behind the port, on weekends the ritzy new marble casino draws well-heeled trippers by the thousand from Marseille, and in summer the quayside is crowded with Euro-visitors who would never dream of taking a room without a bath *en suite* and will happily pay 250 francs for some *nouvelle* menu of tiny bits of fish and vegetable arranged daintily around the plate like Japanese flower patterns.

So, as some people claim, has Provence been irretrievably spoiled? Only partly. It is true that some touristy places and much of the gorgeous coast do suffer severely from their over-popularity and especially from the traffic. Some of the people who work there have grown blasé and irritable from the incessant tourist pressure, and are now almost Parisian in their sharpness, not as helpful and relaxed as most French provincials.

But the wild hinterland, mostly still so empty, has been spoiled far less. In fact, many old villages that were decaying and depopulating have now been lent a new life by the influx of smart summer residents, retired middle-class people, craftsmen and artists, and other Mayle-like immi-grants from the north. This artificial trend might not be in line with one's cozy view of picturesque rural Provence, but it is better than letting these villages die. And in the towns and on the coast, the crowded bustle does at least carry with it an exciting variety of stimulating modern activity. Is the new invasion from the north, then, just the latest of Provence's many absorbing layers of civilization?

INDUSTRY, FARMING AND TOURISM

Agriculture used to be the basis of the region's economy. It remains important, but has now been joined by mass tourism and by modern industry. Only since the war has Provence been developed on any scale as a region of advanced industry. It is true that Marseille, La Ciotat and Toulon have long been centers of shipbuilding and repairing, but their yards are now closed or moribund. Marseille still has some engin-eering, chemicals and food-processing firms.

But since the 1950s the industrial center of gravity has shifted west-ward, to the lake of Berre and the new port of Fos. Here are large oil refineries, petro-chemical works, and Europe's biggest helicopter factory; also steelworks, which have been affected by Europe's general steel crisis. Beside the Rhône north of Avignon, and in the Durance valley, there are important hydro-electric works and nuclear stations (some 70 percent of French electricity comes from nuclear sources).

The Nice/Cannes area has found an entirely new vocation to add to its tourism, for it is now marked out as a pilot zone for high-technology research. In the 1970s the government initiated an "international scientific park" at Valbonne near Antibes, called Sophia-Antipolis, where various firms have built research units and laboratories; and IBM has a large research center nearby. Companies do not find it hard to persuade scientists and executives to migrate to the sunlit south.

Some small-scale traditional industries are still active in Provence, based on exploitation of local resources: bauxite mining near Brignoles, ocher quarrying near Apt, salt works at Hyères and near Aigues-Mortes, cork production in the Maures forests. Not to mention the *pastis* industry of Marseille.

Agriculture is very varied. Sunshine, a fertile soil and good irrigation conspire to make the lower Rhône valley the foremost market garden of France, widely exporting its early fruit and vegetables: melons, strawberries, peaches, asparagus, etc. In the Camargue, rice is cultivated. The chalky soil of Provence is good terrain both for vine and olive: some 450,000 acres are under vine, while Provence is France's leading producer of olives and olive oil, as well as of almonds. In the lush valleys near Cannes, flowers are cultivated on a massive scale (roses, carnations, violets, jasmine etc.) for the cut-flower markets of Europe, although not so much any more for the perfume industry of Grasse.

Lavender is grown on the hills farther west, and lemons on the sheltered coast near Menton. Many upland areas are used for sheep-grazing, where transhumance is still practiced: the flocks spend the winter on the lowlands, and are taken to browse on the plateaux in summer. Bulls are reared in the Camargue. And all along the coast fishermen are active, charging high prices.

Tourism is a major income-earner, more than ever. The Alpes-Maritimes *département* alone has more than 4 million annual visitors, half of them foreigners. The tourists come to bathe or to gamble, to ski or water-ski, to explore the museums and fine buildings, or to enjoy local cuisine — or several of these at once. Some stay in seaside hotels or country inns; but more popular today are the rented villas and farmsteads *(gîtes),* or the crowded camp sites along the coast.

The Côte d'Azur has changed radically since the 19th century when its mild winter climate first made it fashionable as a playground of the rich. Until the 1920s, winter was its smart season, when the leisured and titled would come, with their retinues, to escape the northern climate; in summer, tourists were few. Today, summer is the main season, and the old, elitist visitors are vastly outnumbered by a new mass tourism.

But the Côte is busy all the year, thanks to this and the huge growth of "business tourism" (conventions and incentive trips). It is these visitors, far more than the well-to-do individual visitors, that keep the luxury hotels in business. And what better pretext for combining work with pleasure than to be flown out with your firm, all expenses paid, to attend some seminar or conference in out-of-season Cannes or Monte-Carlo?

Culture, history and background

Historical landmarks

Provence has attracted invaders and settlers like its bright flowers attract bees; from prehistoric times it has been a melting-pot of varied peoples, and its story is one long complex chronicle of wars, brilliant dynasties and cultural splendors.

Almost everyone from Julius Caesar to Brigitte Bardot seems to have come, seen and conquered — or been captivated.

EARLY CELTIC AND GREEK COLONIZERS

The earliest known inhabitants were primitive Ligurian tribes during the Bronze Age (**1800–600BC**). Near the end of this period, Celts came down in large numbers from the north; their peaceful intermarriage with the Ligurians provided the essence of Provence's future population. Around the same time, Phocaeans from Asia Minor were the first of the Greek colonizers, founding Massilia (Marseille) in **c.600BC**, then Nikaia (Nice), Antipolis (Antibes) and small places in the Rhône delta. They built Massilia into a major commercial center that traded as far afield as Brittany; but they were constantly fighting with the Celto-Ligurians, who in **218BC** helped Hannibal from Spain to cross Provence and the Alps into northern Italy.

THE ROMAN ERA

The Romans' colonization was to mark Provence profoundly. Their legions first arrived under Sextius to help their allies, the Greek Massiliots, and in **125BC** near Aix they decisively defeated the Salyans, the main Celto-Ligurian tribe, and wiped out their capital at Egremont. Sextius built a thermal center at what is now Aix. When Teuton warriors moved in from the north, they were in turn defeated in **102BC** by a second Roman general, Marius, who remains a hero in the region today (that's why Marius is still a popular local first name).

After these key victories, the Romans set about systematically colonizing coastal Provence as a *provincia* (hence its name today), i.e., a full part of their empire. Julius Caesar conquered the rest of Gaul (France), then defeated his rival Pompey in a civil war in **49BC**. In this conflict Massilia foolishly allied itself with Pompey and was then punished by losing its power and independence. Instead, the Romans built up Nîmes, Arles and Fréjus as the main towns of their *provincia,* together with Narbonne to the west in what is now Languedoc. Over the next decades, the Romans endowed Provence with a wealth of majestic buildings, many of which still stand today. At Arles, Nîmes and Orange, also at Cimiez (near Nice), Fréjus, Glanum, Vaison and elsewhere, magnificent theaters, temples, arenas and baths were built. The Emperor Augustus settled a large colony of veterans at Nîmes; Vaison became a patrician residential town of some luxury; in **19**BC the mighty Pont du Gard viaduct was erected; and later the Emperor Aurelius built the Aurelian Way from Rome into Spain.

EARLY CHRISTIANS AND THE DARK AGES

From the early 4thC, Nîmes declined and Arles began a golden age as the foremost town of Provence. After the Emperor Constantine's conversion to Christianity, he chose this as his favorite town in the West (balancing Byzantium in the East) and built a massive palace there. Then in **AD400** the Emperor Honorius made Arles the capital of the "three Gauls" (France, Britain and Spain).

Around this period, Christianity spread widely in Provence and abbeys were founded, notably that of St-Victor in Marseille, set up by St-Cassien in **413**. But with the fall of the Roman Empire, barbarian hordes such as Ostrogoths and Vandals drove down from the north, devastating the region, and in **471** proud Arles fell to the Visigoths.

Then in the 7th and 8thC it was the turn of Saracen (Moorish) marauders from North Africa, who raided the coastal towns. As in most of Europe, the Dark Ages were a confused and decadent era of war, piracy and poverty, as local rulers jostled for power and ousted one another.

But Christianity quietly managed to survive the storms. The Frankish dynasty of the Merovingians brought some stability for a while, as did the great Frankish ruler Charlemagne, who at Rome in **800** was crowned Emperor of the West. When his realm was divided between his three grandsons, the eldest of them, Lothair, made Provence into a kingdom in **855**, with his own son Charles as its king.

THE MIDDLE AGES

The Middle Ages were politically an unstable period: but this was also a time of cultural brilliance, when great abbeys and cathedrals were built. After changing hands several times, in **1032** Provence joined the Holy Roman Empire, and was divided into two parts, ruled by semi-autonomous local counts. The area east of the Rhône belonged to the Counts of Provence, who made Aix their capital; the lands west of the river fell within the domain of the powerful Counts of Toulouse. As the region gradually emerged from feudal anarchy, a more prosperous kind of society developed: fine Romanesque churches were built, and some towns became powerful self-governing entities.

When the Cathar heresy spread in the early 13thC, Provence was less affected by it than neighboring Languedoc, and so did not suffer the same degree of retribution from the Capetian monarchy in Paris. It retained its autonomy, whereas Languedoc, after the brutal suppression of the Cathars, was virtually annexed to the French crown. Then in **1307** a remarkable event occurred: the Popes, wearying of the turbulent instability of Rome, moved the Papacy lock, stock and barrel to Avignon.

There they stayed until **1377**, protected by the Counts of Provence and the Kings of France. In **1388**, Nice detached itself from Provence and joined the Earldom of Savoy, in Italy.

In the later 14thC, famine and plague swept through Provence, and the population declined. To make matters worse, parts of the country were in prey to brigands such the cruel Viscount of Turenne, who held sway in the castle of Les Baux.

But in the early 15thC, happier times returned. A university was founded at Aix in **1409**. The civilized Dukes of Anjou had taken control of Provence by marriage, and in **1434** René of Anjou, who was also the exiled King of Naples, became Count of Provence on the death of his elder brother. René was a generous, cultured and convivial man who drew artists to his court at Aix, improved the economy, and generally introduced a golden age. He is warmly remembered to this day as *le bon roi René.* But his nephew Charles of Maine, who succeeded him, incautiously granted the countship to Louis XI of France.

And so finally in **1481**, Provence was subsumed into the kingdom of France, and its long era of semi-independence ended. Although the new Provençal parliament set up at Aix in **1501** had some local powers, in practice Paris never allowed it to wield much influence.

THE WARS OF RELIGION
After the Reformation made its first impact in France around **1530**, Provence like other regions became engulfed by the brutal Wars of Religion during the 16thC. In the Lubéron hills, an ancient Protestant sect, descended from the Cathars and known as the Vaudois, was persecuted, and retorted by attacking abbeys and churches in the area. François 1er ordered a campaign against them, and some 3,000 of them were ferociously massacred in **1545**. However, Protestantism continued to spread in Provence and Languedoc, and for many years Catholics and Huguenots were in regular, bloody conflict.

In **1567**, some 200 Catholic priests and dignitaries were killed in the Protestant fief of Nîmes. Finally, in **1598**, under the Edict of Nantes, Henri IV granted religious tolerance to the Huguenots. But this did not end the problem, and in the **1630s** Richelieu was still repressing the "heretics," destroying castles and ramparts in pro-Huguenot towns such as Les Baux and Uzès.

After this, Provence entered a long period of peace. In the 18thC it became quite prosperous, even though in **1720** a fearful plague, brought in from Syria, killed some 100,000 people, half of them in Marseille.

THE FRENCH REVOLUTION AND NAPOLEON
In **May 1789** the Comte de Mirabeau was elected as member for Aix of France's Etats-Généraux, a sort of parliament. This helped prepare the way for the Revolution, since his powers of oratory and radical ideas made a big impact in Paris. But the Revolution then stripped Provence of what little autonomy it retained, for in 1790 the new Government divided it into three *départements* of the new centralized France, so that politically it no longer existed.

It did, however, play some incidental part in the post-Revolutionary period. In **1792**, 500 Marseillais volunteers marched through Paris singing the newly-composed *Battle Hymn of the Army of the Rhine,* which thus became dubbed *La Marseillaise,* which is today the French national anthem.

Then at the siege of Toulon in **1793** the young Napoléon Bonaparte first won military renown; and in **1815**, returning from exile on Elba, he landed at Golfe Juan near Cannes and marched over the hills to Paris, along what is now called the Route Napoléon.

THE 19TH CENTURY

In this period Provence began to industrialize, and more than most parts of France it increased hugely in prosperity. Marseille developed into one of the world's greatest ports, boosted by the French conquest of North Africa, and by the opening of the Suez Canal in **1869**. While new industry grew around Marseille, farming too began to modernize, although it was damaged by new foreign competition and by the scourge of phylloxera in the vineyards.

The greatest of all these 19thC changes took place in the Nice–Cannes coastal area, thanks to an entirely new phenomenon: tourism. The British named this coast the French Riviera, while the French later called it the Côte d'Azur. After the novelist Tobias Smollett had led the way in the 18thC, some well-to-do English people began to winter at Nice, and in **1822** their growing community financed the building of the Promenade des Anglais, which bore their name.

Then in **1830** Lord Brougham settled almost by chance at Cannes and sponsored its subsequent rise as a resort. After the astute Prince of Monaco built a casino at Monte-Carlo in the 1860s, the titled and the rich of all Europe were soon descending on the Riviera each winter, drawn by the mild, protected climate as much as by the gambling.

In **1860**, the Nice area was reintegrated into France after its long attachment to the Italian House of Savoy.

THE SECOND WORLD WAR

In the late 19th and early 20th centuries, many great artists and writers began to settle in Provence and on the Côte d'Azur (see pages 31–36). But little of note happened politically — save maybe that King Alexander of Yugoslavia was assassinated in Marseille in **1934**.

It was not until **1940** that world events brought dramatic change. After the German victory of that year, the region at first formed part of the Non-Occupied Zone governed from Vichy. But after the Allied occupation of North Africa in **November 1942**, the Germans took over the entire Vichy zone. (Vichy's fleet eluded them by scuttling itself at Toulon.)

In **1943–44** some active resistance developed in hillier areas, but less than in some other parts of France. Then on **August 15, 1944** the Allies landed on the coast around St-Tropez and St-Raphael, and were able to liberate all of Provence within two weeks, for the Germans in northern France were by now in full retreat.

After the Liberation, thousands died in bitter reprisals by Résistants (mainly communists) against suspected collaborators, and this rough justice left a sour taste that persisted for many years.

THE POSTWAR PERIOD

The people of Provence joined actively in France's great task of national renewal after the Second World War, and by the mid-1950s there were many signs of new prosperity. As the farms modernized, thousands of people left the land for new jobs in the towns, and new, modern industries grew. For some years this bright picture was marred by the anguish of the Algerian War (**1954–62**), which had a special impact on Provence, as Algeria was directly across the sea.

In **1962**, when Algeria won its independence, some 800,000 French colonists (*pieds noirs*) came back to France, and many chose to settle in Provence, where the life-style and climate were more familiar to them than in northern France. In those days of economic boom, they easily found new jobs; they had a dynamic, enterprising spirit, and this helped to bring a new vigor to the region.

The dominant figure in postwar Provençal politics has been Gaston Defferre, the socialist leader who was elected mayor of Marseille in **1953** and held the post until his death in 1986. At the national level, as Minister of the Interior from 1981–84, he was also a leading architect of the decentralization reforms that have recently benefitted all French regions. Since **1964**, the 90 or so French *départements* had been loosely grouped into 21 "regions" for economic purposes (six of them were linked to form the Provence–Côte d'Azur region), but these regional bodies had very little actual power.

Then in **1981**, when the socialists took office, Mitterrand gave Defferre the task of promoting real devolution at last. Under these reforms, Provence and the other regions now each have a directly-elected assembly with a real budget and some autonomy. But it was a sad irony for the ageing Defferre, two months before his death, that in Provence these first elections produced a right-wing assembly, in a region where until then the left had been dominant.

When the extreme-right-wing Front National party, led by Jean-Marie Le Pen, erupted into French politics in the mid-1980s, Provence became its prime stronghold. The party won much local support from the *pieds noirs* with their racist dislike of Muslim immigrants, and there were sometimes ugly clashes between the two groups. The upsurge of racism in France in recent years has been more marked in Provence than anywhere else.

In the regional elections of **March 1992**, the socialists once more fared rather badly, seeing their share of the vote fall yet again. The Front National made new advances, achieving its highest figure in any French region. In Nice, where Le Pen himself was elected a councilor, the FN topped the poll with 30 percent. The right-of-center held on to power, with Jean-Claude Gaudin, a "Giscardian," remaining as president of the assembly. To govern, however, it was forced to rely on Front National support.

Provençal tradition and modern life-styles

The power of French centralization has not destroyed the individuality of the regions, and certainly not of Provence. Admittedly, the old Provençal language has almost entirely died out in daily speech, and folk tradition has suffered from the impact of modern life. But the sharp accent of the Midi survives, as do many local words and dialect usages. Many customs and sports remain distinct, and likewise the local architecture, and the cuisine. The red-tiled roofs and floors of Provence have little in common with the granite of Brittany or the half-timbering of Alsace; no Provençal would exchange his *pastis* for the *calvados* of Normandy; and nowhere in northern France will you find bullfights, still so popular around Arles and Nîmes.

Similarly, modern material changes have not greatly affected the basic character and temperament of the Provençaux. Like other meridionals, they are less reserved, more instinctive and maybe more passionate, than northerners.

A Provençal may quickly fly into a temper, but without malice, and minutes later he will have his arm round your shoulder, offering to buy you a drink. He has the quality known as *"bon enfant,"* a good-natured ability to make quick human contact; rather in the Italian manner, he enjoys endless feuding, but without taking it entirely seriously. He works hard (it is a myth that people are lazy in the south) but is not too bothered with punctuality, and is adept at twisting or quietly ignoring rules.

These traits are true especially of the Marseillais, with their earthy humor; also of some country areas where the tempo of life is still slow. In the cosmopolitan resorts of the Côte, it is true, there is now such an admixture of new residents from the north that local temperament has become diluted; and many people have become reserved or short-tempered, made blasé by so much tourism. But a true Niçois remains essentially meridional.

The people of Provence tend to be dark, often swarthy, and stockily-built. They speak French with the twangy accent of the Midi *(mangtenang* for *maintenant),* harsh and grating in the cities, more melodious in country areas. In medieval times their daily language was Provençal, a version of Occitan that was the common tongue of southern France in the Middle Ages: the Papal court at Avignon used it.

After about 1550, pressures from Paris enforced the introduction of French, but this progressed so slowly that the playwright Racine, on a visit in 1661, found that he could not understand the local people. However, by the mid-19thC, Provençal had vanished from daily use in the towns. The poet Frédéric Mistral then made efforts to revive it, but had little success outside literary circles.

Today among local intellectuals there is again a certain vogue for studying Provençal, helped by the fact that government curbs are now eased: it used to be banned in schools, but it is now an option for the *baccalaureat* and can be studied at university. A few books are even published in Provençal. However, public interest is limited. Not only do people find it more practical to speak French, but as at school they must all study English or some other modern language, few have the energy or ability to turn to Provençal as well. So it is dying out as a daily tool, and its preservation has become somewhat artificial. This is sad in a way, for it is a beautiful language — as you can tell by reading Mistral aloud.

A NEW ERA IN THE HILL-VILLAGES

The scores of old fortified villages, standing on hilltops or terraced along mountainsides, form one of the most striking features of Provence's landscape. Some are dramatically situated, such as Èze, perched giddily above the Côte d'Azur, or Saorge, which clings to the side of a cliff near Sospel. And some, like Peillon inland from Nice, lie quite close to the big towns of the coast, yet seem in a different world.

Most are built of local stone, so that they appear to merge into the rocks on which they stand, like Gordes and Les Baux. Some are circled by the remains of ancient ramparts, or are crowned by some half-ruined château. And so steep and narrow are their alleys that cars cannot enter. They present a maze of winding stone steps, vaulted archways, shady arcades, and little squares where fountains play.

Today not all of these charming old places are lively communities of real local villagers. Some are silent, deserted, falling into ruin. But others have been taken over by new inhabitants of a very different kind. They are adorned with a new chic, their alleys lined with tourists' bistros and boutiques, their mellow, stone facades lavishly restored — and the strollers in their streets are less likely to be local peasants than Parisians, Londoners or Rhinelanders. In short, the hill-villages are now undergoing a revolution hardly less dramatic than that which hit the Côte itself a century or so ago. It is causing a kind of death — and a kind of rebirth.

The villages were built on high points for protection, first against Saracen marauders, then against the bandits of medieval times. The peasants would sleep within the ramparts, then venture out by day to till their fields. When conditions became more settled in the 19thC, many preferred to live in farmsteads down in the valleys.

In the past 50 years, farm modernization has led to a mass exodus from the countryside, all over France, so that many more remote villages have been entirely or partly abandoned. Yet the growth of tourism and of urban prosperity have simultaneously lent them a new, very different lease on life. A few villages — Les Baux, Èze and St-Paul-de-Vence are examples — have become major tourist centers, full of souvenir stores and pizza parlors. Their old stone facades have been beautified with neat flowerpots and fancy ironwork, and their rough cobbled alleys tidily repaved.

More significantly, hundreds of other villages have succumbed to the recent middle-class vogue for acquiring rural properties and converting them into homes for weekends, summer vacations or retirement. Parisians and many other city-dwellers, including Britons, Dutch, Germans and others, all in search of the sun and rural peace, have bought up many thousands of such buildings, sending land and house prices rising steeply. Some of these renovated villages are now modish haunts of the intelligentsia, especially places near the coast such as Grimaud and Mougins, and others east of Avignon such as Gordes and the trendy haunts of the Lubéron hills. Here Peter Mayle bought his house outside Ménerbes, and in *A Year in Provence* described how the snobbish Parisian cliques did not mix in too readily with the foreigners. He in turn became none too popular with the locals, for the publicity that his best-selling books gave to the area.

This renaissance of the hill-villages, however artificial, is surely better than letting them die. In many cases, the new influx has revived local commerce: food stores that had closed have reopened, and banks and real-estate agents have arrived. So a former artisan/peasant economy is becoming more suburban or touristic, full of new service industries. However, most of the new residents are there only in summer, and in winter the shops do little trade: so the boom is fragile. And some social tensions have appeared. Some village cafés remain the preserve of locals, mainly old men playing cards, while others are frequented by the newcomers and tourists. One antique dealer from Paris said that superficially he was on friendly terms with the locals, but after ten years he had failed to penetrate their social life and to them was still an outsider.

Not that any of this is surprising. Provençaux remain suspicious of those not from their own area, whom they tend to regard as foreigners (*"les estrangers"* in their *patois*). Some locals feel that the influx has spoiled the nature of village life. Or they dislike the new swimming pools that use up the water much needed by the farms in summer.

FOLKLORE AND FESTIVALS
With the advent of machines and television, many of the old folk traditions have inevitably disappeared from daily life. Only at special fêtes do women now wear the gorgeous old Provençal head-dresses and costumes. At one big hotel in Arles, until recently, the waitresses were required to wear them daily, to please the tourists: but they are no longer prepared to do so, for it takes over an hour to prepare the coiffure for the famous Arlesian bonnet.

And yet, in Provence as in some other French regions such as Brittany, conscious efforts have been made in the past 30 years to revive the old traditions — not for daily life but for special events such as festivals. The Var *département* now has a federation of over 30 folk groups, which compete against one another at major galas and perform at local fêtes. The impetus for this renewal has tended to come less from the old villagers than from teachers, students and other educated people, including the non-Provençal new residents. So this is a self-consciously "cultural" movement rather than an authentic one — but surely it is preferable to allowing the old traditions to die out.

The groups have learned to dance the old *farandole* of Provence, and their musicians to play the *galoubet* (a three-holed flute) and the *tambourin* (a narrow drum), old instruments that are still made locally by one or two artisans. The old embroidered costumes are taken out of cupboards for the festivals; in some places new ones are again being made, for sale to tourists as well as for the folk groups.

Most villages still have their traditional annual fête, usually lasting two or three days, with games and contests of various kinds and a big outdoor communal feast known as an *aïoli* (after its principal dish: see page 47). Often marking some local saint's day, the fête remains the focal point of the village year, but seldom does it excite the villagers as it did in former days when they had few other distractions. The young nowadays go to discos in their cars on weekends, so they feel blasé about the fête, which draws tourists as much as locals. It may well include an afternoon folk-group show, but for the nightly dancing, the music is more likely to come from a modern rock band.

A few of these fêtes, however, do include lavish pageantry, often religious in origin, and dating back centuries. These traditions are dutifully maintained, even in an age that has mainly lost touch with their sacred meaning. Leading fêtes of this kind include the two *bravades* at St-Tropez, where the bust of a local saint is paraded around town by locals in 18thC military uniform; the pageants at Roquebrune, 15thC in origin, where villagers enact the Passion of Christ; the festival of the Tarasque at Tarascon, also 15thC, where a green papier-mâché monster is paraded through the streets; the strange Fête de St-Marcel at Barjols, where a cow is ritually sacrificed and people dance in the church; the big gipsy pilgrimage in May at Les-Saintes-Maries-de-la-Mer; and the Nice carnival and flower-battles (hardly village affairs). In the ARLES and NÎMES area, festivals include bullfights and bull races.

CRIBS AND *SANTONS*

The Christmas crib and the making of *santons* for it are traditions that survive quite strongly, despite the decline of religious practice. The *santon,* a clay-costumed figurine usually some 50 centimeters (20 inches) high, was invented at Marseille in the late 18thC. Initially *santons* represented just the figures of the Nativity story, but soon the range was widened to include Provençal stock types such as the drummer, the *gendarme,* the drunkard, the Camargue cowboy. Many a family still has its *santon* collection, either for a crib at Christmas in the living room or purely as secular ornaments; and *santons* today are still manufactured, for sale to local people as well as to tourists.

Marseille has a big *santon* fair each December. In many churches from Christmas to late January you will find prettily lit cribs full of *santons.* And the folklore museums of Aix, Arles, Marseille and Monaco have fine historical displays of cribs and *santons.* What's more, in a few villages, notably Les Baux and Séguret, the tradition of a "live crib" survives. This is a Midnight Mass on Christmas Eve in the form of a Provençal pageant of the Nativity, with villagers dressed up as the Holy Family and other figures. And in summer, some villages still keep up their annual pilgrimages, usually a costumed procession to the local shrine of a saint.

HANDICRAFTS

The making of *santons* is one of several traditional Provençal crafts to have been revived in recent decades: ceramics, olive-wood sculpture, and the weaving of local fabrics, are others. These activities were in decline, but the arrival of artisans and artists from the north, eager to work in the sunny south, has brought some new impetus. It was in fact Picasso, by spending the years 1947–53 in the ceramics town of Vallauris, who helped to set this trend. These immigrants became as numerous as the native craftsmen, notably in fashionable villages such as Roussillon and Tourettes-sur-Loup. But since the early 1980s, many of them have found it hard to make a living and have departed. The revival of handicrafts, like that of the entire local folk tradition, remains uncertain.

PÉTANQUE AND *BOULES*

Like the drinking of *pastis* (see page 52), the playing of *pétanque*, otherwise known as *boules,* is a local tradition that has survived strongly. It originated in Marseille, and Provence is still its heartland: but it has since spread all over France. It is an early version of the game of bowls, and is generally played by two teams of three or four people each, either on a proper pitch of hard earth or gravel, or on any piece of hard ground. As in bowls, the winning team is the one that gets its balls closest to the jack. *Boules* is played on a longish pitch, *pétanque* on a shorter one with the players standing in a circle, heels together. *Pétanque* has today become far more popular than *boules,* which remains, however, the more usual name for the sport.

You can see these intent little groups of players everywhere, in village squares under the plane trees, in public parks, even on smart promenades. A game nearly always end with a glass or three of *pastis* in a café and a good bitchy gossip.

RURAL ARCHITECTURE

Here the vernacular tradition has managed to survive fairly well, despite some ugly modern excrescences. Provençal villas and farmsteads tend to have stone walls and sloping roofs of terracotta tiles. North walls are often blind, as a protection against the Mistral, the chill north wind. Front doors and windows face south, and as a defense against summer heat are often quite small, so that the interiors are dark and cool, in contrast to the exterior dazzle.

A large farmhouse or rural residence is called a *mas* (from the Latin *mansum,* like *maison* or mansion); similar to it is the *bastide,* a small country house, usually square. Inside these buildings, typical Provençal decor consists of red-tiled floors, beamed ceilings, sturdy wooden furniture, and bare, stone walls often hung with copper pots. This rural style is now studiously imitated by many modern hotels, restaurants and villas, alike in their architecture and decor. The results may be monotonous and contrived, but at least are in keeping with tradition.

A mass of new rural building has been generated by the recent tourist and residential boom. But the landscape has been disfigured less than one might have feared. One reason is that in many areas strict regulations require all new buildings or alterations to conform to traditional styles, so the new villas too have red-tiled roofs and pale stone walls.

Sadly, in some cases, large modern buildings in assorted styles have been allowed to scar the landscape, and some local mayors, less interested in aesthetics than in money from new investment, are lax in enforcing the rules.

Who's who

Assembled here are just some of the well-known people associated with Provence and the Côte-d'Azur: those who were born there, or who settled and lived there.

Other names, including many writers, artists, etc., will be found in later pages. Refer to the INDEX to find them.

Bardot, Brigitte *(born 1934)*
When director Roger Vadim made *And God Created Woman* on location at St-Tropez in 1956, he propelled both his young wife and the resort to stardom. Bardot became the archetypal sex-kitten. Today she spends little time at St-Tropez and devotes herself mainly to wildlife preservation causes.

Bonaparte, Napoléon *(1769-1821)*
The diminutive Corsican began his brilliant military career by driving the British from Toulon in 1793. In 1794 he commanded the defenses of Antibes. When exiled, he sailed to Elba from St-Raphael in 1814, and in 1815 landed again at Golfe-Juan, before marching up what is now known as the ROUTE NAPOLÉON to meet his Waterloo.

Bréa, Louis *(c.1450-1522)*
Pictures by the leading painter of the Nice school of the 15th and 16thC can be seen at NICE, ANTIBES, BIOT, GRASSE and LUCÉRAM, as well as in many other hinterland village churches. They show both the influence of the Avignon school (especially the *Pièta* in the Louvre) and the Italian Renaissance. Bréa's brother Antoine and nephew François were also notable painters.

Brougham, Lord Henry *(1778-1868)*
This leading British politician of his day, renowned as a law reformer and campaigner against slavery, did more than anyone to make the Riviera fashionable. Visiting the fishing-village of Cannes in 1834, he fell in love with it and lived there for over 30 years.

Cézanne, Paul *(1839-1906)*
The leading Post-Impressionist painter, who had a fundamental influence on the art of the 20thC, was a native of Aix, where his father was a wealthy banker. Cézanne spent most of his life in Provence, painting the landscape he loved, particularly around L'Estaque and Mont Ste-Victoire.

Chagall, Marc *(1887-1985)*
The paintings of this Russian-born artist depict a highly personal dream world of color, fantasy and spirituality and have made him one of the most popular of 20thC artists. His later years were spent at Vence, where he died. The Chagall museum at Nice contains some of his most vivid and highly admired works.

Cocteau, Jean *(1889-1963)*
A brilliant and versatile poet, dramatist, painter and film-maker, and a leading figure of the avant-garde, Cocteau had a summer home at Cap Ferrat and spent much of his time in Provence. Frescoes by him are at MENTON and VILLEFRANCHE.

Daudet, Alphonse *(1840-97)*
Born at Nîmes, this writer of humorous stories of Provençal life was hugely successful in his own lifetime. From 1857 he lived in Paris, but he often visited FONTVIEILLE, which formed the setting of his *Lettres de mon Moulin.*

Defferre, Gaston *(1910-1986)*
As socialist mayor of Marseille since 1953, Defferre dominated the politics of postwar Provence. Staunchly anti-communist, he was a suave, wealthy bourgeois, owning Marseille's two main daily newspapers. As Interior Minister in Mitterrand's government from 1981–84, he drew up the devolutionary reforms that gave much new autonomy to the French regions, including Provence. He was also for some years President of Provence's regional council.

Escoffier, Auguste *(1846-1935)*
The great French chef, born at Villeneuve-Loubet near Cannes, won his reputation as a master of *haute cuisine* while working at luxury hotels in London, and became known as "the king of sauces and the chef of kings."

Jean-Claude Gaudin *(born 1939)*
Leading local center-right politician (Parti Républicain), from Marseille. President of the Regional Assembly since 1986.

Jean Giono *(1895-1970)*
The novels of this great Provençal writer are imbued with an almost mystical feeling for nature, for animal life and for the simple virtues of the peasantry, which he tended to idealize. Ecologist and pacifist, he wrote lyrically about the wild, hilly countryside around Manosque, where he lived and died.

The Grimaldi
One of the most powerful feudal families of medieval Provence, the Grimaldi were of Genoese origin. Monaco has been in their hands since the 15thC. The present Grimaldi ruler of this principality, Rainier III (born 1923), is a forceful businessman who has brilliantly revived its fortunes since the 1950s.

Léger, Fernand *(1881-1955)*
This pioneer of abstract painting turned later to scenes of contemporary industrial life, executed in his distinctive, simplified style. He worked first in Paris, then settled at Biot, near Antibes.

Le Pen, Jean-Marie *(born 1928)*

Son of a Breton fisherman, and leader of the extreme-right Front National Party with its racist anti-immigrant views. As the party is especially strong in Provence–Côte d'Azur, Le Pen has recently chosen this as his own stamping-ground, and in 1992 he was elected to the regional assembly in a Nice constituency.

Matisse, Henri *(1869-1954)*

The leading artist of Fauvism, Matisse produced much of his finest work in Provence. He first stayed at St-Tropez in 1904, and lived at Vence and Nice from 1917 until his death.

Jacques Médecin *(born 1928)*

The Médecin family ruled Nice like an elected dynasty for over 60 years. Jean Médecin was mayor from 1928–65, and his son Jacques from 1965–90, when he fled France to escape charges of fraud and corruption. He had run the city with smooth efficiency, mixed with ruthless autocratic wheeler-dealing.

Mirabeau, Count Honoré Gabriel *(1749-91)*

Although unusually ugly, Mirabeau was one of the most effective leaders of the French Revolution, and was a gifted orator. He spent some years in Aix and was elected to the States General as its deputy.

Mistral, Frédéric *(1830-1914)*

Provence's greatest poet, he led a revival of the region's language and culture and wrote only in Provençal, winning the Nobel Prize for Literature in 1904 for his epic poetry. He lived all his life at Maillane, near St-Rémy, and also had close connections with Arles, where he created a famous museum of Provençal folklore.

Nostradamus (Michel de Notredame) *(1503-66)*

The great astrologer and physician was born at St-Rémy and lived mainly at Salon. His rhyming quatrains of enigmatic prophecies had a wide vogue at the time, finding royal favor.

Pagnol, Marcel *(1895-1974)*

Hugely popular as film-maker, playwright and novelist, Pagnol spent his early years in Marseille and the wild country to its east, before moving to Paris. In his comedies set on the Marseille waterfront, and his films about rural life, he shrewdly depicted the Provençal character with a mix of satire and sentimentality. Posthumous remakes of his *Manon* films have recently made him more widely popular than ever.

Petrarch, Francesco *(1304-74)*

The Italian lyric poet and humanist spent many years as a churchman at the Papal court at Avignon, where he sharply criticized its profligacy. Then he lived at nearby Fontaine-de-Vaucluse. Some of his best work was inspired by his unrequited passion for Laura, a virtuous Avignonnaise.

Picasso, Pablo *(1881-1973)*
Although his most creative years were spent mainly in Paris, the Spaniard's genius was nourished by his native Mediterranean and its sensuality. In 1945 he moved permanently to Provence, living and working in Antibes, Vallauris, Mougins, and Vauvenargues near Aix.

Puget, Pierre *(1620-94)*
Provence's greatest sculptor did much of his finest work in his native Marseille and in Toulon, where some of his robust Baroque creations are still on display. He also worked for many years in Italy.

René, King of Naples and Duke of Anjou *(1409-80)*
Excluded from his kingdom, "Good King René" became the most popular and successful Count of Provence, where his reign at Aix and Tarascon was something of a golden age. His daughter married King Henry VI of England.

Renoir, Auguste *(1841-1919)*
After a long career based in Paris, the great Impressionist spent his last 12 years at Cagnes-sur-Mer, still painting with sensuous vigor although crippled with arthritis.

Ricard, Paul *(born 1909)*
Born humbly in Marseille, Ricard amassed a fortune from the making of that favorite Provençal drink, *pastis.* His own huge firm, Ricard, later merged with its chief rival, Pernod. He was a flamboyant self-publicist, philanthropist, arts patron, and creator of Provence's leading racing circuit.

Tapie, Bernard *(born 1943)*
This brilliant and controversial Parisian entrepreneur and media showman acquired one of France's foremost soccer clubs, the Olympique de Marseille. He became a socialist deputy for Marseille in 1989.

Van Gogh, Vincent *(1853-90)*
The son of a Dutch pastor, Van Gogh moved to Paris after he took up painting, and then in 1888 to Provence where he lived at Arles, cut off his ear, and spent time in a mental asylum near St-Rémy. The clear light of the Midi inspired much of his best work.

Vergé, Roger *(born 1930)*
A leading pioneer of *nouvelle cuisine* whose restaurant at Mougins, near Cannes, has long been rated one of the very best in France.

Architecture

The architecture of the region is marvelously varied. Most of the major styles are represented, from Roman to ultramodern. Made mostly of local limestone, the buildings tend to harmonize not only with one another but with the landscape.

See also RURAL ARCHITECTURE on page 24 and the GLOSSARY OF ART AND ARCHITECTURE on pages 32-33.

ROMAN *(1st century BC to 3rd century AD)*

Western Provence and the Nîmes area, the heart of the Roman *provincia,* contain the best-preserved assortment of Roman buildings to be found outside Italy. They include grandiose public structures such as the

theater at Orange, the great arenas at Arles and Nîmes, and a superb example of Roman engineering in the lofty Pont du Gard aqueduct. The Romans were also capable of delicacy: witness the elegant proportions of the Maison Carrée temple at Nîmes and the carvings on the triumphal arches at Carpentras, Orange and St-Rémy. Roman villas and other contemporary domestic architecture can be examined at Vaison-la-Romaine.

The arena at **Nîmes**

GALLO-ROMAN AND MEROVINGIAN *(5th to 8th centuries)*

Virtually all that has survived from the Merovingian period are some octagonal baptistries, notably at Aix, Fréjus, Riez and Venasque. Merovingian Early Christian art was a mixture of the Roman Classical and Germanic-Frankish styles.

ROMANESQUE *(11th and 12th centuries)*

The 12thC was a golden age of Provençal architecture, producing a style of Romanesque that is readily distinguishable from its Norman counterpart and is seen at its purest in the Cistercian abbeys of Sénanque and Thoronet.

The influence of Roman antiquity is clearly visible in the fine limestone masonry (sometimes incorporating fragments from Roman ruins) and some of the carvings.

The churches are generally in the form of a cross, with a semicircular apse at the end of a broad nave, which often has no side-aisles. The few small windows barely dissipate the austere, sparsely decorated gloom, but the tall pillars and barrel vaulting lend a sense of space.

West fronts are sometimes richly sculpted, and notable examples can be seen at St-Sauveur in Aix, St-Trophîme in Arles, and at St-Gilles, also near Arles. Superb carved capitals can be seen in the cloister galleries of St-Trophîme, Montmajour and St-Rémy.

GOTHIC *(12th to 15th centuries)*

The Gothic style, which originated in northern France, is marked by more ornate decoration and the use of pointed arches, ribbed vaulting and flying buttresses. These new techniques made it possible to liberate space for larger windows (often of stained glass), reducing the solidity of the walls and flooding the interior with light. The overall effect is of a soaring, vertical quality, in contrast to the horizontal and rounded lines of the Romanesque. The Gothic style is not well represented in Provence apart from the cloisters at Fréjus and the basilica of St-Maximin. The later phase, ornate and exuberant, is known as Flamboyant Gothic because of its flame-shaped window traceries and columns, best seen in the facades of St-Siffre at Carpentras and St-Sauveur at Aix. Other notable Gothic buildings are the abbey at St-Maximin and the newer part of the Palais des Papes at Avignon.

MILITARY ARCHITECTURE

In the Middle Ages, kings and feudal lords built castles for protection, usually on hilltops (as at Sisteron) but sometimes on the plain (as at Tarascon). Each castle has a keep *(donjon),* turreted battlements, often with machicolation (parapets with apertures for dropping missiles or molten lead on assailants), and maybe a moat too if it is on a plain.

Some early churches, such as St-Victor at Marseille, and that at Les Saintes-Maries, have battlements and a fortress-like look, for they were constructed partly as a refuge against Saracens and other invaders. Aigues-Mortes is a perfect example of a medieval walled city. In the 15thC, the arrival of heavy cannon made this kind of defense obsolete. But then in the 17thC, Louis XIV's great military architect, Vauban, built a series of far more impregnable forts, such as those above Toulon.

RENAISSANCE AND CLASSICAL *(16th to 18th centuries)*

The Renaissance style in France, a synthesis of the French medieval and Italian Renaissance styles, is marked by a return to Greek and Roman forms, with Classical columns, balustrades and pediments. However, despite the proximity of Italy, the style never caught on widely in Provence, although its influence can sometimes be seen in certain facades, courtyards and stairways, as, for example in the fine ducal palace at Uzès.

The ducal palace at **Uzès**: facade

The more ornate Classicism of the 17th and 18th centuries left a much stronger mark, notably in the many *hôtels* (mansions) in the heart of Avignon and Aix. François Mansart built the *hôtels de ville* (town halls) at Arles and Marseille.

ECLECTICISM *(19th century)*

This was an age of stylistic revivals, reflecting the opulent self-confidence (and somewhat dubious taste) of the period. Marseille contains good examples: the New Cathedral and the Basilica of Notre-Dame-de-la-Garde (both Neo-Byzantine) and the Palais Longchamp (Neo-Baroque; illustrated on page 120). In the Belle Époque (late 19thC), the growth of aristocratic tourism on the Côte d'Azur produced such dazzling Neo-Baroque marvels as the Casino and the Hôtel de Paris in Monte-Carlo, followed by grand Edwardian palace-hotels such as the Negresco in Nice and the Carlton in Cannes.

POST-1945

Swiss-born architect Le Corbusier's one seminal work in Provence, the Unité d'Habitation at Marseille (1952), was a huge apartment block on massive supports, intended to form part of the never-completed Cité Radieuse. Once influential, it now looks dated. But its example did help to generate the "neo-gigantism" in vogue in France during the 1960s and early '70s, whose dubious legacy includes the vast curling pyramid blocks of the Marina Baie des Anges near Antibes.

By contrast, other tourist developments of the 1970s — notably Port-Grimaud, and Port-Galère on the Esterel coast — cleverly used a pastiche vernacular style that blends with the landscape. J.L. Sert's designs for the Fondation Maeght museum of modern art at St-Paul-de-Vence show an equal sense of harmony.

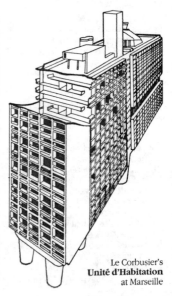

Le Corbusier's
Unité d'Habitation
at Marseille

Artists and writers

Across the centuries, Provence has produced a large number of notable artists and writers — Fragonard, Cézanne and Mistral, to name but three. In medieval times, Nice and Avignon were key centers of religious painting. And more recently, regional literature (witness Daudet, Giono and Pagnol, as well as Mistral) has flourished more robustly here than elsewhere in France. In view of the potent traditions and personality of Provence, this is not surprising.

Nor does it seem odd that Provence's vivid colors and bold light, its climate, people and life-style, should have seduced so many creative

Glossary of art and architecture

The French term is given, in brackets, when it differs significantly from the English one.

Aedicule　Niche framed by columns

Apse *(abside)*　Semicircular or polygonal termination to E end of church

Arcade　Range of arches supported on piers or columns

Atlante　Carved male figure used as a column

Atrium　Central room or court of pre-Christian house; forecourt of early Christian church

Balustrade　Ornamental rail with supporting set of balusters

Baptistry　Building, often separate from church, containing font

Barrel vault *(voûte en tonnelle)*　Continuous vault of semicircular or pointed section

Basilica　Rectangular Roman civic hall; early Christian church of similar structure

Bastide　Provençal traditional farmhouse, smaller than a *mas* (see opposite)

Campanile　Bell tower, generally free-standing

Capital　Crowning feature of a column or pilaster

Cartoon　Full-sized preparatory drawing for a painting, fresco or tapestry

Caryatid　Carved female figure used as a column

Chancel *(sanctuaire)*　Part of church reserved for clergy and containing altar and choir

Choir *(choeur)*　Part of church where services are sung, generally in W part of chancel

Ciborium　Altar canopy; casket for the Host

Cloisters *(cloître)*　Covered arcade around a quadrangle; connects the monastic church to the monastery's domestic parts

Colonnade　Row of columns supporting arches or an entablature

Column *(colonne)*　Vertical cylindrical support, usually with base, shaft and capital

Crenellate *(créneler)*　To indent or embattle

Crossing *(croisement)*　Space at intersection of chancel, nave and transepts in a cruciform church

Diptych　Work of art on two hinged panels

Donjon　Castle keep (inner stronghold)

Entablature *(entablement)*　Upper part of a Classical order, between capitals and pediment

Ex-voto　Work of art offered in fulfilment of a vow

Facade　Exterior of a building on one of its principal sides; usually incorporates main entrance

outsiders. Van Gogh and Lawrence Durrell came to western Provence. And to the Côte d'Azur came many others. Its appeal for great painters — Chagall, Matisse, Picasso, Renoir and others — has bequeathed a splendid heritage of modern art in its museums. Writers have come too, drawn by the beauty of the coast or the sophisticated glamor of the Riviera in what Scott Fitzgerald called "the lost caviar days."

ART: THE SCHOOLS OF NICE AND AVIGNON

Influenced by the Italian Renaissance, Provence developed its own

Faïence Glazed earthenware used for pottery or to decorate buildings; originally from Faenza in Italy

Flying buttress *(pilier d'arc-boutant)* Arch or half-arch built on a detached pier abutting against a building to take the thrust of a vault

Fresco *(fresque)* Technique of painting onto wet plaster on a wall

Greek cross *(croix grecque)* Cross with arms of equal length

Low relief *(bas-relief)* Sculpture that is attached to its background and projects from it by less than half its natural depth

Mas Large traditional mansion or farmhouse in Provence and Languedoc

Mosaic *(mosaïque)* Surface decoration made of small cubes of glass or stone that are set in cement

Nave *(nef)* Main body of a church w of crossing; more specifically, the central space bounded by aisles

Pediment *(fronton)* Triangular gable above window, door or Classical entablature

Pier *(pilier)* Heavy masonry support, like a column but thicker, and often square in section

Pilaster *(pilastre)* Rectangular column projecting from the wall

Polyptych Work of art on more than three hinged panels

Presbytery *(sanctuaire)* Part of cathedral or church E of the choir, in which the main altar is situated

Retable Painted wooden screen above the altar

Ribbed vaulting *(voûte d'ogives)* Arched ribs built across the sides and diagonals of the vaulted bay to support the infilling

Sacristy Repository for sacred vessels in a church

Sarcophagus Stone or marble coffin or tomb, usually decorated with inscriptions or sculpture

Stele Commemorative stone slab, which often bears an inscription

Terracotta *(terre cuite)* Baked unglazed clay used for construction and decoration

Transept Transverse arms of a cruciform church

Triptych Work of art on three hinged panels

Triumphal arch In Roman architecture, monumental arch usually erected in honor of a victorious commander

Trompe-l'oeil Literally, deceive-the-eye: decorative painting that gives false impression of realism, e.g., by painting flat surfaces to give appearance of depth and perspective

Tympanum Triangular space enclosed by a Classical pediment

Vault *(voûte)* Arched ceiling or roof of stone or brick

schools of religious painting. In the late 15thC, a school of "primitives" flourished at Nice, led by the prolific **Louis Bréa** and his brother and nephew. Their works, mainly retables, can be seen in many churches of the Nice hinterland, and some of the best examples of their work are at Lucéram.

Meanwhile, **Enguerrand Charonton** (or **Quarton**) was working at Avignon (his masterly *Coronation of the Virgin* is at nearby Villeneuve), while **Nicolas Froment** was King René's court painter at Aix (his remarkable *Burning Bush* is in its cathedral). These two were among the founders of the so-called Avignon School, which continued in various guises until the 19thC. In the 17thC, its leading lights were **Nicolas Mignard** and the **Parrocel** family, whose works adorn many local churches.

In the 17thC, Provençal artists began to turn to secular subjects. **Pierre Puget** of Marseille, Provence's greatest sculptor, chose Greek Classical themes, like Bernini in Italy to whom he is sometimes compared. His best works are in Paris and Italy, but others are at Marseille and Toulon.

The **Van Loos**, a Dutch family who lived and worked at Aix and Nice in the 18thC, are known for their vividly colored portraits and *genre* paintings: the Musée Chéret at Nice has a good collection. Provence's greatest native painter of the 18thC, **Pierre Fragonard**, was born at Grasse but spent most of his working life in Italy and Paris, devoting himself to whimsical and sensuous subjects that delighted a frivolous age.

ART: FROM IMPRESSIONISM TO MODERNISM

Ever since Impressionism changed the face of art in the 1870s, Provence has been a constant magnet for painters. The Impressionists were much concerned with the effects of light, and under the Mediterranean sun they found an ideal clarity and luminosity.

Paul Cézanne (later to diverge from the Impressionists both in ethos and technique) was born in Aix in 1839, and spent much of his later life there painting the landscape he loved: chalky hills, lone cypresses and red-roofed farmsteads. His searching analysis of color and tone led him to paint again and again, in varying lights, the glowering pyramid of Mont Ste-Victoire. **Van Gogh** likewise was inspired to a savage passion by the sun, sky and scenery around Arles and St-Rémy, where he spent the last two years of his life, in and out of mental institutions. His northern Protestant spirit, however, never took to the local life-style, which he called "rather squalid." None of his work, and more surprisingly very little of Cézanne's, is to be seen in local museums.

Just before the turn of the century, artists moved toward the Côte d'Azur. In 1892 the Neo-Impressionist **Paul Signac** settled in the then unknown fishing-village of St-Tropez, thus setting a trend. **Bonnard, Matisse, Dunoyer de Segonzac** and others would spend their summers in this little port, whose museum today houses many of their lively land- and seascapes. To the east, at Cagnes-sur-Mer, **Renoir** spent the last 12 years of his life until 1919, painting joyously to the end although he was crippled with arthritis.

Then, after 1918, leading artists formed a virtual colony on the Côte. **Matisse** lived at Cimiez (Nice) and Vence from 1917 until his death in 1954. His feeling for color matured here, and it was in his studio at Cimiez that he painted the odalisques and still-life subjects that form his main *oeuvre*. **Picasso** did not settle in Provence until 1945, but his short period at Antibes, 1946–47, was among the most creative of his long career, and works such as *Ulysses and the Sirens* were clearly inspired by the region. His move to the nearby pottery center of Vallauris brought a new outlet for his versatile genius, and he devoted much of his later life to ceramics.

Marc Chagall likewise did not move to the Côte until late in life, but found there a new inspiration: witness the luminous Mediterranean colors of the *Biblical Message* in his museum at Nice, painted at Vence when he was in his seventies. **Léger** and **Vasarely** are other artists who have lived and worked in Provence, although its influence on their work is less direct. **Cocteau** was romantically fascinated by the life of the local fisherfolk, as can be seen from his murals at Menton and Villefranche. **Braque, Vlaminck** and **Dufy** (he lived at Nice) were others who portrayed the vivacity and color of this coast.

LITERATURE: THE NATIVE PROVENÇAL WRITERS

The region's earliest known writers were the troubadours, lyric poets of the 12th and 13thC. The vogue for them flourished all over southern France, more in Gascony and Languedoc than Provence itself, where their main center was the feudal castle of Les Baux. They wrote and sang in Occitan, the old language of the South; they were court poets and musicians attached to noble families, and their theme was love: patient, chaste, courtly love for beautiful women (often their employers' wives). For centuries after their era had faded, Provence produced no notable writers — save **Nostradamus**, the poet and astrologer, in the 16thC.

It was not until 1854 that cultural life in the region was revitalized: a group of young poets in the Avignon/Arles area, led by **Frédéric Mistral**, founded a movement which they named the Félibrige, after a Provençal folk tale. These poets were not nationalists in a political sense, but they resented the suppression of Provençal culture by Napoleon's new centralized France; and passionately they embarked on a new crusade to renew local interest in the region's history, customs, spirit, and above all in its language, which Paris had banned from being taught in schools.

Their success with the language revival was modest: but they did succeed in promoting some wider regional awareness. And they caused a stir in French literary circles, for Mistral himself was a poet of genius. His *Miréio* (*Mireille* in French), the tale of a girl's tragic love-affair on the Crau plain near the Camargue, is the most celebrated of his epic poems of Provençal rural life. It is not easy to assess how great a writer he was, for he wrote only in Provençal (a lovely melodious language akin to Occitan). But as a person he was romantic, full-blooded, handsome and generous, able to fire a visitor with his own fervent love for the land where he spent all his life (in the village of Maillane south of Avignon). A cult grew around him in his lifetime: it remains alive today, although many people regard him as a rather sentimental, reactionary figure. He was awarded the Nobel Prize for Literature in 1904.

Of the region's later writers, few wrote in Provençal, but many were influenced by Mistral — notably **Alphonse Daudet**, who was born in Nîmes. He spent most his adult life in Paris, but remained closely attached to the land that bred and inspired him. Witness his satirical trilogy *Tartarin de Tarascon*, and *Lettres de mon Moulin*, a collection of quirky sketches of rural life centering round an old windmill at Fontvieille, near Arles.

Closer to the present day, the great novelist **Jean Giono**, a serious and philosophical figure, ecologist and pacifist, spent all his life in the Manosque area where he was born, and in those wild and lovely hills he set his lyrical studies of peasants living in close harmony with nature and animal life. **Henri Bosco**, from Avignon, wrote in not dissimilar style about the Lubéron hills and the Durance valley where he lived.

René Char, a noted Surrealist poet, was inspired by the country around his home town of l'Isle-sur-la-Sorgue, near Avignon. As for **Marcel Pagnol**, that hugely popular storyteller, he made his name with the *Marius* trilogy of comic plays, set in Marseille, then made films and wrote racy stories — notably *Jean de Florette* and *Manon des Sources* — about the rural life east of the city, near Aubagne where he was born.

LITERATURE: THE IMMIGRANT WRITERS

The first of an illustrious line of non-Provençal writers to be influenced by the region was the Italian poet **Petrarch**. As a child, he moved with his parents to the Papal court at Avignon in 1312; and although he came to hate the city and the corrupt court in which he worked, he was inspired by the nearby Fontaine de Vaucluse, where he spent 16 years, and by his chaste passion for Laura, a lady of Avignon.

In our own day, Avignon has been vividly described by **Lawrence Durrell** (in his novel *Monsieur or the Prince of Darkness*) who spent his final years in the village of Sommières, near Nîmes.

Among French writers, **Émile Zola** spent his boyhood in Aix (it is the setting for some of his novels), while **Albert Camus** lived the last years of his life at Lourmarin (north of Aix) where he lies buried.

Victor Hugo visited Nîmes on one of his many tours round France. He adored puns and other word games, and one of his cleverest jokes of this kind was this couplet, whose two lines sound identical if spoken fast:

> *Galles, amant de la reine, alla — tour magnanime! —*
> *gallament de l'Arène à la Tour Magne, à Nîmes.*

(The Prince of Wales, lover of the Queen, went — generous feat! — gallantly from the Arena to the Tour Magne, at Nîmes.)

It is to the Côte d'Azur above all that outsiders have been drawn. Among the French, **Colette** lived for a time at St-Tropez, **Guy de Maupassant** and **Prosper Mérimée** came often to Cannes, **Françoise Sagan** set *Bonjour Tristesse* on the Esterel coast, and today **J.M.G. Le Clézio** lives in Nice. But even more it is foreign writers who have descended on the Côte, beginning with **Tobias Smollett**, who wrote luridly about the months he spent in Nice in 1763–65. After the Riviera became fashionable, it attracted writers in droves, and the gaudy expatriate worlds of Nice, Cannes and "Monte" provided settings for numerous novels good and bad (one good one was *The Green Hat* by **Michael Arlen**).

Nietzsche stayed often at Nice. **Somerset Maugham** lived for years at Cap-Ferrat, **Katherine Mansfield** for a shorter time at Menton and Bandol, and both set stories in the area. In the 1920s, *Tender is the Night* by **F. Scott Fitzgerald** recorded the decadent American socialite set of Cap d'Antibes, while **Cyril Connolly** in the 1930s stayed at Haut-de-Cagnes where he located his astringent novel *The Rock Pool*. **Grahame Greene** spent his final years at Antibes, where in 1982 he wrote *J'Accuse*, a polemic against corruption and gang warfare in Nice. And **Anthony Burgess** lived in Monte-Carlo until his death in 1993.

Planning
your visit

Orientation

This guide covers the four *départements* that span the south coast from Aigues-Mortes across to Menton, and the two hinterland *départements* bounded at the outer edge by the towns of Nîmes, Uzès, Orange, Sisteron, Colmars and Brigue.

To help you plan your visit, these *départements* have been divided up into three larger geographical areas.

- **Western Provence**, from Aigues-Mortes in the west to Aix-en-Provence and Marseille in the east and to Orange in the north — the *départements* of **Bouches-du-Rhône**, **Gard** and **Vaucluse**.
- **The western Côte d'Azur and the central hinterland**, from Cassis in the west as far east as St-Raphaël, and north to Sisteron — the *départements* of **Var** and **Alpes-de-Haute-Provence**.
- The **eastern Côte d'Azur**, from the Esterel Massif, inland from Cannes, in the west, to Monaco and Menton in the east and to Auron in the north — the *département* of **Alpes-Maritimes**.

Where to go

Whatever time of year you go, you will find Provence to be a region of dazzling variety, where it is possible to have many different kinds of vacation in one. Medieval mountain villages lie just a few miles from glamorous resorts. There are great castles and cathedrals as well as casinos and palace hotels.

THE WESTERN REGION: THE LOWER RHÔNE
Broadly speaking, the western part of the region is richer than the eastern zone in history and culture. In and around the lower Rhône valley, the heartland of Roman Provence, there are Roman remains and gracious medieval and Renaissance cities full of museums and fine buildings. The landscape is relatively flat, broken by ranges of limestone hills.

FROM MARSEILLE TO THE CÔTE D'AZUR
To the E, the 240-kilometer (150-mile) stretch of coast from Marseille to Menton is hilly, indented with capes and coves, and mostly very beautiful. But its popularity has brought problems. It is heavily built up, and in places spoiled by recent eyesores. This is the French Riviera, today

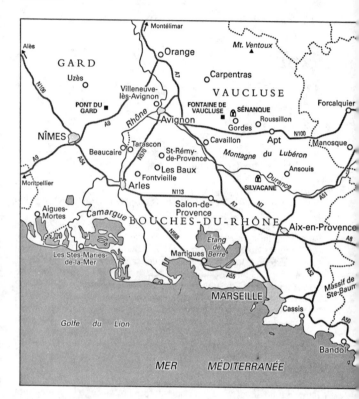

better known by its French name, the *Côte d'Azur*. The eastern part (Cannes, Nice, Monte-Carlo, Menton) has for more than a century been Europe's leading playground of the rich. Its resorts, although today more democratized, remain smart and sophisticated. This coast is one string of towns. Yet only a few miles behind, in striking contrast, lie isolated hill-villages and a wild hinterland.

THE HINTERLANDS

Provence stretches inland for some 160 kilometers (100 miles). From the snowy Alps in the E to the Cévennes uplands w of the Rhône, this is a vast undulating territory of wooded or vine-clad valleys and lime-stone plateaux cut by deep gorges. It contains much of interest, from lonely mountain chapels decorated with vivid medieval frescoes, to modern art museums surprisingly located in old castles.

THE CENTRAL COASTAL REGION: THE VAR

The *département* of the Var is perhaps the most varied in Provence,

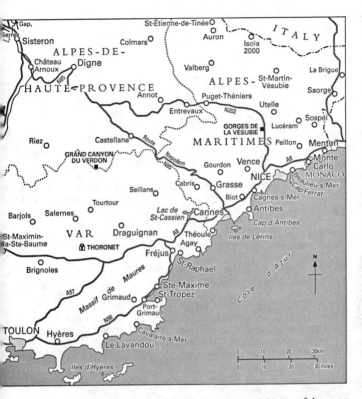

and yet it remains the least well known to tourists. It is one of the most heavily forested areas in France, ranging from the sparsely populated and hilly Haut Var, through the darkly wooded — with pine, cork oak and chestnut — hills of the Maures Massif range (so called from *mauro,* the Provençal word for black), to the coastal resorts sprinkled between Bandol and St-Raphael.

Unlike the eastern Côte d'Azur in the neighboring Alpes-Maritimes, the Var coast has not suffered from unfettered, and often ugly, development. This is in part because the autoroute A8 from Nice runs a long way inland, and partly because much stricter building regulations are in force. As a result, the coastal resorts, although they can be crowded in summer (in the case of St-Tropez, unbearably so), retain more charm and are, on the whole, cheaper than those in the Alpes-Maritimes.

Communications within the Var, rather poor in the past, are improving all the time, not least with the extension of the A57 up from Toulon to the A8. The Haut Var, and beyond it, Haute Provence, are now within an hour's drive of the coast. The area has also seen the development, over recent years, of a number of major golf courses, many of them beautifully sited, making it the center of golf in Provence.

THE HILL-VILLAGES

The mountainous parts of inland Provence are dotted with hundreds of ancient, fortified villages either perched on the crests of hills or terraced along mountainsides. Many of the villages were built in the 8th–10thC, and people lived within their narrow confines for centuries.

In the 19thC, people began to move down into the valleys. Today many of the more remote villages, such as Évenos, are wholly or partially abandoned, and it is fascinating to wander in their ruins.

However, the past 50 years or so have seen an entirely new trend, which is bringing new life back to some villages. A few, such as ÈZE and LES BAUX, have been taken over by the tourist trade and are now filled with cafés and souvenir stores, which give them the semblance of being lived in. Many others — especially near down the coast — succumbed to the postwar fashion for buying up rural cottages and converting them as weekend or summer homes. Such villages have now been smartly restored — an artificial revival, maybe, but better than letting them slip back into ruin. Colonies of artists and craftsmen have settled in some villages.

Whatever their present condition, the hill-villages are well worth exploring. Often you must go on foot, for the alleys are too steep and narrow for cars. You will find a maze of winding stone stairways and vaulted archways, shadowy arcades and tiny squares where fountains play. The villages are built of the local stone, so that some, like GOURDON, seem to merge into the hillside. Some of them still have their old ramparts.

Here are some villages that are particularly worth visiting. Place names in SMALL CAPITALS have their own entry. To find entries for other places use the INDEX.

- Most spectacularly situated: LES BAUX, Évenos, ÈZE, GOURDON, Ste-Agnes and SAORGE.
- Haunts of artists and artisans: Haut-de-Cagnes, ROUSSILLON, ST-PAUL-DE-VENCE, Séguret and TOURETTES-SUR-LOUP.
- Restored, smart, residential: Auribeau, Bormes-les-Mimosas, CABRIS, Le Castellet, Gassin, GORDES, GRIMAUD, MONS, MOUGINS, Peille, PEILLON, ROQUE-BRUNE, SEILLANS and TOURTOUR, as well as some of those above.
- Still lived in by villagers, and largely unrestored: COARAZE, Fox-Amphoux, LUCÉRAM, Roure, UTELLE.

When to go

May and June are ideal months, especially on the coast. The sun is hot, but not uncomfortably so, and the sea is warm enough for bathing. The resorts are alive but not yet too crowded; the countryside is filled with flowers. The adjustment to the clock for French summertime means that in June and July it stays light until nearly 11pm.

The French vacation season is from July to August. During this time the tourist industry swings into high gear, and many resorts offer their full amenities, such as outdoor discos, only in those months. But the crowds are dense, especially on the coast with its tedious traffic jams.

September is a good month. The sun is still hot, but the crowds are thinning out. In the w, however, the cold north wind known as the Mistral has begun to blow. September to October can be a good period for cultural sightseeing. November, although the weather might still be pleasant, is not an ideal time to visit Provence, as many hotels, restaurants and, in particular, museums, close for the month.

Until the 1930s, winter was the fashionable season on the Riviera, its resorts — such as Cannes and Menton — favored for their sheltered, mild climate. Today these resorts are still fairly active in winter, with their own select clientele. This can be a good time for a visit if you don't expect to sunbathe — and there is the advantage of skiing just inland. And the indigenous life of the towns, stripped of their tourist facade, is revealed at this time of the year. But the resorts farther w, like St-Tropez, all but close down in winter, as do many of the hotels in rural areas.

Events in the Provence calendar

See also PUBLIC HOLIDAYS on page 325 and EVENTS in the individual entries. Apart from religious and folk festivals, many of the dates below will change from one year to another, so check with local tourist offices.

JANUARY
Avignon: Horse festival.
Cannes: MIDEM — International Record and Music Publishing Fair.
Monte-Carlo: Automobile Rally.

FEBRUARY
Avignon: Dance festival.
Menton: Lemon festival.
Nice: Carnival (two weeks preceding Lent).
Villefranche-sur-Mer: Antique fair.

MARCH
Antibes: Festival of *café-théâtre*.
Cagnes-sur-Mer: International flower show.
Grasse: Carnival.
Vaison-la-Romaine: Regional automobile rally.

APRIL

Antibes: Antique fair.
Arles: Bullfight festival (Easter Friday to Monday).
Brignoles: Wine fair (first two weeks).
Cannes: MIP-TV television market and festival.
Marseille: Trade fair (early April).
Monte-Carlo: International Tennis Championships.
Mougins: Professional Golf Open.
Nice: Marathon.
Roquebrune: Procession of the Passion (Good Friday).

MAY

Arles: Fête of Camargue *gardians* (May 1).
Beaulieu-sur-Mer: Boat show.
Cannes: Film Festival.
Monaco: Automobile Grand Prix (Formula One).
Nîmes: Feria de Pentecôte — bullfights, folklore events, concerts, etc. (five days of Whit weekend).
St-Tropez: *Bravade*— folk festival (May 16–18).
Les Saintes-Maries: Pèlerinage des Gitanes — gypsy celebration (May 23–27).

JUNE

Cannes: International advertising film festival.
Nice: Sacred music festival.
Nîmes: Music in the Arènes.
Roquebrune-Cap-Martin: Theater festival.
St-Tropez: Spanish *bravade* — folk festival.
Signes: Fête de St-Eloi (Sunday nearest to June 24).
Tarascon: Fête de la Tarasque (last Sunday).

JULY

Everywhere: July 14 is Bastille Day, a French national holiday — parades, street dancing, fireworks.
Aix-en-Provence: International opera and music festival (mid-July to early August). • Dance festival (early July).
Apt: Pilgrimage of Ste-Anne (last Sunday).
Arles: International photography festival. • Festival of music, dance and drama.
Avignon: International drama festival (last three weeks).
Beaucaire: Fête of the Fair (end July to early August).
Cap d'Antibes: Religious procession (first Sunday).
Juan-les-Pins: Jazz festival.
Marseille: Folklore festival.
Martigues: Venetian festival on canals (first Saturday).
Monaco: Firework festival.
Nice: Grand Jazz Parade (festival). • International folk festival.
 • International track and field (athletics) meeting.
Nîmes: Jazz festival. • Gypsy festival.

Orange: International music festival (last two weeks).
La Ste-Baume: Midnight Mass (July 22).
Sisteron: Theater and music festival (mid-July to mid-August).
Vaison-la-Romaine: Theater and music festival (mid-July to mid-August). • Folklore festival in July.
Vence: Music festival.
Villeneuve-lès-Avignon: Summer arts festival.

AUGUST
Antibes: Music festival.
Avignon: Jousting tournament on the Rhône.
Cagnes-sur-Mer: World *boules* championship.
Entrevaux: Two-week music festival.
Menton: Chamber music festival (first two weeks).
Roquebrune: Procession of the Passion (August 5).
Vaison-la-Romaine: Provençal festival.

SEPTEMBER
Cannes: Regatta (last two weeks).
Marseille: Trade fair.
Nîmes: Bullfights (third week).
St-Tropez: Nioulargue yacht race (last week).

OCTOBER
Antibes: Underwater film/photography festival.
Cannes: MIPCOM international communications market.
Monaco: Symphony concert season.
Les Saintes-Maries: Fête of St Mary Salome (weekend nearest October 22).

NOVEMBER
Antibes: Military film festival.
Monaco: Monegasque national holiday (November 19) and fête.

DECEMBER
Antibes: Mountain film/photography festival.
Bandol: Wine festival (first Sunday).
Les Baux: Fête of the Shepherds (December 24). • Christmas Eve Midnight Mass.
Cannes: Antique fair.
Marseille: Fair of *santons* (last two weeks).
Séguret: Christmas Eve Midnight Mass. • Provençal mystery play.

Choosing and reserving accommodation

For advice on choosing and reserving your hotel before you travel to the region, turn to the first section of the next chapter.

The daily necessities

Accommodation

WHERE TO STAY

Hotels range from the ultra-luxurious palaces that line the smart promenades of the Riviera to the functional urban hotels of the kind that are found all over France, comfortable but with no special ambience, to be used purely as a convenient base. In between are the traditional country inns *(auberges)*, many simple, some extremely plush. Owners of small hotels in France take their role seriously, and it is commonplace to find that what was once a simple inn has gradually grown, improving its amenities, its food and its star-rating, and increasing its prices to match.

Suitable more for an overnight stay than a vacation, but excellent none the less, are the recently built chains of utility hotels, usually located along the main roads or on the outskirts of towns. Although some are more enticing than others, they are all reliable. The principal hotel chains are **Altea** (▥), **Ibis** (▢ to ▥), **Mercure** (▥), **Novotel** (▥) and **Sofitel** (▥).

Many privately owned hotels have grouped themselves into associations for joint promotion, and are of comparable quality, submitting to mutual inspection. The most reliable are **Logis de France** (▢ to ▥), in the country or in small towns, and **Relais et Châteaux** (▥ to ▥), which is mainly rural.

See also CAMPING AND CARAVAN (TRAILER) VACATIONS on page 56.

RESERVATIONS

In season (Easter, and mid-June to mid-September), it is essential to reserve well ahead at the better vacation hotels. In July and August, if you try to tour without prior reservations, you may end up spending the night in the car or on the beach. Out of season, things are easier, but many vacation hotels, on the coast and in rural areas, tend to close from about November to March. Other hotels reopen for the period around Christmas and New Year, as many French people choose to celebrate the festive season in a hotel.

PRICES

These tend to be highest in stylish resorts such as Cannes and Monte-Carlo, and lowest in the hinterland. The apparent price category of a hotel can be deceptive, for most hotels have a choice of bedrooms of different kinds across a wide price range; under the same roof, you can pay three times as much for a large room with balcony facing the sea as for a small one at the back with no bath. So, when making reservations, specify the kind of room you want, and then check the price.

You will be charged for the room rather than per head. Thus two people occupying one room pay only slightly more than one person, especially if the room has a double bed, as is usual, rather than twin beds. Beware, also, of large seasonal differences, particularly in coastal resorts. These are nowhere more marked than on the eastern Côte d'Azur, especially in Monaco, when prices rocket during the Grand Prix, and in Cannes during the film festival.

COMFORT

Thanks to the strict national rating system (ranging from 1-star for the most modest hotels to 4-star for first-class hotels, and 4-star-Luxe for the grandest), standards of comfort in French hotels have greatly improved in the past 25 years, and the days of primitive French plumbing are long gone. Even our cheapest recommendations have at least some rooms with bath or shower. And if you want to economize by foregoing this amenity, you will always find a communal bathroom down the corridor.

Pillows may at first present a problem, for many hotels provide the traditional French bolster *(traversin)*. But, if you ask, the hotel will usually supply a softer square or rectangular-shaped pillow *(oreiller)*.

If in doubt about how to choose your hotel, you will be safest, in terms of both comfort and budget, in a 3-star hotel.

MEALS IN HOTELS

Especially in country areas, food in hotels tends to be every bit as good as in restaurants; in many cases, the *patron* of an *auberge* sees himself foremost as a restaurateur and only secondly as a hotelier. In season, particularly in small towns or isolated areas, some vacation hotels require residents to take at least one main meal a day *(demi-pension)*, if not both *(pension complète)*. It is wise to check this beforehand, especially if you intend to have a culinary spree and eat out frequently. The *menu pension* included in these terms may well be simpler, and with less choice, than the hotel's more elaborate menus, but for an extra payment you can order special dishes.

The French tend to be rather frugal when it comes to breakfast; most hotels provide just coffee, bread, *croissants* and small prepacked portions of butter and jam. Fruit juice or a boiled egg will come if you ask, but you must pay extra. In the smartest hotels, of course, you can have anything you like — but at a price. A few more modern hotels are moving over to a Dutch-style cafeteria buffet-breakfast with cold meat, cheese, cereals and fruit, but this is still rare.

VOCABULARY

For useful words and phrases to be used when reserving ahead or when staying in a hotel, and including a sample reservation letter, see the WORDS AND PHRASES chapter at the end of the book.

UNDERSTANDING OUR HOTEL ENTRIES

- Look for the ✿ symbol throughout the book.
- **Symbols:** The symbols show price categories and credit cards, as well as giving a résumé of available facilities. See the KEY TO SYMBOLS on page 7 for an explanation of the full list.
- **Prices:** The price categories given for each hotel are intended as a rough guide to what you can expect to pay, and are **based on average charges for two people staying in a double room with bathroom/ shower, inclusive of Value-Added Tax** (*TVA* in French). Charges for one person are not much cheaper. Breakfast is usually charged extra, and can cost between 40–100 francs.

Although actual prices will inevitably increase, our relative price categories are likely to remain the same.

Symbol	Category	Current price
▥	very expensive	more than 1,500 francs
▥	expensive	700–1,500 francs
▥	moderate	400–700 francs
▥	inexpensive	200–400 francs
▢	cheap	under 200 francs

Eating and drinking

Of France's great regional cooking styles, *cuisine provençale* is probably the one with the strongest personality. It is a spicy, Mediterranean cuisine of bold, clean flavors, leaning heavily on garlic, on local herbs such as thyme, basil and fennel, and on olive oil, which generally replaces butter in cooking. Garlic enhances the natural flavors of the food, but is used so carefully that it rarely leaves any unpleasant mark.

The cooking is wonderfully varied — a blend of the traditions of mountain people and fisher folk, as befits an area where the Alps sweep down to the sea. In a region richly endowed by nature, it draws lavishly on local produce: fish of all kinds, game from the hinterland, lamb, and an abundance of fresh fruit and vegetables in season, for Provence is France's foremost market garden. Artichokes, asparagus, eggplant and tomatoes are especially delicious.

Not least because of an influx in recent years of Italian tourists, there has been an increasing Italian influence on the Provençal cooking in many restaurants, particularly the use of pasta. This has always been true east of Nice, but the trend has spread westward.

SOME TYPICAL DISHES

As an appetizer, a meal might begin with *tapenade,* a purée of chopped black olives and anchovies. Starters include a range of salads and *crudités,* the commonest being *salade niçoise,* a rich mixture of eggs, olives, anchovies and tomatoes.

At lunch some restaurants offer a cafeteria-style buffet of spicy *hors d'oeuvres;* others bring a basket of crispy raw vegetables with mustard and vinaigrette dips. The best soups are *pistou,* a thick vegetable soup with a paste of garlic and basil, and the ubiquitous *soupe de poissons,* made from a pungent stock of many fish including shellfish, and served with toast crusts, grated cheese and *rouille,* a strong garlic sauce. At its best, probably in some unpretentious bistro near the fishing boats, it can be superb.

On and near the coast, fish holds pride of place. *Bouillabaisse,* star of the Provençal kitchen, is a garlicky stew made from various rock- and shellfish; *rascasse,* a spiky fish unique to this part of the Mediterranean, is the essential ingredient — as is saffron. The delicate taste depends on the right combination of fish, and on the amalgamation of oil and water by correct boiling. The result looks alarming, as the fish in their orange, saffron-flavored stew are gruesomely cadaverous, and the strong taste might scare the novice, although he will soon succumb to its spell.

The true home of *bouillabaisse* is MARSEILLE (see page 115), but you can find it elsewhere. It usually needs to be ordered in advance, for very few restaurants keep it on their daily *carte,* so hard is it to prepare. Be warned: it is very expensive, as are many other of the best fish dishes, such as *bourride,* a simpler garlic stew made with white fish, and *loup au fenouil,* sea bass grilled with fennel.

Cheaper fish are *rouget* (red mullet), now a staple on many menus, and *daurade* (John Dory), usually cooked richly with tomatoes and herbs; inland you can find trout and *écrevisses* (crayfish), the latter often in a rich sauce. To tackle this dish, you are usually swathed by the waiter in a white napkin to catch the drips. At least once you must try *aïoli,* a garlic mayonnaise, whose very name sends the Provençaux into fits of lyricism (the poet Mistral once founded a local newspaper called *L'Aïoli*). It often forms the main dish at village feasts, and is served either as a sauce, with boiled cod and vegetables, or pounded into a *purée* with the cod, when it is called *brandade de morue.*

VOCABULARY

For a 7-page **food and drink vocabulary and menu guide**, plus a section on Provençal words, see the WORDS AND PHRASES chapter at the end of the book.

NOUVELLE CUISINE

Although the true *cuisine bourgeoise* of Provence is still the norm in most restaurants, a number of more ambitious or modish places have continued, in recent years, to be influenced by the vogue for *nouvelle cuisine,* which has swept France since the 1960s. It is characterized by a move to a lighter, purer manner, spurning most heavy sauces and relying on very fresh ingredients, rapidly cooked in their own juices, almost in the Chinese manner, to bring out their full flavors; vegetables are served crispy, half-cooked. The chef is encouraged to deviate from classic recipes and try out daring new blends.

In the wrong hands, the results can be absurd, with ridiculous combinations of ingredients and niggardly portions. But France's best modern chefs have worked wonders with *nouvelle cuisine,* and some of its leading exponents are in the region: notably Roger Vergé at MOUGINS, Louis Outhier at LA NAPOULE and Jacques Maximin, formerly in Nice, now in JUAN-LES-PINS. These chefs are true masters, and at their restaurants you will sample marvelously inspired food using the local produce of the region. In fact, while some of Provence's grandest restaurants stick within the classic repertoire, a majority today flirt with *nouvelle cuisine,* which is almost always expensive; you will not find it in a modest *auberge.*

Nouvelle cuisine is not so much a break with the classic tradition as an adaptation of it, to suit a calorie-conscious age, and one that demands purity and requires first-class ingredients to speak for themselves. Similarly, it is not so much turning its back on regional cuisine as seeking to re-explore it. Thus, in Provence, many of the best chefs are using traditional Provençal dishes as a basis for their own innovations — and the results, at their best, are a subtle blend of the old and the new. They give their dishes long and complex names, and are constantly changing their menus or adding new inventions: so the specialities we quote for restaurants can be no more than a rough guide.

THE CELEBRITY CHEF
Many top chefs in the region have been experimenting with the use of spices and Oriental cooking methods, to add further interest to familiar local ingredients. They are often very successful with these culturally hybrid dishes, but, once again, their less talented imitators are to be avoided.

The *patron* or his staff will usually be eager to unravel for you the mysteries of his baffling bill of fare, and in many restaurants the chef himself will make an appearance to ask you if you liked your meal. Chefs in France have long enjoyed a celebrity only now being accorded to their American or British counterparts and, with France's tradition of gastronomy, it is perfectly possible to find a complete social mix among the clients of even the grandest restaurants — from blue-collar workers to millionaires — all making pilgrimages to gastronomic shrines.

LOCAL VARIATIONS
In **the hinterland**, meat predominates. Here you will find *agneau de Sisteron:* lamb whose aromatic flavor comes from grazing on wild herbs on upland pastures. Like beef, it is often served grilled on a wood fire, with more herbs sprinkled on it. Rabbit *(lapin)* is common, cooked either in a mustard sauce or *à la provençale* (in a tomato and garlic sauce); chicken and frogs' legs also come *à la provençale.* In winter, wild game is prepared in dozens of ways — try *civet de lièvre* (jugged hare), *pâté de grives* (thrush pâté) or *sanglier* (wild boar).

And all year, as in other French country areas, you will find meat stewed deliciously in red wine and herbs, such as *boeuf en daube* or (in the Camargue area) *boeuf gardianne.* But beware of the fact that Provençal beef in general, particularly when not stewed, is not of high quality. The best restaurants obtain their meat from Burgundy or Lyons, or even Scotland. Arles is famous for its salami-style sausages, while Marseille offers *pieds et paquets,* a kind of tripe, which can be an acquired taste. Truffles, too, when in season (which ends in March), are an important feature of Provençal cuisine.

Within the Provençal tradition, **the Nice area** has its own distinctive cuisine. It is closer to the Italian style, reflecting the town's former association with Italy. Many of its special dishes are served, like pasta, as starters: *anchoiade* (anchovy tart), *pissaladière* (a kind of pizza), *socca* (a pancake of ground chick peas), *tian* (a grill of rice, vegetables and grated cheese), and *ravioli,* more delicate than the Italian kind. *Mesclun* is a dressed salad of coarse lettuce and dandelion. And *ratatouille* (a stew of eggplant, peppers and other vegetables in olive oil) is a local dish which — like *salade niçoise* and *soupe au pistou* — has spread far beyond the Nice area.

Provence's **cheeses** are few, and not among France's greatest, but pleasant in their way. They are often, as *chèvre,* made from goat's milk. Try *cachat,* made from sheep's milk and often marinated in brandy and herbs, or *banon,* soaked in wine and wrapped in chestnut leaves.

Desserts, except in some luxury restaurants, lack imagination or finesse; but fresh fruit is plentiful in season — notably the sweet pink melons of Cavaillon, the sweet green figs of the Marseille area, and local cherries, peaches and grapes. Apt is known for its crystallized fruits, and Aix for its *calissons* (tiny almond cakes).

In the restaurant

Generally it is less expensive to choose a fixed-price menu than to eat *à la carte,* where exactly the same dishes can cost twice as much. In provincial restaurants, much more than in Paris, the French still expect to eat a *prix-fixe* meal of four or even five courses; the only exceptions are in modern downtown brasseries or snack bars or, at the other end of the spectrum, in some luxury restaurants where special dishes are often only to be found on the *carte.*

WHEN AND WHERE TO EAT
You will often find, in both hotels and restaurants, including the grandest, that set menus at lunchtime are bargains compared with the evening. So, if you want to eat at a serious or celebrated restaurant and your budget is limited, go there for lunch.

It is an unfortunate fact of French life that, over the last few years, many small, family-run restaurants, once one of the joys of eating in Provence, have lowered their standards and raised their prices. However, it is still possible to have a good meal at a very reasonable price if you know where to go.

If in doubt, go where the local people go with their families. If a restaurant is full of people from the town or village, there is usually a good reason — even if you don't find it listed in this guide or any other. It is extremely common in France to eat *en famille,* particularly on

Sunday lunchtime, so try to reserve ahead, as any good restaurant in a small town or village is certain to be full for Sunday lunch.

Although southerners, the *Provençaux* tend to lunch early, unlike the Spaniards. Service begins at noon or so, and in most places ends at 2pm. As for dinner, many places in large resorts are open till midnight, although many rural restaurants stop serving as early as 9pm. Most restaurants have space for eating outdoors (look for the 🍴 symbol throughout this book), but at the first breath of a cold wind they will close their terraces or gardens and make you eat indoors.

THE MENU

The most noticeable difference on a French menu is that cheese is eaten before dessert. Meat is not smothered indiscriminately with several vegetables in the Anglo-Saxon manner, but is usually served with just one vegetable, selected by the chef to give his dish the right balance of tastes. If you want another vegetable, it will come later as a separate course. As for steak, the French prefer to eat it rare *(saignant)* or semi-rare *(à point),* and a serious restaurateur may even refuse to serve a "barbarian" who insults him by asking for it well done *(bien cuit).*

Restaurants generally display their menus outside, and may offer three or four different *prix-fixes,* varying greatly in price. No one will mind if you order the lowest; on the other hand, the best specialities (notably fish) may well only be on the highest. For an inexpensive, light snack, there are plenty of pizzerias and *crêperies,* while most larger cafés serve simple hot snacks such as *croque-monsieur* (toasted cheese) or *un sandwich* (half a *baguette* filled with cheese, pâté, ham or salami).

UNDERSTANDING OUR RESTAURANT ENTRIES

- Look for the ▬ symbol throughout the book.
- **Symbols:** The symbols show price categories and credit cards. See the KEY TO SYMBOLS on page 7 for an explanation of the full list.
- **Times:** Times are specified when restaurants are **closed**, but it is always best to check ahead.
- **Prices:** The price categories given for each restaurant are intended as a rough guide to what you can expect to pay, **based on the approximate cost of a meal for one person, inclusive of wine, Value-Added Tax** (*TVA* in French) **and service**.

Although actual prices will inevitably increase, our relative price categories are likely to remain the same.

Symbol	Category	Current price
▨	very expensive	more than 500 francs
▨	expensive	300–500 francs
▨	moderate	150–300 francs
▨	inexpensive	100–150 francs
▢	cheap	under 100 francs

What to drink

Although the region has few great wines compared with Burgundy or Bordeaux, there is a fine variety, and nearly all local wines are palatable.

In the Rhône valley, **Châteauneuf-du-Pape** red wine is warm, long-lived and full-bodied. The white is heavy: at best rich, almost sweet. Some of the nearby **Côtes-du-Rhône** are excellent too, notably the strong red **Gigondas** and **Vacqueyras**. From the same area comes the famous **Muscat de Beaumes-de-Venise**, a sweet and very pleasant fortified dessert wine, also drunk as an aperitif.

Tavel, NW of Avignon, produces a strong, dry rosé, although it is rather expensive; cheaper and lighter is **Listel** *gris-de-gris,* a cloudy rosé from vines growing on sand near the sea s of Nîmes. From the Nîmes area itself come the very drinkable and reasonably priced **Costière de Nîmes** wines.

From the area E of Marseille come two fruity reds, **Bandol** (try the excellent although expensive **Château Pibarnon**) and **Château Simone**, as well as the dry white wine of **Cassis**, ideal for drinking with shellfish or *bouillabaisse.* The area also produces light, fruity rosés.

To the N and E of Toulon is the steadily improving **Côtes-de-Provence** sector. Labels to look for here are **Pierrefeu**, **Château Minuty**, **Belieu**, **Château de Rasque** and **Château Barbeyrolles**, while **Ott** is a prolific but reliable grower. The hill slopes of Nice itself produce **Bellet**, a rare, select and fashionable wine, which comes as red, rosé or white. The white is dry, and goes well with shellfish.

Wine from the **Lubéron**, and the **Côtes-du-Ventoux** area near Carpentras, is also very acceptable: heady reds and decent rosés, although the whites are somewhat less successful, a problem with Provençal wines generally. The wines labeled **Coteaux d'Aix-en-Provence** are also improving, and some of them are organically produced.

Remember that although you can buy a perfectly reasonable bottle of local wine for a very few francs in a shop, the markup in a restaurant can often be outrageous, and better known non-Provençal wines will be much more expensive. In order to pick a good bottle at a fair price, it is wise to know something of the classification of French wines.

The four classifications of wines are *Appellation Contrôlée,* VDQS *(Vin Delimité de Qualité Supérieure), Vin de Pays* and *Vin de Table.* None of these is a guarantee of quality: they simply mean that each category must conform to certain criteria of origin, vinification and grape variety. The criteria are more strict for *Appellation Contrôlée* than VDQS, and so on down the scale, and prices reflect this. Good value, however, can be found in each category. House wines in most reputable restaurants are rarely less than acceptable, and usually much cheaper than the next couple of wines on the list.

The reputation of the grower, château or *négociant* (wine merchant) is another very important criterion, particularly with Burgundies. If a name is not familiar, it is often wiser to choose according to the year, because a good vintage VDQS can often be of better quality, and value, than a mediocre vintage of an *Appellation Contrôlée.* Most wine in the lower categories is blended by the shippers and does not carry vintage dates.

Vin de Table is commonly served in carafes or jugs called *pichets.* It is a simple matter to order a small *pichet,* then a second if it is good.

Apart from buying wine from shops and supermarkets, you can purchase from *Vinicoles,* where different wines are blended. A *cubitaine* is usually good value from one of these co-operatives. The sign *vente au détail* at vineyards means you can purchase the château-bottled wine retailed at source.

Among aperitifs, by far the most popular local drink is *pastis,* aniseed-flavored, not unlike the *ouzo* of Greece. It is drunk chilled with ice and diluted with water, which makes it go cloudy, and on a hot day it is most refreshing — as well as being heady stuff. **Ricard** and **'51** are both dry; their rival **Pernod** is sweeter. It is fashionable to mix pastis with syrups *(sirop),* resulting in such concoctions as *perroquet* (with mint), *tomate* (with grenadine) and *mauresque* (with almond and orange syrup).

If you want to drink beer, it is almost always cheaper to drink French brands (such as **Kronenbourg**) than imported ones. The cheapest is draft beer. Ask for *un pression* or *un demi* ($\frac{1}{3}$ liter).

Shopping

As befits France's affluent society, every main town of Provence has modern stores, to meet all daily needs. In some resorts, such as Cannes, the boutiques are among the smartest in Europe. See PRACTICAL INFORMATION on page 325 for shopping hours.

WHAT TO BUY

The main **regional specialities** are ceramics, glasswork, olive-wood sculpture, silk-painting, weaving, and *santons.*

Villages with boutiques specializing in such products include the following. Place names in SMALL CAPITALS have their own entry. To find entries for other places, use the INDEX.

BIOT Pottery, glassware	GORDES Stained glass
CABRIS Olive-wood sculpture, *santons*	**Moustiers-Ste-Marie** *Faience*
La Cadière-d'Azur Pottery, weaving	ST-PAUL-DE-VENCE Murals
	SALERNES Enamel tiles
COARAZE Enamel sundials	**Seillans** Pottery
Cogolin Carpets, furniture, pipes	SOSPEL Olive-wood sculpture
	TOURETTES-SUR-LOUP Ceramics, silk-painting, puppets, etc.
ÈZE Jewelry, ironwork	VALLAURIS Pottery

Many boutiques in the towns, too, sell the output of the villages, but often at higher prices. In the area around LES BAUX and ST-RÉMY you will find some of the best **olive oil** not only in Provence, but the whole of France.

Provençal fabrics make a memorable buy. Provence is the home of

Souleiado (Provençal for sunbeam), a company founded in the 1930s to revive the widespread 17thC style of printing on calico using pear tree wood blocks. The traditional *Indiennage* patterns were, as the name suggests, originally Indian-inspired. Souleiado fabrics are available throughout Provence, although the company's base, and museum, is at TARASCON. A rival company, **Les Olivades**, is based near ST-RÉMY.

If you are tempted to buy **clothes**, the international differences in clothing sizes can be confusing. Refer to the useful **clothing sizes chart** near the end of the book.

WHERE TO BUY
Hypermarkets   More than any other European country, France has followed the American model of giant superstores on the outskirts of towns. The French call them *hypermarchés*. The range of goods is wide, with seductively lavish food counters. All have free parking lots, and many stay open till 10pm. **Carrefour**, **Leclerc** and **Casino** are the leading chains in Provence.

There is one absurdity, however. Because of the central buying systems of large chains, you will often find produce from other regions of France, or even from abroad, when the local produce on sale in open-air markets is markedly superior.

Open-air markets   Markets are a lively aspect of the local daily scene. Almost every town, large or small, has its outdoor market in some shaded square or avenue, where farmers come in to sell their produce. Some markets are open daily, some weekly (mainly on Saturday); most operate in the mornings only. Their food is often fresher and a little cheaper than in the shops. Prices are marked, and bargaining will rarely bring dividends.

Some markets, such as the ones at L'ÎSLE-SUR-LA-SORGUE, CARPENTRAS and ARLES (and even in villages such as Bédoin), are real events, with a festive air and a huge variety of produce — with perhaps twenty types of olives, and dozens of other local specialities. They are also fine places for picking up snacks or food for a picnic.

SHOPPING VOCABULARY
It is essential to communicate clearly when you're shopping. Turn to WORDS AND PHRASES at the end of the book, for a host of typical words, questions, responses and requests in French and English.

Family leisure activities and sports

The French are an energetic, sport-loving nation, and Provence is especially well organized for most sports. The majority of clubs accept temporary members, while many resorts run courses for beginners. For details ask at the local tourist office.

BICYCLING
Bicycles can be rented by the hour, day or week. Ask at the **Gare SNCF** at Antibes, Cannes, Juan-les-Pins, Aix and Avignon. In Nice, try **Deux Roues Location**, and in Monte-Carlo **Autos-Motos-Garage**.

BOULES
Boules (and its local variant *pétanque*) is a very popular traditional game all over France, especially in the s (see page 24). It is played with small metal balls on an earth court. You'll see the locals playing it intently in every dusty village square.

Why not set up your own game? A set of *boules* is not expensive, and the rules are simple. First throw the small ball (called the *cochonnet* or little pig). Divide into teams. There are three pairs of balls in a set, and the aim is for one team to finish nearest to the *cochonnet*. Touching it, or even displacing it, is allowed. Play continues with the small ball in its new position.

BULLFIGHTS
Real bullfights (where the bulls are killed) take place in NÎMES and ARLES. The bulls and matadors come from Spain, although most of the toreadors are local. There are also less lethal *courses à la cocarde,* where amateur toreadors compete to snatch rosettes from the animals' horns.

CASINOS
The "sport of kings" is today democratized (and some would say debased). American games are almost as common as continental ones, bringing more than a touch of Las Vegas. Provence's best casinos are at ANTIBES, CASSIS, CANNES, JUAN-LES-PINS and NICE.

MONTE-CARLO, however, is still the liveliest gambling center in the South of France. Casinos are obliged by law to provide a high standard of entertainment and dining and are open year round, except public holidays. You must be over 21 and must produce a passport or identity card.

CHILDREN
Hotels in France rarely make special provision for children (though some have reduced rates). Children are expected to take all meals with their parents and to eat the same food. But most hotels have a number of large bedrooms with several beds, and you can economize by sharing.

The French have a typically Latin love of small children — tiny tots are welcome even in the smartest restaurants. Some hotels have children's playgrounds, ping pong, etc. A few hotels and beach lidos (ANTIBES, MONTE-CARLO) employ trained *moniteurs* to take charge of small children.

FISHING

Plenty of scope in the numerous rivers and lakes — mostly trout, also carp and perch (a permit is needed). Contact the local tourist office or the **Fédération Départementale des Associations de Pêche** *(34 av. St-Augustin, 06000 Nice ☎ 93-72-06-04).*

GARDENS

There are *jardins exotiques* with fine collections of Mediterranean and tropical plants at ÈZE, HYÈRES, MENTON, MONACO and CAP D'ANTIBES.

GOLF

There are numerous clubs — the best are at MONTE-CARLO, CANNES, **Valescure** (ST-RAPHAEL), and the area between AIX and MARSEILLE.

There are no fewer than 14 golf courses in the Var, now the center of golf in Provence. There are courses in the **Massif Esterel**, and at STE-MAXIME, LE LAVANDOU, BANDOL, **Nans-les-Pins**, **Roquebrune-sur-Argens** and near BRIGNOLES. Inquire at the local tourist office for full information.

SKIING

Most people think of the Côte d'Azur in connection with sun, sea and sand. But in early spring it is quite possible to be sunning oneself on the beach at Nice, and an hour later to be skiing high in the mountains. There are several small ski stations in the Nice hinterland, but the three best resorts are at AURON, ISOLA 2000 and VALBERG. All have extensive *pistes* and lifts and ski schools, with provision for children. Skiing equipment can be bought or rented on the spot.

SWIMMING

There are beaches for swimming all along the coast. But remember that they are only sandy to the w of Antibes: the coast E from Antibes to Italy is gravel, apart from some coarse imported sand at Menton and Monte-Carlo. A recent campaign against pollution has produced results. Only in the industrial zones w of Marseille and in some pockets between Nice and Menton do beaches tend to be dirty. Most smart hotels, however, have swimming pools (some heated), while every town has its *piscine municipale.*

Beaches are usually free, apart from the fashionable ones at St-Tropez, Cannes, Nice and Monte-Carlo. Some of the more exclusive hotels have private beaches. As for dress (or, rather, nondress), topless bathing is now universally accepted — indeed, it is the norm.

TENNIS

Many better hotels have their own courts, but tennis clubs and public courts are numerous. All courts are hard. The **Monte-Carlo Country Club** and the **Tennis École** at VILLENEUVE-LOUBET organize tennis courses.

WALKING AND RAMBLING

Many tourist offices in the Alpes-Maritimes organize summer excursions into the mountains (SOSPEL, ST-ÉTIENNE-DE-TINÉE, ST-MARTIN-VÉSUBIE and St-Laurent-du-Var). For further information contact the **Fédération Française de Randonnées Pédestres** *(8 av. Marceau, 75008 Paris* ☎ *(1) 47-23-62-32)* and the **Club Alpin Français** *(15 av. Jean Médecin, 06000 Nice* ☎ *93-87-95-41)*.

WATER SPORTS

Sailing, waterskiing and wind surfing are available at all main resorts, scuba diving and underwater fishing at some, parascending at major ones. Ask at the local tourist office.

There are good marinas and seaport centers at **Port-Camargue**, **Bendor** and **Embiez islands** (see BANDOL), PORT-GRIMAUD, LA NAPOULE, CANNES and MONTE-CARLO.

For information about sailing schools, contact the **Centre d'Informations Jeunesse Nice-Côte d'Azur** *(Espl. des Victoires, 06000 Nice* ☎ *93-80-93-9)*.

ZOOS AND DOLPHINARIUMS

ANTIBES has a marine park, and BANDOL, MONACO, ST-JEAN-CAP-FERRAT, TOULON and MARSEILLE have zoos. The CAMARGUE has a nature reserve (open only to authorized visitors), and FRÉJUS has two safari parks.

Camping and caravan (trailer) vacations

CAMPING

All official camp sites in France are graded with one, two, three or four stars according to regulations laid down by the government. Prices in three- and four-star categories are not standardized.

In this part of France, prices vary enormously, depending on how close the site is to the coast. In high season, camp sites nearer the coast resemble high-class refugee camps rather than vacation centers, with thousands of people milling among hundreds of closely-pitched tents. Lower prices, peace and quiet and the beautiful countryside are the advantages of camping in the hinterland.

All those sites listed in the following pages (alphabetically by town, with the name of the site and postal code following) are in the three- or four-star category and will be an enclosed area, marked out in pitches *(emplacements)* and guarded 24 hours a day. There will be a communal area with washing facilities, often including a restaurant and/or shop. Many camp sites have excellent sports and other facilities.

The French Government Tourist Office *(international addresses on page 318)* will supply you with a list of sites recommended by the **TCF (Touring Club de France)**. Many camp sites require reservation in advance, although for those sites run by the TCF, this is only possible if you are a member of their club or affiliated to it.

For camping on farmland, contact the **Fédération Nationale des Gîtes Ruraux de France** *(35 rue Godot-de-Mauroy, 75009 Paris* ☎ *(1) 49-70-75-75)*.

For forest camping, contact the **Office National des Forêts**; ask at the local **Syndicat d'Initiative** for the address. You must be able to produce an insurance certificate or camping permit.

CARAVANS (TRAILERS)

Bringing a caravan into France may be accomplished without formality unless you plan to stay for more than six months. However, certain traffic rules must be complied with:

- You must have an adequate rear-view mirror.
- You must maintain a distance of at least 50 meters (55 yards) between yourself and the car ahead.
- You may not drive through Paris while towing a caravan.
- You may not travel in the fast lane on the autoroute.
- If the towed weight is more than 30 percent greater than the weight of the towing vehicle, a limit of 45kph (28mph) must be observed. You must also display a plate indicating this on the back of the caravan.
- For further information, contact the **French Government Tourist Office** *(see international addresses on page 318)* or your camping club.

AGAY (Var)
Esterel Caravaning, 83700 St-Raphael. Map 13G13 ☎94-44-03-28 ⇌ ⋘ ♨ ⛵
Closed Oct–Easter.
A small, quiet camp site for caravans only, 4km ($2\frac{1}{2}$ miles) NW of Agay and close to the sea. There are a number of other camp sites nearby.

AIX-EN-PROVENCE (B.-du-R.)
Chantecler, 13100. Map 10G7
☎42-26-12-98 ⇌ ⋘
Large, well-shaded camp site, 3km (2 miles) SE of Aix, with caravans to rent. A library, organized entertainments for adults and games for children are available.

AVIGNON (Vaucluse)
Pont St-Bénézet, Île de la Barthelasse, 84000. Map 9D4 ☎90-82-63-50 ⇌ *in summer* ⛅ ⋘
A large and shady site on the Île de la Barthelasse, affording a superb view of the Palais des Papes. Additional sports are available nearby in the town itself.

CAGNES-SUR-MER (Alpes-Mar.)
Camping de l'Oasis, av. de Grasse, 06800. Map 15F15 ☎93-20-75-67 ⋘
A well-run camp site, away from the sea but equipped with a swimming pool.

CAVALIÈRE (Var)
Les Mimosas, 83980 Le Lavandou. Map 13I12 ☎94-05-82-94 ⇌ *Closed early Oct to Easter.*
This quiet, shady camp site near the sea is open to caravans only, and it is essential to reserve ahead.

CHÂTEAU-ARNOUX (Alpes-du-H.-P.)
Les Salettes, 04160. Map 7C10
☎92-64-02-40 ⛅ ⋘ ➤
A comfortable, well-equipped camp site run by the TCF and only 1km ($\frac{1}{2}$ mile) from a lake where you can sail and fish.

GIENS (Var)
La Presqu'île, 83400 Hyères. Map 12I10
☎94-58-22-86 ⇌ ⛅ *Closed Oct–Mar.*
A small, well-shaded camp site where you can rent tents and caravans. Swimming pool and riding facilities nearby. Although close to the sea, Giens is not quite as frenetic as the rest of the coast in summer.

GRASSE (Alpes-Mar.)
Caravan-Inn, 06650 Le Rouret. Map 15F14
☎93-77-32-00 ⇌ ⋘ ♨ *Closed Nov.*
A small and attractive shady site for caravans, only 8km (5 miles) E of Grasse at Opio, within easy reach of Cannes yet providing a peaceful retreat from the

bustle. Booking is advised in high summer. Games provided for children.

GRIMAUD (Var)
Camping-Caravaning A-C.F., St Pons-les-Mures, 83310 Cogolin. Map 13H12
☎94-56-34-71 ═ ≪ ≋ ✿ *Closed Dec.*
An attractive and comfortable site 6km (3¼ miles) E of Grimaud and very close to the sea. Entertainments are provided for both children and adults, and sports include riding, sailing and swimming.

LE LAVANDOU (Var)
Le Domaine, 83230 Bormes-les-Mimosas. Map 12I11 ☎94-71-03-12 ═ ℘
Closed Nov–Mar.
A vast site able to accommodate 1,200 caravans or tents, yet has surprisingly few facilities for its size. However, the site is alongside the beach, and swimming is one of the attractions.

MANDELIEU-LA NAPOULE (Alpes-Mar.)
Les Cigales, 06210. Map 15G14
☎93-49-23-53 ᚼ ✿
The appearance of this pretty site rates higher than its facilities, making it a good base for a vacation if you are prepared to seek out your own entertainment. Caravans can be rented. It is advisable to reserve in high summer.

MAUSSANE-LES-ALPILLES (B.-du-R.)
Les Romarins, 13520. Map 9E4
☎90-97-33-60 ᚼ ℘ *Closed Oct to mid-Mar.*
A small, quiet camp site with modern facilities. A popular hinterland site where reservation is recommended.

ST-PAUL-EN-FORÊT (Var)
Le Parc, 83440 Fayence. Map 13F13
☎94-76-15-35 ═ ≋ ℘
A small and peaceful site in an attractive setting. Caravans and bungalows are available for rent.

ST-RAPHAEL (Var)
Douce Quiétude, 83700. Map 13G13
☎94-95-55-50 ᚼ ≋ ℘ *Closed Oct–Mar.*
As its name suggests, this camp site, set in an attractive wooded area, is beautifully quiet, although conveniently close to St-Raphael. Organized games for children and a discotheque are among the more unusual attractions, although they don't disturb the peace unduly. Caravans can be rented.

SOLLIÈS-TOUCAS (Var)
Les Oliviers, 83210 Solliès-Pont. Map 12H10 ☎94-28-95-39 ═ ≋ ℘ ►●
Open mid-June to mid-Sept.
This small, attractive and decently equipped site makes a good base for seeing the art exhibitions and workshops that are such a feature of this area. Reservations are advised. Tents can be rented.

UZÈS (Gard.)
Le Moulin Neuf, 30700. Map 8D3
☎66-22-17-21 ═ ᚼ ≋ ℘ *Closed Oct–Easter.*
This is a comfortable and quiet site, just outside Uzès in the Provence hinterland. It is wise to reserve. For those without caravans, bungalows can be rented.

Western Provence

The rich historical heritage of this area, in the Bouches-du-Rhône, Vaucluse and Gard *départements,* includes the Roman monuments at ORANGE, PONT DU GARD, NÎMES, ARLES and ST-RÉMY; these are all within a 32-kilometer (20-mile) radius. You should also visit the museums, palaces and churches of Provence's three proudest cultural cities, the three As: AIX, ARLES and AVIGNON (it is only an hour by autoroute from Avignon to Aix). And do not miss some smaller, equally historic towns: AIGUES-MORTES, TARASCON, UZÈS and VILLENEUVE-LÈS-AVIGNON.

Go northeast of AVIGNON, to the stunning scenery around MONT VENTOUX, the cathedral at CARPENTRAS, and the Roman town at VAISON. Or southeast to the equally spectacular LUBÉRON mountain, with its hill-villages and the abbeys of SÉNANQUE and SILVACANE. The area has some interesting curiosities; these include the gushing waters of the FONTAINE DE VAUCLUSE, the odd stone dwellings of **Les Bories** at GORDES, and the château at ANSOUIS. LES BAUX, a ruined hilltop feudal stronghold, is one of France's most remarkable sights; nearby, the white rocky spurs of **Les Alpilles** are worth exploring.

The CAMARGUE to the south of ARLES and northwest of MARSEILLE — a strange marshy plain full of birds, bulls and wild horses — is like nowhere else in France. The seaport of MARSEILLE, second city of France, may be strident and shabby; but it is lively and full of historic interest. And those interested in modern France may care to visit the big new oil-based industries of ÉTANG DE BERRE and **Fos** nearby.

AIGUES-MORTES
Map 8F2 (Gard). 42km (26 miles) sw of Nîmes. Postal code: 30220. Population: 5,000 ℹ Porte de la Gardette ☎66-53-73-00.

Approached from the D979, built on the site of the original causeway to the town, Aigues-Mortes presents an unexpected and extraordinary sight: a perfect example of a medieval fortified town, still completely enclosed by four walls, above which no building or church spire is visible. This strange, lovely and rather melancholy town stands amid flat salty marshes and lagoons (the name means dead water, from the Roman *Aquae Mortuae*). The only external aspect that has changed is the moat, now filled in; inside, the ancient streets preserve their original grid pattern. The population has dropped from 15,000 in the days of the Crusades to approximately 5,000 today.

Aigues-Mortes developed from a sleepy fishing village. It was once by the sea, but the waters have since silted up, and it lies some 8 kilometers (5 miles) inland. Louis IX (St-Louis) chose this spot from which to set sail on the Seventh Crusade in 1248. While preparing for the voyage, he built the city fortress, the **Tour de Constance**. After his death from the plague on the Eighth Crusade (also begun from Aigues-Mortes), his son, Philip the Bold, completed the main ramparts. In **place St-Louis** there stands a statue of his father.

● **MARKETS** These are on Wednesday and Sunday.

WHAT TO SEE IN AIGUES-MORTES
Tour de Constance et Remparts 🏛 ☆
📷 ◀€ 🗶 *available July–Aug. Open Oct–Mar 10am–noon, 2–5pm; Apr–Sept 9am–noon, 2–6pm.*

The imposing circular keep is 27 meters (90 feet) high, and consists of two vaulted rooms, one above the other. In the lower room, the **Oratory of St-Louis** is built into the 5.5-meter/18-foot-thick walls; here a showcase holds early illuminated manuscripts and other documents of St-Louis at Aigues-Mortes.

The upper room is devoted to souvenirs of the long period between the 14th–18thC, when the tower was used as a political prison, first for Templars, later for Huguenots and victims of religious oppression. You can see the brave inscriptions left on the walls by the 18thC Huguenots: notably the words *"au ciel, résistez,"* carved by Marie Durand, who entered the prison aged eight and was released 38 years later, physically a wreck but morally triumphant.

The Protestants of the Nîmes area still venerate this tower for the sufferings of their martyrs. The summit of the tower affords a fine view over the strange countryside around, and from the tower you can walk around the ramparts.

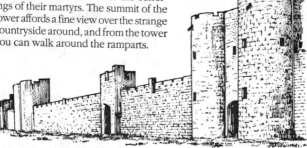

�')= LES REMPARTS
6 pl. Anatole-France, 30220 Aigues-Mortes
☎ 66-53-82-77 🎫 *20 rms* 🖼 ⟴ 𝔸𝔼 ⊕
⊙ 𝕍𝕀𝕊𝔸 ⌂ ዿ ▢ 🖵 🎿

Location: Just inside the ramparts, facing the Tour de Constance. An 18thC mansion has been converted into a sophisticated little hotel of some character (although the ambience is slightly

frosty), with comfortable period furniture offsetting the gray stone walls.

You can choose between eating in the elegant dining room, or on the terrace with a view of the ramparts (🎫 *to* 🎫 ⌂ ▮ 🚗 *last orders 10pm, closed Wed (except July-Aug), mid-Nov to mid-Dec, last two weeks in Jan).* The *carte* is over-priced, but the set menu is a much better value, with various local dishes.

⇌ LA CAMARGUE

19 rue de la République ☎*66-51-86-88* ⅢⅡ *to* ⅢⅡ ☐ ■ 🚗 ▣ *Last orders 10pm. Closed Tues (except July–Aug); Nov to mid-Dec.*

Well known and touristy, but fashionable too, La Camargue has hit on a surefire formula for revelry by night: a gargantuan six-course set menu — *crudités* with *bagna cauda*, fish with *rouille*, log-fire-grilled steaks, salad, cheeses, homemade tarts, unlimited wine—eaten by candlelight in the 17thC stone-walled house to the vibrant accompaniment of gypsy guitarists and singers, often including Manitas de Plata. The name plates on the banquettes bear witness to the famous faces that have dined here; Pompidou, Romy Schneider, Alain Delon, Princess Radziwill *et al.* Lunches are simpler and quieter.

🐦 ⇌   Other hotels/restaurants: **St-Louis** *(10 rue Amiral Courbet* ☎*66-53-72-68* Ⓕ*66-53-75-92* ⅢⅡ *hotel closed Jan to mid-Mar; restaurant closed for lunch (except Sun) Nov to mid-Apr);* **Arcades** *(23 blvd. Gambetta* ☎ *66-53-81-13* Ⓕ *66-53-75-46* ⅢⅡ *hotel closed Feb; restaurant closed Mon, except for dinner in July, Aug).*

PLACES NEAR AIGUES-MORTES

Salins du Midi *(just s of Aigues-Mortes).* These huge saltworks produce 500,000 tons of salt from the surrounding marshes *(✗ visits July-Aug, Tues-Fri afternoons).*

Le Grau-du-Roi *(6km/4 miles to the sw).* This is a charming old fishing village, crowded in summer. Cheap, fairly good restaurants line its quays.

Port-Camargue *(10km/6 miles to the sw).* This is the most easterly of the chain of modernistic resorts that line up along the Languedoc coast. (**La Grande Motte** is another, only 8 kilometers/5 miles from Aigues-Mortes, although geographically it is not within Provence.) Carved out of a marshy strip of deserted coast in the 1970s, it is a vast residential marina for 3,000 boats, so designed that every villa has its own mooring. It is superficially comparable to PORT-GRIMAUD, but whereas the latter is in mock-traditional style, Port-Camargue is unashamedly modern, and more spacious.

For villa rental and boat moorings, apply to: **Carrefour 2000** *(BP49, 30240 Port-Camargue* ☎*66-51-41-71).*

🐦 ⇌ LE SPINAKER

Pointe du Môle, 30240 Port-Camargue ☎*66-53-36-57* ⅢⅡ *21 rms* ▤▤ 🚗 ⇌ *VISA* 🔥 ☐ 🖂 《 ≈ ▲ *Closed Jan to mid-Feb. Location: On a broad grass jetty in the heart of the marina.* This well designed and cheerful little hotel would make a good base for a sailing vacation (it has ten moorings, free to residents). The Cazals are charming hosts, and each bedroom has its own terrace, with a view of the port.

Excellent fish dishes from Jean-Pierre Cazals are served in the light dining-room *(*ⅢⅡ ■ 🚗 *July-Aug* 🚗 *VISA closed Sun dinner, Mon from Oct-May, Jan to mid-Feb, last orders 9pm)* overlooking the port. Buffet lunches are served by the swimming pool in summer. *Specialities: Escalope de mérou poêlée au basilic, bouillon de crustacés à l'estragon, râble de lapin farci en crépinette.*

🐦   Other hotel: **L'Oustau Camargen** *(3 Route des Marines, Port-Camargue* ☎*66-51-51-65* Ⓕ*66-53-06-65* ⅢⅡ *closed Nov to mid-Mar).*

•   See also: LA CAMARGUE and LES SAINTES-MARIES-DE-LA-MER.

AIX-EN-PROVENCE

Map 10G7 (B.-du-R.). 31km (19 miles) N of Marseille. Postal code: 13100.
Population: 125,000 **i** *pl. du Général-de-Gaulle* ☎42-26-02-93. **Bus station**
☎42-27-17-91. **Railway station** ☎91-08-50-50.

Aix is many people's favorite French town. More than any other in the
French provinces, it has the same aristocratic grace as certain noble
Italian cities, such as Florence or Verona. From the 12th–18thC it was
Provence's brilliant capital — today, capital no more, it is still a center
of learning and the arts, and still wears a proud patrician air. Its many
lovely buildings of the Classic period somehow harmonize with its
modern student ambience; and so intense and vivid is the life of its
womb-like nucleus of narrow streets that you hardly notice its wider
setting — on the edge of the plain of the Rhône delta, with Cézanne's
beloved hills rising steeply from the eastern suburbs.

As at other towns called Aix, such as Aix-les-Bains, its name (pronounced "aches") comes from the Latin *aquae* or waters, for there are
springs here. In 123BC the Roman consul Sextius, after subduing a local
Ligurian tribe, founded a thermal station and named it after himself,
Aquae Sextiae (today called the **Thermes Sextius**). Until 1990, some
8,000 people a year still came here to be treated by the supposedly healing
waters. Aix soon became a major Roman center and for a while was
capital of this part of Gaul. It then went into a long decline, to revive in
the 12thC when the Counts of Provence made it their capital.

Aix knew its greatest splendor under "Good King René" from 1442–80.
He was really a count, but as exiled King of Naples and Duke of Anjou
he kept his royal title. Patron of music and the arts, linguist and mathe-
matician, René was a true Renaissance man. He did much for Provence's
economy, introducing the silkworm and the muscat grape. He was also
a genial man with the common touch, who loved chatting with his
subjects and organizing festivals for them. Today he still enjoys popularity
and is something of a cult figure in Aix: you will see shops, cafés, even
driving schools and dry-cleaners, all bearing the name *Au Roi René.*

Soon after his death came the union of Provence with France, but until
1790 much autonomy remained in Provence, and Aix was the seat of its
parliament and courts of justice. This is how the city acquired its elegant
17th and 18thC mansions, built by wealthy nobles, magistrates and
prelates.

Then in the 19thC, with the rise of Marseille, Aix went into relative
decline, and today it is a mere sub-prefecture. But the population has
grown enormously since 1945, with new suburbs and industries spreading across the plain. The new campuses of its important university
(founded in the 15thC) are also in the suburbs. But Aix is very much a
university town, thronging with over 30,000 students, many of them on
exchange visits. The relationship between Aix and Marseille is rather like
that between Bath and Bristol, Edinburgh and Glasgow, or even San
Francisco and Los Angeles.

The old part of the town is compact, a mere 730 meters (800 yards)
across, and is best visited on foot. Its central avenue, and focus of local
life, is the famous **Cours Mirabeau**. Here, even outside university

AIX-EN-PROVENCE

| 0 | 100 | 200 | 300m |
| 0 | 100 | 200 | 300 yds |

sessions, the sidewalks and cafés are crowded with people who seem to retain a rare natural grace. The Aixois seem in many ways more Northern Italian than French. They are relaxed, they dress with chic, they have pride. It is a town that exudes culture and a deeply-rooted stylishness very different from the imported gloss of, say, Cannes.

But the town has not been entirely free of intrusions from the real world. In October 1992, a Corsican political group set off a bomb outside the main entrance of the Palais de Justice, which, however, continues to function inside.

Work on the new **Sextius-Mirabeau** suburb began in 1991, and should finish by the end of the century. The design competition was won by Oriol Bohigas, who was also responsible for Barcelona's Olympic village. Plans for the area include a new theater, a convention center and new bus and railway stations. The latter, most important for the town and its inhabitants, will allow the high-speed TGV to stop at Aix (the nearest TGV station at the moment is in Marseille.)

- **EVENTS** • Last two weeks in June, **street festival** of free outdoor concerts. • Early July sees a **Dance Festival** and a **Provençal festival**. • From mid-July to mid-August, Aix stages one of the leading **annual music festivals** in Europe. There are also a number of "fringe" performances in the streets and elsewhere, and a **jazz festival** in August. High-priced opera (there are only 1,600 seats) is performed in the courtyard of the former Archbishop's palace, which now houses the Tapestry Museum. For details apply to the Bureau du Festival *(Palais de l'Ancien Archevêché, 13100 Aix* ☎ *42-17-34-00)*. • For other festivals contact the Comité Officiel des Fêtes *(Espace Forbin, Cours Gambetta, 13100 Aix* ☎ *42-63-06-75)*.
- To find out what's on locally, pick up the tourist office's comprehensive *Le Mois à Aix,* or the local weekly *Le Courrier d'Aix.*

WHAT TO SEE IN AIX-EN-PROVENCE
Atelier Cézanne
9 av. Paul Cézanne ☎*42-21-06-53* 🔲 📷 *Open June–Sept 10am–noon, 2–6pm; Oct–May 10am–noon, 2–5pm. Closed Tues.*

Cézanne's austere, obsessive personality emerges forcefully in this untidy studio, which has been reconstructed to look just as it did at his death in 1906. He lived down in the city, at rue Boulegon: but each day he would come to paint in the first-floor room of this small house in the N suburbs, with its wide, N-facing windows.

Of his own works there are just two drawings and a gouache; but you can see his easel and palette, his chair, hat and cloak, clay pipe and other personal effects, as well as photos and letters. Here too are some of the actual objects that he painted: wineglasses, bottles and skulls (only the onions are recent).

The effect is more than a little macabre, far removed from the sense of family warmth and life-affirming lyricism that pervades Renoir's house at CAGNES-SUR-MER.

Cours Mirabeau ☆
Aix's central avenue, built in the 17thC on the site of the old ramparts, and later named after the Marquis de Mirabeau, is still one of France's noblest streets, although a mere 450 meters (500 yards) long. It is shaded by four rows of tall plane trees, which form a green arbor.

The two sides of the street have distinctly different atmospheres. The N side, full of social activity, is lined with bookstores and cafés, of which the most famous is **Les Deux Garçons** *(#53).* "Les Deux Gs," as it is known to habitués, founded in 1792, has a mirrored and gilded interior and has been fashionable with intellectuals — and a place to see and be seen in — since World War II. It has become rather touristy and over-priced, although things have improved somewhat since a change of ownership in 1992.

The s side of the Cours is more down-to-earth and businesslike, full of banks and real-estate agents — although it is still mainly a preserve of 17th and 18thC mansions. Note the bearded, half-naked atlantes supporting the balcony of **#38**, now a university building.

The Cours has four fountains. To the w, the giant three-tiered **Fontaine Grande**, with traffic swirling around it in the wide place du

Général-de-Gaulle; then the **Fontaine des Neufs-Canons** (1691); then the squat, moss-covered **Fontaine d'Eau Chaude**, with running warm spring water; lastly, the **Fontaine du Roi René**, with a 19thC statue of the king holding muscat grapes.

Espace Culturel Méjanes
8–10 rue des Allumettes ☎ *42-26-66-75.*
A major cultural center opened in the late 1980s in an old match factory. There is a cafeteria, a videotheque specializing in recordings of opera performances, and regular exhibitions. The famous **Méjanes library**, 300,000 volumes bequeathed in the 18thC by the Marquis of Méjanes, has been relocated here from the town hall. Its many rare books from the 15th–16thC are kept locked away, but can be consulted by scholars. The **Fondation St-John Perse**, devoted to that poet's life and works and containing a legacy of his own letters, photographs and manuscripts, has also been moved here.

Granet, Musée ☆
Pl. St-Jean-de-Malte ☎ *42-38-14-70* ▨ *Open 10am–noon, 2–6pm. Closed Tues.*
This former Priory of the Knights of Malta (17thC) now houses one of the most excellent and varied, if badly displayed, art collections in Provence. The museum is named after the early 19thC Aixois painter François Granet, who was a leading donor, as was the aristocratic Gueidan family, which bequeathed its family portraits to the museum in the late 19thC.

On the first floor are French paintings of the Renaissance and of the Fontainebleau and Provençal schools. Provence is represented notably by Granet himself, as well as by Van Loo and Le Nain, and by a large colorful 19thC canvas of *King René Signing a Reprieve,* by Guillemot.

The eight Cézanne canvases are minor works. But there is a fine Ingres: *Jupiter and Thetis* (1811). On the second floor are mainly Dutch and Flemish works, including a De Hooch interior, a small Rembrandt self-portrait, Teniers' charming *Night Fête in a Village,* some works by Rubens, and Vinckboons' strange *Wedding in Cana.* Curiously, and infuriatingly, the museum has no catalog of its permanent collection.

The museum mounts special exhibitions each year *(open until 8pm except Sat and Sun).* In 1990, after the great fire on Cézanne's much-painted Mont Ste-Victoire the previous year, the museum held a Cézanne exhibition, and around Aix you will see small brass plates in the sidewalk marking a trail to places associated with the great Impressionist. These include the school, the **Collège Bourbon** (around the corner from the Musée Granet), attended by both him and his friend Emile Zola. The friendship lasted until 1886 when Zola published *L'Oeuvre.* In this novel, the character of the painter Claude Lantier was based on Cézanne, a portrait the latter thought was somewhat unfair. A map of the walk, the **Circuit Cézanne**, is available from the tourist office.

The large archeology section in the basement has Greek and Roman sculptures (as well a Roman columns and a Roman tiled floor) and Egyptiana, including a mummy of the Twelfth Dynasty, with elaborate, colored inscriptions. There is also a unique collection of **Celto-Ligurian sculptures** from Egremont, mostly excavated in the 1940s. They include death masks, low reliefs and warriors' torsos, and are all very primitive yet detailed in their carving. They are the earliest known pre-Roman sculptures in France.

Mazarin Quarter

Just SE of Cours Mirabeau, this once aristocratic quarter was built in the 17thC by Michel Mazarin, Archbishop of Aix. It is a grid of narrow streets, harmonious but severe. Worth seeing are the 17thC **Fontaine des Quatre Dauphins**; the **Musée Paul Arbaud** of local art and history (▨ *open 2-5pm, closed Sun);* and the lovely 13thC interior of the **St-Jean-de-Malte church**, next to the Musée Granet.

Ste-Marie-Madeleine ✝

Pl. des Prêcheurs. Closed Mon–Sat 11.30am–3pm, Sun afternoon.

This large 17thC church has a dull, modern W facade, but inside it is very ornate. There are paintings by Rubens and Van Loo, and an 18thC marble *Virgin* by Chastel at the far end of the right aisle. The treasured work of art is the 15thC *Annunciation,* believed to be the work of Jean Chapus of Avignon. It is the centerpiece of a triptych, the side panels of which are in Belgium and the Netherlands, although copies are here in the sacristy.

St-Sauveur, Cathédrale ⎗ ✝ ☆

Rue J-Laroque ▣ *Open daily 8am–noon, 2–6.30pm.*

This cathedral, rich in works of art, shows a great jumble of architectural styles, from the 5th–16thC. The right aisle was the nave of an old Romanesque church, later incorporated into the Gothic cathedral. The W facade, too, has a Romanesque section on the right, while the rest is 16thC Flamboyant Gothic. Of its original sculptures, all were destroyed in the Revolution save the central *Virgin,* spared because someone stuck a cap of Liberty on her head. The other statues are 19thC replacements.

The cathedral's main treasures are kept locked away, for safety, but the sacristan will open them up and explain them. First, the elaborate 16thC wood carvings on the W doors, depicting 12 pagan sibyls and four prophets. Next, Nicolas Froment's famous triptych, *The Burning Bush* (☆), painted for King René in 1475.

The cathedral's magnificent set of 15 Brussels tapestries is not now on view, alas. They were woven in 1511 for Canterbury Cathedral in England, then sold by Oliver Cromwell, and finally bought by a canon of Aix for a paltry 2,200 *écus.* Off the right aisle is a large 5thC Gallo-Roman baptistry, similar in style to that at the Cité Épiscopale at FRÉJUS.

Beside the cathedral is a delightful Romanesque **cloister**. Unlike those at ARLES and FRÉJUS it is roofed over.

Tapisseries, Musée des

Ancien Archevêché ☎ *42-21-05-78* ▨ 𝕩 𝕏 *available. Open 10am–noon, 2–6pm. Closed Tues.*

The former archbishop's palace, with its chandeliers and marble walls, houses this celebrated collection of 18 Beauvais tapestries dating from the 17th–18thC. They were discovered in the roof in 1849, having possibly been hidden there during the French Revolution. Nine of them, from designs by Natoire, are lively scenes from the life of Don Quixote, seen as a gangling figure with startled eyes.

Vasarely, Fondation ☆

Av. Marcel-Pagnol, 4km (2½ miles) sw of Aix ☎*42–20–01–09* ◼ *Open 9.30am–12.30pm, 2–5.30pm. Closed Tues (except July, Aug).*

This ultramodern museum stands alone on a hill in the w suburbs. The Hungarian-born artist, not the most modest of men, created it himself in 1975 to house his own works, and has included tributes to his "genius" by Le Corbusier and other contemporaries.

The display is very striking, and will fascinate admirers of Vasarely's idiosyncratic innovations. Seven open-plan hexagonal cells, cleverly lit, display a range of his huge geometric murals, as well as tapestries, rotating glass sculptures, polychromatic tiled mosaics and much else. Dazzling colors integrate with mathematical complexities, to provide insights into Vasarely's experiments with the illusions of light and movement. Upstairs, a set of automatic sliding panels explain his oeuvre to the uninitiated (as he has also done in his museum in the château at GORDES). The Foundation also acts as a research and seminar center.

Vendôme, Pavillon de

32 rue Célony ☎*42-21-05-78* ◼ *Open June–Sept 10am–noon, 2–6pm; Oct–May 10am–noon, 2–5pm. Closed Tues.*

Lying just outside the Old Town, this gracious mansion with its formal garden was built in 1667 as a summer home of the Cardinal of Vendôme, governor of Provence. It later belonged to the Aixois painter Van Loo. The facade, a fine example of the 17thC local style, has atlantes supporting its balcony. Inside can be seen furniture and paintings of the period, and an imposing double stairway.

Vieil Aix ☆

The oldest part of Aix, between Cours Mirabeau and the cathedral, is a delightful place for a walk, especially as many of its narrow streets are now traffic-free. Although lined with lovely old buildings, Vieil Aix is more than a museum piece: it is a vibrant center of the city's present-day life, full of smart stores and shoppers. Here the comparison with Florence is most apt.

Of the many fine 16th–17thC houses, several are now museums. The **Hôtel Boyer d'Éguilles** *(6 rue Espariat)* now houses the **Muséum d'Histoire Naturelle** *(* ◼ *open 10am-noon, 2-6pm, closed Sun am).* Next door, the calm and enchanting little **place d'Albertas** (☆) is a tiny, cobbled square with a fountain in the middle, lined with gray 18thC houses, with not a shop or café to be seen.

To the N, via rue Aude and rue Maréchal Foch, is **place de l'Hôtel-de-Ville** with its colorful flower market. The former corn-market building, now a sub-post office, has splendid 18thC carvings by the sculptor Chastel. The **Hôtel de Ville** itself (17thC) has a fine wrought-iron entrance gate. The early 16thC **Tour de l'Horloge** (clock tower) beside the town hall is unusual, for in the belfry at its top are four statues representing the seasons, which rotate, each one showing its face in turn for three months.

From here it is just a few yards to the **Musée du Vieil Aix**, the cathedral of **St-Sauveur**, and the **Musée des Tapisseries**. In the NW corner of the old town is a spa center, or *établissement thermal*, built in the 18thC beside the old Roman baths.

Vieil Aix, Musée du

17 rue Gaston de Saporta ☎ *42-21-43-55* 🚇 🚾 *Open daily Apr–Sept 10am–noon, 2.30–6pm: Oct–Mar 10am–noon, 2.30–5pm. Closed Mon.*

Occupying the ground floor of a fine 17thC mansion, this is one of the best folklore museums in Provence, noted for its collections of *santons*, nativity cribs, and mechanical dolls and puppets, all once used in local traditional fêtes. The *santons* are of clay and the puppets of cardboard, but all are so richly costumed you can hardly spot the difference.

At the back is a pretty boudoir with a frescoed ceiling; in it is a chest that Louis XIV left behind on a visit to this house. Note also the unique paintings worked on velvet by the Aixois artist Grégoire (1751–1846).

✒ WHERE TO STAY IN AIX

DES AUGUSTINS

3 rue de la Masse ☎ *42-27-28-59* ▥ *to* ▥ *35 rms* 🖼 ▦ 🅰🄴 🔾 🚾 ✳ 🗆 🗀 ✺ 🕭 🏖

Location: Just off Cours Mirabeau. This is a converted 12thC convent with a very convenient location. It used to be known locally as a hotel "with a four-star lobby and two-star rooms," but it changed ownership in 1992, and has been much improved, with bright new furnishings, and good, well-equipped, bathrooms. There is no restaurant, but this is now a comfortable hotel, and one of the best choices in town. You can have breakfast in the garden.

CARAVELLE ✿

29 blvd. du Roi René, 13100 Aix-en-Provence ☎ *42-21-53-05* 🄵🄰*MI42-96-55-46* ▥ *to* ▥ *32 rms* 🅰🄴 🔾 🚾 ✳ 🗆 🗀 ✺ 🏖

Location: Fairly central, on a main street SE *of Cours Mirabeau.* This neat, modern hotel makes a useful base. The staff are attentive and helpful, and the prices modest for such comfort.

MERCURE PAUL CÉZANNE 🏨

40 av. Victor-Hugo, 13100 Aix-en-Provence ☎ *42-26-34-73* 🄵🄰 *42-27-20-95* ▥ *55 rms* ▦ 🚗 🖼 🅰🄴 🔾 🚾 ✳ 🗆 🗀 ✺ 🖼

Location: Central, on a main street facing the station. The Cézanne's prices are justified, for the hotel has real character. Each bedroom is strikingly different, some modern, some classic in style. Some even have the added luxury of four-poster beds, and the feeling is that of a private hotel. Only one complaint on our visit: the reception staff did not overwhelm with their helpfulness.

NÈGRE COSTE

33 Cours Mirabeau, 13100 Aix-en-Provence ☎ *42-27-74-22* ▥ *to* ▥ *37 rms* 🖼 🅰🄴 🔾 🚾 ✳ 🕭 🗆 🗀

Location: Central. This former 18thC residence is now a sedate little hotel, the discreet elegance of which is fully suited to Aix's famous main avenue. The spacious rooms are decorated, if somewhat dully, in Louis XV style, and much of the hotel's ornate furniture consists of genuine period pieces.

LE PIGONNET ✿

5 av. de Pigonnet, 13100 Aix-en-Provence
☎42-59-02-90 ⓕ 42-59-47-77 ▦ to ▦
50 rms ▣ ⒶⒺ ⓞ ⓦⓢⒶ ⌂ ⚡ ♿ ▢ ◰ ☙
▧ ♨ *For* ☰ *see LE PIGONNET, overleaf.*

Location: Toward the outskirts. This is one of Aix's most seductive hotels: a handsome, ivy-covered mansion with true Provençal decor and an air of intimate chic. Bedrooms are spacious, with pretty wallpaper and antique furniture; some have large balconies, facing the hills that Cézanne loved. The large, ornate garden with its fountains and rose arbors could belong to some grand Edwardian villa, and is suffused with romantic melancholy.

PULLMAN ROI RENÉ

24 blvd. du Roi René ☎42-37-61-00
ⓕ42-37-61-11 ▦ to ▦ *134 rms* ▤ ▣
☰ ⒶⒺ ⓞ ⓞ ⓦⓢⒶ ⚡ ▢ ◰ ♿ ♨ Ⓨ ▢
Location: Central; not far from Cours Mirabeau. A good business hotel with a selection of differently decorated modern rooms that vary in price according to the facilities offered. The best rooms are first-class. The hotel's restaurant, **La Table du Roi**, is one of the best in town, well run, with friendly service, if a little impersonal in atmosphere. There is a good wine list, and prices are moderate. Chef Dominique Frérard's cuisine is imaginative, if a little on the heavy side, and uses good, fresh ingredients, with an emphasis on Provençal specialities.

VILLA GALLICI ⌂

Av. de la Violette (Impasse des Grands Pins) ☎42-23-29-23 ⓕ42-21-29-23 ▦
17 rms ▤ ⒶⒺ ⓞ ⓞ ⓦⓢⒶ ⌂ ▢ ◰ ♿ ☙
▧ Ⓨ ▢
Location: Not far from the center of Aix, N of Cours Mirabeau. This is probably, in terms of stylishness, and comfort, the best hotel in Aix — an 18thC building,

with rooms each differently, cheerf[...] and imaginatively decorated with rea[...] verve, and even wit. It isn't cheap, and nor does it have a restaurant (although you can eat light meals by the pool). The hotel does, however, have an arrangement with the neighboring CLOS DE LA VIOLETTE (see ☰ overleaf). Service is friendly, and the atmosphere is relaxed and charming. The hotel's decorative style probably won't appeal to those with conventional or old-fashioned tastes.

✍ Other recommended hotels are: • **Novotel Aix Beaumanoir** *(3km/2 miles SE beside A8* ☎42-27-47-50▦*).* • **Le Manoir** *(8 rue d'Entrecasteaux* ☎42-26-27-20 ▦ *to* ▦*).* • **Le Prieuré** *(2km/1½ miles NE on Route de Sisteron* ☎ 42-21-05-23 ▦ *to* ▦*).*

✍ Hotels near Aix: • **Mas d'Entremont** *(Montée d'Avignon, 13090 Aix-en-Provence* ☎ 42-23-45-32 ▦*),* a converted farmhouse 2km (1½ miles) NW of Aix, with delightful gardens and a pretty swimming pool. • **Château de la Pioline** *(Les Milles, 13290* ☎42-20-07-81 ⓕ42-59-96-12 ▦*),* an 18thC château 3km (2 miles) from Aix, with high-quality facilities. • **Domaine de la Cride** *(Le Puy-Ste-Reparade, 13610* ☎ 42-61-96-96 ⓕ42-61-93-28 ▦ *),* in the hills 14km (9 miles) N of Aix. Very comfortable, more like a family house than a hotel. • **Mas de la Bertrande** *(Chemin de la Plaine, Beaurecueil, 13100* ☎ 42-66-90-09 ▦ *to* ▦*),* a pretty, peaceful little hotel in the countryside 10km (6 miles) E of Aix. There are views of Mont Ste-Victoire, and a good restaurant, although there was a recent change of chef. • **Relais Sainte-Victoire** *(Beaurecueil, 13100* ☎42-66-94-98 ▦ *),* a pleasant hotel with a fine restaurant.

☰ EATING AND DRINKING IN AIX

L'ABBAYE DES CORDELIERS

21 rue Lieutaud ☎42-27-29-47 ▦ *to* ▦
▢ ■ *Last orders 9pm. Closed Mon–Thurs (Oct–Feb); Tues–Wed (Mar–Sept).*

A quiet and select establishment, housed in a former abbey. Known for reliable, traditional cooking, although the restaurant recently changed ownership.

...lly

‖ ♦

...ne ☎42-38-22-88 ⊞

🌐 Closed Sun dinner;

... Last orders 10.30pm.

Bruno Ungaro, the young and enthusi-astic chef, is a relation of the celebrated dress designer, and his smart but re-laxed restaurant is certainly stylish enough. His cuisine is basically Proven-çal, with a light touch and good presen-tation. Try the *blanquette d'agneau* or the *charlotte de sole*. The set menus are good value.

LE CLOS DE LA VIOLETTE △

10 av. de la Violette ☎42-23-30-71 ▥
⊞ ▱ ▰ ▰ ♠ AE ◑ ▦

Jean-Marc Banzo (formerly at the now-defunct Caves Henri IV) owns, along with his wife Brigitte, the best (and, with its garden, probably the prettiest) restaurant in Aix. Banzo learned his craft in some of the top restaurants in the region, such as HIÉLY in Avignon, and his cooking is sunny, fresh and inventive, using the finest local ingredi-ents. The menu changes regularly, and there is a fine selection of local wines.

AL DENTE

14 rue Constantin ☎42-96-41-03 ⊞
Closed Sun; Mon lunch. Last orders 11pm.
Quick service and very reasonable prices at this lively Italian restaurant, popular with young people, which spe-cializes in various kinds of fresh pasta.

LES FRÈRES LANI

Rue Victor Leydet ☎42-27-76-16 ▥ ⊞
▱ ▰ AE ▦ Closed Sun; Mon lunch. Last orders 10.30pm.
The Lani family own a hotel and res-taurant outside Aix, but the eponymous

brothers have branched out to open this rather more formal restaurant with good, friendly service, conveniently near Cours Mirabeau. They cook with flair, if sometimes rather too elabor-ately, and care about flavor and presen-tation. Prices on the *carte* are rather high, although the set menus are rela-tively good value.

LE PIGONNET

5 av. de Pigonnet ☎42-59-02-90 ▥ to
▥ ▱ ▰ ♠ ▰ AE ◑ ◐ ▦ Closed
Sat lunch; Sun out of season; Nov; early Feb. Last orders 9.30pm.
This hotel dining-room is elegant but somewhat formal, but on fine days it is a delight to dine out on the wide terrace under the chestnut trees. Service is polished, and the classic cuisine very reliable. *Specialities: Terrine de St-Pierre, aiguillettes de canard aux griottes, estouffade de boeuf provençal.* (See ❧ LE PIGONNET, above.)

▭ Some other recommended res-taurants: • **A La Cour de Rohan** *(pl. de l'Hôtel de Ville* ☎ 42-96-18-15 ⬚ to ⬚)*, a long, cozy tea room, with pale, exposed stone walls and wooden beams. Light meals and a lively atmos-phere. • **Chez Gu et Fils** *(3 rue Frédéric Mistral* ☎ 42-26-75-12 ▥)* offers an eclectic menu. • **Le Clam's** *(22 Cours Sextius* ☎ 42-27-64-78 ▥ to ▥)* specializes in fish and seafood. • **Le Grillon** *(49 Cours Mirabeau* ☎ 42-27-58-81 ⬚)* is the best café in Cours Mirabeau. The food is good (if simple), the service efficient, and the prices reasonable, and as a result, the propor-tion of locals to tourists eating and drinking here is unusually high.

🌙 NIGHTLIFE IN AIX

The **Casino Municipal** *(2bis av. Napoléon Bonaparte* ☎42-26-30-33, open 3pm-2am)* has 1920s decor. A move is expected at the end of 1994. Jacket required.

Aix has more than a dozen discos. • Try the **Mistral** *(3 rue Frédéric Mistral* ☎42-38-16-49, open 11pm-8am; closed Sun, Mon)*, **Le Damier** *(av. des Infirmeries* ☎42-26-52-74)* or the trendy **Les Mandragores** *(Chemin Aubère* ☎42-21-28-28, open 11pm-8am; closed Sun, Mon, Tues)*.

The best **jazz clubs** in Aix are **Hot Brass** *(Route d'Eguilles-Célony* ☎ *42-20-67-98, open 10.30pm-8am; closed mid-Aug to Sept)* and **Le Scat Club** *(11 rue de la Verrerie* ☎ *42-23-00-23, open 10.30pm-4am; closed Sun, Mon).*

La Chimère *(Montée d'Avignon* ☎ *42-23-36-28)* is a gay club open 10.30pm–5am. • **La Rotonde** *(2 pl. Jeanne d'Arc* ☎ *42-26-01-95)* is a piano bar/brasserie open 10pm–2am.

Apart from a number of conventional theaters, Aix also has some studio spaces, a restaurant-theater, **Théâtre de la Fonderie** *(14 Cours St-Louis* ☎ *42-63-10-11)* and a café-theater, **La Fontaine d'Argent** *(5 rue Fontaine d'Argent* ☎ *42-38-43-80, open from 9pm; closed Sun, Mon).*

SHOPPING IN AIX

Several streets in the old town, N of Cours Mirabeau, are full of antique stores and boutiques selling Provençal handicrafts and food specialities, namely rue Gaston de Saporta, rue Granet, rue Jaubert, rue Mathéron and place des Cardeurs. The same area (in streets such as rue Thiers) is also full of big-name and designer clothes stores.

At **Carcassonne** *(rue Chabrier, open Tues-Sat)* you will find high-quality Provençal fabric.

Bechard *(12 Cours Mirabeau)* and **Brémond Fils** *(36 Cours Mirabeau)* are two *confiseries* specializing in *calissons,* the marzipan biscuits for which Aix is famous.

* **MARKETS** There is a delightful open-air **food market** each morning, in place Richelme, near the post office. • There is a **flower market** in place de l'Hôtel de Ville *(Tues, Thurs, Sat mornings).* • A **flea market** is held in place du Palais de Justice *(Tues, Thurs, Sat mornings).*

PLACES NEAR AIX-EN-PROVENCE

Aqueduc de Roquefavour *(11km/7 miles W of Aix).* This vast three-tier aqueduct was built in 1842–47 to carry the waters of the Durance to Marseille. It is nearly twice as high as the PONT DU GARD, and 90 meters (100 yards) longer.

Entremont *(3km/2 miles N of Aix).* In pre-Roman days, a group of Celto-Ligurian tribes had their base on this plateau. Recent excavations have revealed the remains of their sizeable *oppidum,* which was sacked by the consul Sextius in 123BC. Parts of the ramparts, a gateway and some house walls are visible.

Meyrargues *(20km/13 miles NE of Aix).* A village in the Durance valley, dominated by a 12thC château-hôtel (details follow).

☞ CHÂTEAU DE MEYRARGUES

13650 Meyrargues ☎ *42-57-50-32* ⓕ *42-63-43-99* ▥▥ *to* ▥▥▥ *14 rms* ➡ ⇌ 🖨 ▣ ▦ 🗀 ▱ ✒ ◈ ♨ *Closed Nov–Jan.*
Location: Perched on a high hill above the village, set in its own 12-acre park. The perfect place for lovers of baronial grandeur, this may look like the set of

an old Errol Flynn movie, but it's real. The stately 12thC château, restored in the 17thC, has been converted into an elegant little hotel, with all the right touches — tapestries, beamed ceilings, genuine Louis XV furniture in the bedrooms, and lordly stone chimneypieces where log fires are lit on chilly days. The entrance is high romance: a steep flight of steps, a massive stone gateway, and a charming inner courtyard, open on one side to a dizzying view across the valley below. The hotel recently changed hands, so check with the local tourist office before making your reservation.

Mont Sainte-Victoire *(8km/5 miles E of Aix).* This high limestone ridge is the mountain that Cézanne loved and painted so often, in so many varied hues. Seen head-on from Aix, as he saw it, it looks like a great white cone. In reality, as seen from the A8 autoroute to the S, it is a long, 16-kilometer (10-mile) wall of rock, rising more than 1,000 meters (3,300 feet).

From Aix, take the D10 to Vauvenargues. Just beyond a string of artificial lakes, leave the car at **Les Cabassols** for a stiff 2-hour hike up a mule-track, past the chapel of Ste-Victoire to the monument of **Croix de Provence** on the summit. From here there are superb views, from the Alps to the sea.

At **Vauvenargues** is the 17thC château owned for a while by Picasso; he lies buried in its park. Near **Pourrières**, at the E end of the ridge, is the site of the Roman general Marius' victory over the Teuton hordes in 102BC. Here 100,000 invaders are said to have been slain — hence, it is thought, the mountain's name.

- See also: MARSEILLE.

ANSOUIS

Map **5**E7 (Vaucluse). 29km (18 miles) N of Aix. Postal code: 84120. Population: 600.

A tiny hill-village, just S of the LUBÉRON mountain, which is dominated by its **Château de Sabran** *(✉ open 2.30-6pm, closed Wed from Nov to end Feb ✗ compulsory: approx. every 30 minutes).* Heavily fortified, part medieval and part 17thC, the château has belonged to the same ducal family since the 13thC. The interior is baronial and impressive, notably the dining hall with its Flemish tapestries and the guard room with its armor. There are also many impressive family portraits (the present Comte de Sabran-Pontèves, who lives there, is a banker — in contrast to his many military forebears). Do not miss the curious hanging gardens.

The kitchen (the room has had the same use since the end of the 11thC) is a favorite with many visitors, and the count still takes his lunch there.

The village **church** is an old Romanesque fortified chapel. Nearby is the little **Mazoyer museum** *(open 2-7pm, closed Tues)* of Provençal furniture, paintings and seashells, the latter an odd subject for a museum in a hill-village.

PLACE NEARBY

La Tour d'Aigues *(8km/5 miles E of Ansouis).* In the village are the ruins of a fine moated 16thC castle, burned in 1780. The stately Corinthian entrance gate gives some idea of the building's quality in its heyday. Attractive views.

≈ ⇌ **LES FENOUILLETS** ■
Quartier Revol ☎*90-07-48-22*
[Fx]*90-07-34-26* ▢ *to* Ⅲ *10 rms* ➡ [AE]
[VISA] & ▢ ☑ ✇ ⛵ *Closed mid-Feb to
mid-Mar. Last orders in restaurant 9pm.*

This is a good, simple hotel. The restaurant specializes in the cuisine of the southwest of France, and menus range from simple grills to duck dishes. Unpretentious but satisfying food.

• See also: LUBÉRON, MONTAGNE DU; SILVACANE, ABBAYE DE.

APT
Map **5***D7 (Vaucluse). 52km (33 miles)* E *of Avignon. Postal code: 84400.
Population: 11,600* ℹ *pl. de la Bouquerie* ☎*90-74-03-18.*

A busy, if not particularly exciting, town set in the valley N of the LUBÉRON mountain, and now creeping up the surrounding hillsides with new high-rise apartment blocks. Apt is a center for the quarrying of ocher (see also ROUSSILLON). It also makes crystallized fruits and lavender essence, and it is a center of the truffle trade in winter.

Apt was an active place in Roman days too, and some traces still remain. Roman baths lie beneath the sub-prefecture, while part of the Arena can be reached underground from the museum.

Ste-Anne, mother of the Virgin, has long been venerated in Apt, for, according to legend, her body was brought here. The town was the site of the first shrine dedicated to her in France, and there is still an annual pilgrimage *(last Sunday in July)*. In the apse of the 11thC **ex-cathedral of Ste-Anne** *(closed Mon, Sun pm)* is a 14thC stained-glass window representing the saint, while a reliquary bust of her is above the altar in the first chapel in the N aisle. This chapel's **sacristy** *(open July, Aug 2.30-5pm, closed Sun, Mon)* houses treasures including 11th and 12thC manuscripts, 12th and 13thC enamel reliquaries, the "shroud of Ste-Anne," and an 11thC Arab standard brought back from the First Crusade.

WHAT TO SEE IN APT
La Maison du Parc
1 pl. Jean Jaurès ☎*90-74-08-55. Open Mon–Fri (Sat also, June–Sept) 8.30am–noon, 1.30–6pm.*
This 18thC house doubles as an information office and small museum of the Lubéron national park. Here you can find maps, details of walks and other outdoor activities in the LUBÉRON, and facts about local natural history. During the summer, there are tastings of regional produce.

There is also a small **Museum of Paleontology** (▨ ✱) covering the local area, with interactive displays.

Musée Archéologique
Pl. Carnot ☎*90-74-00-34* ▨ *Open summer 10am–noon, 2.30–5.30pm; winter 10am–noon, 2.30–4.30pm. Closed Tues.*
The museum contains Roman objects found in local excavations: coins, pieces of mosaic, sarcophagi, and oil lamps of the 2ndC BC. There is also Provençal faïence of the 17th–19thC.

≈ ⇌ **AUBERGE DU LUBÉRON**
17 Quay Léon Sagy ☎*90-74-12-50*
[Fx]*90-04-79-49* Ⅲ *16 rms* ➡ [AE] ▢ ▣

[VISA] ▢ ☑ ⛷ *Closed first week in July.
Location: In the center of town, by the river.* A serviceable old auberge, with

small but well-equipped rooms. Its restaurant, the **Peuzin** *(▦ ⬤ ▢ ▦ ☺ closed Sun, Mon, first week in July, last orders 9.30pm),* is probably the best in town. Its menu centers on Provençal specialities like red mullet, duck *foie gras* with garlic, and pigeon. Desserts also feature. There is a pleasant terrace.

☞ ⚍ Good hotel/restaurant near Apt: **Relais de Roquefure** *(Roquefure, 84400, Apt ☎ 90-04-88-88 ▢ closed Jan to mid-Feb; last orders in restaurant 9.30pm, closed Mon out of season).* Expect a warm welcome from M. and Mme Rousset to their charming, cheap and comfortable country hotel.

PLACE NEAR APT

Colorado de Rustrel *(11km/7 miles NE of Apt).* This is a series of enormous ocher quarries, some still being exploited. To view this unusual sight, leave the car on the main road, D22. It is then about a 50-minute walk to reach the terraces overlooking the partially man-made canyon.

• See also: LUBÉRON, MONTAGNE DE; ROUSSILLON.

ARLES ★

*Map 9F4 (B.-du-R.). 36km (22 miles) SW of Avignon. Postal code: 13200. Population: 53,000 i Esplanade des Lices ☎90-18-41-20. **Railway station** ☎90-96-43-94.*

The mellow city of Arles stands astride the wider of the two arms of the lower Rhône, on the N edge of the plain of the CAMARGUE. It is a museum town *par excellence.* Although no individual building can equal, say, Avignon's Palais des Papes or Orange's Théâtre Antique, the ensemble of Roman and early Christian splendors in Arles is more rich and varied than that found in many French cities. It is also the capital of Provençal folk tradition.

> Arles is so fortunately placed, its commerce is so active and merchants come in such numbers that all the products of the universe are channeled there; the riches of the Orient, perfumes of Arabia, delicacies of Assyria.
>
> (Honorius, Roman Emperor, writing in AD418)

Arles became a key Roman center thanks to its geographical position. After the consul Marius dug a canal to the sea near Fos, around 100BC, it grew into a major maritime port. Being at the southernmost point where the Rhône was bridgeable, it also carried much of the land traffic from Italy to Spain, and was at the junction of the Aurelian Way leading W and the Agrippan Way leading N to Lyon. When Julius Caesar punished Marseille for siding with Pompey, Arles supplanted it in influence and for a while became capital of Roman Provence.

Under the later Roman Empire, it grew into an important industrial and trade center. Constantine the Great built himself a palace here in the 4thC, and in AD400 the Emperor Honorius made Arles the capital of the "three Gauls" (France, Spain and Britain).

After the Roman era, Arles became a vital focus of early Christianity. It was here in 597 that St Augustine was consecrated first Bishop of

Canterbury by the Bishop of Arles. But the town suffered terribly from the Barbarian invasions of the Dark Ages and never recovered its status, even though in the 9th–10thC it was the capital of a kingdom of Provence. From that date on, it played a minor role compared with Aix or Avignon.

In more modern times, Arles has held a strong appeal for writers, artists and musicians. Bizet wrote the music here for Daudet's play *l'Arlésienne.* Van Gogh lived in Arles between 1888–90, painting with a furious fecundity and subsiding into madness; it was here that he cut off his ear. Alas, the Arles that he painted has also been disfigured. His *Café du Soir,* on the E site of place du Forum, later became a furniture store below the VACCARÈS restaurant, but was happily reopened as a café in 1993. The house he shared with Gauguin in place Lamartine, and painted as *The Yellow House,* was bombed in 1944. And his bridge, the *Pont de Langlois,* s of Arles, was pulled down and moved to another canal nearby.

The **Espace Van Gogh** *(rue Président Wilson* ☎ *90-49-39-39)* is the hospital where the painter was taken after he cut off his ear, and which he subsequently painted. It is now a library, a teaching center and an exhibition space. There are annual exhibitions there of the work of artists with an Arles connection. The Espace Van Gogh should not be confused with the **Fondation Van Gogh** *(26 Rond-point des Arènes* ☎ *90-49-94-04),* a private gallery that sometimes mounts major exhibitions, but has no connection with Van Gogh himself.

This country seems to me as beautiful as Japan for clarity of atmosphere and gay color effects. Water forms patches of lovely emerald or rich blue in the landscape, just as we see it in the crepe-prints. The pale orange of the sunsets make the fields appear blue.
(Letters, 1888–90, Vincent Van Gogh)

Today, artists in Arles are few, and folklore is for museums and festivals. The lovely old costumes and bonnets of the Arlésiennes are no longer part of daily wear. As a modern town, Arles is a quiet place, except for its tourist trade, with little of the intense inner-city animation of Aix or Avignon. But its old streets have their own sleepy charm. Apart from the **Alyscamps** to the SE, all the main sights are close together in the town center, between **boulevard des Lices** and the broad majestic Rhône (there is a promenade above the river, past the back of the **Musée Réattu**).

The heart of the town is **place de la République**, where stand the former cathedral of **St-Trophîme** and Mansart's imposing 17thC **Hôtel de Ville**. Just to the N, the small **place du Forum** is not quite on the site of the old Roman forum, but the two Corinthian columns at its SE corner are the remains of a temple that adjoined the forum. In the square is a statue of the poet Mistral, around whom the tiresome north wind of the same name often swirls.

Some of the town's main museums are being relocated to the **IRPA** (Institut de Recherches sur la Provence Antique) research center being built by the excavation site of the old Roman Circus on the N outskirts of town. The research center, designed by Henri Ciriani, strikes some as rather unattractively resembling a factory, but others admire its modern

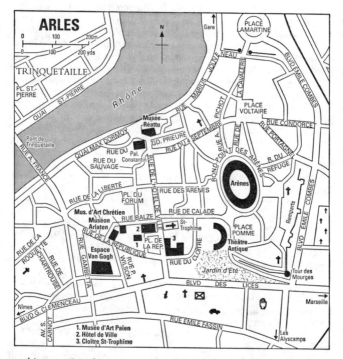

1. Musée d'Art Païen
2. Hôtel de Ville
3. Cloître St-Trophîme

architecture. It is due to open some time late in 1994, and will house the museums of Christian and Pagan Art (their present sites will probably become exhibition spaces). The **Musée Camarguais** is due to move to LES SAINTES-MARIES-DE-LA-MER, 38 kilometers (24 miles) away.

• **EVENTS** • On May 1, there is a **fête** of Camargue *gardians* (people who tend the wild horses and bulls).

• In July, there is an international **festival of music, dance and drama** in the Théâtre Antique. • Also in July is an international photography festival, the **Rencontres Internationales de la Photographie** *(10 Rond-point des Arènes* ☎ *90-96-76-06).* It can be very difficult to find a hotel room during this period. • In August is the unusual, indeed bizarre, **Festival du Film Peplum**: screenings of movie epics set in ancient times at the Théâtre Antique.

• From mid-December to mid-January, a **trade fair** of *santons* is held in the town.

• **Bullfights** (normally in the Provençal style, where the bull is not hurt, but also in the Spanish style: to the death) are held in the Roman arena approximately two Sundays in every month, from April to November.

• There is a four-day **bullfight festival** from Easter Friday to Monday *(*☎ *90-96-03-70).* Reservations are taken as early as January, and at the time of the festival, the hotels are always full.

• There are major **art exhibitions** for most of the year, with a major new exhibition opening at the Espace Van Gogh every spring.

WHAT TO SEE IN ARLES

Various combination tickets are available for admission to the sights in Arles. Details from the tourist office or from any of the attractions.

Les Alyscamps

Rue Pierre-Renaudel ▱ *Open June–Sept 9am–12.30pm, 2–7pm; Mar, Apr, May, Oct 9am–12.30pm, 2–6, 6.30 or 7pm; Jan, Feb, Nov, Dec 9am–noon, 2–4.30 or 5pm.*

This wide path lined with sarcophagi, in the SE suburbs, is the remnant of what was formerly one of Christendom's greatest cemeteries. The Romans first established it as a necropolis on the Aurelian Way (Alyscamps is thought to mean Elysian Fields). During early Christian times it became a prestigious burial ground, remaining so until the 12thC.

Almost 2 kilometers (1 mile) long and half as wide, it contained thousands of tombs. Many of these were given away as gifts during the Renaissance, but some have found their way into the museums of Arles. Today a few second-rate tombs remain on the site, which preserves a strange, faded and peaceful atmosphere, even though factories and a railway now insensitively abut it. At the end of the path is the ruined Romanesque church of **St-Honnorat**.

Les Arènes ▥ ☆

Rond-point des Arènes. For entry details and opening times see LES ALYSCAMPS ◁€

Built in the 1st century BC, this is one of the earliest arenas of the Roman world, as well as one of the largest. It could hold some 21,000 spectators. Fights with wild beasts were often held here, as is clear from the height of the wall surrounding the ring, and from the tunnels that led to their cages. For gladiatorial combat, a raised wooden floor was temporarily inserted, to give the lower spectators a better view (you can still see the sockets of its supports in the wall).

After the fall of the Roman Empire, the arena was turned into a fortress, with a church and some 200 houses inside. Its own stones were used for this construction, so it suffered badly and was not restored until the 19thC. Today the arena is in fairly good shape, although unlike the arena at NÎMES, it lacks a third story, which would have held a canopy-like roof. The three towers were added as a defense in the 7th and 8thC. From the top of the tower by the entrance you get a good bird's-eye view of the arena, and of Arles and the country around.

Today, bullfights and festivals are frequently held here (see opposite).

Arlaten, Museon ☆

Rue de la République ☎ *90-96-08-23* ▱ ✗ *Open summer 9am–noon, 2–5pm (7pm July, Aug); winter 9am–noon, 2–5pm. Closed Mon.*

This marvelously vivid and varied museum of Provençal traditional life was founded in 1896 by the poet Frédéric Mistral, who installed it in this 16thC house. He spent many years building up this great collection, helped at the end by the money from his 1904 Nobel Prize for Literature, and many of the exhibits are labeled and explained in his own hand. The museum is an intensely personal creation. Every one of its 30 rooms is suffused with Mistral's passion for the people, language and culture of his native Provence.

The whole museum, particularly the first floor, holds a splendid profusion of exhibits, which merit hours of study. From traditional costumes and coiffures to a green spiky monster, the Tarasque, from the famous procession at TARASCON, and from life-sized tableaux of traditional scenes to the golden tresses of a girl found in a tomb at LES BAUX, the museum is a marvelous insight into the cultures and traditions of Provence.

Art Chrétien, Musée d' (Museum of Christian Art)
Formerly in rue Balze. Due to relocate during 1994 to the new IRPA building (see page 75). Check opening details with tourist office.
This collection of richly carved early Christian sarcophagi is the world's finest after that of the Lateran Museum in Rome. It includes three splendid 4thC tombs found in 1974 at Trinquetaille in the NW suburbs of Arles, and a fascinating tomb of a married couple, known as the **tomb of the Trinity**, with a medallion of the couple below friezes of Old Testament scenes. Also on view are sarcophagi from LES ALYSCAMPS.

Art Païen, Musée d' (Museum of Pagan Art)
Formerly in rue de la République. Due to relocate during 1994 to the new IRPA building (see page 75). Check opening details with tourist office.
This is a rich collection of Greek and Roman art — statues, tombs, mosaics — all found locally. A fine sarcophagus of **Hippolytus and Phaedra**, a Greek work from the 2ndC AD, comes from the villa excavated at Trinquetaille.

The statue of *Augustus* stood at the THÉÂTRE ANTIQUE. The two statues of *Venus* are casts of the famous *Venus of Arles,* also found in the theater, in 1651, broken in three pieces and with both arms missing. The original, much restored, is in the Louvre. Of the two copies here, the one made in the late 17thC, just before the Restoration, has a pristine purity that is missing in the later model, more complete but more contrived.

The Grecian or Greek-influenced works here are noticeably more sophisticated than those in the parallel Christian Art museum, and show a far greater understanding of the human form and how to portray it.

Réattu, Musée ☆
Rue du Grand Prieuré ☎90-49-37-58. Open June–Sept 9am–12.30pm, 2–7pm; Feb–Apr 10am–12.30pm, 2–7pm; Oct 10am–12.30pm, 2–6pm; Nov, Dec, Jan 10am–12.30pm, 2–5pm.
Formerly the Priory of the Knights of Malta, this graceful 15thC building belonged for a while to the local painter Jacques Réattu (1760–1833). It is now a spacious museum of art, varied and eclectic, and uneven in quality. Many of the works by minor 19th and 20thC painters are mediocre, including most of those by Réattu himself. But there are wonderful things, too.

On the ground floor, pieces of Roman masonry stand beside an arresting modern tapestry by the Spaniard Grau Garriga. But most of the exhibits are in a suite of 12 rooms on the first floor. Here, two collections stand out: first, five 17thC **Brussels tapestries** showing a quirkily imaginative view of five of the Seven Wonders of the World; second, an intriguing set of colored **sketches by Picasso**, donated by him in 1971. Most are in cartoon style, like playing-card figures, with an impish sense of humor. One room is devoted to Lurçat, with a fine tapestry, *Early Dawn.* There is a notable Léger, *The King of Hearts.*

The second floor houses a display of 19th and 20thC photographs, mostly views of Arles. Special exhibitions are held here every summer.

St-Trophîme ⅲ † ☆
Rue de l'Hôtel-de-Ville. Open 10am–noon, 2–7pm.
This former cathedral, now demoted to a church, is dedicated to St-Trophîme, who was said to have been sent by St Peter to evangelize Provence. Although much rebuilt in the 11th, 12th and 15thC, the original church was Carolingian. This is evident from the w facade, where the lowest part is Carolingian, while the 12thC **portal** above is purest Provençal Romanesque, in startling contrast to the plainness of the upper facade. The stone carvings, once somber and weather-beaten, were cleaned in 1993, and are very rich. Above a row of stern-looking saints is a curious frieze: to the left, a row of the elect, fully clad, advance toward Christ in the center; to the right, the damned are led off, naked and chained together, to be cast into hell.

Inside, the Romanesque nave is unusually high and narrow. Its simplicity contrasts with the Gothic flamboyance of the choir. In a chapel off the N aisle is a 4thC sarcophagus now used as a font; farther on, another sarcophagus, representing the crossing of the Red Sea, is now an altar. Note also two paintings by Finsonius: an *Annunciation,* in the left transept, and an *Adoration of the Magi* in a chapel off the s aisle.

St-Trophîme, Cloître (St-Trophîme Cloister) ⅲ ☆
Pl. de la République. Entrance through the porch next to the Palais de l'Archevêché. Open June–Sept 9am–12.30pm, 2–7pm; Apr–May 9.30–12.30pm, 2–7pm; rest of year 9.30 or 10am–12.30pm, 2–5.30 or 6pm.
Its serene beauty, and its ornate and detailed carvings, have made this the most renowned of all the cloisters in Provence. Its graceful arcades, with their slender marble pillars, surround a little garden of cypresses. The N and E arcades (12thC) have barrel vaulting, while those to the w and s, with ogival arches, are 14thC Gothic. The capitals are decorated with scenes from the Bible and from Provençal legends, including, on the s side, the strange low relief of St Martha and the Tarasque dragon (the legend is fully explained in the TARASCON entry on page 151), and the pillars themselves carry elaborate carvings of Christ and saints. The richest are to be found at the NW and NE corners.

A chapel off the N side contains three superb 17thC Aubusson tapestries of the *Life of the Virgin,* and three smaller 17thC Flemish tapestries of the Hebrews.

Théâtre Antique (Roman Theater)

Rue du Cloître. For entry details and opening times see LES ALYSCAMPS.

Built under the Emperor Augustus, the theater today is far more of a ruin than the arena. In the Dark and Middle Ages, it was pillaged and used as a quarry to provide building materials for churches, houses and the city ramparts. Of the stage wall, once so elaborate with its rows of statues, just two tall columns and a few lesser fragments survive; but the foundations of the stage are still visible.

Twenty rows of seats survive too, from a theater that once held nearly 7,000 people. Open-air spectacles are held here in summer (see page 76).

Thermes de Constantin, Palais Constantin (Baths of Constantine) ▥

Rue D. Maïsto, opposite MUSÉE RÉATTU.

These Roman baths, the largest in Provence, are all that visibly survive of Constantine's great imperial 4thC palace. Although partly ruined, the sheer size, 98 meters (320 feet) by 45 meters (148 feet), is impressive. Unlike earlier Roman buildings, the baths are constructed of narrow alternate layers of brick and stone.

✆ WHERE TO STAY IN ARLES

ARLATAN ♣

26 rue du Sauvage, 13200 Arles
☎90-93-56-66 ⟨Ex⟩90-49-68-45 ▥ to ▥
50 rms ▦ ▣ AE ⊙ ⊙ ▥ ⌂ ≷ ⊌ ▢
▢ ☀ ⵖ ▣

Location: On a quiet side street, in the Old Town. One of the loveliest hotels in Arles. Its Arcadian garden is under the high Roman wall of Constantine's palace; beside it is an equally charming patio where breakfasts and drinks are served. The building, 15th–17thC, was the ancestral home of the Counts of Arlatan, and has been converted with consummate taste by the Desjardin family, which runs the hotel with the civilized and friendly warmth that the setting deserves. The red-tiled floors, beamed ceilings and 18thC furniture, all so common in Provence, are most elegant; many of the rooms have the original walls exposed, as well as other features of architectural interest. Some have four-poster beds. Five rooms overlook the garden, and a number of others have a view of the courtyard. The hotel was enlarged and its facilities were improved in 1989, when it acquired a neighboring building. One extraordinary feature of this new area is that, under part of the floor (covered by toughened glass), you can see relics of the old Roman forum, which date back to the 1stC BC.

LE CLOÎTRE

16 rue du Cloître, 13200 Arles
☎90-96-29-50 ▥ *33 rms* ⊟ AE ⊙ ▥
⌂ ▢ ▢

Location: Very central, in a narrow street of the Old Town. Some bedrooms of this quiet little hotel overlook the lovely cloister of St-Trophîme. The hotel has few amenities, but is efficient and comfortable enough.

JULES CÉSAR ⌨ ▥

Blvd. des Lices, 13200 Arles
☎90-93-43-20 ⟨Ex⟩90-93-33-47 ▥ *55 rms* ▦ ▣ AE ⊙ ⊙ ▥ ₺ ▢ ⌂ ⊌ ⌐
☀ ⵖ ▣ *Closed Nov to mid-Dec. For* ⊟
see LOU MARQUÈS, below.

Location: On the town's main boulevard. This 17thC Carmelite convent is now a sedate hotel, particularly popular with well-to-do Americans. Its best feature is the flowery, tree-lined cloister garden, where you can take breakfast or bask in the sun. The lobby is too grand for many tastes, and the mock-Imperial Roman facade is, perhaps, a misjudgment. But the large Baroque chapel, now used for receptions and exhibitions, is genuine enough. Bedrooms are most pleasantly decorated with Provençal furniture and Souleiado fabrics, and bathrooms are very well appointed. The charmingly efficient owners, Monsieur and Madam Albagnac, are hoteliers very much of the old school. The food is varied and excellent.

MAS DE LA CHAPELLE
Petite Route de Tarascon, 13200 Arles
☎90-93-23-15 ⊠90-96-53-74 ▥ 16 rms ⇔ ≒ AE ⊙ ⊚ VISA ⌂ ▢ ⌸ &
❦ ⛾ ≈ ♪° ▱ *Closed Feb.*
Location: Off the N570, w of Arles. This lovely old farmhouse, set in an eight-acre park, has very good facilities, including three tennis courts and a pool. It is a most relaxing place, and tastefully decorated with tapestries. The restaurant is housed in a 16thC chapel of the Knights of Malta.

NORD-PINUS
Pl. du Forum, 13200 Arles ☎90-93-44-44
⊠90-93-34-00 ▥ to ▥ 24 rms ▱ ≒ AE VISA ✦ ▢ ⌸ ▱ *Closed Jan.–Feb.*
Location: Centrally positioned, near the Hôtel de Ville. Eccentric, eclectic decor (bull-fighting posters, trophies, mementos of Picasso and Cocteau) but a very good hotel, with strong literary

connections, recently taken over by young owners. An unusual, slightly raffish, ambience, with large, comfortable rooms and good bathrooms. Many of the matadors appearing in Arles stay here, as have many famous names. It is one of the favorite hotels of local boy Christian Lacroix. Its brasserie/restaurant has a good reputation. In the summer you can sit outside (in the shade) in place du Forum.

PRIMOTEL CAMARGUE
Av. 1ère-Division-Française-Libre
☎90-93-98-80 ⊠90-49-92-76 ▥ 147 rms ▱ ▤ ≒ AE ⊕ ⊙ VISA ✦ ▢ ⌸ ❦ ≈ ♪° ⛾ ☸
Location: Near the convention center. A serviceable, if rather bland, modern business hotel. Attractions include a tennis court and a large pool.

❧   Other hotels in Arles: **Calendal** *(22 pl. Pomme* ☎90-96-11-89 ▱ *to* ▥ *)*, a modest hotel that offers good value; **Camargue** *(45 av. Sadi-Carnot* ☎90-99-40-40 ⊠90-93-32-50 ▥ *)*, a good, modern hotel, which was formerly a member of the Mercure group; **Mireille** *(2 pl. St-Pierre* ☎90-93-70-74 ▥ *)*, situated across the Rhône from the main part of town; and **Le Forum** *(10 pl. du Forum* ☎90-93-48-95 ▥ *to* ▥ *)*.

≒ EATING AND DRINKING IN ARLES

L'ESCALADOU ☻ ♥
23 rue Porte de Laure ☎90-96-70-43
▥ MI to ▥ ▭ ■■ *No cards. Closed Wed. Last orders 11.30pm.*
Situated in a side street not far from the Arena, this place is what the locals would call *typique*. An authentic, no-frills restaurant, it is packed with Arlésians of all types, having a thoroughly good time eating large helpings of food, which, if not cooked or presented with delicacy, is at least flavorful and served with enthusiasm. Old-fashioned down-to-earth places like this, with their reasonable prices, and pleasant (if leisurely) service and ambience, are becoming increasingly difficult to find in

Provence. Try the *soupe de poisson,* the Arles sausage, or the *boeuf gardian.* The latter is the famous spicy Camarguais beef stew with olives.

HOSTELLERIE DES ARÈNES ☻ ♥
62 rue du Réfuge ☎90-96-13-05 ▱ ■■ ⊙ VISA ⌸ *Closed Wed; Tues dinner out of season. Last orders 9pm (10pm in summer).*
Location: Opposite the Arènes. Tourists and Arlésians alike flock to this simple family-run *auberge* and pizzeria. It's often crowded, but the value is remarkable and the food excellent. *Specialities: confit de canard, salade Arlésienne, côte d'agneau grillé.* You can eat on the terrace in summer.

LOU MARQUÈS
Hôtel Jules César, Blvd. des Lices
☎ 90-93-43-20 ▢ to ▢ ▢ ▆ ▆ ▆
▬ AE ▣ ▣ ▨ *Last orders 9.30pm.*
Closed Nov to mid-Dec.

Alas, the waitresses no longer wear Arlésienne costume, but their service remains skilled and smiling, and a meal here is a joy, either in the spacious dining room or (especially) on the front terrace. There are a number of menus (including a specifically Provençal one, a quick lunch menu, and one for children), and chef Pascal Renaud shows great skill with specialities such as *pigeon de grain au miel de lavade et au rhum, filet de loup rôti au jus de volaille, noisette d'agneau de Sisteron et son ragout fin d'artichauts et d'olives noires.* The wine list is excellent, although not cheap. (See ☞ JULES CÉSAR, above.)

LE MEDIÉVAL
9 rue Truchet ☎ 90-96-65-77 ▢ ▆ ▆
🏠 ▣ ▨ *Closed Wed; Nov–Feb. Last orders 10pm.*

This is a most unusual place, in a tiny side-street near place du Forum. The genial chef-patron Guido Ballestera hails from Cortona in Italy, but the food is firmly Provençal, as are the reasonably-priced wines. The small dining room with its open fire (all year round) is a vaulted room, once part of a 12thC abbey. Both the decor and the cooking are simple, the clientele youngish and the atmosphere casual and jolly. The main courses are, perhaps, a tad overpriced, but the food is good and fresh,

and you can eat well here. In the summer, a few tables are put outside. Gentle classical music plays in the background, making way, from time to time, for occasional visits from serenading guitarists.

LE TAMBOURIN
65 rue Amédée-Pichot ☎ 90-93-13-32 ▢
▢ ▆ AE ▣ ▨ ▨ *Closed Mon. Last orders 10.30pm.*

A place with friendly service, soft lighting and family cooking. Fish and seafood are the specialities here.

LE VACCARÈS
Pl. du Forum ☎ 90-96-06-17 ▢ to ▢ ▢
▆ ▆ 🏠 ▣ ▨ *Closed Mon; Sun (dinner); Jan. Last orders 9.30pm.*

Le Vaccarès is a lake in the Camargue, and Bernard Dumas' excellent and varied cuisine closely reflects the traditional dishes of the region, as well as including some flourishes of his own. Equally excellent is the wine list, well balanced and very reasonably priced. The chic and spacious restaurant faces the Roman Forum, and there is a small outdoor terrace. *Specialities: Soupière de baudroie camarguaise, pieds et paquets, filets de sandre à la poutargue.*

▬ Other recommended restaurants in Arles: **Le Tourne-Broche** *(6 rue Balze* ☎ *90-96-16-03* ▢ *),* where meals are served in a vaulted 17thC room; or **L'Olivier** *(1bis rue Réattu* ☎ *90-49-64-88),* which is one of the fanciest restaurants in town, with prices to match.

SHOPPING IN ARLES
E. Ferriol *(2bis, Chemin de Barrol)* makes and sells *santons;* the workshop is open to visits 10am–8pm, except Sunday. **M. Deville** *(66 rue de Chartreuse)* sells ceramics. You can buy Provençal *Indiennage* fabrics from **Souleiado** *(4 blvd. des Lices)* or **Les Olivades** *(2 rue Jean Jaurès),* and traditional Arles lace and other local items from **L'Arlésienne** *(12 rue Wilson).*

- **MARKETS** There is a bustling **food market** (the place to get Arles sausage) Wednesday and Saturday mornings along the town's main street, the Boulevard des Lices. • The **Saturday market** is very much a jolly local event. • An **antiques market** takes place there on the first Wednesday of the month.

🔊 NIGHTLIFE IN ARLES

For bars, try the lively **place du Forum** (the bar **Le Paris**, for example).
• The main disco is **Le Plantation** *(outside town at Albaron on the N570 ☎90-97-11-26)*. • **Le Tropicana** *(7 rue Molière ☎90-93-34-70)* is a piano bar. • **Acte Sud/Le Méjan** *(quai M. Dormay ☎90-93-33-56)* is a lively arts and cinema complex with a bar and a restaurant *(closed mid-July to end Aug)*.

PLACES NEAR ARLES

Montmajour, Abbaye de (Ⅲ ✝) *(5km/3 miles) NE of Arles, beside D17 to Fontvieille* 🔁 *open Apr-Sept 9-11.45am, 2-7pm, Oct-Mar 9-11.45am, 2-5pm, closed Tues, Wed)*. The former Benedictine abbey of Montmajour was founded in the 10thC, on a low hill which then was an island surrounded by marshlands beside the Rhône. In the Middle Ages it was rich and powerful, owning priories all over Provence: its annual *pardon* would draw up to 100,000 pilgrims. But the abbey gradually fell into decline, and after the Revolution was sold off cheaply by the State and partially demolished.

Today, it is only partly restored. The towering, crenelated *donjon*, built for defense against marauders, dates from the 14thC. Below it stands the 12thC Romanesque church of **Notre-Dame**, cross-shaped, with an unusually wide nave. From here, steps lead down into the crypt, partly raised and partly built out of the rock. The **cloister** with its marble pillars and ancient well is particularly charming. Note the carvings of bears, camels and other animals on the capitals of the columns.

The unusual little burial-ground chapel of **Ste-Croix** *(keys at the abbey)* lies 180 meters (200 yards) along the Fontvieille road. It is shaped in the form of a Greek cross and is surmounted by a campanile.

St-Gilles *(15km/9 miles w of Arles, on N572)*. In the Middle Ages this town on the edge of the Camargue was an important center for pilgrims, who came to venerate the tomb of St-Gilles the Hermit. It was also en route to Santiago de Compostela, and a port of embarkation for the Crusades.

An abbey was founded here by St-Gilles in the 7thC, but the present abbey-church dates from the 12thC. It was badly damaged during the Wars of Religion, but its broad **west front** (✪) survives as one of the finest ensembles of medieval sculpture in Provence. Its three arched portals are decorated with scenes from the life of Christ and with animals such as lions, camels and even a centaur. The central doorway was carved by 12thC artists from Toulouse; the side doorways are the work of early 13thC sculptors from the Paris area.

The abbey-church's 11thC **crypt** is a spacious Romanesque church in its own right, one of the earliest in France to have ogival vaulting. Here the **tomb of St-Gilles** was unearthed in 1865 and is believed to be authentic. The E part of the abbey-church is in ruins, save for a solitary bell tower: this contains a famous spiral staircase, known as **Le Vis** (the "screw"), unusual because the steps are roofed over with stone, giving the effect of a curving funnel *(crypt and staircase* 🔁 ✗ *on the hour 9-11am, 3-6pm, half-hourly July-Aug, closed Jan-Feb)*.

Nearby is a **museum**, with lapidary remains from the church.

- See also: LES BAUX, BEAUCAIRE, LA CAMARGUE, FONTVIEILLE, ST-RÉMY-DE-PROVENCE, TARASCON.

AVIGNON ★

*Map **9**D4 (Vaucluse). 100km (63 miles) NW of Marseille. Postal code: 84000. Population: 91,500* **i** *41 Cours Jean-Jaurès* ☎*90-82-65-11, and small office near Pont St-Bénézet.* **Airport** ☎*90-81-51-51.* **Railway station** ☎*90-82-50-50.*

Avignon, like AIX-EN-PROVENCE, is a sophisticated modern city with a glorious historical legacy. But whereas Aix's history focuses on the intimacy of the 17thC, Avignon's great period was the grander 14thC. Today, the full circuit of the ramparts above the Rhône remains, even if four-fifths of the town spreads outside them. Dominating it all is the colossal palace that the Popes created here. It is perhaps the most impressive medieval building in Europe.

Well placed at the confluence of the Rhône and Durance, Avignon had been a trading center since pre-Roman times. Yet mere chance led to its becoming a major city, for it was indeed chance that led the Papacy to move here.

In 1307, the Papacy found that life in Rome was becoming impossible, owing to the endless feuding between rival noble families. It already possessed the lands of the Comtat Venaissin just to the N of Avignon, but these had no town suitable to be its capital. Avignon was in the earldom of Provence, then on friendly terms with the Church; and it was in fact the French king, Philippe le Bel, who persuaded the newly elected Clément V, a French Pope, to make the move here, in the hope of increasing French influence over the Papacy.

Clément and his successor ruled from the episcopal palace. Then Benedict XII, elected in 1334, decided to make the move from Rome more permanent by building the **Palais des Papes**, which was completed in 1352 by his successor, Clément VI. Thus began Avignon's brief golden age as the capital of Christendom, at a time when the Papacy enjoyed pomp and high living, flaunted its great wealth ostentatiously, and was tolerant of fleshly weaknesses.

Avignon became a town of gaiety and luxury, even of vice and crime, to the horror of some of the more straitlaced members of the papal entourage, including the Italian poet Petrarch: ". . . an abode of sorrows, the shame of mankind, a sink of vice. . . a sewer where all the filth of the universe has gathered. There God is held in contempt, money is worshiped, and the laws of God and man are trampled underfoot. Everything there breathes a lie: the air, the earth, the houses and above all the bedrooms."

By 1377, seven Popes had ruled in Avignon, all of them French; then, at last, Gregory XI was persuaded to return to Rome. But some Cardinals disputed the move and decided to remain in Avignon, where they elected their own Pope — or Antipope. Thus began the Great Schism of the West, as Popes and Antipopes flung insults and excommunications at one another, and wrangled over Papal lands and revenues. Avignon's last

Antipope was expelled by force in 1403, but he continued the fight in his native Spain, and the Schism did not end until 1449. Avignon was then governed by a Papal legate until the Revolution, when it was finally united to France.

> I climbed the green-fringed ramps which led up into the marvellous hanging gardens of the Rocher des Doms. From this vantage point one can look down on three sides to see the loops and curls of the Rhône carving out the embankments of its bed in the carious limestone, sculpting the soft flanks of the nether hills. A frail sun shone upon distant snowlines leading away towards the Alps. Mont Sainte-Victoire stood up in the distance, erect as a martyr, tied to its stake of ice.
>
> (*Monsieur or The Prince of Darkness,* 1974, Lawrence Durrell)

The focus of the town's life today is still the area within the ramparts, which were built in the 1350s by Innocent VI, then much restored by the architect Viollet-le-Duc in the 19thC. Avignon lies on a plain surrounded by suburbs and other towns, and so is less spectacular as a walled city than Carcassonne or AIGUES-MORTES. But the network of old streets within the ramparts is fascinating and full of animation. Here the main avenue is **rue de la République**, leading from the station to **place de l'Horloge**, the center of social life.

Avignon is one of the most fashionable French towns outside Paris: the shops are smart, and so are the people, who since Papal days have kept their reputation for ebullience and gaiety. The town lives late. Even out of season, the cafés in place de l'Horloge are crowded long past midnight with young people. And Avignon's July theater festival is one of Europe's great annual cultural events.

PARKING IN AVIGNON
The old town of Avignon, with its one-way systems and pedestrianized areas, is a nightmare for drivers. The best advice is to park outside the city walls at the gate nearest your destination and then walk. If you get lost, walk or drive around the outside of the walls until you find the correct gate.

- **EVENTS**   At the end of January is the **Cheval Passion**, a three-day horse festival. • In February there is a **dance festival** and an **antique fair**. • In April is a **festival of Provençal Baroque art**. • In August a **jousting tournament** on the Rhône makes a colorful and exciting spectacle. • An **international drama festival** takes place for a month from mid-July, one of Europe's leading events of its kind, created in 1947 by Jean Vilar and Gérard Philippe. It presents some 50 productions in all, including many on the "fringe." Main productions are staged in the Great Courtyard of the Palais des Papes. Apply to the Bureau du Festival *(BP 92, 84006 Avignon)*. The festival's headquarters are at the Hôtel de Crochans *(8bis rue de Mons* ☎ *90-82-67-08)*.

- The high-tech and efficient tourist office produces a list of events, titled *Rendez-Vous,* every two weeks.

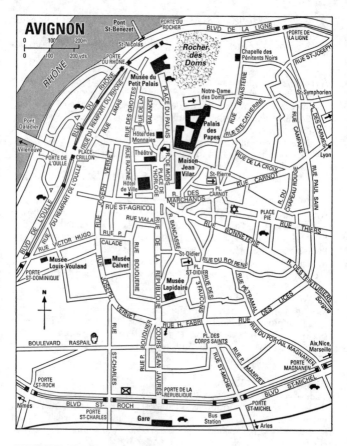

WHAT TO SEE IN AVIGNON
Calvet, Musée

Rue Joseph Vernet ☎ *90-86-33-84* 🔳 📷 *Open 9am–noon, 2–6pm. Closed Tues. The museum has been closed for renovation, but will partially reopen during 1994.*

The ground floor of this 18thC mansion houses an oddly diversified museum of art. One large room contains hundreds of pieces of wrought iron and locksmiths' work — one of Europe's leading collections of its kind. Next door is the Hellenic room: vases, sculptures and stelae dating back to the 4thC BC.

The lion's share of the museum is given over to a display of French painting from the 16th–20thC (as well as two Brueghels), remarkable more for its range than its high quality. The early Avignon School is here in force, led by Mignard and de Chalons; landscapes by the 18thC Joseph Vernet of Avignon share rooms with paintings by Géricault, Toulouse-Lautrec, and a good Corot. Of the modern artists, Vlaminck, Dufy and Utrillo are outshone by a lesser-known painter, Albert Gleizes, whose three vivid canvases recall Picasso.

The museum surrounds a courtyard that is full of peacocks, where — so says an inscription — Stendhal once liked to stroll.

Lapidaire, Musée
27 rue de la République ▨ *(▣ Nov–Apr). Open 10am–noon, 2–6pm. Closed Tues.*

Housed in a former 17thC Jesuit chapel, the museum contains a few Renaissance sculptures, but is devoted mainly to local Roman and pre-Roman remains. Note especially the *Venus of Pournières,* found near Aix, and the *Tarasque of Noves,* a statuette of a man-eating lion, dating from the Second Iron Age.

Palais des Papes ▥ † ★
Pl. du Palais ☎ *90-27-50-00* ▨ ▣ ◁ *ⲭ all year round in French, and from mid-Mar to end Oct in various other languages. Open daily for guided or unguided visits: Apr to mid-Aug, Oct 9am–7pm; mid-Aug to end Sept 9am–8pm; Nov–Mar 9am–noon, 2–6pm.*

At first sight, with its massive walls and turreted towers rising to 45 meters (150 feet), this great building looks more like a fortress than a palace of the Church. Inside, it is a labyrinth of halls, chapels and corridors.

In fact there are two adjacent palaces, built within 20 years by two very different Popes. **The Old Palace** to the N is simple and sober, reflecting the austere spirit of Benedict XII, a former Cistercian monk. The **New Palace** to the S, built by Clément VI, a lover of the arts and of high pomp, is much more ornate.

During the French Revolution, the building was damaged and its furniture removed; from 1810 until 1906 it served as a barracks, and many of the frescoes were vandalized. Today it has been restored as far as possible; but it is still bare of much of the sumptuous decor and furnishings that must have lent it such splendor in its great days.

The conducted tour begins in the **Grand Courtyard** and proceeds first to the **consistoire**, where the Pope received important visitors, conferred with his cardinals, and passed judgment in trials. Little is left of its lavish decoration, save for some fine but faded frescoes by Simone Martini of Siena. It is now hung with 18thC portraits of the nine Avignon Popes. Off this room is the **chapel of St-Jean**, its upper part covered with bright frescoes showing scenes from the lives of the two St Johns, by Matteo Giovanetti, painter to Pope Clément.

The tour then leads upstairs to the long **Banqueting Hall** (le Grand Tinel), where 150 people would sit down to a meal that lasted as long as 8 hours, accompanied by minstrels and jugglers. The hall today is hung with six Gobelins tapestries: the best, early 18thC, are based on works by Raphael. Off the hall is the tiny **chapel of St-Martial**, its upper walls and ceilings lined with beautiful dark blue frescoes by Giovanetti, showing the miracles of St-Martial.

Steps lead down from the hall to the **Papal Antechamber**, where traces remain of the original vaulted roofing, badly damaged by a fire in 1413. This room contains a scale model of the palace as it was in the 14thC. The Pope's **bedroom** (☆) is small and richly decorated. Note that its blue-and-gold frescoes of birds, squirrels and foliage are entirely secular: so they probably date from Clément VI, not Benedict XII. The brightly-colored tiled mosaic floor is a recent copy of the original, which was found beneath existing flooring and is now in the palace museum.

Pope Clément's study is known as the **Room of the Deer** (☆) because of its intriguing frescoes of hunting and fishing scenes, swimming and games, which offer more evidence of the worldly tastes of Clément and his court. Steps lead to the N sacristy of the **Grand Chapel**, containing statues of Popes, cardinals and kings, copies of originals in various museums. The Grand Chapel itself has 17thC paintings by Mignard and Parrocel. In its s sacristy are casts of the tombs of Clément VI and other popes.

The tour here ends, and the visitor is left to explore other rooms himself. At the top of the staircase leading from the Grand Chapel is the **Indulgence Window**, from which the Pope would give his blessing to pilgrims in the courtyard below. The stairs lead down to the **Grand Audience Hall**, a majestic state room where tribunals were held. On the way out, do not miss the lovely vaulted **Gallery of the Conclave**. This leads to the Conclave itself, where the cardinals were locked up to elect a new Pope, as still happens in the Vatican today.

In summer, there is an open-air cafeteria, with very good views of Avignon. The **gardens of the Rocher des Doms**, next to the Palais des Papes, are very pleasant, and also afford magnificent views of Avignon, the Rhône, and the surrounding area.

Petit Palais, Musée du ☆
Pl. du Palais ☎ *90-86-44-58* ■■ *Open 9.30–11.50am, 2–6pm. Closed Tues.*
Built in 1317, this is the former palace of the Archbishops of Avignon, whose famous guests included Cesare Borgia and François 1er. It is now a museum with 20 rooms, very well laid out, housing a remarkable collection of 13th to 16thC works of art of the Avignon and Northern Italian schools. Avignon is represented by frescoes and sculptures and by two rooms of paintings, notably a beautiful retable by Enguerrand Charonton. Especially impressive are the compelling Italian Primitives: a *Virgin and Child* by Taddeo di Bartolo of the Siena school; and a *Virgin in Majesty* by an unknown Pistoia artist. There is a room of fine Florentine paintings (note the lovely triptych by Lorenzo Monaco, the vividly-colored miniatures by Ambrogio di Baldese, and Botticelli's *Virgin and Child*), and among the best of the Venetian works are a triptych by Antonio Alberti and a *Holy Conversation* by Carpaccio.

Also in place du Palais is the cathedral of **Notre-Dame-des-Doms**, dating from the 12thC. It contains an archbishop's throne in white marble, and, in a chapel off the sacristy, the Flamboyant Gothic tomb of Pope John XXII. The gilt *Madonna* on the steeple was added in 1859.

Just to the N of the cathedral and the Palais des Papes is the **Rocher des Doms**, a rocky plateau overlooking the Rhône, which has been transformed into an attractive, rose-filled garden with a little lake and fine views. Also in place du Palais is the **Hôtel des Monnaies**, a large 17thC mansion with a highly decorated facade.

Pont St-Bénézet
Open Apr to end Sept, 9am–6.30pm; Oct to end Mar, 9am–1pm, 2–5pm. Closed Tues.
Built in the late 12thC, this famous bridge originally stretched for 900 meters (985 yards) across the river to the foot of the Tower of Philippe le Bel in VILLENEUVE-LÈS-AVIGNON. As one of the then very few solid bridges over the lower Rhône, it helped bring prosperity to the town. But most of it was carried away by floods in the 17thC, and today just four arches remain, on the Avignon side. Beside one of them is the small **chapel of St-Nicolas**, Gothic above, Romanesque below.

This is the "Pont d'Avignon" of the ancient nursery rhyme. Built for pedestrians and horses, it was, in fact, far too narrow for people to "dance in a circle" on it: more probably the dancing was *sous* (under) *le pont*, on the Île de la Barthelasse, which was a traditional recreation place for the Avignonnais.

Vieille Ville (Old Town)
The central district of Avignon, within the ramparts, is best explored on foot, for parking is not easy. The honeycomb of narrow streets contains a number of churches and mansions, some from the time of the Popes and others from the 16thC, when this was a prosperous city under the tolerant rule of the Papal legates. Most of the churches and chapels have paintings by Parrocel and the Mignards, of the Avignon school.

To the NE of the Papal Palace, the **Chapelle des Pénitents Noirs** *(rue Banasterie; ask for key at tourist office)* has a facade, remodeled in the 18thC, with ornate sculptures of angels carrying the head of John the Baptist; inside are more rich carvings in wood and marble.

The **church of St-Symphorien** *(pl. des Carmes)* is notable for its 16thC gilded wood sculptures. To the s of the palace, the **Maison Jean Vilar** *(Hôtel de Crochans, rue de Mons)* is a small museum likely to appeal to anyone interested in postwar French theater. It was inaugurated in 1981, in honor of Jean Vilar, the great director who founded the Avignon Festival and led the revival of interest in French drama in the 1950s. To the E, the **church of St-Pierre** has sumptuous Renaissance carvings on its interior folding doors, and fine sculptured woodwork in the choir. To the s, **rue des Marchands** and other little streets nearby are now an elegant pedestrian zone full of smart stores.

Turning E off rue de la République, the 14thC **church of St-Didier** has superb late 14thC frescoes. In the first chapel on the right is the famous **retable** (★) of the *Bearing of the Cross* (15thC), by Francesco Laurana of Dalmatia, with movingly realistic looks of anguish on the faces of The Virgin and other bystanders. To the E of the church are **rue Roi René** and **rue des Teinturiers**, an old cobbled street beside the river Sorgue; the old paddle wheels were still used until the late 19thC to power the local textile workshops.

A number of Avignon's churches now only open on Sunday because of a series of thefts.

The **Musée Louis-Vouland** *(17 rue Victor-Hugo ☎ 90-86-03-79; open June to end Sept 10am-noon, 2-6pm, rest of year only 2-6pm; closed Sun, Mon),* on the w side of the town, is an interesting little museum of decorative arts, local ceramics and furniture of the 17th and 18thC.

✑ WHERE TO STAY IN AVIGNON

ANGLETERRE
29 blvd. Raspail, 84000 Avignon
☎90-86-34-31 🖾90-86-86-74 ▥ 40
rms ☛ ⏹ ᵂᴵˢᴬ ✿ ☐ ⏢ ✿ ☙ Closed mid-Dec to end Jan.
Location: Fairly central, on a quiet boulevard within the ramparts. A cut above the average utility town-center hotel, offering good value for simple facilities.

BRISTOL
44 Cours Jean-Jaurès, 84000 Avignon
☎90-82-21-21 🖾90-86-22-72 ▥ to ▥
67 rms ▦▦ ▱ ᴬᴱ ⏹ ⏹ ᵂᴵˢᴬ ☐ ᴷ ✿ ⏢
☙ Closed Nov–Feb.
Location: Very central, on the main street, near the station. The bedrooms are comfortable and the staff friendly, so do not be put off by the hotel's hum-drum appearance. It is much in demand by foreign tourist groups, and was recently redecorated.

CLOÎTRE SAINT-LOUIS ▥
20 rue Portail Bouquier, 84000 Avignon
☎90-27-55-55 🖾90-82-24-01 ▥ 80
rms ☛ ≕ ᴬᴱ ⏹ ᵂᴵˢᴬ ✿ ☐ ⏢ ᴷ ☙ ☚
☙ ᵞ ⏢
Location: Near the main railway station, toward the town center. This good and rather unusual new hotel was originally built in 1589 as a Jesuit seminary, and was consecrated in 1611 (the beautiful chapel is still, occasionally, in use for weddings). It later became a hospice. The original interior remains largely intact, and well kept, and the cool, modern decor and furniture work very well in the context of stone walls

and tiled floors. The restaurant is currently in a vaulted room, but will move into the glazed-in cloisters. Some of the rooms, however, are rather dark. The hotel has a new, high-tech extension, the work of none less than the high-flying architect Jean Nouvel, who designed the Institut du Monde Arabe in Paris. There is a rooftop swimming pool, where buffet meals are served. The genial new boss, Laurent Poggi, has some very firm ideas and — if he is given his head — should turn it into a first-class hotel. Prices are competitive, and there are few more interesting hotels in town.

EUROPE 🏨

12 pl. Crillon, 84000 Avignon ☎ *90-82-66-92* ⨎ *90-85-43-66* ▥ *47 rms* ▤ ▨
▨ ▢ ▣ ▨ ≉ ⚲ ▢ ▱ ⚲ ▾ ▭ ⇌
For ⇌ see *VIEILLE FONTAINE, below.*
Location: A square just inside the ramparts, near the Palace. This 16thC building, once the home of the Marquis de Graveson, was already in use as a hostelry when Napoleon stayed here in 1799. It is beautifully kept: the spacious bedrooms have beamed ceilings and period furniture, mostly Louis XV. The formality of the public rooms, with their marble floors, may not suit all tastes, but the Gobelins tapestries lend a touch of softness, while the piano-bar adds a cheerful, individual note.

MERCURE PALAIS DES PAPES

Quartier de la Balance, 84000 Avignon ☎ *90-85-91-23* ⨎ *90-85-32-40* ▥ *86 rms* ▤ ▨ ▢ ▣ ▨ ≉ ▢ ▱ ⚲ ▾
Location: Central, in a side-street behind the Petit Palais museum. An efficient upper-medium-priced modern hotel, part of one of the leading French hotel chains. Efficient service and good sound-proofing. The hotel has no restaurant.

LA MIRANDE 🏨

Pl. de l'Amirande, 84000 Avignon ☎ *90-85-93-93* ⨎ *90-86-26-85* ▥ *20 rms* ▤ ▨ ⇌ ▨ ▢ ▣ ▨ ≉ ▢ ▱ �&
⚲ ⁕ ⌂ ⚲ ▭
Location: A fine old house in the center

of town, very near the Pa...
This luxurious boutique ho...
stylishly converted by archite...
Grégoire and decorator Franç...
seph Graf. Owned by retired Ger...
civil engineer, Achim Stein, it is witho...
doubt the best (and the most expensive) hotel in town. The inner courtyard has been turned into a lovely winter garden. The bedrooms and bathrooms are all large, and are sumptuously decorated with excellent taste and attention to detail, as are the public areas. The restaurant, in a lovely room, has improved beyond measure, and the quality of the cuisine matches up to the rest of the hotel.

NOVOTEL

Route de Marseille, 84000 Avignon ☎ *90-87-62-36* ⨎ *90-88-38-47* ▥ *79 rms* ▤ ⇌ ▨ ▢ ▣ ▨ ≉ ▢ ▱ ⚌
▾ ▭
Location: On the outskirts. This relatively new, medium-sized hotel, with swimming pool, is suitable for individual visitors, although it is also frequented by businessmen and by tour groups.

PRIMOTEL HORLOGE

1 rue Félicien David, 84000 Avignon ☎ *90-86-88-61* ⨎ *90-82-17-32* ▥ *70 rms* ▤ ▨ ▢ ▣ ▨ ≉ ▢ ▱ �& ⚲
Location: In place de l'Horloge, very near the Palais des Papes. A very well-located, unpretentious and brightly decorated hotel, which is modern although in an old building. The rooms are well equipped. This is a good budget choice.

⚓ Other good hotels: **Auberge de Cassagne** *(450 Allée de Cassagne, 84130 Le Pontet* ☎ *90-31-04-18* ⨎ *90-32-25-09* ▥ *to* ▥ *)*, a smart hotel on the outskirts of town, with excellent food; **Blauvac** *(11 rue de la Bancasse* ☎ *90-86-34-11* ⨎ *90-86-27-41* ▥ *)*, a charming small hotel; **Danieli** *(17 rue de la République* ☎ *90-86-46-82* ⨎ *90-27-09-24* ▥ *)*, a very good, recently renovated hotel in a 19thC building.

is des Papes.
r has been
t Gilles
is-Jo-

7 ▥ 🖃 ▭
; *Sun; Nov;*

...nt around a
...yard with a large plane tree. It is
bright, cheerful, and attractively furnished. The food is simple, with an emphasis on fish and seafood.

CAFÉ DES ARTISTES
21bis pl. Crillon ☎ *90-82-63-16* ▭ *to* ▭
▭ 🍽 🛋 *Closed early Jan; Sun*
(except July). Last orders 11pm.

A modish, informal bistro where in fine
weather you can eat outdoors in a pretty
square. Reliable cooking, which includes dishes such as *pot-au-feu en
gelée, lapin à l'ail, loup vapeur en vinaigrette.*

CHRISTIAN ETIENNE ⬠
10 rue de Mons ☎ *90-86-16-50* ▥ 🖃 ▭
🍽 �︎ 🛋 *AE* ⊙ *VISA Closed Sun dinner;
Mon; mid- to end Aug; mid-Feb to Mar. Last
orders 9.30pm.*

This is a very special restaurant, situated
right next to the Palais des Papes, in a
building that once housed papal legis-
lators. It is generally considered to be
the best restaurant in Avignon, and you
can sense that it knows exactly what it
is about, without needing to resort to
frills or pretention. The main room, with
its beamed ceiling, stone walls, flowers
on the tables and gentle side-lighting,
has a mellow atmosphere. Service from
the young team is friendly, impeccable
yet unpompous. The same can be said
of the excellent cuisine, with its traditional but light use of sauces. The *carte*
is short, the menus (including one for
vegetarians) well-priced for the quality.
There is a good selection as well of
Rhône wines. In summer, you can sit
outside. *Specialities: Rouget rôti au
coulis d'olives noires, agneau rôti au
jus de ratatouille, homard juste poêlé
au jus.*

LA FÉRIGOULO
30 rue Joseph Vernet ☎ *90-82-10-28* ▥

🖃 ▭ 🍽 *AE* ⊙ *VISA Closed Mon out of
season; Sun (except during theater festival).
Last orders 10pm.*

Here is the kind of post-1960s "bistro"
one associates with St-Germain-des-
Prés or Chelsea — modern decor and
informal service; youthful clientele. The
food is traditional and not at all bad.
*Specialities: Truite aux amandes,
daube Avignonnaise.*

LA FOURCHETTE II ♣
17 rue Racine ☎ *90-85-20-93* ▥ ▭ 🍽
*VISA Closed Sat; Sun; mid-June to July. Last
orders 9pm.*

Robert Hiély (brother of Pierre HIÉLY,
see below) proves that a stylish setting
plus good food need not necessarily
equal high prices, so it is small wonder
that his delightful restaurant is often
fully booked days ahead. The pretty
decor is breezily modern; flowers and
ivy lend a rural air. Here, graceful young
ladies serve Avignon's *beau monde*
with a set menu that is not only great
value but full of interest and originality,
for M. Hiély blends local tradition with
his own fascinating innovations. *Specialities: Haricots blancs en anchoïade,
terrine à la confiture d'oignons, boeuf
cuit à la manière des anciens mari-
niers du Rhône.*

HIÉLY-LUCULLUS ♣
5 rue de la République ☎ *90-86-17-07* ▥
🍽 �︎ 🖃 ⊙ *VISA Closed Tues lunch and
Mon out of season; Jan; mid-June to July.
Last orders 9.30pm.*

Not, perhaps, quite what it once was,
but still one of Avignon's best restaurants, Hiély-Lucullus is designed for
the dedicated gourmet — a first-floor
room in the heart of town, simply but
tastefully furnished, where the service
is impeccable, the atmosphere old-
fashioned, and Madame Hiély's welcome always courteous. Her husband
Pierre, although no longer in the kitch-
en, remains loyal to his family's 60-year
tradition of serving a single set menu
with wide choice, and no *carte*. The
cuisine is classic but not over-conven-

tional and the quality irreproachable. *Specialities: Cassoulet de moules aux épinards, tourte chaude et cailles au foie gras, râble de lapereau farci.*

JARDIN DE LA TOUR

9 rue de La Tour ☎90-85-66-50 ▥ to ▥ ▢ ■ ♿ AE ⊙ ⊙ ₥ *Closed Sun dinner; Mon; mid- to end Aug. Last orders 10.15pm (later, in July and Aug).*

This restaurant, in a small alley near the Porte St-Lazare, was once a factory. The long main room has a relaxed but lively ambience, with gentle French pop music playing in the background (occasionally there is live entertainment in the summer months). The chef, Jean-Marc Larrue, who runs it with well-known local figure Rose Requead, takes his job very seriously, and his cuisine, although sometimes lacking subtlety, is rich, flavorful and interesting.

LE VERNET

58 rue Joseph Vernet ☎90-86-64-53 ▥ to ▥ ▢ ■ ♿ ⊙ ⊙ ₥ *Closed Sun; Mon lunch (out of season); Feb. Last orders 9.30pm.*

It's evident that Claude Chareton, the ambitious *patron,* wants to be considered a great restaurateur, and there is just a hint of pretentiousness about his admittedly very elegant restaurant in this 18thC mansion. The intimate dining room achieves its effect with soft lights, low music and romantic modern paintings. For summer dining, there is a shady and spacious garden, complete with a statue of *Diana.* As in many similarly ambitious restaurants, the cuisine blends the *nouvelle* with the regionally traditional, generally with great success. The *menu gastronomique* comes with English and German translations. *Specialities include: Aigo boulido, compôte froide de lapereau, l'agnolade d'Avignon, sartanado de rognons de veau.*

VIEILLE FONTAINE ⌂

Hôtel Europe, 12 pl. Crillon ☎90-82-66-92 ▥ to ▥ ▢ ■ ≡ ♿ ⇦ AE ⊙ ₥ *Closed Sat lunch; Sun; Jan–Mar. Last orders 10pm.*

In summer you can dine beside the restaurant's namesake, an old fountain in a lovely courtyard where lamps glow on every table. The indoor *salle* is more severely classical. The *cuisine,* among the best in Avignon, is sunny, flavorful and hard to fault. *Specialities: Rizotto de pigeon aux truffes, tarte fine à la tomate fraîche et au basilic.* (See ❧ EUROPE above.)

≡ Other good restaurants: **Brunel** *(46 rue de la Balance* ☎90-85-24-83 ▥ to ▥ *closed Sun, Mon out of season),* in the center of town, very high-quality cuisine; **L'Isle Sonnante** *(7 rue Racine* ☎90-82-56-01 ▥ *closed Sun, Mon)* and **La Table de Patrick** *(22 rue du Chapeau Rouge* ☎90-82-66-99 ▢ *to* ▥ *),* both good and cheap; **Les Domaines** *(28 pl. de l'Horloge* ☎90-82-58-86 ▥ *);* and **Le Petit Bedon** *(70 rue Joseph Vernet* ☎90-82-33-98 ▥ *to* ▥ *closed Sun, Mon dinner),* for Provençal cuisine.

❧ ≡ HOTELS/RESTAURANTS NEAR AVIGNON

AUBERGE DE NOVES ▥

13550 Noves ☎90-94-19-21 ⒻⓍ90-94-47-76 ▥ *23 rms* ➔ ▢ AE ⊙ ⊙ ₥ ⌂ ♿ ‡ ▢ ▢ ⚓ ❅ ≈ ♨ ℘ ♟ ⊙ ▢ ■ ≡ ♿ *Closed early Jan to mid-Feb* ≡ *closed Wed lunch (and dinner, mid-Oct to Apr); last orders 10pm.*
Location: In its own wooded park of 22 acres off D28, 4 kilometers (2½ miles) w of Noves, which is 13km (8 miles) SE of Avignon. This is a most impressive hotel, one of the best in the region, converted from a 19thC manor house. It has a rambling garden planted with pines and cypresses, and the spacious rooms, with tiled floors, are vividly decorated with local Olivades fabric in the traditional Indiennage style. The very modern tiled bathrooms in the chapel annex are splendid. All is stylish and welcoming: there are caged songbirds in the lobby, and a lounge with pale-green decor and cozy modern sofas. The rooms in the main building are

traditional, with some good pieces of furniture. They might, ideally, be spruced up a little, but the many regular clients like them the way they are. André Lalleman, a cultured and amiable host, speaks perfect English. He is justly proud of his chic country hotel, with its top-notch facilities and reassuringly old-fashioned service.

The bright, elegant dining-room is so full of flowers that if the Mistral blows, one hardly feels disappointed at being deprived of the lovely, shaded terrace. The kitchen is now in the very capable hands of Robert Lalleman, the owner's son, who trained with such luminaries as Troisgros, Pic and Chapel. The restaurant had three stars a couple of decades ago, and Robert is well on the way to restoring its reputation as one of the finest in Provence. The cuisine marries *nouvelle* and regional. *Specialities: Salade de homard à l'huile de noisettes, royale de tourteaux aux pointes d'asperges, filet de rouget, noisettes d'agneau aux pignons de pin.* The cellar boasts some 65,000 bottles.

L'ERMITAGE-MEISSONNIER ⌂ ♣

Route de Nîmes, Bellevue-lès-Angles (4km/2½ miles w of Avignon)
☎ 90-25-41-68 ▥ to ▥ 16 rms ☐ ▬
▬ AE ⦿ ▥ *Closed Sun dinner (winter); Mon (except dinner, in July and Aug).*
L'Ermitage-Meissonnier is a hard-work-

ing family affair, and Paul Meissonnier's son Michel (almost as accomplished a chef as his father) has now taken over the kitchen. The restaurant lacks the *hauteur* of some top-class establishments, and prices for the set menus start very reasonably. The wine list has some excellent Côtes du Rhône; the cheeses are superb; and the food is, on the whole, light, inventive and delicious. There are 16 very comfortable, inexpensive and extremely well-appointed rooms situated across the garden.

HOSTELLERIE LES FRENES ▥

645 av. des Vertes-Rives, Monfavet, 84140 Avignon ☎ 90-31-17-93 ▣ 90-23-95-03
▥ to ▥ 19 rms ▤ ▬ AE ⦿ ⦿ ▥ ⌂
✴ ☐ ▱ & ♨ ⋘ ☷ ≋ ☞ ‧/ ☝ ⚘
Closed mid-Nov to mid-Mar ⊸ closed Nov–Apr; last orders 9pm.
Location: At Monfavet, 5 kilometers (3 miles) e of Avignon on D53. A lovely hotel set around a rather grand 19thC house with a shady 2-acre park. The whole place is most tastefully decorated in a variety of antique styles. The rooms and service are excellent, the bathrooms large. The restaurant has a high reputation and fairly reasonable prices. The chef is Antoine Biancone, who trained at HIÉLY-LUCULLUS. *Specialities: Sandre à la fondue morilles, cassoulette d'escargots à la fondue provençale.*

◪ NIGHTLIFE IN AVIGNON

For an evening in a piano bar, visit **La Tâche d'Encre** *(22 rue des Teinturiers),* or **La Caf'Conce** *(25 rue Carnot).* • There is a jazz club at **AJMI** *(Théâtre du Chêne Noir, 8bis, rue Ste-Catherine* ☎ 90-85-46-03). • Disco: **Club 55** *(Porte St-Roch* ☎ 90-85-46-76).

SHOPPING IN AVIGNON

Good boutiques and shops include: for regional fabrics and clothing, **Souleiado** *(rue Joseph Vernet);* for local food products, **Les Olivades** *(rue des Marchands);* for *santons* and other local handicrafts, **Gattini** *(rue de la République);* and an attractive antiquarian bookstore, **Roumanille** *(19 rue St-Agricol).* There are also numerous antique stores off rue Joseph Vernet, and many smart clothes stores in rue St-Agricol.

- **MARKETS** The famous covered food market **Les Halles** *(pl. Pie)* is open Tuesday to Sunday *(mornings).* • At place des Carmes, there is a **flower market** *(Sat morning)* and a **flea market** *(Sun morning).*
  • A **junk/antique market** takes place in place Crillon on Saturdays.

PLACE NEAR AVIGNON
Barbentane *(10km/6 miles sw of Avignon).* An old fortified village on the northern slopes of the Montagnette hills. Its handsome **17thC châ-teau** (■ *open daily Easter-Nov, except Wed Oct-July; Nov-Easter open Sun only),* owned by the Duc de Barbentane, is more in the style of the Île-de-France than of Provence; the ceilings are ornate, and the rooms are sumptuously decorated, some with Louis XV and XVI furniture.

In the village, the **Maison des Chevaliers**, with a loggia gallery running the length of the facade, the 12thC Romanesque **church of Notre-Dame-de-Grace**, and the **Tour Anglica** — the keep of a 14thC castle, from which there are good views of Avignon — are also worth a visit. There are also beautiful views of the Rhône Valley from the nearby 18thC **Moulin de Bretoul**, a windmill set in pine woods.

• See also: BEAUCAIRE, L'ISLE-SUR-LA-SORGUE, ORANGE, ST-RÉMY-DE-PROVENCE, TARASCON and VILLENEUVE-LÈS-AVIGNON.

LES BAUX ☆
Map 9E4 (B.-du-R.). 19km (12 miles) NE of Arles. Postal code: 13520. Population: 450 i Grand' Rue ☎90-54-34-03.

Les Baux-de-Provence, most celebrated of all Provençal hill-villages, stands on a southerly spur of the craggy limestone range of Les Alpilles. It is a haunting, mysterious place — a half-ruined, half-deserted village, nestling below the grisly remains of a castle with a long and tormented history. The best views of Les Baux are from the hill road to the NW (D27) or the valley road to the E (D5). Here the whitish-gray castle walls seem to be part of the great white rock on which it stands. The name Les Baux comes from the Provençal *baou,* meaning rock, and has given its name to bauxite, which was first discovered here in 1822 but is now no longer quarried.

> At other times we would arrange to meet at the town of Les Baux, that dusty pile of ruins, sharp rocks, and old emblazoned palaces, crumbling, quivering in the wind like high eagles' nests. . . .
> (*Lettres de mon Moulin* [Letters from my Windmill], 1868, Alphonse Daudet, translated by Frederick Davis)

From the 11thC, the lords of Les Baux were among the strongest and most arrogant feudal families of France, claiming descent from the magus Balthazar. At one time, their realm extended over 79 townships of Provence, including ORANGE, and as far afield as Sicily and Albania. In the 13thC, Les Baux was a great "court of love," where the troubadours played for lovely women. But in 1372 it fell under the rule of the sadistic Viscount Raymond de Turenne, a high-class brigand whose favorite sport was to kidnap people from neighboring towns, then force them to jump to their deaths from his clifftop castle. The sight of their agony made him weep with laughter. Finally, in 1400, the king led an army to crush this "scourge of Provence," and he was encircled near Tarascon and drowned while trying to cross the Rhône.

Incorporated into the earldom of Provence in the 15thC, Les Baux later became a Protestant enclave under its seigneurs, the de Manvilles. Such private strongholds displeased Louis XIII and Cardinal Richelieu, who, in 1632, demolished the castle and ramparts and fined the citizens 100,000 *livres*. Les Baux, or what was left of it, then became a fiefdom of the Grimaldis of Monaco until the Revolution.

Thus ended the great days of Les Baux, which in its prime had 6,000 inhabitants, and today just over 450. But more than a million tourists a year now invade this eyrie, crowding its crumbling alleys, jostling its souvenir stalls. The village was very firmly put on the tourist map as the result of the success of one restaurant, the legendary OUSTAU DE BAUMA-NIÈRE (see below), which was owned, until his death in 1993, by Raymond Thuilier, former mayor of Les Baux.

You would be advised to come very early in the day, or right out of season — or, best of all, explore the ghost realm by moonlight.

Les Baux is terrifyingly lonely: the midnight silence is shattered merely by the baying of some stray dog at the moon, or by the echo of a church bell as the church clock strikes the hour. Below you in the valley you can hear the gross coarse croaking of the bull-frogs in the ponds.

(*Aspects of Provence,* 1952, James Pope-Hennessy)

Park in the valley below, and enter the village on foot by the Porte Mage. The 16thC **Hôtel de Manville** houses a **Musée d'Art Moderne**. All around are other half-ruined Renaissance mansions, such as the **Hôtel des Porcelets**, now the **Musée Archéologique**; above it is the former **Protestant chapel** (1571) built by the de Manvilles. Overlooking the tiny place St-Vincent is the charming 12thC church of **St-Vincent**, the scene of the famous Nativity pageant (see EVENT below).

From the terrace by the church, the view extends over the valley, with its row of luxury hotels. Among them, incongruously, is the tiny **Pavillon de la Reine Jeanne** (accessible by a path from the Porte Eyguières), built in 1581 in memory of the second wife of King René, who owned Les Baux for a time before the de Manvilles.

The narrow **rue Turcat**, hewn out of the rock, leads up to the 14thC **Tour de Brau**, now a small **Musée Lapidaire** with a well-presented display of locally-excavated finds. Here you buy tickets for the castle ruins. First, a path leads to the barren s end of the spur, where stands a memorial to the Provençal poet Rieu: here the view offers a dramatic contrast between the wild peaks of the Alpilles and, at their feet, a lush pastoral landscape of vines and olive groves.

The path then doubles back to the N end of the spur and the castle ruins, crowned by the 13thC keep where de Turenne watched his victims leap into the abyss. Even without this memory, the acres of gaunt wreckage are a macabre spectacle.

- **EVENT**   Every year since the 16thC, a Midnight Mass in the form of a **Provençal pageant of the Nativity** has been held in the church of St-Vincent on Christmas Eve. It is still enormously popular: do arrive early.

☎ ☰ HOTELS/RESTAURANTS IN LES BAUX

☎ ☰   BENVENGUDO

13520 Les Baux-de-Provence
☎ 90-54-32-54 Fx 90-54-42-58 ▥ 20
rms ━ ▤ ▣ ▥ ⌂ ▢ ▨ ❦ ⟨⟨ ⇝
♨ *Closed Nov–Feb.*

Location: In glorious country, 2 kilometers (1 mile) sw of Les Baux, off D78F. An old ivy-covered farmhouse, now an elegant little hotel with more than a touch of glamor. Excellent for a quiet but civilized rural vacation: idyllic garden, snug Provençal salon with log fire for winter, bedrooms prettily decorated with local furniture. The hotel recently changed hands, and is now owned by the former chef of LA CABRO D'OR (where he had a Michelin star) and his wife. Expect a warm welcome. Ten of the rooms have air conditioning.

In the restaurant (▥ ▭ ▬ ☰ *closed Sun, lunch, Nov–Feb, last orders 9.30pm),* dinner is served on the beautiful patio, gently lit at night, or in the rustic-style dining room, with rather ornate furniture. *Specialities: Salade Landaise au magret de canard, médaillons de lotte au safran, cassoulette du pêcheur au cerfeuil.*

☎ ☰   LA CABRO D'OR

Les Baux-de-Provence, 13520 Maussane
☎ 90-54-33-21 Fx 90-54-45-98 ▥ 22
rms ▤ ━ ⌂ ▣ ▣ ▣ ▨ ⌂ ⚓ ▢
▣ ❦ ⟨⟨ ♨ ♥ ♣ ♨ *Closed mid-Nov to mid-Dec.*

Location: In the open valley sw of Les Baux. For those who cannot quite manage Oustau de Baumanière's prices, that establishment also runs the "Golden Goat." It is a spacious, modern hotel, built to resemble a Provençal *mas;* bedrooms, furnished in period style, are in villas spread around the huge, ornate garden, where swans glide in neat pools. The accent here is on sports: tennis, riding, and a large, luxurious swimming pool. Service is attentive, and the ambience, although sophisticated, is quite informal. In the restaurant *(closed Mon; Tues lunch in winter),* the food, while not in the same class as the Baumanière's, is still distinctive.

☎ ☰   MAS D'AIGRET

13520 Les Baux-de-Provence
☎ 90-54-33-54 Fx 90-54-41-37 ▥ 15
rms ━ ☰ ▣ ▣ ▣ ▨ ⌂ ▢ ▬
❦ ⟨⟨ ⇝ ♨ ♥ ♈ *Closed Jan to end Feb.*
Restaurant closed Wed lunch.

Location: Just below the old town, on D27A. Owned by a British former journalist, who took it over in 1987. All the simple but bright rooms (two of which are cut into the rock behind the hotel) have books in them, and a number of them have tiny private terraces where you can take lunch. There are freshly cut flowers around the hotel, and family mementos line the walls of the lobby. This is a hotel with personality; it is well-located, and is good value for the area. The cuisine here has a good reputation.

☎ ☰   OUSTAU DE
BAUMANIÈRE ▥ ⌂

Les Baux-de-Provence, 13520 Maussane
☎ 90-54-33-07 Fx 90-54-40-46 ▥ 24
rms ▤ ━ ▣ ▣ ▣ ▨ ⌂ ▢ ▣
⟨⟨ ⇝ ♨ ♥ ♣ *Closed mid-Jan to Mar.*
Location: At the foot of craggy cliffs, where the valley narrows into a gorge NW of Les Baux. Proven to be a place fit for a queen when Elizabeth II and The Duke of Edinburgh dined here on their state visit to France in 1972, L'Oustau (hostelry) de Baumanière has long held a place of honor as one of the grandest of French hotels and restaurants, as did its owner, the seigneurial Raymond Thuilier, a talented painter who even designed the crockery. He continued to appear at the restaurant until his death, aged 96, in 1993.

For some years the hotel has actually been run by his grandson Jean-André Charial. Pampered guests stroll in the cypress groves of the large garden, bask by the fine pool, or sip cocktails on the elegant terrace. The ornate salon may seem somber, but the illuminated rocks behind the hotel are a soothing sight. Bedrooms are suitably regal. It is also possible to rent apartments within the hotel itself. Even if you cannot afford to stay here, you can visit the shop attached to the hotel, where there is a selection of Baumanière-labeled products.

In the restaurant (🎞 ⬜ ■ ➡ 🚗 *closed mid-Jan to Mar, Wed, Thurs lunch in winter, last orders 9.30pm)*, luxury is the keynote, whether in the vaulted *salle* amid tapestries, silver candlesticks and bouquets of flowers, or on the lovely shaded terrace. The menu carries a design contributed by Jean Cocteau. In the 1950s and '60s, *patron* and chef Raymond Thuilier built this into one of the world's greatest restaurants, visited, like the hotel, by royalty, politicians and celebrities.

Today, the cooking, while lighter than it used to be, is no longer at the zenith (it recently lost a Michelin star), yet it still ranks among the best in France. The *cave* comprises over 90,000 bottles and includes an 1865 Château Lafitte Rothschild. *Specialities: Filet de rouget au basilic, pigeon rôti et son ragoût de blettes aux truffes, gigot d'agneau en croûte, tourte de ris de veau braisés aux champignons, olives vertes et épinards.*

⇌ Recommended restaurant: **Le Riboto de Taven** *(Val d'Enfer, 2km to the NW of Les Baux* ☎ *90-54-34-23* 🎞 *to* 🎞 *).*

PLACES NEAR LES BAUX

Les Alpilles   Les Baux lies on the southern edge of a range of arid hills, the Alpilles, which run for 32 kilometers (20 miles), from the Rhône to the Durance. Nowhere do the hills rise above 450 meters (1,500 feet), although the jagged white peaks give a mountainous and prehistoric air. On the lower slopes are olive and cypress trees, and higher up, sheep graze the scrub and rough grass.

The highest point is **La Caume**, with fine views. The approach is a road that leads up off the D5, s of St-Rémy. Some of the wildest scenery is in the **Val d'Enfer** (Hell Valley), a rocky gorge 2 kilometers ($1\frac{1}{4}$ miles) NW of Les Baux, where Jean Cocteau filmed *Le Testament d'Orphée.*

Maussane *(5km/3 miles s of Les Baux).* A small village on the southern edge of Les Alpilles, which reputedly produces the finest olive oil in France. The picturesque local oil mill *(Coopérative Oléicole de la Vallée des Baux* ☎ *90-54-32-37)* is worth a visit, although the oil might well be sold out. You can, however, find the slightly pungent oil of the Vallée des Baux in local shops.

❧ ⇌ NEARBY

❧   **L'OUSTALOUN** ✿
Pl. de l'Église, 13520 Maussane-les-Alpilles ☎ *90-54-32-19* 🎞 *12 rms* ➡ 🖼 ⇌ 🆎 🎞 ⬜ ▱ ✇ *Closed Jan to mid-Feb.*
Location: On the square in the village center. After the glamor and formality of the establishments around Les Baux, it is pleasant to find this modest but comfortable *auberge.* A converted 16thC chapel, it is run by the charming and cultivated Bartolis. In the dining room, which is lined with paintings, there is good country cooking, delicious chocolate cake, and homemade jam for breakfast.

⇌   **LE BISTRO DU PARADOU**
Av. de la Vallée-des-Baux, Le Paradou ☎ *90-54-32-70* 🎞 *Closed Sun.*
A simple place on the D17 just outside Maussane. There is only one menu (the price includes wine), which changes daily. In effect, you eat what you are given. There is a log fire in winter, and the place is usually packed with colorful local people.

⇌   **OU RAVI PROVENÇAU**
34 av. de la Vallée-des-Baux, Maussane-les-Alpilles ☎ *90-54-31-11* 🎞 ⬜ ■ 🚗 🆎 🖾 *Closed Mon eve (winter); Tues; mid-June; mid-Nov to mid-Dec. Last orders 10.30pm.*

Situated in the center of Maussane, this restaurant is a local favorite, particularly at lunchtime, when it gets full even on a winter weekday. Aurore Richard lavishes just as much attention to the cheerful and lively front of house, with its bright decoration, as her husband Jean-François does in the kitchen. He provides very good Provençal food, with specialities such as *lapin sauté au thym, noisettes d'agneau aux épices* and *morue fraîche à la crème d'ail doux.*

- See also: ARLES, BEAUCAIRE, FONTVIEILLE, ST-RÉMY, TARASCON.

BEAUCAIRE
Map 9E4 (Gard). 25km (16 miles) sw of Avignon. Postal code: 30300. Population: 13,400 i 24 Cours Gambetta ☎66-59-26-57.

Beaucaire and TARASCON, each with its mighty castle, face each other across the Rhône, linked by a long bridge. For centuries, they were rivals, for Beaucaire historically is in Languedoc, as Tarascon is in Provence.

Beaucaire's **château** was built in the early 13thC by Count Raymond VI of Toulouse, who also instituted the town's annual Trade Fair. This became the greatest one in Western Europe, drawing as many as 300,000 people and 800 boats, every July, from all over the Mediterranean and much of Europe. The fair survived until the mid-19thC, when it died out with the arrival of the age of rail. The fair was held in the broad meadow between the castle and the river.

Try the local speciality, *pattisoun* — pastries filled with dried fruits.

- **EVENTS** An annual **fête** at the end of July to early August to commemorate the old fair. • **Bullfights** are held occasionally in summer, in the bullring below the castle.

WHAT TO SEE IN BEAUCAIRE
Château
☎ ◀ *Open Apr–Sept 10am–noon, 2.15–6.45pm; Oct–Mar 10.15am–noon, 2–5.15pm. Closed Tues.*

The castle is reached via a steep flight of steps, leading to a promenade above the town. Partly demolished by de Richelieu in 1632, the castle is half-ruined, and little attempt has been made to restore it. But its high *donjon* still stands, and you can still climb up inside, to the top of its unusual triangular tower. There are fine views, although in the foreground, the romantic towers of the château at Tarascon are hardly less noticeable than the tall chimneys of two huge factories by the river.

The **vieille ville**, below the castle, is attractive: note the late 17thC **Hôtel de Ville**, and the 18thC church of **Notre-Dame-des-Pommiers**. The **Musée du Vieux Beaucaire** *(27 rue Barbès ☎ opening times variable)* contains souvenirs of the history of the fair. The **Musée Lapidaire** *(rue de Nîmes)* contains local Roman finds.

❧ ☎ NEARBY

❧ ☎ ROBINSON ✿
Route de Remoulins, 30300 Beaucaire
☎66-59-21-32 ▯ to ▯ 30 rms ➤ ☎
▢ ☎ ❧ ⚘ ✍ *Closed Feb.*

Location: In a garden beside wooded hills, 2.5 kilometers (1½ miles) to the NW of Beaucaire, just off the D986. A spacious family hotel that is good for a short stay; neither smart nor alluring, but with a large garden and plenty of amenities. Most bedrooms are in annexes around the garden. The hotel's emphasis is on food, which it serves at low prices in a large dining room (☐ to ☐☐ ☐ ■■ last orders 9.30pm). Locals pack out the place and are served reliable *cuisine familiale*.

☜ ☰ Other good hotels/res-

taurants in Beaucaire are: **Les Doctrinaires** *(quai Gén.-de-Gaulle ☎66-59-41-32* Fx*66-59-31-97 ☐ to ☐☐ restaurant closed Sat lunch, Sun dinner in winter),* a 17thC building with a pretty courtyard; **Les Vignes Blanches** *(Route de Nîmes ☎66-59-13-12* Fx*66-59-40-97 ☐ to ☐☐ restaurant closed for lunch, except July, Aug).*

• See also: LES BAUX, ST-RÉMY-DE-PROVENCE, TARASCON.

BERRE, ÉTANG DE
Map 10G6 (B.-du-R.). 32–40km (20–25 miles) NW of Marseille.

This vast and placid salt-water lake, separated from the sea by the Estaque mountain range, covers 155 square kilometers (60 square miles), yet is only 10 meters (30 feet) deep.

Its shores have been colonized since Roman times. Today they are heavily industrialized, especially on the SE and SW sides, where the glittering factories and blazing flares make a powerful sight at night. There are four big oil refineries, as well as factories for petrochemicals and other derivatives; and the terminal of the South Europe Pipeline, carrying crude oil to the refineries of eastern France and southwestern Germany.

PLACES OF INTEREST NEAR THE ÉTANG DE BERRE
Marignane is the site of Marseille's international airport. Next to it is Europe's largest helicopter factory, part of the State-owned Aérospatiale group. It is famous in France for having successfully pioneered a system of labor relations based on small autonomous work groups, similar to earlier ventures by car manufacturers Volvo and Fiat.

The town of Marignane has an interesting château and church.

☜ Good hotels at Marignane include the following: **Novotel** *(Z.I. les Estroublans, 13700, 9km/5 miles N on N113 ☎42-89-90-44* Fx*42-79-07-04* ☐☐*); **Sofitel** *(13700 ☎42-78-42-78* Fx*42-78-42-70 ☐☐*); **Primotel** *(13127 Vitrolles ☎42-79-79-19* Fx*42-89-69-18 ☐☐*).

Martigues Here a 6-kilometer (4-mile) canal links the lake to the sea at the giant oil complex of Port-Lavéra.
Miramas-le-Vieux A village on a rocky spur at the N tip of the lake, with good views; 15thC church and 13thC ruined castle.
Pont-Flavien A fine 1stC Roman bridge.
St-Blaise Beside a 12thC chapel is a major archeological site. Excavations have revealed a Greek fortress dating from the 7thC BC, and possibly the oldest Greek colony in France. There are traces too of an early Christian settlement.

OTHER PLACES NEARBY
Fos (✪) *(10km/6 miles W of the lake).* This gigantic modern port and industrial estate, covering 103 square kilometers (40 square miles) and

able to handle ships of up to 400,000 tons, has been developed since 1965 by the Port of Marseille Authority. It is in fact an extension of MARSEILLE's own port, 40 kilometers (25 miles) to the E, which is cramped for space and now in decline.

In the boom years before 1973, Fos was a trailblazer of France's role as a new industrial superpower. After this, it was hit by the world recession and has not grown as fast as planned. Even so, it has a number of sizeable refineries, steelworks, and chemical and other factories.

At **La Fossette** *(8km/5 miles inland beside the N568 to Arles)*, the **Centre de la Vie** is an information and exhibition center *(open Mon-Fri 9am-noon, 1-5pm)*, with large-scale models of Fos and details of its activities. It will arrange guided tours of Fos with prior warning *(☎42-05-03-10)*.

- See also: MARSEILLE, MARTIGUES.

CAMARGUE, LA ★

Map 8F3 (B.-du-R.). Area approx. 770sq.km (300sq. miles). For **i** *see ARLES or LES SAINTES-MARIES-DE-LA-MER.*

The symbols of the Camargue are pink flamingos, black bulls and white horses, and they inhabit this mysterious and marshy plain, an area like no other in France, and a sharp contrast to the mountains and rocky coasts of the rest of Provence. The animals, half-wild, roam free, and are tended by tough, gypsy-like men and women called *gardians*, who live mostly out on the marshes in isolated thatch-roofed cottages, each with a cross on top. Outside the tourist season, the Camargue can be a very lonely place indeed; apart from its so-called "capital," the seaside village of LES SAINTES-MARIES-DE-LA-MER, it has no locality larger than a hamlet.

The Camargue consists of 770 square kilometers (300 square miles) of the Rhône delta between ARLES and the sea, stretching from the Grand Rhône on the E to AIGUES-MORTES on the W. Here, land and water meet in a mesh of lagoons and salty meadows, attracting a rich variety of flora and fauna.

The sector to the N, toward Arles, has been desalinated since World War II, and today is given over to rice-growing. To the S, the large **Étang de Vaccarès** and the maze of islands that screen it from the sea are now a **nature reserve**, where scores of species of birds live amid an equal variety of rare plants and flowers. The plain around the lake is divided into some 30 ranches, each owner having his mixed herd *(manade)* of black fighting bulls and sturdy white horses, stocky but surefooted and extremely compliant.

The best time to see the Camargue is in spring or early summer, before the high season; in autumn mosquitoes can be troublesome, and in winter the Mistral can make things miserable. There are many good roads, including one along the N and E shores of the lake, but although, from a car, it is possible to spot plenty of bulls and horses, bird-watchers may be disappointed. Most of the bird wildlife is inside the reserve, which is open only to accredited naturalists and students *(apply in advance, giving reasons, to the Réserve Nationale, La Capelière, 13200 Arles* ☎ *90-97-00-97).*

However, it is possible to get close to the reserve, and thus see something of the birds and flowers, by driving beyond the SE corner of the lake, then turning W to the road's end at the lighthouse of **La Gacholle**; from here you can take a long, bracing walk along the dike (impassable in wet weather) to Les Saintes-Maries. The migratory flamingoes come in summer to the lagoons around the lighthouse, and are a wonderful sight as they rise up from the water's edge in a cloud of pink. To see them, try to arrive early in the morning, or late afternoon.

> It is a profound passion, almost a religion, a faith, *La fé di biou,* or the belief in the bull, and to satisfy it, the *Gardian* will brave the elements, endure the worst fatigue and even risk his life. . . . it is a race of men apart.
>
> (*En Camargue,* Gérard Gadiot)

The Camargue is ideal for a riding vacation. The ranch-hotels have their own horses (see LES SAINTES-MARIES-DE-LA-MER); and numerous local establishments *(details at any tourist office)* take groups for long excursions on horseback through the marshes, led by *gardians,* although this is not cheap. For nonriders, there are tours by Land-Rover.

Alternatively you can see something of the Camargue's animal life by taking a 75-minute boat trip up the Petit Rhône from a landing-stage 3 kilometers (2 miles) W of Les Saintes-Maries *(Apr-Oct* ☎ *90-97-81-68).* The public can also attend a *ferrade:* a ranch ceremony where the young bulls are branded by *gardians.*

At **Gines**, 5 kilometers (3 miles) N of Les Saintes-Maries on the N570, the **Camargue Information Center** has photographs, documents and a free slide show *(closed in winter).* Next door is a small outdoor aviary, rather run-down. More interesting is the **Musée Camarguais** (▨ *closed Tues from Sept-Apr),* installed in a handsome old farm building at the Pont de Rousty, 10 kilometers (6 miles) SW of Arles on the N570, where details of Camargue history, folklore and daily life are well set out. From the museum, there is a 3-kilometer (2-mile) signposted footpath that leads walkers into the marshes.

Domaine de Méjanes is a ranch on the NW shore of Lake Vaccarès, owned by *pastis* tycoon Paul Ricard, and run by him as a vacation center (☎ *90-97-10-10).* It is commercialized but lively: horseback riding, scenic railway, mock bullfights, equestrian displays and *ferrades.*

• See also: ARLES, LES SAINTES-MARIES-DE-LA-MER.

CARPENTRAS

Map 4C5 (Vaucluse). 24km (15 miles) NE of Avignon. Postal code: 84200.
Population: 25,000 i 170 Allée Jean Jaurès ☎ *90-63-57-88.*

From 1320 to the time of the Revolution, Carpentras was the capital of the **Comtat Venaissin**, an area E of the Rhône corresponding roughly to the modern Vaucluse. It was annexed by the Papacy in 1274 and did not rejoin France until 1791.

Today, Carpentras is the center of a prosperous farming district. The town is ringed by a series of boulevards on the site of the old city ramparts, of which nothing now remains save the Porte d'Orange.

WHAT TO SEE IN CARPENTRAS

There is much of interest in the center of Carpentras. Just to the N of the town's main sight, the cathedral of ST-SIFFREIN, is a small Roman municipal **arc de triomphe**, built at the same time as that at ORANGE: its E side is decorated with curious low reliefs of two captives, one wearing a tunic, the other wearing an animal skin. Nearby is the oldest **synagogue** in France, built in 1367 and rebuilt in the 18thC; its interior *(open 10am-noon, 3-5pm, closed Sat, Sun)* is richly decorated. Note the purification baths and the oven for unleavened bread. The synagogue was the center of a major Jewish colony, especially influential when the Jews were financiers to the Avignon Popes.

Of the town's museums, the **Musée Duplessis** *(Hôtel d'Allemand, blvd. Albin Durand* ☎ *closed Tues)* is devoted to local history and folk art. Also housed in the 18thC city mansion, the Hôtel d'Allemand, is the **Bibliothèque Inguimbertine**, with a collection of 200,000 books and manuscripts.

The vast 18thC **Hôtel-Dieu** *(av. Victor-Hugo, open Mon, Wed and Thurs mornings)*, with its handsome central stairway, is notable for its 18thC **pharmacy**, still much in use by hospital staff; its cupboards contain Moustiers faïence, and are decorated with comic paintings of monkey apothecaries.

St-Siffrein † ☆
Rue de la République.

In the heart of the Old Town, this former cathedral has a Renaissance W door, but the entrance is by the S door, an example of the Flamboyant Gothic style. It is known as the **Porte Juive**, as Jewish converts to Christianity went through it to be baptized. The interior of the church is ornately decorated with some fine works of art. In the choir and behind the altar are exuberant, gilded sculptures by Jacques Bernus; in the chapels of the N aisle, paintings of saints by Mignard and Parrocel; to the left of the altar, a triptych of St-Siffrein (the town's patron) from the 15thC Avignon School. More precious objects are in the **Trésor** *(to view, apply to the Bibliothèque Inguimbertine)*.

Carpentras also has a museum devoted to the history of the Comtat Venaissin, the **Musée Comtadin**. The **Musée Sobirats**, also worth a visit, is an 18thC house with a preserved period interior. *(Both closed Tues.)* The **Palais de Justice** (law court) is housed in the old (17thC) episcopal palace, and contains a number of fine rooms and interesting paintings.

Walking around the town, you will notice a number of 17th and 18thC *hôtels particuliers* — large town houses — with impressive facades.

- **EVENTS** • In July and August, a **festival of music, dance and theater**. • In November, a second-hand and antique **fair**. • In December, a *santons* **fair**.

- **MARKETS**   Carpentras is in the middle of a rich agricultural area. There is a particularly good **general market** every Friday. • Also a **truffle market** from November to March.

❧   SAFARI
1 av. J.H. Fabre, Route d'Avignon
☎90-63-35-35 ⨍90-60-49-99 ▢ 42
rms ▦▣▭▤ AE ◉ ▣ ‡▢▭ ⸙ ❧
☟ ♨ ▰ ♛

Location: On the outskirts of town, in its own grounds. This very serviceable, recently refurbished hotel offers a wide range of facilities. The restaurant, too, achieves a decent standard.

❧   Also recommended: **Hotel du Fiacre** *(153 rue Vigne* ☎90-63-03-15)*, a pleasant, elegant and comfortable hotel in an 18thC building in the town center; **Forum** *(24 rue du Forum* ☎90-60-57-00 ⨍90-63-52-65).

▭   L'ORANGERIE
26 rue Duplessis ☎90-67-27-23 ▢ *to* ▢▢
▦▤▢ ▭ AE ◉ ▥ *Closed Sat lunch. Last orders 10pm.*

This pleasant restaurant, with its garden and 1930s-style decor, has a range of menus to suit all pockets. Try the *gratinée de filets de poisson,* or the *rognons de veau au gingembre et poires.*

▭   Another good restaurant: **Vert**

Galant *(12 rue Clapies* ☎90-67-15-50 ▢▢ *closed Sat lunch, Sun).* Probably the smartest place in a town not famed for its restaurants.

❧ ▭ NEARBY

HOSTELLERIE DE CRILLON-LE-BRAVE
▱
Pl. de l'Église, Crillon-le-Brave, 84410
☎90-65-61-61 ⨍90-65-62-86 ▢▢ *to* ▢▢▢
22 rms ▬▭ AE ◉ ▣ ▭ ≪ ▰ ⸙
☟ ♛ ♨ *Closed Jan–Apr.*

Location: In the village of Crillon-le-Brave, 14 kilometers (9 miles) NE of Carpentras, off D974. Based around a large old presbytery and a number of adjoining houses, in a hill-village near the base of Mont Ventoux, this hotel — run by a Canadian — is the most luxurious in the area. The rooms, many with views of vineyards and olive groves, are cheerful, and furnished with antiques and bright Souleiado fabrics. The effect is altogether soothing and most comfortable. The restaurant, which specializes in truffles, lamb and freshwater fish, is in a vaulted room; the standard of the cuisine is commendable.

PLACES NEAR CARPENTRAS
Pernes-les-Fontaines *(6km/3$\frac{1}{2}$ miles s of Carpentras).* Capital of the Comtat before Carpentras, this ancient and picturesque town has a number of graceful fountains. The most pleasant spot is where the Porte Notre-Dame stands beside a former castle keep, opposite a 16thC bridge with a tiny chapel built on it. The **Tour Ferrande** is notable, and worth a visit for the 13thC frescoes in its third-floor room.
Venasque *(11km/7 miles sw of Carpentras).* This old village on the foothills of the Vaucluse plateau preceded Carpentras as the bishopric of the Comtat Venaissin, to which it gave its name. As well as being well-restored, and as pretty as a picture to wander through, it is also one of the most stunningly located villages in the whole of Provence. Built on a spur of rock, it seems to float on a cloud of trees as you approach it from the direction of Carpentras — and it offers lovely views over the plain, with MONT VENTOUX visible in the distance.

Adjoining its 13thC church is a 7thC Merovingian baptistry, not unlike those at RIEZ and FRÉJUS, except that it has only four sides. Slim marble columns with Classical capitals support its vaulted apsidioles. The chapel of **Notre-Dame-de-la-Vie** *(2.5km/1½ miles to the N on the D4)* contains the tombstone of Bohetius (died 604), said to have been Bishop of Venasque and Carpentras. It has several fine Merovingian sculptures.

Venasque tends to be full of tourists in the summer, although quiet for the rest of the year. Cherries are an important part of the local economy, with daily **markets** in May and June.

⚭ ⇶ **AUBERGE DE LA FONTAINE**
Pl. de la Fontaine, 84210 ☎*90-66-02-96*
Fx*90-66-13-14* 〰 *5 rms* ▦ 〰 ▰ ⇶
♪ ☐ ⌂ *Restaurant closed Sun dinner;*
Wed. Last orders 10pm. Reservation
necessary.
Location: In the center of the village. A charming hotel in an 18thC manor house, whose rooms are well equipped and furnished. The restaurant specializes in game, and good country cooking. Once a month, there are chamber music concerts with dinner.

⚭ **LES RAMPARTS** ▰
Rue Haute, 84210 Venasque

☎*90-66-02-79* ☐ *5 rms* ⇶ 〚AE〛 ⊙ 〚VISA〛
⟨⟨ *Closed Nov–Mar. Restaurant closed*
Wed out of season. Last orders 9.30pm.
A simple hotel where the view is the main thing. An inexpensive restaurant serves basic, adequate Provençal dishes.

⚭ **LA GARRIGUE**
Route de l'Appie, 84210 Venasque
☎*90-66-03-40* 〰 *15 rooms* ⇝ ⇶ 〚VISA〛
⌂ ⌂ ⚘ *Closed end Oct–Mar.*
A good, basic, little country hotel just outside Venasque, and surrounded by ancient, dry-stone *bories*. There are large, comfortable bedrooms leading out to a flower-filled garden.

• See also: VENTOUX, MONT.

CAVAILLON

*Map **4E5** (Vaucluse). 27km (17 miles) SE of Avignon. Postal code: 84300.*
Population: 23,000 i 79 rue Saunerie ☎*90-71-32-01.*

France's leading market center for fruit and vegetables (notably sweet pink melons) lies in a very fertile stretch of the lower Durance valley. In Roman times, too, this was an important trading center, as can be seen at the **Musée Archéologique** *(closed Tues),* with its varied collection of local discoveries (pottery, coins, funeral urns). In Boulevard du Clos is a small **Roman arch**.

The former cathedral of **Notre-Dame-et-St-Véran** *(closed mornings Sun and Mon)* has a Romanesque nave and cloister, with later additions; in the side chapels are 17thC gilded wood carvings and paintings by Mignard and Parrocel. The nearby **synagogue** *(closed Sat)* houses a small **museum** of the Jewish community, once so strong in Vaucluse.

A climb up the steep path to the 12thC (with 17thC alterations) **Chapelle St-Jacques** *(closed Tues)* and its nearby hermitage affords a panoramic view of the Vaucluse Plateau, the LUBÉRON mountain and MONT VENTOUX.

The area immediately around Cavaillon is quite industrialized, and there is a lot of heavy traffic on the roads.

⚭ **Christel** *(Digue des Grands-Jardins* ☎*90-71-07-79* Fx*90-78-27-94* 〰 ⇶*)*, a modern hotel 2km (1 mile) outside town near the autoroute; **Parc** *(pl. Clos* ☎*90-71-57-78* Fx*90-76-10-35* 〰*)*, basic but centrally located.

Prévôt *(353 av. de Verdun* ☎*90-71-32-43* ▦*),* the best in town; **Fin de Siècle** *(46 pl. Clos* ☎*90-71-12-*

27 ▦ *closed Tues dinner, Wed);* **Nicolet** *(Cheval Blanc, Route de Pertuis* ☎*90-78-01-56* ▦*).*

● See also: AVIGNON; LUBÉRON, MONTAGNE DU.

FONTAINE-DE-VAUCLUSE ☆

Map **5***D6 (Vaucluse). 30km (18 miles) E of Avignon. Postal code: 84800 L'Isle-sur-la-Sorgue. Population: 600* **i** *Chemin de la Fontaine* ☎*90-20-32-22.*

In winter or spring, especially after heavy rain or when snows are melting, the fountain is a magnificent sight. Set in a cavern where the river Sorgue emerges at the foot of a high limestone cliff, the waters surge up over a rocky barrier in a roaring cascade of spray. In the dry season, though, the water flows normally and there is nothing special to see. Nevertheless, the fountain attracts well over a million visitors every year.

It is a short walk from the village of the same name, which is, not surprisingly, tourist-oriented. Little is left of the romantic serenity that persuaded the Italian poet Petrarch to live here. He is commemorated with a stele, erected in 1804 to mark his fifth centenary, and with a small **museum** *(closed Tues Apr-Oct, Jan, Feb; rest of year open weekends only)* of his works, on the site of the house where he lived from 1337–53.

There is also a **speleological museum** *(closed Nov to late Jan, and Mon, Tues except in summer),* where some fine stalactites can be viewed, the small Romanesque **church of St-Véran,** and a ruined **castle** overlooking the village.

● **EVENT** A *son et lumière* show is held daily at the fountain from mid-June to mid-September at 9.30pm.

▦ ❧ LE PARC

Les Bourgades, Fontaine-de-Vaucluse, 84800 ☎*90-20-31-57* ▦ *to* ▦ ◥ ▭
■ ✿ ▣ ◉ ▦ *Closed Wed; Jan to mid-Feb. Last orders 9.15pm.*
Straightforward food served in the large garden by the river, or in the vast *salle.* The creeper- and rose-covered *auberge* also has comfortable bedrooms.

▦ ❧ HOSTELLERIE DU CHÂTEAU

Quartier Petit Prince, Fontaine-de-Vaucluse,

84800 ☎*90-20-31-54* ▦ ▭ ■ ▣ ◉
▦ *Closed Mon eve; Tues. Last orders 8.30pm.*
A very friendly, well-kept place in the center of town, with a glass-covered dining area overlooking the river and bridge. The restaurant offers good value: the food is unpretentious, using decent ingredients, particularly lamb and freshwater fish. The Hostellerie also has a number of simple but pleasant bedrooms.

● See also: AVIGNON, CAVAILLON, GORDES, L'ISLE-SUR-LA-SORGUE, ROUSSILLON.

FONTVIEILLE

Map **9***E4 (B.-du-R.). 9.5km (6 miles) NE of Arles. Postal code: 13990. Population: 3,500* **i** *at Mairie* ☎*90-97-70-01.*

A small town beneath the plain of Arles and the Alpilles range, chiefly visited for its famous mill.

Moulin de Daudet

2km (1 mile) s of Fontvieille, off the D33 🚗 ✗ *available. Open daily 10am–noon, 2–5pm (Oct–June), 9am–noon, 2–7pm (June and Sept), 9am–7pm (July, Aug); weekends only in Jan.*

The windmill that 19thC writer Alphonse Daudet found so inspiring is indeed impressively situated, on a bare rocky hill with pine woods behind, amid views of the Alpilles and the Rhône valley. Despite the name of Daudet's best-selling book *Lettres de mon Moulin* (Letters from my Windmill), he never owned the building; the letters were written in Paris where he lived, and he only used to visit the mill when staying with friends in the village. But he would go there to think for long hours, and to listen to the miller's tales, many of which he then used as his published *contes*.

❧ ═ LA RÉGALIDO

Rue Frédéric-Mistral, 13990 Fontvieille
☎90-54-60-22 ▥ *14 rms* ➟ 🖃 🗚 💷
🖭 ▥ 🖛 ☐ 🖾 ❧ *Closed Dec–Jan.*
Location: Set back from a village side-street. Umbrella pines, fig trees, roses and magnolias, trimly-cut lawns: the beautifully-kept garden is the best feature of this luxurious little *auberge,* converted from an old oil mill. The interior is graciously intimate and inviting. Roses abound indoors, and each of the rooms is named after a flower or plant. The flowery patio, gently lit at night, makes a romantic setting for a meal, or you can choose the more formal elegance of the vaulted dining room (▥ ■ ═ 🍴 *closed Mon except in summer, Tues lunch, Dec-Jan).* Here is a talented chef who can produce

light variations on classic cuisine. The menu is short and concentrates on fish. Good local Côteaux-de-Baux wines. *Specialities: Mousseline de loup au beurre blanc, nage de loup à l'huile d'olive et gros sel, tranche de gigot aux gousses d'ail confites, magret de canard au myrtilles.*

❧ LE VALMAJOUR

Route d'Arles, 13990 Fontvieille
☎90-54-62-33 🖷90-54-61-67 ▥ *32 rms* ═ 🖃 🗚 💷 🖛 ☐ 🖾 ✿ ❧ ⁓
🍴 👥 *Closed Jan to mid-Mar.*
Location: On the w fringe of the town, just off the Arles road (D17). A modern ivy-covered hotel, attractively designed in the style of a local *mas.* Spacious and comfortable, plenty of amenities and good views, but not much ambience.

• See also: ARLES, LES BAUX, ST-RÉMY-DE-PROVENCE.

GORDES

Map 5D6 (Vaucluse). 38km (24 miles) E of Avignon. Postal code: 84220. Population: 1,600 𝒊 *place du Château* ☎90-72-02-75.

One of the largest and best-known of Provençal hill-villages, Gordes, with its paved alleys, stands on a steep, rocky hillside overlooking the rolling landscape between the Vaucluse plateau and the Coulon valley. Rows of old stone houses rise sharply up to the Renaissance château on the top, which is visible from many miles away. Numerous craftsmen work and exhibit in Gordes: potters, weavers, painters on silk, and the like.

Gordes has now been officially designated as one of "Les plus beaux villages de France." The rather off-hand locals are fully aware of this — and do their best to make the most of it financially. It has also become a magnet for trendy Parisians and foreigners, many of them in the media. The imposing town hall has become a favorite for fashionable weddings. The 18thC **church of St-Firmin** is gaudily decorated inside, and looks more like a drawing-room than anything else. Most of the village is a pedestrian mall.

WHAT TO SEE IN GORDES
Château et Musée Vasarely
■■ *Open 10am–noon, 2–6pm. Closed Tues.*

Although the fortified château, with its two round towers, looks austere from the outside, inside it is full of elegant Renaissance touches: the fine gateway in the courtyard, the moldings on the ceiling of the main stairway, the ornate chimney piece on the first floor.

Victor Vasarely, one of many artists and intellectuals who have spent the summer at Gordes, restored the château in return for permission from its owners, the town council, to install there his **musée didactique** — and didactic it certainly is, even more so than his Fondation at AIX-EN-PROVENCE. Sliding panels give an exposé of his theories, which come alive in the two rooms filled with his vividly colored geometric designs in the form of mosaics, tapestries and sculptures. An upper room, by contrast, contains some of his early figurative work of the 1930s.

Musée du Vitrail (Museum of Stained Glass)
5km (3 miles) s of Gordes ■■ *Open 10am–noon, 2–7pm; weekends only Nov–Jan.*

A modern building beside the 16thC Bouillons olive-oil mill houses a museum created by Frédérique Duran, an artist who has pioneered new techniques with stained-glass tiles. Part of the museum is devoted to the history of stained glass; part is a gallery where the work of Duran and other artists is exhibited and sold.

Village des Bories ☆
3km (2 miles) sw of Gordes, off the D2, down a 2km (1-mile) rough track ■■

A *borie* is a beehive-shaped primitive hut made, without mortar, of rough stones. In France, they are unique to the southern slopes of the Vaucluse plateau and the northern slopes of the LUBÉRON mountain, where they stand singly or in clusters. Some are thought to date from Ligurian times, but some have also been inhabited as recently as the 18thC, and one theory is that they were sometimes used by town dwellers fleeing from the plague.

This village consists of a group of a dozen *bories,* the last dwellers of which left in the early 19thC. It has now been converted into a museum of traditional rural life, and is well laid out and interestingly documented.

Five kilometers (3 miles) to the N of Gordes is the abbey of SÉNANQUE.

❧ ⇶ IN GORDES

❧ ⇶ LA BASTIDE DE GORDES 🏰

Rue de la Combe, 84220 Gordes
☎90-72-12-12 ⊠90-72-05-20 ⅢⅠ to ⅢⅡ
18 rms ▦ ▦ AE VISA ✱ ☐ ⏰ ♿ ☀ 《
꩜ ✍ 🏊 🍴 ⇶ Closed Nov–Mar.
Once the local village *gendarmerie*, and, with its views of the Lubéron and its top-notch rooms and facilities, now certainly the best hotel in the village. The restaurant, run by a former pupil of Alain Ducasse, has few local rivals.

❧ ⇶ LES BORIES

Route de Sénanque, 84220 Gordes ☎90-72-00-51 ⊠90-72-01-22 ⅢⅠ to ⅢⅡ
▢ ▀ ▦ ▦ AE ⏰ VISA 🖙 ✱ ☐ ⏰ ♿
☀ 🍴 🏊 ꩜ ✍ Closed Dec to mid-Jan.
Location: On a stony plateau, 3 kilometers (2 miles) N of Gordes. A group of ancient *bories* have been transformed with great originality into a chic, intimate hotel in a lovely location. At first the hotel had only two rooms (hovel-like from the outside, they are attractively furnished, with all modern facilities). It has now upgraded, with a swimming pool and new rooms. The restaurant, with its dim lighting, white walls and comfortable chairs, is distinguished and often original. *Specialities: Filet de rouget, selle d'agneau à l'ail, game (in season).* Last orders 9.30pm.

❧ ⇶ HOSTELLERIE LE PHÉBUS

Route de Murs, 84220 Joucas
☎90-05-78-83 ⊠90-05-73-61 ⅢⅠ 16 rms ▦ ▦ AE ⏰ ☐ ⏰ ☀ 《 🏊
꩜ ✍ Closed Nov to mid-Mar.
Location: Outside Joucas, 6 kilometers (4 miles) E of Gordes on D102. A very pleasant, quiet hotel, with large, attractive rooms and an enchanting setting. The restaurant hits high standards: try *royale de loup sur son lit de pétragone et basilic* and *médaillons de ,. croûte de truffes.*

❧ ⇶ MAS DES HERBES BLANCHES 🏰

Route de Murs, 84220 Joucas
☎90-05-79-79 ⊠90-05-71-96 ⅢⅡ 19 rms ▬ AE ⏰ ⏰ VISA ⏰ ☐ ⏰ ☀ 《
꩜ ✍ 🚶 Closed Jan to mid-Mar.
Location: Outside Joucas, 6 kilometers (4 miles) E of Gordes on the D102. Built in the form of a traditional dry-stone *mas,* this is one of the most celebrated hotels in the region. It has tasteful, restrained decor, and the feeling is of staying as a guest in a private house. Most rooms have good views of the Lubéron. The commendable restaurant serves food that is light and flavorsome.

❧ LA MAYANELLE ♣

84220 Gordes ☎90-72-00-28
⊠90-72-00-28 ⅢⅠ 10 rms AE ⏰ ⏰ VISA
⏰ ⏰ ☐ Closed Jan–Feb.
Location: Near the main square. This sleek little hotel occupies a part-12thC, part-17thC mansion. The decor is bare wooden floors and antique furniture — gracious, but not cozy. The dining room *(closed Tues)* serves good local dishes. Prices are modest. There are fine views.

❧ Also good: **La Gacholle** *(Route de Murs* ☎90-72-01-36 ⅢⅠ; **Domaine de L'Enclos** *(Route de Sénanque* ☎90-72-08-22 ⊠90-72-03-03 ⅢⅠ to ⅢⅡ ⇶); **Le Gordos** *(Route de Cavaillon* ☎90-72-00-75 ⅢⅡ); **Domaine Le Moulin Blanc** *(Chemin du Moulin, Les Beaumettes* ☎90-72-34-50 ⊠90-72-25-41 ⅢⅡ),* smart, with good views.

⇶ Try too: **Le Mas Tourteron** *(Les Imberts* ☎90-72-00-16 ⅢⅠ to ⅢⅡ); **Domaine de l'Enclos** *(Route de Sénanque* ☎90-72-08-22 ⅢⅡ).

SHOPPING IN GORDES

Gordes has its fair share of up-to-the-minute stores, including a Souleiado boutique, **Vivement l'Été** (for glassware and pottery), **La Maison de l'Hélicanthe** (for Provençal souvenirs), **Le Miel Peyron** (for honey and jams) and **Cassiopée** (for jewelry).

- See also: APT; ROUSSILLON; LUBÉRON, MONTAGNE DU; SÉNANQUE, ABBAYE DE.

RGUE ☆

23km (14 miles) SE of Avignon. Postal code: 84800.
place de l'Église ☎90-38-04-78

, but attractive town, with running streams and grassy, , lies at the place where the river Sorgue divides into five bra... s church has a richly decorated 17thC Baroque interior, and a retable of the Assumption. The old hospital *(open daily)* has 18thC woodcarvings in its chapel and Moustiers faïence in the pharmacy. There are a number of old water wheels along the river, and some fine old town houses.

- **MARKETS** There are large, bustling **general markets** on Thursdays and Sundays. There you will find salt cod (the basis of the Provençal dip *brandade*), local cheeses such as Banon, and 20 types of olives combined with such flavorings as garlic, pimentos and fennel. • The Sunday morning market is also a magnet for "**antique**" dealers. Among the bric-a-brac, you will come across ancient muskets, old glass, outmoded farm implements, and rustic furniture — all haphazardly displayed, and all to be haggled over. • In March there is a full-scale **antique fair**.

On market days, the fin-de-siècle **Café de France**, near the church, is the place for a snack or a coffee.

Good restaurant/hotel: **Mas de Cure Bourse** *(Route de Caumont ☎90-38-16-58)* is 2km (1 mile) out of town, and has a pleasant setting.

- See also: AVIGNON, CAVAILLON, FONTAINE-DE-VAUCLUSE.

LUBÉRON, MONTAGNE DU ☆

Map **5***E7 (Vaucluse). 24–80km (15–50 miles) E of Avignon*

This remarkable range of hills runs for 56 kilometers (35 miles) from W–E between the Durance and Coulon valleys. To the E is the higher and wilder stretch, the **Grand Lubéron**, now a national park. The peak of **Mourre Nègre**, at an altitude of 1,100 meters (3,690 feet), is accessible by car; from the top, there are dizzying views, from the Alps to the Rhône delta. To the W of the Apt–Cadenet road is the **Petit Lubéron**, a fertile plateau full of vineyards, lavender fields and beehives. From Bonnieux down to CAVAILLON, a fine scenic road runs along the crest of the hills, past a forest of giant cedars.

From the 13th–16thC, the Lubéron was the stronghold of an early Protestant sect, the Vaudois. These "heretics," if devout, were also often violent; bands of them would burn and pillage churches in the region. Finally, in 1545, François 1er launched a crusade against the Vaudois, killing or capturing over 2,000 of them.

Bonnieux

This hill-village on a N-facing spur of the Petit Lubéron (as are **Ménerbes** and **Oppède-le-Vieux**) has views across the Coulon valley. On the summit of the hill is a 12thC church, which is now little used. The large 19thC church down the hill is of no beauty, but is worth visiting for the four remarkable 15thC **German paintings** (☆) behind the main altar. They depict the *Martyrdom of Christ*. Painted on wood panels in vivid reds and greens, they are fresh and well preserved. Formerly they were in the old church.

✍ ⇶ L'AIGUEBRUN

84480 Bonnieux ☎*90-74-04-14* ▥ *8 rms* ⬤ ▦ ▣ ▨ ⌂ ⌂ ❧ ⊀ ⬤ ⅋ *Closed mid-Nov to mid-Mar.*

Location: Isolated, by a stream in a narrow valley, just off the D943, 5 kilometers (3 miles) E of Bonnieux. A small 19thC manor, owned by a Parisian artist and ex-couturier, and furnished with taste. The enchanting setting and the tranquility attract people who come to paint, write or read. The chic little restaurant (▥ *to* ▥ ▭ ■ ⇶ ⇔ *closed Mon lunch, mid-Nov to mid-Jan, last orders 10pm)* looks onto the valley, or you can choose to eat under the plane and fir trees in the garden. Meals are certainly not cheap, but the young chef shows real talent. *Specialities: Figues fraîches à la crème de fenouil, gentille de saumon au beurre de tomate, poulet au safran.*

⇶ **Hostellerie du Prieuré** *(rue J.B. Aurard* ☎*90-75-80-78* ▥ *to* ▥*)*. This is an extremely pleasant hotel in an 18thC building at the foot of the town's ramparts. Meals can be taken in front of the open fireplace or in the garden.

Fort de Buoux

A ruined fortress on a rocky peak above the rugged Buoux gorge. As a natural defense point, it was used in turn by Ligurians, Romans and Protestants. The **Aigue-Brun** valley, just to the E, has Paleolithic cave dwellings.

⇶ AUBERGE DE LA LOUBE

Quartier La Loube ☎*90-74-19-58* ▥ ⬤ ■ ⇔ ▦ *Closed Thurs; Jan. Last orders 9.30pm.*

High in the hills near Buoux, this simple restaurant is a great local favorite. Since Peter Mayle mentioned it in *A Year in Provence,* it has also become a site of pilgrimage for visitors. In the summer, tourists brandishing Mayle's book turn up and order the very lunch he describes in its pages. Later, they often seek an autograph from the jolly chef, Maurice Leporati, a star of the book. But don't let that put you off: the 150f menu (there is only one price), with its splendid array of hors d'oeuvres (including *tapenade,* the Provençal paste of olives, anchovies and capers) and hearty rustic specialities like lamb laced with garlic and local herbs, is very good, and the ambience is cozy and seductive. Perfect for a relaxed lunch, which you can eat either inside or in the garden.

Lacoste

The ruined 11thC castle was once the home of the Marquis de Sade and is described in his *Justine* and *120 days of Sodom*. Before that, it was owned by local grandees, the Simiane family. Now partly restored, the castle is in the hands of a retired teacher and devotee of de Sade, who will (sometimes) show you around. The 17thC belfry is also well worth a visit.

Part of this charming, well kept and wealthy village is given over to an American art school. There are concerts of early music in August.

✍ **Le Simiane** *(rue Basse* ☎*90-75-83-31* ▥*;* **Marquis de Sade** *(rue Sous Barri* ☎*90-75-83-21* ▥*).*

⇶ **Le Relais du Procureur** *(rue Basse* ☎*90-75-82-28* ▥*),* a 17thC building with a pool.

Lourmarin

This village on the southern slopes of the Lubéron has an imposing château, part-15thC, part-Renaissance, which has a fine main stairway and chimney pieces; classical concerts are held here in summer. The novelist Albert Camus lies buried in the village cemetery.

⇒ LA FENIÈRE
9 rue du Grand-Pré ☎90-68-11-79 ⊞ ▦
▢ ▪ ⇒ ▦ ◈ ◉ ▦ *Closed Sun dinner; Mon; Tues lunch (July to end Sept); 1st week Oct; last week Jan. Last orders 9.30pm.*

Down a small side-street, this unexpectedly smart restaurant is surely the best in the locality. The interior is light and bright, embellished by a large mural. It is run by a husband-and-wife team and the service is very smooth and helpful. The modern Provençal cooking is inventive, light and very well presented. Ingredients are all local, as are many of the wines on the comprehensive list. Try the *bouillabaisse d'asperges* or the *tian de St-Jacques* as starters, and the *carré d'agneau* or the *pigeonneau rôti* as a main course. In season, there is a menu (not inexpensive) in which *every* course contains truffles.

⇒ **Le Bistrot** *(2 av. Philippe de Girard* ☎90-68-29-74 ⊞*).*

☞ ⇒ **Le Moulin de Lourmarin** *(rue du Temple* ☎90-68-06-69 ⊞*),* a very attractive and well-equipped hotel with an excellent restaurant.

Ménerbes

Standing amid rocks above the valley, Ménerbes is an old village with a lively colony of artists and craftsmen. In the 16thC, it was the final stronghold of the local Protestants. There is a 14thC church, and a 13thC fortress (rebuilt by the Huguenots in the 16thC, restored again in the 19thC, and over the last 20 years by its present owner). The painter Nicholas de Staël lived in the village, but it is probably now best known because of the frequent mentions in *A Year in Provence.* Peter Mayle lives somewhere nearby.

⇒ PASCAL ☞
Rue Clovis Hugues ☎90-72-22-13 ▢ ▢
☞ ◆ *No cards. Lunches only (last orders 2pm). Closed Nov–Easter.*

Boisterous parties of Vauclusiens descend on this splendid village *auberge* to enjoy the lavish food and mountain views. There's a shady garden and three large, plain dining rooms — all very down to earth, yet professional. Such is their popularity that the Pascals close for dinner; they say they couldn't cope with the invasion twice a day. The simple country cooking can rarely be faulted, and the five-course set menus are excellent value.

☞ HOSTELLERIE LE ROY SOLEIL
Route des Beaumettes, 84560 Ménerbes
☎90-72-25-61 ▤90-72-36-55 ⊞ 14
rms ◆ ▦ ▢ ▢ ▢ ⚹ ❅ ☀ ▦ ☞
☞✓ ▦ ⇒

This is a well-located, well-equipped, tastefully decorated and restful hotel, in a converted 17thC building standing amid vineyards and cherry trees. In the restaurant *(closed mid-Nov to mid-Mar),* the food is distinctly respectable, with specialities such as *daube de baudrois à la Provençale, minute de loup grillé à la peau* and *filet de boeuf à la lit de Châteauneuf-du-Pape et à la moelle.*

Oppède-le-Vieux

Although this medieval village, on a rocky spur overlooking the Coulon valley, had fallen into ruin (abandoned by its inhabitants in 1910), artists, writers and others started to buy up some of the houses after World War II. Particularly around the village square, many have been restored, and life has gradually returned to Oppède. The village has a ruined castle, and a 13thC church with 16th and 19thC additions.

MAS DES CAPELANS
84580 Oppède-le-Vieux ☎*90-76-99-04*
[Fax]*90-76-99-29* ▥ *10 rms* ━ ═ [AE] [VISA]
▱ ▱ ❧ ❮ ▲ ≈ *Closed Sun; mid-Nov to mid-Feb.*

A pleasant little hotel with large rooms, in the 18thC former home of a silkworm breeder. The restaurant is open only to residents. The garden, where you can eat, is shaded by mulberry trees.

• See also: ANSOUIS, APT, GORDES, ROUSSILLON.

MARSEILLE

Map 10H7 (B.-du-R.). 777km (485 miles) s of Paris; 188km (117 miles) w of Nice. Postal code: 13000. Population: 800,550 **i** *4 La Canebière* ☎*91-54-91-11.* **Airport:** *at Marignane, 27km (17 miles)* NW ☎*42-78-21-00.* **Railway station:** *Gare St-Charles* ☎*91-50-59-18.*

France's foremost port, second city, and capital of the Provence–Côte d'Azur region, is handsomely situated around a wide bay, circled by high limestone hills. It is a powerful city with a strong draw — noisy, congested, in places ugly, but with much to offer. It contrasts strongly with the nearby elegant smaller towns such as AIX and ARLES.

The Marseillais are proud and hot-blooded — proud of their past, for this is the oldest town in France. Founded in 600BC by the Greeks from Phocea in Asia Minor, Massilia — as it was then called — soon became the main Greek colony in the west, and was to play a sizeable role in Roman history, siding with Rome against Hannibal and then (to its misfortune) with Pompey against Caesar.

Marseille has always lived on commerce: the period of the Crusades brought it great prosperity, when it became a trading rival of Genoa and Venice and set up posts all over the Levant. In 1721 it suffered heavily from a plague, contracted from Syria, which wiped out 50,000 people. After 1789, the town welcomed the French Revolution and sent soldiers to Paris, where so lustily did they sing the new *Battle Hymn of the Army of the Rhine,* composed in Strasbourg by Rouget de l'Isle, that the song was dubbed *La Marseillaise.* The nickname has stuck.

The French conquest of North Africa in the mid-19thC, and the opening of the Suez Canal in 1869, gave Marseille its greatest era of commercial prosperity, and most of the grand buildings in the city date from that period. In this century, the port has gone into relative decline, due partly to the loss of France's overseas empire and in recent years to the world shipping slump. Repair yards have closed, some docks lie idle, and unemployment is above the national average.

Yet this is still an active city, which was long governed with lordly *panache* by Gaston Defferre, the socialist mayor from 1953 until his death in 1986, and Provence's most powerful politician at the time. In 30 years he did much to modernize and develop the city: witness the Métro (1977), the tunnel under the Vieux Port, and the unlovely but much-needed apartment blocks that rise on all the city's hills. There are large universities and research centers, and many industries (chemicals, engineering, food products and, of course, *pastis*), although recently many firms have moved to surrounding towns such as Vitrolles and Aubagne, attracted by tax incentives.

Like other great Mediterranean cities — Naples, Athens, Alexandria — Marseille is a town of contrasts: beautiful setting, superb history, and brash modern workaday reality. In its crisscross of drab commercial streets, the traffic jams are among Europe's worst, while the climate varies from torrid midsummer heat to the icy blasts of the winter Mistral. The Marseillais are industrious, volatile, rough-mannered and earthily humorous — just as the writer Marcel Pagnol described them.

However, the rise of racial tension in France has been sharpest in Marseille (Jean-Marie Le Pen's right-wing Front National party has its greatest support here), and the city still lives up to its reputation for violence, shady dealing and Mafia-style gangsterism. The famous local soccer team, **Olympique de Marseille**, is owned by the colorful entrepreneur and socialist politician Bernard Tapie, who resigned amid a financial scandal as a minister in the French government. True to the spirit of Marseille, OM, as the team is known, was faced with allegations of bribery after winning the European Champions Cup in 1993 and was eventually stripped of the trophy.

> A fine town, Marseille. This human ant-heap, this smutty vulgarity, this squalor. They don't kill each other as much as it's said, in the alleys of the Vieux Port — but it's a fine town all the same.
> (*Eurydice* [translated as *Point of Departure*], 1942, Jean Anouilh)

Sprawling Marseille is divided into 16 districts or *arrondissements*. Its life focuses around the main boulevard, **La Canebière**, which slopes down to the **Vieux Port**, used today mainly by fishing and pleasure craft; the modern port is to the N. To the S of the Vieux Port, housing development covers the slope of a broad hill around whose western side the coastal highway, **Corniche Président-Kennedy (☆)**, winds for miles past rocks, sandy coves and the rich villas of the bourgeoisie.

Atop the hill stands the city's most famous and evident landmark, the 19thC **Basilica of Notre-Dame-de-la-Garde** *(open summer 7am-7.30pm, winter 7.30am-5.30pm)*, which is to Marseille what the Sacré-Coeur is to Paris, only more so. Built in Neo-Byzantine style, it is crowned by a large statue of *The Virgin*, which is floodlit at night. Inside is a fascinating array of sailors' votive offerings — one reason for going up (by car or trolley-bus) to this hideous church; the other is the superb view (☆) from its terrace over the city, the coast and surrounding hills.

PUBLIC TRANSPORT IN MARSEILLE
There is a good bus link, every 20 minutes, between the international airport at Marignane (France's third-largest) and St-Charles station. Marseille has good bus and subway services: information from **RTM** (Réseau de Transport Marseillais) *(6-8 rue des Fabres ☎ 91-91-92-10)*.

Tickets are transferable between the two modes of transport, and can be bought singly or in books of six. **Fares** are flat-rate, but note that the **Métro** runs only from 5am–9pm (unless the OM soccer team is playing at night), and **buses** from 6am–9pm (although there are some night bus routes that operate until midnight).

Good **coach services** head northward, or along the coast from the **Gare Routière** *(pl. Victor-Hugo* ☎ *91-08-16-40)* behind the railway station. Or take either TGV or slower **trains**, northward from Gare St-Charles.

- **EVENTS** End of November to beginning of January, a picturesque *santons* **fair** on La Canebière. • Early April and last two weeks of September, **international trade fair** at Parc Amable-Chanot.

BOUILLABAISSE

Bouillabaisse is the Marseillais dish, an invention of local fishermen who, while sorting through fish for the market, would put aside choice pieces for their families. There is considerable mystique attached to the dish, and much argument about precisely what *une vraie bouillabaisse* should contain. There is even a Charte de la Bouillabaisse, to which various local restaurateurs are signatories, guaranteeing authenticity.

Experts say that *bouillabaisse* should include a minimum of four types of fish — which must be as fresh as possible — including *rascasse* (the ugly scorpion fish is considered to be essential), *Saint-Pierre* (John Dory), *lotte* (anglerfish/monkfish), *rouget grondin* (red gurnard), *araignée* (spider crab) and *congre* (conger eel). The fish is cooked with salt, pepper, onions, saffron, olive oil, garlic, fennel, parsley, potatoes and tomatoes.

The dish is traditionally served in two parts: the fish comes separate from the broth (which is eaten with the garlic mayonnaise, *rouille,* and croutons). You are, however allowed to mix the two components if you feel like it.

AREAS TO EXPLORE
La Canebière

In the days before air travel, when Marseille really was "the gateway to the East," this was one of the world's great streets. Its big terrace-cafés, with their orchestras, were a chic rendezvous for the princes, sultans and maharajahs who used the port on their way to or from Paris or London; and so there was a grain of sense in the fanciful local boast, "If Paris only had a Canebière it would be quite a little Marseille."

Today, the rich and mighty bypass Marseille, and the orchestras are gone. There is now little reason to be proud of this humdrum boulevard, lined with cut-rate stores, movie houses and seedy bars and cafeterias. But it is still the main thread that draws the city together.

At the port end, in front of the Bourse, is a reminder that political terrorism is no monopoly of our postwar age: here in 1934, a Macedonian shot dead King Alexander of Yugoslavia. The **Bourse** itself houses a maritime museum, **Musée de la Marine et de l'Économie de Marseille** *(Métro: Vieux Port* ☎ *91-39-33-33; open 10am-noon, 2-6pm, closed Tues),* with models of sailing ships and steamships. In the new **Centre Bourse** shopping mall is the **Musée d'Histoire de Marseille** *(☎ 91-*

90-42-22, open noon-7pm, closed Sun), which displays the archeological discoveries found in the JARDIN DES VESTIGES, including a wrecked Roman ship from the 3rdC AD, and other exhibits relating to Marseille's history.

On rue Grignan, 450 meters (500 yards) to the S, is the MUSÉE CANTINI. The area S of La Canebière is tolerably smart, while that to the N, around rue Thubaneau, is today a squalid red-light district, sinister at night. A massive new high-tech regional government building (designed by Will Alsop) is being erected near the **Porte d'Aix**, a 19thC triumphal arch off Cours Belsunce, N of the Vieux Port end of La Canebière.

Le Port Moderne
☎91-91-90-66 📷 ♣ ✗ *Sun and public holidays only: Apr–Sept 7am–9pm, Oct–Mar 7am–6pm. Entry by gate #2 (Arenc). No cars. Métro: Joliette.*

Work on the great port began in 1844. Today it contains 19 kilometers (12 miles) of quays, and stretches for 6 kilometers (4 miles) N from the VIEUX PORT area. Activity has declined, but it still handles some 20 million tons of goods a year and 800,000 passengers, mostly Algerian "guest-workers." The port is closed to tourists, but there is a bird's-eye view by car from the elevated Autoroute du Littoral, the fast N568B.

Vestiges, Jardin des
Rue Henri-Barbusse 📷 *Open 8am–sunset. Métro: Vieux Port.*

After years of excavation, the remains of the Greek port and town of the 3rd–2ndC BC have now been ingeniously transformed into a small public garden close to the NE corner of the VIEUX PORT. You can walk on lawns amid the ruins: quays, ramparts, towers and a reservoir, all Greek, with some Roman additions. There are clear explanatory panels. It is a most attractive restoration, beautifully floodlit at night.

Vieux Port ☆
This quay-lined inlet, full of small boats, was the port of Marseille from Phocaean days until the 19thC; and today it is still, in a sense, the heart of the city. At its mouth stand two old fortresses: **St-Jean** to the N and **St-Nicolas** to the S, the latter built by Louis XIV to keep the unruly Marseillais under control. To the E of this fort is the **Basilique St-Victor**; to the NW, facing the sea, the public **Parc du Pharo**, the château of which once belonged to the Empress Eugénie. From there, a fine view of the port can be had.

There is a **fish market** every morning on quai des Belges, at the head of the Vieux Port. The area around Cours d'Estienne d'Orves is pedestrianized and full of restaurants, bars and cafés. There is also a large underground parking garage in the vicinity.

The district of narrow alleys to the N of the old port, an ancient and once aristocratic area, had by the 1930s declined into a slum. In January 1943, the occupying Germans, finding it uncontrollable, turned out 40,000 of its inhabitants overnight and blew up the area between rue Caisserie and the old port.

After the war it was rebuilt, with rows of soulless gray rectangular

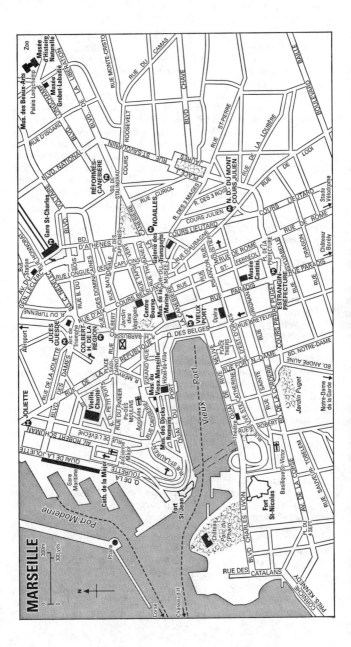

MARSEILLE

0   300m
0   300 yds

Zoo

Musée d'Histoire Naturelle

Palais Longchamp

Mus. des Beaux-Arts

Musée Grobet-Labadié

RUE MONTE-CRISTO

RUE DU CAMAS

RUE D'ISOARD

BLVD DE LA LIBERATION

BLVD NATIONAL

RUE ST-PIERRE

BLVD CHAVE

RUE DE LODI

BOULEVARD BAILLE

RUE DE LA LOUBIERE

Gare St-Charles

BLVD

RUE ST-SAVOURNIN

RUE ROOSEVELT

PLACE STALINGRAD

RÉFORMÉS-CANEBIÈRE

Sq. de Stalingrad

RUE CONSOLAT

RUE CURIOL

R. DES 3 MAGES

R. DES 3 ROIS

NOAILLES

COURS JULIEN

N. D. DU MONT

COURS LIEUTARD

RUE DE ROME

Stade Vélodrome

Château Borély

AV. DU Station Bus

GEN LECLERC

BD. D'ATHENES

RUE LONGUE

RUE NATIONALE

DES CAPUCINES

PL. DES CAPUCINES

RUE D'AUBAGNE

RUE FERREOL

Musée Cantini

RUE DE LA

H. DU TURENNE

RUE B. DU BOIS

RUE DES DOMINICAINS

RUE D'AIX

COURS BELSUNCE

RUE THUBANEAU

Galerie des Transports

MUSÉE

RUE MOUSTIER

PL. DE LA PREFECTURE

PREFECTURE

RUE DRAGON

Airport

JULES GUESDE

Arc de Triomphe

COLBERT-

H. DE LA RÉGION

RUE COLBERT

Jardin des Vestiges

Centre Bourse

Mus. de la Marine

CANEBIÈRE

Opéra

RUE PARADIS

RUE GRIGNAN

ESTRANGIN-PREFECTURE

COURS PIERRE PUGET

JOLIETTE

BLVD DES DAMES

PLACE SADI CARNOT

RUE DE LA RÉPUBLIQUE

H. BARBUSSE

GRAND RUE

Mus. du Vieux-Marseille

Hôtel-de-Ville

QUAI DU PORT

O. DES BELGES

VIEUX PORT

PLACE THIERS

RUE BRETEUIL

RUE ST-FERREOL

RUE PARADIS

BD. NOTRE-DAME

BD. ANDRE AUNE

RUE D'ENDOUME

Gare Maritime

AV ROBERT SCHUMAN

QUAI DE LA JOLIETTE

RUE DE L'EVÉCHÉ

Vieille Charité

R. DU PANIER

PL-DES MOULINS

Accoules

Mus. des Docks Romains

RUE CAISSERIE

QUAI DU PORT

Vieux   Port

Théâtre QUAI DE RIVE NEUVE

RUE SAINTE

RUE FORT N-DAME

BD. DE LA CORDERIE

Jardin Puget

Notre-Dame de la Garde

Port Moderne

Cath. de la Major

Ancienne Major

O. DE LA TOURETTE

RUE ST-LAURENT

Fort St-Jean

Vieux Port

RUE ST-CATHERINE

RUE ROBERT

Basilique St-Victor

RUE SAUVEUR-TOBELEM

BLVD CHARLES LIVON

Château Parc du Pharo

Fort St-Nicolas

RUE D'ENDOUME

Corse

Château d'If

Phare

Port Moderne

RUE DES CATALANS

BLVD PLOU 4 SEPT

AV. DE LA CORSE

CORNICHE PRES KENNEDY

N

blocks. However, the area N of **rue Caisserie** survives intact: you can glimpse alleyways where five-story houses are festooned with washing like faded bunting. Around the perimeter are some beautiful buildings: the **Mairie** with its 17thC facade; the **belfry of the Accoules**, a relic of a church dating from the 12thC; the HOSPICE DE LA VIEILLE CHARITÉ; also the MUSÉE DES DOCKS ROMAINS and the MUSÉE DU VIEUX MARSEILLE.

Just to the NW, near the new port, are the twin **cathédrales de la Major**, side by side and as different as chalk from cheese. The newer one is a vast, late 19thC Neo-Byzantine folly with cupolas and striped stone; it resembles a marzipan wedding-cake. Nestling in its shadow is the enchanting little **Ancienne Major** (✫): pure 12thC Romanesque. In its dim interior you can make out the porcelain low relief by Della Robbia and, over in the left transept, a 15thC altar of St-Lazarus, finely sculpted (☎ 91-90-53-57 𝘟 *available; both churches open daily May-Sept, 9am-noon, 2-6pm, otherwise 9am-noon, 2-5pm; closed Mon).*

WHAT TO SEE: MUSEUMS AND CHURCHES
Arts-Décoratifs, Musée des   See CHÂTEAU BORÉLY.

Beaux-Arts, Musée des ✫
Palais Longchamp, blvd. Longchamp ☎91-62-21-17 🖭 Open 10am-5pm (in summer, Sat-Sun noon-7pm).
This museum, set in the left wing of the PALAIS LONGCHAMP, houses the city's art collections. On the first floor, the central hall displays works by Provençal painters such as Guigou and François Duparc. Here the eye is caught by Michel Serre's two vast canvases of Marseille during the plague of 1721: the streets, full of the dead and dying, are graphic social documents, with an immediate impact.

Foreign artists (the core of the collection was booty amassed during Napoléon's campaigns) on exhibit include Rubens (including an *Adoration of the Shepherds*), Annibale Carracci (a lively *Village Wedding*) and Jan Brueghel (*l'Air*, a fantasy with cupids). Two adjoining rooms are devoted to the great Marseillais sculptor Pierre Puget: details of his life and his never-realized town-planning schemes for the city; some small original works; and, notably, casts of six of his greatest sculptures (the originals are in the Louvre and in Genoa).

On the second floor are works by French artists: Corot, Courbet, Millet, etc., and notably Daumier (who was born in Marseille), with vitriolic caricatures of Louis Philippe's supporters. On the stairways between the two floors are two lively cartoon-like murals by Puvis de Chavannes, showing Marseille as a Greek colony and as the gateway to the East.

In winter, you may find some rooms closed for renovation.

Cantini, Musée ✫
19 rue Grignan ☎91-54-77-75 🖭 Open 10am-5pm (in summer, Sat-Sun noon-7pm). Métro: Estrangin Préfecture.
This old mansion houses a major collection of modern art, including works by Bacon, Balthus, Braque, Dubuffet, Dufy, Ernst, Le Corbusier, Léger, Miró and Picasso. The collection is sufficiently large for only a

part of it to be displayed at any one time. There are also major temporary exhibitions. At the time of writing, the museum also housed a good display of Provençal faïence (some of it dating back to the 17thC) and work by the modern Marseille sculptor César.

Both these collections will move, the former to the CHÂTEAU BORÉLY museum and the latter to a new museum, **Musée César**, celebrating the sculptor's work, and due to open in 1994 in place du Mazeau.

César, Musée
Pl. du Mazeau. Due to open in 1994. Ask tourist office for details.
A new museum of work by the contemporary Marseille sculptor César.

Château Borély/Musée des Arts Décoratifs ☆
Promenade de la Plage or av. Clot-Bey 🚾 *Métro: Rond-point du Prado.*
Built as the home of a rich local merchant, Louis de Borély, this handsome late 18thC mansion, to the s of the city, stands in a corner of the formal Parc Borély, which includes a botanical garden. The château was due to reopen as a museum of decorative arts in late 1993 (check with tourist office), and should also house the ceramic collection of the MUSÉE CANTINI, as well as the *Feuillet de Borsat,* a collection of 18thC French drawings (slight but charming works by Greuze, Fragonard and Ingres) previously on display there. Two of the museums formerly housed at the château have been transferred to the VIEILLE CHARITÉ museum.

Two kilometers (1 mile) E of here, on Boulevard Michelet, is **L'Unité d'Habitation** (or Cité Radieuse), the 17-story "dwelling unit" with over 300 apartments. Built on piles (without a ground floor — see the illustration on page 31), it was designed in the late 1940s by Le Corbusier as an experiment in communal living. It was a great pioneering work in its day, with many imitators around the world (although it was very unpopular with Marseillais), and is one of the few buildings that the architect ever created in his adoptive land. There is now a small hotel, the **Le Corbusier**, in the building (see page 123), which is often fully booked.

Château-Gombert, Musée de
5 pl. des Héros 🕿 *91-68-14-38. Open Sat, Sun, Mon 2–6pm; Wed 3–6pm.*
A display of popular art and folklore includes *santons,* furniture, glassware, musical instruments, and reconstructions of traditional rooms.

Docks Romains, Musée des
28 pl. Vivaux 🕿 *91-91-24-62* 🚾 *Open Mon–Fri 10am–5pm; Sat–Sun noon–7pm. Métro: Vieux Port.*
The Roman docks of Massilia first came to light when the area N of the **Vieux Port** was destroyed during the war. An apartment block was built on top of them; but this museum on its ground floor cleverly comprises the original docks in their actual setting — so it is less a museum than a real Roman remain. You can see the quay, and the *dolia* (grain storage jars) just as they were. Roman anchors and amphorae have been added, mostly taken from wrecks found offshore.

The museum has clear, informative maps and models of Massilia's commercial role in Greek and Roman days, and details of the retrieval of ancient wrecks carried out since 1952 under Jacques Cousteau.

Galerie des Transports

Pl. du Marché-des-Capucins ☎ *91-54-15-15* ▦ ✱ *Open Tues–Fri 10am–5pm; Sat noon–7pm. Closed Sun–Mon. Métro: Noailles.*

A former railway station, now a museum of public transport history in Marseille since 1840, from the horse-drawn omnibus to the Métro.

Grobet-Labadié, Musée

140 blvd. Longchamp ☎ *91-62-21-82* ▦ *Open 10am–5pm (in summer, Sat–Sun noon–7pm). Métro: Longchamp/Cinq-Avenues.*

Local musician and art lover Louis Grobet owned this charming little 1870s house in the open space at the end of Boulevard Longchamp. On his death in 1919 he bequeathed it, with its remarkable contents, to the city of Marseille. The small, intimate rooms are richly furnished with the varied treasures that Grobet and his wife collected: French and Flemish tapestries of the 16th–18thC, Oriental carpets, porcelain, old musical instruments, German 15thC paintings, works by Murillo and Greuze; and much else.

Despite the diversity, the overall effect is one of harmony, a reflection of the Grobets' taste. A free leaflet gives full details of all the exhibits.

Histoire Naturelle, Musée d'

Palais Longchamp, blvd. Longchamp ☎ *91-62-30-78* ▦ ✱ *Open 10am–noon, 2–6pm. Closed Tues and Wed am.*

A small aquarium of gaudy tropical fish; a large main hall with the huge skeletons of whales, elephants, rhinoceroses, etc.; stuffed animals of every kind; and fossils and prehistoric remains.

Palais Longchamp ☆

Blvd. Longchamp. Métro: Longchamp/Cinq-Avenues.

Built at the end of the Durance–Marseille canal, the palace is typical of the grandiose style of the period. It was designed by the Provençal architect Henri Espérandieu between 1862 and 1869.

A central colonnade links its two wings, each housing a museum (BEAUX-ARTS to the left, NATURAL HISTORY to the right). In the middle, a mighty, mossy fountain sends its waters cascading into a wide pool.

St-Victor, Basilique ☷ ✝ ☆

Rue Sainte 🖾 *(crypt). Crypt open Mon–Sat 10am–noon, 3–5pm; Sun 3–5pm.*

Early Christian history comes vividly to life in this ancient church. It was first built by St-Cassien in the 5thC, in honor of the 3rdC martyr, St-Victor. This was wrecked by the Saracens, and the existing fortified Gothic church was erected above it in the 11th–12thC; with its crenelated tower, it does indeed resemble a fortress.

Stairs lead down from the upper church to the large **crypt**, which is St-Cassien's original church, gracefully restored and still much in use as a place of worship. Here are catacombs with both early-Christian and pagan sarcophagi (some have been transferred to the CHÂTEAU BORÉLY). Here too, beside the main chapel, is the **tomb of two 3rdC martyrs**. This was long known to have existed, but only in 1965 were the skeletons and other relics unearthed, and dated by experts to AD250. The martyrs are thought to be Volusianus and Fortunatus, two obscure gentlemen. But a legend from the Dark Ages holds that St Lazarus and St Mary Magdalene took refuge in the grotto that is now this crypt, after bringing Christianity to Gaul (see LES SAINTES-MARIES-DE-LA-MER).

Vieille Charité, Hospice de la

2 rue de la Charité ☎ *91-56-28-38* 🖾 *Open Mon–Fri 10am–5pm; Sat–Sun noon–7pm. Métro: Joliette.*

With a Baroque chapel built by Pierre Puget, court architect to Louis XIV, this 17thC hospice (although the Classical facade is 19thC), built of pink and white stone from the Couronne quarry N of Marseille, contains one of Europe's best collections of Egyptian antiquities. The exhibits include mummies, Etruscan bronzes, Greek and Roman ceramics, and even a Minoan wine pitcher of the 15thC BC.

The museum also has a rich diversity of Greek, Roman and medieval relics. Its showpiece is a reconstructed pre-Roman sanctuary of the 3rdC BC, built up of finds made recently at the Celto-Ligurian burial place of Roquepertuse, w of Aix: note the two-headed Hermes and the portico decorated with skulls. There are also collections of Oceanian and American Indian artifacts.

The Vieille Charité is one of the city's main arts centers, with major temporary exhibitions every three months (including photography) in the chapel, and video shows. The courtyard is used for musical performances. A museum dedicated to Puget is also planned. The museum, which has a small café and a highbrow arts bookstore, is situated in a rather unsalubrious area, near the port, in which not everyone will feel comfortable walking.

Vieux Marseille, Musée du

Rue de la Prison ☎ *91-55-10-19* 🖾 *Open 10am–5pm (in summer, Sat–Sun noon–7pm). Métro: Vieux Port.*

An absorbing folk-art museum housed in the 16thC Maison Diamantée ("diamond-studded"), so called because of its faceted facade. On the ground floor is Provençal 18thC furniture, porcelain, etc. On the first floor, a whole room full of *santons* and Nativity cribs of all shapes and sizes, both Provençal and Neapolitan. Mostly they are 18th and 19thC; but there is also a huge, colorful tableau of traditional local life, with hundreds of tiny *santons* made by Georges Prost.

On the second floor, there is a delightful collection of Camoin playing cards. On all floors are to be found maps, models and paintings of Marseille life through the centuries. The main stairway has a superb coffered ceiling that is richly carved.

❧ WHERE TO STAY IN MARSEILLE

CONCORDE PALM-BEACH 🏨

2 promenade de la Plage, 13008 Marseille
☎91-16-19-00 ᴇ᙭91-16-19-39 ▥ᴵ *146*
rms ▤▤ ▣ ⇥ ᴀᴱ ⊙ ⊚ ᴠᴵˢᴬ ▱ ✦ ⅋ ▢
▢ ⅏ ⟨⟨ ⋙ ⅊ ⍬ ⌐ ⅃ ⅄ ⍟ ⊡ ⊙ *Open all year.*

Location: Right by the sea, below the corniche road, 4 kilometers ($2\frac{1}{2}$ miles) s of the city center, but easy to drive past thanks to poor signposting. A large, quite smart, modern hotel (built in 1976), part of France's Concorde group but with American overtones. It is much used by business and professional people, not least because the convention center is nearby; the hotel itself has a 345-seat conference theater. The hotel also usefully combines the amenities of a seaside vacation with the proximity of the city — and it is sheltered from the Mistral. Off-season, though, you might well have to fight your way through convention delegates and company display stands in the lobby.

Next door is a club and school for sailing, wind surfing and scuba diving. A pianist plays at the hotel bar, which opens onto a wide terrace. Many bedrooms have balconies, and all have sea views; there is one self-contained apartment, often used by Bernard Tapie to house new signings to Olympique de Marseille. There is a soundproofed disco.

The hotel is on the site of a 19thC spring-water thermal cure center: the Source du Roucas Blanc spring, surrounded by exposed rock, can still be seen in the middle of the hotel. Within the hotel is **Les Voiliers**, a good cafeteria-style restaurant, and **La Réserve**, for more formal meals. Buffets are served by the pool in summer.

CONCORDE PRADO

11 av. de Mazargues, 13008 Marseille
☎91-76-51-11 ᴇ᙭91-77-95-10 ▥ᴵ *100*
rms ▤▤ ▣ ⇥ ᴀᴱ ⊙ ⊚ ᴠᴵˢᴬ ✦ ▢ ▢ ⅃
⅏ ⋙ ⅄ ⊡ ⅊

Location: A modern hotel near the convention center. The hotel has very good facilities (residents are allowed to use the sporting amenities of the nearby CONCORDE PALM-BEACH) and well-designed rooms with good bathrooms. A bedside button allows you to open the door for breakfast without stirring. The decor throughout is bright and relaxing. The hotel has a buffet restaurant and a shopping arcade. Off the bar is a pretty terrace, but views from the bedrooms are generally uninteresting.

MERCURE-CENTRE

Rue Neuve-St-Martin, 13001 Marseille
☎91-39-20-00 ᴇ᙭91-56-24-57 ▥ᴵ *to* ▥ᴵ
199 rms ▤▤ ▣ ⇥ ᴀᴱ ⊙ ⊚ ᴠᴵˢᴬ ✦ ▢
▢ ⅃ ⋙ ⅄ ⊡ ⅊ ⌐ *Open all year.*

Location: Close to La Canebière and the Vieux Port, and next to the Bourse shopping center and the A7 autoroute. Typical of the modern hotels in the Mercure chain. Like the others, this one is geared mainly to business needs, with a number of seminar and conference rooms, but it could also suit the well-heeled tourist. Outside, it is a brash, brown cube of glass and steel, but inside all is smart, with full amenities and efficient service. This is a well-run and comfortable hotel with nicely decorated bedrooms (including family rooms with sofabeds) and good marble-lined bathrooms. Some of the bedrooms overlook the Vieux Port; others the Jardin des Vestiges. Its restaurant, **L'Oursinade**, was once one of the best in town. Although still good, it is now geared to simpler gastronomic needs.

NEW HÔTEL BOMPARD ♥

2 rue des Flots Bleus, 13007 Marseille
☎91-52-10-93 ☒91-31-02-14 ▥ 46 rms ▤ ▰ ᴀᴇ ⊙ ⊞ ⌂ ‡ ⌂ ▢ ⌂ ✿
🖾 Open all year.
Location: A quiet road on the high hill s of the Vieux Port, 2.5 kilometers (1½ miles) from the city center. What a pleasant surprise to find a hotel of rural charm, secluded in its own extensive grounds, so close to downtown Marseille — and at bargain price. The hotel is functional inside, but has a pleasant English-style paneled bar and idyllic wide patio under the sophora trees. Twelve rooms are bungalows with their own kitchenettes. Most rooms have balconies. There is no restaurant.

LE PETIT NICE ▦

160 Corniche Kennedy, 13007 Marseille
☎91-52-25-92 ☒91-59-28-08 ▥ 16 rms ▤ ▰ ᴀᴇ ⊙ ⊞ ⌂ ‡ ⌂ ▢ ⌂ ✦ ⧫ ≈ᴎ
🖾 Ⴤ ▣ For ⬝ see *LE PETIT NICE* below.
Location: By the sea, on a small headland between two coves, just off the corniche road, 2.5 kilometers (1½ miles), sw of the city center; reached by a narrow side road. Miraculously situated on an isolated strip of rocky coast, yet deep within the conurbation, this is by far the best hotel in town. Marseille is a city short of hotels of character and quality; but Le Petit Nice can hold its own with almost any small hotel in Provence. Built as a private villa in the 19thC by the Passedat family, who are still in charge, it has been a hotel now for 70 years. Understandably so, for this little hotel is a model of refined enchantment: a sumptuously decorated Hellenic-style villa with a pretty garden above the rocky shore.

Rooms in the main building were redesigned in ultramodern style by architect Eric Klein, with bright colors, and shapes reminiscent of the work of Philippe Starck. They are more like chic apartments than hotel rooms, the best of them very spacious, each with a Jacuzzi and large French windows

overlooking the sea. There is also a bedroom annex with elegant, Classical-style rooms. This is the perfect tranquil hotel.

PULLMAN BEAUVAU

4 rue Beauvau, 13001 Marseille
☎91-54-91-00 ☒91-54-15-76 ▥ to ▥ 72 rms ▤ ▰ ⬝ ᴀᴇ ⊙ ⊞ ‡ ▢ ⌂ ⧫
⧫ 🖾 Ⴤ ▣ Open all year.
Location: Very well situated just behind the Vieux Port. The large rooms in this 19thC building (where George Sand and Chopin stayed) are well equipped, with good bathrooms. Many rooms have good views of the old port. However, the decor lacks charm and rooms could be better maintained. Nonetheless, the hotel, with its cozy bar and friendly service, is a good choice for either business or pleasure in a city short of good hotels.

ST-FERRÉOL'S HOTEL

19 rue Pisançon, 13001 Marseille
☎91-33-12-21 ☒91-54-29-97 ▥ to ▥ 19 rms ▤ ▰ ⊙ ⊞ ‡ ▢ ⌂ Ⴤ
Location: Well positioned in the heart of the St-Ferréol pedestrianized shopping district, and an easy walk away from the old port, La Canebière, and the Musée Cantini. This is a little hotel of undoubted charm, with stylish individually decorated bedrooms. The facilities are good, and include marble bathrooms and satellite TV. No restaurant, but otherwise one of the best choices in town.

🖾 Other good hotels: • **Alizé** (*35 quai des Belges, 13001* ☎*91-33-66-97* ☒*91-54-80-06* ▥ *to* ▥), in the old port, with double glazing and very good views. • **Le Corbusier** (*280 blvd. Michelet, 13008* ☎*91-77-18-15* ▥ ▦), an architectural curiosity in Le Corbusier's prototype tower block, L'Unité d'Habitation. • **Genève** (*3bis rue Reine Elisabeth, 13001* ☎*91-90-51-42* ▥ *to* ▥), an old hotel with comfortable rooms. • **Holiday Inn** (*103 av. du Prado, 13008* ☎*91-83-10-10* ☒*91-79-84-12* ▥), in the Prado business district; a smart hotel (opened 1992) with very comfortable rooms. • **Novotel Marseille Centre** *(4 blvd. Ch. Livon, 13007* ☎*91-59-22-22* [Fx]*91-31-15-48* ▥*)*, with good views. • **Sofitel Vieux Port** *(36 blvd. Ch. Livon, 13007* ☎*91-52-90-19* [Fx]*91-31-46-52* ▥ *to* ▥*)*, modern, very comfortable, with good views.

⇌ EATING AND DRINKING IN MARSEILLE

LES ARCENAULX

25 Cours d'Estienne d'Orves, 13001
☎*91-54-77-06* ▥ ▤ ▢ ▰ ⇌ ⊕ AE
⊕ ⊙ ▨ ⇀ *underground nearby. Closed Sun. Last orders 12.30am.*

A most unusual place, this. The dream of publisher Jeanne Lafitte, it combines bookstore, exhibition space and restaurant, in a pedestrianized area off the old port. You eat in a book-lined room, and can mingle with the local intellectuals. No prizes for exceptional cuisine, but still worth going for the lively ambience. You can also take tea in the afternoon.

MAURICE BRUN: AUX METS DE PROVENCE

18 quai de Rive Neuve, 13007
☎*91-33-35-38* ▥ ▰ ▢ ⇌ AE ⊕ ▨
Closed Sun; Mon. Last orders 9.30pm.

A visit *chez Brun* is unmissable; it's the most idiosyncratic restaurant in town, and the best at keeping alive the traditions of classic Provençal cuisine. There is no sign outside, save a modest nameplate: you climb up a gloomy stairway, in an old house opposite the Vieux Port, to find the door opening into a graceful and comfortable dining room. Here the founder's son, Frédéric Brun, plays *restaurateur* — if you light a cigarette or otherwise break the rules, you risk his instant wrath.

There was once no choice of food, just a single unchanging menu, without variations. Now there is a short *carte*, but most people prefer to stick to the menu. And what a meal! For two solid hours, the awestruck guests eat their way through a lavish succession of superb local dishes — from the multiple hors d'oeuvres to the spit-roasted chicken and the *boeuf en daube* to sorbets, dessert and Provençal pastries. The prices seem high, but it's undoubtedly worth every *centime*.

CHEZ ANGÈLE ▰

50 rue Caisserie ☎*91-90-63-35* ▢ *to* ▢
▢ ▰ *Closed Mon; Christmas to early Jan. Last orders 10.30pm.*

In a back street just N of the Vieux Port. One of the very few cheap eating places in town that are worth recommending. A small, animated bistro, filled to bursting with jovial habitués, provides Italo-Provençal cooking: simple, but tasty and copious.

MICHEL (LES CATALANS)

6 rue des Catalans ☎*91-52-30-63* ▥ ▢
⇌ AE ⊙ ▨ *Closed Tues; Wed; July. Last orders 10pm.*

The *bouillabaisse* here is as good as any in Marseille — therefore in the world — at this much-praised brasserie facing the coast on the W side of town. The accent is entirely on serious eating, and certainly not on ambience. Only the view of the sea from some of the tables can possibly distract you from the task at hand, which is to relish Jeanne Visciano's superb classical rendering of fresh local fish.

NEW YORK/VIEUX PORT

7 quai des Belges ☎*91-33-91-79* ▢ *to*
▥ ▢ ▰ ⇌ AE ⊕ ⊙ ▨ *Closed Sun. Last orders 10pm.*

A handsome, well-established, fish restaurant and bar, much in vogue, with well-spaced tables, pretty lighting at night, and by day a front-of-stalls view of the bustle around the Vieux Port (mainly cars). The usual local fish specialities are on offer; or try the memorable *selle d'agneau*. Sometimes service can be slow.

LE PETIT NICE ⌂

160 Corniche Kennedy ☎*91-52-25-92* ▥
to ▥ ▢ ▰ ⇌ ⇀ AE ⊙ ▨ *Closed Sat lunch; Sun (from Nov–Mar). Last orders 10.30pm.*

Greek statues stand guard in the cool, elegant dining-room, with its marble floor, where a pretty, curving picture-window overlooks the sea and the Château d'If. The celebrated cooking of Jean-Paul Passédat (and his son Gérald, who is following in his footsteps) is superb: imaginative, inspired, beautifully presented and most flavorful. Service, although stylish, can be inattentive at times. Desserts are impressive, as is the wine list.

Specialities: Compressé de bouillabaisse port d'orient, gâteau de grenouilles aux pieds et museau de porc, salade de truffes fraîches, blinis de supions au caviar sevruga, dorade grillée à la peau, tronçon de loup comme l'aimait Lucie Passédat, côte de veau de lait aux lentilles blondes. (See ✎ LE PETIT NICE on page 123.)

⇌ Other recommended restaurants: • **Chez Etienne** *(43 rue de Lorette* 🎫*),* a relaxed atmosphere; they serve the best pizzas in town. • **Au Panier des Arts** *(3 rue du Petit Puits* 🎫*91-56-02-32* 🎫 *to* 🎫*),* near the Vieille Charité: good local dishes at very reasonable prices in a pleasant ambience. • **Bistrot Gambas** *(29 pl. aux Huiles* 🎫 *to* 🎫*),* where scampi is the speciality.

La Baie des Singes *(Cap Croisette* 🎫*91-73-68-87* 🎫 *closed Nov-Mar),* for decent fish dishes. • **Le Chaudron Provençal** *(48 rue Caisserie* 🎫*91-91-02-37* 🎫 *closed Sat lunch, Sun),* for seafood and fish. • **Jambon de Parme** *(67 rue La Palud* 🎫*91-54-37-98* 🎫 *closed Sun dinner, Mon, mid-July to end Aug),* mainly Italian. • **La Ferme** *(23 rue Sainte* 🎫*91-33-21-12* 🎫*).* • **Miramar** *(12 quai du Port* 🎫*91-91-10-40* 🎫 *closed Sun, Aug),* fish specialities, among the best in town, including impeccable *bouillabaisse.*

Le Patalain *(49 rue Sainte* 🎫*91-55-02-78* 🎫 *closed Sat lunch, Sun, July–Sept),* a smart restaurant where Suzanne Quaglia offers superb *cuisine Marseillaise.* • **Chez Madie** *(138 quai du Port* 🎫*91-90-40-87* 🎫 *closed Sun dinner, Mon),* seafood and a very good view. • **Les Échevins** *(44 rue Sainte* 🎫*91-33-08-08* 🎫 *closed Sat lunch, Sun, mid-July to mid-Aug),* for Gascon specialities and fish. • **Cousin-Cousine** *(102 Cours Julien* 🎫*91-48-14-50* 🎫 *closed Sun, Mon),* for light, fresh, imaginative cooking. • **Peron** *(56 Corniche Kennedy* 🎫*91-52-43-70* 🎫 *closed Sun dinner, Mon, Jan, early May),* ocean-liner decor, excellent views and first-class fish cuisine, including very good *bouillabaisse.*

⚫ NIGHTLIFE IN MARSEILLE

The city's nightlife is hardly distinguished, but it has improved somewhat in recent years.

If you want to find out more, Marseille has a listings magazine, *Taktik,* and the tourist office also issues a free list of events in *Atout Marseille.* The local newspapers *La Marseillaise, Le Provençal* and *Le Méridional* also all carry entertainment listings. The weekly *Marseille Poche* is a free magazine.

Bars The area around the Vieux Port, particularly Cours d'Estienne d'Orves, is full of colorful bars, open till late. Cours Julien is also quite lively. • At **Au Son des Guitares** *(18 rue Corneille* 🎫*91-33-11-47* ❦ *open 11pm-8am, closed Sun, mid-July to mid-Sept),* Corsicans sing and play guitar music; you can also dance. • **L'Abbaye de la Commanderie** *(20 rue Corneille* 🎫*91-55-52-78, open 10.30pm-8am, closed Sun-Mon)* is a comfortable bar, where they sing typical Marseillais songs and tell ribald jokes. You need to know the *patois.*

Best discos **L'Ascenseur** *(22 pl. Thiers* 🎫*91-33-13-27, open 11pm-4am),* mainly for teenagers. • **Club 116** *(rue de Chantier* 🎫*91-33-*

77-22, open Thurs-Sat 11pm-8am), for all ages, but mainly for students.
• **London Club** *(73 Corniche Kennedy* ☎*91-52-64-64, open daily 10.30pm-4am),* quite elegant. • **Quai 9** *(9 quai de Rive Neuve* ☎*91-33-34-20, open 11.30pm-8am, closed Sun-Mon),* modern and trendy.

Jazz and blues **May Be Blues** *(2 rue Poggioli* ☎ *91-42-41-00, open 7pm-2am except Wed),* **Les Nuits des Thés** *(21 rue Poggioli* ☎*91-48-34-34, open 7pm-2am, closed Sun, Aug)* or **Le 31** *(31 pl. Jean Jaurès* ☎*91-47-61-07, open daily 8pm-2am)* for jazz and blues. • **Maison de l'Étranger** *(8-16 rue Antoine Zattara* ☎*91-95-90-15)* for music from around the world.

And also. . . The **Espace Julien** arts center *(33 Cours Julien* ☎*91-47-09-64)* has dance, jazz and rock performances.

PERFORMING ARTS

Opera and dance The **Opera House** *(pl. Reyer* ☎*91-55-14-99)* puts on good provincial performances of opera and ballet all year except summer. Despite its august presence, the streets around the opera are full of dim bars and lolling women.

Theater Marseille also has a number of theaters. Worth looking out for are: • **Théâtre National de Marseille** *(30 quai de Rive Neuve* ☎*91-54-74-54).* • **Théâtre Le Merlan** *(av. Raimu* ☎*91-98-28-98),* some way out, in N Marseille. • The **Théâtre Massalia** *(60 rue Grignan* ☎*91-55-66-05),* a puppet theater, with shows for children during the day, and adults in the evening.

SHOPPING IN MARSEILLE

The streets with the smartest modern stores are the pedestrianized **rue St-Ferréol** (and the small streets off it) and **rue de Rome**, both leading S from LA CANEBIÈRE. The **Centre Bourse**, just N of La Canebière, next to the Hôtel Mercure-Centre, is a big, new, indoor shopping center with 70 boutiques, including **Habitat**, **Dior**, and the excellent **FNAC** music-and bookstore, which is well worth a visit.

Regional foods Some traditional stores selling local produce: • **Bataille** *(18 rue Fontange),* a luxury delicatessen, similar to Fauchon in Paris, selling Provençal wines and food products, including takeout *bouillabaisse*. • **Marrou** *(15 pl. Castellane),* selling all regional food products. • **Four des Navettes** *(rue d'Endoume),* behind the S side of the old port; the oldest bakery in Marseille, founded in 1787.

Fabrics and santons **Les Olivades** *(rue Moustier),* for Provençal fabrics, *santons* etc. • *Santons* also at **Marcel Carbonel** *(47 rue Neuve Ste-Catherine),* where they also show you how they're made.

Best hairdressers **J.L. David** *(1 pl. Général-de-Gaulle* ☎*91-33-71-13).* • **Hervé** *(12 pl. Castellane* ☎*91-37-74-61).*

* **MARKETS** Good open-air markets include: • Avenue du Prado for **food**, **flowers** and **clothing** *(Mon-Sat mornings).* • A **food market** for food, coffee, spices, etc. at rue Longue des Capucins *(Mon-Sat, all day).*
  • A **fish market** along the quays of the Vieux Port *(Mon-Sat mornings).*
  • There are also markets in Cours Julien and Place Sébastopol.

PLACES NEAR MARSEILLE

Aubagne *(map 11 H8, 17km/10 miles E of Marseille).* Just w of this industrial town, off the D2 to Marseille, the **French Foreign Legion** has its HQ, following its departure from Algeria in 1962. There is a **museum** *(open June-Sept daily; Oct-May Wed, Sat, Sun)* where documents, photos and other souvenirs recall the Legion's many exploits.

Carry-le-Rouet *(27km/17 miles w of Marseille).* This is the smartest of a string of little resorts along the s side of the Estaque range (see below): well-to-do Marseillais have villas here, and there is a pretty fishing port.

☰ L'ESCALE ⌂

Promenade du Port, Carry-le-Rouet
☎42-45-00-47 ▥ ▭ ◼◼ ▤ ⊛ AE VISA
Closed Sun dinner; Mon (except July–Aug); Nov–Feb. Last orders 9.30pm.

This is a top-class, sophisticated restaurant opened by the charming Dany and Gérard Clor in the 1970s. The bright, airy dining room, full of flowers, and decorated with a real eye for detail, has a most pleasant view of the bay and fishing-port. Primarily a fish restaurant (meat dishes on the menu tend to be simple), with light, fresh, appetizingly presented dishes based on traditional Provençal recipes adapted with flair. The service is friendly and unpretentious. Good cheese board and Provençal wines. L'Escale is a member of the Relais & Châteaux group. *Specialities include: Tartare de loup aux huîtres, casserole de poissons, feuilleté d'asperges et truffes, dos de loup, suprême de Saint-Pierre et ragoût de tagliatelles aux crustaces, homard rôti au beurre de corail.*

Château d'If *(◼◼ ▣ ✗ available; open June-Sept 8am-noon, 1.30pm-sunset, Oct-May 10am-4pm; frequent motorboat departures from quai des Belges, Vieux Port, connect with the opening times; the round trip, including a visit to the castle, takes about 90mins).* An ever-popular excursion is the boat trip to this notorious fortress on a limestone islet 3 kilometers (2 miles) offshore. It was built in 1524 by François 1er as part of Marseille's defenses, and was then used for many years as a state prison. Its many inmates included the "Man in the Iron Mask" (see **Îles des Lérins** under CANNES) and (in fiction) Dumas' *Count of Monte Cristo.*

You can see the carvings left by Huguenot prisoners brought here in thousands, and the memorial since erected to them; also a ghastly, windowless cell, where those with life sentences were flung and left to perish. It is not for the squeamish — but don't miss the view of Marseille from the highest terrace. The larger **Frioul islands** to the w now make up a sailing and sports center.

Estaque, Chaîne de l' Another of the rugged limestone ranges that circle Marseille: 24 kilometers (15 miles) long, it separates the Berre Lagoon (see BERRE, ÉTANG DE) from the sea. Its wild scenery — whitish rocks and dark pines — much impressed Cézanne, who painted it several times.

In 1920, the 6-kilometer (4-mile) **Canal du Rove** was tunneled under the mountain, in order to provide a shipping link from Marseille to the lake, but because of danger from landslides it has been out of use for 30 years.

Étoile, Chaîne de l' Marseille is hemmed in to the NE by this limestone range, which has several points of interest: **Allauch**, with old windmills and a fine view over the city; splendid vistas from the **Col Ste-Anne**; **Château Goubert** with its interesting museum of Provençal folk art *(open Mon, Sat, Sun pm);* and the **Grottes de Loubière**, with multicolored stalactites and stalagmites *(open all day Sun, Mon, Wed-Sat pm only; closed Tues).*

Marseilleveyre massif These stark and craggy limestone hills frame the S side of the bay of Marseille. The corniche road leads around to the fishing hamlet of **Callelongue**. At **Montredon**, hardy walkers can strike inland by a stiff 90-minute climb to the highest peak at 430 meters (1,425 feet), and there be rewarded with tremendous views of city and coast.

From **Mazargue**, in the SE suburbs, other rough walks lead to the lovely creeks *(calanques)* of **Sormiou** and **Sugiton** (see also CASSIS).

- See also: BANDOL; BERRE, ÉTANG DE; CASSIS; MARTIGUES.

MARTIGUES

*Map **10**G5 (B.-du-R.). 40km (25 miles) W of Marseille. Postal code: 13500. Population: 42,700 **i** quai Paul-Doumer ☎42-80-30-72.*

The former fishing village has today grown into a sizeable commuter suburb, being close to the new oil-based industries of Lavéra and Berre L'Étang. But its old quarter, where pretty houses line the canals, has not lost the charm that drew Ziem and Corot to paint it in the 19thC. The **Musée Ziem** *(☎42-80-66-06 open July-Aug 10am-noon, 2.30-6.30pm, closed Tues; Sept–June 2.30-6.30pm, closed Mon, Tues)* has a collection of Félix Ziem's work, as well as that of various 19thC Provençal painters.

The prettiest spot is the **Pont St-Sébastien** on the central Île de Brescon, where there is also the 17thC **church of Ste-Madeleine**, fronted by Corinthian pillars, which has a fine organ loft and Baroque decor.

In the W suburbs, an imposing modern suspension bridge, 292 meters (330 yards) long, carries an autoroute over the canal. Just N of the town, above a new hospital, the **Chapelle de Notre-Dame-des-Marins** stands alone on a hilltop; from here there are views over the vast industrial complex of **Berre** and **Fos**, and the limestone ranges beyond.

- **EVENT** There is a sardine festival, the **Sardinades**, in July and August, when plates of fresh grilled sardines are offered free to all and sundry.

St-Roch *(Route d'Arles ☎42-80-19-73 AE Visa),* a modern *concrete hotel, very comfortable, mainly for businessmen; pleasant garden with an olive-oil mill.*

La Gousse d'Ail *(42 quai Général-Leclerc ☎42-07-13-26 closed Sun, Aug 24 to mid-Sept).* An animated bistro facing the lake, this is one of the few eating places round here that is popular with local people; it does good *crudités,* but the service can be a little impersonal.

- See also: BERRE, ÉTANG DE.

NÎMES

Map 8E2 (Gard). 121km (75 miles) NW of Marseille. Postal code: 30000.
Population: 129,000 **i** *6 rue Auguste* ☎*66-67-29-11.* **Airport:** *at Garon, 8km*
(5 miles) to S ☎*66-70-06-88.* **Railway station:** *blvd. Talabot* ☎*66-23-50-50.*

Nîmes likes to call itself "the Rome of France." The parallel may be far-fetched, but the city does contain two of the best-preserved buildings of Classical Rome: the ARÈNES, and the temple known as the MAISON CARRÉE. The Romans came across a gushing spring here, and so founded a town. Then Augustus, after defeating Antony at Actium, settled a large colony of veterans here from the Egyptian campaign: hence the crocodile chained to a palm tree which the city still bears on its crest.

Nîmes lies at the frontier of Provence and Languedoc, and really belongs to both. Like the rest of Languedoc, it has always been strongly hostile to the central power in Paris. In the 16thC it was the headquarters of the Huguenot "heretics," and played a large role in the Camisard revolt after the revocation of the Edict of Nantes in 1685. Much blood was spilled — and the Nîmois have neither forgotten nor forgiven.

Today, this is a large commercial city of sprawling new suburbs and dusty boulevards. Apart from a small, well-restored sector of the Old Town, it is not a very elegant place. But it has a lively cultural life, even though it is not a university town. In the last decade or so, the city has benefited from the energy of its dynamic mayor, Jean Bousquet, former head of the Cacharel fashion company, who has used top architects and designers such as Philippe Starck (a bus shelter in avenue Carnot, completed in 1987), Jean Nouvel (the Nemausus I housing project in avenue Gen. Leclerc), Jean-Michel Wilmotte (the town hall, covered market and other buildings) and Norman Foster (the Carré d'Art), to add sparkle to new building projects and renovations. The CARRÉ D'ART project in particular is calculated to build Nîmes into a major destination on the contemporary cultural and artistic map.

The construction of the autoroute (A54) between Nîmes and Arles has also made the city more easily accessible. Its major industries include fruit canning, shoemaking and textiles. A rough, twilled cloth for overalls was first manufactured here in the 19thC and marketed abroad as *"de Nîmes";* the name was contracted to "denim."

- **ℵ** Guided tours of Nîmes take place daily in July and August and from time to time during the rest of the year. Details at the tourist office.
- **EVENTS** • At Whitsun, **Feria de Pentecôte** (Whitsun Festival): five days *(Thurs–Mon)* of bullfights, bull races, folklore displays, concerts, dancing in the streets, etc.; one of the great festivals of Provence *(box office: Bureau des Arènes, rue Alexandre Ducros* ☎*66-67-28-02).* • In the third week of July, an **international jazz festival**. It is preceded by the **Mosaïques Gitanes**, a festival of gypsy music and dance. • Also in July and August, an **international folklore, music and dance festival**. • From May to October, **bullfights** take place two or three times a month in the Arènes, mostly on Sunday afternoons. The toreadors are both local and Spanish. The bulls are from the Camargue, and are fought to the death. • There are also **bullfights** during the last weekend of February. • The last weekend in September features a **wine festival, bull races** and **folklore displays**.

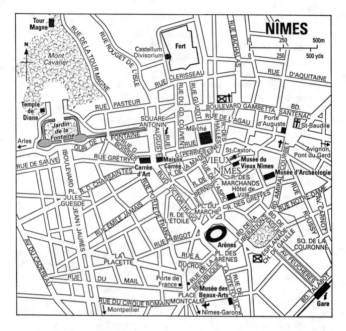

• As for year-round events, Nîmes is a lively and interesting cultural center, especially for music. All summer there are frequent **outdoor concerts** in the Jardin de la Fontaine or in local churches and mansions. • Sometimes **operas** are staged in the Arènes. From November to March, there are operas in the municipal theater.

WHAT TO SEE IN NÎMES

One ticket covers admission to the ARÈNES, MAISON CARRÉE, JARDIN DE LA FONTAINE ET TEMPLE DE DIANE and the TOUR MAGNE.

Arènes (Arena) 🏛 ☆
Blvd. Victor-Hugo ☎66-76-72-77 Ticket also admits to MAISON CARRÉE, JARDIN DE LA FONTAINE ET TEMPLE DE DIANE and TOUR MAGNE ✗ obligatory Oct to end Apr. Open summer 9am–7pm; winter 9am–noon, 2–5.30pm.

This majestic arena (illustrated on page 29) is slightly smaller (it once held up to 23,000 people) than the one at ARLES but is otherwise very similar. It is one of the best preserved of the 70 extant arenas of the Roman world. In the 5thC it became a fortress, and afterward the headquarters of an autonomous corps of knights.

From the 13thC, it became a tenement inhabited by 2,000 poor people, who built 150 houses. The Romans used it for chariot races, and for combats where gladiators fought with one another or with wild beasts.

Today there are frequent bullfights there in summer, and at other times of the year. Since 1988, the arena has been covered by inflatable temporary roofing from October to April.

Carrée d'Art et Musée d'Art Contemporain ☆

Carrée d'Art ☎66-76-35-35; open 10am–8pm; closed Mon. **Musée d'Art Contemporain** ☎66-76-35-70; open 11am–6pm; closed Mon. Charges and separate opening times for special exhibitions.

Just across from the MAISON CARRÉE is the new médiathèque, designed by the British architect Norman Foster, opened in 1993 as a contemporary arts center not unlike the Centre Pompidou in Paris. Although built of glass, concrete, steel and aluminum, it uses slender pillars to echo those of the Maison Carrée. The danger, though, is that its sheer scale may diminish the older building. The 400-million-franc building, the brainchild of mayor Jean Bousquet, took nine years to see through from brief to completion.

The Carrée d'Art contains a contemporary art museum, housing nearly 300 works, mostly French and created after 1960, exhibition spaces, an auditorium, and a library with over 360,000 books, records and videos.

Jardin de la Fontaine et Temple de Diane ☆

Quai de la Fontaine. Garden open daylight ⏺ see ARÈNES.

The garden was created in the 18thC, in typically French ornamental style — all urns and statues, pools and curving balustrades. At its top end, on the slopes of Mont Cavalier, the **Fontaine de Nemausus** gushes into a basin of clear water. Here the Romans built baths, a theater and a temple; little of all this now remains, save the massive ruin of the temple, dedicated to the goddess Diana, with its great vaulted arch.

Maison Carrée ☆

Blvd. Victor-Hugo. Open winter 9am–5.30pm; summer 9am–7pm ⏺ see ARÈNES.

The so-called "square house" is in fact rectangular. It is a temple, built in Hellenic style by Agrippa in c.20BC, and is generally regarded as the loveliest of all surviving Roman temples, as finely proportioned as those of Classical Greece itself. It is well preserved, too, despite its checkered history. Since the Middle Ages, it has been used in turn as the town hall, a private residence, a stable, a church, and now a museum. At night it is beautifully floodlit. It now houses three huge works by the no longer fashionable American contemporary artist Julian Schnabel.

The Maison Carrée stands on a raised platform, facing what used to be the Forum. Steps lead up to its peristyle of fluted columns, where the carving is superbly delicate, both on the capitals and on the frieze above them. The *cella* (interior) is walled in, and now contains a collection of local Roman finds. Among them is an imposing statue of *Apollo,* and the *"Venus of Nîmes,"* found in fragments and pieced together. The original mosaic centerpiece of the floor of the *cella* is in remarkable condition.

Tour Magne

Open winter 9am–5.30pm; summer 9am–7pm ◁€ 📷 *see* ARÈNES.
This massive Roman tower stands high on the wooded hill of Mont Cavalier, behind the JARDIN DE LA FONTAINE. From these gardens, only the top of the tower is visible: the best view is from rue Mallarmé to its E.

Probably built as a watch-tower near the end of the 1stC BC, the tower was part of the city wall. Originally 36 meters (118 feet) high, it has lost its upper ten meters (33 feet). From the platform on top of the tower, there are splendid views of the city, the mountains of western Provence, and even the Pyrénées, on a clear day.

Vieux Nîmes ☆

The W quarter just N of the ARÈNES is as elegant and picturesque a *vieille ville* as almost any in Provence — a contrast to the rest of dusty, workaday Nîmes. Here a few streets, notably **rues de l'Aspic, de Bernis** and **des Marchands**, are now a pedestrian zone, beautifully restored, lined with smart boutiques, and full of interesting surprises.

Push open the door of **#14 rue de l'Aspic**, and you find yourself in a private courtyard, flanked by a strikingly handsome 17thC double stairway. Look, too, at the Renaissance gateway of **#8** and the charming 15thC facade of **#3 rue de Bernis**. The **Passage des Marchands**, off #12 rue des Marchands, is a lovely Renaissance gallery with low vaulted arches and balustrades. It is now full of handicraft and antique stores.

Close by, the 11thC **cathedral of St-Castor** was largely rebuilt in the 19thC. On the facade frieze, the scenes (left) from Genesis are originals; the rest are copies. Next door is the **Musée du Vieux Nîmes** (📷 *open 11am-6pm, closed Mon),* housed in the former Bishop's Palace. It has furniture, pottery and costumes, and two rooms devoted to bullfighting.

The **Musée Archéologique** (📷 *open 11am-6pm, closed Mon)* has Greek pottery dating from the 8thC BC and a display of objects evoking the daily life of a Gallo-Roman family. Just to its N is the Roman **Porte d'Auguste**, built in 15BC.

The **Musée des Beaux-Arts** *(rue de la Cité Foulc* 📷 *open 11am-6pm, closed Mon)* contains some unremarkable works by Rubens, Poussin, Rodin and many others. Its star exhibit, in the center of the ground-floor room, is a huge Roman mosaic found at Nîmes in 1883 and thought to represent the marriage of Admetus.

➷ � IN NÎMES

➷ �   **LE CHEVAL BLANC** 🏨
1 pl. des Arènes ☎66-76-32-32
🖷66-76-32-33 ▥ 26 rms ▦ ➡ � AE
📷 📷 📷 🏠 ⚄ ☐ 🕭 ◁€ 🏋 🍸 📷

Location: Situated opposite the Arènes: a number of rooms have an excellent view of it. A new luxury hotel (opened late 1991) owned by the great nightclub queen, Régine. One might expect it to be flashy or vulgar. In fact it is by far the best hotel in Nîmes, for design, quality of service and food. The interior, by Jean-Michel Wilmotte, if not to everyone's taste, is strikingly modern, and remarkably confident in its use of large doors, roller blinds and wooden shutters, as well as vividly-colored modern furniture and clever side-lighting, to offset the building's original stone walls.

Service, from the young and friendly staff, is charming. And, the main restaurant, in a semicircular room built around the stairwell, under chef Thierry Marx, is the best in town: delicate, fresh and inventive cuisine. The *Menu Découverte* (which includes wine) is a true bargain. This is not a cheap hotel, but nor is it expensive considering the standards of comfort and cuisine on offer. There is a low-calorie breakfast, and a casual restaurant **Bistrot des Costières**, cheaper than the main one, where there is live music on Friday and Saturday nights.

Other recommended hotels in Nîmes: • **La Baume** *(21 rue de l'Agau* ☎ *66-76-28-42* [Fx] *66-76-28-45* ▥ *)*, formerly part of the Mercure group, a 17thC house with a fine period staircase, and modern, somewhat arty rooms. • **Impérator** ▥ *(quai de la Fontaine* ☎ *66-21-90-30* [Fx] *66-67-70-25* ▥ *)*, part of the prestigious Concorde group, with a pompous Victorian lobby and luxuriant garden behind; recently redecorated, the rooms are very well appointed and comfortable, although the atmosphere is somewhat impersonal. • **Louvre** *(2 sq. de la Couronne* ☎ *66-67-22-75* ▥ *)*, a well-modernized hotel in a 17thC building; service is uneven. • **Michel** *(14 blvd. Amiral-Courbet* ☎ *66-67-26-23* ▢ *to* ▥ *)*, functional but friendly, with a sidewalk terrace.

Relais du Moulin Royal *(1973 av. Pierre Mendès-France* ☎ *66-84-30-20* [Fx] *66-29-45-99* ▥ *)*, on the outskirts of town, a smart little hotel with good facilities, in an old mill. • **Novotel Atria** *(5 blvd. de Prague* ☎ *66-76-28-*

42 [Fx] *66-76-26-36* ▥ *)*, conveniently located near the Arènes, well-designed and comfortable. • **Novotel Nîmes-Ouest** *(124 chemin de l'Hostellerie* ☎ *66-84-60-20* [Fx] *66-38-02-31* ▥ *)*, an excellent modern motel, attractively designed, with an inviting atmosphere.

L'Orangerie *(755 rue Tour de l'Évêque* ☎ *66-84-50-57* [Fx] *66-29-44-55)*, a very pleasant, villa-style hotel set among plane trees. • **Plazza** *(10 rue Roussy* ☎ *66-67-24-89* [Fx] *66-67-28-08* ▢ *to* ▥ *)*, a 19thC house recently converted to a comfortable hotel decorated in 1930s style.

Royal *(3 blvd. Alphonse Daudet* ☎ *66-67-28-36* ▢ *to* ▥ *)*, a rather trendy, eccentrically decorated little hotel near the Maison Carrée, whose casual atmosphere appeals to artists and performers. • **Solotel** *(510 chemin de l'Hostellerie* ☎ *66-62-04-04* [Fx] *66-29-24-44* ▥ *)*, a modern hotel with swimming pool, suitable for families.

Good restaurants in Nîmes are few. • One is at the **Hôtel Impérator** *(quai de la Fontaine* ☎ *66-21-90-30* ▥ *)*, for good classic cuisine served on the lovely terrace or in the dining-room. • Another (and probably the best: see above) is at the hotel **Cheval Blanc** *(*☎ *66-76-32-32* ▥ *)*, where the chef is building up a good reputation. • **Le Magister** *(5 rue de l'Agau* ☎ *66-76-11-00* ▥ *)* is one of the smartest restaurants in town, with prices to match and imaginative cooking. • **Le P'tit Bec** *(87bis rue de la République* ☎ *66-38-05-83* ▥ *)* offers particularly good value at lunch, and has a garden. • **La Belle Respire** *(12 rue de l'Étoile* ▥ *)*, situated in the center of town, is good value. • At **Lou Mas** *(5 rue de Sauve* ☎ *66-23-24-71* ▢ *)* you will find hearty meals in a rustic setting.

NEARBY

L'Hacienda *(Chemin du Mas de Brignon, 30320 Marguerittes* ☎ *66-75-02-25* [Fx] *66-75-45-48* ▥ *)*, *8km/ 5 miles NE off the N86)*, a very pleasant and well-equipped former farmhouse, with a sauna and other good leisure facilities. The food, which you can eat outside near the large pool, attains a decent standard.

=== **ALEXANDRE**
Garons (8km/5 miles SE of Nîmes) ☎*66-70-08-99* ▥ ▆ ▀ ▟ ▄ ▦ ▧ ▨
Closed Sun dinner; Mon; last week in Aug; 1st week in Sept; Feb. Last orders 9.30pm.

A luxurious restaurant beside the airport, set in its own park. You may find the dining room's period elegance too formal, in which case eat in the lovely garden, if it is not a windy day. Michel Kayser's cuisine is arguably the best in the Nîmes area. Dishes change seasonally but may include *île flottante aux truffes noires* or *pieds et langues d'agneau mijotés dans leur jus.*

▶ **NIGHTLIFE AND PERFORMANCES IN NÎMES**

Of the ten discos and dance halls in town, the best are probably **Le 86** *(RN86 Route d'Avignon* ☎*66-27-48-63 15)*, **Cotton Club** *(sq. de la Couronne* ☎*66-76-10-19)*, **Le Marinella** *(150 Route de Sauve* ☎*66-64-78-67)* and **Le Médiatic** *(3 rue Corneille* ☎*66-67-28-52)*.

The **Théâtre de Nîmes**, near the Maison Carrée *(box office: 1 pl. de la Calade* ☎*66-36-02-04)*, offers a particularly strong program of drama and dance, and all types of music, from jazz to orchestral to opera.

SHOPPING IN NÎMES

Boutique Souleïado *(5 pl. de la Maison Carrée)* sells Provençal fabrics and costumes, including Arlesian skirts, and Camargue *gardians'* outfits. **Boutique les Olivades** *(3 rue de l'Hôtel de Ville)* is similar. **Don Quichotte** *(10 rue de l'Horloge)* sells local handicrafts, olivewood carvings, ceramics, copper and *santons.* **L'Huilerie** *(10 rue des Marchands)* sells olive oils, olive-oil soaps and local food products. There is a **FNAC** music- and bookstore in rue des Halles.

In the Old Town, E of the Maison Carrée, are many other boutiques ofering the same type of goods.

• **MARKETS** **Food markets** take place daily on avenue Jean Jaurès, with a **flower** and **junk market** on Friday. • There is a **clothes market** on boulevard Gambetta on Monday. • A **flea-market** is at the Stade Costrières on Sunday morning. • There is also a covered **food market** *(rue des Halles).*

PLACE NEAR NÎMES

Source Perrier *(14km/9 miles SW of Nîmes, off N113* ▣ **✗** *lasting 50mins, Mon-Fri at 9am, 10am, 1.30pm, 3.30pm).* Perrier, the sparkling mineral water, comes from an underground spring here and from nowhere else. It was first commercialized by an Englishman, St-John Harmsworth, of the newspaper family. He bought the spring in 1903, and modeled the tapering green Perrier bottle on the Indian clubs that he used for remedial exercises after a car accident. Today, a French firm owns the spring and sells over 500 million bottles a year, half of them for export. The guided tour starts with a film *(in French, English or German)* showing production processes, including the quarrying of sand from Mont Ventoux to make the bottles. There follows a cursory visit to the plant, where 2,000 people work.

• See also: PONT DU GARD.

ORANGE ☆

*Map 4C4 (Vaucluse). 31km (19 miles) N of Avignon. Postal code: 84100.
Population: 26,500* **i** *Cours Aristide Briand* ☎ *90-34-70-88.* **Railway station:**
av. Frédéric Mistral ☎ *90-34-17-82.*

On the site of an old Celtic capital, the Romans founded a town called
Arausio, and this is the origin of the name Orange. The town lies amid
vineyards on the plain of the Rhône valley — a pleasant place, with
avenues of plane trees and a nucleus of narrow streets, dominated by
the Roman theater and triumphal arch, two of the greatest monuments
of the Roman world. The Romans settled a colony of veterans here,
and by the time of Augustus, it was a thriving city with temples, baths,
an arena and stadium.

Later it suffered from the Barbarian and Saracen invasions, and in the
13thC became a tiny principality, an enclave within the Comtat Venaissin
(see CARPENTRAS). Finally, in the 16thC, it was inherited by William, Prince
of Nassau, forebear of the present Dutch family. He found the town so
agreeable that he called his dynasty the House of Orange, the title it bears
to this day. And so it is, through former Dutch connections abroad, that
the name of Orange is borne today by a river and state in South Africa,
by towns in the US, and by the Protestant movement of Ulster.

The principality was annexed to France in 1713 by the Treaty of
Utrecht. By then, its Roman buildings had suffered heavily: when Prince
Maurice of Nassau set about fortifying his city, in 1622, he used stones
from the temples, baths and arena to build his château, which is why little
remains of them today. The theater and arch were spared, for they formed
part of his defense system.

It is worth remembering that Orange, in the heart of the Côtes-du-
Rhône area, is an important center for the local wine trade, and is a good
base from which to explore it.

- ◖€ For the best bird's-eye view of theater and town, drive up the Montée
  des Princes d'Orange-Nassau to the top of the *colline* St-Eutrope.
- **EVENT** • Last two weeks of July, and early August, an **international
  music festival**, the Chorégies — operas and classical concerts — in the
  Théâtre Antique *(details from Maison du Théâtre, pl. des Frères-Mounet,
  84100* ☎ *90-34-15-52).* • There is also a **photography and
  contemporary art exhibition** during the summer. • An **antique fair**
  takes place in August.
  • Since 1993, the Roman theater has been the scene of **major musical
  events** during the summer (jazz, rock and popular classics).
- **MARKET**   There is a market on Thursdays.

WHAT TO SEE IN ORANGE
Arc de Triomphe ☆
Av. de l'Arc de Triomphe.

This most impressive arch was built to celebrate Julius Caesar's victories over local Gauls and over the Greek fleet of Massilia (Marseille),
which had sided with Pompey. It is the third-largest extant Roman
triumphal arch and one of the best-preserved, notably the N side with
its elaborate low reliefs. The frieze high above the central arch depicts

battles with Gauls, while nautical emblems (anchors, prows and ropes) above the side arches mark the naval victory.

Musée de la Ville ★

Rue Madeleine-Roch ☎ *90-51-18-24* ▨ *Open Oct–Apr 9am–noon, 1.30–5.30pm; Nov–Mar Mon–Sat 9am–7pm, Sun 9am–noon, 2–6.30pm.*
Situated opposite the Roman theater, the museum contains exhibits (including portraits) relating to Orange's Dutch connections and Roman past (including marble fragments of a cadastral land survey from 77AD — the only surviving example of its kind).

There is also, oddly, a collection of works by Sir Frank Brangwyn, a Welsh pupil of William Morris, well known at the turn of the century.

Théâtre Antique ★

Pl. des Frères-Mounet ▨ ✗ *available. Open Apr–Oct 9am–6.30pm; Oct–Apr 9am–noon, 1.30–5pm.*
Orange possesses the finest, best-preserved Roman theater in existence, and the only one whose facade still stands. Viewed from either side, it is an immensely stirring sight: a great wall of reddish-brown sandstone, 35 meters (120 feet) high by 90 meters (295 feet) long.

On the inner side, the three tiers of statues and columns have gone, but the original 3-meter (11-foot) statue of Augustus with his general's baton was returned to its central niche in 1935. Above, the stone blocks once supported the masts carrying awnings to protect the spectators from the sun. The theater held over 7,000 people, and its acoustics were — and remain — superb, as testified by the musical events still held here.

On the w side, recent excavations have laid bare the foundations of a temple, the largest found so far in Gaul, and the remains of a sports field thought to have been 365 meters (400 yards) long. On the slopes of the hill above stood the majestic capital; the traces of three temples are still visible. This whole ensemble of buildings must have been the most grandiose in Gaul, and a powerful reminder of the might and superiority of the Roman Empire.

❧ There are no very exciting hotels in Orange, but **Arène** *(pl. de Langes* ☎ *90-34-10-95* ▨ *90-34-91-62* ▢ *closed Nov to mid-Dec)* is worth mentioning, as is the **Altéa Orange** *(Route de Caderousse* ☎ *90-34-24-10* ▨ *90-34-85-48* ▢*)* a lively, well-equipped modern hotel with spacious grounds on the outskirts of town, 3km (2 miles) sw of Orange, just w of the entrance to the autoroute; **Mas des Aigras** *(Chemin des Aigras* ☎ *90-34-81-01* ▢ *to*▢*)* is a comfortable, pretty country hotel.

═ **LE BEC FIN**
14 rue Segond-Weber ☎90-34-14-76
▢ to ▢ ▭ ▬ Closed Mon (except

summer). Last orders 9.30pm.
After a long drive down from the N, this little *auberge* opposite the Théâtre may provide the first taste of the cuisine and ambience of Provence. The hungry traveler could do far worse, for it is a good example of its genre, animated, unpretentious, with authentic local dishes. *Specialities: Poutargue provençale, coq au vin de Châteauneauf-du-Pape, lapereau aux trois moutardes.*

═ **LE PARVIS**
3 Cours Pourtoules ☎90-34-82-00 ▢ to ▢ ▨ ▭ ▬ ▬ ▥ ◉ ◎ ▨ Closed Mon (except July, Aug); mid-Nov. Last orders 9.30pm.

Monsieur Berengier's family-run restaurant is in a converted blacksmith's forge with beamed ceilings and large windows. The food is interesting, well presented, flavorful and generally very enjoyable. Specialities include pheasant salad, mushroom salad with saffron, and good lamb, pigeon and guinea fowl dishes. There is an extensive selection of Châteauneuf-du-Pape wines.

⌘ ⊟   Nearby is the **Château de**

Rochegude (Rochegude, 26790 (in Drôme) **☎** 75-04-81-88 ⓕ 75-04-89-87 ▥ closed Mon and Tues lunch out of season, Jan-Mar), 14km (9 miles) from Orange, an imposing château in its own grounds, with all the comfort you would expect of a Relais & Châteaux establishment, including pool and tennis court. It provides an excellent base from which to explore the local wine country. The cuisine is top-quality.

PLACES NEAR ORANGE

Châteauneuf-du-Pape (13km/8 miles s of Orange). The vineyards growing around the village once belonged to the Popes of Avignon (hence the name) and today produce one of the finest and most celebrated **Côtes-du-Rhône** wines. In 1923, the local winegrowers won a legal battle for the right to impose regulations enabling them alone to market their wine as **Châteauneuf-du-Pape**. This led to the present system of *Appellation Contrôlée,* used throughout France to guarantee the origin of good wines and to protect their quality. In the village is a small wine museum, the **Caves du Père Anselme**.

Of the summer residences built here by the Popes, only one high tower remains. From its top there is a splendid view of the Palais des Papes in Avignon, set dramatically against a backdrop of the Alpilles.

⌘ ⊟   Château des Fines Roches (**☎** 90-83-70-23 ⓕ 90-83-78-42 ▥ to ▥ ⊙ ▦ closed Sun dinner, Mon, Jan, Feb) is an excellent restaurant with very fine local wines, good views, and seven smart rooms, 3km (2 miles) s of Châteauneuf-du-Pape. The château, run by the Estevenin family, is mock-medieval. It was once a popular meeting place for Provençal writers such as Frédéric Mistral and Alphonse Daudet.

⌘   Logis d'Arnavel (Route de Roquemaure **☎** 90-83-73-22 ▥), a comfortable, unfussy hotel with a swimming pool.

Sérignan (8km/5 miles NE of Orange). Here is the villa where the great entomologist J.H. Fabre (1823–1915), a friend of Charles Darwin and John Stuart Mill, spent the last 40 years of his life. It is now a vivid museum (**▨** closed Tues) housing his varied collections. The large, wild garden, originally planted by Fabre himself, contains over a thousand species, including some botanical rarities.

• See also: VAISON-LA-ROMAINE; VENTOUX, MONT.

PONT DU GARD ▥ ✭

Map 8D3 (Gard). 25km (16 miles) w of Avignon. Postal code: 30210 Remoulins
i **☎** 66-37-00-02.

One of the noblest monuments left to the world by the Roman Empire, this celebrated bridge was built across the Gardon by Agrippa in 19BC, as part of the 48-kilometer (30-mile) aqueduct carrying water from the

Eure to Nîmes. Today, after some restoration during the 19thC, it is still in a near-perfect state.

It consists of three tiers of arches, of golden local stone, harmonizing with the landscape of rocks and forests. The lower tiers each have large arches; the uppermost tier, which carried the water, is a suite of 35 smaller arches. The bridge is 275 meters (900 feet) long and 50 meters (165 feet) high, and its blocks of stone weigh up to 6 tons each. An awe-inspiring sight, its construction is still a source of wonder to engineers.

The best view of the bridge is from the entrance to the Château de St-Privat, just 90 meters (98 yards) upstream on the right bank. From near here, a path winds up to the E end of the upper tier, which can easily be walked across by those not afraid of heights. A road bridge, built in 1747, runs level with the lower tier of the Roman bridge.

There have recently been attempts to pep up the Pont du Gard as an attraction, with a new parking lot, a store, and other improvements.

≈ ≈ **Le Vieux Castillon** (*Castillon-du-Gard, 30210 Remoulins* ☎*66-37-00-77* Ex*66-37-28-17* ▥ *to* ▥ ▥ *closed Jan-Mar*), a luxurious Relais & Châteaux establishment converted from a number of old buildings in a medieval hill-village just NE of the Pont du Gard on the D192. There is a pool, and even a hair salon. Musical evenings are a feature. Fishing is available. The restaurant is one of the finest in the area: **Le Vieux Moulin** (*30201 Remoulins* ☎*66-37-14-35* ▥ *closed mid-Nov to mid-Mar*), a converted old mill near the river, close to the Pont du Gard (with views of it). Comfortable, with reasonable food and pleasant, shaded terraces.

• See also: UZÈS.

ROUSSILLON

Map 5D7 (Vaucluse). 48km (30 miles) E of Avignon. Postal code: 84220 Gordes. Population: 1,300.

This is the heart of the ocher country (see also APT), where pines and heather strike their roots into the bright red earth, and the red rocks jut out for miles around. Roussillon (meaning "russet") is a most pretty, ancient village, on a hilltop between the Coulon valley and the Vaucluse plateau. Its houses of local stone are in every shade of pink, red and orange, and have long attracted artists. All around are ocher quarries, where many cliffs have been slashed into strange shapes and consequently been given fancy names such as "Giant's Causeway" and "Needles of the Fairy Vale."

The American sociologist Laurence Wylie lived in Roussillon and made it the subject of his well-known book, *Village in the Vaucluse*

(1961). He described a sleepy peasant community awakening to the modern world. Nowadays it is not so sleepy and has become a modish center of writers, painters (who hold frequent art exhibitions), well-to-do summer visitors and plenty of tourists.

✿ ≡ MAS DE GARRIGON

Route de St-Saturnin d'Apt, 84220
☎90-05-63-22 ⊠90-05-70-01 ▥ to ▥
9 rms ━ ≡ AE ◉ ▥ ⌂ ▢ ⌁ �&ᴗ
《 ⇔ ♨ ☙ ❍ Restaurant closed Sun dinner, Mon mid-Nov to end Dec.
Location: 3 kilometers (2 miles) N of Roussillon on D2. An excellent, extremely charming and comfortable hotel with very well-decorated rooms. Every room has its own little terrace looking out on the pine-filled garden, with Roussillon in the distance. The feeling is of peace and privacy, almost as if you are staying in a house party — and Madam Rech is a most competent and solicitous host. There is a small library, and a log fire in the lounge. The bright restaurant overlooks the sheltered swimming pool (you can eat outside if you wish), and the cuisine, although not cheap, is of a high standard. Specialities include: Soupe de truffes, rouget de roche au coulis de poivron rouge, daube mitonnée à l'ancienne, pigeonneau au miel.

✿ RÉSIDENCE DES OCRES

Route de Gordes, 84220 Gordes
☎90-05-60-50 ▥ to ▥ 16 rms ▦
━ ▥ ⌂ ⌁ ❧ Closed Feb; mid-Nov

to mid-Dec; mid-Jan to mid-Feb.
Location: On the edge of the village, beside a main road. A small modern hotel, neat and well cared for. A reasonable base for exploring the area.

≡ DAVID

Pl. de la Poste ☎90-05-60-13 ▥ ⌷ ▰
⊕ Closed Mon; Tues; end Nov to mid-Dec; Feb to early Mar. Last orders 9.30pm.
A smart, spacious village restaurant with views over the valley and the ocher cliffs. Garden dining in summer. The cuisine is classic and well-presented. Specialities: Feuilleté d'écrevisses, aiguillettes de pintade aux cerises, cassoulette de moules, borcette d'agneau, brouillade de truffes, coq en pâte.

✿ ≡ Nearby: **Mas de La Tour** (Gargas ☎90-74-12-10 ⊠90-04-83-67 ▥), a newish hotel in a restored old mas in the countryside, with good rooms, and simple, well-prepared food in a pleasant dining room; **Les Voyageurs** (pl. Gambetta, St-Saturnin d'Apt ☎90-75-42-08 ▢ to ▥), a place with few frills, but cheap and very much of this region, serving large helpings of hearty local food such as jugged hare or wild boar.

- See also: GORDES; LUBÉRON, MONTAGNE DU; APT.

ST-RÉMY-DE-PROVENCE

Map **9**E5 (B.-du-R.). 21km (13 miles) s of Avignon. Postal code: 13210. Population: 10,000 **i** pl. Jean Jaurès ☎90-92-05-22.

The pleasant town of St-Rémy is a thriving greenmarket center, situated in a fertile plain. It was the birthplace of Nostradamus, astrologer and seer, who later lived in SALON-DE-PROVENCE.

The town has two museums. One, the **Musée Archéologique** (Hôtel de Sade, rue du Parège ☎90-92-13-07 ▦ visits by 𝄞 only, open daily from Apr to end Dec) is housed in the former home of relatives of the sadistic marquis, and contains a display of interesting finds of the Gallo-Greek and the Gallo-Roman periods from Glanum.

The other, the **Musée des Alpilles**, across the street (▦ open 10am to noon, 2 to 5, 6 or 7pm depending on season, closed Jan-Mar), is devoted to local folk art: costumes, *santons* and souvenirs of Mistral and Nostradamus. There is also the **Centre d'Art Présence Van Gogh** *(8 rue Estrine* ☎*90-92-34-72),* a gallery in an 18thC house, where there is a Van Gogh display and regular exhibitions of modern art.

St-Rémy has one of the few remaining factories where crystallized fruits are still made in the traditional way (APT, the center of production in the region, is now heavily industrialized). Ask the tourist office for details of visits to the local factory. Above all, however, St-Rémy is known for its nearby Roman monuments.

> On the plain of Maillane and St-Rémy the sky can sometimes seem more important than the earth, for here above the low green land the dawns and sunsets quiver — magenta changing to pale apple-green; scarlet to deep yellow — and at midday the sky is as blue as in the tropics.
>
> *(Aspects of Provence,* 1952, James Pope-Hennessy)

- **EVENTS** • May 1, a **horse and junk fair**. • Whit Monday, the **Fête de la Transhumance**, during which shepherds bring up to 2,000 animals into town, before they are sent to the hills for summer. Also on Whit Monday, **antique/junk fair**). • There is a **wine festival** at the end of July.
  • August 15, the Carretto Ramado, a **harvest festival**. • Last Sunday in September: **concerts**, a **bull run** (also on July 14, August 15), a *boules* **tournament**, and other festivities. • There is a **festival of organ music** from July to September.

WHAT TO SEE IN ST-RÉMY
Aromes de Provence, Musée des
34 blvd. Mirabeau ☎*90-92-48-70. Open daily Mar–Oct 10am–noon, 3–6pm.*
A privately-owned museum with an exhibition of old stills used to distill scent, and a collection of perfume bottles and other curiosities.

The visit is free *(✘ on request),* and there is a small shop attached to the museum where you can buy soap, essential oils and scent.

Glanum and Les Antiques 🏛 ☆
2km (1 mile) s of St-Rémy, beside the D5 ☎*90-92-23-79* 🚾 *Open Apr–Sept 9am–7pm; Oct–Mar 9am–noon, 2–5pm.*
Lying at the foot of the Alpilles, this former Gallo-Roman settlement has been widely excavated since 1920 and is of particular interest because it shows the diverse impact of first the Greeks and then the Romans in Provence. In the 6thC BC it was a Gaulish settlement. Although it was never a Greek colony, the influence of the Greeks at Marseille is clear, for by the 2ndC BC the houses were being built to Greek designs.

When Caesar colonized Provence, the Romans settled at Glanum, and have left evidence of extensive building, including their customary forum, baths and temples. In the 3rdC AD the town was completely destroyed by Barbarian invaders, so that today nothing is left standing more than a few feet high; but traces of the ground layout are clearly discernible.

To the w of a Roman-built street are Greek-style houses, notably the house of Antes and the house of Atys, each with columns, peristyle and fine mosaics. To the e are the Roman buildings: baths with a covered gallery and swimming pool, a sizable forum, with temples near its sw corner. Farther s is a nymphaeum, still filled with fresh spring water, and beside it six altars dedicated to Hercules. The Romans are thought to have used Glanum as a hill station and spa.

Across the way from the entrance to Glanum stand **Les Antiques**, the two most memorable and inspiring Roman monuments in Provence. They were obviously a part of Roman Glanum (both date from c.20BC) but somehow managed to escape destruction in the 3rdC. They are not enclosed, and can be inspected at any time.

The **arch**, the oldest in Provence, is decorated with sculptures of captives chained to a tree and of garlands of fruit and flowers. The top part is missing.

The **cenotaph**, however, is in a marvelous state of preservation after 2,000 years. It was long thought to have been a mausoleum, but scholars today hold the view that it was a memorial erected in honor of Augustus' grandsons, Caius and Lucius, who died young (the fine portrait bust of their mother, Julia, is to be seen in the **Musée Archéologique** in St-Rémy: see above). The square base of the cenotaph carries elaborate low reliefs of battles involving infantry and cavalry, a boar hunt, and various marine emblems. Beneath the cupola are the toga-clad statues of the two young Roman men.

There is a small **museum** with models, historical explanations and copies of statues.

●   ✗   Guided tours of Glanum are available on request to the tourist office (☎ 90-92-05-22).

St-Paul-de-Mausole
Just n of Glanum, e of the D5. Open daily 9am–noon, 2–6pm.
A former monastery, this fine building, named after the Glanum mausoleum, has been a mental institution since 1605. It was here that Van Gogh spent a year as a patient in 1889–90, after cutting off his ear in ARLES. His cell is now closed to visitors, but you can see the bust of him in the drive, and the quiet flowery garden where he painted, among others, his famous paintings, *The Sower, Starry Night* and *Cypress Trees,* for his artistic powers did not diminish during the last year of his life. The beautiful cloister and the Romanesque chapel, both 12thC, are worth a visit in their own right. The chapel has become a favorite for fashionable weddings.

Nearby, there is the imaginative Promenade Van Gogh. The signposted walk marks various points from which Van Gogh painted some of his best-known late works, with reproductions of the paintings at the appropriate vantage points. You can walk about by yourself, but there are also guided walks lasting around $1\frac{1}{2}$ hours (✗ *at 9am on Tues, Thurs, Sat from Apr to mid-Oct),* which set off from the tourist office.

The local tourist office also arranges a walking tour in the footsteps of Nostradamus from May to the middle of October.

❧ WHERE TO STAY IN ST-RÉMY

❧ LES ANTIQUES
15 av. Pasteur, 13210 St-Rémy
☎90-92-03-02 ▨90-92-50-40 ▥ to ▥
27 rms ⟶ Ⓐ Ⓔ ⑩ ⱳ ⌂ ☐ ⌁ & ✿ ⚒
⚲ ⚓ ☐ Closed mid-Nov to end Mar.
*Location: In lovely grounds near the
center of town.* In this well-converted
19thC mansion, you can stay in the main
building or in an outbuilding. The decor
is tasteful, sometimes rather grand, and
the rooms large — although some of the
bathrooms could be improved.

❧ ⇌ DES ARTS ☙
30 blvd. Victor-Hugo, 13210 St-Rémy
☎90-92-08-50 ▥ 17 rms ⌁ ✿ ⱳ
Closed early Nov; Feb. For ⇌ see below.
*Location: On main street in the center
of town.* This cheerful café-pension is
aptly named, for it attracts visiting artists
and writers as well as students and locals to gossip, drink and play cards.
Beamed ceilings, a pretty patio and an
ivy-hung terrace add to the atmosphere.
Bedrooms have been modernized,
while retaining their rustic charm.

❧ ⇌ LE CASTELET DES ALPILLES
6 pl. Mireille, 13210 St-Rémy
☎90-92-07-21 ▨90-92-37-32 ▥ 18
rms ⌂ ⇌ Ⓐ Ⓔ ⑩ ⱳ ⌁ ✿ ⚒ Closed
late Oct to Apr. For ⇌ see below.
*Location: On the main road, just s of
the town center.* A turn-of-the-century
villa converted to a sympathetic little
family hotel, run by a friendly local
couple. The lounge is plain, but the
flowery tree-lined garden is lovely.
Some bedrooms are in Louis XVI style,
and some have balconies facing the Alpilles.

❧ LE CHÂTEAU DES ALPILLES ▥
Route Départementale 31, 13210 St-Rémy
☎90-92-03-33 ▨90-92-45-17 ▥ 20
rms ⟶ ▤ ⇌ Ⓐ ⑩ ⑩ ⱳ ⌂ ✦ ☐
⌁ & ✿ ⚔ ⚒ ⚲ ⚘ ⚓ ⚓ ☐ Closed
mid-Nov to end Mar.
*Location: On the D31, 2 kilometers (1½
miles) w of the town center.* This lovely
early 19thC manor (where Lamartine
and Chateaubriand both stayed) is set

in its own 10-acre grounds. It has been
well converted into a refined luxury
hotel, and there is an annex (a former
barn), as well as the main building. The
rooms, furnished with antiques, are
large, the bathrooms well appointed,
and decorations tasteful and splendid
throughout. Residents can order from a
short, light but interesting menu in the
beautiful dining room. There is a poolside barbecue in summer.

❧ CHÂTEAU DE ROUSSAN
Route de Tarascon, 13210 St-Rémy
☎90-92-11-63 ▨ 90-9237-32 ▥ 22
rms ⌂ ⇌ Ⓐ ⱳ ⌂ ⌁ ✿ ⚔ Closed
early Nov to end Dec.
*Location: In its own 15-acre park, 2.5
kilometers (1½ miles) w of St-Rémy, off
the N99.* The Roussels, from Montpel-
lier, owned this superb, small 18thC
château for 100 years as their summer
residence. Then, to make ends meet,
they accepted paying guests. The château is now a hotel, although still
owned by the family; it is slowly being
renovated, but the atmosphere of a private home remains, and the interior,
with its Louis XV furniture and red-tiled
floors, is most gracious. Only the bathrooms are modernized. Browse in the
library, explore the 16thC farmhouse
once lived in by Nostradamus, or stroll
around the rambling garden. This is a
noble house and park, steeped in romantic melancholy, a favorite with
Americans, some of whom have married or gone on honeymoon there. A
19thC annex has been renovated and
will provide extra rooms, but it lacks the
genuine charm and style of the main
part of the house.

❧ ⇌ DOMAINE DE VALMOURIANE
Petite Route des Baux, 13210 St-Rémy
☎90-92-44-62 ▨90-92-37-32 ▥ 12
rms ▤ ⟶ Ⓐ ⱳ ⌂ ☐ ⌁ ✿ ⚔ ⚓
⚘ ⚓ Closed Jan.
*Location: 5 kilometers (3 miles) sw of
St-Rémy, off the Tarascon road (D99)
on the D27.* This 18thC *mas* has been
turned into a most comfortable, even

luxurious, hotel with individually decorated rooms and first-class facilities including a video library. There are also many extras in the large and well-appointed bathrooms. The British owners, Brian and Judy McHugo, also run the CHÂTEAU DE ROUSSAN. There are a number of leisure activities on offer within the 6-acre grounds of the hotel, including tennis, archery, golf, putting and billiards.

The restaurant serves palatable, if not particularly inventive Provençal cuisine.

🐚 🍴 HOSTELLERIE DU VALLON DE VALRUGUES 🏨

Chemin Canto Cigalo, 13210 St-Rémy
☎90-92-04-40 📠90-92-44-01 ▥ 49
rms ▦ ▣ AE ◉ ◎ VISA ▱ ✱ ▯ ▨ ♿
♨ ⟨⟨ ♨ ♒ ⸫ ♔ ⟨⟩ ⦂ ♘ ♈ ▣ ♞
☛ *Closed Jan–Mar.*
Location: At the E outskirts of the town.
This tries to be a very smart hotel indeed, shaded by mulberry trees and with views of the Alpilles and olive groves. But it feels a little out of place in the middle of the countryside. The rooms (some with beams, all with a whirlpool bath and a terrace) are very well equipped, but the decorative styles seem jumbled. The public rooms (including the restaurant) seem to belong to another hotel altogether, and are too ostentatious for many tastes. There is a large swimming pool, a gym, sauna, a *boules* pitch, a billiards room and putting green. This hotel is not for everyone, but it is rather fun if you think you can cope with the pretension. The service is both good and friendly, and the facilities provided are pretty well beyond criticism.

The cuisine (chef Jacky Morlon trained with both Michel Guérard and Michel Lorain) is among the best in the area. The set menus at lunchtime are good value. Try to get a table outside. *Specialities: Rouget parfumé au basilic, selle d'agneau aux senteurs des garrigues.*

🐚 Other good hotels: **L'Amandière** *(av. Théodore Aubanel* ☎90-92-41-00 📠90-92-38-52 ▥)*, a very well kept and pretty little hotel, with comfortable, nicely-decorated rooms; **La Reine Jeanne** *(12 blvd. Mirabeau* ☎90-92-15-33 📠90-92-49-65 ▥)*, a good small hotel with an above-average restaurant; **Soleil** *(35 av. Pasteur* ☎90-92-00-63 📠90-92-61-07 ▥)*, centrally located, with pleasant rooms and a swimming pool; and **Ville Verte** *(av. Fauconnet* ☎90-92-06-14 📠90-92-38-52 ▥)*, not brilliantly decorated, with few amenities, and street-side rooms that are rather noisy; it is nonetheless the best budget choice in town.

🍴 EATING AND DRINKING IN ST-RÉMY

🍴 DES ARTS ✿

30 blvd. Victor-Hugo ☎90-92-08-50 ▯ to
▥ ▱ ▪ AE VISA *Closed Wed; early Nov to Feb. Last orders 9.30pm.*
It's usually a question of scrambling or lining up to get a table in this ever-animated and extremely popular dining room where, despite the pressure, *la patronne* Nicole Caritoux serves her husband's *cuisine familiale,* such as *cuisses de grenouilles provençale* and *côte de boeuf aux cèpes.*
(See 🐚 above.)

🍴 LE BISTROT DES ALPILLES

15 blvd. Mirabeau ☎90-92-09-17 ▥▱

▪ ▬ ♞ AE ◉ VISA *Closed Sun; Nov. Last orders 9.30pm (10pm in summer).*
A very attractive bistro/brasserie in the center of town, with a pleasant atmosphere, charming service, and good Provençal food. A pianist plays on winter Fridays, and there is jazz from time to time in the summer. Try the *gigot d'agneau de pays à la ficelle,* cooked suspended by a string over a wood fire.

🍴 LE CASTELET DES ALPILLES

6 pl. Mireille ☎90-92-07-21 ▥ to ▥ ▱
▪ ♞ ⟨⟩ AE ◉ VISA *Closed Mon (except dinner in summer); Tues lunch; Nov–Apr. Last orders 9pm.*

In summer, try to eat on the pleasant terrace by the garden. Cheerful service and traditional *cuisine*. *Specialities: Bourride, gratin de crustaces, daube provençale*. (See ❧ above.)

☰ LA GOUSSE D'AIL

25 *rue Carnot* ☎90-92-16-87 ▥ ▭ ▰
◉ ▱ *Closed Wed. Last orders 9.30pm.*
Small, with a charming ambience, enhanced by a collection of dolls, *bric à brac* and a beamed ceiling. It is run by a young husband-and-wife team (Dutch/French); the menu is short, the cuisine Provençal. The restaurant specializes in *bouillabaisse* on Tuesdays, with a good selection of local wines.

☰ Other recommended restaurants are: **Marceau** *(13 blvd. Marceau* ☎*90-92-37-11* ▥ *closed Wed, Thurs lunch, Jan)*, smartly decorated; **Jardin de Frédéric** *(8 blvd. Gambetta* ☎*90-92-27-76* ▥ *closed Wed)*, one of the best restaurants in town; **Le France** *(2 av. Fauconnet* ☎*90-92-11-56* ▥ *closed Nov-Feb)*; **La Reine Jeanne** *(12 blvd. Mirabeau* ☎*90-92-15-33* ▥ *closed Thurs, Dec-Mar)*, a surprisingly good restaurant for a simple hotel; and **Croque Chou** *(pl. de l'Église, Verquières* ☎*90-95-18-55* ▥ *closed Mon, Tues)*, an excellent restaurant, one of the best in the area, 11 kilometers (7 miles) NE via the D30.

SHOPPING IN ST-RÉMY
Many shops in St-Rémy open on Sundays, and therefore often close on Mondays.

* **MARKET**   There is a picturesque market in the old town on Wednesday mornings.

PLACE NEAR ST-RÉMY
Maillane *(6km/4 miles NW of St-Rémy)*. In this pretty village the poet Mistral was born, lived much of his life and died: he lies buried in the cemetery. The house where he lived from 1876 till 1914 is now the **Muséon Mistral**, where rooms have been preserved as they were at the time of his death.

* See also: ARLES, AVIGNON, LES BAUX, BEAUCAIRE, CAVAILLON, FONTVIEILLE, SALON-DE-PROVENCE, TARASCON.

LA SAINTE-BAUME, MASSIF DE ★
Map 11H9 (B.-du-R. and Var). Approx. 32km (20 miles) E of Marseille. Area approx. 130sq.km (50sq. miles).

The most spectacular of all the craggy limestone massifs of Provence also breathes the mystery of early Christian legend. Its name comes from the Provençal *baoumo* (cave): here St Mary Magdalene is said to have retreated alone to a cave on the heights and spent the last 30 years of her life (see opposite and ST-MAXIMIN-LA-SAINTE-BAUME).

Arid and bare on its S slopes, richly forested to the N, the range runs for 16 kilometers (10 miles) between Aubagne and ST-MAXIMIN. The best excursion through its wild heart is the D2 from **Gémenos**, E of Aubagne. You soon pass, on the right, the **Parc de St-Pons**, with its varied, beautiful trees and remains of a 13thC Cistercian abbey. From there, the narrow road loops up and up into a blasted landscape of toothy white crags. Here is the gaunt pinnacle of the **Fourcade rock**, and the sugarloaf **Pic de Bertagne** crowned by a domed white observatory. All around are majestic views, toward Marseille to the w, the coast of Cassis to the s, and, far to the n, the Mont Ste-Victoire above AIX.

As you reach **Plan d'Aups**, there's a sudden change of landscape: a mild upland plateau with neat farmsteads and cultivated fields. A little farther on, to the right, is an old hostelry now run by Dominicans as a religious and cultural center: it has a Renaissance chimney piece and statues of Louis XI and his wife. Here too is the **Forêt de la Ste-Baume**, famous for its giant beeches, trees rarely found in southern France.

To the s, the view sweeps up to the high crest of the massifs, where a stone monument crowns its topmost peak, **St-Pilon**, 1,150 meters (3,800 feet). This is holy ground, for Mary Magdalene's alleged cave is a few yards w of St-Pilon: in the 14thC, kings, popes and princes would make the pilgrimage to this lonely spot, where Midnight Mass is still celebrated every July 22 in a chapel in the cave.

From the hostelry on the main road, you can walk through the lovely forest and up, along well-marked paths, to the cave and St-Pilon (views that take in MONT VENTOUX, 104 kilometers/64 miles to the n). From the hostelry, the main road winds on down through woods of silver-green trees to **Nans-les-Pins**.

🌤 **Relais de la Magdeleine** *(on N396, Gémenos* ☎*42-32-20-16* Ⓕ*43-32-02-26* ⅢⅢ *closed Nov-Mar),* a most comfortable and attractive hotel with many amenities, in a lovely 18thC building.

* See also: CASSIS, MARSEILLE, ST-MAXIMIN-LA-SAINTE-BAUME.

LES SAINTES-MARIES-DE-LA-MER ☆
Map 8G3 (B.-du-R.). 39km (24 miles) sw of Arles. Postal code: 13460. Population: 2,250 **i** *av. Van-Gogh* ☎*90-47-82-55.*

The only town or village in the Camargue — and hence its self-styled capital — Les Saintes-Maries-de-la-Mer is today a popular seaside resort, strung out between the lagoons and the sand dunes with their miles of fine beaches. The nucleus of old alleys around the church is appealing, notably the traffic-free **avenue Victor-Hugo**. Here the **Musée Baroncelli** *(* ☎ *closed Wed, Nov)* is devoted to the wildlife and customs of the Camargue.

But folklore at Les Saintes-Maries is not relegated to museums; it is more a part of daily life than in almost any other town in Provence. Provençal is still spoken, folk groups are active, and the year revolves around the great traditional festivals.

The town is a place of pilgrimage, officially at the end of October, for it is at the heart of the legends relating to the arrival of Christianity in Provence. According to a 9thC legend, a boat without sails or oars left the Holy Land and drifted ashore here, bearing St Mary Jacobe, the Virgin's sister, St Mary Salome, the mother of James and John, St Mary Magdalene, Saints Martha, Maximin, Lazarus and Sidonius, and Sara, their African servant. The legend relates that the saints then split up to evangelize Provence — Martha went to TARASCON, Lazarus to St-Victor at MARSEILLE, Maximin and Sidonius to AIX (see ST-MAXIMIN), and Mary Magdalene to LA

SAINTE-BAUME. The two other Marys and Sara stayed on here — hence the town's name — where they built an oratory, and were buried on the spot where the great church now stands.

- **EVENTS** May 24–25, **Pèlerinage des Gitanes** (gypsy pilgrimage). This famous festival is the great event of the gypsy year. Gypsies converge here in their thousands from all parts of France, and other countries too (mainly Spain), bringing their caravans, which today are all motorized, not horse-drawn. However, the gypsies themselves are still an exotic sight, with their dusky good looks and bright clothes. On May 23, they hold a night vigil in the church crypt in honor of Ste-Sara, whom they chose long ago as their patroness. The next day, the reliquary of the two Marys is lowered from its high chapel, in a special service.

  Then on May 25 comes the pilgrimage: a procession of clergy, gypsies, *gardians*, Arlésiennes and flute players, all in fine costume, carries the blue and pink statues of the two saints, in their little boat, as far as the sea. They are solemnly taken back to the church in the afternoon. The next two days are given over to Provençal fêtes, with bull races, horsemanship and folk dancing. • The **same pilgrimage** also takes place on the weekend nearest October 22 and the first Sunday in December, but these are less colorful.

  In March and April, the town hosts the **world speed windsurfing championship**. • There is a **fête** at the end of June, and a **horse fair** in mid-July.

Church ▥ ✝ ☆
Pl. de l'Église ◁≡ *Crypt open Apr–Sept 7.30am–noon, 2–7.30pm; Oct–Mar 7.30am–6pm.*

Built in fortified style as a defense against Saracen and other attackers in the 11thC, this strange-looking church does resemble a fort, with its massive walls and crenelated parapet. Above is a high five-arch belfry, visible from afar across the plain, and definitely worth climbing up for the view.

The simple, somber nave is almost bare of decoration, save for the showcase of naive *ex-votos* and, to the left of the altar, the "boat of the Saintes-Maries," carried in procession in the festivals. The reliquary holding the bones of the saints is in a chapel above the apse, kept closed. But you can visit the 15thC crypt, where the reliquary of Sara stands across the altar from an elaborately dressed statue of the grave-faced lady. The rows of burning candles show how much she is still venerated.

☜ L'ÉTRIER CAMARGUAIS
Chemin bas des Launes, 13460 Les Saintes-Maries-de-la-Mer ☎ 90-97-81-14 ⊞ 90-97-88-11 ▥ 27 rms ☛ ≕ 🏨 AE ⊡ ⊙ ▥ ⊟ ⅙ 🗔 🖾 ⍾ 🐎 ⅋ 🚶 ☜
Closed Nov–Apr.
Location: In its own park, in the Camargue, 3 kilometers (2 miles) N of town, just off N570. The corner of the Camargue just N of Les-Saintes-Maries has a dozen or so modern ranch-hotels, where the accent is on riding and other sports.

L'Étrier ("the stirrup") is one of the best: spacious, lively, youthful, informal. Dogs pad about in the huge log-cabin lounge with its cozy leather chairs, the barman wears a local cowboy hat, and *l'après-cheval* proves it can be as relaxing and amusing as *l'après-ski*. The hotel has 25 horses, for hire by the hour, as well as a big swimming pool and lido, romantically lit at night with pink and orange lamps. Bedrooms, rustic and spacious, are in bungalows spread across the park.

Meals are served on the patio by the pool, or in the large dining room, where the log fire is used for grills. The hotel's own disco, **La Brouzetière**, just nearby, although out of earshot, is the best in the area.

❧ MAS DE LA FOUQUE 🏨

Route d'Aigues-Mortes, 13460 Les-Saintes-Maries-de-la-Mer ☎ *90-97-81-02* Ⓕⓧ *90-97-96-84* 🎟 *to* 🎟🎟 *14 rms* 🛏 ➡ 𝔸𝔼 ⊙ ⊙ 🖵 🖴 ⛓ ⬜ 🖵 🦆 ⦔ ⚓ ℘ 🏌 🗡 🏊 𝕐 🖃 *Closed Jan to late Mar.*

Location: 5 kilometers (3 miles) NW of town, off D38, in its own big park beside a Camargue lake. Another modern ranch-hotel: this one is smaller and more luxurious than the ÉTRIER, a little more formal, with an older clientele. The restaurant has large windows overlooking the lake, as does the attractive lounge; lunches are served by the heated swimming pool in summer. The decor is mostly Camarguais, with modern touches.

❧ Other recommended hotels in the area include: **Cavalière** *(Route d'Arles* ☎ *90-97-88-88* Ⓕⓧ *90-97-84-07* 🎟 *to* 🎟🎟 *open all year);* **L'Estelle** *(Route du Bac du Sauvage* ☎ *90-97-89-01* 🎟 *closed mid-Nov to mid-Dec, Jan to late Mar);* **Le Galoubet** *(Route de Cacharel* ☎ *90-97-82-17* Ⓕⓧ *90-97-71-20* 🎟 *closed mid-Jan to mid-Feb);* and **Pont des Bannes** *(Route d'Arles, Pont des Bannes* ☎ *90-97-81-09* Ⓕⓧ *90-97-89-28* 🎟 *to* 🎟🎟 *closed Jan-Apr).*

➡ **Brûleur de Loups** *(av. Gilbert-Leroy* ☎ *90-97-83-31* 🎟 *to* 🎟🎟 *closed Wed, mid-Nov to mid-Mar)* is an attractive restaurant overlooking the sea, serving delicate, if ambitious *cuisine.* **Pont de Gau** (♣) *(Pont de Gau* ☎ *90-97-81-53* 🎟 *to* 🎟🎟*)* is a down-to-earth *auberge* serving authentic *cuisine Camarguaise.*

There are several lively, inexpensive restaurants around place Esprit Pioch.

- Camarguais specialities include *boeuf gardian* (chunks of beef stewed in red wine and garlic), *salade de tellines* (very small shellfish with a garlic mayonnaise) and *poutargue* (red mullet roe). Also, eels from the Vaccarès: *catigot d'anguilles* (stewed in red wine) and *bouriroun* (an omelet made with young eels).

- See also: ARLES, LA CAMARGUE.

SALON-DE-PROVENCE
*Map **10**F6 (B.-du-R.). 55km (34 miles) NW of Marseille. Postal code: 13300. Population: 34,000* 𝓲 *56 Cours Gimon* ☎ *90-56-27-60. Railway station: av. Emile Zola* ☎ *90-56-00-47.*

A busy market town, its main streets lined with plane trees, this has been a center of the olive-oil industry since the 15thC. Today it has military connections: not only is the French Air Force's officer-training school here, but a museum of French Army history, the **Musée de l'Empéri** *(* ☎ *90-56-22-36* 🖾 *10am-noon, 2.30-6 or 6.30pm, closed Tues),* is installed in the 12thC **Château de l'Empéri**, former residence of the archbishops of Arles, lords of Salon. The museum contains some 10,000 army souvenirs dating from Louis XIV's day to 1918.

Close nearby is a **museum** *(11 rue Nostradamus* ☎ *90-56-22-36* 🖾 *open mid-June to mid-Sept 10am-noon, 3-8pm; mid-Sept to mid-June 10am-noon, 2-6pm),* devoted to the astrologer Nostradamus, in the house where he spent the last 19 years of his life. He is buried in the 14thC church of St-Laurent.

There is also a wax museum, the **Musée Grévin**, *(pl. du Puits de Jacob* ☎*90-56-36-30* ▨ *open mid-June to mid-Sept daily 10am-noon, 3-8pm; mid-Sept to mid-June 10am-noon, 2-6pm).* Its lifelike tableaux capture the region's many historical figures.

Beside the N7, 53.5 kilometers (33 miles) N, is a **memorial** to the greatest of French Resistance heroes, **Jean Moulin**, tortured and killed by the Gestapo, whose tomb lies in the Panthéon in Paris.

* **MARKET** There is a market on Wednesdays.

✎ ≡ **ABBAYE DE STE-CROIX** ⌂
*Route du Val de Cuech, 13300
Salon-de-Provence* ☎*90-56-24-55*
▨*90-56-31-12* ▥ *to* ▥ *24 rms* ◼ ▨
◻ ◻ ▥ ◻ ◻ ◻ ◻ ◻ ◻ ◻ ◻ ◻
▣ ▽ ▤ *Closed Nov–Mar.*
Location: Spectacularly located, and secluded in its own large grounds, on a hillside 5 kilometers (3 miles) to the NE of Salon. A carefully restored 12thC abbey, furnished with antiques. There are stone stairways to the unusually attractive bedrooms. Many of the rooms are spacious; some look over the pretty Romanesque cloister, others over the distant hills and the shimmering valley below, and offer one of the most stunning views in Provence. Some rooms have private terraces, others small gardens. The owner, Catherine Bossard, speaks excellent English, and runs the place efficiently.

The hotel's restaurant *(*▥ ◻ ◼ ◼ *closed Mon lunch, last orders 9.30pm)* is a graceful, stone-walled, candlelit room, overlooking the valley. It produces excellent food: lavish, intelligently balanced, and generally light. *Specialities: Gigotin de lotte pané aux truffes, roulade de lapereau à l'anchois, gâteau de courgettes et saumon mariné.*

✎ ≡ **Domaine de Roquerousse**

(Route d'Avignon, 13300 Salon-de-Provence ☎*90-59-50-11* ▨*90-59-53-75* ▥*),* on a large estate 4km (2½ miles) along the N538 from Salon. Hunting is available, and there is a good restaurant, specializing, appropriately, in meat dishes.

✎ Hotels that are more central include: **Sélect** (◼) *(35 rue Suffren* ☎*90-56-07-17* ▥ *to* ▥*)* and **Midi** *(518 Allées de Craponne* ☎*90-53-34-67* ▨*90-53-37-41* ▥*).*

≡ **FRANCIS ROBIN** ♣
1 blvd. Clémenceau ☎*90-56-06-53* ▥ *to* ▥ ◻ ◼ ▨ ◻ *Closed Sun dinner; Mon; Feb. Last orders 9pm.*
Not a cheap place, but smart and comfortable, with exceptionally good modern cooking, including featherlight pâtisseries. *Specialities: Millefeuille d'agneau aux légumes nouveaux, aiguillette de canard aux mangues.*

≡ **Craponne** *(146 Allées de Craponne* ☎*90-53-23-92* ▥ *to* ▥ ▥ *);* **La Mas du Soleil** *(38 Chemin St-Côme* ☎*90-56-06-53* ▥ *closed Sun dinner, Mon);* **Le Poêlon** *(71 Allées de Craponne* ☎*90-53-31-38* ▥ *closed Sun in summer, Wed in winter, early Aug, early Jan).*

PLACES NEAR SALON
Château de Barben *(8km/5 miles E of Salon).* The medieval château *(*☎*90-55-19-12* ▨ *closed Tues)* contains paintings by Van Loo, as well as the Empire-style boudoir of Pauline Borghese, Napoléon's sister, who once lived there.

In the château grounds are a zoo, aviary and aquarium.

≡ **La Touloubre** *(La Barben* ☎*90-55-16-85* ▥ *to* ▥ ▨ ▨ *closed Sun dinner, Mon, mid- to end Nov, end Feb to early Mar).*

Lambesc *(16km/10 miles E of Salon).* An old town of great charm. Beyond it, a narrow road climbs steeply onto the **Chaîne des Côtes**, a former French Resistance stronghold, where a monument now stands to those killed here by the Nazis. There is an 18thC church, which has a 14thC bell tower.

Vernègue *(11km/7 miles NE of Salon).* A hilltop village devastated by an earthquake in 1909. The site affords spectacular views over SW Provence.

- See also: AIX-EN-PROVENCE; ARLES; BERRE, ÉTANG DE; MARSEILLE; MARTIGUES; ST-RÉMY-DE-PROVENCE.

SÉNANQUE, ABBAYE DE ▥ † ☆

Map 5D6 (Vaucluse). 42km (26 miles) E of Avignon ☎ 90-72-02-05 ▥
✗ available July–Aug. Open July, Aug 10am–7pm; Sept–June 10am–noon, 2–6pm; weekends only in Jan.

Of Provence's three beautiful 12thC Cistercian abbeys, SILVACANE, THORONET and Sénanque, the last exemplifies best that austere order's love of isolated sites. It stands alone in a lovely, wild and narrow valley filled with lavender. The access route, over rocky hills from Gordes, is far from easy, but offers a stunning view. Built in 1148, Sénanque is also the best-preserved of the "three sisters," perhaps because it has had the quietest history. Its only serious drama came in 1544, when it was attacked and damaged by Protestants from the nearby Lubéron, who hanged some of the monks.

Later it was repaired, then sold during the French Revolution, like most monasteries. But the Cistercians acquired it again in 1854; they still own and run it today, from their base on the Île St-Honorat.

The main buildings are all intact, unchanged since the 12thC apart from some restoration. The arcaded cloister is enchanting; so are the chapter house and monks' dormitory, with their Romanesque vaulted ceilings. In the Cistercian manner, the large and graceful church is bare of ornamentation. But it has carpets, rows of new chairs and other signs that today it is very much in use for services and concerts.

Indeed, Sénanque's ambience is strikingly different from that of its two sisters, locked in their mystical medieval bustle, for it is particularly well kept, and today houses a thriving lay and religious cultural center. There are exhibitions of contemporary art, concerts, mainly of Gregorian music, and lectures and study groups on historical and religious subjects. The former refectory has a display of Cistercian history, as well as an imaginative sequence of "symbolic photographs" where bizarre landscapes are counterpointed by biblical and philosophical quotations.

Above all, strange as it might seem, the **Collections Sahariennes** (Center for Saharan Studies) has a fascinating **museum** here: details of the Tassili N'Ajjer cave paintings, of Touareg arts and life-styles, and more.

The finances of the abbey are boosted by an excellent book and souvenir store, selling books about Provence, Sénancole liqueur, lavender essence, soaps, and cassettes of religious music.

• See also: GORDES; LUBÉRON, MONTAGNE DU.

SILVACANE, ABBAYE DE 血 † ☆

Map 10E7 (B.-du R.). 28km (18 miles) NW of Aix ☎42-50-41-69 ▨ ✗ available. Open 10am–noon, 2–5 or 6pm (depending on season). Closed Tues; Jan 1; May 1; Nov 1 and 11; Dec 25.

Another of the celebrated trio of 12thC Cistercian abbeys in Provence (see SÉNANQUE and THORONET), Silvacane's setting, in the broad and ugly valley of the Durance, is less secluded and appealing than that of its sisters; but the harmonious purity of the abbey's Romanesque architecture is almost a match for theirs, and it follows a similar style.

The high-vaulted **church**, typically Cistercian, is quite plain inside (the side chapels and sanctuary are rectangular, and not the more usual apsidal or semicircular shape). The **chapter house**, built about 50 years later than the church, shows early Gothic influence in its vaulting; next door is the large, handsome **refectory**, rebuilt in the 15thC. The little **cloister**, with its vaulted arcades, exudes the same quiet charm as many Provençal cloisters of the period.

The abbey's name derives from *silva* (wood) and *cane* (reed), for it was built beside reed-filled marshes. In the late 12thC, with 110 monks, it was the most important of the "three sister abbeys," but its subsequent history was stormy. In the early 13thC the Benedictines briefly took over by force.

Then in 1357 it was pillaged by vagabonds and in 1590 was seized by bandits. For long periods it was no more than a village church. Today it belongs to the State, which is overseeing its restoration.

• See also: ANSOUIS; APT; LUBÉRON, MONTAGNE DU; SALON-DE-PROVENCE.

TARASCON

Map 4E4 (B.-du-R.). 23km (14 miles) SW of Avignon. Postal code: 13150. Population: 13,100 𝒊 59 rue des Halles ☎90-91-03-52. Railway station: blvd. Gustave-Desplaces ☎90-91-04-82.

Until the death of Good King René in 1480, the Rhône was the frontier between independent Provence and the kingdom of France to the W.

Tarascon, lying on the Rhône's E bank, was a key stronghold: hence its fortified château. Here, René (see AIX-EN-PROVENCE) spent much of his later life. It was he, a lover of popular festivity, who introduced the Festival of the Tarasque for which the town has since been famous.

The tale of **the Tarasque** is woven into the 9thC legend that the three St Marys landed in Provence, having been set adrift in an open boat some years after Jesus' death. Ste-Marthe (Martha), one of the party, made her way to Tarascon, then terrorized by an amphibious dragon, the *Tarasque*, which would emerge from the Rhône to devour children and abduct their mothers. The knights of Provence had failed to subdue this creature, but the saint did so, with the sign of the Cross. She ordered the Tarasque back to its cave in the river, and it was never seen again. Ste-Marthe remained in Tarascon, and is said to be buried in the church named after her.

Tarascon has also passed into literary history: the author Alphonse Daudet made it the home town of his comic antihero Tartarin, in his trilogy of satiric novels. At the time, the Tarasconnais felt insulted, but today Tartarin has passed harmlessly into local folklore, even playing a role in the annual parade of the Tarasque. The **Maison de Tartarin** *(55bis blvd. Itam ☎ 90-91-05-08 ⊠ open winter 9.30am-noon, 1.30-5pm, summer 9.30am-noon, 2-7pm)* celebrates the fictitious figure with wax models, rooms decorated in late 19thC style to fit descriptions in the books, and memorabilia from plays and films.

- **EVENT** Last Sunday in June, **Fête de la Tarasque**. Fascinating as a festival that has survived in a genuine form since the 15thC, the parade has its focal point in the green, scaly papier-mâché monster whose head and tail are manipulated by young men walking inside. Costumed figures walk beside it, and there is much celebration.

- **MARKET** There is a market on Tuesday mornings.

WHAT TO SEE IN TARASCON
Château ★
Blvd. du Château ☎ 90-91-03-52 ⊠ ✗ at 10 and 11am, 2, 3 and 4pm (also 5 and 6pm Apr–Sept). Closed Tues.

The massive walls and turreted towers of King René's castle stand proudly above the Rhône, looking across to BEAUCAIRE and its own castle. The foundations and some walls are 12thC, but the main part of the château was built by the king in the 15thC. For centuries it was used as a prison, indeed as recently as 1926. Yet it has survived almost intact, and has needed little restoration. From the outside, and even more so from within, it impresses as a perfect example of a medieval feudal castle, and is well worth a visit.

Surrounded by a moat, the castle is in two parts: the wide lower courtyard has square towers, while the *logis seigneurial* (royal dwelling) is a high, compact fortress with two round towers and two square ones. Here, the little inner court, elegant and intimate, has a first-floor restored loggia from which the king and his queens would watch miracle plays, jugglers and minstrels; the castle was a great center for troubadours. The minstrels' gallery gives onto both the court and the chapel, and was used for religious services and secular singing.

From the court, a stone spiral stairway leads to the series of beautiful rooms on the three upper floors. The large banqueting hall has a fireplace for roasting, and a wood ceiling covered with tiny paintings, all 15thC. But the curious graffiti on the walls, in this and other rooms, are of a later date: they are the work of prisoners, some of them English seamen captured in the 18thC. One sad little inscription reads: "Here be three Davids in one mess/prisoners we are in distress. . ." Upstairs is a priest's bedroom, with a hole in the wall for baking bread, and farther up, a chapel with separate oratories for the king and queen, built into walls that are up to 3 meters (11 feet) thick.

Finally, you arrive on the roof terrace; it was from here that supporters of Robespierre were hurled into the Rhône in 1794, when he fell from power.

Cloître des Cordeliers
Pl. Frédéric Mistral. Open 10am–noon, 2–5.30pm (winter); 10am–noon, 3–7pm (summer).
This well-restored 15thC Franciscan cloister is mainly used for exhibitions of art.

Ste-Marthe † ☆
Blvd. du Château.
Close to the castle entrance, this is a graceful 12thC building, restored after bomb damage in 1944. In the crypt, the 5thC sarcophagus is venerated as being the tomb of Ste-Marthe; above it can be seen a lovely marble sculpture of the saint, a 17thC Genoese work. On the stairway is the fine Renaissance tomb of King René's seneschal, Jean de Cossa.

Souleiado, Musée
39 rue Proudhon ☎90-91-08-80. Visits by appointment only.
A museum celebrating *Souleiado* (Provençal for sunbeam), the fabric design business that is now a worldwide name. The company was founded in the 1930s to revive the once widespread Provençal industry, dating from the 17thC, of printing on calico using pear tree wood blocks. The characteristic and traditional *Indiennage* patterns were, as the name suggests, originally Indian-inspired.

♋ **Échevins** *(26 blvd. Itam ☎90-91-01-70* ⌁ ▥ *closed Jan);* **Mazets des Roches** *(Route de Fontvieille* ☎*90-91-34-89* ▥ ⌁ *closed Nov-Apr);* **Provence** *(7 blvd. Victor Hugo* ☎*90-91-06-43* 🅵🆇*90-43-58-13* ▥ *closed late Dec to Jan);* **Terminus** (🍴) *(pl. du Colonel-Berrurier ☎90-91-18-95* ⌁ ▢ *to* ▥ *closed mid-Feb to mid-Mar).*

PLACE NEAR TARASCON
Abbaye de St-Michel-de-Frigolet *(6km/4 miles NE of Tarascon, off D81 ✗ daily).* Founded in the 10thC by the monks of Montmajour (see ARLES), the abbey was rebuilt in the 19thC in a richly ornate style. It is still in active use, and visitors can also attend the services, where the singing is very fine. The 11thC chapel to the left of the nave has gilded wooden sculptures, a gift from Anne of Austria in 1638.

The abbey lies in a beautiful valley just w of **La Montagnette**, a range of rocky hills not unlike the Alpilles to the SE.

- See also: ARLES, AVIGNON, LES BAUX, BEAUCAIRE, FONTVIEILLE, ST-RÉMY-DE-PROVENCE.

UZÈS ☆

*Map 8D3 (Gard). 25km (16 miles) N of Nîmes. Postal code: 30700. Population: 7,650 **i** av. de la Libération ☎66-22-68-88.*

The history of Uzès, a charming town of lofty towers and narrow streets, is bound up with that of its great ducal family, the House of Uzès, dating back to the time of Charlemagne. In 1632, Louis XIII proclaimed it "the premier duchy of France," a title it is still entitled to flaunt, even in today's Republican age. The family continues to live in its fairytale castle in the heart of the old town, at the hub of a network of arcaded streets lined with noblemen's houses.

Towers were a great symbol of power in medieval times, and Uzès, once heavily fortified with ramparts, has several of them. But the town was a Huguenot hotbed, and this led Cardinal Richelieu to pull down its ramparts. A circular boulevard now takes the route of the old ramparts.

Jean Racine (1639–99) lived here for a year in his youth, sent by his family to keep him away from Paris and poetry, in the hope that his uncle, the local Vicar-General, could persuade him to take holy orders. He failed, and Racine became one of France's greatest playwrights, his time in Uzès inspiring him to write his only comedy, *Les Plaideurs.*

The town was used as one of the locations for Jean-Paul Rappeneau's recent film version of *Cyrano de Bergerac* starring Gérard Depardieu.

- **EVENTS** • In the last three weeks of July, a **festival of classical and modern music** takes place. • Amusing **country fairs** are held in place aux Herbes: first Saturday in February, a **pig fair**; second Saturday in April, a **spring fair**; June 24, a **garlic fair**; first and second Saturday in August, a **wine fair**; August 14, a **general fair**; October 11, a **sheep fair**; November 17, a **horse and poultry fair**.

WHAT TO SEE IN UZÈS

The many lovely buildings around the Château du Duché include the 12thC **Tour de l'Horloge**; the **Hôtel Dampmartin**, with its round tower, Renaissance facade and elegant staircase; the 18thC **Hôtel de Ville**, with a fine courtyard; the **Crypte**, where one low relief figure has glass eyes; and the 18thC colonnaded **Hôtel du Baron de Castille**.

Across the road from here is the former **Cathédrale of St-Théodorit** (17thC), with a fine organ. It is flanked by a spectacular 12thC campanile, the **Tour Fenestrelle** (☆) — all that remains of the Romanesque cathedral destroyed by the Huguenots. This circular six-story tower is unique in France, although of a kind familiar in N Italy. From the **promenade Jean-Racine** to the s (so called because the dramatist spent part of his youth in Uzès) there is a good view over the valley.

Place aux Herbes (☆) in the Old Town is a pretty square, with broad stone arcades, plane trees and a small fountain. Just to the s, in avenue

Foch, **Muséon di Rodo** (⬛ ⬛ *closed Tues, Easter-Oct, open Sun pm only Oct-Easter*) is a vintage car and model railway museum.

- **MARKET** There is a market on Saturday in place aux Herbes.

Château du Duché 🏛 ☆

⬛ ✗ *available. Open 10am–noon, 2.30–5pm (6.30pm May–Sept). Closed Mon.*
The duke's flag flies proudly in the red and gold Occitan colors on the massive turreted castle. The building is a mixture of several different epochs and styles, as is clear on entering the courtyard. On the left is the 11thC *donjon*, the **Tour Bermonde**; next to it, the 14thC **Tour de la Vicomté**; on the right, the stately Renaissance facade of the living quarters (pictured on page 30). The chapel is Gothic, but the roof of colored tiles, emblazoned with the ducal crest, is a 19thC addition.

❧ ☰ CHÂTEAU D'ARPAILLARGUES: HÔTEL D'AGOULT 🏛 ⬛

Arpaillargues, 30700 Uzès ☎ *66-22-14-48* 🖷 *66-22-56-10* 🎴 *to* 🎴 *27 rms* ⬛ ⬛ ☰ 🅰🄴 ⊙ ⊙ 🎴 ⬛ ⚅ ☐ ⬛ ⚘ 《 ∾ ♨ ⚓ *Closed mid-Nov to mid-Mar.*
Location: In its own park, 5 km (3 miles) w of Uzès. The stately 18thC château d'Arpaillargues belonged to the d'Agoult family (hence the double name), from which came Liszt's lover, Marie d'Agoult. Today it is a luxurious country hotel, furnished with antiques, stylishly managed. A sophisticated clientele comes here to enjoy the tennis and the large swimming pool, the views over the rolling hills, and the well-stocked library.

On fine days, meals (☐ ⬛ ⚓ *closed Wed, mid-Oct to mid-Mar, last orders 9.30pm)* are served by the pool or on the lovely terrace. On cooler days, a log fire is lit in the baronial dining-hall. Elegance reigns supreme, and the cuisine makes a fair bid to compete with the setting, though quality can be erratic. *Specialities: Terrine de saumon aux poireaux, volaille de Bresse au Gigondas.*

❧ ☰ ENTRAIGUES

Pl. de l'Évêché, 30700 Uzès ☎ *66-22-32-68* 🖷 *66-22-57-01* 🎴 *19 rms* ⬛ 🅰🄴 ⊙ ⊙ 🎴 ☐ ⬛ ⚘ ⚓ *Open all year.*

Location: Central, in a narrow street of the Old Town. The owner of the CHÂTEAU D'ARPAILLARGUES saw scope for a cheaper hotel in Uzès, and converted this 15th–16thC mansion, once the home of a general. The result is supremely aesthetic, although hardly cozy; soft-hued stone, bare floors, and dimly-lit low-vaulted ceilings. And the hotel is enclosed, with not much of a view. Bedrooms are carpeted and attractively decorated in creams and browns. The food is deliberately simple: grills, salads, a *plat du jour,* served under 17thC beams.

❧ Other hotels: **Le Mas d'Oléandre** *(Saint-Médiers, 30700 Uzès, 6km/ 4 miles NW of Uzès via D981* ☎ *66-22-63-43* 🎴 *closed mid-Oct to May, no cards).* A peaceful, simple and very prettily located hotel, with a swimming pool but no restaurant (some rooms have kitchenettes). **Hostellerie Le Castellas** *(Grand Rue, 30210, Collias, 8km/5 miles SE via D981* ☎ *66-22-88-88* 🖷 *66-22-84-28* 🎴 *closed Jan-Mar).* An extremely comfortable, well-appointed and decorated hotel converted from two 19thC houses, with many period features. There is a pool, and the restaurant *(closed Wed out of season)* is reputable, with a good cellar.

PLACES NEAR UZÈS

To the s of Uzès is **Garrigues** country, typical of the southern foothills of the Cévennes. *Garrigues* are low limestone hills, covered with sparse foliage. The 13thC **Pont St-Nicolas**, 10 kilometers (6 miles) s of Uzès on the D979, is in a most attractive spot. At the **Moulin de**

Charlier, near Arpaillargues *(5km/3 miles w of Uzès)* is the **Musée 1900,** a collection of artifacts from that era.

The region is well known for its pottery and ceramics, best found at **St-Quentin-la-Poterie,** NE of Uzès. Some parts of the fortified **Château de Castelnau** *(on a rocky spur 19 kilometers (11½ miles) w of Uzès via the D982)* date from the 12thC, others from the 17th and 19thC. There is a stunning view, and rooms furnished in various period styles.

VAISON-LA-ROMAINE ☆

*Map 5B6 (Vaucluse). 47km (30 miles) NE of Avignon. Postal code: 84110. Population: 5,900 **i** pl. du Chanoine-Sautel ☎90-36-02-11.*

Some of the most fascinating reminders of the Roman occupation in France can be found at Vaison. Even in pre-Roman days it was a town of importance, the capital of a civilized Ligurian tribe, the Voconces. When the Romans took over, they developed it, as Vasio Vacontiorum, into one of the wealthiest places in Gallia Narbonensis. As excavations reveal, it was a residential center with luxurious patrician villas, rather than a city of large public building such as ORANGE or ARLES.

At the beginning of the Christian era, Vaison became a major religious center, and later an important bishopric. The envy of the powerful Counts of Toulouse was aroused, and in the 12thC, they seized the church's territory and built their own castle on the hill across the river. In the 13th and 14thC, the population would take refuge here from marauders, and gradually a medieval town grew up on the castle slopes. Later the inhabitants drifted back, and built the present 18th and 19thC town on the N bank, beside the Roman quarter.

So Vaison today consists of three distinct entities, from three epochs; and they are not, as has happened at NÎMES and FRÉJUS, jumbled on top of one another. This has made it easier to excavate the Roman town, where, as at Pompeii, a life-style now lies revealed.

Tourism in Vaison took a knock in September 1992, as a number of people died when the river Ouvèze overflowed its banks during heavy storms. But such occurrences happen once in a lifetime.

- **EVENTS** • In March, a regional **automobile rally**. • In April and May, a biennial **print show**. • In early July, an **international folklore festival**. • In mid-July to September, a **theater and music festival** in the Roman theater. • In August, every third year (next one in 1995), a **choral festival** at Séguret. • First Sunday after August 15, **Provençal festival**. • December 24, **Provençal mystery play** and Midnight Mass.
- **MARKET** There is a market on Tuesday mornings.

WHAT TO SEE IN VAISON

You can buy one ticket to visit all the major monuments.

- ✗ The same ticket also entitles you to join a guided tour if you wish. There is one a day in winter, from the tourist office, normally leaving at 11am. In spring and autumn there are two a day, and five a day in summer; check times with the tourist office.

  English-language tours are only available in July and August.

Haute Ville

This is the medieval part of Vaison, across the river, where terraces of narrow, cobbled streets line the hillside below the castle. By the middle of this century, the quarter was derelict and almost empty; now it has been revived, thanks to the vogue for restoring old Provençal houses as summer homes.

The lower part, by the river, is still in decay; but the upper streets, such as rue des Fours, are now most elegant, with their flowerpots, vines and neatly renovated facades. From here a steep path leads up to the 12thC **château**: it is empty and closed, but from beside it there is a stunning view over Mont Ventoux and the Ouvèze valley.

Notre-Dame, Ancienne Cathédrale de Ⅲ †

Av. Jules-Ferry. Closed noon–2pm.

The former cathedral stands by itself to the w of Quartier La Villasse. It is 12thC Romanesque, austerely graceful, built on the clearly visible foundations of a 6thC Merovingian church. The marble high altar, table-shaped, is pre-Romanesque, and behind the present apse are traces of an arcaded 6thC apse.

The attractive cloister now houses a small museum of early Christian art *(opening times as the RUINES ROMAINES).*

Les Ruines Romaines Ⅲ ☆

✗ *available. Open Mar–May, Sept, Oct 9.30am–12.30pm, 2–5.45pm; June–Aug 9am–12.30pm, 2–6.45pm; Nov–Feb 10am–noon, 2–4.30pm.*

Two areas in the Roman town have been excavated: the Puymin quarter and the Villasse quarter. The former is just E of the tourist office, the latter nearer the river, by the post office.

Quartier de Puymin   The **Maison des Messii**, the home of a rich local family, has mosaic floors and tall columns. Its layout, with atrium, salon, baths, latrines and kitchen, is clearly discernible. Next door, the **Portique de Pompée** is an elegant colonnade with three statues; once it had a central garden with paving, murals and many more statues. Beyond are the remains of servants' and common people's houses; and above it is the **Nymphée**, a covered basin above a spring that supplied the town's water.

Nearby, a Roman tunnel leads to the theater, built on the hillside facing N, away from the town. The stage, of which little survives, was cut out of the rock; the amphitheater, better preserved, retains its rear colonnade.

The modern **museum** (☆) *(open Nov–Mar 10am–noon, 2–4.30pm; Apr–June, Sept, Oct 10am–1pm, 2.30–6.15pm; July–Aug 10am–1pm, 2.30–7.30pm),* which contains the main finds from the local excavations, is superbly laid out, with full details in French, English and German. Look out for the marble statue of an armor-clad emperor (thought to be Domitian); statues of Hadrian and his wife Sabina; the silver bust of the owner of the villa in the Villasse quarter; and a delightful double-faced statuette, one side a laughing satyr, the other a bearded noble. The collection of coins, ceramics and utensils gives some idea of the daily life of the times.

Quartier de la Villasse   Here is a central street with pavements parallel to a narrower colonnaded street that was once lined with shops. Next door is the huge **Maison de la Buste en Argent**, an elegant villa with paved hall, baths and peristyle. Behind it are vestiges of hanging gardens. To the w, the **Maison du Dauphin** is similar in style.

❀❧ ☎   **LE BEFFROI** ❀
Rue de l'Évêché, Haute Ville, 84110
Vaison-la-Romaine ☎*90-36-04-71*
🖼*90-36-24-78* 🔳 *20 rms* 🛏 AE 💿 🔲
📺 🔳 🖼 ⟨⟩ 🌿 *Closed Jan to*
mid-Mar.
Location: In the medieval part of town,
up a steep cobbled street, beside an old
belfry. No charm has been lost in converting this 16thC mansion with beamed ceilings and uneven stone floors into a comfortable, if rather folksy, little hotel. The plumbing is modern, but the antique furnishings are genuine. Informal family atmosphere, and good views from some of the rooms.

Meals (🔳 ■■ 🍴 *closed Mon, Tues lunch (except July–Aug), Jan to mid-Mar, last orders 9.30pm)* are served in the cheerful red and yellow dining-room or on the panoramic terrace. Try the *râble de lapereau à l'estragon* or *filet de pintade de la Drôme en demi-croûte.*

PLACES NEAR VAISON
Dentelles de Montmirail *(approx. 13km/8 miles s of Vaison).* The outer foothills of the Ventoux range have formed sharp, spiky crests — hence the name, meaning lace point. The lower slopes of this range are covered in gorse, and oak and pine forests, and make splendid terrain for hiking.

Séguret *(10km/6 miles sw of Vaison).* On the edge of the Dentelles de Montmirail, this is a tiny village of cobbled streets, beneath a steep rock. It has a 12thC church and a fine 15thC fountain. On the plain to the w and sw lie the vineyards of some of the best Rhône Valley *appellations,* including Gigondas.

■■ ❀❧   **LA TABLE DU COMTAT**
Séguret, 84110 Vaison-la-Romaine
☎*90-46-91-49* 🖼*90-46-94-01* 🔳 ■■ 🛏
🔳 ■■ 🍴 💿 🔲 📺 *Closed Tues dinner*
and Wed (except July–Aug); late Nov to
early Dec. Last orders 9pm.
The house is 15thC, finely converted, and the setting is spectacular: on a steep hill above the Rhône vineyards, with splendid views of the valley and of the jagged peaks of the Dentelles de Montmirail. Fully worthy of this setting, the cooking by *patron* M. Gomez is among the best in the region, and is well-priced for its quality. *Specialities: Coq au vin de Gigondas, millefeuille de saumon à l'oseille, gigot d'agneau en croûte.*

The Comtat also has eight cozy bedrooms (🔳) and the advantage of a swimming pool.

VENTOUX, MONT
Map 5C6 (Vaucluse). 63km (40 miles) NE of Avignon.

Mont Ventoux's lonely, lofty pyramid, 1,900 meters (6,260 feet) high, dominates the E side of the Rhône valley and is visible for a number of miles. It is the tallest southwestern spur of Europe's alpine massif, and is Provence's highest peak apart from the Alps themselves, 16 kilometers (10 miles) away to the E on the Italian frontier.

Beside the panorama point on the summit (⟨⟩) are a meteorological station, a TV transmitter and a military radar post. Good roads lead up, both from CARPENTRAS or VAISON-LA-ROMAINE to the W, and from **Sault** to the E. The drive is well worth it, for this is the greatest viewpoint in all Provence, if not in France. The whole region lies before you, from the higher Alps to Marseille and the Cévennes: on a very clear day you can even make out the Pyrénées, 257 kilometers (160 miles) away. At night, lighthouses flash along the coast.

In summer, the best time to ascend is early morning or late afternoon, for at midday the summit is often wrapped in haze. In winter, skies may be clearer, but the Mistral howls as ferociously as the name ("Windy Mount") implies. In winter, there is skiing at **Chalet-Reynard** and **Mont-Serein**; in July, some years, the Tour de France sends cyclists panting to the top.

The slopes are cloaked in the usual Provençal foliage, but near the summit are alpine flowers and even polar ones, such as the hairy poppy of Greenland.

PLACES NEAR MONT VENTOUX
Bédoin *(at the foot of Mont Ventoux)*. A picturesque village with a 12thC chapel and an interesting church. There is a very lively **market** (with live jazz) every Monday.

Gorges de la Nesque *(8–24km/5–15 miles SW of Sault)*. The gorges are deep, wild and dramatic. A good road runs along the N cliff, with parking points for views over the gorge and the jagged **rocher de Cire** on the S side. Both S and SW from here stretches the limestone **Plateau de Vaucluse**, pitted with some 200 caves, and a paradise for speleologists. The S edge of the plateau dominates the Coulon valley (see GORDES and APT).

Sault *(18km/12 miles SE)*. A village on a rocky spur above the Nesque valley, known for its lavender and honey. Its 12thC church has a finely vaulted Romanesque nave.

• See also: CARPENTRAS, VAISON-LA-ROMAINE.

VILLENEUVE-LÈS-AVIGNON ☆
Map 4D4 (Gard). 3km (2 miles) NW of Avignon. Postal code: 30400. Population: 10,750 ℹ *1 pl. Charles David* ☎*90-25-61-33.*

Villeneuve lies directly across the Rhône from AVIGNON (*lès* in French place-names means "near"). The French kings used it as a fortress town in the 13th–15thC, when the river was the frontier between France and independent Provence to the E: this explains the presence of its two great military posts, the Fort of St-André and the Tower of Philippe le Bel. But this did not prevent the cardinals of the 14thC, when the Popes ruled in Avignon, from turning "foreign" Villeneuve into a wealthy residential suburb. Finding their own city overcrowded, they built 15 grandiose mansions *(livrées)* here. Only two survive, one of them in rue de la République.

Today this is a quiet little town with some splendid buildings, notably the great Charterhouse *(chartreuse)*. The **Tour de Philippe le Bel** *(admission details as for MUSÉE MUNICIPAL)*, on a rock above the river, was begun in 1293 and its watchtower added in the 14thC. There are excellent views from the top, especially of AVIGNON and the great Palais des Papes, best seen in the late afternoon sun. The **Fort St-André**, late 14thC, is a fine example of medieval military architecture, with its twin round towers and proud gateway. From here too there are marvelous views.

- **EVENT** In July, the **International Summer Festival** takes place all month in the Chartreuse, with ancient and modern music, dancing, theater, poetry, art exhibitions, and workshops. There are also **cultural exhibitions**, which continue until the end of September. For details apply to Centre National des Écritures du Spectacle *(BP 30, 30400 Villeneuve-lès-Avignon* ☎ *90-25-05-46* 🖷 *90-25-05-46).*

- **MARKET** There is a market in place Charles David on Thursday mornings.

WHAT TO SEE IN VILLENEUVE

Chartreuse du Val de Bénédiction 🏛 ✝ ☆
Rue de la République 🚌 *Open Apr–Oct 9am–6.30pm; Nov–Mar 9.30am–5.30pm.*

Covering six acres, this is the largest charterhouse, or Carthusian monastery, in France, founded in 1356 by Pope Innocent VI. In its heyday, it housed hundreds of monks of the Carthusian Order, with its strict emphasis on solitary prayer. After the Revolution, the monks were evicted and their huge monastery was sold by lots.

Today it is being restored, and has an odd variety of uses. The SW sector inside the main entrance, including the largest cloister, is today a municipal housing property, full of shops and apartments. The sector to the E and N, containing the main religious buildings, is owned by the State, which runs it both as a historic monument and as a scientific and cultural center, popular for seminars. So, on your visit, you are quite likely to find, say, doctors or engineers sipping aperitifs beside the tomb of the Pope. It is a little unnerving.

Here, everything is very well laid out and documented, with explanatory panels in French, English and German, and pictures and diagrams of the life of the monastery in its prime. The highlights are the graceful **tomb of Innocent VI** with its white marble effigy, the 14thC **frescoes** by Matteo Giovanetti in the chapel of Innocent VI, the two **cloisters**, and the **monks' quarters** with washhouse, bakery and barbershop.

The cultural center mounts theatrical, musical and other artistic events throughout the year.

Municipal, Musée ☆
Rue de l'Hôpital 🚌 🅿 *Apr–Sept 10am–12.30pm, 3–7.30pm; Oct–Mar 10am–noon, 2–5pm. Closed Tues (mid-Sept to mid-June); Feb.*

Many of the items in the small museum, housed on the first floor of a 17thC palace, are from the CHARTREUSE: for example, a 17thC cupboard, made by the monks, the doors of which have rich paneling on their inner sides. In the same room, a 17thC engraving shows the completed

Pont St-Bénézet at AVIGNON soon before its destruction. Among the best of the paintings are a *Crucifixion* by de Champaigne, an *Entombment* by de Châlon, and a gruesome Mignard, depicting the monks being summarily hanged.

The museum's treasure is a painting of great power that stays vividly in mind. It is the *Coronation of the Virgin* (✪) by Enguerrand Quarton (or Charonton), often regarded as the masterpiece of the 15thC Avignon School. At the center are The Virgin, Father and Son, all in robes of gold and crimson. Flanking them are worshipers, in strict hierarchy: saints, prophets, popes, kings and commoners. In a Flemish-influenced landscape (the artist was from Laon, in Picardy) of mountains and cities kneels the white-robed figure of St-Bruno, founder of the Carthusian Order. Below is a panorama of hell, the devil and the damned.

Notre-Dame †

Pl. J. Meissonier 🔲*to sacristy. For entry, ring bell on left of altar. Opening details as for* MUSÉE MUNICIPAL.

Founded in 1333, the church — once the chapel of a *livrée* — has paintings by the Avignon artists de Champaigne and the Mignards, and a marble relief of *Christ Entombed* on the 18thC high altar. Its chief glory is in the sacristy: a 14thC polychrome ivory statuette of *The Virgin and Child* (✪) richly carved from an elephant's tusk. The line of the statuette follows the curve of the tusk, which is why the Virgin is leaning uncomfortably sideways.

☙   L'ATELIER ❀

5 rue de la Foire, 30400 Villeneuve-lès-Avignon ☎*90-25-01-84* 📠*90-25-80-06* 🔲 *26 rms* AE 🔘 💲 🎦 🚾 🖂 🔲 🖃 ⚓ *Closed Nov–Mar.*

Location: Central, in a side street of the Old Town. A quiet and gracious hotel in a 16thC building, although some may find its enclosed position and severity a little oppressive. The large bedrooms have beamed ceilings and antique furniture; the lounge has bare stone walls and a log fire. At the back, there's a paved patio with fig trees, where breakfasts are served.

☙ 🚃   LA MAGNANERAIE

37 rue Camp de Bataille, 30400 Villeneuve-lès-Avignon ☎*90-25-11-11* 📠*90-25-46-37* 🔲 *to* 🔲 *27 rms* 🖃 🖂 AE 🔘 💲 🖂 🔲 🖂 ⚓ ✿ ❄ ⚓ ≋ ♒ ☕ 🖃 🍷

Location: On the fringe of town, across the river from Avignon on the Nîmes road. This hotel, in a 15thC former *livrée,* has been improved over the years and is now a relaxed spot with a spa-

cious, immaculately tended garden (where you can have breakfast or lunch), a large pool and tennis courts. Some of the views down to Villeneuve are lovely. A modern annex adjoins the old building. The dining room, which opens onto the garden, is most elegant, and Gérard Prayal's cuisine (he trained with Roger Vergé) vies with the more expensive PRIEURÉ as the best in town.

☙   LE PRIEURÉ ⌂

Pl. du Chapître, 30400 Villeneuve-lès-Avignon ☎*90-25-18-20* 📠*90-25-45-39* 🔲 *to* 🔲 *36 rms* 🖃 ⚓ 🖂 🚃 AE 🔘 💲 🚾 🖂 ✈ 🔲 ✿ ≋ ♒ 🍴 *Closed Nov to mid-Mar.*

Location: Central, in a side street close to the church. Most amenities of a country hotel are available at this center-of-town converted 16thC priory: swimming pool and lido, tennis courts, shady patio and a beautiful garden. Bedrooms in the old building have tiled floors and antiques; those in the modern annex, **l'Atrium,** are larger and more expensive, with deep, comfort-

able sofas and wide loggias.
(See ⇌ below.)

✑ Choose also from: **Résidence Les Cèdres** *(39 av. Pasteur-Bellevue* ☎ *90-25-43-92* Fx *90-25-14-66* ▢ *to* ▥ *closed mid-Nov to mid-Mar)*, a 17thC building, surrounded by cedar trees, with a restaurant (dinner only) and pool; **Beauséjour** *(61 av. Gabriel Péri* ☎ *90-25-20-56* ▢ *to* ▥ *closed Jan)*, a good budget choice.

⇌ **LE PRIEURÉ** ⬗
Pl. du Chapître ☎*90-25-18-20* ▥▥ *to* ▥▥
▢ ■ ⇌ ⊕ ⟿ AE ⊙ ⓒ VISA Closed

Nov to mid-Mar. Last orders 9.30pm.
Everything is perhaps a little too slick for any lasting impressions to shine through, and although the mainly classic food with modern touches is good, the prices are high. But it's a joy to eat on the lawn at lunch, or in the beamed dining room in the evening, and Ronald Searle's hilarious illustration on the menu will keep you happily amused until the food (very quickly) arrives. Try Serge Chenet's lobster and prawn lasgne, or pigeon with a *foie gras mille-feuille*. Desserts are also much to be recommended.

(See ✑ opposite.)

• See also: AVIGNON, BEAUCAIRE, ORANGE.

Western Côte d'Azur and the central hinterland

A 128-kilometer (80-mile) stretch of fascinating coast, mostly in the Var *département*. **CASSIS** and **BANDOL** are the best of the resorts to the west: visit the creeks *(calanques)* near Cassis. **TOULON**, France's leading naval base, is unexpectedly absorbing and strikingly located, with grandiose scenery to its north. Off the coast farther east lie the lovely islands of Hyères (see **HYERES, ÎLES D'**), which can be visited by boat.

The Maures coast, between Toulon and **FRÉJUS**, is beautiful too, backed by the wooded **MAURES MASSIF**. The most famous of its resorts is the flamboyant **ST-TROPEZ**, a former byword for the sybaritic life. In its hinterland are some smartly restored hill-villages. And don't miss **PORT-GRIMAUD**, that modern miracle of pastiche. **FRÉJUS** is worth a visit, for its cathedral ensemble and its Roman ruins.

There is a broad swath of attractive hill country to be found to the east of the north–south line marked by **AIX-EN-PROVENCE**, **MONTAGNE DU LUBÉRON** and **MONT VENTOUX**, and inland from **TOULON** and **ST-TROPEZ**: you can reach any part easily in one- or two-day trips from these or other towns.

It has, first of all, some splendid scenery: the **GRAND CANYON DU VERDON**, the haunting **MASSIF DE LA SAINTE-BAUME**, and picturesque **ENTREVAUX** and the **Cians gorges**. Farther north is more fine country, all the way to **SISTERON** and its stern citadel in the remote Alpes-de-Haute-Provence *département*.

It contains, too, some lovely and interesting buildings: the 12thC Cistercian sister abbey of **THORONET**, the abbey at **ST-MAXIMIN-LA-SAINTE-BAUME**, and some oddities such as the museum in the castle at **Entrecasteaux** devoted to the work of the Scottish Surrealist Ian McGarvie-Munn.

AGAY

Map 13G13 (Var). 9km (5½ miles) E of St-Raphael. Postal code: 83700 St-Raphael
i blvd. Mer, N98 ☎94-82-01-85.

An animated bathing resort on the Esterel coast, set in a deep bay with gently sloping sides crowned by the red crags of the Rastel d'Agay. The bay makes a perfect anchorage, and Roman pottery dug up from the seabed indicates that it has harbored boats for well over 2,000 years. A long, sandy beach curves around the bay, and there are several smaller creeks and coves.

At **Le Dramont**, 1 kilometer (½ mile) to the sw, a slab by the main road marks the landing at this spot of the 36th US Infantry Division on August 15, 1944. To the E of Le Dramont beach is a headland surmounted by a semaphore from where there is a spectacular view of the coast and the red Esterel massif behind.

Agay is very much a place for families rather than high life or nightlife.

- **EVENT**   There is a **fête** during the last weekend of July.
- **MARKET**   There is a market every Wednesday morning.

☙   BEAU SITE
Camp-Long, Agay, 83700 St-Raphael
☎94-82-00-45 ⧉94-82-71-02 ▭ 20
rms ⬛⬛⬛⬛⬛⬛⬛⬛⬛⬛⬛
Closed Nov to mid-Dec.
Location: Just s of Agay, across the main road from an attractive sandy cove. A neat, German-owned *pension;* most guests are German. The leafy forecourt has a replica of Brussels' *Manneken Pis.* No lunches.

☙   SOL E MAR
Le Dramont, Route de la Corniche d'Or, 83700 St-Raphael ☎94-95-25-60 ▭ 45
rms ⬛⬛⬛⬛⬛⬛⬛⬛⬛⬛⬛⬛⬛
Location: Right by the sea at Le Dramont, 1.5 kilometers (1 mile) sw of Agay. A very comfortable hotel, and

relatively secluded. There is a superb view from its panoramic restaurant, which has a sliding sun-roof. The pleasant rooms have balconies facing the sea. Amenities include two seawater swimming pools, solarium, and a well-equipped private beach.

⧋ NEARBY

LES FLOTS BLEUS ☙
Anthéor, 4km (2½ miles) E of Agay
☎94-44-80-21 ▭ ▭ ⬛ ⬛ *Closed mid-Oct to Feb; Mon from Mar–May and Sept–Oct. Last orders 9pm.*
Here are some reasonable fish soups, as well as tasty local fish dishes. A good place to stop for lunch, where you can eat under plane trees on a pleasant outdoor terrace in summer.

- See also: FRÉJUS, ST-RAPHAEL.

ANNOT

*Map **14**D12 (Alpes-de-H.-P.). 32km (20 miles) NE of Castellane. Postal code: 04240. Population: 1,050 ℹ pl. du Revely ☎92-82-23-03 (winter), 92-83-21-40 (summer); inquiries also at Mairie ☎92-83-22-09.*

Annot has attracted many painters, for this graceful little town has much charm and is one of the most pleasant summer resorts of the eastern hinterland. Stroll down the winding, neatly paved alleys of the Old Town, full of little streams, ancient archways and tall Renaissance houses. The main square, archetypally Provençal, is shaded by lofty old plane trees. Annot lies in a valley that in summer is full of scents and colors: lilac and lavender, lime and chestnut. The hills close by, easily reached on foot, are famous for their curious sandstone rock formations, eroded into bizarre shapes.

☙⧋   AUBERGE LA CIGALE
Blvd. St-Pierre, 04240 Annot
☎92-83-20-24 ▭ 8 rms ▭ ⬛ ⬛
Location: 30 meters from the main square of the town. A simple but sympathetic little country inn, with two dining-rooms, a room for dancing and a terrace where meals are served in sum-

mer. Helpings here are generous. *Specialities: Pâté de truite, filet de sanglier ou de chevreuil (in season).*

☙   HONNARATY
Les Scaffarels, 04240 Annot
☎92-83-22-03 ▭ 12 rms ⬛ ⧋
Closed mid-Dec to Feb.

Location: 2 kilometers (1¼ miles) from Annot on the Nice road. A modest family hotel but with comfortable rooms. There is a serviceable restaurant with a choice of two inexpensive menus (🍴).

✎ Other simple hotels in Annot: **Avenue** *(av. de la Gare* ☎*92-83-22-07* 🅵🆇*92-83-34-07* 🖤*)* and **Beauséjour** *(pl. du Revely* ☎*92-83-21-08* 🖤*).*

PLACES NEAR ANNOT

Méailles *(8km/5 miles NW of Annot).* This is an attractive hilltop village, beyond which there are good views from the **Col de la Colle-St-Michel**, leading into the upper Verdon valley toward COLMARS.

To the E of Annot, along the N202, lies ENTREVAUX; to the SW is the GRAND CANYON DU VERDON.

• See also: CASTELLANE; COLMARS; ENTREVAUX; VERDON, GRAND CANYON DU.

BANDOL

Map 11I9 (Var). 17km (11 miles) W of Toulon. Postal code: 83150. Population: 7,450 **i** *Allées Vivien* ☎*94-29-41-35.*

Bandol is a delightful and sophisticated resort with a style of its own; it has sandy coves, a lively yachting and fishing harbor, and an elegant, palm-lined promenade with a fashionable café. The only blemishes are the ugly new row of concrete vacation apartments on the hill behind, and an unsightly modern casino. A very attractive resort during the fall and early winter, when the crowds have departed.

• **EVENT** There is a colorful **wine festival** in the town, usually during the first Sunday in December.

WHAT TO SEE IN BANDOL
Jardin Éxotique et Parc Zoologique ☆

Beside the B52 autoroute, 3km (2 miles) NE of Bandol (clearly signposted) ▰▰ ✿
Open 8am–noon, 2–7pm in summer. Closed Sun mornings.

Not a large zoo, but arguably the most attractive and well-kept of the dozen or so on the Côte. The animals look happy and well-cared-for. They share their habitat with a variety of exotic plants and pretty trees, spread across a carefully landscaped garden.

There are no large animals here, but plenty of small species such as monkeys and lemurs, as well as brightly-colored birds; and there are puppy-like Saharan fennec foxes, with their big ears, and, often to be found rolling in the mud, two charmingly hideous Vietnamese pigs called Romeo and Juliet.

✎ **ÎLE ROUSSE** 🏨
Blvd. Louis-Lumière, 83150 Bandol
☎*94-29-46-86* 🅵🆇*94-29-49-49* 🖤 *55 rms* ▤▤ ◛ ⇌ 🅰🅴 ◉ ⓪ 🎞 ⌂ ✦ ⅙ ▢
▣ ⇜ ⩙ ⛵ 🏊

Location: On a narrow isthmus, just off the town center. This is a stylish, luxury vacation hotel in a modern idiom: every amenity is on hand, and soft pop music plays in the spacious *salon.* The bedrooms are in period style, some with four-poster beds, but the decor is not always very new.

The restaurant, **Les Oliviers**, in a not overly-enticing room, tends to err on the ambitious side. In summer there are two cheaper restaurants on the beach.

☙ MASTER HÔTEL
Rue Raimu, 83150 Bandol ☎94-29-46-53
[Fx]94-32-53-54 ▥ *20 rms* ⬛️ 🚗 🔌 ▨
⬛️ ▢ 📷 ☕ ⚓ ⛄ 🍴 🛎

*Location: On a cliff, 45 meters (150
feet) above the beach, in the quiet w
part of the town.* This beguiling beach
hotel was built as a private villa by the
great Provençal actor Raimu. The hotel's
former name, Ker-Mocotte, was his
own in-joke, for his wife came from
Brittany, where *ker* means "house,"
while *mocotte* is Provençal slang for
inhabitants of Toulon, Raimu's home
town. In summer there are *soirées* for
the residents, while water sports are on
hand at the hotel's private beach (children can be left with a trained *moniteur*).

☙   Other good hotels in Bandol include: **La Baie** *(62 rue Docteur-Marçon*
☎94-29-40-82 ▥), **Les Galets**
(2km/1 mile E of town ☎94-29-43-46
[Fx]94-32-50-39 ▥) and **Provençal**
(rue des Écoles ☎94-29-52-11 [Fx]94-
29-67-57 ▥ *to*▥).

☙   Hotel nearby: **Frégate** *(Route de
Bandol, 83270 St-Cyr-sur-Mer* ☎94-
29-39-39 [Fx]94-29-39-40 ▥) is a
very good, brand-new hotel with an
emphasis on sporting activities: a gym,
riding, tennis and golf.

🍴   Some decent restaurants are:
Auberge du Port *(9 Allée Jean-Moulin*
☎94-29-42-63 ▥), **Parc** *(Corniche
Bonaparte* ☎94-32-36-36 ▢ *to*▥)
and **Réserve** *(Route de Sanary* ☎94-
29-30-00 ▥).

🌙 NIGHTLIFE IN BANDOL
Bars   Two bars are worth mentioning. • **Tchin-Tchin** *(Allée Jean-
Moulin)* is a highly sophisticated place, with soft lights and a smart
clientele. Whiskey, champagne and cocktails are the only drinks
served; also *foie gras* and caviar. • **Le Bistrot du Port** (near the
Mairie) is a bar with a lively terrace and a jolly atmosphere.
Clubs   There is a nightclub, **Stars Circus**, at the Casino. • Another,
much in vogue, is the **Maï Taï**, on the Sanary road *(reservations advised).*
Casino   The casino itself *(*☎94-32-45-44, *open 4pm-4am daily)* has
the usual blackjack and roulette tables, as well as craps.

SPORTS AND ACTIVITIES IN BANDOL
Auto racing   **Circuit Paul Ricard**, *(18km/12 miles N of Bandol, just
off N8).* Auto racing is one of the great passions of Paul Ricard, who
has built the best track in Provence; it stages several major races each
year, notably the **Moto Journal 200** (early April) and the **Bold d'Or**
(mid-September). Nearly every weekend there is an event of some
kind. The circuit also includes a **museum of vintage racing cars**, and
a **karting center**. Anyone can run his own car or motorcycle on the
track for an hourly fee. For details contact **Circuit Paul Ricard** *(83330
Le Beausset* ☎94-93-55-19).
Amusement park   **OK Corral** *(RN8 Cuges-les-Pins, 28km/17 miles N
of Bandol* ⬛️ 💺 ⚑ *open daily Apr-Sept 10am-6.30pm, Mar-Oct Wed,
Sat, Sun only, closed Nov-Feb).* A Dutch-owned amusement park with
ghost train, Wild West train, shooting galleries, big wheel etc., as well
as live shows where actors play out the exploits of Buffalo Bill and
other heroes. Plenty of excitement, and fun for kids.
Water sports   Bandol has a number of diving clubs including **Lato-
niccia Club** *(200 blvd. des Graviers* ☎94-29-76-59); *also* **Centre de**

Plongée *(2 blvd. Victor Hugo* ☎*94-29-41-57)*. • For sea fishing, there is the **Sport Fishing Club** *(3 rue Pierre Toesca* ☎*94-29-53-15)*. • For sailing, try the **Société Nautique de Bandol** *(* ☎*94-29-42-26)*.

Tennis/cycling/riding   Make contact with the **Tennis Club de Bandol** *(av. Albert 1ᵉʳ* ☎*94-29-55-40)*. • For details of local cycling trips and riding stables, ask at the tourist office.

PLACES NEAR BANDOL

Bendor, Île de *(frequent boat trips from Bandol)*. This tiny island just 2 kilometers (1 mile) from Bandol was rocky and deserted until 1955, when it was bought by Paul Ricard, the flamboyant *pastis* tycoon. He transformed it into a tourist-cum-cultural center.

The boat moors beside an imitation Provençal fishing port, a miniature forerunner of PORT-GRIMAUD. Close by is an "artisans' village" with potters, jewelers and lacquer painters. There is also an excellent art gallery, devoted to exhibitions of contemporary artists. However, the island's *pièce de résistance* is its **World Museum of Wines and Spirits** *(* ☒ *closed Wed)*, which has a collection of wines from 50 nations, and a fine array of glasses.

Paul Ricard has a villa on Bendor, and his island is now attractively planted with pines, flowers and creepers. It has three hotels, restaurants, a convention center and a thriving **Nautical Club** *(apply to Club Nautique, Île de Bendor, 83150 Bandol* ☎*94-29-47-15)*.

✎   **DELOS** 🏨
Île de Bendor, 83150 Bandol ☎*94-32-22-23*
🖷*94-32-41-44* 🎟 to 🎟 55 rms ⊟ 𝔸𝔼
🔲 🔲 🎞 ⌂ ◻ 🖵 ⚡ ⚓ ⟨⟨ ≋ ☄ 🏊
Location: On the rocks above the sea, on the E tip of the island. Pseudo-Moorish clashes with pseudo-Classical at this bizarrely decorated 1960s hotel. If you can take the surroundings, you'll find the service attentive and the rooms comfortable. The situation is romantic, and waves lash on the rocks below.

La Cadière d'Azur *(9km/6 miles N of Bandol)*. An unspoiled hill-village where dogs laze in the sun, fountains play and beaded curtains rustle in the shop doorways. Several artists work and sell their goods here, notably **Martine Kistner** *(Route de St-Côme)*, a potter and weaver. All around is a lush landscape of vine, olive, pine and cypress, spoiled a little by the fact that the A57 runs below the village.

✎ ⊟   **HOSTELLERIE BÉRARD** ♣
Rue Gabriel Péri, 83740 La Cadière d'Azur
☎*94-90-11-43* 🖷*94-90-01-94* 🎟 to 🎟
40 rms ⌂ ⊟ 𝔸𝔼 🎞 ⚡ ⟨⟨ ≋ 🏊
⌷ ■ ⊟ *Closed Jan.*
Location: Near the village center, overlooking the valley. One of the best country hotels in the area: a 19thC auberge, (partly 10thC), with red-tiled floors and white, vaulted ceilings. The bedrooms are well modernized, especially in the annex (a converted monastery). Good Provençal cooking, charming reception and service from the family, and a log fire for spit-roasts. Very much a centre of village life.

Le Castellet *(11km/7 miles N of Bandol)*. Perched high on a hilltop, close to La Cadière, this ancient village is more a half-deserted show-piece, and less lived-in than its neighbor, whose inhabitants scorn it as not a real village. There are ramparts, a 12thC church, and the remnants of an 11thC castle. It is certainly a magnet for tourists: you can tell by the many "art" and craft stores and the two large parking lots on its outskirts.

⇌ ✑ CASTEL LUMIÈRE

Le Castellet ☎ 94-32-62-20
☒ 94-32-70-33 ▥ ☐ ▆ ⇔ Closed Sun dinner; Mon; Nov. Last orders 9.30pm (10.30pm in summer).

This is an elegant little restaurant, once upon a time the home of the Lumière brothers, pioneers of the cinema, beside the medieval gateway to the village. There are lovely views over the valley, both from the outdoor patio and from the indoor *salle* with its Provençal antique furniture. *Patron* Bernard Laffargue offers interesting Provençal cooking, which perhaps sometimes tries too hard to be different. The service and ambience are formal. There is an extensive wine list, with Provençal wines a speciality.

The restaurant also has six pleasant rooms, some with fine views (▥ 🗚🗚 ◉ 𝘝𝘐𝘚𝘈).

Embiez, Île des *(just offshore from Le Brusc)*. This 240-acre island also belongs to the Paul Ricard empire and has been developed as a sea-sports center. It has a big, modern marina for sailing and power-boats, a repair shipyard, a luxury hotel and apartments, and sports facilities. Above all, the island houses the **Fondation Océano-graphique Ricard**, a research center directed by Alain Bombard, the famous marine biologist, with a small museum and aquarium *(ⓘ Île des Embiez, 83140 Le Brusc ☎ 94-25-02-49)*.

Les Lecques *(10km/6 miles NW of Bandol)*. A family resort with a good sandy beach. **Musée le Tauroentum**, built on the foundations of a Roman villa, has 1stC mosaics and other Gallo-Roman relics.

✑ **Grand** *(☎ 94-26-23-01 ▥ to ▥)*.

Sanary *(5km/3 miles SE of Bandol)*. A pleasant sailing and fishing port, with a sandy beach and some modest family hotels. Aldous Huxley used to live here, as have many other writer and artists, and it was the home of Jacques Cousteau. The place has an unspoiled, very French feel to it: you almost expect Monsieur Hulot to come stumbling along. Farther S, **Le Brusc** is a not-too-spoiled village amid a landscape of rocky cliffs and pines.

• See also: CASSIS, TOULON.

BARJOLS

Map **12**F10 (Var). 22km (14 miles) NW of Brignoles. Postal code: 83670.
Population: 2,100 ⓘ blvd. Grisolle (summer only) ☎ 94-77-20-01, and at Mairie ☎ 94-77-07-15.

A small market town enclosed by hills, and full of fountains, running springs and shady trees. The plane tree by the town hall, 12 meters (40 feet) in circumference, is said to be the largest in France. The church, founded in 1060, rebuilt in the 16thC, has an early 12thC tympanum on its Gothic facade.

Barjols is the only town in France still making the traditional *galoubets* (three-holed flutes) and *tambourins* (narrow drums) that accompany Provençal dances.

- **EVENT**　On January 16, the **Fête de St-Marcel** is celebrated every fourth year, with dancing inside the church. • There are *boules* **tournaments** in April and June.

- **MARKETS**　There are **food** and **flower** markets on Tuesdays and Thursdays at place Capitaine Vincens.

🍴　**Pont d'Or** (🏠) *(Route St-Maximin ☎94-77-05-23 ▢).*

- See also: ST-MAXIMIN-LA-SAINTE-BAUME, SALERNES.

BRIGNOLES

Map 12G10 (Var). 57km (36 miles) E of Aix. Postal code: 83170. Population: 11,250 i pl. St-Louis ☎94-69-01-78.

Wines, bauxite and marble have brought affluence to this busy little market and industrial town on the old N7 Aix–Nice highway. It lies in a valley full of vineyards and is one of the main wine-producing centers of Provence. It is also France's leading center for bauxite extraction (2 million tons a year), and white marble has been quarried nearby since Roman times.

In the *vieille ville,* the remains of the 11thC château of the Counts of Provence today house the small **Musée du Pays Brignolais** (🖼 *closed Mon, Tues),* with a 3rdC sarcophagus. The church of **St-Sauveur** has a fine Romanesque doorway and a *Descent from the Cross* by Parrocel, much of whose work can be seen at Avignon, but who died at Brignoles.

🍴 ☴ **NEARBY**

LE MAS LA CASCADE 👄
La Celle, 83170 ☎94-69-01-49
🅵ₓ*94-69-07-17 ▢ to ▢ 10 rooms ➡*
▤ 🏠 ◻ 🖼 ☕ ♀ 🎿 *Closed Tues–Wed (except July–Aug); Feb. Last orders in ☴ 9.30pm.*
Location: on the D554, 3km (2 miles) sw of Brignoles. A charming, atmospheric family-run hotel with a small stream and waterfall running past most of the rooms. Service, whether in the large bar, with its wooden beam, or the restaurant, with its picture windows overlooking the waterfall, couldn't be friendlier. The rooms are surprisingly comfortable and well-decorated for the price, and the food is decent and unpretentious. The family keep geese and ducks, which add to the rustic charm of the place. Breakfasts are generous.

PLACE NEAR BRIGNOLES
Montagne de la Loube *(8km/5 miles SE of Brignoles).* A strenuous 70-minute walk from the D5 brings you to the summit, from where there are views of the whole region and far beyond.

- See also: THORONET, ABBAYE DU.

CASSIS

Map 11H8 (B.-du-R.). 23km (15 miles) SE of Marseille. Postal code: 13260. Population: 7,900 i pl. P-Baragnon ☎42-01-71-17.

The most westerly resort on the Côte d'Azur, and also one of the most attractive, Cassis lies secluded in a deep bay, surrounded by the high limestone cliffs and hills that give this part of the coast its distinctive character. Like ST-TROPEZ, it has kept its charm as an old fishing port, even if today it is submerged by tourists, and on weekends by Marseillais; many well-to-do Marseillais have villas on the lovely pine-clad slopes to the W of the port. Sadly, the hillside to the N is scarred by ugly new vacation apartments, but the port area is now a pedestrian zone. The **Musée Municipal** is interesting.

Cassis has often attracted artists: Dufy, Matisse and Vlaminck, among others, have painted it. The town is also known for its white wine, which has a faintly greenish tint and is ideal for drinking with the excellent local fish and shellfish.

- **EVENTS** First Sunday in September, **wine-harvest festival**.
  - July: **Music and dance festival**.

✍ 🍽 LIAUTAUD

2 rue Victor-Hugo, 13260 Cassis
☎42-01-75-37 ▦ *32 rms* ▣ ▦ ≉ ₫
▢ ▱ ⚡ ⫷ ➡ 🚗 Closed Nov to mid-Dec. For 🍽 see LIAUTAUD, below.
Location: Very central, on the quayside. A busy and friendly vacation hotel, much modernized in recent years, but run by the Liautaud family for a century. The adjoining bar-café is popular with locals, so not all bedrooms are totally quiet, but the front ones have balconies facing the harbor.

✍ LES ROCHES BLANCHES

Route de Port-Miou, 13260 Cassis
☎42-01-09-30 ▦42-01-94-23 ▦ *32 rms* ➡ 🍽 ▣ ▦ ▦ ≉ ₫ ₫ ▢ ▱ ➰
⫷ ➡ 🚗 ➡ 🎣 Closed mid-Dec to Feb.
Location: 1.5km (1 mile) SW of Cassis, alone on a rocky, pine-covered headland. A most civilized hotel, with sophisticated owners and discerning guests. This is a beautifully located, white, ivy-covered late 19thC villa (it became a hotel in the 1930s), with a spacious garden sloping down to the sea, where there is a private stone sun-terrace with diving board (no sand, deep water). There are enchanting views of the port, bay and hills from the dining room and bedrooms alike. A pity that the bedrooms' modern decor is not more alluring.

✍ Other recommended hotels:

Clos des Arômes (*10 rue Abbé Paul Mouton* ☎42-01-71-84 ▦); **Jardins du Campanile** (*rue Favier* ☎42-01-84-85 ▣42-01-32-38 ▦); **Grand Jardin** (*2 rue P-Eydin* ☎42-01-70-10 ▦); **Plage du Bestouan** (*Plage du Bestouan* ☎42-01-05-70 ▣42-01-34-82 ▦); **Rade** (*av. des Dardanelles* ☎42-01-02-97 ▦).

🍽 EL SOL

23 quai des Baux ☎42-01-76-10 ▦ ▱
◼ 🚗 ▣ ▦ Closed Wed; mid-Dec to Jan.
Last orders 11pm (summer), 10.30pm (winter).
One of the few reasonably-priced restaurants along a quayside lined with expensive ones. With rustic decor and an open terrace facing the port, it is always thronged, especially by Germans, and menus are in German as well as French. Service is rapid, the cooking average, with Provençal dishes as well as some Lyonnais and Norman ones.

🍽 LIAUTAUD

2 rue Victor-Hugo ☎42-01-75-37 ▦ ▱
◼ ➡ ▦ Closed Nov to mid-Dec. Last orders 10pm.
The hotel's dining room, simple but cheerful, has wide windows overlooking the port. First-class *bouillabaisse*, which does not have to be ordered in advance. Other Marseillais dishes are on the menu, including *pieds et paquets*. (See ✍ above.)

🍽 Other acceptable restaurants: **Le Presqu'île** (*Route de Port-Miou* ☎42-

01-03-77 ▥ *closed Sun dinner, Mon except July, Aug)*, the smartest restaurant in town; **Gilbert** *(quai des Baux* ☎ *42-*

01-71-36 ▥ *closed Tues lunch in season, Tues, Wed in winter, Jan-Mar)*, for dependable fish specialities.

◪ NIGHTLIFE IN CASSIS
Casino Municipal
Av. du Professeur Leriche, 13260 Cassis ☎ 42-01-78-32 ☿ ⊛ ♫ ⊌ *and revues. Open daily 3pm–2am.*

In refreshing contrast to most of the Côte's turn-of-the-century casinos, that at Cassis is the most active, successful and modern on the entire coast from Cannes to Spain: the Marseillais, its main clientele, are great gamblers. The luxurious building, which opened in 1977, has marble floors, modern sculptures and a floodlit Japanese garden spread out in front — a suitably sybaritic atmosphere in which to gamble.

- ◉ Discos in Cassis include **Big Ben**, near the harbor *(pl. Clémenceau* ☎ *42-01-93-79, open 11.30pm-8am, nightly in summer, Thurs-Sat in winter)*, which attracts a young crowd, and **Le K 6** *(2 rue Ventron* ☎ *42-01-17-85, open nightly in summer, Fri-Sat in winter)*.

- **MARKETS** There are markets on Wednesday and Friday on the Parking du Marché.

PLACES NEAR CASSIS
Les Calanques (★) *Calanque* means a deep creek like a small fjord, and there are several along the rugged coast w of Cassis. Flanked by limestone cliffs covered with gorse and heather, they are very beautiful. The creek of **Port-Miou** can be reached by road from Cassis. The white rock here is quarried; its hard stone was used to build parts of the Suez Canal. From here you must continue on foot, along well-marked paths, to reach the **Port-Pin** and **En-Vau** creeks, 2 kilometers (1 mile) farther w. Or you can take one of the frequent boat excursions from Cassis — the best way to see the creeks.

Cap Canaille *(6km/4½ miles SE of Cassis)* Dominating the bay of Cassis to the E, this craggy limestone cliff rises 360 meters (1,200 feet) sheer above the sea. From Cassis, the narrow D41 leads to the top; then you can drive along the **Corniche des Crêtes** to the **Grande Tête**, 396 meters (1,320 feet), down to La Ciotat. These cliffs are the highest in France, with wonderful views.

La Ciotat *(12km/7½ miles E of Cassis)* Once a Greek colony, La Ciotat is a sizeable town (population: 30,000), with shipyards that can build or repair vessels of up to 60,000 tons. Today, like so many in Europe, the yards are partly idle, but they are an impressive sight, with their giant cranes lit up at night, and behind them the strange sugarloaf outlines of Cap de l'Aigle. The area beyond the shipyards is now the cliff-top **Parc du Mugel**, which has varied vegetation *(closed Dec)*. The **Musée Ciotaten** *(open summer: Mon, Wed, Sat 4-7pm, Sun 10am-noon; winter: 3-6pm, Sun 10am-noon)* shows the history of shipbuilding in the town, from ancient times to the present day. Excursions can be made to the offshore **Île Verte**, with its little fort.

- 🐟 There are good beaches at the resort of **La Ciotat-Plage**, 3 kilometers (2 miles) to the NE.

- **EVENT** The Lumière brothers showed the first motion picture here in September 1895 (three months before they did so in Paris), and there is an annual **film festival** in July. • There is also a **chamber music festival**.

🐟 Some hotels in La Ciotat are: **Miramar** *(3 blvd. Beaurivage ☎42-83-09-54 ℻42-83-33-79 Ⅲ)*, which has the town's best restaurant, **Les La-** **vandes** *(38 blvd. de la République ☎42-08-42-81 Ⅲ to Ⅲ)* and **La Rotonde** *(44 blvd. de la République ☎42-08-67-50 Ⅲ)*.

- See also: BANDOL, CASSIS, MARSEILLE.

CASTELLANE
Map 14E12 (Alpes-de-H.-P.). 63km (40 miles) NW of Grasse. Postal code: 04120. Population: 1,350 i rue Nationale ☎92-83-61-14.

Whether you are traveling from Digne or from Grasse, the N85 winds for miles over empty highlands, then dips into the VERDON valley close to the famous gorge to enter this lively little market town and tourist center. **Place Marcel-Sauvaire** is the center of village life, with its terrace-cafés, shops and large buildings.

The church of **St-Victor** was built in the 12thC (the aisles are 16th–17thC) by monks from the abbey of St-Victor in Marseille *(ask for key at tourist office)*. Behind it stands a high pentagonal tower, a vestige of the old ramparts. Castellane is dominated by a sheer 180-meter (590-foot) rock, on top of which is the pilgrim chapel of **Notre-Dame-du-Roc**, accessible by a 30-minute footpath climb starting behind the parish church *(for entry to chapel, apply for key to presbytery in the town)*.

🐟 ☰ MA PETITE AUBERGE ☛
8 blvd. de la République ☎92-83-62-06 ▭ to ▭ 16 rms ◙ Ⅶ ▱ ◈ Closed Nov–Easter.
Location: In the main square. A typical small-town Provençal *auberge,* as much a lively meeting place for locals as a tourist hotel. Suitable for a stopover on the way to or from the coast.

Dine in the rustic-style dining room *(▭ to Ⅲ ▭ ▬ 🐟 closed Wed (except July–Aug), Nov–Easter, last orders 9.30pm)*, with red tablecloths, or the sizeable terrace garden, under lime trees. Either makes a pleasant setting for the local cuisine of *patron/*chef M. Tardieu, who offers a wide range of menus and prices.

PLACES NEAR CASTELLANE
Castillon, lac et barrage *(5km/3 miles N of Castellane).* The building here in the 1940s of a large hydro-electric dam has widened the upper Verdon river into an 11-kilometer/7-mile-long artificial lake of bright green water that is suitable for swimming. For the best views of it, leave Castellane by the D955, then take the hill road (D102) that climbs up from the dam to Demandolx, which then descends in narrow hairpin bends to the high **Chaudanne dam**, 3 kilometers (2 miles) E of Castellane.
St-André-les-Alpes *(21km/12 miles N of Castellane).* At the N end of Lac Castillon, and on one of the two main Digne–Nice roads, this

village is a pleasant and popular summer resort, set amid orchards and lavender fields in a wide mountain valley with hills all around. There is swimming, riding and tennis; it's ideal hiking country.

CLOSERAIE BAGATELLE ▰
Route d'Allos, 04170 St-André-les-Alpes
☎93-89-03-08 ▢ 10 rms ▱ ✿ *Closed Oct, Mar.*
Location: Down a quiet road on the edge of the village. For those seeking rural peace and simplicity, this is a family *pension,* with a large garden shaded by fir and lime trees. Bedrooms are basic but gaily decorated; there is a minuscule TV lounge. Sound *cuisine familiale,* supplied by the amiable *patronne* and chef, Mme Dubois, is

served either in the garden or the cheerful restaurant *(▢ to ▢ ▭ ▰ ▱ closed Mon (Nov-May), Sun dinner, Oct, Mar, last orders 9pm).*

Other good hotels in St-André: **Clair Logis** *(Route de Digne* ☎92-89-04-05 ▢ *to* ▢*)*, **Le Colombier** *(Route d'Allos* ☎92-89-07-11 [Fx]*92-89-10-45* ▢*)*, **Grand** *(by the station* ☎92-89-05-06 ▢*)* and **Lac et Forêt** *(by the lake to the s* ☎92-89-07-38 ▢ *to* ▢*)*.

Senez *(20km/12 miles NW off Castellane, just off N85).* Believe it or not, this ancient, tiny village, with a population of 200, was the seat of a bishopric from the 5thC until 1790. All that today remains of its former glory is the little **ex-cathedral**, typically Provençal Romanesque in style, with 17thC pulpit and choirstalls and 16th–18thC Flanders and Aubusson tapestries — all slightly decrepit now that its many worshipers and priests have long since departed. *(For entry, ask for the key from the curé at Barrème, 5km/3 miles to NW, or attend Sunday Mass at 11am.)*

• See also: VERDON, GRAND CANYON DU.

CAVALAIRE-SUR-MER

Map **13**I12 *(Var). 18km (11 miles) SW of St-Tropez. Postal code: 83240. Population 4,200* **i** *sq. de Lattre-de-Tassigny* ☎94-64-08-28.

A popular, if unremarkable, seaside resort on the Maures coast, backed by hilly forests of oak, pine and mimosa. There are several sandy beaches, both public and private, a yachting port, and various sports and festivities all summer.

RAYMOND
Av. des Alliés, 83240 Cavalaire
☎94-64-07-32 ▢ *to* ▢ 35 rms ▬ ▣
▣ ▱ ✿ ▰ *Closed Oct-Easter.*
Location: On the w fringe of the resort, set back from the main road and close to the beaches. The owner's white parrot helps to set the tone of relaxed informality at this rambling and unassuming vacation hotel. Eat, if you can, on the side terrace rather than in

the airy but dull dining room. The whole Meunier family gears itself to the streamlined service of copious food at fair prices *(▢ to*▢ ▭ ▰ ▱ *closed Wed (Sept, Easter to June), Oct–Easter, last orders 9.30pm).*

Other recommended hotels: **Calanque** *(rue de la Calanque* ☎94-64-04-27 ▢ *to*▢*)* and **Pergola** *(av. du Port* ☎94-64-06-86 ▢*)*.

PLACES NEAR CAVALAIRE-SUR-MER
La Croix-Valmer *(6km/4 miles NE of Cavalaire).* The village, set high

among wooded hills, obtained its name from the vision that Constantine the Great is said to have had there, when marching to Italy to win the Empire over to Christianity: a cross appeared in the sky, with the words "Thou shalt conquer by the sign." The spot is marked by a stone cross beside the N559, 2 kilometers (1 mile) sw of the village.

A few kilometers to the E around **Gigaro** are some lovely secluded beaches.

❧ PARC

83420 La Croix-Valmer ☎ *94-79-64-04*
🖷 *94-54-38-91* ▨ *to* ▨ *33 rms* ▰ ▣
🖾 ✦ ▱ ✿ ⚓ ◁ *Closed Oct–Easter.*
Location: In its own park just outside the village, on the D93 Ramatuelle road. At first sight, this vast white mansion looks like yet another of the Côte's turn-of-the-century palace-hotels, but the institutional air and long corridors

reveal the hotel's true origins — a girls' boarding school, built in 1903. Comfortably converted, with charming staff and lovely views.

❧ ➡ At Gigaro, to the E, is **Souleias** (▨) (☎ *94-79-61-91* 🖷 *94-54-36-23* ▨), a luxury hotel with a fine setting, first-class food and all modern facilities.

• See also: LE LAVANDOU.

CHÂTEAU-ARNOUX

*Map 7C10 (Alpes-de-H.-P.). 25km (15 miles) w of Digne. Postal code: 04160.
Population: 5,100 ℹ rue Victorin-Maurel* ☎ *92-64-02-64.*

A small town on the Durance at the intersection of the highways from Marseille and Nice to Grenoble. The town has the remains of an old château, flanked by five 15thC towers. The Durance valley here is ugly, the brown river flowing sluggishly between wide mud flats in the dry season. Industrial buildings dot the landscape, notably the large chemical and electrical works at St-Auban.

Three kilometers (2 miles) to the N is the pretty hill-village of **Volonne**, crowned by two tall towers of another feudal castle.

❧ ➡ LA BONNE ÉTAPE

Chemin du Lac, 04160 Château-Arnoux
☎ *92-64-00-09* 🖷 *92-64-37-36* ▨ *to* ▨
18 rms ▰ ▤ 🖾 ▣ ◉ ▨ □ ▱
⚓ ◁ ≈ ♨ ⚐ *Closed early Jan to mid-Feb; early Dec.*
Location: On the main road in the town, but looking over open fields in back. An 18thC coaching inn has been converted into this luxurious but unpretentious hotel, one of the most sympathetic in the famous Relais et Châteaux association. The Anglophile Gleize family, owner for three generations, provides all the right touches, such as homemade jams and croissants on a breakfast tray of regal elegance. Sumptuous bedrooms in the Louis XIII and

XV styles; heated swimming pool.

To crown this delightful place, the food ranks as some of the best in all Provence. Joint *chefs de cuisine* are Pierre Gleize and his son Jany (who has trained with Guérard, Troisgros and other modern masters), who create light and subtle variations on local dishes. The dining room is most attractive, with its painted silk lampshades and exquisite porcelain. Excellent wine cellar. (▨ *to* ▨ □ ■ ▰ *closed Sun dinner, Mon in winter, early Jan to mid-Feb, also early Dec, last orders 9.30pm).*
Specialities: Omelette fraîche de legumes à tapenade, salade tiède de homard, agneau de Sisteron.

COLMARS ☆

*Map **14**C12 (Alpes-de-H.-P.). Postal code: 04370. 71km (44 miles) NE of Digne, 124km (75 miles) NW of Nice. Population: 350 i at Mairie ☎92-83-41-92.*

Set in the high alpine valley of the upper Verdon, against a backdrop of peaks and pine forests, Colmars is a little town bristling with fortifications and completely enclosed by 17thC ramparts. Even the town's name is warlike — it comes from a temple to the god Mars, which once stood on the nearby hill, *Collis Martis.* War remained Colmar's vocation, hence the ramparts and the massive medieval **Fort de Savoie** *(open July-Aug)* to the N and its twin **Fort de France** to the S, which guarded the town in the 14thC when it was on the frontier of Provence-Allos and the Barcelonnette valley, after it had been annexed by the Duke of Savoy.

Today Colmars is quite at peace, and makes a popular summer resort. It is a delightful place, full of tiny, traffic-free squares, each one with a sparkling drinking water fountain.

✿ 🚆   **Chamois (▣)** *(☎92-83-43-29 ▢).*

PLACES NEAR COLMARS

From Colmars, the road curves on up the valley, past the village of **Allos**, with a Romanesque church, and the brash ski resort of **La Foux d'Allos**. Beyond La Foux the road then loops and twists giddily upward to the **Col d'Allos**, and down again to Barcelonnette. Narrow, with hairpin bends, this pass road is closed in winter, and even in summer the drive demands quick reflexes and a Monte-Carlo Rally spirit. For those thus equipped, there is the reward of stunning views of distant peaks and valleys from the top of the pass.

DIGNE

*Map **7**C11 (Alpes-de-H.-P.). 153km (96 miles) NW of Nice. Postal code: 04000. Population: 16,100 i 2 blvd. Victor-Hugo ☎92-31-42-73.*

True to its name, Digne is a dignified little spa town, capital of the Alpes-de-Haute-Provence *département.* The thermal baths, to the SE, are recommended for rheumatism, and the town's hotels are often full of elderly *curistes.* It was in Digne that the first chapters of Victor Hugo's *Les Misérables* were set.

Digne's main boulevard is shaded by tall plane trees, and close by is a pedestrian zone of old narrow streets. The **Musée Municipal** *(▨ open 10am-noon, 2-6pm (5pm Sun), closed Mon)* contains a good collection of local natural history and archeology, as well as paintings by local artists. Digne's most interesting building, on the D900 in the NE outskirts, is the yellowish 12th–13thC **Notre-Dame-de-Bourg** *(for admission see cemetery keeper),* an ex-cathedral now used only for funerals: it has a graceful nave in Provençal Romanesque style, a Lombard portal and a pretty rose window.

Digne also has a **Musée de la Seconde Guerre Mondiale** *(rue Colonel Payan ☎92-31-00-53; open May-Sept 3-6pm, closed weekends;*

Oct-Apr Wed only 2-5.30pm), a privately-owned museum of the town's history during World War II, during which it was occupied by both Italians and Germans.

A privately-owned railway line, the **Chemin de Fer de Provence**, runs between Nice and Digne from the Gare de Sud France (☎ *92-31-01-58; in Nice: 33 av. Malausséna* ☎ *93-88-28-56).*

- **EVENTS** There is a **cinema conference** in April, a **sculpture symposium** in July, a **women's film festival** in September, a **lavender and honey fair** in August, and an **accordion festival** in October.

- **MARKETS** There are markets on Wednesday and Saturday.

✎ L'AIGLON
1 rue de Provence, 04000 Digne
☎*92-31-02-70* ✉*92-32-45-83* ▭ *27 rms* ▦ ⇌ 🏠 🅰🅴 🄾 🅾 🆅🆂🅰 ‡ ▢ ▱
▨ *Closed late Nov to late Dec.*
Location: On the Route Napoléon. A straightforward little place of no special charm, but suitable for a night or two's stay in the area. In the bedrooms, wallpaper and bedspreads clash merrily. The hotel's name echoes Digne's Napoleonic associations, and an assertive mural of the dance of the eagle fills one wall of the dining room. Sound Provençal cooking.

✎⇌ GRAND PARIS
19 blvd. Thiers, 04000 Digne ☎*92-31-11-15* ✉*92-32-32-82* ▭ *31 rms* ▦ 🅰🅴 🄾 🅾 🆅🆂🅰 ‡ ♿ ▢ ▱ ▨ *Closed late Dec to Mar.*
Location: In the center of town, facing a parking lot. A 17thC monastery of the Brothers of the Trinity has been converted into a cozy hotel of some character. It is spotlessly clean and extremely well run, with spacious, well-equipped rooms, although the rather somber predilection for dark colors and velvet might not suit all tastes.

The best food in Digne is served either in a formal dining room (▥ *to* ▥ ▱ ▦ ⇌ 🕏 *closed Sun dinner, Mon, mid-Dec to Mar, last orders 9.30pm)* or, in fine weather, on a ter-race under shady trees. Prices are not low, but the *patron* and chef, J.J. Ricaud, deserves his accolades. Try the Lirac or Vignelaure wines. Good service, friendly atmosphere. *Specialities: Mousseux de poireaux James, truite à la crème de poivrons, pigeon en bécasse.*

✎ MISTRE
65 blvd. Gassendi, 04000 Digne
☎*92-31-00-16* ▭ *to* ▥ *19 rms* ▦ ⇌
(last orders 9pm, closed Sat) ▢ ▱ ▨
Closed mid-Dec to mid-Jan.
Location: In the town center, on the main street. Although the bedrooms and bathrooms have been modernized, this sedate and spacious old hotel has the air of being a little past its prime; but it is friendly and comfortable, and popular with the elderly French people who come to Digne for cures. The brochure in English lauds its "insonorous rooms" and "thrush pie." Pleasant dining patio for summer.

⇌ LA CHAUVINIÈRE
56 rue de l'Hubac ☎*92-31-40-03* ▥▢ ▱
▰ 🕏 *Closed Sun dinner; Mon (Oct–Mar); second half of June; first week July; second half of Nov. Last orders 9.30pm.*
The accent is on well-prepared Provençal cooking with a number of additions from northeastern France. Mellow lighting, soft music, quiet. *Specialities: Raclette, fondue.*

PLACES NEAR DIGNE
Two roads, the D900 and D900A, wind N through the impressively wild and arid **Pré-Alpes de Digne** to the **Col de Maure** and **Seyne**, on the way to Barcelonnette. Of the two, the westerly route on the D900A via the *clues* (clefts) of **Barles** and **Verdaches** is the more spectacular.

DRAGUIGNAN

Map **13***F12 (Var). 65km (45 miles) w of Cannes. Postal code: 83300. Population: 31,200* **i** *9 blvd. Clémenceau* ☎*94-68-63-30.*

This dignified old market town has broad avenues and a floodlit fountain; the narrow streets of the old quarter are now a pleasant traffic-free zone, and above them stands the impressive 17thC **tour d'horloge** with its wrought-iron campanile. The **museum** contains some Gallo-Roman remains, and Flemish and Italian paintings. Nearby, there is a major military base.

Two kilometers (one mile) to the E, on D59, an **Allied war cemetery** holds the graves of those killed in the battles that followed the parachute drop of 10,000 men at Le Muy on August 15, 1944. Two kilometers (one mile) to the NW, on D955, is the **Pierre de la Fée**, a curious monolith two meters (6 feet) high, perched on three stones.

☜ ⊨ **Le Col de l'Ange** (*Route de Lorgues* ☎*94-68-23-01* ▥), **Victoria** (*54 av. Carnot* ☎*94-47-24-12* ℻*94-68-31-69* ▥ *to* ▥) and **du**

Parc (*21 blvd. de la Liberté* ☎*94-68-53-84* ℻*94-47-11-92* ▥) are all adequate, the Victoria being the best of the three.

PLACES NEAR DRAGUIGNAN

Les Arcs (*10km/6 miles s of Draguignan*). The village has a Roman bridge, and in its **church**, a lovely 16thC retable divided into 16 panels.

☜ ⊨ **LE LOGIS DU GUETTEUR** ▥
Pl. du Château, 83460, Les Arcs-sur-Argens
☎*94-73-30-82* ▥) ℻*94-73-39-95* ▥
10 rooms ⬛ AE ⊡ ▥ ⬛ □ ⬛ ≪ ⬛
≋ ♈ ⦂/ ⦂ ⬛ ⬛ ⬛ *Closed Fri (out of season); Nov 15 to Dec 15. Last orders in* ⊨ *9pm.*
Location: Overlooking the Argens Val-

ley and the Maures Massif. The word *guetteur* means "lookout" in French, and this stunningly situated hotel, converted from part of an 11thC castle, is not only true to its name, but also very comfortable, well decorated and well run. The food is good, with game a speciality, and the service is efficient.

Chapelle Ste-Rosaline (☆) (*4.5km/3 miles E of Les Arcs*). Formerly attached to an 11thC abbey, the recently-restored chapel contains 17thC gilded wood retables, 16thC choir stalls, and modern works of art, notably two by Giacometti: a lectern, and a bronze low relief relating the life of Ste-Rosaline.

Lorgues (*12km/7½ miles sw of Draguignan*). This pleasant small town, spreading up a slope, has fortified 14thC gateways, some pretty houses, and a huge 18thC church, built by Bishop Fleury of Fréjus, who later became a minister and a cardinal during the reign of Louis XV. The area around Lorgues is good wine country, and is a center of olive-oil production.

⊨ **CHEZ BRUNO** ⌂
Route de Vidaubon, 83510 Lorgues. 13km (8 miles) sw of Draguignan ☎*94-73-92-19*
▥ ▤ ⬛ □ ⊨ ⬛ AE ▥ *Closed Mon;*

Jan. Last orders 8.30pm (9pm in summer).
You will either love this place or hate it. The ursine Bruno Clément is a local celebrity, as he will make quite clear

given the opportunity. The lengthy menu is only there for guidance: he cooks according to the market and his own mood. And his mood is usually for truffles in every conceivable guise. The food is rich, dedicated to local produce such as lamb, the service formal, and the place polished.

- See also: THORONET, ABBAYE DU.

Some people will find Bruno and his menu overpowering — others will simply sit back and enjoy the work of a passionate chef.

≠ Restaurant nearby: **Les Pignatelles** *(726 Route de Bagnols, 83920 La Motte* ☎ *94-70-25-70* ▥▯*).*

ENTREVAUX
*Map **14**D13 (Alpes-de-H.-P.). 72km (45 miles) NW of Nice. Postal code: 04320. Population: 700* ℹ *near bridge, at entrance to village* ☎*93-05-46-73.*

This remarkable fortified village is not on a hilltop, like most in Provence, but stands beside the rushing river Var and the Nice–Digne road and railway. Vauban, Louis XIV's military engineer, built its ramparts in 1695, when the Var was France's frontier with ducal Savoy. Entrevaux has changed little in appearance since. It has moats and three gates, through one of which you must pass to enter the old village with its steep, shady alleys, all pleasantly unspoiled. Some buildings date from the 11thC. It is worth climbing up to Vauban's fort on the hill behind.

- **EVENTS** Culture and folklore are very much alive in Entrevaux. One high point is the **Fête of John the Baptist** on the weekend nearest to June 24, when locals in traditional costume process to a chapel 12 kilometers (8 miles) away.

Ancienne cathédrale † ☆
✗ *available. Open daily all year.*
Although it was built as a cathedral in the 17thC, this richly ornate church was demoted during the Revolution. It forms part of the 17thC ramparts, although the adjoining bell tower was the work of the Knights Templar in the 11thC. As with many Provençal churches, the exterior is plain, even austere, and there is just one nave and no aisle. But the interior has much to please the eye: note the chancel and choir stalls, the good 17thC paintings, the antique silver ornaments and the fine altarpiece of St John the Baptist.

❧ **Vauban** (◼) *(by the main road, 4 pl. Moreau* ☎ *93-05-42-40* ▢*)* offers acceptable Provençal food and simple lodging.

PLACES NEAR ENTREVAUX
Gorges de Daluis *(16km/10 miles N of Entrevaux).* From Daluis at its S end to **Buillaumes** (see VALBERG for details) at the N end, the D2202, by means of hairpins and tunnels, ascends the left side of the magnificent and giddying gorge, providing many stunning views of the towering cliffs of red rock, studded with green.

- See also: ANNOT.

FAYENCE

Map 13F13 (Var). 27km (17 miles) w of Grasse. Postal code: 83440. Population: 3,500 **i** *pl. Léon-Roux* ☎94-76-20-08.

A small, very pretty town spiraling up a hilltop, which provides a good base from which to explore the Haut Var, its spectacular countryside and its pretty medieval hill-villages. The name derives from the Latin *faventia loca,* or favorable place. Local crafts include pottery, wood-carving and leatherwork. There is a large 18thC church built in the Classical style, and some attractive houses in the old town.

- **EVENT** In late October, there is a high-quality **chamber music festival** in the various old churches in the locality.

↝ MOULIN DE LA CAMANDOULE
Chemin Notre-Dame-des-Cyprès
☎94-76-00-84 94-76-10-40 11
rms ↝ ≡ ▦ ▨ ◳ ☐ ◪ ↯ ⟨⟨ ⤫

Location: Beside a river, in a 4-acre park. A 17thC olive-oil mill converted into a delightful, restful hotel. There is a simple but satisfying cheap *menu prix-fixe.* Large swimming pool, pretty bedrooms (but avoid the uncomfortable single rooms). There are plans to build rooms by the river. There's a poolside barbecue in summer, and the pool is open to non-residents for a minimum charge. The food is good *(demi-pension obligatory from mid-Mar to end Oct).* The English owners, Wolf and Shirley Rilla, took over in 1986: he used to be a well-known film director, so there are often actor friends staying.

↝ Les Oliviers *(Quartier La Ferrage* ☎94-76-13-12 94-76-08-05).

⊟ FRANCE ✿
1 rue du Château ☎94-76-00-14 to ◳ ■ ⚬ *Closed Tues eve and Wed in winter. Last orders 9.30pm.*

Food is cooked and presented with care and represents real value. There is a simple but satisfying cheap *menu prix-fixe.* Eat on the terrace overlooking the street or in the calm of the neat provincial dining-room. After dinner, wander across to the main square. Something often seems to be happening, be it a *fête* or some other cause for hilarity. *Specialities: Poulet sauté pignons, manchons de canard en confit, brouillade aux truffes.*

⊟ Other restaurants worth a look are **Le Castellras** *(Route de Seillans* ☎94-76-13-80) and **Le Relais du Castel** *(Quartier St-Eloi* ☎94-76-07-48).

PLACE NEAR FAYENCE
Mons
41km (25 miles) w of Grasse; 14km (8½ miles) N of Fayence. 83440 Fayence, Var.
It is worth a detour to Mons, which is one of the most exhilarating of the hinterland villages. Superbly situated at a high altitude, with marvelous views, it has steep steps and tiny alleys leading into little courtyards.

⊟ **Auberge Provençale** (☎94-76-38-33): simple food, marvelous views.

- See also: SEILLANS.

FORCALQUIER

Map 6D9 (Alpes-de-H.-P.). 59km (31 miles) sw of Digne. Postal code: 04300. Population: 3,950 **i** *pl. Bourguet* ☎92-75-10-02.

The town, an important feudal capital in the 12thC, is finely situated on the slopes of a steep hill, overlooking the lush surrounding countryside. In the central square, the stately Romanesque **church of Notre-Dame** stands opposite a small local **museum**. Nearby, the 13thC **Couvent des Cordeliers** was one of the first Franciscan monasteries in France.

The town's main curiosity is its **cemetery**, 1 kilometer ($\frac{1}{2}$ mile) up the hill to the N: its terraces are partitioned by tall box hedges of clipped yew, forming archways — a rare sight in France.

- **EVENT**   **Festival of Haute-Provence**, end of July to early August.
- **MARKET**   There is a market on Mondays.

Hostellerie des Deux-Lions *(11 pl. Bourget* ☎*92-75-25-30* [Fx] *92-75-06-41* ▥ *to* ▥ *closed Sun dinner, Mon in winter, mid-Nov to mid-Dec, Jan, Feb)* offers very acceptable food.

PLACES NEAR FORCALQUIER

Lure, Montagne de *(32km/20 miles N of Forcalquier)*. This lofty ridge runs 1,800 meters (5,994 feet) from W to E. From St-Étienne, a road leads through dense forest to the crest. From there, a strenuous 15-minute walk leads to the **Signal de Lure**, with fantastic panoramic views as far as the coast and the Cévennes.

Observatoire de Haute Provence *(13km/8 miles to the SW of Forcalquier* ✗ *on Wed between 2.15-3.45pm and first Sun of month Apr-Sept between 9-11am)*. This is a major state-run astronomical research center, with powerful telescopes. The site was chosen because of the purity of the atmosphere here.

- See also: MANOSQUE.

FRÉJUS

Map 13G13 (Var). 40km (25 miles) SW of Cannes. Postal code: 83600. Population: 41,500 i 325 rue Jean Jaurès ☎94-17-19-19. Airport (open July–Aug only) ☎94-51-04-07. Railway station ☎94-95-16-90.

Lying a mile inland, on a plain just W of the MAURES MASSIF, Fréjus contains some of the most fascinating traces of the Roman era in France, and a remarkable cathedral and 5thC baptistry. As a modern town, it has few attractions apart from the beaches of Fréjus-Plage.

Founded by Julius Caesar in 49BC, Fréjus *(Forum Julii)* became an important and highly efficient naval base under Augustus; here he moored the warships captured from Antony and Cleopatra at Actium in 31BC. Fréjus was by then a flourishing Roman town, its population of 25,000 only a little smaller than it is today. But gradually, with the decline of Roman influence, the port lost its significance, and by the 3rdC AD had silted up.

In the 10thC Fréjus was destroyed by Saracens, then rebuilt by Bishop Riculphe, who elevated it to an episcopal city of some rank. Although Fréjus is more or less contiguous with the neighboring town of ST-RAPHAEL, there is a considerable civic rivalry between the two places.

- **EVENTS**   The *bravade* **costume procession** takes place on the third Sunday after Easter. • There are **bullfights** in summer in the Arena.

WHAT TO SEE IN FRÉJUS
Cité Episcopale ⏷ † ☆
Pl. de Formigé 🚻 *for cloister, baptistry and museum* ✗ *available. Open Apr–Sept 9am–7pm; Oct–Mar 9am–noon, 2–5pm. Closed Tues in winter.*

At the entrance to this rich ensemble in the center of town, the guide opens the shutters protecting the fine **Renaissance doors** on which are carved 16 walnut panels showing scenes of the life of The Virgin and of Saracen massacres.

To the left is the remarkable 5thC baptistry, one of the oldest in France. It is octagonal, with a sunken font and two doors. Baptisms in those days were conducted by bishops and reserved for adults. Catechumens would enter by one door; the bishop would wash their feet, immerse them and anoint them with oil; then, white-robed, they would pass out through the other door to their first communion in the cathedral.

The elegant little 12thC **cloister** has a colonnade of twin, slender marble pillars, in the style that is common in Provence; in its middle is a garden with rose trees and a well. The beamed ceiling of its arcade was decorated, in the 15thC, with 1,200 tiny painted panels of animals and grotesques; many of these were destroyed in the French Revolution, but 400 of them remain. Above the cloister rises the graceful bell tower, which is part 13thC, its steeple covered with patterned, colored tiles.

The rooms above the cloister house a **musée archéologique**, devoted to local Roman finds: a mosaic, discovered in 1921, and Roman sculptures and a sarcophagus. Most attractive, however, are the small Greek vases, exquisitely shaped and decorated, which the Romans brought with them on their travels. The two-headed marble bust of Hermes, discovered in 1970, has been adopted as the town's symbol.

The cathedral, part 10thC, part 12th–13thC, is of lofty and graceful dimensions, but rather austere. It has a 16thC painted wooden crucifix, and a 15thC retable of *Ste-Marguerite* above the sacristy door.

Cité Romaine
The sea has receded since Roman days; Augustus's port was close to the modern town center, just s of avenue Aristide-Briand. It is thought to have had quays 2 kilometers (1¼ miles) long, with a lighthouse, shipyards and warehouses.

Although little remains today, there are relics enough to imagine *Forum Julii* in its prime. It lay astride the Aurelian Way, the highway from Rome to Arles, and was girt by 3 kilometers (2 miles) of ramparts. Its w entrance was the **Porte des Gaules**, of which one tower survives.

Outside was the **arena** *(rue H. Vadon* ☎ *94-51-34-31; open Oct-Mar, 9am-noon, 2-4.30pm; Apr-Sept, 9.30am-noon, 2-6.30pm, closed Tues),* the oldest in Gaul and built to seat 10,000. Today, modern seating has been installed, and it is still used for bullfights and pop concerts. Inside the ramparts was a **theater**, which is still partly standing.

On the low hill to the SE are traces of the Roman military headquarters, while the **Porte d'Orée** *(just SE of the new town)* was probably part of the old baths. The **Lanterne d'Auguste**, just E of the modern town and s of the railway, is a medieval tower built on a Roman base that is thought to have stood by the harbor entrance.

✎ Hotels worth recommending in Fréjus are: **Les Palmiers** *(blvd. de la Libération* ☎ *94-51-18-72* ▥ *)* and **Les Résidences du Colombier** *(Route de Bagnols* ☎ *94-51-45-92* ⟨Fx⟩ *94-53-82-85* ▥ *).* The latter hotel is modeled on the Club-Med idea, where the accent is on sport and get-together jollity; bed-rooms are in bungalows spread about the garden.

🍴 **La Toque Blanche** *(394 av. Victor Hugo* ☎ *94-52-06-14* ▥ *).*

🍴 **Auberge du Vieux Four** *(46 rue de Grisolle* ☎ *94-51-56-38* ▥ *).*

🏖 BEACHES NEAR FRÉJUS

There are 5 kilometers (3 miles) of sandy public beaches at **Fréjus-Plage**, 1.5 kilometers (1 mile) SE of the town center.

PLACES NEAR FRÉJUS

Beside the D4 road to **Bagnols-en-Fôret** stands a **mosque**, built in World War I by soldiers from the former French Sudan. A replica of the famous Missiri mosque at Djenne, it is now empty and uncared for, and with its red paint and squat designs, looks for all the world like a large raspberry fruitcake.

Better cared for is the **Buddhist pagoda** *(3km/2 miles SE of Fréjus, beside the N7),* built as a shrine in the cemetery of 5,000 Annamite soldiers killed in World War I. Down a turnoff to the Tour de Mare estate, 3 kilometers (2 miles) farther up the N7, the modern chapel of **Notre-Dame-de-Jerusalem** *(often closed)* was decorated by Jean Cocteau.

Also off the D4 Bagnols road *(the turning is 3km/2 miles out of Fréjus, just before the autoroute)* is the **Safari de l'Esterel** *(*🐘 *closed Tues in winter)* and the **Parc Zoologique** (🐘), both with a wide variety of animals and birds in a natural environment. In the barricaded section of the safari park, which contains fierce animals, mainly tigers, visitors must remain in their cars with windows shut.

Malpasset, barrage *(11km/7 miles N of Fréjus; turn left down a track off the N7).* A terrible tragedy occurred in December 1959 when this dam burst, causing flood water to sweep down through Fréjus, killing hundreds of people and causing appalling damage to the town. The ruins of the vast structure, and the enormous pieces of reinforced concrete strewn below it where they were swept by the flood, are an eerie and forbidding sight.

Roquebrune-sur-Argens *(11km/7 miles W of Fréjus).* A pretty hill-village, to the W of which is the high rocky crest of the **montagne de**

Roquebrune, an outcrop of the MAURES MASSIF, from where there are good views (the summit is accessible on foot). On the N part of the same circular road (which joins with the D25), parallel with the autoroute, is the chapel of **Notre-Dame-de-la-Roquette**, which has an excellent view.

St-Aygulf *(6.5km/4 miles s of Fréjus)*. A bustling family resort full of camp sites, and stores selling buckets and spades. Pine forests fringe the bay, and the beaches are sandy.

✤ **Catalogne** *(☎94-81-01-44* Fx *94-81-32-42* ▥*)* is comfortable. It has a pool, but no restaurant.

⊨ **La Galiote** *(St-Aygulf plage)*

• See also: ST-RAPHAEL.

stands among a string of beach restaurants. At this one, the best, you can emerge from the sea to a plateful of enormous prawns *(gambas)*, deliciously grilled in butter and herbs.

GRIMAUD

Map 13H12 (Var). 10km (6 miles) w of St-Tropez. Postal code: 83360. Population: 3,300 i pl. des Écoles ☎94-43-26-98.

This dignified, very pretty and well-kept hill-village stands on the wooded slopes of the Maures mountains, facing ST-TROPEZ, and its modern counterpart, PORT-GRIMAUD. Its steep and ancient alleys have been neatly restored, for many of these houses are now weekend or summer residences of the well-to-do. The village is crowned by the ruins of a feudal castle, once a Grimaldi stronghold (which is how Grimaud got its name), the towers of which are visible for miles around. The ruins can be explored at any time.

Take a look, too, at the 11thC **Templar church** and the arcaded **House of the Templars** beside it, and at the **Folklore Museum**. There is also a recently restored **windmill**. The views from Grimaud are spectacular, and the village is well worth a visit, to escape the hurly-burly of the coast. There are a number of good craft stores open in season.

✤⊨ **COTEAU FLEURI**
Pl. des Pénitents, 83360 Grimaud
☎94-43-20-17 Fx94-43-33-42 ▥ 14
rms ➡ ᴁ ⊡ ⊙ ⅦⅢ ⊡ ⊡ ❦ ⋘
Closed Dec; Jan.
Location: On a side road in the w outskirts, facing the hills. A quiet, cozy, typically Provençal little *auberge* with tiled floors, a log fire in winter, and a piano that guests can use. There is a small garden on a slope, with mimosa and olive trees, while from the bedrooms and the dining room there are terrific views over the MAURES MASSIF. The hotel's refined local cuisine, cooked by a young chef trained by Troisgros, is reliable.

✤ Also recommended: **La Boulangerie** *(Route de Collobrières* ☎*94-43-23-16* Fx*94-43-28-27* ▥*)*.

⊨ **LES SANTONS** ⌂
Route Nationale, 83360 Grimaud
☎94-43-21-02 ▥ ⊏ ▮▮ ▰ ➡ ⊙ ⅦⅢ
Closed Wed (except dinner in summer);
Nov–Mar. Last orders 10.30pm (summer),
9pm (winter).
Silver candlesticks, red roses and an elegant Provençal decor makes a worthy setting for what is arguably the finest cooking between Marseille and La Napoule. Service too is very stylish. Claude Girard wins rapturous praise for a subtle blend of classic and *nouvelle*

cuisine, and menus change constantly. *Specialities: Pâté de lapereau aux pistaches, goujonettes de St-Pierre au champagne, pigeonneau au miel.*

≡ LA BRETONNIÈRE
Pl. des Pénitents ☎94-43-25-26 ▥ ⊏⊐
■■ ≋ *No cards.*
A very good, but expensive, comfortable, and beautifully decorated res-

taurant. The owner, Monsieur Rabud, is also the chef, and much in evidence. Try the *mignon d'agneau* with honey and pepper. There is a very good selection of cheeses. Desserts, from a bulging trolley, are a speciality.

≡ Also recommended: **Le Gacharel** *(7 rue du Gacharel* ☎ *94-43-24-40* ▥ *to* ▥*).*

PLACES NEAR GRIMAUD

Cogolin *(3km/2 miles s of Grimaud).* One of the liveliest centers of practical handicrafts in Provence, Cogolin has kept alive an interesting variety of traditional cottage industries: carpets, corks, briar pipes (which are famous throughout France), as well as furniture, fishing rods and clarinet pipes. **Girodengo** *(av. Clémenceau)* is a carpet factory *(✗ on Mon-Fri).*

❧ Clémenceau *(pl. de la République* ☎ *94-54-62-67* ▣ *94-54-58-21* ▥ *to* ▥*).*

La Garde-Freinet *(10km/7 miles NW of Grimaud).* From Grimaud, a wide road winds up through cork forests to this unspoiled village in the heart of the MAURES MASSIF. The ruined castle on the hill above (a 30-minute walk) was the last stronghold of the Saracens, who ravaged the coast in the 10thC until finally driven out, in 973, by Count William the Good. Yet the Saracens were not just vandals: they taught medical skills to the Provençaux, and showed them how to utilize the bark of cork oak.

Today, cork is still the main local industry. La Garde-Freinet is also popular with writers and actors; Jeanne Moreau, among others, has a villa here.

≡ FAÙCADO
31 blvd. de l'Esplanade ☎94-43-60-41 ▥
⊏⊐ ■■ ⇔ ▦ *Closed Tues except dinner July–Aug; mid-Jan to early Mar. Last orders 10.30pm.*
Behind a high wall in the main street lies a pretty garden where you can dine

under parasols amid roses and wisteria, with views over the valley below. Friendly service and sound local cooking: try the *civet de porcelet à l'estouffade de pigeonneau.* There are set menus for lunch, but dinner is *à la carte* only.

* See also: PORT-GRIMAUD, ST-TROPEZ.

HYÈRES

Map 12I10 (Var). 18km (11 miles) E of Toulon. Postal code: 83400. Population: 48,000. **Airport:** *Toulon/Hyères, 4km (2½ miles) to SE* ☎94-57-41-41 **i** *av. de Belgique* ☎94-65-18-55.

Hyères is the oldest resort on the Côte d'Azur: it dates from the 18thC, and was once particularly popular with the British. Queen Victoria, Robert Louis Stevenson, Napoléon Bonaparte and Leo Tolstoy have all been among its devotees. Today, however, it has gone out of fashion, although the broad avenues shaded with date palms, and the grand casino, remain as reminders of its past glory. The town may well see a revival, however, if Toulon/Hyères airport is eventually opened up to international flights, as the local authorities would like. This will be subject to the agreement of the French military, which has a number of bases in the area.

The town's full name is Hyères-les-Palmiers, and it is known for production of palm trees (many of them, ironically, exported to the Middle East) and potted plants. It has much to offer, for it is a town that has more to it than tourism alone.

It has, for example, been a favorite location of a number of French movie directors including Jean-Luc Godard *(Pierrot le Fou)*, Agnès Varda *(L'Une chante, l'autre pas,* titled in English as *One Sings, the Other Doesn't)* and François Truffaut, with his last film, *Vivement Dimanche/ Confidentially Yours (US)/Finally Sunday (UK)*.

Of most interest is the old, medieval part of the town, lying 5 kilometers (3 miles) inland, on a hill. The 19thC resort and modern town stretch s and E toward the sea.

Both the Greeks and Romans colonized the coast at Hyères: their archeological remains can be seen in the **Musée Municipal** *(pl. Lefèvre, closed Tues).* In the Middle Ages, the town was used as a port of departure for journeys to the Holy Land; St-Louis stayed here on his return from the Seventh Crusade in 1254.

The sea, in those days, came much closer to the town, and the port was in a place that has long since silted up. Vestiges of the town's importance in medieval days can be seen in the *vieille ville,* notably around place Massillon, where a bustling market is held every morning. Here is the handsome 12thC **Tour St-Blaise**, part of a former fortified church of the Templars.

Steep, narrow streets lead up behind the tower to the 12thC church of **St-Paul**, flanked by an elegant turreted Renaissance house that was built above one of the medieval city gates. There are two buildings *(in av. Jean-Natte and av. de Beauregard)* in the North African style, designed by the architect Chapoulart and built in the 1880s, reflecting the 18th and 19thC vogue for the Orient.

In the SE suburbs, the 16-acre **Jardin Olbius-Riguier** is rich in exotic plants. W of Hyères, the main road to Toulon passes just below the high rocky crest of **Le Fenouillet** at 292 meters (960 feet): you can climb to the summit along a footpath off the D554 to Le Crau.

- **EVENTS** In May, a **French music week**. • In June, a **Provençal festival**. • In July, a **jazz festival**. • In August, a *santons* **fair**. • In October, a **theater festival**.

- A bustling market is held every morning, in place Massillon.

MERCURE
19 av. Amboise Thomas, 83400
☎94-65-03-04 94-35-58-20 84

rms ▦ ◛ ⇌ AE ⊚ WSA ☐ ⌂ ⌄ ▲
⌁ ⅋

A good, serviceable, modern hotel in a

commercial area not far from the town center and 3 kilometers (2 miles) from the beach.

🏨 Other hotels: **Le Paris** *(20 av. de Belgique* ☎ *94-65-33-61* Ⅲ) and **Les Pins d'Argent** *(Port St-Pierre* ☎ *94-57-63-60* Ⅲ).

=≡ **LES JARDINS DE BACCHUS**

32 av. Gambetta ☎ *94-65-77-63* Ⅲ 📧
▢ ▆ ᴬᴱ ₩ⁱˢᵃ Closed Sat lunch (summer); Sun eve (winter). Last orders 10pm.
One of the better restaurants in town, run and owned by Jean-Claude Santioni. The menu offers rich, traditional cuisine with a strong Provençal touch.

=≡ Another to try: **Chez Marius** (♣) *(pl. Massillon* ☎ *94-35-83-13* Ⅲ).

PLACES NEAR HYÈRES

Presqu'île de Giens *(11km/7 miles s of Hyères)*. The Giens peninsula would be one of the hilly ÎLES D'HYÈRES, except that it is now linked to the mainland by two strips of sand, each carrying a road. The E strip is relatively broad, covered with pines and bordered by a splendid beach on its seaward side. Here is the thriving resort of **La Capte**, where the campers' orange and yellow tents fill the pine forests.

The village of **Giens** stands on a hill in the center of its lovely wooded peninsula, crowned by a ruined castle: there are marvelous views from its terrace. At **La Tour Fondue** to the SE, where boats leave for Porquerolles, is a small fortress built under Cardinal Richelieu. The poet St-John Perse used to live at Giens.

🏨 **LE PROVENÇAL**

Giens, 83400 Hyères ☎ *94-58-20-09*
ᶠˣ*94-58-95-44* Ⅲ 45 rms ▅ =≡ ᴬᴱ ◉
◎ ₩ⁱˢᵃ ▢ ☀ ⚓ ▱ ⚘ ≪ ⌂ ℡ ⚲ ♨
Closed Nov–Apr.
Location: On a hill at the edge of the village, looking down across a large garden that slopes down to the sea. Spacious, elegant and wonderfully located, this is a large, modern building, with a snugly furnished *salon* and views from the wide balconies over the rocky coast below. The hotel has plenty of amenities and a breezy vacation atmosphere. There is a private beach (not sand), where lunches are served in summer; or there is a panoramic restaurant serving reasonable food.

Hyères-Plage The plain between Hyères and the sea is remarkably ugly, but full of activity. It is an important green-market center (fruit, spring vegetables, flowers) owing to the warm climate. Here is Toulon/Hyères Airport; here, too, is a string of brash new swimming resorts, notably Hyères-Plage.

Just to the s, on the isthmus leading to Giens, are the large Pesquier saltworks with their high, white piles of salt. There is a yacht marina at **Port d'Hyères**.

=≡ **BRASSERIE DES ÎLES**

Le Port Saint-Pierre, 83400 ☎ *94-57-49-75*
Ⅲ ▢ ▆ ᴬᴱ ◉ ₩ⁱˢᵃ Last orders 10pm.
Overlooking the marina, this cheerful restaurant is in two parts: a bright glassed-in area (with a palm tree growing through the middle) and a comfortable, even cozy indoor section. It is justly popular locally, offering generous, well-presented portions of good, fresh fish and seafood. There are meat dishes, of more variable standard, for insistent carnivores, but fish is the thing here. Try the *plateau de fruits de mer* or the *loup* (sea bass) with fennel, and *pistou* sauce. On offer is a good selection of Bandol, Côtes-de-Provence and other local wines.

HYÈRES, ÎLES D'

Map **12***J11. Frequent* **boat services** *all year (crossing takes 20 minutes) between La Tour Fondue and Porquerolles; other services (mainly in summer) from Toulon, Hyères-Plage, Le Lavandou and Cavalaire to all three islands; for* **information** ☎*94-66-21-81, 94-71-01-02 or 94-92-49-64.*

These three strange and beautiful islands, where the lushly subtropical blends with the wildly rugged, are known as the Îles d'Or, from the yellowish glint of their steep cliffs in the sunlight. Geologically, they are a breakaway from the MAURES MASSIF to the N. In the 16thC, criminals and convicts were granted right of asylum here, but many became pirates, and the islands were not finally pacified until the late 17thC.

Porquerolles

To the w, this is the largest of the islands. Its one village, on the N coast, was built in the 19thC as an army garrison, and has a broad main square with the same air of a military compound as one finds all over former French North Africa. In the little church there is a sequence of Stations of the Cross, sculpted in wood with a penknife by a soldier with sophisticated artistic gifts.

The N coast has sandy coves, good for swimming; the s is sheer and rugged. The island is covered with pines, heather and myrtle; it is ideal for walking, or you can rent a bicycle.

☞ ⚏ MAS DU LANGOUSTIER 🏨

83400, Île de Porquerolles ☎*94-58-30-09* 🅵🆇*94-58-36-02* ▥ *57 rms* AE ● ● VISA ▦ ♣ □ 🖼 ☙ ⟪ ♨ 🔥 ℘ *Closed mid-Oct to May.*

Location: 3km/2 miles w of the village. A very tranquil, recently upgraded and modernized hotel, with first-class cuisine served in a restaurant with lovely views. Fish dishes, including those Provençal favorites red mullet and *bouillabaisse,* are a speciality.

☞ RELAIS DE LA POSTE

Pl. des Armes, Porquerolles, 83540 Hyères ☎*94-58-30-26* ▥ *30 rms* ▦ 🖼 ✿ 🔥 *Closed Oct–Apr.*

Location: In the village square. A quiet, old-fashioned *auberge* run by the same family since 1880. The atmosphere is homely and the 19thC Provençal decor is genuine, not a modern imitation.

⚏ ☞ ARCHE DE NOÉ

Pl. des Armes ☎*94-58-30-74* ▥ *to* ▥ □ ▰ 🔥 *Closed Nov to mid-Mar. Last orders 9.30pm.*

Madame Bourgue talks with wistful pride of the days when her late husband ran this famous old 19thC inn, and she will eagerly show you the visitors' book with its dazzling signatures: King Baudouin, Chaplin, Mountbatten. . . . Today, Noah's Ark may be past its prime, but it still provides many a humble visitor with an honest meal — on the shady terrace, facing the square, or else in the ornate, dark-paneled dining room, with its great, central archway surmounted by frescoes of fish. Fish is the theme on the menu too, for example *langouste au whisky.*

The attached **Hôtel Arche de Noé** (▥) has 15 spacious bedrooms, some with large balconies facing the sea.

Port-Cros ★

In the middle, this is the loveliest, most mysterious of the three islands. It is hilly and thickly wooded: the presence of springs explains its lush vegetation. From the tiny port, with its fishermen's cottages and few small restaurants, you can walk to the **Vallon de la Solitude** or the cove of

Port-Man, through groves of shrubs and trees of every shade of bright green. Smoking is forbidden everywhere except at the port.

Port-Cros is more for the student of nature than the casual sightseer, and it has few beaches. It is also of literary interest, having inspired several novels. D.H. Lawrence once stayed here, as the guest of a young, well-bred Englishwoman who told him of her earthy affair with a local laborer. Lawrence then changed the locale — but not the theme — for his most famous novel.

- ✗ Port-Cros is owned by the State as a national park and nature reserve, and staff run unusual guided tours from June to September (☒). These include botanical rambles, and underwater explorations with scuba masks, to see the marine flora and fish life. For information ☎94-65-32-98 or 94-05-90-17.

☙ LE MANOIR D'HÉLÈNE

83145 Île-de-Port-Cros ☎*94-05-90-52*
☒*94-05-90-89* ▥ *20 rms* ◷ ⌂ ▣ ❧
Closed early Oct to May.
Location: By a creek close to the port and secluded in its own park. Pierre Buffet's family used to own the whole island. Today he is left with this graceful 18thC manor house, which — to make ends meet — he runs as a hotel, although it still seems far more like a private home: no reception desk and no sign at the gate save *propriété privée.*

M. Buffet and his wife are charming, cultivated hosts; their regular visitors include theatrical directors, actors, writers and musicians. The atmosphere is precisely that of a cultured house party, not a hotel. Bedrooms are simple and spacious, with 19thC furniture; food is plain but well cooked; there are few seaside amenities, save wind surfers and motor dinghies. An air of calm and romantic melancholy pervades, more Celtic than Latin, despite the palm trees.

Île du Lévant

This island, to the E, has high cliffs all around and dense foliage. The main part of the island belongs to the French Navy and is closed to visitors. But on the w side is the famous village of **Heliopolis**, one of the early pioneers among European naturist colonies, and still popular.

- See also: LE LAVANDOU, TOULON.

LE LAVANDOU

Map 12I11 (Var). 41km (26 miles) E of Toulon. Postal code: 83980. Population: 5,200 ℹ quai Gabriel Péri ☎*94-71-00-61.*

The old fishing port of Le Lavandou has today swollen into a sizeable seaside vacation resort, and the charm of the attractive harbor has been somewhat eroded by the rows of high-rise apartments. It is not a sophisticated place, but what compensates is the coast, with miles of good sandy beaches, notably to the E around **Cavalière** and **Le Rayol**. The wooded hills of the MAURES MASSIF behind make fine walking country.

☙ ➔ IN LE LAVANDOU

☙ ➔ LES ROCHES ◷ ❧

1 av. des Trois Dauphins, Aiguebelle Plage, 83980 ☎*94-71-05-07* ☒*94-71-08-40*

▥ to ▥ *42 rms* ▤ ◢ ▦ ◉ ▨ ▭
▢ ▣ ❧ ✦ ⛊ ☜ ⌁ ⌇ ⅄ ▣ ◪
Closed mid-Nov to mid-Dec; Jan to end Mar.

Location: At Aiguebelle, 3 kilometers (2 miles) along the coast road (D559) E *of Le Lavandou.* One of the finest hotels (and restaurants) in the area, with beautiful sea views, large bathrooms and excellently appointed, comfortable rooms, decorated with antiques in a Provençal style. Some of the larger rooms and suites have magnificent picture windows. Most rooms have balconies, and those that don't are right above the sea. The feeling (quite deliberately in the hotel's public areas) is of a 1930s cruise liner. There are shops, selling the chef's specialities, antiques, porcelain, and Souleiado products, and a discotheque, open to residents and their guests. English is spoken throughout the hotel. Service is polite, efficient, but very friendly. A sailboat is available in summer.

Breton chef Laurent Tarridec's light but carefully flavored cuisine is celebrated in the region. His strengths are fish, seafood, and specialities like duck or pigeon, with an extensive and well-tended selection of cheeses. Barbecues and buffets near the pool in summer.

☞ BELLE-VUE

Blvd. du Four des Maures, St-Clair, 83980 Le Lavandou ☎94-71-01-06 ⓕ94-71-64-72 ▥ *to* ▥ *19 rms* ▤ ⓐ ⓞ ▥ ⌂ ☎ ⋟ ⛾ ⌖ ⋢ ❦ ⋍ ⛾ *Closed Nov–Apr.*

Location: At St-Clair, just E *of Le Lavandou, on an open hillside just above the beach.* An entrancing little villa-hotel with a feminine touch, run by Mme Clare and her three daughters. The bedrooms, simple but pleasant, have wide balconies with tables and deck chairs and views of the sea, and the bathrooms are unusually attractive. Inside, the hotel is filled with flowers; outside, blue parasols are dotted about the garden. The food is reasonable but hardly exciting, and the *menu pension* offers no choice.

☞ ≡ LA CALANQUE

62 av. Général-de-Gaulle, 83980 Le Lavandou ☎94-71-05-96 ⓕ94-71-20-12 ▥ *to* ▥ *37 rms* ⋒ ▤ ⓞ ⓞ ▥ ⋢ ⌖ ⌂ ⋟ ⋍ ❦ ⋈ ⋍ ⛾ *Closed Jan to mid-Feb.*

Location: Overlooking the harbor. A long, white Provençal villa. The rooms are comfortable, and all have sea views; the service is attentive. The large dining room and its terrace both overlook the sea (▥ ⌂ ⋈ ⋍ *closed Wed, Jan to mid-Feb, last orders 10.30pm in summer).* The food is better than average, with flourishes of individuality. *Specialities: Navarin de loup, mousseline chaude de rascasse et saumon à la menthe fraîche.*

☞ Other recommended hotels in Le Lavandou include: **Éspadon** *(pl. Ernest-Reyer* ☎94-71-00-20 ⓕ94-64-79-19 ▥), **La Lune** *(10 av. Général-de-Gaulle* ☎94-71-04-20 ▥) and **Neptune** *(26 av. Général-de-Gaulle* ☎94-71-01-01 ⓕ94-64-91-61 ▥).

≡ LA BOUÉE

Rue Ch.-Cazin ☎94-71-11-88 ▥ *Last orders 9.30pm.*

Friendly service, careful cooking and good value. Lobster is a speciality.

≡ AU VIEUX PORT

Quai Gabriel-Péri ☎94-71-00-21 ▥ ⌂ ⋈ ❦ ⊞ ▤ ⓞ ▥ *Closed Wed off-season; Oct to mid-Mar. Last orders 10.30pm.*

The English *patron* and his chef from Alsace conspire to serve an excellent *bouillabaisse* and other local fish dishes, at this gaily decorated little restaurant facing the port. The menu changes often; desserts are especially good.

▶ NIGHTLIFE IN LE LAVANDOU

Much the best disco in the area is **Le Tropicana** *(on the beach at Le Rayol, 13km/8 miles to the* E ☎94-05-61-50).

PLACES NEAR LE LAVANDOU

Bormes-les-Mimosas (☆) *(5km/3 miles* NW *of Le Lavandou).* One of the most elegant of all Provençal hill-villages, Bormes-les-Mimosas stands on a hilltop amid mimosa and eucalyptus groves, with commanding views of the sea. The houses are painted in pastel shades of blue, yellow and pink — a change from the austere air of most other hill-villages, with their streets of ancient gray stone.

✅ LE MIRAGE

Route du Stade, 83230 Bormes-les-Mimosas ☎94-71-09-83 📠94-64-93-03 ▥ 35 rms ⬅ ≕ ▣ ⬇ ◉ ▥ ☐ ▱ 🍴 ⚓ ⟨⟨ ♨ ≈ ♒ ⛾

Location: Just to the SE of Bormes, 2.5km (1½ miles) away, on an open hillside facing the sea. Built in a modern, functional style, this recently upgraded hotel is a delightful vacation spot, cheerfully run and superbly located. It has a garden with a lawn, and a pleasant bar beside the heated swimming pool. The brightly decorated rooms nearly all have wide balconies with views over the coast and islands.

≕ LA TONNELLE DES DÉLICES

Pl. Gambetta ☎94-71-34-84 ▥ ▥ ☐

■ ⚓ *Closed Nov–Apr. Last orders 10pm.* The name means "arbor of delights" — a fitting one for this serene and intimate little place, screened from the main village square by a vine- and rose-bower. No longer the defiantly Provençal restaurant it was; the new owner is trying hard to make the fare more "modern."

≕ **L'Escoundudo** (*2 Ruelle du Moulin* ☎94-71-15-53 ▥) serves authentic Provençal cooking in a pleasant ambience.

≕ Other recommended restaurants: **La Cassoule** (*1 Ruelle du Moulin* ☎94-71-14-86); **Le Jardin de Perlefleurs** (*100 Chemin de l'Orangerie* ☎94-64-99-23).

PLACES NEAR LE LAVANDOU

Cabasson (*8km/5 miles SW of Le Lavandou*). A hamlet on the W side of the high promontory of Cap Bénat with its wild rocky coast, best seen on a boat excursion from Le Lavandou. (Part of the Cap belongs to the military and is closed to the public.)

Farther S from Cabasson, the fortress of **Brégançon**, built by Vauban, stands in solitary grandeur by the sea; it is now an official summer residence of the President.

✅ ≕ LES PALMIERS

240 Chemin du Petit Fort, Cabasson, 83230 Bormes-les-Mimosas ☎94-64-81-94 📠94-64-93-61 ▥ to ▥ 21 rms ⬅ ▣ ⬇ ◉ ▥ ⌂ ♨ ▱ ♒ ☎

Location: Near the beach, on a relatively undiscovered part of the coast. A good choice for a quiet, simple seaside vacation. This is a family hotel run with real warmth, and once a week or so there is a *soirée-surprise* with a visiting orchestra or folk group. The comfortable bedrooms overlook a garden that is filled with many different species of tree, including weeping willow, blue cedar, orange and palm. TV in many rooms. The large Provençal dining room (☐ ■ ▤ ⚓ *last orders 10pm*) offers good views, honest cooking and good set-menu value.

Cavalière (*8km/5 miles E of Le Lavandou*). A small resort in a sheltered bay, backed by pine forests and with a splendid sandy beach.

✅ LE CLUB 🏠 △

Plage de Cavalière, 83980 Le Lavandou ☎94-05-80-14 📠94-05-73-16 ▥ 32 rms ▤ ⬅ ≕ ▣ ⬇ ▥ ⌂ ♨ ☐ ▱

♒ ⟨⟨ ♨ ☎ ♒ ≈ ⛾ ▣ *Closed Oct–May.*

Location: By the beach. The most fashionable address on the coast between St-Tropez and Marseille is aptly named, for the ambience is that of an exclusive, highly sophisticated club, with a private beach and dancing at night by the sea. Bedrooms are predictably luxurious, some in separate bungalows with their own patios.

The sumptuous dining room of the hotel (▥ ▭ ▬ ▬ ▲ ▤ *closed*

Oct-May, last orders 10pm) and seaside terrace provide fit settings for the excellent *cuisine*. The set menu (dinner only) is not unduly expensive, but expect to pay handsomely for chef Patrick Beekes's best creations, using first-class ingredients, on the *carte*. Try the tuna fish, or the pasta with squid and pesto.

• See also: CAVALAIRE-SUR-MER, HYÈRES.

MANOSQUE
Map 6E9 (Alpes-de-H.-P.). 53km (33 miles) NE of Aix. Postal code: 04100. Population: 19,100 i pl. Dr. P.-Joubert ☎92-72-16-00.

Medieval Manosque, now a lively agricultural center, spreads itself on a slope above the Durance valley. As at CARPENTRAS, a circular boulevard has replaced the old ramparts, but two fortified 14thC gateways survive: the high **Porte de la Saunerie**, floodlit at night, is a fine sight. Inside is a maze of narrow streets, lined by tall, typically Provençal town houses. Some of the streets are paved and closed to traffic.

The novelist Jean Giono lived here earlier this century, and both the town and the region influenced much of his writing.

• **EVENT** There is a **jazz festival** in late July.

❧ **François 1er** (▬) *(18 rue Guilhempierre ☎92-72-07-99 ▥ ◼ ▥)*, a clean and friendly commercial hotel, will open up for very late arrivals.

▬ **André** *(21bis pl. du Terreau ☎92-72-03-09 ▥ closed Mon, June)*, a family-run *auberge*, popular with the locals, serves regional cooking.

▬❧ **NEARBY**

▬❧ **LA FUSTE** ⌂
Route de Barrème, La Fuste (6km/4 miles E of Manosque) ☎92-72-05-95 ▥ ▭ ▬

▬ ▲ ▬ ▣ ◼ ▣ ▥ *Closed Sun dinner; Mon (mid-Sept to June); Jan–Mar.*
A 17thC coaching inn, standing in its own park, has become a well-known luxury restaurant, run with style by the Jourdan family. It feels remote, but is close to a main highway and attracts a sophisticated international clientele. Daniel Jourdan's fine cooking is an imaginative version of more traditional regional cuisine. *Specialities: Truite à la nage, gigot de poulette au gingembre.* There are nice bedrooms at the *hostellerie,* all gracefully furnished and very popular (▥).

PLACES NEAR MANOSQUE
Cadarache *(16km/10 miles SW of Manosque).* On the Durance, the Cadarache hydroelectric dam stands adjacent to one of France's leading nuclear research centers (closed to the public).
Gréoux-les-Bains *(14km/9 miles SE of Manosque).* A small spa town on the river Verdon, where rheumatism, arthritis and chest troubles are treated. The waters are thought to have been used for thermal cures even in pre-Roman times. A Roman votive inscription can be seen in the modern baths.

• See also: LUBÉRON, MONTAGNE DU.

MAURES MASSIF
Map 12H11. Var.

The wooded mountain range of schistous rock follows the coast for 56 kilometers (35 miles) from HYÈRES to FRÉJUS. It is almost as ancient as the Esterel massif to the NE, and very much larger. Its name comes from Greek and from the Provençal word *maouro,* meaning "dark," on account of its somber woods of Aleppo pine and chestnut; it is not derived, as is often supposed, from *Les Maures* — the Moors (or Saracens), who occupied and ravaged the region in the 9th–10thC, having already colonized Spain.

Until the tourist boom of the 20thC, this part of the coast was unpopulated, except for the old fortified port of ST-TROPEZ. Today, it is an unbroken string of swimming resorts, the high-rise buildings of which have only partly spoiled the lovely scenery, seen at its best on the **Corniche des Maures** between LE LAVANDOU and CAVALAIRE-SUR-MER, and around STE-MAXIME (see also GRIMAUD and PORT-GRIMAUD). The wild interior of the massif is still remarkably unspoiled and little-known. It is covered with a profusion of rare plants and flowers, as well as with great forests of chestnut and cork oak which provide the area with two of its industries: the making of *marrons glacés* and of corks for wine bottles.

Several scenic roads wind through the heart of the massif, offering majestic views of the coast and mountains. Take, for example, the road from Le Lavandou via the **Col de Babaou** to **Collobrières** and thence to Grimaud, with a detour to the ruined 18thC monastery of the **Chartreuse de la Verne** *(open daily, closed Tues from Oct-June).* Or from Collobrières drive up close to **La Sauvette**, the massif's highest peak, 780 meters (2,550 feet) high, and then by way of La Garde-Freinet to Plan-de-la-Tour and back to the coast at Ste-Maxime. Or, from Bormes-les-Mimosas, drive up to the rocky peak of the **Pierre d'Avenon** above Le Lavandou.

PORT-GRIMAUD ☆
Map 13H12 (Var). 7km (4 miles) w of St-Tropez. Postal code: 83310.

Port-Grimaud can well claim to be one of the most dazzling architectural achievements in postwar France, a triumph of the current return to the vernacular. On the shore of the bay of St-Tropez, the Alsatian architect François Spoerry has built a graceful small-scale Venice on the site of a former swamp — a luxury vacation village where there are no roads, only broad canals and little alleys, linked by pretty, arched bridges. The houses are in Provençal fishing-port style, painted in a variety of bright colors and no two looking alike. Viewed from a boat on the canals, the design is pleasing and ingenious, and achieves harmony. Other developments along the coast have tried to ape Port-Grimaud, with much less charm and success.

The houses, individually owned, appeal especially to sailing enthusiasts, for each has its own mooring by the front door. Spoerry has also conceived Port-Grimaud as a real village: around its little main square are shops, banks, cafés, a post office, and an interdenominational church.

Unlike Port-Galère (see THÉOULE), the village is open to tourists, although only on foot. Climb the tower of the church for a fine view over ST-TROPEZ, the bay and the mountains, and the port at your feet. Or tour the canals by renting an electric self-drive boat *(80f for a 30-minute ride for two)* or taking one of the regular sightseeing cruises.

Denise Spoerry, the architect's wife, has an expensive but interesting interior design store at the entrance to the village, selling lamps, statues and vases designed by her and her husband.

GIRAGLIA

Pl. du 14-Juin ☎ 94-56-31-33
94-56-33-77 48 rms AE Closed Oct to mid-Apr.

Location: On an outer arm of the new port, between a quiet canal and the beach. This glamorous, modern seaside hotel, in rural Provençal style, is part of the master design for Port-Grimaud. It is built around a lovely swimming pool and beside its own private beach of fine sand (there are facilities for wind surfing, waterskiing, etc.). The luxurious bedrooms are in various period styles, and the general decor is sympathetic and sophisticated. Artificial the Giraglia may be, but what it does, it does well.

The hotel's restaurant, **Amphitrite** (*last orders 10pm),*

- See also: GRIMAUD.

is a cheerful dining room with views across the bay of St-Tropez. In summer, tables are set out under parasols around the pool. The cuisine is a creative blend of variations on traditional themes. *Specialities: Panaché de poisson en bourride, caneton braisé au miel, pigeon with pine nuts and chestnuts, capon stuffed with olives.*

Other recommended hotel: **Hôtel du Port** *(pl. du Marché ☎ 94-56-36-18 to),* in a picturesque location right by the port.

LA TARTANE

8 rue de l'Octogone ☎ 94-56-38-32 Closed Nov–Mar.

An attractive place, with a view over a canal. You can enjoy *poulet de Bresse aux morilles* or baked sea bass.

RIEZ

Map 7E10 (Alpes-de-H.-P.). 25km (16 miles) E of Manosque. Postal code: 04500. Population: 1,700 **i** pl. de la Colonne ☎ (Mairie) 92-77-80-21.

Here is another pleasant and unassuming Provençal town that once knew days of far greater importance, being, in both Roman and early Christian times, an important religious center. Reminders of those days include the remains of a Roman temple standing in a meadow on the town's w side: four gray granite columns with white marble Corinthian capitals.

Close by, across the river, is a 5thC Merovingian **baptistry**, not unlike those at AIX and FRÉJUS: its hexagonal interior has eight granite columns with marble capitals *(key available from tourist office).* The *vieille ville,* once surrounded by ramparts, is attractive with its long alleys.

To the w stretches the wide plateau of **Valensole**, France's principal region of lavender cultivation. It is at its best in July, when the fields and hills are a blaze of fragrant purple lavender.

- **MARKET**   There is a market on Wednesday.
- See also: VERDON, GRAND CANYON DU.

ST-MAXIMIN-LA-SAINTE-BAUME

*Map 11G9 (Var). 43km (27 miles) E of Aix-en-Provence. Postal code: 83470.
Population: 9,600 ℹ Hôtel de Ville ☎94-78-00-09.*

A lively little market town with some pleasant old streets, known above all for its famous basilica.

- **EVENTS**   Second weekend of June, **horse fair**. • First weekend of July, **antique market**. • End of July, **Fête de Ste-Marie Madeleine**. • Late September, **organ festival**. • Last weekend of November, *santons* and **craft fair**.

- **MARKET**   There is a market on Wednesday morning.

Ste-Marie-Madeleine, Basilique 血 † ☆
🚶 *Open 9–11.45am, 2–7pm.*

The basilica is the finest Gothic building in Provence, in the town named after Maximin, the saint who, according to the legend, accompanied the three Marys from Palestine to LES SAINTES-MARIES-DE-LA-MER and was then martyred in Aix, where he had gone to evangelize. The tombs in its crypt have been venerated as his and Mary Magdalene's. This crypt was covered over for safety during the Saracen period, then rediscovered in 1279; and it was soon after this, in 1295, that the building of the abbey began, on the orders of Charles II of Anjou. The construction took more than two centuries, and even today the facade is not complete.

The abbey was saved from demolition during the French Revolution through the lucky chance that Napoléon Bonaparte's young brother Lucien was stationed in the town and took the building over as a military warehouse.

The vaulted nave, rising to 18 meters (60 feet), and the polygonal apse, with its high windows, are both of great beauty. Unlike many in Provence, the church has a feeling of light and space and its many fine art works can be seen to good effect. Among them, note the 17thC choir screen in sculpted wood, the fine 18thC organ, and the great 18thC pulpit carved out of a single piece of wood. Above all, to the left of the high altar, is an unusual 16thC retable by Antonio Ronzen of the Venetian school: his 16 painted panels portray the life and Passion of Christ against such backgrounds as the Colosseum at Rome, St Mark's, Venice, and the Palais des Papes at AVIGNON.

The crypt was originally the burial vault of an early 5thC Roman villa. Its four sarcophagi are among the oldest Christian relics in France — even if there is little historical substance in the legend that they are the tombs of saints. A 19thC gilt-bronze reliquary holds a skull that has long been worshiped as that of St Mary Magdalene.

≡ **Chez Nous** (🍲) *(3 blvd. Jean-Jaurès* ☎*94-78-02-57* ▭ *closed Wed),* a simple *auberge* on the main road, serving Provençal dishes such as *noisettes d'agneau au jus de basilic,* and good game.

- See also: AIX-EN-PROVENCE, BARJOLS.

ST-RAPHAEL

*Map **13**G13 (Var). 43km (27 miles) sw of Cannes. Postal code: 83700.*
*Population: 26,000 **i** rue Waldeck-Rousseau ☎94-19-52-52. **Railway station:***
*rue Waldeck-Rousseau ☎94-95-16-90. **Airport:** at Fréjus (open July–Aug only)*
☎94-51-04-07.

The sizeable, long-established swimming resort of St-Raphael looks across the Gulf of Fréjus to the MAURES MASSIF and is sheltered by the Esterel massif. It is a rather sedate place, but good for families, with its miles of public sandy beach, lively sea front and excellent marina. It is also popular for conferences.

Offshore lie the strangely-formed twin red rocks of the **Lion de Terre** and **Lion de Mer**.

St-Raphael was settled by the Romans at the same time as adjacent FRÉJUS. Roman villas, of which no traces remain, once stood on the site of the modern casino.

It was in the harbor here that Napoléon Bonaparte disembarked on his return from Egypt in 1799, then later set sail for exile in Elba in 1814. St-Raphael was then a mere fishing village. It was first developed as a resort in the 1860s, thanks largely to the Parisian journalist Alphonse Karr, ex-editor of *Le Figaro,* who settled here and encouraged his friends to come too. One who responded was Gounod, who composed *Roméo et Juliette* here in 1866.

Set up to take in interesting finds of local diving clubs, the **Musée d'Archéologie Sous-Marine** *(rue des Templiers ☎94-52-22-74 ▨ open mid-June to mid-Sept 10am-noon and 3-6pm, closed Tues; mid-Sept to mid-June 10am-noon, 2-5pm, closed Sun)* contains old ships' anchors, an array of Classical amphorae, and, in the garden, two 18thC warships' cannons and other objects. Next to the museum is the 12thC **Église des Templiers**, a single, vaulted Romanesque building of austere simplicity.

☙ LA POTINIÈRE

Route des Plaines, 83700 St-Raphael
☎94-95-21-43 ▣94-95-29-10 ▥ to ▥
25 rms ➡ ▦ ▣ ▥ ➩ & ◻ ▢ ♥
♨ ≈ ♠

Location: In its own wooded park near the beach, 4 kilometers (2½ miles) E of St-Raphael in the residential suburb of Boulouris. A modern vacation hotel run by the Hotte family. The atmosphere is youthful and sporty, if a little stark. Several villas are spread out in a small park full of pines and mimosa. The modern rooms may not inspire you, but they have balconies with deck chairs, and you can park, motel-style, right by your door. The hotel has its own 8-seat motor yacht with skipper, which is available for fishing parties and short cruises. The bright restaurant is pleasant enough, but neither the food

nor the service really stands out.

☙ Other reasonable hotels to look at in St-Raphael include **Beau Séjour** *(promenade René-Coty ☎94-95-03-75 ▣94-95-06-75 ▥), **Excelsior** (blvd. Félix Martin ☎94-95-02-42 ▣94-95-33-82 ▥ to ▥), **Provençal** (197 rue de la Garonne ☎94-95-01-52 ▥)* and **Les Relais Bleus** *(Port Santa Lucia ☎94-95-31-31 ▣94-82-21-46) ▥).*

═ Other restaurants: **L'Arbousier** *(4 av. Valescure ☎94-95-25-00 ▥ to ▥),* **L'Orangerie** *(promenade Réne-Coty ☎94-83-10-50 ▥),* **Pastorel** *(♣) (54 rue de la Liberté ☎94-95-02-36 ▥ to ▥)* and **La Voile d'Or** *(1 blvd. Gén-de-Gaulle ☎94-95-17-04 ▥).*

⬛ NIGHTLIFE IN ST-RAPHAEL

Casino

☎94-95-10-59 ❍ ❀ ♪ ☙ *Dancing with orchestra July–Aug nightly 10pm–3am; rest of year Sat, Sun only. Joker disco open all year from 10pm. Casino open daily. Closed Nov to mid-Dec.*

For a resort lacking sparkle, the casino complex is very lively in season.

Discos **La Réserve** *(promenade René-Coty* ☎94-95-02-20*)* is the smartest disco in town. **Le Toukan** *(Plage de Boulouris* ☎94-95-21-66)M *is also popular.*

Piano bars Try **Le Kilt** *(rue Jules-Barbier* ☎94-95-29-20*)* or **Embassy** *(blvd. F. Martin* ☎94-95-02-19*)*.

PLACE NEAR ST-RAPHAEL

Valescure *(3km/2 miles N of St-Raphael).* High on the slopes of the Esterel massif, this is a residential zone of properous villas scattered amid a pine forest. Valescure used to be favored by wealthy English people as a winter health resort, but times have changed, and its barracks-like turn-of-the-century hotels now stand empty, or are used as apartments. However, the famous golf course is still popular (the Grand Duke Michael founded it in 1891): for membership details consult the GOLF HÔTEL.

❧ GOLF HÔTEL

Valescure, 83700 St-Raphael
☎94-82-40-31 ⬛94-82-41-88 ▥ 40 rms ▤ ➴ ≈(last orders 9.15pm) ᴀᴇ
▣ ▣ ▥ ⌂ ≵ ♿ ▢ ⟠ ☙ ≋ ♒ ✔
🏊 *Closed mid-Nov to Feb.*

Location: Next to the golf course, in a pine wood at an altitude of 550 meters (1,800 feet). The old Golf Hôtel, built in the 1890s, closed some years ago, and in 1981 there opened in its place this comfortable, modern super-motel, geared particularly to sporting vacations. It owns the golf course, and the surrounding countryside is excellent for walking. Green fees are cheaper for residents.

❧ ═ SAN PEDRO

Av. du Colonel Brooke, 83700 St-Raphael
☎94-83-65-69 ⬛94-40-57-20 ▥ to ▥
27 rms ▤ ➴ ᴀᴇ ▣ ▥ ⌂ ≵ ▢ ☙ ✿
🏊 ≋ ♥ ✔ ⚲ ♈ ▱ *Closed Jan.*

Location: Near the Valescure golf course and tennis club, on the road from St-Raphael. The extraordinary, almost operatic decor in some of the hotel's public areas may not suit everyone, but the bedrooms are comfortable and well-appointed, and the setting, among pines, is pleasant. Chef Philippe Troncy's cuisine is interesting, light and well executed, and smartly served. You can eat, or have a pre-dinner drink outside, near the pool. *(Last orders 9.45pm.)*

• See also: AGAY, FRÉJUS.

ST-TROPEZ

Map 13H12 (Var). 69km (43 miles) E of Toulon. Postal code: 83990. Population: 5,750 ℹ *quai Jean-Jaurès* ☎94-97-45-21.

That legend of our times, St-Tropez, is what you make of it. For some, it remains a charming old fishing port, loved by artists, cradled by green hills and facing out across its blue bay toward the Maures mountains. For others, it is a haunt of high society; or a stage for trendily bohemian eccentrics; or a commercialized fairground beset by touristy mobs that come in hapless quest of that elusive legend. There's no doubt that the legend has grown distinctly jaded, since the far-off days when, along with Haight-Ashbury and Carnaby Street, St-Tropez embodied the Swinging Sixties.

St-Tropez' propulsion into limelight at that time was spearheaded by a movie director and his young starlet wife, but its true beginnings stemmed from less pleasant happenings. It was named after Torpes, a Roman officer martyred under Nero for his Christian beliefs, whose headless body is said to have found its way across the sea to this spot; he is venerated to this day by a bust in the main church and by the annual *bravade* festival.

Destroyed by the Moors in 739, St-Tropez was finally rebuilt in the 15thC by the Genoese, and for nearly 200 years was semi-autonomous. Its citizens had a flair for naval warfare, putting a Spanish fleet to rout in 1637, so it is fitting that France's greatest admiral, the Bailli de Suffren, should have been born here. His statue is to be found on Quai de Suffren.

St-Tropez' status as a center of culture did not begin until the late 19thC, when Guy de Maupassant discovered it by chance. In 1892 the painter Paul Signac settled here, and was quickly followed by Bonnard, Matisse and others who came for the summer. Between the wars, the town became a kind of *Montparnasse plage,* full of artists and writers, such as Colette, taking summer breaks from Paris. In August 1944 the retreating Germans blew up the port: the pretty pink, white and yellow houses that line the quay today are clever copies of the old ones.

In 1957, St-Tropez's postwar fortunes took another sharp change of direction. Roger Vadim brought the little-known Brigitte Bardot on location here, to make *And God Created Woman.* The film was a *succès fou* and started a cult for both Bardot and St-Tropez.

Today, despite St-Tropez' tarnished reputation, it still attracts enough lovely ladies and smooth young men from the milieu of fashion, showbiz and the media to keep its trendy flavor; and a surprising number of truly rich, distinguished and famous remain loyal to St-Tropez. Among those with villas in or near town are Bardot, wife-and-husband Charlotte Rampling and Jean-Michel Jarre, and Gunter Sachs. Other celebrities line up their yachts, stern-to, along the quay, among them Harold Robbins and Jack Nicholson.

In summer, St-Tropez can be unbearably crowded. In winter, it almost shuts down. But a visit out of season, if you're lucky with the weather (alone among the Côte d'Azur's resorts, it faces N, wide open to the driving Mistral), can be extremely pleasant, and gives some idea of why the place became so popular in the first place. Prices in restaurants, bars and hotels also fall to about half their summer levels.

Traffic and parking problems can be unbearable in summer, with the 20-kilometer ($12\frac{1}{2}$-mile) journey along the coast to Ste-Maxime taking as much as 2 hours. So, do what the locals do and take the ferry service that runs between the two towns, every half-hour from 7am–1am.

- **EVENTS** The folk festivals known as *bravades* are peculiar to this part of France, and the two at St-Tropez are especially famous. May 16–18 sees the **Bravade de St-Torpes**, dating from the 16thC. The bust of the saint is taken from the church and carried in procession around the town, with a guard of 100 men in 18thC uniform, amid music, mirth and firing of blank cartridges. Visitors are welcome to join in. • On June 15, there is the **Fête des Espagnols**, a more modest *bravade,* to commemorate the victory over the Spanish fleet in 1637. • In June there is also an **open tennis tournament**. • In July and August, there are **classical concerts** about once a month in the citadel. • At the end of September or the beginning of October is the **Nioulargue**, a major local race for old sailing-boats.

WHAT TO SEE IN ST-TROPEZ
Annonciade, Musée de l' ☆
Pl. Georges-Grammont ☎ *94-97-04-01* ▨ *Open June–Sept 10am–noon, 3–7pm; Oct, Dec–May 10am–noon, 2–6pm. Closed Tues; Nov.*
St-Tropez's turn-of-the-century heritage as a leading artistic center has resulted in one of France's finest collections of paintings from that period. It was donated to the town in 1955 by local connoisseur Georges Grammont. Spacious and beautifully lit, the museum — a former 16thC chapel — has marble and bronze sculptures by Maillol and Despiau, and some 100 canvases, both by St-Tropez artists such as Signac, Matisse and Bonnard, and by many others.

There are charming Van Dongen portraits of girls, attractive bathing scenes by Manguin, cheerful Dufys, and colorful Provençal landscapes from Vlaminck and Braque. St-Tropez itself appears time and again — in a colorful Camoin, a subtle pointilliste Signac, and drawings and gouaches by Segonzac.

Citadelle
▨ *Open June–Sept 10am–6pm; Oct–May 10am–5pm. Closed Thurs; Nov.*
This 17thC fortress stands on a hill just E of the town, surrounded by ramparts and a moat. In its *donjon* is a **maritime museum**, with a

reconstructed Greek galley, 17thC maps of the Mediterranean, engravings of old St-Tropez and details of the 1944 Liberation.

It's well worth strolling around the **Ponche** area of the old town, to get an idea of what it was that attracted French intellectuals to St-Tropez in the first place. The district is dilapidated now, but atmospheric nonetheless (the feeling is rather Southern Mediterranean), with some fine architectural details. Rue des Ramparts is lined with small restaurants, and leads you to a view of the coast. Round the corner, in pretty place de l'Ormeau, you will find an 18thC church with a restored bell tower.

✎ WHERE TO STAY IN ST-TROPEZ

BYBLOS 🏨
Av. Paul-Signac, 83990 St-Tropez
☎94-97-00-04　📠94-97-40-52　▥ 103
rms ▦ ▤ AE ⊡ ⊙ ▥ ⊡ ✻ □ ⧠
❦ 《 🛥 ⚓ ♈ ▣ ⊙ 🛎 ○　Closed Oct–
Mar. For ⚌ see LE CHABICHOU, opposite.
Location: On a hillside below the Citadel, 450 meters (500 yards) from the port. One of the most fashionable hotels on the Côte d'Azur, this exotic fantasy was the dream child of a wealthy Lebanese, Proseper Gay-Para. He built it in 1967 and named it after the ancient Phoenician city that once stood on his native shore. The hotel is a pastiche of a Provençal hill-village, with little white-walled, red-roofed houses grouped intimately around the swimming pool. Inside is an ingenious labyrinth of patios, alcoves and archways where enough ancient and modern *objets d'art* have been assembled to fill a museum, mostly from Lebanon and Syria, with Greek and Roman touches. Everything, from bedrooms individually furnished with opulent Oriental fabrics and European antiques, to the *salon Arabe,* transferred intact from a Beirut palace, attains a level of studied glamor that comes near to setting new records even for the Côte d'Azur.

LA FIGUIÈRE
Route de Tahiti, 83350 Ramatuelle
☎94-97-18-21　▥ to ▥ 38 rms ⚌ ⊡
□ ⧠ ❧ ❦ 🛥 ♒ ♈　Closed Oct–Apr.
Location: In open country, amid vineyards, close to Tahiti Beach. Modern villas have been grouped around a converted 18thC farmhouse to form a delightful country hotel that seems all the more peaceful for its proximity to St-Tropez.

LOU TROUPELEN
Chemin des Vendanges, 83990 St-Tropez
☎94-97-44-88　📠94-97-41-76　▥ 44
rms ➤ AE ⊡ ⊙ ▥ ♒ □ ❧ ❦
Closed Nov to mid-Apr.
Location: Amid vineyards on the SE fringe of town. A hotel designed in the style of an old, pink-walled Provençal *mas,* and set in a pretty garden. Rooms are simple but comfortable, and the atmosphere is cheerful and cozy.

LE MAS DE CHASTELAS 🏨
Route de Gassin, 83990 St-Tropez
☎94-56-09-11　📠94-56-11-56　▥ 31
rms ➤ AE ⊡ ▥ ♒ □ ⧠ 🛥
♒ 🛎　Closed Oct–Easter. For ⚌ see LE
MAS DE CHASTELAS, *on page 200.*
Location: Amid pine woods and vineyards, 3 kilometers (2 miles) w of St-Tropez. A 17thC farmhouse, formerly used for breeding silkworms, converted into a select little hotel, is very much in vogue with celebrities who remain loyal to St-Tropez but seek refuge from the harbor area. The visitors' book is filled with eye-catching names from the arts world: Sagan, Depardieu, Nastassia Kinski. Certainly the hotel is beautiful, with the exact ambience of a private house party, where guests easily strike up friendships and return every year. There are few greater pleasures than sitting by the lovely pool, or in the graceful salon, sipping an exquisite *champagne framboise.* Amenities at this delightful hotel include a Jacuzzi and a children's playground.

LE SUBE

Quai de Suffren, 83990 St-Tropez
☎94-97-30-04 ☒94-54-89-08 ▯▯ to ▯▯
30 rms ▦ ▭ ▣ ◉ ◎ ▨ ▢ ◹ ◁ ☯
*Location: The only hotel on the quay-
side, overlooking St-Tropez harbor, just
behind the statue of Admiral Suffren.*
A good, friendly, very well-located
hotel. Even if you don't have a room
with a view of the port and its moored
gin-palaces, you can go to the lively bar
(a focal meeting point in season) and
admire it from there. You will certainly
get the feel of St-Tropez life here.

RÉSIDENCE DE LA PINÈDE ▥

Plage de la Bouillabaisse, 83990 St-Tropez
☎94-97-04-21 ☒94-97-73-64 ▦ *36*
rms ▦ ▬ ▣ ◉ ◎ ▨ ◻ ✿ ▢ ◁ ⚿
☙ ◁ ▲ ⚘ ✓ ♈ ▣ *Closed Oct–Mar.*
*Location: One kilometer w of St-Tropez
on the D98.* Shaded by pines, with its
own beach and a panoramic view of the
coast around St-Tropez, this old villa
has long been one of the most popular
hotels in the area. Its restaurant is as
renowned as the hotel itself, and you
can eat outside on the lovely terrace.

VILLA DE BELIEU ▥

Domaines de Bertaud-Belieu, 83580 Gassin
☎94-56-40-56 ☒94-43-43-34 ▦ *18
rms* ▦ ▣ ⇆ ▣ ▨ ▢ ◻ ☙ ◁
▲ ⚭ ☌ ♈ ✓ ♈ ▣
Location: Up a tree-lined drive, 3.5 km

(2 miles) w of St-Tropez on the N98.
One of the most extraordinary hotels on
the whole coast, with the highest standards of luxury and a well-earned reputation for exclusivity — at appropriately
high prices. It is the fantasy creation of
its millionaire owner, and has appealed
to the likes of Joan Collins, Roger Moore
and Clint Eastwood. No expense has
been spared in designing the rooms in
completely different styles, almost as if
they were stage- or film-sets: one is
decorated in Art Deco fashion; another
as a library; a third as an art gallery. All
bathrooms have Jacuzzis, and there is
an expensive but first-class restaurant
(open to nonresidents), with formal service, specializing in imaginative fish
dishes. Helicopter transfer for guests
from Nice airport. Nearby is the hotel's
own Bertaud-Belieu vineyard, which
produces some of the best Côtes-de-
Provence wines in the area.

☙ Other good hotels: **La Bastide
de St-Tropez** *(Route des Carles* ☎*94-
97-58-16* ☒*94-97-21-71* ▦*),* **La
Mandarine** *(Route de Tahiti* ☎*94-97-
21-00* ☒*94-97-33-67* ▦*),* **La Ponche** *(pl. du Revelin* ☎*94-97-02-53*
☒*94-97-78-61* ▯▯ *to* ▦*),* **Treizain**
*(Domaine du Treizain, Route de Gas-
sin* ☎*94-97-70-08* ☒*94-97-67-25*
▦*)* and **Le Yaca** *(1-3 blvd. d'Aumale*
☎*94-97-11-79* ☒*94-97-58-50* ▦*).*

▰ WHERE TO EAT IN ST-TROPEZ

LE CHABICHOU ◮

Hôtel Byblos, Av. Paul-Signac
☎94-54-80-00 ▦ *to* ▦ ▦ ▬ ▣
◉ ◎ ▨ ▭ ▢ ◼ ▰ *Closed mid-Oct
to mid-Apr; lunch July–Aug. Last orders
10pm.*
The luxurious restaurant of the BYBLOS
hotel (see ☙ above) serves its dazzling array of guests with some of the
best food to be found in the area, with
prices to match. Chef Michel Rochedy's
cuisine is up-to-the-minute and quite
complex. *Specialities: Tatin de thon au
caramel d'épice, rôti de turbot sur
l'arête, mitonée de langue et pied de
veau "paquet."*

TABLE DU MARCHÉ

38 rue Georges-Clémenceau ☎*94-97-
85-20* ▯▯ ▭ ▣ ◉ ▨ *Closed Mon
except in season; mid-Nov to mid-Dec.*
One of the trendiest restaurants in town,
just off place des Lices. Smart waiters in
claret aprons serve mostly simple, well-
presented food from a short menu in
this nicely decorated bistro. Try chef/
patron Christophe Leroy's pigeon salad,
or spaghetti with lobster and clams.

CAFÉ DES ARTS

Pl. des Lices ☎*94-97-02-25* ▯▯ ◼ ❧ ▨
*Closed mid-Oct to mid-Apr. Last orders
11.30pm.*

A simple local café until it was taken up by the St-Tropez *beau monde* in the early 1960s, the Café des Arts has remained chic and shabby ever since. It packs them in, not for the food, which is quite ordinary, but simply as a place to see and be seen and to have fun.

CHEZ NANO

Pl. de l'Hôtel-de-Ville ☎9497-91-66 ▥ ▭
🍴 ▣ ▣ ▥ *Closed Tues (except July–Aug); mid-Jan to end Mar. Last orders midnight.*
Another intensely Tropézien place, opposite the *hôtel de ville*, crowded alike with tourists and the chic-Bohemian set. Pretty lighting, exuberant service, deafening chatter (even on the terrace). The *carte* is short, simple and so-so; but food isn't the main reason for being there.

LE MAS DE CHASTELAS

Route de Gassin ☎94-56-09-11 ▥ 🍴
▤ 🍴 ▤ ▣ ▣ ▥ *Closed Oct–Easter. Last orders 10.30pm.*
Lunches (residents only) are light and delicious meals served by the pool. Dinner, also served by the pool when the weather is fine, is more elaborate and open to nonresidents. Excellent cooking, fresh and full of taste. The menus change frequently. *Specialities: Volaille au citron et sa barigoule de légumes, filet de boeuf à la crème d'ail doux.* (See ☜ LE MAS DE CHASTELAS, above.)

≈   Other good restaurants include:
• **Le Boeuf sur la Place** *(pl. des Lices* ☎94-97-60-50 ▥ to ▥). • **Chez Fuchs** *(7 rue des Commerçants* ☎94-97-01-25 ▥ to ▥). • **La Maison du Ravi** *(38 rue du Portail Neuf* ☎94-97-88-27 ▥). • **La Mandarine** *(Route de Tahiti* ☎94-79-06-66 ▥ to ▥).
• **L'Olivier** *(Hôtel La Bastide de St-Tropez, Route des Carles* ☎94-97-58-16 ▥ to ▥). • **La Ponche** *(pl. du Revelin* ☎94-97-09-29 ▥). • **La Renaissance** *(pl. des Lices* ☎94-97-02-00 ▥ to ▥). • **La Romana** *(Chemin des Conquettes* ☎94-97-18-50 ▥).
• **Villa de Belieu** *(Domaines de Bertaud-Belieu* ☎94-56-40-56 ▥): see ☜ VILLA DE BELIEU, above.

▣ CAFÉS IN ST-TROPEZ

The **Sénéquier**, **Le Café de Paris** and **Le Gorille**, all on the harbor, are all quintessential Tropézien cafés: they are open late and attract the young (at heart, at least) and beautiful.

SHOPPING IN ST-TROPEZ

You will find a selection of high-priced boutiques in **rue Allard**.

▣ NIGHTLIFE IN ST-TROPEZ

Places to see and be seen are at: **Café des Arts** *(pl. des Lices);* **L'Escale**, a piano bar *(quai Jean-Jaurès);* **Nano**, also a piano bar *(4 rue Sybille).*

Discos

Les Caves du Roy, in the Hotel Byblos, is the Côte's most fashionable disco, along with Jimmy'z at Monte-Carlo; dress very modishly if you want a chance of being allowed in *(open mid-June to mid-Sept from 10.30pm).* **Le Papagayo** *(Nouveau Port)* is for anyone. **Le Pigeonnier** *(11 rue de la Ponche)* is moderately trendy, mostly gay and always crowded. **L'Esquinade** *(rue du Four)* is open late, in summer.

🏖 BEACHES NEAR ST-TROPEZ

St-Tropez owes much of its attraction to its fantastic sandy beach — an unbroken 6 kilometers (4 miles), SE of the town along the **Baie de**

Pamplonne. As at Cannes, almost the whole beach is parceled into 30 privately-run sectors where you must pay. There is no road along the shore, and the beaches are accessible only via winding lanes, not always well signposted. Some free beaches do exist, mostly farther s, beyond Cap Camarat.

St-Tropez beaches are a case-study in exotic hedonism. All are topless, some are bottomless; some of the sights are wonderful, others unmentionable. The beaches include: **Tahiti**, since the 1960s one of the most famous beaches in the world, although today its chic is tinged with decadence, like a late Roman orgy; **Moorea**, now more *à la mode* than Tahiti; **La Voile Rouge**, very chic; **Club 55**, also select, if less so than Moorea; and **Blouch**, for naturists.

⇥ **LE CLUB 55**

Blvd. Patch, Plage de Pamplonne, 83350 Ramatuelle ☎ *94-79-88-28* ▯▯ ⬥ ▭ ⊟
▣ ◉ ▣ ▨ *Closed early Nov to end Mar. Lunch only.*

It is deliberately not signposted. Nor is it a club in the technical sense, although the restaurant certainly has a dedicated following. But there are few more enjoyable places to eat a lingering lunch outdoors in or around St-Tropez. The clientele is very chic, even jet-set, and many of the customers are personal friends of the owner, Patrice Colmont, a popular local figure; yet the atmosphere is casual and relaxed. The food is simple (anything from fried egg to lobster. . .) but excellent, particularly the *salad niçoise* and the steaks.

If you eat at what Patrice Colmont calls his "hotel without rooms," you may also use the beach.

PLACES NEAR ST-TROPEZ

Gassin *(8km/5 miles sw of St-Tropez)*. A well-known village perched high on a ridge above the plain, with marvelous views all around. Its church, floodlit at night, is a landmark for miles around. The village used to be a lookout point in the defense against Saracen pirates.

Ramatuelle *(6km/4 miles s of St-Tropez on D93)*. The lovely Ramatuelle peninsula stretches s of St-Tropez, its hillsides cloaked in vineyards and lush woodland of oak and pine. It remains remarkably unspoiled, despite the influx of tourists to the area. Ramatuelle itself is a pleasing village on a low hill, with quiet old alleyways and a simple 17thC church. The name, a reminder of the Saracen presence, is said to come from the Arabic *Rahmatu'llah* (God's gift). The noble elm in its main square was planted in 1598.

The three ruined **Moulins de Paillas** stand 3 kilometers (2 miles) NW of Ramatuelle, on a high hilltop next to a radio tower. It is worth driving up here for the view, which is the best in the region.

- **EVENT**   Ramatuelle has a 500-seat open-air theater, where a **jazz festival** is staged in July and a **theater festival** in August. Both events are of a high standard, with ticket prices to match.

❧ ⇥ **Le Baou** *(at Ramatuelle* ☎ *94-79-20-48* ☏ *94-79-28-36* ▯▯▯*)*, a sophisticated, stunningly located modern hotel, externally in the style of a Provençal *mas*. The 41 rooms are cheerily comfortable, furnished and equipped to a high standard, and all with a balcony or terrace with a sea view. There is a heated swimming pool and a good restaurant.

- See also: GRIMAUD, PORT-GRIMAUD.

STE-MAXIME

Map 13H12 (Var). 61km (38 miles) sw of Cannes. Postal code: 83120.
Population: 10,000 **i** *promenade Simon-Lorière* ☎94-96-19-24.

Ste-Maxime's tree-lined promenade, with its glittering lights and busy terrace-cafés, is an elegant sight at night. It is the main focus of this sizeable, modern bathing resort, which, compared with its neighbors, is decidedly more fun than St-Raphael, if less exotic and interesting than St-Tropez just across the bay. Ste-Maxime has a faithful clientele of young people, and of families who are drawn by the sheltered climate and the miles of public sandy beaches.

It is not an expensive place. Seaside tourism is its sole industry, and there's plenty to do. Sports include waterskiing, wind surfing, yachting (there is a good marina) and golf (9-hole course at Beauvallon, 5km/3 miles to the w). There is also a casino and six nightclubs; numerous fêtes and festivals take place during the summer.

Recommended hotels in Ste-Maxime: • **La Belle Aurore** *(4 blvd. Jean-Moulin* ☎94-96-02-45 [Fx]94-96-63-87 [▥]), a small hotel, but probably the best in town. • **Calidianus** *(blvd. Jean-Moulin* ☎94-96-23-21 [▥]), a quiet and very attractive modern vacation hotel. • **L'Ensoleillée** (♣) *(av. de la Gare* ☎94-96-02-27 [▥]), a clean, comfortable *pension,* where meals are not obligatory except in July and August. • In a lovely garden, **Marie-Louise,** *(Hameau de Guerrevieille* ☎94-96-06-05 [▥]), a white villa with small, spruce bedrooms, a pretty dining room and a serene, rather wistful atmosphere.

The best restaurants in Ste-Maxime are: • **Le Gruppi** *(av. Charles-de-Gaulle* ☎94-96-03-61 [▥]), a rather expensive, formal restaurant on the promenade, where very fresh fish is classically served. • **L'Amiral** *(Le Port* ☎94-43-99-36 [▥]), one of the best and most expensive restaurants in town, specializing in fish, seafood and lamb dishes. • **La Réserve** *(pl. Victor-Hugo* ☎94-96-18-32 [▥]), for good regional dishes. • **Sans Souci** (♣) *(34 rue Paul-Bert* ☎94-96-18-26 [▥]), a shining example of the sort of small family restaurant at which the French excel: simple, in a pretty setting, with swift, smiling service and competent local cuisine. • **Le Clocher Provençal** *(rue Jean-Ricard* ☎94-96-24-73 [▥]), a modestly decorated restaurant with unassuming Provençal food and affordable prices.

PLACE NEAR STE-MAXIME

Between Ste-Maxime and St-Aygulf lies a string of tiny resorts. At **Les Issambres**, the coast is beautiful, with sandy coves enclosed by rocks and umbrella pines waving in the breeze. The hotels are spread out at intervals, retaining their privacy.

VILLA ST-ELME

Corniche des Issambres (N98), 83380 Les Issambres ☎94-49-52-52 [Fx]94-49-63-18 [▥] 12 rms [▤][▤][▤][AE][▥][▥]♦♦[▢][▥] ♠♥♦♣♠♠♠♦♦♠ *Closed Jan–Apr.*
One of the best opened recently on this coast is this charming, bright and delightfully decorated hotel, in a restored villa, owned by a Swiss couple. Standards are high, most rooms face the sea, and the elegant main restaurant, with its fabulous sea view, lives up to the rest of the place in both ambience and quality of cooking. *Specialities include: Salade de caille aux épices et confiture d'oignons, aiguillettes de bar tièdes au basilic frit, rouelles de canette aux noix et morilles.*

La Réserve *(Les Issambres* ☎ *94-96-90-41* ▥) is a beautifully sited *auberge* above the sea, serving high-quality, high-priced dishes, such as *marmite de pêcheur, escargots au pistou* and *foie de veau au vinaigre vieux.*

Le Saint-Pierre *(Les Issambres* ☎ *94-96-89-67* ▥). Ernest Loudet's formal restaurant is hardly cheap, but it serves excellent fish and seafood, with imaginative twists, and offers a superb sea view.

• See also: GRIMAUD, PORT-GRIMAUD, ST-TROPEZ.

SALERNES

Map ***12****F11 (Var). 23km (15 miles) w of Draguignan. Postal code: 83690. Population: 3,000* ℹ ☎*94-70-69-02.*

Owing to its local clay deposits, this little town has a thriving traditional industry: the making of colored enamel tiles for bathrooms and other domestic uses. At some of the workshops, visitors can watch the tiles being made, and can buy samples. Among the best are **Emphoux** on the Draguignan road and **Polidori** on the Entrecasteaux road. The leading local firm, **Pierre Boutal**, has a large showroom and sales-room, but the factory is closed to visitors.

Allègre *(rue J-J Rousseau* ☎ *94-70-60-30* ▢ to ▥).

Le Vieux Soufflet *(Route de Draguignan* ☎ *94-70-72-72* ▢).

PLACES NEAR SALERNES

Cotignac *(13km/8 miles sw of Salernes).* A little town lying at the foot of a brown cliff, pockmarked with a number of curious caves, some of them once inhabited. To the s and e stretch miles of vineyards.

Lou Calen *(1 Cours Gambetta* ☎ *94-04-60-40* ⨏*94-04-76-64* ▥ *closed Wed, except July-Sept, Jan to mid-Mar).* The name means "the place of the oil lamp" in Provençal, and this simple hotel and its restaurant are ap-propriately welcoming, if a little down-at-heel.

Le Mas de Cotignac *(Route de Carces* ☎ *94-04-66-57* ▢ to ▥ *closed Mon-Tues, Oct-Nov, Feb).*

Entrecasteaux *(8km/5 miles s of Salernes).* A medieval village in a narrow valley, with a 13thC humpback bridge and Gothic fortified church. The village is dominated by its great château, in front of which lies a formal garden by André Le Nôtre, designer of the Tuileries and Versailles gardens. It is now communal property.

Château ☆

☎*94-04-43-95* ■ *Open daily: Apr–June, Sept 10am–1pm, 2–6pm; July–Aug 10am–8pm; Oct–Mar 10am–noon, 2–6pm.*

The austere, prison-like castle, once strongly fortified, has experienced a bizarre history, not least in recent years. It belonged to local *seigneurs,* one of whom, in the 18thC, killed his young wife and then vanished into a Portuguese jail. This event brought the family into such disrepute and poverty that gradually the château fell into ruin.

Finally it was bought in 1974 by Ian McGarvie-Munn, avant-garde painter, Scottish nationalist, soldier and adventurer, ex-commander-in-chief of the Guatemalan navy and married to the granddaughter of a former president of that country.

McGarvie-Munn patiently restored the château at his own expense. He died in 1981, and the castle is now run by his son as a museum of his father's collections, which are at least original, if stupefyingly eclectic. On the ground floor are Scottish bagpipes, pre-Columbian ceramics, 17thC Chinese watercolors on silk, and Murano goblets designed by the artist. In the basement is a collection of Provençal kitchenware. Upstairs are McGarvie-Munn's own lurid surrealist paintings. A permanent exhibition is devoted to Admiral d'Entrecasteaux, who died in 1793 during an expedition to the Pacific.

Visitors enter through the château's shop (where you can buy books, crafts and various other assorted objets) and are free to wander through the living rooms. In summer, classical concerts are held on the castle's lovely terrace, and there are regular art exhibitions and seminars.

-   ❖ The château has two large bedrooms (with kitchenettes) on its top floor, available for paying guests on a bed-and-breakfast basis. However, staying there, while undoubtedly an interesting and unusual experience, isn't cheap when compared with hotel accommodation of a similar standard.

Fox-Amphoux *(13km/8 miles w of Salernes).* Superb views over great forests of pine and oak are to be enjoyed from this old hill-village on a high plateau.

❖ =   **AUBERGE DU VIEUX FOX**
Pl. de l'Église, Fox-Amphoux, 83670 Barjols
☏ 94-80-71-69 □ to □ 10 rms ⎯ AE
◉ VISA ▢ □ ▣ ❄ ✯ Closed mid-Dec to mid-Feb.
Location: *In the village square, with marvelous views looking over the Ste-Victoire and Ste-Beaume ranges.* This 16thC presbytery, once semiderelict, was restored with great taste, and became a hotel in 1975. It has since established itself as one of that rare breed of really special hotels that stand out for an intimate quality only their owners can provide. Bedrooms here, inevitably small but each different, are decorated in warm colors, and even the bathrooms have 16thC beams. Downstairs is a cozy salon with a log fire.

The dining room (□ □ ■ ✈ *closed mid-Dec to mid-Feb, mid-Nov to Easter, last orders 8pm),* filled with flowers, is delightful, and the atmosphere is convivial. Specialities of the chef include Verdon lamb, and lamb with tarragon.

-   See also: BARJOLS; DRAGUIGNAN; THORONET, ABBAYE DU; VERDON, GORGES DU.

SEILLANS

Map **13**F12 (Var). 31km (19 miles) w of Grasse. Postal code: 83440 Fayence. Population: 1,700 **i** ☏ 94-76-85-91.

A quiet and lovely old medieval village facing SE across a valley toward the Esterel hills. It has a 12thC ruined château, fountains, and steep, paved alleyways. The ramparts of the château were once used for defense against Saracen invaders, and indeed, the name Seillans derives from the Provençal word meaning a pot of boiling oil.

Today's more peaceful invasion is of well-to-do owners, who find this one of the most delightful corners of Provence. Max Ernst used to live and paint here.

✿ ☞ DEUX ROCS

Pl. d'Amont, 83770 Seillans ☎*94-76-87-32* ▢▢ *15 rms* ▨▨ ▢▢ ▢▢ ▨ ▢▢
Closed Nov to mid-Mar.

Location: In a small square, opposite two rocks that stand by a gateway to the old village. A former biochemist from Paris, the delightful and ever-present Lise Hirsch has converted this 18thC *maison bourgeoise* into a chic and intimate little hotel. Its cream walls and brown shutters are fronted by miniature fir trees and geraniums, and, in summer, the tables outside encircle a fountain, in the same square as the HÔTEL DE FRANCE. Inside, the bedrooms are gaily decorated with unusual fabrics and wallpapers.The dining room *(last orders 9.30pm)*, where the food is usually reliable, is heavily beamed and inviting; a small private room with deep sofas leads off it.

✿ ☞ HÔTEL DE FRANCE

Pl. du Thouron, 83770 Seillans
☎*94-76-96-10* ▯▯*94-76-89-20* ▢▢ *20 rms* ▢▢ ▨▨ ▢▢ ▨▨ ▢ ▢▢ ▨ ▨ Closed Jan.*

Location: Conveniently situated near the center of the village. The rooms of this long-established hotel are comfortable, if rather characterless, and there is a swimming pool in back. The hotel's popular restaurant **Clariond** *(▢▢ ▢▢ ▨▨ ▨▨ closed Wed (Sept-May), Jan, last orders 9pm)* is set in a charming square. In summer, tables are put out under plane trees and beside the old fountain. Lunch here is a joy. M. Clariond's cooking, in the sound tradition of the hinterland, suits the mood very well. *Specialities: Civet de lièvre, poulet aux écrevisses, feuilleté de lotte, saumon soufflé, noisettes de chevreuil à la groseille.*

SHOPPING IN SEILLANS

Several artisans work and sell their goods here. Among the best workshops are **Castel Jehanne d'Arc** *(in the village),* for pottery and weaving, and **Poterie du Vieux Moulin** *(1km/ $\frac{1}{2}$ mile along the Mons road, the D53).*

PLACES NEAR SEILLANS

Bargemon *(13km/8 miles sw of Seillans).* Amid equally glorious woodland scenery, this village is less quaint than Seillans, but livelier and equally popular with summer residents (the British almost outnumber the Parisians). Plane trees line its avenues, fountains play in its little squares, and there are 12thC fortified gateways.

The 14thC **church of St-Étienne**, built into the ramparts, has three 17thC retables (the best is on the second side altar on the left). The sculpted heads of angels on the high altar are by Puget.

☞ CHEZ PIERROT

Pl. Philippe-Chauvier ☎*94-76-62-19* ▢▢ *to* ▢▢ ▢▢ ▨ ▨ ▢▢ ▨▨ *Closed Sun dinner (Nov–Apr); Mon (except June–Sept); Feb. Last orders 10pm (summer), 9.30pm (winter).*

In the village center, this is a typical *auberge,* where you can eat in the country dining room, or out on the square under the plane trees and watch local life go by. M. Pierrot is no pantomime figure but a serious cook who serves basic Provençal dishes (mostly meat and poultry; there is little fish on the menu), and some Périgourdin ones such as *magret de canard au poivre vert ou aux baies de cassis* and *confit de canard.*

≡ MAÎTRE BLANC

☎94-76-60-24 ▭ to ▭▭ ▭ ■■ ▦ ▣▣ ▣
▣ ▣ *Closed Wed; Jan. Last orders 9pm.*
Considered by local connoisseurs to be the area's gastronomic leader, Maître Blanc is nonetheless an ordinary village

restaurant intent on serving good local food. Sunday lunch is a great institution here. Local families, from great-grand-mothers to babes-in-arms, pile in for uproarious meals that last most of the afternoon.

* See also: FAYENCE.

SISTERON ☆

Map 6C9 (Alpes-de-H.-P.). 39km (25 miles) NW of Digne. Postal code: 04200. Population: 6,600 **i** *rue des Arcades* ☎92-61-12-03.

The ancient town of Sisteron forms the natural gateway to Provence from Grenoble and the Dauphiné region. It is impressively located, at a point where the river Durance forces its way through a defile between high rocky hills. On the crest of the hill to the W stands the mighty **citadel**, while opposite is the fearsome, toothy precipice of the **Rocher de la Baume**.

On August 15, 1944, the day of the landings in Provence, Sisteron was heavily (and some say needlessly) bombed by the Allies: 400 people were killed and many old houses destroyed. Much of the town is thus modern, but a few old, medieval streets survive between place du Dr. Robert and the river. At rue Saunerie *(#20)* is the *hôtel* where Napoléon breakfasted on March 15, 1815, on his return along the ROUTE NAPOLÉON from Elba. The church of **Notre-Dame**, a former cathedral, is a fine example of 12thC Provençal Romanesque architecture, with a graceful nave and a portal in Lombard style. Beside it stand three isolated towers, remains of Sisteron's 14thC ramparts.

* **EVENT**   From mid-July to early August, an annual **festival of drama, dancing and music** takes place in an open-air theater on the N slope of the citadel hill. • There is also an **art show** during the same period.

* **MARKETS**   There is a market on Wednesday and Saturday.

La Citadelle ▥ ☆

▩ *Open 9am–7pm. Closed mid-Nov to mid-Mar.*
"The most powerful fortress in my kingdom," said Henri IV of this massive stone edifice, towering on its rock above the town. Built in the 13th–16thC, it was badly damaged by the 1944 bombing but has since been partly restored. The long, steep climb up to the top is well worth making, if only for the sweeping views from the upper terrace. It is clear that Sisteron has long been a natural frontier point: to the S are the plains and hills of Provence, and to the N, the rolling Dauphiné with its alpine backdrop.

Points of interest in the citadel are the **tour de l'horloge** (once a prison), the 15thC Gothic **chapel** (almost totally rebuilt since 1944, with attractive modern stained glass), and the amazing **Guérite du Diable** (Devil's Watchtower) perched precariously above the river. Free leaflets (in English, French or German) tell the citadel's story, but French-speakers may also wish to listen to the dramatized record of its history, broadcast continuously from the terrace. In summer the citadel is splendidly floodlit at night. At its entrance, the guardroom where French patriots were imprisoned by the Germans in 1940–44 is now a small museum of the local Résistance.

☞ **Grand Hôtel du Cours** *(pl. de l'Église* ☎ *92-61-04-51* 🔲 *92-61-41-* 73 🔳 *to* 🔳*);* **Tivoli** (🔺) *(pl. Tivoli* ☎ *92-61-15-16* 🔲 *to* 🔳*).*

PLACES NEAR SISTERON
Haute Vallée du Vançon   Cross the bridge over the Durance, turn left, then immediately turn right along the D3, a narrow mountain road that winds up to the **Défile de la Pierre Écrite**. At the far end of this little gorge, to the left of the road beside a bridge, is a Roman inscription in honor of the Consul Dardanus, who opened up this route in the 5thC. The road winds on via Authon to a dead end at the pass of Fontbelle. The terrain of this upper valley is spectacularly mountainous.

THORONET, ABBAYE DU 🏛 ✝ ★
*Map **12**G11. 17km (11 miles) NE of Brignoles* ☎ *94-73-87-13* 🚩 *✗ available from mid-July to late Aug. Open Apr–Sept 9am–7pm; Sept–Apr 9am–noon, 2–5pm. Closed Sun noon–2pm.*

In the 12thC, the Cistercian monks chose three isolated spots in Provence and built the abbeys of SÉNANQUE, SILVACANE and Thoronet. The sublimely beautiful Abbaye du Thoronet reflects best of all, and to perfection, the austere and humble spirit of the order, through its architectural style of great purity and simplicity. The result is a Provençal Romanesque ensemble of exceptional harmony.

In the Cistercian manner, the **church**, with its high vaulted ceiling, is entirely devoid of furnishings or decoration, except for some frescoes added in the 17thC and now largely faded. The church, which has superb acoustics, is in the shape of a Latin cross, with narrow side-aisles opposite the altar. Outside, on the S wall, is a curious niche where local people could place their dead.

On the N side, a door leads to the delightful little **cloister**, entirely unadorned and very graceful, with cypresses and a hexagonal washhouse in the middle. Next door is the **chapter house**, early Gothic, with ribbed vaulting; beyond are the refectory, library and dormitories. Each room is finely proportioned.

The abbey has not always been in such an excellent condition. It fell into disrepair after the monks were expelled in the Revolution. In 1854, it was bought by the State, and it has been superbly restored by the Service of Historic Monuments, using the same reddish-gold stone as the original, from a nearby quarry that was reopened for the purpose.

In its secluded sylvan setting, the abbey exudes a sense of peace that visitors may find deeply spiritual. It is seen at its best in late afternoon, when the sunlight falling through bare windows gives the golden stone a soft glow. Visitors are welcome to attend vespers *(Mon-Sat 5.30pm,*

Sun 5.45pm), in a plain but elegant chapel beyond the cloister. There is a 2-hour service at the abbey at noon on Sundays.

Good restaurants nearby: **Le Gourmandin** *(8 pl. Louis-Brunet, 83340 Le Luc-en-Provence* ☎*94-60-* *85-92* 🔲 *to* 🔲*);* **Hostellerie du Parc** *(12 rue Jean-Jaurès, 83340 Le Luc-en-Provence* ☎*94-60-70-01* 🔲*).*

• See also: BRIGNOLES, DRAGUIGNAN, SALERNES.

TOULON ☆

Map 11I9 (Var). 64km (40 miles) E of Marseille. Postal code: 83000. Population: 167,600 **i** *8 av. Colbert* ☎*94-22-08-22.* **Airport:** *at Hyères, 21km (13 miles) to E* ☎*94-38-57-57.* **Railway station:** *pl. Albert 1ᵉʳ* ☎*94-91-50-50.*

France's leading naval base is a busy, commercial city in a theatrical setting around a deep natural harbor, sheltered by a ring of high hills crowned by Vaubanesque forts. It may at first seem a dull, workaday place; but it soon reveals itself as an exciting town of real character, especially in the old quarter by the port, where sailors from many nations frequent the little bars and bistros, some less innocent than others.

Although not a place for a full vacation, Toulon is fun to visit, and a superb center for excursions, and prices are the lowest on the coast. It is now trying hard to attract more young people to the town, by siting various educational institutions there. If it succeeds, Toulon's entertainment amenities and cultural life should receive a significant boost.

The oldest part of the port, the *darse vieille,* dates from the 16thC. But it was Louis XIV who turned Toulon into a great naval base by building the arsenal to the W, the *darse neuve.* Here, in the 17thC and 18thC, convicts, blacks and political prisoners, such as Huguenots, were forced to become galley slaves, rowing the royal galleys, chained to their seats and whipped by their masters into action if they slackened their pace. Passers-by would stare and laugh at them as they shuffled, shackled together, through the streets of Toulon.

It was at Toulon in 1793 that a young unknown artillery captain, Napoléon Bonaparte, first made his military reputation. The town had declared for the Royalists against the Revolutionary government and was under the protection of an English fleet, which set up a seemingly impregnable stronghold at Tamaris, on the SW of the harbor. But Bonaparte directed on the English such a hail of cannon fire that he forced them to withdraw. He was promptly promoted to brigadier-general.

Toulon has figured more recently in military annals. In November 1942, after the Allied landings in North Africa, the Vichy fleet of 60 ships was scuttled by its own crews, to avoid falling into German hands. The port was then heavily damaged by Allied bombing in 1943–44, and in August 1944, after the Allied landings in Provence, the Germans blew up the citadel and most of what was left of the harbor, before surrendering.

Modern Toulon is divided in two by a broad boulevard running W–E *(blvd. Général-Leclerc, blvd. de Strasbourg).* To its N is the commercial district around the station, to its S the areas of tourist interest: the Old Town and the harbor.

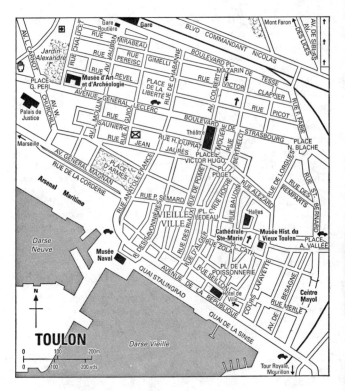

- **EVENTS** Main annual festivals in Toulon include an April **flower parade**, a **music festival** from late May to early July, a **youth theater festival** during June, and a **festival of films about the sea** in November. There is also a **fair** of *santons* (Provençal clay figures) in November. Toulon has a good **theater and opera** house *(pl. Victor-Hugo)* where frequent performances are held in winter.

- **MARKETS** Each morning there is a teeming **food market** where you can buy fish, mushrooms and olives, among other local produce, in Cours Lafayette. • A **flea market** happens regularly, near the beach.

Toulon has become a major conference venue, and now has a large, state-of-the-art conference center, the **Palais Neptune** *(Centre Mayol, 83000 Toulon* ☎ *94-03-83-83* Fx *94-03-83-62)*, attached to a shopping complex and with its own hotel (see below).

TRANSPORT IN TOULON

There are TGV connections to Marseille and Nice from the railway station, as well as local trains. From the *gare routière,* near the train station, you can get buses along the coast or inland. Now that the A57 autoroute has been completed, you can drive N from Toulon right into the heartland of the Var and northern Provence in little more than an hour (or, if you want, to the A8 to take you in the direction of either Aix or Nice).

In summer, there are boats to Corsica (daily) and to Sardinia (weekly) (☎94-41-18-38). You can also go on boat tours of the harbor, surrounding coast and **Îles d'Hyères** (Les Bateliers de la Rade ☎94-31-21-36) for most of the year from quai Stalingrad.

WHAT TO SEE IN TOULON
Art et d'Archéologie, Musée d'/Musée de Toulon
Blvd. Général-Leclerc ☎94-93-15-54. Open 1–7pm. Closed public holidays.
The paintings on display range from the 13th–20thC, with good works by Caracci, Van Loo, Fragonard, Vlaminck, Friesz and Ziem, and contemporary art too. One room is devoted to Oriental art, from the Levant to Japan. Others deal with archeology and include some interesting Gallo-Roman remains from Provence.

Cathédrale Ste-Marie †
Pl. de la Cathédrale. Open 6am–noon, 3–7pm.
The imposing, if somewhat gloomy, cathedral was originally built in the 11thC, in the Romanesque style, but contains a mixture of later architectural modes, mostly as a result of its enlargement and the construction of a Classical facade in the 17thC. There are a number of works of art by, among others, Pierre Puget, one of whose pupils designed the Baroque altar.

Le Port
Few buildings here survived the devastation of 1943–44, and today **quai Stalingrad** along the harborfront is lined with hideous gray rectangular apartment blocks that were thrown up hurriedly just after the war. Even so, it is a lively and amusing area, full of little bars and cafés, and high-spirited sailors on shore leave. From the quai there are frequent guided tours by boat all around the large harbor, to **St-Mandrier, La Seyne** and back. On the 3-hour trip, the dry docks, arsenal and other installations, almost all of them modern, are explained.

This is still the headquarters of the French Mediterranean fleet, and also has some commercial traffic. The **Musée Naval** (▨ closed Tues), housed in the Maritime Prefecture, has model ships, paintings of sea battles, and other naval mementos.

Toulon, Musée de   See ART ET D'ARCHÉOLOGIE, MUSÉE D'.

Tour Royale
Pointe de la Mitre ☎94-24-91-00 ▨ ✖ ✗ available ✿ Open Mar–May 3–6pm; June to mid-Sept 2–7pm; mid-Sept to Oct 2–6pm. Closed Mon; Nov–Feb.
Built in the 16thC as part of the harbor defenses, this sturdy stone tower stands strategically on a promontory to the east of the harbor en-

trance, 3 kilometers (2 miles) s of quai Stalingrad. Long used as a prison, today it is an annex of the **Musée Naval** and more interesting than its parent. There are two large black atlantes, taken from men-of-war, and the cannon used by Lafayette against the British at Rhode Island. The tower's terrace provides fine views over the harbor and the coast.

Vieille Ville (Old Town)

Mercifully, the Allied bombers were accurate enough to hit the harbor and miss the mass of old alleyways that stretch behind, it, N of quai Stalingrad. Today most of this area remains intact: part has now been turned into an elegant pedestrian mall, with boutiques and cafés, and little paved squares with flowers and potted palms. In **place Puget** there is the amusing 18thC **Fontaine des Trois-Dauphins**, 3 meters (10 feet) wide and overgrown with dense foliage.

To the E is the somber **cathedral**, and E again the leafy **Cours Lafayette**, with its busy market. Here the **Musée Historique du Vieux Toulon** (▣ *open pm only, closed Sun*) might be worth a quick look: souvenirs of local history, old weapons, the works of Toulon painters, etc. Turning E again, the sadder and more sordid side of life becomes evident; here washing hangs across the alleys, and Algerian children play in dirty courtyards.

• **MARKET** There is a busy and excellent market each morning (except Monday) at **Cours Lafayette**.

❧ ═ LA CORNICHE

1 Littoral Frédéric-Mistral, 83000 Toulon
☎94-41-35-12 ⊠94-41-24-58 ▥ 22
rms ▤ ▥ ᴀᴇ ⊕ ⊚ ▦ 🛋 ‡ ▢ ⌧
❧ ⟨⟨ ☏ ⏛ ▣

Location: Facing the tiny harbor at Le Mourillon, 3 kilometers (2 miles) SE of the city center. The central core of this excellent, cunningly designed little hotel is a stone-flagged patio with flowering shrubs and mimosa. The whole place exudes a homely, family atmosphere, enhanced by the attention to detail and good taste of its owners, Patrick Suere and his English wife Rebecca. Several rooms have balconies and sea views, and all have good, old oak furniture and first-rate appointments.

The main restaurant is constructed around three huge umbrella pines, whose broad trunks push up through the middle of the room with extraordinary effect. The food, served quite formally, is well-presented, and prices are reasonable, with fish and Provençal specialities to the fore. There is a well-compiled and comprehensive wine list,

with a good selection of local wines and some classic Bordeaux. Downstairs, there is a cheaper bistro, serving grills and other simple food. *(Main restaurant closed Sun dinner, Mon; bistro closed Sun, Mon lunch.)*

❧ DU PALAIS

Centre Mayol, 83000 Toulon
☎94-03-83-83 ⊠94-03-83-55 ▥ 150
rms ⇌ ⇌ ═ ᴀᴇ ⊕ ▦ ‡ ▢ ⌧ ♟ ⚓
⏛ ▣

Location: Part of the Centre Mayol conference and shopping complex. This is a very new and comfortable hotel, ideal for business visitors. As a vacation hotel, its location and slightly functional air may perhaps make it less attractive, but its standards are high enough.

❧ LA TOUR BLANCHE

Blvd. Amiral-Vence, 83000 Toulon
☎94-24-41-57 ⊠94-22-42-25 ▥ 92
rms ⇌ ▤ ═(last orders 11pm) ᴀᴇ ⊕
⊚ ▦ ⌂ ‡ ⚕ ▢ ⌧ ❧ ⟨⟨ ⛰ ♟ ⏛ ▣
Location: High on the slopes of Mt. Faron, at the foot of its funicular, 2.5

kilometers (1¼ miles) N *of the city center.*
A member of France's Altea group until
1993, this is a well-located hotel. The
smell of pines is in the air, and the views
of Toulon and its bay are breathtaking,
whether from the bedroom balconies,
the outdoor bar-terrace or the airy restaurant, where the service and local
cuisine are equally good. The hotel
caters with equal smoothness to brisk
businessmen and more leisurely vaca-
tioners. A 2-year refurbishment is under-
way, to bring the hotel right up to date.

✍   Other functional and efficient
hotels worth considering: **Amirauté** *(4
rue A.-Guiol* ☎*94-22-19-67* ▥*)* and
Europe *(7bis rue de Chabanne* ☎*94-
92-37-44* ▥*).*

➡   **LE DAUPHIN**
21bis rue Jean-Jaurès ☎*94-93-12-07* ▥
▤ ▭ ◼ ◩ ▦ *Closed Sat lunch; Sun;*

early Aug. Last orders 9.45pm.
At the edge of the old town, chef-patron
Alain Biles offers a selection of refined
dishes such as *filets de Saint-Pierre à la
poêlée de champignon, emincé de
pommes chaudes à la cannelle* and *foie
gras de canard cuit en terrine.*

➡   **AU SOURD**
10 rue Molière ☎*94-92-28-52* ▥ ▭ ◼
◩ ▦ 🍴 *Closed Sun; Mon; Aug.*
A very pleasant restaurant, one of the
oldest in Toulon, where Francis Garino
serves local fish specialities like
bouillabaisse, bourride or squid in ink.

➡   Also recommended: **Le Cha-
made** *(25 rue Denfert-Rochereau*
☎*94-92-28-58* ▥ *closed Sat lunch,
Sun, Aug); **Gros Ventre** *(279 Littoral
Frédéric-Mistral* ☎*94-42-15-42* ▥
closed Thurs lunch, Wed), for seafood
and fish.

PLACES NEAR TOULON

Toulon is backed by an exceptionally wild and mountainous hinterland, much of which makes for excellent excursions. At **Ollioules**, just
off the N8, a narrow, steep road winds up along the great ridge of **Le
Gros Cerveau** (✰), where the views are spectacular, both over the
coast and the country inland toward the MASSIF DE LA STE-BAUME. North of
Ollioules, the main N8 goes through the dry and stony **Gorges d'Ollioules**, emerging within sight of the craggy rocks of the Grés de
Ste-Anne, to the W.

Farther along the N8, a turnoff to the E leads up to the ruined, ghostly
village of **Évenos** (✰), perched on a rocky cliff and watched over by its
ruined castle above. From there the D62 winds on E to the 800-meter
(2,640-foot) summit of **Mont Baume**, the highest peak in the area, with
wonderful views. The D62 then zigzags back, through pretty scenery, to
Toulon. Directly behind Toulon rises the 550-meter/1,800-foot-high limestone ridge, **Mont Faron**.

From beside the hotel LA TOUR BLANCHE, a funicular climbs almost to
the top *(operates 9-11.45am, 2.15-6.15pm).* Or you can drive up and
up, along a steep, winding road amid pines and rocks. The view from the
top is one of the grandest in Provence. All Toulon lies spread out, its great
harbor full of gray warships and brown tankers, like children's toys. To
the W are the ÎLES D'HYÈRES; to the E stretches the coast as far as BANDOL.

Just below the summit, in an old fort, is Provence's counterpart to the
D-Day Museum at Arromanches in Normandy. The **Mémorial National
du Débarquement** (✰) *(▧ ◼ 🍴 open 9-11.30am, 2-5.15pm)* gives
a full and vivid, if overblown, picture of the Allied invasion of Provence
in August 1944, its preparation, and the battles that followed. Close by is

a small **zoo** (*☒ open 9.30am-noon, 2pm-dusk*), with monkeys and other animals.

Solliès-Ville (*13km/8 miles NW of Toulon, just to the W of the N97*) is an old village with a remarkable Romanesque church. It has fine 14thC and 17thC retables, and an enormously tall ciborium by the high altar. The organ, in sculpted walnut, dates from 1499 and is one of the oldest in France.

* ⛱ There are sandy beaches at **Le Mourrillon** in the SE suburbs, and at **Tamaris** and **Les Sablettes** in the SW suburbs.

🚆 At **Solliès-Toucas** (*3km/2 miles NW of Solliès-Ville on the D554*), the very commendable **Le Lingousto** (*☎ 94-28-* 90-96 ▢ *to* ▢) offers particularly good value even on its cheapest set menu.

* See also: BANDOL, HYERES.

TOURTOUR
Map 12F11 (Var). 20km (12 miles) w of Draguignan. Postal code: 83690 Salernes. Population: 450.

Amid rolling woodlands of oak and olive, pine and cypress, this medieval village stands on a hill, with wide vistas on all sides. Tourtour today is a smart residential center; it has been neatly restored and is something of a showpiece. Its pristine houses of local golden-brown stone have all been carefully cleaned. In the main square are two giant elms, which were planted in 1638 to mark the birth of Louis XIV.

St-Pierre-de-Tourtour, 3 kilometers (2 miles) E, is a new vacation estate of chic private villas, with swimming pool, tennis courts and other amenities. Built in the local style, and carefully landscaped, it recalls **Castellaras** near MOUGINS. Close by are several smart hotels.

Although not quite in the same gastronomic league, Tourtour has certainly become the Upper Var's answer to MOUGINS.

☜ 🚆 AUBERGE ST-PIERRE ✿
St-Pierre-de-Tourtour, 83690 Salernes
☎ 94-70-57-17 ▥ 18 rms ☟ No cards
🏠 🖻 ◀€ ⛐ ☝ ☞ ♈ Closed mid-Oct to Apr.
Location: In its own 175 acres of farmland, amid glorious countryside, 3 kilometers (2 miles) E of Tourtour. René Marcellin and his family preside over one of the most unusual hotels in Provence, most suitable for those who love animals, sports and the countryside. The solar-heated pool lies beside a wide meadow, where horses and antelope graze. Close by is the home farm, and good riding facilities are available. The hotel itself, a low-ceilinged, stone-floored 18thC manor house, is countrified and attractive, with some amusing touches such as the chapel-turned-TV-room, complete with font, and the alcoves in the lounge filled with groups of *santons*.

The dining room (*▦ ⛾ closed Thurs, mid-Oct to Apr, last orders 8pm*) has good views and contains a mossy fountain (it was once the manor's courtyard). M. Marcellin's cheeses and all his meat come fresh from his farm, and the menus combine Provençal dishes, such as *pieds et paquets*, with his own dishes. *Specialities: Salade de jambon cru d'agneau truffée, jambonette de chapon avec julienne de légumes.*

☜ 🚆 LA BASTIDE DE TOURTOUR 🏨
Tourtour, 83690 Salernes ☎ 94-70-57-30
🖾 94-70-54-90 ▥ to ▥ 25 rms ☟ 🆎

▣ ▣ ▦ ⌂ ⚡ ▢ ◪ ☖ ⟨⟨ ♨ ⛟ ⚲
♈ ♈ ▣ Closed Nov to early Mar.

Location: In its own pinewood grounds, 2 kilometers (1 mile) SE of the village. The word *bastide* is Provençal for "farmhouse" — definitely a misnomer for this rather inelegant, château-style hotel, which was actually built in the late 1960s using local honey-colored stone. Inside, the effect is spacious and stylishly baronial (18thC tapestries hanging on the walls, etc.). The setting is superb and the service gratifyingly attentive. *Patron* Étienne Laurent enjoys showing his guests his intriguing collection of 200 peasant hats and bonnets.

The heavily-vaulted dining room, with its beamed ceiling (▥ ▭ ▰ ▰ ▰ *closed Mon, Tues lunch, Mon evening out of season, Nov to early Mar; last orders 9pm),* is an effective medieval pastiche; or you can take lunch outdoors on the terrace. Chef Alain Anstett, who trained with the Troisgros brothers at Roanne, smoothly blends

classic, *nouvelle* and regional cuisine. Try his *tian de légumes, rougets farcis* or *paupiettes de volaille.*

✑ Also recommended: **La Petite Auberge** (☎ 94-70-57-16 Ⓕ 94-70-54-52 ▭ to ▥), a family-run hotel with comfortable rooms, and good views and facilities.

⚏ **LES CHÊNES VERTS**
Route de Villecroze ☎ 94-70-55-06 ▥ ▭
▰ ▰ ⚏ 🚗 No cards. Closed Tues dinner; Wed; Jan to mid-Feb. Last orders 9pm.

A temple to *nouvelle cuisine,* this tiny modern dining room has just five tables, and little in the peaceful setting will disturb diners from the serious business of eating. The results justify Paul Bajade's dedication to his art — and his prices. The menus offer no choice, but are carefully thought out. They often change, but might include *feuilleté d'asperges au sabayon de morilles* or *blanc de turbot.*

• See also: DRAGUIGNAN, SALERNES.

VERDON, GRAND CANYON DU ★

Map 7E11 (Alpes-de-H.-P.). Approx. 62km (45 miles) NW of Grasse.

No canyon in Europe is so deep, so long, nor so wildly impressive as Verdon, 700 meters (2,500 feet) deep and 21 kilometers (13 miles) long. It was caused by an ancient fault in the limestone plateau that rolls for miles over this part of upper Provence. Through it, the river Verdon rushes on its way to join the Durance.

The bed of the canyon is impassable. Tourist roads wind along the clifftops on both sides, and there are frequent places where you can park safely and then peer giddily into the depths to where the greenish waters swirl. The roads, in some places unprotected by railings, are not broad, so cautious driving is vital. Drivers wary of precipices are advised to take the S road from W–E, or the N road from E–W. The canyon can be approached from Moustiers or Aups to the W, or from CASTELLANE or Comps to the E. Allow a couple of hours to drive round the canyon.

On the S side of the canyon, the road from Moustiers winds up through Aiguines, offering initial views over the canyon at the **Col de l'Illoire** and the **Cirque de Vaumale**. It then follows the **Corniche Sublime**, with superb viewpoints at the **Falaise des Cavaliers** and the **Tunnels de Fayet**. But the best view of all is at the **Balcons de la Mescla**, just beyond the Pont de l'Artuby: from this parapet you look vertically down at the point where the Artuby and Verdon gorges meet.

On the N side, coming from Castellane, the first good view of the E part of the canyon is at the **Point Sublime**. Farther on, a turning to the left takes you along the **Route des Crêtes** (cliff road), with its 15 belvederes overlooking the gorge.

At the Point Sublime, a footpath leads down the cliff and then winds its way along a series of ledges above the river, to rejoin the Route des Crêtes at the Châlet de la Malène. This dizzily exciting walk can be made in either direction. Either way, it is an 8-hour trek, recommended only for tough, experienced hikers not afraid of heights. They should take warm clothing, climbing boots and flashlights, for tunnels are numerous. The bed of the canyon by the river is negotiable only by trained sportsmen or mountaineers, and with an official guide.

PLACES NEAR THE GRAND CANYON DU VERDON
Aiguines   A village on the edge of the plateau, with vistas over the lake below and the plain of Valensole to the W. The pretty 17thC château has a multicolored tiled roof. *(i ☎94-70-21-64.)*

☜ ⇌   **Altitude 823 (☸)** *(☎94-70-21-09 ▢ to ▥):* basic bedrooms, good Provençal food, and views of the lake from the terrace.

Comps-sur-Artuby *(16km/10 miles E of the canyon).* The old village stands on the bare plateau, circled by rocky escarpments. On a hill close by is a little gray limestone 13thC church in primitive Gothic style. To the S of Comps, the large military camp of **Canjuers** stretches for miles across the plateau, with smart, new military housing visible from the road.

☜ ⇌   **GRAND HÔTEL BAIN ☗ ☸**
83840 Comps-sur-Artuby ☎*94-76-90-06*
[Fax]*94-76-92-24* ▢ *to* ▥ *18 rms* ⟵ ▣
[VISA] ▢ ▢ ▱ ✔ ⟪ *Closed mid-Nov to end Dec.*
The name may imply some stately spa hotel, but this is a modest rural inn, owned and run with true country hospitality by the delightful Bain family. If you don't mind simple bedrooms, the

Bain should make you a very good base for touring the Verdon area. In the dining room *(▢ ▨ closed Wed dinner, Thurs out of season, last orders 8.30pm),* the three rows of white-clothed tables are usually filled to bursting with hungry tourists. Service is lighthearted and swift in the face of this onslaught, and Mme Bain's country dishes are most satisfying.

Moustiers-Ste-Marie *(6km/4 miles N of the W end of the canyon).* This 15thC village is strikingly situated at the foot of a ravine 150 meters (500 feet) deep. Between its cliffs, there hangs a 210-meter (700-foot) iron chain with a gilded star in the middle: it is said to have been put there by a local knight in fulfillment of a vow, on his return from the Crusades after a long captivity.

Moustiers is known for its **faïence**, which is the best in Provence. The secret of its white glaze is reputed to have been brought by an Italian monk from eponymous Faenza. In the 17th–18thC Moustiers was a leading pottery center; in the 19thC the industry dwindled away, but was revived in the 1920s and today can be said to be flourishing modestly.

Several shops sell the local produce, while the **Faïence Museum** *(open Apr-Oct)* has a display covering the 17th–20thC.

A 10-minute climb from the village leads to the **Chapel of Notre-Dame**, up inside the ravine. It has a Romanesque porch and tower, and a Renaissance door of sculptured wood.

Ste-Croix, Lac de   At the W end of the Verdon Canyon the river widens into an artificial lake 11 kilometers (7 miles) long, formed in the 1960s by a new hydroelectric dam at its far end.

Trigance *(8km/5 miles E of the canyon)*   A tiny village on the plateau, amid grandiose mountain scenery.

☙ ≕ **CHÂTEAU DE TRIGANCE**
Trigance, 83840 Comps-sur-Artuby
☎94-76-91-18 Ⓕ94-47-58-99 ▥ to ▥
10 rms ⬛ Ⓐⓔ ⊙ ⊙ ▥ ⌂ ◻ ⌖ ⦉
Closed early Nov to late Mar.
Location: On a rocky hilltop above the village, circled by barren mountains.
To reach this 9th–11thC fortress (converted in 1965), you must climb a steep rocky path. You will be greeted with bonhomie by the hotelier and *seigneur,* Jean-Claude Thomas, a former Parisian executive. Any luggage goes up by pulley. The cozy bedrooms have marvelous views of the mountains, as do the castle's numerous terraces, and are stylishly furnished.

You might find the assertive medievalism in the candle-lit dining room *(closed Wed lunch except summer)* a little oppressive; but the cooking is inventive, unpretentious and enjoyable, if not always even. Try the duck with asparagus, mushrooms and red cabbage. Service is friendly.

The hotel is part of the Relais et Châteaux group.

☙ ≕ **Ma Petite Auberge** *(☎94-76-92-92* Ⓕ*94-47-58-65* ▥ *to* ▥*)*
is a pleasant, airy, fairly new hotel just beneath the CHÂTEAU DE TRIGANCE, run by the château's former chef. Good modern decor and simple food. The hotel, with its pool, supplements the facilities at the château.

Eastern Côte d'Azur and Nice's hinterland

From the Esterel Massif to Menton stretches one of the world's most luxurious strips of coast, in the Alpes-Maritimes *département,* saturated with glamor but interesting for many other reasons too. To the east lies the startling Esterel Coast with its jagged red rocks. Then at **CANNES** begins the classic Riviera — each resort a household name, and each quite different from the other. First, Cannes itself, glossy and cosmopolitan, a small-scale Paris-on-Sea; a little to the east is the youthfully boisterous **JUAN-LES-PINS.**

Next, by contrast, is the leafy elegance of exclusive **CAP D'ANTIBES**; then **ANTIBES**, an old seaport. From here to Nice the coast is ugly, but in the hill-villages just behind (**VALLAURIS, BIOT, ST-PAUL-DE-VENCE, CAGNES-SUR-MER**) are museums devoted to the work of the great artists who lived in this area, such as Picasso and Renoir. **NICE**, the Côte d'Azur's capital, is a sophisticated city of manifold fascination. **ST-JEAN-CAP-FERRAT**, to its east, is worth a visit too.

The tiny state of **MONACO** is a must for its museums, princely palace and the pleasure haunts of **MONTE-CARLO**. Beyond, lies the wistfully old-fashioned resort of **MENTON**. The steep coast between Nice and Menton is of spectacular beauty and includes two fine hill-villages, **ÈZE** and **ROQUEBRUNE**.

Travel just a dozen miles inland from the crowded coast, and you enter another world: a wild, mountainous environment in the foothills of the Alps, where old hill-villages and scattered vacation chalets are almost the only signs of habitation. One good excursion is to **LA BRIGUE** and the curious **Vallée des Merveilles** cradled by snowy Alps. Farther west, there is fine sub-alpine scenery around **ST-MARTIN-VÉSUBIE**. Inland from **CANNES**, you should visit **GRASSE**, the perfume town, and the hill-villages nearby. The immediate hinterland of Cannes is beautiful, although rather overbuilt. However, farther north you come to wild, grandiose scenery: take the circuit of the *"clues"* from **VENCE**.

ANTIBES ☆

*Maps **2**D3 and **15**F14 (Alpes-Mar.). 11km (7 miles) NE of Cannes. Postal code: 06600. Population: 72,000* **i** *11 pl. de Gaulle* ☎ *92-90-53-00.* **Railway station:** *av. Robert-Soleau* ☎ *93-99-50-50.*

Founded by the ancient Greeks as a trading post, Antibes today is still bustling and commercial, with sprawling suburbs and dense traffic. The Greeks called it Antipolis, "the city opposite," for it faced their colony at Nice across the Baie des Anges. This geographical factor has dominated much of the town's history. From the late 14thC, Antibes was the frontier fortress town of the kings of France when their enemies, the dukes of Savoy, held sway in Nice. Of the town's fortifications only the seafront and the giant 16thC **Fort Carré**, located just N of the harbor, remain. As a young general in command of coastal defenses, Napoléon lived here with his family in 1794 — in penury it seems, for his revolutionary masters were slow with their paychecks.

Today you can walk along the sea ramparts and take in the fine views of the coast, of NICE and the Alps. Behind them is the famous **Musée Picasso**, and the narrow streets of the small **Vieille Ville**, full of atmosphere and charm. Antibes is not the best choice for a beach vacation (although the gravel to the E here turns to sand and the beach is usually very crowded), but culturally it is fascinating. It is also younger and more casual in atmosphere than nearby Cannes, and is fairly lively all year round, with far less reliance on the tourist and conference trade than its neighbor. Its harbor, Port Vauban, is one of the most important in Europe for pleasure craft.

The gleaming, state-of-the-art new business park, fancifully called **Sophia-Antipolis** *(N of Antibes off the D103),* has attracted such international giants as IBM, Toyota and Air France to its 24 high-tech square kilometers. Often referred to as the Silicon Valley of France, it is, indeed, inspired by the Californian model and is intended to make the Côte d'Azur less reliant on tourism.

The park's fast and furious expansion has meant the disappearance of much greenery in the cause of commerce and progress. You can take a cab there, or a bus from Antibes railway station (a Métro connection with Nice is also planned). See also VALBONNE on page 308.

- **EVENTS**   In March, a **festival of religious art**, and a **café-theater festival**. • In April, an **antique fair**. • In May, **bridge and badminton competitions**, a **young soloists' festival**, and a **car rally**. • In August, the **Musique au Coeur**, a classical music festival. • In October, an **international underwater film and photography festival**. • In November, a **military film festival**. • In December, a **mountain film/ photography festival**.

WHAT TO SEE IN ANTIBES
Cathédrale †
Antibes' parish church, the **Église de l'Immaculée Conception**, is still referred to as a cathedral, although the bishopric was removed to Grasse as far back as 1244 and is now at NICE. The nave is mainly 17thC Baroque, and although the building dates back to the 12thC, only the choir and apse show its Romanesque origins. The church stands right by the sea wall, on what is thought to be the site of a Roman temple. Inside, the elaborate altarpiece *Madonna with Rosary,* at the end of the right aisle, is by Louis Bréa (1515).

Histoire et d'Archéologie, Musée d'
Bastion St-André ☎ *93-34-48-01* ✉ *Open 9am–noon, 2–6pm. Closed Sat; Sun.*

This museum is just to the s of the Château Grimaldi, along the coastal promenade in the **Bastion St-André**, part of Vauban's original fortifications. Here, 4,000 years of the town's history are revealed, in pottery, money and other discoveries, including those recovered from beneath the sea.

Picasso, Musée ☆

Château Grimaldi, Vieille Ville ☎93-34-91-91 🔳 𝘟 *available. Open summer 10am–noon, 2–7pm; winter 2–6pm. Closed Tues; Nov.*

The 13th–16thC castle of the Grimaldis, for centuries the rulers of Antibes, is today a municipal museum, housing one of the world's finest Picasso collections.

After spending the bleak war years in Paris, Picasso returned to his adored Mediterranean in 1945, but he was handicapped by the lack of a proper studio — until the curator offered him the museum for this purpose. Here Picasso worked for several months with joyous inspiration, and afterward, in gratitude, he left his entire prodigious output of that period on permanent loan to the museum, together with some 200 of the vivid ceramics he later produced at nearby VALLAURIS.

The museum's first floor is filled with works that have been inspired by the sea and Greek mythology: here are numerous centaurs, fauns, fish and fishermen, and some of the artist's famous large-scale paintings such as *Ulysse et Les Sirènes* and *La Joie de Vivre,* an exuberant fantasy with dancing satyrs.

The second floor houses temporary exhibitions, and works by other modern artists including Ernst, Modigliani, Mirò and de Staël. There are tapestries by Léger and Lurçat, as well as Jean Cocteau's *Judith and Holofernes.* On the terrace facing the sea are four statues by Germaine Richier.

The museum also shows archeological exhibits dating from the Roman occupation of Antibes. The museum's exhibits are labeled in Braille and, as an additional help for the blind, there are representations of various pictures in relief.

✑ BLEU MARINE

Rue des Quatre-Chemins, 06600 Antibes
☎93-74-84-84 ℻93-74-46-36 Ⅲ *to* Ⅲ
18 rms ➡️ 🆎 🅾️ 🅾️ 🎲 ‡ 🔲 ⬜ 🌱 🐾
Closed Dec to mid-Jan.
Location: 2km (1¼ miles) N of Antibes, between the N7 and the sea. This is a newish hotel; most of its rooms have sea-facing balconies. There is no restaurant.

✑ MAS DJOLIBA

29 av. de Provence, 06600 Antibes
☎93-34-02-48 ℻93-34-05-81 Ⅲ 14
rms ➡️ ≡ 🆎 🅾️ 🅾️ 🎲 🔲 ⬜ 🔲 🌱
Location: On a quiet street in the s suburbs, near the beach. This villa-hotel

stands in its own large garden and has something of the air of a private house. Rooms are comfortable, although service can be a little vague. No lunch; dinner (for residents only) is served in a vine arbor in fine weather.

✑ Other hotels: **Auberge Provençale** (*61 pl. Nationale* ☎93-34-13-24 Ⅲ), a pleasant small hotel. • **Chrys** (*50 Chemin de la Pourouquine* ☎93-74-32-48 ℻93-74-93-23 Ⅲ *to* Ⅲ). • **L'Étoile** (*2 av. Gambetta* ☎93-34-26-30 ℻93-34-41-48 Ⅲ). • **Josse** (*8 blvd. James-Wylie* ☎93-61-47-24 ℻93-61-97-62 Ⅲ). • **Mas de la Pagane** (*15 av. du Mas Ensoleillé* ☎93-

33-33-78 ▥▯), in a pretty 18thC building. • **Petit Castel** (22 Chemin des Sables ☎93-61-59-37 Fx 93-67-51-28 ▥▯ . • **Relais du Postillon** (8 rue Championnet ☎93-34-20-77 ▥▯). • **Royal** (blvd. Maréchal-Leclerc ☎93-34-03-09 Fx 93-67-51-28 ▥▯). • **Teranga** (2 rue Marcel-Paul ☎93-67-40-93 Fx 93-67-27-93 ▥▯). • **Thalazar** (770 Chemin des Moyennes Bréguières ☎93-74-78-82 Fx 93-65-94-14) ▥▯ to ▥▯), which offers thalassotherapy facilities.

▱ L'ÉCURIE ROYALE
33 rue Vauban ☎93-34-76-20 ▥▯ AE ●
● ▥ Closed Sun eve; Mon; mid-Jan to mid-Feb; mid-Nov to Dec; lunch June to mid-Sept.

A Belgian couple, the Xhauflairs, show flair indeed in running their rustic-style restaurant, warm and welcoming, with excellent cooking. Specialities: Foie de canard au torchon maison, suprême de pintade aux épinards.

▱ LA PAILLE EN QUEUE
42 blvd. Wilson ☎93-34-39-89 ▥▯ AE ●
▥ Last orders 10pm. Closed Sun eve; Wed.

The decor is Louis XVI, and the owners, the Niesor brothers, come from the island of La Réunion, which explains the spicy exoticism of some of their dishes. Specialities: (from Réunion) agneau au massale, samoussas sambos; (French) brouillade d'aubergine à la menthe fraîche.

▱ LES VIEUX MURS
Promenade Amiral-de-Grasse
☎93-34-06-73 ▥▯ to ▥▯ ▤ ▰ ▱ ▰
▰ ▰ AE ● ▥ Open daily. Last orders 10.30pm.

This restaurant near the Musée Picasso has established itself as one of the best in Antibes. The vaulted ceiling, exposed stone walls and tiled floor make it pleasantly cool on a warm day, and the view of the bay is a further bonus. Service from the blue-liveried staff is smooth but friendly (they even have valet parking), and the light, modern cooking, with strong Provençal and Mediter-

ranean influences, is excellent. Fish is a speciality.

▱ Other decent restaurants in Antibes are: • **Auberge Provençale** (pl. Nationale ☎93-34-13-24 ▥▯ closed Mon, Tues lunch). • **Café des Chineurs** (27 rue Aubernon ☎93-34-57-58 ▱ closed Tues out of season), a charming café in the old town, good for lunch. • **Clafoutis** (18 rue Thuret ☎93-34-66-70 ▥▯). • **Le Dauphin** (8 blvd. Maréchal-Leclerc ☎93-34-03-09 ▥▯). • **Le Marquis** (rue de Sade ☎93-34-23-00 ▥▯ closed Mon), serving Provençal food. • **Le Michelangelo** (2 rue des Cordiers ☎93-34-04-47 ▥▯), a new restaurant in the old town, specializing in Provençal and Italian cuisine, with excellent antipasti. • **L'Oursin** (16 rue de la République ☎93-34-13-46 ▥▯ closed Sun eve, Mon). • **Le Transat** (Residence du Port Vauban, 17 av. du 11 Novembre ☎93-34-20-20 ▥▯), for Provençal and fish specialities. • **Le Vieux Four** (22 rue Thuret ☎93-34-40-25 ▥▯ closed Sun and Wed eve), specializing in brochettes, grills and pizzas, and offering good value and friendly service.

There are a number of interesting eating places in Boulevard Aguillon, in the old port area, including **Chez Félix** (☎93-34-01-64), the restaurant where the late Graham Greene used to go daily for lunch (other customers included Picasso and Jacques Prévert), and **Latino**, a tapas bar. There are several small restaurants in place Nationale where you can eat outside. **Pims** is a trendy bar in rue de la République.

▱ NEARBY

LA BONNE AUBERGE ⌂
RN7, La Brague (4km/2½ miles N of Antibes)
☎93-33-36-65 ▥▯ ▱ ▰ ▰ ▰ ▰ AE
● Last orders 10pm. Closed Mon lunch; Mon eve Sept–June; mid-Nov to mid-Dec.

Under the supervision of Philippe Rostang, son of its brilliant patron and former chef, Jo Rostang, this spacious pink auberge just N of Antibes remains near the top of the Côte's gastronomic league, and is besieged by the rich and famous. Flowers on every table, a shady arbor for summer dining: all is near perfection, including the food, which, under Philippe (who trained with the Troisgros brothers and Alain Senderens), has changed its style and become more traditional than before. Picture windows separate kitchen from dining room, so that some tables have a front-row view of the spectacle as the *maître* and his acolytes prepare their delights. Service and presentation rate highly.

⬛ NIGHTLIFE IN ANTIBES

The best nightlife in the area is just outside town at **La Siesta** *(N98, La Brague, 4km/2½ miles N of Antibes* ☎*93-33-31-31* ☿ ○ ❀ ❧ *open June to mid-Sept 10am–5am, dancing from 9pm)*, a huge and exotic beach nightclub for the Côte's *jeunesse dorée*.

By day it's a beach resort, with every watersport, specially imported sand, a supervised children's area, and even a restaurant for dogs. By night there is a network of open-air bars and dance floors where waterfalls are illuminated by flaming torches. There is an extraordinary wave-shaped casino.

SHOPPING IN ANTIBES

La Colombelle, opposite the Musée Picasso, sells good, locally-made jewelry, pottery and handicrafts. **Rue James-Close** has many little boutiques.

* **MARKETS**   Just behind the Musée Picasso, in place Masséna, is the open-air **fruit**, **vegetable** and **fish market**, open every morning except Monday. • There is an **antique** and **junk market** on place Jacques Audiberti on Tuesday and Saturday.

PLACE NEAR ANTIBES

Marineland (✩) *(RN7, La Brague* ☎*93-33-49-49* ▣ ▣ ✽ *)*. Performing dolphins, sea lions and huge Icelandic whales. The zoo also contains penguins and an aquarium, and there's a children's play area. Amusing and, inevitably, crowded.

ANTIBES, CAP D' ✩

Maps **2***E3 and* **15***F15 (Alpes-Mar.). 2km (1 mile) s of Antibes. Postal code: 06600* **i** *11 pl. de Gaulle, Antibes* ☎*92-90-53-00.*

The name Cap d'Antibes refers to the whole of the beautiful pine-forested peninsula to the S of ANTIBES and JUAN-LES-PINS, although the Cape proper is its southernmost tip. A haven of calm, it is, like ST-JEAN-CAP-FERRAT, a favorite haunt of the rich, and much of it is divided into private estates with imposing villas and subtropical gardens. But there is much for the ordinary visitor too: sandy beaches, splendid views, reasonably-priced hotels and restaurants, botanical gardens and other curiosities.

The best beaches charge a fee: to the E, **Plage de la Garoupe**; to the W, **Port Gallice**.

WHAT TO SEE IN CAP D'ANTIBES
La Garoupe, Sanctuaire de ☆
La Garoupe 🚋 ◁€ *Open Easter–Sept, 9.30am–12.30pm, 2.30–7pm;*
Oct–Easter 10am–noon, 2.30–5pm. Ask porter for key.

Standing by a lighthouse on a hill in the center of the peninsula, this curious sailors' chapel is famous for the votive offerings hung on its walls: paintings by amateurs, executed in fulfillment of a vow or in thanksgiving for deliverance from death. Their naivety is fascinating and rather touching. One aisle is filled with sailors' offerings, including a self-portrait by a convict seen giving thanks to Our Lady for helping him escape to Martinique from the Toulon jail.

The second aisle is devoted to the miraculous escapes of landlubbers: a man falling from a tree in 1865, another from a ladder, another saved from an irate dog. A particularly vivid one depicts a road accident. The car lies on its back in a ditch, while the family — somewhat foolishly, you might think — kneels in the middle of the road and gives thanks to Our Lady, who has appeared in the sky.

After this high drama, it may come as an anticlimax to learn that the chapel also has a fine 14thC Russian icon and a Russian silk painting, both spoils of the Crimean War.

Next to the chapel is a vantage point with marvelous views of the coast. The lighthouse is one of the most powerful on the Côte d'Azur.

Naval et Napoléonien, Musée
Blvd. J.-F.-Kennedy ☎*93-61-45-32* 🔲 ◁€ *Open 9.30am–noon, 2.15–6pm.*
Closed Sat pm; Sun.

Housed in the **Batterie du Grillon** are many models of 17th and 18thC men-of-war and mementos of Napoléon's landing at nearby Golfe-Juan on his great return from Elba in 1815. There are splendid views of the Alps and Corsica on a clear day, from the top of the **Sella tower**.

Thuret, Jardin
w of La Garoupe Chapel. Open 8.30am–noon, 2–5.30pm. Closed Sat; Sun.

Containing a fine array of exotic trees and flora, the 12-acre gardens were founded in 1856 as one of the first centers in Europe for the acclimatization of tropical vegetation, much of which is now established on the coast. There are around 2,000 different species today.

❧ ⇌ HÔTEL DU CAP EDEN-ROC 🏨
Blvd. J.-F.-Kennedy, 06604 Antibes
☎*93-61-39-01* 📠*93-67-76-04* ▥ *130 rms* 🍽 ⬛ 🖥 No cards ⬛ ♨ ♿ ▢ 🔲
🌺 ⛵ ◁€ ⛰ ♒ ⚓ ⮌ 🛥 *(out of season). Closed Nov–Easter.*

Location: At the s tip of the Cap d'Antibes peninsula, in its own 15-acre park. There are more famous ghosts than there are bedrooms to haunt at this, the proudest and most stylish of all the Côte's luxury palaces. This was the

hotel in F. Scott Fitzgerald's *Tender is the Night;* and from its opening in 1870 until recent times, it was the very smartest rendezvous for royalty and celebrities alike, from Haile Selassie to Betty Grable and J.F. Kennedy to G.B. Shaw.

Nowadays, the hotel has married tasteful, modern decor with the opulence of that bygone age: marble floors, airy salons, spacious bedrooms, and, beneath the handsome cream-colored palace, a splendid garden of flowers, pines and palms that sweeps down to the sea and beach club. There are five tennis courts and a heated sea-water pool. Every room has a sea view.

The hotel's famous restaurant, the **Pavillon Eden-Roc** (〰 ⌷ 🍴 🎐 *last orders 10pm, closed Nov-Easter)*, stands apart from the hotel at the foot of the garden, overlooking the rocky shores and glittering sea. Here the bright young things of the 1920s enjoyed some of their wildest times. Today's ambience is more sober, but the idyllic setting can still set the head spinning, whether you dine on the terrace or just take a drink at the open bar. The food has never been remarkable, but it has been revitalized in recent years by chef Poette Arnaud, and includes a lavish buffet.

🍴 ≡ LA GARDIOLE

Chemin de la Garoupe, 06600 Cap d'Antibes ☎93-61-35-03 📠93-67-61-87 〰 *21 rms* ⊞ ⒜ ⊡ ◎ 💳 🖂 � ⌷ 🎐 ❧ 🐟 ≈ *Closed Nov-Mar.*
Location: High in the center of the peninsula, with a sandy beach close by.

Set in a pine forest in its own flowery garden, this is a delightful, medium-priced hotel with a civilized family ambience. Rooms are simple and fresh, many with private terraces. Service, it has to be said, can at times be a little disorganized. The large terrace, overhung with wisteria and surrounded by flowers, provides a delightful setting for a meal (♥) in fine weather (〰 ⌷ 🍴 🎐 *last orders 10.30pm).* Service may be slow, but the Provençal cooking is copious and good value. *Specialities: Soupe de poissons, papillotte de saumon.*

≡ BACON ⌂

Blvd. de Bacon ☎93-61-50-02 〰 *to* 〰 ⌷ ⒜ ⊡ *Last orders 9pm. Closed Mon; Sun eve (except July, Aug); mid-Nov to Feb.*
Many connoisseurs consider the *bouillabaisse* here to be the finest E of Marseille. Prices are high, but that's justified by the quality of the fish cuisine, and the luxurious setting of the restaurant, which enjoys wide views of the Baie des Anges and the Alps. *Specialities: Salade de poissons crus, langouste "nage de légumes."*

• See also: BIOT, JUAN-LES-PINS, VALBONNE, VALLAURIS, VILLENEUVE-LOUBET.

AURON

Map 15B14 (Alpes-Mar.). 98km (61 miles) NW of Nice. Postal code: 06660 St-Étienne-de-Tinée i in the town square ☎93-23-02-66.

Auron is a natural choice for a winter ski resort and has a genuinely alpine flavor. It stands imposingly on a circular plateau at 1,600 meters (5,250 feet) and is surrounded by an amphitheater of peaks rising to 2,474 meters (8,120 feet). The resort has a feeling of space and grandeur that the other "Ski Azur" villages of VALBERG and ISOLA 2000 lack. Various hotels, snack bars and shops have grown up around the large, informal square, and there are plenty of facilities behind the square, such as tennis courts, swimming pool and cinema.

Despite these, and other summertime activities, Auron remains very much a winter resort, and most of the hotels are closed in summer.

St-Érige, Chapelle † ☆
Just off main square. Apply to tourist office for key.
This richly decorated chapel, according to legend, was established in a place previously only inhabited by a few shepherds in summer. In the late 6thC, St-Érige, Archbishop of Gap, was returning from Rome. His mount evidently tired of the journey and leaped over the Tinée valley in a single bound. A chapel was built on the spot where the horse

landed. In fact this chapel, dating from the 12thC, is another sign that ST-ÉTIENNE-DE-TINÉE was an important religious center. It has a simple larch interior, with two parallel apses covered in arresting and wonderfully vivid 15thC frescoes depicting St Mary Magdalene (said to have lived in Provence: see STE-BAUME, MASSIF DE), St-Denis (martyred in Paris in AD250) and St-Érige. Best of all is the fresco of Christ, wearing a mantle decorated with birds and animals.

✅ ST-ÉRIGE

06660 St-Étienne-de-Tinée, Auron ☎93-23-00-32 ✉93-23-04-06 💷 *16 rms* 🍽 🖭 🔟 🖂 🔲 🖾 *Closed May–June; Oct–Nov.*
Location: On boulevard Georges-Pompidou. The St-Érige has the advantage of being run by the welcoming Mme Rubini and her family, who in fact built the hotel. The bedrooms, although small, have a pleasant, old-fashioned feel to them, and you can eat heartily in the wood and stone "hunting lodge"

dining room, complete with assorted stuffed beasts. Mme Rubini, who adores animals, welcomes pets.

✅ Other recommended hotels in Auron: **Las Donnas** (☎*93-23-00-03* ✉*93-23-07-39* 💷 *to* 💷*);* **L'Heure Mauve** (☎*93-23-00-21* 💷 *to* 💷*);* **Le Pilon** (☎*93-23-00-15* 💷 *to* 💷*).*

🍽 The **Piscine** restaurant provides reasonable food.

SPORTS AND ACTIVITIES IN AURON

With 120 kilometers (74 miles) of *pistes* over the steep-sided slopes of two valleys, Auron offers far more adventurous skiing than its main rival, ISOLA 2000. It has the advantage of plenty of sun, but the drawback that good snow isn't always guaranteed. Whereas Isola and VALBERG are good for beginners, Auron is the choice for more advanced skiers. In summer, it has good pony trekking with guides, as well as walking and climbing. A cable car rises almost to the summit of **Las Donnas**, at 2,256 meters (7,400 feet), where the views are excellent. It operates in summer and winter *(daily 9am-5.30pm, closed May-June, Oct-Nov).*

• See also: ST-ÉTIENNE-DE-TINÉE.

BEAULIEU-SUR-MER

Maps 3C4 and 15E15 (Alpes-Mar.). 10km (6 miles) NE of Nice. Postal code: 06310. Population: 4,300 ℹ pl. Georges-Clémenceau ☎93-01-02-21.

Once one of the most fashionable resorts on the coast, Beaulieu has lost much of its glamor but, with its floodlit palms, still retains a certain elderly chic. Handsome villas abound: the **Villa Namouna** belonged to Gordon Bennett, the owner of the *New York Herald,* who commissioned Stanley to find Livingstone; the **Villa Léonine** was designed and built in the late 19thC by the British prime minister, the Marquess of Salisbury.

Open to the public is **Villa Kérylos** (✩) *(av. Gustave-Eiffel* ☎*93-01-01-44* 🎦 *open July, Aug 2.30-6.30pm, Sept-June 2-6pm, closed Mon, Nov).* Standing on its little headland, this villa is a faithful reconstruction of an ancient Greek villa, and was built between 1902 and 1908 by archeologist Theodore Reinach. The **library** contains a collection of ancient art. Beware, signposts to the villa are confusing.

Beaulieu's sheltered setting makes it one of the warmest places on the Côte d'Azur, especially in winter. To keep yourself amused, there is a lively **casino** *(open daily 3pm-3am)* and a large **marina**; but the beach is stony. By Promenade Maurice-Rouvier at the w end of Baie des Fourmis you can walk along the sea to ST-JEAN-CAP-FERRAT.

✆ MÉTROPOLE 🏨

Blvd. Maréchal-Leclerc, 06310 Beaulieu-sur-Mer ☎ 93-01-00-08 ☒ 93-01-18-51 ▥ 53 rms ▤ ▨ AE ▣ ▦ ▨ ☀ ₺ ⚓ ⚓ ▧ ❧ 《 ≈ ☀ ☿ Closed late Oct to late Dec. For ☰ see below.

Location: In the town, but overlooking the sea and its own private beach. A *fin-de-siècle* hotel founded in 1892, among the earliest on this coast, which has been in the hands of one family ever since. It has been modernized with some sensitivity, although the garish carpet in the public areas lowers the tone somewhat. Spacious, bright and luxurious, the hotel is set in a large, neat garden, with a delightful heated swimming pool alongside a private beach formed of sheer stone. The bedrooms and bathrooms are elegant, some perhaps a little small, but they all have beautiful views, and the service is smooth, polished and personable. The atmosphere is gratifyingly old-fashioned: no mini-bars in the rooms, no conferences at the hotel. . . . The guests, many of them regulars, are mostly European.

✆ LA RÉSERVE 🏨

Blvd. Maréchal-Leclerc, 06310 Beaulieu-sur-Mer ☎ 93-01-00-01 ☒ 93-01-28-99 ▥ 40 rms ▤ ⚓ ☰ AE ▣ ▣ ▦ ▧ ☀ ⚓ ▧ ☿ ❧ 《 ☀ ≈ ☿ ▤ Open all year. For ☰ see below.

Location: In the town center and right on the sea. When it was founded by Gordon Bennett around a century ago, La Réserve was one of the half-dozen most exclusive hotels on the Côte. For today's tastes, its ambience may be somewhat stiff, and the rival MÉTROPOLE has a more relaxed atmosphere, but it remains flawlessly luxurious, with fine sea views.

✆ Other reasonable hotels: **Carlton** *(7 rue Édith-Cavell* ☎ 93-01-14-70 ☒ 93-01-29-62 ▥); **Frisia** *(2 blvd. Eugène-Gauthier* ☎ 93-01-01-04 ☒ 93-01-31-92 ▥); **Le Havre Bleu** *(29 blvd. Maréchal-Joffre* ☎ 93-01-01-40 ☒ 93-01-29-92 ▥), near the station.

☰ AFRICAN QUEEN

Port de Plaisance ☎ 93-01-10-85 ▥ AE ▣ ▥ ⚓ ⚓

A lively, popular place by the port, with equally good views of the yachts from its terrace and from indoors. *Specialities: Curry de poissons avec légumes crus, salade de ratatouille froide au jambon de canard.*

☰ MÉTROPOLE ⚓

Hôtel Métropole, Blvd. Maréchal-Leclerc ☎ 93-01-00-08 ▥ ▧ ▦ ▨ ⚓ ⚓ Last orders 11pm. Closed end Oct to end Dec.

The gracious dining room of the Métropole, with its large terrace overlooking the sea, offers some of the finest cuisine on the coast. Although the dishes are classic, they are far from heavy, and combine the lightness of *nouvelle* with traditional French cuisine, to achieve first-class results. The *terrine de bouillabaisse en gelée* is an imaginative speciality worth trying. *Other specialities: Soupe de poissons de roche, calmars et St-Jacques sautés aux poivrons rouges doux.* (See ✆ above.)

☰ LA PIGNATELLE ✿

10 rue de Quincenet ☎ 93-01-03-37 ▥ ▧ ▦ ⚓ Last orders 9pm (winter), 10pm (summer). Closed Wed; mid-Oct to mid-Nov.

A very popular little *auberge* in the town center, with a pretty patio for dining outdoors. Honest Niçois family cooking is served, at very reasonable prices for this part of the coast.

☰ LA RÉSERVE ⚓

Blvd. Maréchal-Leclerc ☎ 93-01-00-01 ▥ to ▥ ▧ ▦ ⚓ ⚓ Last orders 10pm *(winter),* 10.30pm *(summer).*

The formal, Renaissance-style dining room, with its paintings, chandeliers and huge Venetian mirrors, looks right onto the sea. Both cuisine and service are in the grand old style — in short, little seems to have changed over the years, but the talented new chef, Joel Garault, has made discreet innovations, and is building a reputation. (See ☜ above.)

☷   Other restaurants: **Les Agaves** *(1 av. Maréchal-Foch* ☎ *93-01-12-90* ▥*);* **Le Maxilien** *(43 blvd. Marinoni* ☎*93-01-47-48* ▥*).*

* See also: ÈZE, ST-JEAN-CAP-FERRAT, LA TURBIE, VILLEFRANCHE.

BIOT

Maps **2***D3 and* **15***F14 (Alpes-Mar.). 8km (5 miles)* NW *of Antibes. Postal code: 06410. Population: 5,500* **i** *pl. de la Chapelle* ☎*93-65-05-85.*

Overlooking a valley growing table grapes, carnations and roses for the market, Biot is a lively and attractive village with an arcaded square and 16thC gates and ramparts. The church contains two 15thC retables of the Nice school; one, depicting *Our Lady of Mercy* in eight panels, is by the prolific Louis Bréa.

Due to the rich clay deposits around Biot, the village has, since ancient times, been a major center of pottery and ceramics. The industry is thriving, as is the old Provençal tradition of glass-making. One of the finest glassworks is **Novaro**, opposite the turning to the **Musée Léger** on the D4. Also worth a visit is the **Verrerie de Biot**, at the entrance to the village, as is the local history museum *(6 pl. de la Chapelle* ☎ *93-65-54-54, open 2.30-5.30pm during summer, Wed, Sat, Sun in winter, closed in Nov).*

The nearest railway station is at **La Brague** *(an uphill 4km/2½-mile walk away),* but there are regular buses from Antibes.

* **EVENTS**   There are *boules* **tournaments** in May, June and August.
  * A **music festival** takes place in June.

Fernand Léger, Musée ☆

☎*93-65-63-61 or 93-65-63-49* ☒ *Open summer 10am–noon, 2–6pm; winter 10am–noon, 2–5pm. Closed Tues.*

Built by Léger's widow, Nadia, soon after his death in 1955, this was the first major museum in France created specifically to house the work of one artist. The handsome building stands on a hillside among pines and cypresses, the front facade dominated by a startling, vividly-colored mosaic representing sport. The interior is functional and spacious, with large windows designed to attract the maximum of sunlight.

More than 300 of Léger's distinctive works are displayed here, a dazzling array of cubes, cogs, girders, machines and massive, robot-like figures frozen in movement. Léger's evolution can be traced through the permanent collection of paintings: from his early dabbling with Impressionism (*Portrait de l'Oncle,* 1905), through his creation, with Picasso and Braque, of Cubism (*La Femme en Bleu,* 1912, *Contrastes des Formes,* 1913), to his increasing preoccupation with machinery, its harsh impersonality, ordered movements and primary colors.

Later in life, his canvases became jollier, although still involving mechanics (*Les Loisirs sur Fond Rouge*, 1949; *Les Oiseaux sur Fond Jaune*, 1955). In the garden are a number of large mosaics and sculptures, executed to Léger's design by his followers.

❧ ☰ **LES ARCADES** 🛏

16 pl. des Arcades, 06410 Biot ☎*93-65-01-04* 🎴 *12 rms* ☐ ◄€ *Closed Nov.*
Location: In a small, arcaded square in the village center. Owner André Brothier sets the tone for the truly bohemian atmosphere at his 16thC inn-cum-art gallery-cum-lively meeting place for local people. The bedrooms, with their antique furniture and views of the hills and sea, are charming, and though the trappings are old, the plumbing is modern.

Brothier is a friend and collector of modern artists, and, among others, Braques and Mirós adorn the walls of the simple, countrified dining room (🎴 ☐ ■ 🍴 *last orders 9pm, closed Mon lunch, Nov*). Or you can eat under the arcades on the sidewalk. Visitors have sometimes found the approach too take-it-or-leave-it, but they are rewarded by sound Provençal cooking.

☰ **AUBERGE DU JARRIER**

30 Passage de la Bourgade ☎*93-65-*

11-68 🎴 *to* 🎴 ☐ 🛏 🍴 *AE* *CB* *VISA*
Last orders 9.15pm. Closed Mon eve; Tues out of season; Tues and Wed lunch, July and Aug; mid-Nov to mid-Dec.
Delicious *nouvelle cuisine* and a friendly welcome at this charming *auberge*, which has a garden. The *patron/chef*, Christian Metral, spent five years with Alain Senderens in Paris. *Specialities: Gâteau chaud de foie de volaille, pigeonneau rôti aux pois gourmands et aux fèves.*

☰ **LES TERRAILLERS**

11 Route Chemin Neuf ☎*93-65-01-59* 🎴 *to* 🎴 🍴 ☐ ■ 🍴 *AE* *CB* *VISA* *Closed Wed out of season, and Thurs lunch in July, Aug; first week Mar; Nov. Last orders 10pm.*
This restaurant, in a 16thC pottery, vies with the AUBERGE DU JARRIER as the best in town, although it is a little formal. There is a good selection of set menus. Try the *salade de homard et ravioles de chèvre*, the *soufflé de coquilles St-Jacques* or the *ris de veau braisé aux truffes noires.*

• See also: ANTIBES, VALLAURIS, VILLENEUVE-LOUBET.

LA BRIGUE

*Map **16**C17 (Alpes-Mar.). 38km (24 miles) NE of Sospel; 82km (51 miles) NE of Nice. Postal code: 06430 Tende. Population: 600.*

Once the private hunting ground (for chamois and wild boar) of the kings of Italy, the region around La Brigue and Tende was ceded to France as recently as 1947. The unrestored medieval village of La Brigue has vaulted and cobbled streets, and its Romanesque **church**, with a Lombard belfry, contains two good primitive paintings, by Bréa and Fossano.

Above the village is the ruined **castle** of the Lascaris, who were the local *seigneurs* until the 18thC.

Notre-Dame-des-Fontaines, Chapelle de ☆
4km (2½ miles) E of La Brigue. Ask at any hotel in La Brigue for key.
Standing alone in a fertile mountain valley full of streams, orchards and grazing sheep, this beautiful sanctuary is the goal of pilgrims and tourists alike. The exterior is quite plain, but inside is a dazzling, richly decorated interior. The walls are covered with 15thC frescoes by Gio-

vanni Canavesio, a Piedmontese priest, depicting with realism and poignancy the Life of Christ. Most memorable is the agonized portrayal of *Judas Iscariot.*

MIRVAL

06430 La Brigue ☎ 93-04-63-71 ▭ 18 rms ▱▱▱▱▱▱▱▱▱▱▱
Closed Nov–Feb.
Location: On the w edge of the village, across the river from the main road. The friendly and helpful owners have

modernized their simple, unpretentious country hotel; the bedrooms are fresh and neat, some with fine upland views. In the restaurant (▱ ▱ ▱ *last orders 8.30pm),* the sound, country cooking includes homemade pasta and fresh trout.

PLACES NEAR LA BRIGUE

Vallée des Merveilles (★) *(24km/15 miles w of La Brigue; signposted roads to near valley, then well-marked paths; no guide needed; jeeps can be rented from any hotel in the region, but this is expensive; the valley is only accessible June-Oct, due to snow).* The aptly named Valley of the Marvels is one of the most haunting and bizarre places in all France. Set beneath the eerie **Mont Bégo**, in a majestic circle of the Alps, the forbidding, rock-strewn landscape makes the visitor feel very remote from the Côte d'Azur. Yet more mysterious are the 30,000 engravings of bulls, daggers and totems cut all over the rock faces. Discovered in 1896 by an American archeologist, they are believed to have been made by Iron- or Bronze-Age tribesmen, who came in pilgrimage to Mont Bégo and its valley.

If you decide to see the valley properly on foot, you should allow 8 hours for the round trip. The **Valmasque path** leads past a string of deep alpine lakes, each, strikingly, a different color.

Although it is on the tourist track, there is a remarkable feeling of awe and isolation when ascending to this remote domain. At the s end of the valley is a **climber's hostel**, with dormitory beds and simple food *(open July to mid-Oct).*

AUBERGE MARIE-MADELEINE

Casterino, 06430 St-Dalmas-de-Tende
☎ 93-04-65-93 ▭ 11 rms ▱▱▱
Closed Nov–May.
Location: 8km (5 miles) NW of Vallée des Merveilles at Casterino. An excellent place to stay on a visit to the *vallée:* a

simple alpine inn, in a glorious open setting amid pastures and wooded hills. Friendly owners; boisterous French family parties; and a large garden, with a playground. Expect *cuisine niçoise* in the restaurant (▱ ▱ ▱ ▱), as well as alpine dishes such as *raclette* and *fondue.*

• See also: SAORGE.

CABRIS ☆

Maps 2D1 and 14F13 (Alpes-Mar.). 5km (3 miles) w of Grasse. Postal code: 06530 Peymeinade. Population: 650 **i** *rue de l'Horloge* ☎ 93-60-55-63.

A very scenic route (the D4) leads w from Grasse to this beautiful old village on the spur of a hill, dominating the lush valley of the Siagne. From the terrace beside the ruined **castle**, and from other vantage points, the view is superb: CAP-FERRAT, CAP D'ANTIBES, the Lérin Islands, the Ésterel and MAURES MASSIFS.

Like ST-PAUL-DE-VENCE, and other of the Côte's hinterland villages, Cabris is a sophisticated place, its narrow medieval streets lined with carefully restored houses. It has long been a favorite venue for writers, actors and other intellectuals, including André Gide, Herbert Marcuse and Jean Marais.

☜ L'HORIZON ☙

06530 Cabris ☎93-60-51-69
Fx93-60-56-29 ▥ to ▥ 22 rms ☜ ☳
AE ⊙ ◎ ▦ ⌂ ⌂ ≈ ☀ ✿ ✿ ⫷
Closed mid-Oct to end Mar.

Location: Overlooking the valley, on a quiet road on the w fringe of the village.
Sartre, Camus, Saint-Exupéry and Leonard Bernstein were among past famous guests here. Surely it was the heart-stopping views, enough to revive the most flagging inspiration, and the lovely patio garden with its acacias and luxuriant creepers, where Bernstein would sit and compose, that drew them to such a modest hotel. Jean Roustan, the cultured owner, talks eagerly to his guests about music, books and local history. His hotel is neat and modernized; bedrooms lack character, but many have balconies with that superb view. Simple family cooking is served

* See also: GRASSE, VALBONNE.

on the patio in summer; *pension* terms are excellent value.

▤ LE VIEUX CHÂTEAU

Pl. du Panorama ☎93-60-50-12 ▥ to ▥ ▢ ▥ ♨ ☜ ⊙ ▥ Closed Thurs (in winter); end Nov to mid-Dec; Feb. Last orders 9pm.
This ravishingly pretty *auberge* has been built out of part of the village 11thC castle ruins. You can eat well-cooked regional dishes, Provençal and others, in the vaulted *salle* or on the vine-covered terrace, with the mighty panorama in front.

▤ Cheap outdoor restaurants and pizzerias can be found on the N side of the village, beside the Grasse road. Among them, **Le Petit Prince** *(15 rue Frédéric-Mistral* ☎ *93-60-51-40* ▥ *to* ▥*)* is perhaps the best.

CAGNES-SUR-MER ☆

*Maps 2D3 and 15F15 (Alpes-Mar.). 13km (8 miles) sw of Nice. Postal code: 06800. Population: 41,000 i 6 av. Maréchal-Juin ☎93-20-61-64. **Railway stations** ☎93-22-46-47, at Cagnes-sur-Mer and Cros-de-Cagnes.*

Cagnes-sur-Mer straggles inland from the sea in three distinct parts, becoming increasingly interesting as it does so. The coastal resort of **Cros-de-Cagnes**, once a little fishing village, is today a conglomeration of highways, hypermarkets and high-rise apartments. Together with nearby VILLENEUVE-LOUBET, this is the least attractive stretch of the whole Côte d'Azur, and has little of interest to offer save the famous **hippodrome** (racetrack).

Two kilometers (1 mile) inland is **Cagnes-Ville**, notable for its MUSÉE RENOIR, and, just above, the tiny hilltop village of **Haut-de-Cagnes (☆)**, crowned by its medieval château. Haut-de-Cagnes, like so many of the region's perched villages, is squeezed tightly into its walls, creating twisting alleys and steps. Cagnes is still popular with artists, although the pace of tourism is more frenetic than in Renoir's days.

The journeys to both by local train from Cannes, Antibes and Nice are swift and cheap. Haut-de-Cagnes is difficult to reach by car, as the roads are very narrow, but there is parking just outside the village.

- **EVENTS**   In April, an **international flower show** and a **wine fair**, both at the Hippodrome. • On May 1, a **fête** at Haut-de-Cagnes. • In June, a **music festival**. • From July to September, an annual **international festival of art** is held in the château (☎ *93-20-87-29).* • Also in July (to end August), there are evening **race meetings**. • In August, a **sea festival** at Cros-de-Cagnes, **medieval evenings** at place du Château, and the **World Boules Championship**. • In September, an **antique fair**. • In December, start of the winter **horse-racing season**.

- **MARKETS**   There is a **market** in Cagnes-sur-Mer every morning apart from Monday. • An **antique/second-hand market** takes place every Sunday in place du Château.

WHAT TO SEE IN CAGNES-SUR-MER
Château Musée
Haut-de-Cagnes ☎ *93-20-85-57* ✉ *Open summer 10am–noon, 2.30–7pm; winter 10am–noon, 2–5pm. Closed Tues.*

This attractive and diverse museum is housed in the castle, which dominates Haut-de-Cagnes. Built as a hill-fortress in the early 14thC by a branch of the Grimaldi family, rulers here until 1789, it was converted by Henri Grimaldi in 1620 into an elegant Louis XIII château. In the 19thC it was bought and restored by a private purchaser, and in 1939 it was acquired by the town and turned into a well-laid-out museum.

Soft music plays as the visitor enters the castle via a delightful triangular inner courtyard dating from Henri Grimaldi's day; there is a 200-year-old peppertree growing on one side. Several ground-floor rooms are devoted to a **museum of the olive tree**, with old olive presses and many photographs, maps and books dealing with the olive industry. On the first floor, the 17thC **Salle des Fêtes** has a high ceiling with a *trompe l'oeil* fresco of the *Fall of Phaeton* (✰) by the Genoese Carlone, the perspective of which gives the impression that Phaeton, together with his chariot and horses, is about to come crashing to the floor.

The second floor, once the Grimaldis' private apartments, brings another abrupt change of subject. This is the **Musée d'Art Moderne Méditerranéen**, featuring the work of artists who were either born near or drawn to the Mediterranean. They include Chagall, Dufy, Vasarely and Kisling. The former boudoir of the Marquise de Grimaldi houses a memorable oddity: 40 portraits of Suzy Solidor, the cabaret singer, by 40 different artists, including Cocteau, Dufy, Foujita and Van Dongen. The flamboyant, free-living Solidor, never one to shun publicity, retired to Cannes in her later years. She inspired the popular song *If you knew Suzy, like I know Suzy.*

Finally, yet another change of scene can be had by climbing up to the castle's 19thC **tower** for a sweeping view of sea and hills.

Notre-Dame-de-Protection
Below château on NE side. Open June–Oct 2.30–6pm; Nov–May 2–5pm. Closed Tues; Fri.

In 1641 Henri de Grimaldi persuaded his cousin Honoré II of Monaco to change his allegiance to France from Spain, by signing the Treaty of Peronne. To celebrate his success, he had the chapel enlarged and dedicated to Our Lady of Protection. It stands outside the walls of the town, below the castle. It was already decorated with interesting 16thC **frescoes** by an unknown although probably local artist, judging by their primitive style.

Renoir, Musée ☆
Les Collettes, av. des Collettes, Cagnes-Ville ☎*93-20-61-07* ▨ *Open June to mid-Oct 10am–noon, 2–6pm; mid-Nov to May 2–5pm. Closed Tues; mid-Oct to mid-Nov.*

The world is full of the former homes of the great, now turned into museums; very few evoke as vividly and poignantly as this one the spirit of the man of genius who lived there. Les Collettes is a simple villa in a large garden full of olive trees, of which Renoir was particularly fond. Here, the artist spent the last years of his life from 1907–19. He had rheumatoid arthritis, and his brushes were tied to his paralyzed fingers so that at least he could paint with the movements of his arm.

> This was the wretched and splendid period of suffering and glory, of magnificent inventiveness. The paintbrush was slipped between his gnarled, deformed fingers. He painted nonstop, pell-mell — flowers, fruit, landscapes, nymphs, naiads, goddesses, garlanded necks, bounding bodies, expressed with a harmony ever more bold and vibrant.
> (*Citation* by Georges Besson, on Renoir's final years, translated from the French)

Renoir's studio has been reconstructed just as it was, with his wheelchair and easel, his invalid sticks, his coat and cravat. The only addition is a life portrait of the artist at work in the same room with the same equipment, giving an eerie sense of time warp. The museum contains only one of Renoir's canvases, but there are several of his drawings and sculptures, including a bronze bust of his wife and, in the garden, his bronze *Venus*. There are also letters and photographs of his friends and family including his son Jean, the movie director, and Gabrielle, his devoted maidservant and favorite model.

This quiet house is wrapped in a serene nostalgia; it attracts, so it seems, not numbers of impatient sightseers, but only the discerning and caring visitor.

❧ LE CAGNARD ⌂
Rue Pontis-Long, 06800 Cagnes-sur-Mer ☎*93-20-73-22* ⊠*93-22-06-39* ▥ *to* ▥ *28 rms* ▤ ▣ ⌷ ⊡ ⊙ ▥ ⌂ ✱ ☐ ⌂ ❧ ⟨⟨ ⚓ ♉ ▣ *For* ⇌ *see below.*
Location: In a narrow, winding alley in Haut-de-Cagnes, where large cars will have difficulty. This well-known and highly sophisticated little hotel, run by the Barel family, has been cleverly converted from some 14thC houses near the ramparts of the medieval village. Some may find it claustrophobic, but it is highly picturesque, and the bedrooms combine an excellent standard of modern comfort with stylish decor.

Some bedrooms are small; others are expensive suites. The hotel offers a restful but conveniently located retreat from the coast, although the formerly excellent views are, unfortunately, being spoiled by housing and industrial development. Saint-Exupéry and Sartre are among the many famous figures who have in the past sought repose here.

✥ LES COLLETTES

38 av. des Collettes, 06800 Cagnes-sur-Mer ☎ *93-20-80-66* ▥ *13 rms* ▬ ▣ ▣ ▣ ▥ ▭ ▱ ▵ ⟨ ⟩ ⟨ ⟩
Closed Nov to end Dec.

Location: On the NE outskirts of Cagnes-Ville, close to the Renoir museum. Les Collettes is very modern and functional, in motel style; but the rooms are spacious, cheerful and thoughtfully equipped, with glass doors and balconies facing the sea. Most rooms have kitchenettes attached — a very useful feature indeed in the absence of a hotel restaurant.

⇛ LE CAGNARD △

Rue Pontis-Long ☎ *93-20-73-22* ▥ ▭ ▮
▬ ▬ ▬ ▣ ▣ ▥ *Closed Thurs lunch; Nov to mid-Dec. Last orders 10pm*

(winter); 10.30pm (summer).

Dine either on the s-facing terrace, with lovely views over the rooftops, or in the elegant candlelit room that was once the castle guardroom. The roof slides open on warm days. Well-executed and presented, chef M. Johany's cuisine is light and flavorful, but essentially simple, with Oriental touches. Good selection of local wines. *Specialities: Foie gras de canard frais, salade de grosses crevettes aux asperges et son croustillant de coriandre, loup de pays cuit à la peau, pigeon fermier doré en cocotte.* (See ✥ above.)

⇛ JOSY-JO

Pl. du Planastel, Haut-de-Cagnes
☎ *93-20-68-76* ▥ *to* ▥ ▣ ▥ *Closed Sat lunch; Sun; mid-July to mid-Aug. Last orders 10.30pm.*

An attractive spot, where you can dine on a terrace under an arbor of vines. Honest cooking. *Specialities: Grillades au feu du bois (T-bone steak, etc.), farcis "grand-mère."*

⇛ La Cagne Haute (♣)

(65 Montée de la Bourgade ☎ *93-20-81-52* ▥ *closed Wed),* a pleasant bistro with excellent *plats du jour.*

▐ NIGHTLIFE IN CAGNES-SUR-MER

The town's nightlife is centered around the castle square in Haut-de-Cagnes. There, apart from cafés, you will find nightclubs such as the fashionable (and expensive) **Jimmy'z**, and other spots including **Le Vertigo** and **La Tourelle**. In Cagnes itself, **Le Liberty** *(52 av. de la Gare* ☎ *93-20-69-17)* is a lively piano bar where you can dance.

- See also: NICE, ST-PAUL-DE-VENCE, VILLENEUVE-LOUBET.

CANNES

*Maps 2E2 and 15F14 (Alpes-Mar.). 33km (22 miles) sw of Nice. Postal code: 06400. Population: 68,700. **Cannes-Mandelieu Airport** ☎ 93-47-11-00. **Helicopter service** ☎ 93-43-11-11 or 93-47-25-51 i at the main station ☎ 93-99-19-77, and at Palais des Festivals, blvd. de la Croisette ☎ 93-39-24-53. **Railway station:** ☎ 93-99-50-50.*

The size and splendor of Cannes' tourist industry gives the town the air of a metropolis, even though its year-round population is only one-fifth that of its rival, Nice. It lays claim to being the very smartest of the world's larger resorts, and certainly all the trappings of high sophistication are much in evidence, especially along **La Croisette**. Palm trees wave serenely in the sea breeze, and elegantly bejeweled ladies slip in and out of the luxury hotels and shops. Yet in high summer, and at festival time, the image becomes decidedly tarnished. Then the town, much as any on the Côte, is crowded and hot, its graciousness ruffled, making it more human, if less chic.

Unlike Nice, Cannes has little history. It was still no more than a fishing village on the day in 1834 when Lord Brougham, a British ex-chancellor, was forced to halt there on his way to the Italian Riviera, as the frontier w of Nice had been closed following an outbreak of cholera. So enchanted was he with the pretty setting and warm climate that he built a villa where he spent the next 34 winters. Thus he created Cannes as we know it, for hundreds of other aristocrats and members of royalty soon followed his example. The Russian Czar and the Prince of Wales were frequent visitors. A modern port was built, and the great hotels grew up along La Croisette. Cannes outshone all its rivals on the Côte, and by the 1920s was arrogantly chanting the rhyme: "Menton's dowdy, Monte's brass, Nice is rowdy — Cannes is class!"

The town is in two parts. To the w is the port and the old quarter, crowned by the hill of Le Suquet with its 11thC tower, romantically floodlit at night. To the E is modern Cannes, where La Croisette sweeps round the bay to the **Palm Beach Casino** on a headland. There are miles of sandy beaches, and two marinas filled with vast, opulent yachts. The wooded hills that shelter Cannes have been marred by numerous blocks of high-rise, high-priced flats, many of them occupied by Parisians for only a few weeks in the summer. The traffic in summer is the worst element: La Croisette then is an endless, chaotic swarm of cars.

Not only in summer, but all year round, Cannes hums with festivals, trade fairs, conventions, regattas, tournaments, flower battles, concerts and galas. The most famous of these is the **Film Festival**, although it is not now the glamorous affair it used to be, but little more than a trade fair like any other. Its headquarters is the new **Palais des Festivals** in the vast **Centre des Congrès**, which opened in 1982 between the port and La Croisette. This ultramodern, if ugly, center has two auditoriums, a theater and 14,000 square meters of exhibition space. In winter Cannes relies much on the conference trade, but it also retains a certain faithful clientele of aristocrats and genteel *rentiers* to echo former days.

Perhaps more than anywhere else on the Côte d'Azur, Cannes is a place in constant flux: this year's most fashionable club may no longer be hot the year after next; a hotel that seems past its prime might suddenly be restored to its former splendor, at a cost of millions. Yet old institutions are less sacrosanct than practically anywhere else on the coast. The Palm Beach casino, for example, has, at least temporarily, closed down; the old Palais des Festivals has been knocked down to make way for a new HILTON HOTEL; and the fine Malmaison building on La Croisette has been turned into a museum *(47 La Croisette* ☎ *93-38-55-26* 📧*)* to house major temporary art exhibitions.

The town's policy is to pull out all the stops to maintain Cannes as a center for major international cultural and business events (it is already second only to Paris, with more than 400 events a year attracting over

100,000 participants). Cannes is proposing to become an even more important media city, with plans to open television and movie studios to the w of the town (which is twinned with Beverly Hills) sometime in 1994. Closer links are being forged with the high technology Sophia-Antipolis business park at ANTIBES, and plans are advanced for a new 30,000-square-meter/320,000-square-foot exhibition hall.

Efforts have also been made to improve the services offered by the town, and the number of hotel beds has doubled in the past 10 years. Prices, too, are now a little more sensible, partly as a result of the recession, and partly thanks to official discouragement of the hefty price increases imposed during major festivals by hotels, restaurants and bars. That said, nobody, with the best will in the world, could ever accuse Cannes of being inexpensive.

- **EVENTS**   In January, **MIDEM** (International Record and Music-Publishing Fair) is a major event. • In February, an international **festival of games** (bridge, chess, etc.) and an international **music festival**. • In April, **MIP TV** (international market of television programs), a biennial **festival of Japanese art**, and an **open golf tournament**. • In May, the **International Film Festival** and a **gymkhana**. • In June, the **Café-Théâtre Festival** and an international **advertising film festival**. • In July/August, the **"Nuits des Lérins,"** and **concerts and opera** on Île Ste-Marguerite. • Also in August, a **fireworks festival**. • In September, an international **yachting festival**.

    This is only a small selection of the numerous events taking place in Cannes. For a fuller list or more details, contact **SEMEC** *(Boulevard de la Croisette, BP262, 06403 Cannes* ☎*93-39-01-01* 🖷*93-99-37-34).*

WHAT TO SEE IN CANNES
La Castre, Musée de ☆
Le Suquet ☎*93-38-55-26* 🖾 🖼 *Open July–Sept 10am–noon, 3–7pm; Oct–Mar 10am–noon, 2–5pm; Apr–June 10am–noon, 2–6pm. Closed Tues.*
In the 11thC, the monks of St-Honorat built a refuge and watchtower on the hill of Le Suquet. Today it is a museum of antiquities and ethnography, donated in 1873 by Baron Lycklama Nijeholt, a Dutchman. It contains Egyptian mummies, Chinese porcelain, vases and other objects of Persian, Greek, Roman and Etruscan origin, Polynesian and pre-Columbian artifacts, and even an Inca-inspired ceramic vase by Picasso, as well as two imposing portraits of the Baron in Oriental dress.

Chapelle Bellini
Parc Fiorentina, 67bis av. de Vallauris ☎*93-38-61-80* 🖾 *Open Mon–Fri 2–5pm. Closed Sat; Sun.*
Built in Florentine-Baroque style by Count Vitali in 1880, this was a painter's studio for more than 30 years, now open to the public. A tranquil spot, it stands in a park of cypresses, palm trees and cedars.

La Croisette ★
Europe's most elegant sea promenade, signposted in gold letters, is far more the central focus of Cannes than Promenade des Anglais is of Nice. Two long rows of palms, pines and other subtropical trees are on

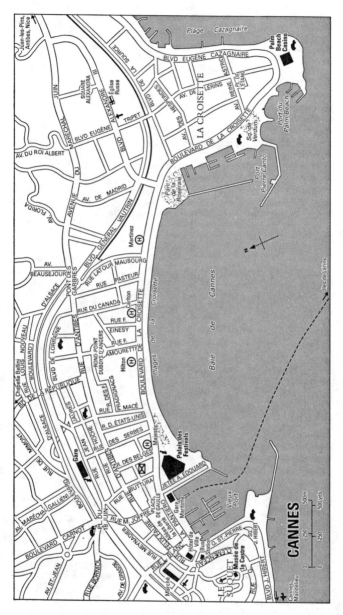

one side flanked by silver beaches, on the other by smart shops, cafés, apartments, and hotels such as the MARTINEZ, the CARLTON and the MAJESTIC. The wide central reservation is also filled with trees and flowers.

Whereas the inhabitants of Nice have deserted Promenade des Anglais as a place to see and be seen, the locals of Cannes still flock to La Croisette. So do the tourists in summer, and the boulevard is at its best out of season, when the residents take their morning strolls. Three blocks inland is **rue d'Antibes**, Cannes' main shopping street.

Super-Cannes ☆

In NE suburbs, 3km (2 miles) from town center. Leave Cannes by av. Isola-Bella and follow signs.

Sadly, the old observatory is no longer open, but one of the finest views in the Côte d'Azur can be had from this area, on the hill of La Californie, where the very richest of Cannes' inhabitants live in their villas. Go to the Chemin des Collines, where, on a fine day, you can see the coast from Italy to St-Tropez — and Cannes set out at your feet.

✥ WHERE TO STAY IN CANNES

AMERICA

13 rue St-Honoré, 06400 Cannes
▥93-68—36-36 ▣93-68-04-58 ▥ 30 rms ▤ ▣ ▣ ▥ ✱ ▢ ▢ ▟ ▼ ▣
Location: At the w end of La Croisette, just behind the Majestic. A pleasantly-decorated modern hotel, with few frills but good facilities.

CARLTON INTERCONTINENTAL ▦

58 blvd. de la Croisette, 06406 Cannes
☎93-68-91-68 ▣93-38-20-90 ▥ 354 rms ▤ ▰ ▣ ▣ ▣ ▣ ▥ ✱ ▵ ▢ ▱
◖ ≋ ▦ ▟ ▣ ❦ ▱ ▼ ▣ ▣ ❀ For ▭ see below.
Location: Halfway along La Croisette, overlooking the sea. The Carlton Hotel is almost as renowned as Cannes itself; its name is synonymous with grandeur and luxury. Built by the famous M. Ruhl of Nice in 1912, it is perhaps the most magnificent among the vast wedding-cake palace-hotels of the Côte. Like the NEGRESCO in Nice, it was built when the town was at the height of its *Belle Époque* glory. Times have changed, and so has the clientele, but the Carlton, now Japanese-owned, continues to provide unashamed luxury. The decor of the bedrooms and suites may be a little garish for some tastes (and the bathrooms disappointingly small for

such a grand hotel), but their comfort is faultless and the views superb. The hotel was completely refurbished in 1989, and reopened with a new restaurant (**La Côte**, one of the best in town), a top-class gym and health club on the top floor (for which there is an extra charge, even for residents), and a casino, separately run, which also boasts one of the finest restaurants in town (**La Belle Otéro**) and a nightclub.

For so august a place, the ambience is remarkably relaxed, and the guests are an unstuffy mixture. The bar is Cannes' leading socialite center. The hotel has its own private beach, but no garden.

HORSET SAVOY

5 rue François-Einesy, 06400 Cannes
☎92-99-72-00 ▣93-68-25-59 ▥ to ▥ 106 rms ▤ ▰ ▭ ▣ ▣ ▣ ▥ ✱ ▢ ▱ ▵ ▟ ≋ ▼ ▣
Location: Behind the Carlton hotel. A thoroughly renovated hotel on the site of the old Savoy, and now part of the Horset group, this is a good choice if you want to shield your bank balance from the traumas that the neighboring Carlton might cause. Centrally located and providing a high standard of comfort, it has the additional benefit of a rooftop swimming pool.

MAJESTIC 🏨

Blvd. de la Croisette, 06403 Cannes
☎93-68-91-00 ☒93-38-97-90 ▥ to ▥
287 rms ▦ ▬ ▣ ▣ ▣ ▥ ☎ ‡
⟡ ☐ ☒ ⚓ ⟨⟨ ⚏ ⚐ ⚑ ⛾ ☒ ▣ *Closed
early Nov to late Dec. For ☰ see below.*
*Location: At the w end of La Croisette,
set back and well screened by trees.* It
lacks the Carlton's cachet as a social
rendezvous, and its public rooms are
less elegant, but for all that the Majestic
remains a worthy rival. Its great advantage is its setting, lying well back from
La Croisette, but enjoying the same
views, with its own heated swimming
pool surrounded by a garden full of
subtropical trees in front. Its location is
also now the most convenient of all
Cannes' grand hotels for the Palais des
Festivals, and the bar is a favorite rendezvous for conference delegates. The
bedrooms are luxurious, with modern
furniture in 18thC style, and they have
spacious marble bathrooms. Many
rooms have wide sea-facing balconies.
Built in 1926, the Majestic is no great
beauty from the outside, but it still man-
ages to live up to its name.

MARTINEZ 🏨

73 blvd. de la Croisette ☎92-98-73-00
☒93-39-67-82 ▥ to ▥ 430 rms ▦
▬ ▣ ▣ ▣ ▣ ▥ ☎ ‡ ☐ ☒ ⟡ ⟨⟨
⚑ ⚏ ⚐ ⚓ ⟳ ⛾ ☒ ▣ ↻ *Closed mid-Nov
to mid-Jan. For ☰ see below.*
Location: At the e end of La Croisette.
After being the Cinderella of Cannes'
grand hotels for some years, the Martinez, built in 1929, has come fighting
back, following much investment and
management changes, to become perhaps the grandest, most stylish of them
all. Its location may be slightly less convenient than the Majestic or the Carlton,
but standards of comfort and service are
unsurpassed. The bar and lobby were
redesigned in 1989. The rooms are decorated with bright fabrics and have huge,
marble bathrooms. Most rooms have
excellent sea views and balconies (although those at the back, unprepos-
sessing view apart, are generally less
satisfactory). Public areas still have an
Art Deco feel. The main restaurant, LA

PALME D'OR, has also become one of the
two or three top spots in town. This is a
place that is currently firing on all cylin-
ders. Even the conference and banqueting areas are kept deliberately separate
from the main part of the hotel, so that
guests aren't disturbed by delegates.
The piano bar is a local favorite, and the
hotel's private beach (with daytime restaurant) is the largest in Cannes. Service
is friendly and obliging.

MONDIAL

77 rue d'Antibes, 06400 Cannes
☎93-68-70-00 ☒93-99-39-11 ▥ 58
rms ▦ ▣ ▣ ▣ ▥ ‡ ☐ ☒ ⟡ ⚑ ▣
Location: Central, in the main street.
Perhaps better suited to businessmen
than to families on vacation. Some rooms
are rather small, but beds are large and
comfortable. Service is efficient.

NOGA HILTON 🏨

50 blvd. de la Croisette, 06400 Cannes
☎92-99-70-00 ☒92-99-70-11 ▥ 225
rms ▬ ⇋ ▣ ▣ ▣ ▥ ‡ ☐ ☒ ⟡ ⟨⟨
⚑ ⚏ ⚐ ⚓ ⛾ ☒ ▣
*Location: Centrally positioned on La
Croisette.* The Noga Hilton couldn't be
better located, for it stands on the site of
the old Palais des Festivals. But although the hotel, with its excellent sea
views, private beach (alone among
Cannes' luxury hotels, it has a tunnel
under La Croisette to get you there) and
state-of-the-art facilities, including a
gym and a casino, has many advantages, it lacks charm, personality and
any real style. It was only opened in
1992, but the decor already looks a little
dated and more in keeping with a
standard business hotel than one of the
most expensive in town. The hotel
boasts three restaurants; the most lively
of these is probably the brasserie **Le
Grand Bleu**, on La Croisette itself.

NOVOTEL MONTFLEURY 🏨

25 av. Beauséjour, 06406 Cannes
☎93-68-91-50 ☒93-38-37-08 ▥ 181
rms ▦ ▬ ▣ ⇋ ▣ ▣ ▣ ▥ ☎ ‡ ⟡
☐ ☒ ⚓ ⟨⟨ ⚏ ⚐ ▣
*Location: At the foot of La Californie hill
in Parc François-André, just inland*

from La Croisette. For those who wish to distance themselves from the madding crowd on the seafront, and crave luxury, yet wish to do more than lounge on the beach, this is the hotel to choose. The well-designed, dazzling white building, set in a 10-acre park, is complemented by lovely terraced gardens. Inside, it is modern and stylish, with every facility. Guests have free access to the adjacent **Montfleury Sports Club**: ten illuminated tennis courts, two heated swimming pools, ice rink (in winter), gymnasium, sauna and more. There are three restaurants with reasonable food, a coffee shop open all day and an outdoor patio.

TOURING
11 rue Hoche, 06400 Cannes
☎93-38-34-40 [Fx]93-38-73-34 □□ to □□
29 rms ◙ ◙ ✱ □ ◚ ◙
Location: Near the Palais des Festivals, just behind rue d'Antibes. This is one of the best budget choices in Cannes: the hotel is salubrious and comfortable, although it offers few luxuries.

UNIVERS
2 rue du Maréchal-Foch, 06400 Cannes
☎93-39-59-19 [Fx]92-98-68-59 □□ 68

⇶ WHERE TO EAT IN CANNES

LA BOUCHON D' OBJECTIF ➥ ✿
10 rue de Constantine ☎93-99-21-76 □
to □□ ◙ ◙ ➥ ▰ ◚ *Closed Sun. Last orders 10pm.*
Cannes is no tourist trap if this little restaurant is anything to judge by. The neat kitchens and dining room are run with zest and enthusiasm. The cooking is exemplary, the place always packed. *Specialities: Aïoli, coq au vin, tarte au citron.*

LA BROUETTE DE GRAND-MÈRE
9 rue d'Oran ☎93-39-12-10 □□ ▤▤ ▰
▰ *Dinner only. Closed Sun; first half of July; Nov to mid-Dec. Last orders 11pm.*
A favorite bistro with local people. It has *fin-de-siècle* decor and a single menu of classical cuisine; the wine is served ad lib. *Specialities: Pot-au-feu aux cinq*

rms ▦ ▭ ⇶ ▣ ◙ ◙ ▨ ✱ ◦ □ ◚
◈ ➴ ▣
Location: Central, on the corner of rue d'Antibes, close to the Palais des Congrès and the w end of La Croisette. The sixth-floor roof terrace is the main attraction of this well-equipped hotel, which is regularly filled to overflowing all year round with tourists or convention-goers. The hotel's restaurant is adequate.

Other recommended hotels in Cannes:
• **Beau Séjour** *(5 rue des Fauvettes* ☎93-39-63-00 [Fx]92-98-64-66 □□ *to* □□). • **Century** *(133 rue d'Antibes* ☎93-99-37-64 [Fx]93-68-26-03 □□ *to* □□). • **Château de la Tour** *(10 av. Font-de-Veyre, Cannes-La Bocca* ☎93-47-34-64 [Fx]93-647-86-61 □□).
 • **Cristal** *(Rond-point Duboys d'Angers* ☎93-39-45-45 □□ *to* □□). • **Gray d'Albion** *(38 rue des Serbes* ▦ ☎92-99-79-79 [Fx]93-99-26-10 □□).
 • **Ligure** *(5 pl. de la Gare* ☎93-39-03-11 [Fx]93-39-19-48 □□). • **Ruc** *(15 blvd. Strasbourg* ☎93-38-64-32 [Fx]93-39-54-18 □□ *to* □□). • **Sofitel-Méditerranée** *(2 blvd. J-Hibert* ▦ ☎93-99-22-75 [Fx]92-99-73-29 □□ *to* □□).

viandes, langue sauce piquante.

CARLTON INTERCONTINENTAL ⌂
58 blvd. de la Croisette ☎93-68-91-68 □
▰ ⇶ ▰ ▣ ▭ ▣ ◙ ◙ ▨ □□ *La Côte (last orders 10.30pm)* □□ *Café Carlton (last orders 11.30pm).*
There are two restaurants in this lavish hotel, or three, if you count the highly-rated and very expensive **La Belle Otéro** in the casino on the 7th floor *(* ☎93-39-69-69, last orders midnight)*. Both the grand **La Côte** and the attractive and less expensive **Café Carlton** opened after the hotel's refurbishment in 1989, as did the casino. The Carlton's food came under heavy fire from critics until recently, but La Côte, under chef Sylvain Duparc, and La Belle Otéro (which is under separate management and di-

rected by chef Francis Chauveau) are now regarded as two of the best *haute cuisine* stops in town. (See also ✇ above.)

FRATELLI

17 rue des Frères Pradignac
☎93-38-70-07 ▥ ▤ ▭ AE ◉ ▨
Closed Sat lunch; Sun eve; Nov–Jan. Last orders 11pm.

A pleasant Italian restaurant between La Croisette and rue d'Antibes, with bright decor (much blue-stained wood), a lively atmosphere, and good food. The menu is short but interesting, and the standard of cooking commendable. Go for the first-class selection of antipasti, the lightly battered *picatta*, or the *filet "Fratelli,"* served with a *salade roquette* and pine nuts. There is a reasonable selection of Italian wines. A few tables are set outside in summer.

MAJESTIC ⌂

Blvd. de la Croisette ☎92-98-77-41 ▥ *restaurant* ▥ *grill* ▭ ▬ ☰ ♠ ▰ ▢ AE ◉ ◎ ▨ *Closed Nov to mid-Dec. Last orders (restaurant) 10.30pm.*

Of the hotel's two restaurants, one, formal and classical, **Le Sunset**, aims at very *haute cuisine,* with worthy if sometimes uneven results. The other, the **grill**, is a little less expensive and less ambitious, with tables spilling out around the pool. Lovely for an outdoor lunch, in your bathing suit if you wish. *Specialities (main restaurant): Tourte de pigeon aux herbes, mille-feuille de saumon frais, filet de volaille aux morilles.* (See ✇ above.)

LA MÈRE BESSON

12–13 rue des Frères Pradignac
☎93-39-59-24 ▥ ▭ AE ◉ ◎ *Closed Sun; Mon (winter). Last orders 10.30pm (summer), 9.30pm (winter).*

This down-to-earth little place behind La Croisette is still usually full to overflowing. The decor is spartan, but the customers noisily provide the ambience. For fresh air and leg-room, try to get one of the few sidewalk tables. Each weekday has its special dish (for example, *aïoli* on Friday), explained in

English on the menu. Provençal cuisine is the thing here. *Specialities (always available): Soupe au pistou, bouillabaisse, pieds et paquets, salade de mesclun.*

LE MONACO ➡ ♣

15 rue du 24 Août ☎93-38-37-76 ▭ ▭ ▰ *No cards. Closed Sun; Nov to mid-Dec. Last orders 10.30pm.*

Georges Peisino's trattoria may be a trifle cramped and crowded, but the service is swift and amiable, the food is copious and the amazingly low prices prove that Cannes is by no means exclusively for the rich. The food is a mixture of Italian and Provençal, with a good *bouillabaisse* prepared to order. *Specialities: Pasta, fish dishes, osso bucco, couscous.*

RADO PLAGE

☎93-94-20-68 ▥ ▭ ▭ ▬ ♠ *Closed end Nov to mid-March. Lunch only.*

Located on the beach, close to the Martinez hotel, this is one of the best of the beach restaurants not owned by the large hotels. The food is fresh, of good quality, reasonably priced, well presented and served in impressive quantity. Service is friendly, if a little on the slow side — but that's something you can forgive if you're sitting in the sun, or under a parasol enjoying a glass or two of rosé from the decent selection of local wines.

LE RÉFUGE

13 quai St-Pierre ☎93-39-34-54 ▭ ▭ ▬ ♠ ◉ ▨ *Closed mid-Nov to mid-Dec. Last orders 10pm.*

Facing the port, this large bistro with its tables spilling onto the sidewalk is a good spot to rest amid the bustle of the seafront. The Provençal cooking, although not special, is good value, particularly the fish dishes.

LA PALME D'OR

Hôtel Martinez, 73 blvd. de la Croisette
☎92-98-74-14 ▥ ▥ ▤ AE ◉ ◎ ▨ ▰ ▭ ▬ ☰ ♠ *Closed Mon; Tues (except dinner in season); mid-Nov to mid-Jan. Last orders 10.30pm.*

The dining room of this fine hotel has a broad terrace giving onto the swimming-pool and La Croisette, and offering a fine view. The decor is somewhat Art Deco, and the atmosphere is pleasantly relaxed. Chef Christian Willer's subtle and inventive, essentially Provençal, cooking (although he likes to use spices from time to time) is about the best in Cannes, but not cheap. Fish is his speciality, but he excels across the board. Service is surprisingly friendly for such a swanky place. The set lunch menu especially (not Sunday), and the cheapest evening one, represent good value. *Specialities: Lapin confit au foie gras, salade de St-Jacques grillées, rougets en filets poêlés à la fondue d'olives noires, le T-bone de veau de lait cuisiné en cocotte, festin d'agneau en fricassée pastorale.*

ROYAL GRAY

6 rue des États-Unis ☎93-99-79-60 ▥
▤ ▦ ▣ ▦ ▨ ▰ ▢ ▰ ➤ *Closed Sun; Mon; Feb. Last orders 10pm.*

Jacques Chibois trained with such great French chefs as Michel Guérard and Roger Vergé, and today in his own right he is one of the gastronomic stars of the Côte d'Azur. His cooking lends highest distinction to this serious luxury restaurant in a rather flamboyant luxury hotel. *Specialities: Velouté d'asperges aux lames de truffes, sauté de langoustines aux fèvettes et aux morilles, St-Pierre rôti au fumet de fenouil, feuillantine de cacao à la crème de poire et zestes d'oranges.*

▱ Other good restaurants: • **Au Bec Fin** (*12 rue du 24 Août* ☎93-38-35-86 ▥ *to* ▥), a cheerful, amusing bistro. • **Chez Astoux** (*43 rue Félix-Faure* ☎93-39-06-22 ▥), fish and seafood. • **L'Éléphant Bleu** (*4 rue Batéguier* ☎93-38-32-72 ▥ *to* ▥), Thai cuisine. • **La Hacienda** (*18 Blvd du Midi, Cannes La Bocca* ☎93-47-08-15 ▥), Spanish food. • **Jade** (*24 rue Pasteur* ☎93-94-33-49 ▥ *to* ▥), Vietnamese. • **Le Palais Oriental** (*10 rue Jean-Hibert* ☎92-98-99-98 ▥), Moroccan cuisine. • **La Pizza** (*3 quai St-Pierre* ☎93-39-22-56 ▥), reputedly the best pizzas in town. • **La Poêle d'Or** (*23 rue des États-Unis* ☎93-39-77-65 ▥), high-quality cuisine. • **Rescator** (*7 rue Maréchal-Joffre* ☎93-39-44-57 ▥). • **Xuan "Le Printemps"** (*14 rue du Batéguier* ☎93-38-08-55 ▥), Vietnamese.

◪ NIGHTLIFE IN CANNES

Nightlife in Cannes is livelier, more sophisticated and daring than in Nice. Some *boîtes* and discos exert a much stronger pull on the fashion-conscious than others.

Discos Try the **Whisky à Gogo** (*115 av. de Lérins* ☎93-43-20-63, open 11pm-dawn), a big place, packed out with very trendy teen-agers. • At **Jane's** (*in the Hôtel Gray d'Albion* ☎92-99-79-59, open 10.30pm-dawn), you can dine as well as dance, although the floor is rather small. • Two of the latest and smartest hot spots in town are **Jimmy'z**, owned by Régine and situated by the Casino Croisette (*Jetée Albert Edouard* ☎93-68-00-77, open 11pm-dawn), and **L' Opéra** (*7 rue Lecerf* ☎93-99-09-01, open 11pm-dawn). • For somewhere more relaxed, try **Brummel's**, off rue d'Antibes (*3 blvd. de la République* ☎93-39-07-03, open 10.30pm-dawn), where service is very good and prices are acceptable: this is both a piano bar and a discothèque.

Bars/piano bars The **Martinez** hotel has a piano bar, open until 1am. • Or you could try the famous, and often jam-packed, **La Chunga** across the road, where you can eat as well as drink (*72 La Croisette* ☎93-94-11-29, open 8.30pm-dawn, closed Mon*). • **La Ragtime**, a cocktail bar, is another popular venue (*1 La Croisette* ☎93-68-47-10, *open 9pm-2.30 am).* • **Le Petit Carlton**, although no more than a bar *(93 rue d'Antibes ☎93-39-27-25)* is one of the most casual — and crowded — meeting places during festivals.

Zanzi-Bar *(85 rue Félix-Faure ☎93-39-30-75)* and **Blitz** *(22 rue Macé ☎93-39-31-31)* are predominantly gay bars. • **Disco 7** *(7 rue Rouguière ☎93-39-10-36),* like Blitz, has a transvestite cabaret.

It is a measure of how rapidly places go in and out of fashion in Cannes that Studio Circus, now renamed **Brasserie des Artistes** *(48 blvd. de la République ☎93-43-25-72, open 11pm-dawn, May, July-Aug),* once one of the trendiest discos in town, is now a karaoke nightclub.

Casinos   That former legend, the **Palm Beach Casino** *(pl. Franklin-Roosevelt (☎93-43-91-12),* was closed at the time of writing, for legal and other reasons, with no foreseeable reopening date. It's a large white building, opened in 1929, which looks, as Archibald Lyall in the *Companion Guide to the South of France* (Collins, 1963) put it, "rather as though a Foreign Legion fort had had a flirtation with the Doges' Palace." As is usual on the Côte, it housed casino, cabaret and disco under one roof.

Other casinos in Cannes: The **Carlton Casino Club** on the 7th floor of the Carlton hotel *(☎93-68-00-33, gaming rooms open from 4pm-4am, until 5am Fri and Sat),* which also boasts a top-class restaurant (La Belle Otéro) and a nightclub. • **Casino Croisette**, part of the ugly Palais des Festivals complex, with Jimmy'z disco next door *(Jetée Albert-Edouard ☎93-38-12-11, gaming rooms open from 5pm).* • **Grand Casino** *(Noga Hilton hotel, 50 La Croisette ☎93-68-43-43).* The last two are the least smart.

Always take your passport: casinos insist on evidence of identity.

SHOPPING
The most fashionable boutiques are to be found on **La Croisette** (including designer names and the main jewelers), on **rue d'Antibes** and on the streets between. Here are shops as chic as any in Paris. There are also some excellent shops, including Souleiado and Hermès in the **Hôtel Gray d'Albion** *(rue des Serbes).* There are also shops in the NOGA HILTON hotel complex.

For traditional and specialized shops, go farther w to rue **Meynadier,** a narrow, animated, traffic-free street behind the old port. Food stores here include **Ceneri** *(#22),* one of the greatest cheese stores in France. It has 300 different types of cheese, ranging from a Franche-Comté monster down to tiny *boutons de culotte* (trouser-button) goats' cheese. The cellars where M. Ceneri matures his young cheeses are open to visitors in the afternoon. At **Aux bons Raviolis** *(#31),* a marvelous range of pastas is made on the premises. **Ernest** *(#52)* is an outstanding *charcutier.* Around the corner, in rue Louis-Blanc *(#2),* the same family makes and sells superb *pâtisseries* and ices. Opposite is the inexpensive and colorful **Forville market** *(open mornings only Tues-Sun).*

🐟 BEACHES NEAR CANNES
Cannes possesses miles of fine sandy beach, both centrally, at **La Croi-**

sette, as well as to its w and E. La Croisette has one section of free public beach near the w end, but the rest is parceled into over 20 paying beaches, each with its tidy row of colored parasols and mattresses.

Several belong to the big hotels, but are open to nonresidents. The **CARLTON'S**, opposite the hotel, is the most fashionable, followed by that of the **Gray d'Albion**. The **MAJESTIC, NOGA HILTON** and **MARTINEZ** also have private beaches, that of the Martinez being the biggest in Cannes. Several beaches offer swimming lessons, wind surfing and waterskiing.

For more free beaches, you need to go a little way out of town.

PLACES NEAR CANNES
Îles de Lérins (✫) *(boat services from Gare Maritime, Cannes* ☎ *93-39-11-82, approx. ten times daily in summer, five times daily in winter; crossing times: 15mins to Ste-Marguerite, 30mins to St-Honorat).* **Ste-Marguerite** and **St-Honorat**, the two low-lying, thickly wooded islands just off the coast, have remarkable histories and are full of interest. They were first settled by the Greeks, then by the Romans.

Île St-Honorat   At the end of the 4thC, the monk St-Honorat founded one of the first French monasteries on the island that bears his name *(*☎*93-38-82-82* ▨ *open summer 9.40am–4.40pm, winter 10.40am–3.30pm).* Pilgrims flocked there, and by the 7thC it was one of the most powerful monasteries in Christendom, with 4,000 monks and a fine library; it was a major center of religious learning during the Dark Ages.

The monastery produced 600 bishops and 20 saints, including St Patrick of Ireland, who trained there. It owned some 100 priories and castles on the mainland, and until 1788 the village of Cannes was within its ownership. By then the monastery was in decline, and it closed. In 1869 it was bought by Cistercian monks from SÉNANQUE who rebuilt it and still keep it going.

·   Île St-Honorat is the smaller of the two islands, 1.5 kilometers (1 mile) long. On the s side of the island, the 11thC *donjon* (✫) of the old fortified monastery stands alone by the sea, looking like a toy castle in a fairy tale. Here, the monks used to take refuge when Saracen marauders were sighted. Inside are 14thC arcaded cloisters, a Roman marble cistern, and a chapel with a high, vaulted ceiling *(open June-Sept, 10am-noon, 2-5pm).* Excellent views of the surrounding coast may be gained from the battlements.

There is a reasonable fish and seafood restaurant on the island, **Chez Frédéric** *(* ☎ *93-48-66-88, lunch only).*
Île Ste-Marguerite   The larger island is 4.5 kilometers (3 miles) long, covered in pine forests and ideal for picnics. It is now mostly uninhabited but has three restaurants, including **L'Escale** *(*☎*93-43-49-25, lunch only except summer),* which has good fish dishes and also simple bedrooms.

The island takes its name from St-Honorat's sister, who headed a nunnery there. Her brother, so legend has it, only visited her once a year, when an almond tree by the beach blossomed in answer to Marguerite's prayer that it would do so.

Considerably closer to fact, and our own epoch, is the story of the 17thC **fort** (☎ *93-43-45-47, open 8am-6pm, closed July 15-Aug 15)* built by Cardinal Richelieu, which for centuries was a state prison. The most famous inmate was the Man in the Iron Mask (velvet, in fact), who was shut up between 1687–98. No one knows who this mysterious figure was — one theory holds that he was the illegitimate brother of the Sun King, Louis XIV, the ruling monarch.

A later prisoner was the cowardly Marshal Bazaine, who in 1870 surrendered Metz to the Prussians; he escaped by bribing his guards and disguising himself as a woman. Visitors are shown the cells of both Bazaine and the Masked Man, and also the statue in memory of six Huguenot pastors locked in solitary confinement after the Revocation of the Edict of Nantes in 1685; all but one went mad.

In summer, **son-et-lumière** shows are held at the fort *(check with tourist office for dates)*.

Today the fort is used as a **youth, sports and cultural center**: in July and August it is reserved for 14- to 17-year-olds, who come either individually or in groups; there are courses in sailing, wind surfing, scuba diving, theater and dance. The rest of the year *(closed Jan 6 to Feb 10)* it plays host to groups of eight or more. Bed and board are provided. For full details contact the **Office Municipal de la Jeunesse** *(2 quai St-Pierre, 06400 Cannes* ☎ *93-38-21-16)*.

The **Musée de la Mer** (☎ *93-43-18-17* ◪ *open winter 10.30-11.45am, 2.15-3.45pm or 4.45pm; summer 9am-12.30pm, 2-6pm or 6.45pm; closed Tues, Jan, Feb)*, opened in the Roman foundations of the fort, contains finds from excavations on the island. Roman and Arab pottery also emerged during underwater research around the island; other exhibits include historical documents.

- See also: MOUGINS, LA NAPOULE, THÉOULE.

COARAZE ☆
Maps 3B4 and 15D15 (Alpes-Mar.). Postal code: 06390 Contes. 27km (17 miles) N of Nice. Population: 330 ℹ *at Mairie* ☎ *93-79-08-07.*

Steep, narrow alleys crisscrossed overhead by vaults and arches, a village square enlivened by brightly enameled sundials — Cocteau designed the one by the *Mairie* — and a 14thC church on the hilltop with fine views from its terrace, all make Coaraze one of the most enchanting of the hill-villages above Nice.

Craftsmen in particular are attracted to the place; just below the church you will find **Rousselot**, a local artist who makes enamel tiles and Coaraze's modern speciality, sundials.

❧ ⇌ **Auberge du Soleil** *(Coaraze, 06390 Contes* ☎ *93-79-08-11* ▥ *to* ▥*)* is a small, well-modernized hotel at the top of the village: it is peaceful, with a fine location, a swimming pool and good traditional food. You can eat on the terrace and revel in the lovely view.

- See also: LUCÉRAM.

CORNICHES OF THE RIVIERA ☆

Maps 3C4–5 and 15E15–16E16 (Alpes-Mar.).

Corniche means a road along the side of a cliff, and refers here to the three famous coastal routes linking NICE, MONACO and MENTON. The lowest, the **Basse Corniche**, N98, built by the prince of Monaco in the 19thC, follows the contours of the coast. The **Moyenne** (middle) **Corniche**, N7, built between 1910 and 1914, runs past the hill-village of ÈZE, and has fine views. The **Grande** (upper) **Corniche**, the D2564, also panoramic, was first built by Napoléon on the track of the Via Aurelia constructed by the Romans. It is now a modern highway like the others, and climbs up to LA TURBIE before dropping down to Menton.

All three *corniches* are connected in places by steep, zigzagging minor roads. A fourth and even higher through-road was added in the 1970s: the A8 autoroute connecting the Côte d'Azur with Italy.

ÈZE

Maps 3C4 and 15E15 (Alpes-Mar.). 12km (7 miles) NE of Nice. Postal code: 06360. Population: 2,450 ℹ pl. Général-de-Gaulle ☎93-41-26-00.

No other hill-village on the Côte d'Azur is as well-known, or as tourist-jammed, as Èze. There are two reasons: first, its accessibility, close to the coast by the Middle Corniche, and second, because the setting really *is* spectacular, on a rocky outcrop 390 meters (1,300 feet) almost sheer above the sea.

Èze may have become a tourist trap, but it is a good one. It has been scrupulously restored, and its numerous art and souvenir stores are not too brashly vulgar. Parking is near the entrance to the ancient village; then visitors must climb its narrow alleys on foot. If you can squeeze through the throng, climb to the summit where the remnants of a castle stand just above the **Jardin Exotique**, full of cacti (☎ *open daily until nightfall).* Here the coastline lies spread before you.

The only other attractions are the **Chapelle des Pénitents Blancs** on place du Planet, with its 13thC Catalan crucifix and 14thC *Virgin and Child,* and the **Fragonard perfume and soap factory** (*free ✗) on the outskirts of the village.

Today, Èze is a museum, albeit a fascinating one. But for a real look at Provence's hill-villages, you must venture farther into the hinterland.

✥ CHÂTEAU DE LA CHÈVRE D'OR 🏨

Rue du Barri, 06360 Èze-village
☎93-41-12-12 [Fx]93-41-06-72 ▦ 24 rms ▦ ➤ 🆑 ⊡ 🆚 ⊖ ◻ 🆎 ❄ ⊀ ⅄ ▣ *Closed Jan–Mar. For* 🍽 *see opposite.*
Location: High in the old village, facing the sea. A medieval château artistically converted into a small luxury hotel, the Chèvre d'Or has become as celebrated as many of its guests (such as Elizabeth Taylor and Roger Moore) and has gradually expanded over the years into neighboring houses. It is run with suave efficiency by its new Iranian owner: soft music plays as you sip champagne cocktails by the pool, gazing at Cap-Ferrat far below, and the bar surely offers one of the best views in the Côte d'Azur. If some of the lavishly furnished bedrooms are cramped, blame the 11thC architect, although the 20thC redesigners have done their ingenious best.

Rooms near the kitchens may be noisy. The hotel has two pools, and plans are now afoot to add to the luxury by providing a conference room and fitness center.

✒ CHÂTEAU EZA 🏨

06360 Èze-village ☎93-41-12-24
[Fx]93-41-16-64 🔲 *8 rms* ▦ ◢ 〓 AE
🔲 🔲 🔲 🔲 🔲 ‹‹ *Closed Nov–Easter.*

Location: In the village. Perched high above the sea, this is a delightful place in which to stay, with first-class food (fish and seafood in particular) from Bruno Cirino, born in Nice and trained by Jacques Maximin, Alain Ducasse and Roger Vergé, no less.

✒ ÈZE COUNTRY CLUB 🏨

Route de La Turbie, 06360 ☎93-41-24-64
[Fx]93-41-13-25 🔲 *80 rms* ▦ ◢ 〓 AE
🔲 🔲 🔲 🔲 ‡ 🔲 🔲 ％ ❦ ‹‹ ₪
♪○ ⚑ ℗ 🔲 *Closed mid-Nov to mid-Dec.*

Location: Peacefully located in its own grounds, 1.5 kilometers (1 mile) NE of Èze village. A modern luxury hotel, built in the late 1980s, with excellent fitness and sporting facilities (including golf practice). The rooms have balconies and terraces with sea views and are extremely comfortable and well appointed. The restaurant is very good, and you can eat outside.

✒ NEARBY

✒ CAP ESTEL 🏨

06360 Èze-bord-de-Mer ☎93-01-50-44
[Fx]93-01-55-20 🔲 *46 rms* ▦ ◢ 〓 🔲
🔲 ‡ ₺ 🔲 ₺ ％ 🔲 ❦ ‹‹ ₪ *Closed Nov–Apr.*

Location: Just off the Lower Corniche, by the sea, on a promontory in a large, elegant garden. A handsome white villa, formerly the home of a prince, has been turned into a beautiful if rather formal luxury hotel, where apartments may also be rented; the amenities are generous. Although fair, the cooking does not equal the setting: by the pool, on the terrace, or in a Louis-XVI-style dining room. *Demi-pension* is obligatory in season.

✒ MIMOSAS COTTAGE

06360 Èze-bord-de-Mer ☎93-01-54-82
🔲 *40 rms* ◢ 〓 🔲 🔲 ₺ ❦ ‹‹ 🔲
Closed Nov–Mar.

Location: Beside the Lower Corniche, close to the beach. Small, simple rooms, most of them in annexes dotted around a subtropical grove of orange and lemon, palm, cedar and even banana trees. Minus points: the railway is very close, and the beach is less than idyllic. Plus points: buffet breakfasts, hors d'oeuvres and good local fish dishes are served on the terrace.

〓 CHÂTEAU DE LA CHÈVRE D'OR ⌂

Rue du Barri ☎93-41-12-12 🔲 *to* 🔲 🔲
■ 〓 ◢ AE 🔲 🔲 *Closed Wed (Oct–Easter); Jan–Mar.*

A beautiful in-hotel restaurant filled with equally beautiful people. The chef, Elie Mazot, has worked with the Troisgros brothers, and his delicate cooking shows their influence. Wines and cheeses are excellent. This is an ambitious operation: when the completely new kitchen was installed in 1989, the ovens were lifted in by helicopter. . . .
Specialities: Noix de St-Jacques grillés sur embeurrée de choux chinois, filets de rougets grillés sauce au vin de Bellet rouge, suprêmes de pigeonneau cuits en cocotte, sauté d'agneau minute en charlotte de feuilles de blettes.
(See ✒ opposite.)

The hotel also boasts three other restaurants: **La Taverne**, a grill; **Le Café Jardin**, a poolside café and snack bar; and **À Votre Èze**, situated near the entrance of the village, which offers Provençal cuisine.

〓 NID D'AIGLE

Rue du Château ☎93-41-19-08 🔲 🔲 ■
🐝 *Closed Thurs; mid-Nov to mid-Dec. Last orders 9pm.*

For those who do not care for La Chèvre d'Or's high prices, this is a modest but pleasing alternative. It is perched at the top of the old village, just below the Jardin Exotique. Good local cooking, such as *bourride* or *lapin aux herbes;* copious hors d'oeuvres trolley.

SHOPPING IN ÈZE

Many artists and artisans live in Èze and sell their work there; some have studios open to the public. Among the best are **José Benito** *(rue Principale)* for colored glass and jewelry, and **A. Aicardi** *(pl. du Planet)* for wrought-iron work.

- See also: BEAULIEU, MONACO, LA TURBIE.

GOURDON ☆

Maps 2C2 and 15E14 (Alpes-Mar.). 14km (9 miles) NE of Grasse. Postal code: 06620 Le Bar. Population: 250 ℹ at Mairie ☎93-42-50-17.

Perched high on a rock, 420 meters (1,400 feet) above the Gorges du Loup, Gourdon vies with SAORGE and LES BAUX for the title of Provence's most dramatic hill-village. Seen from far below, its old gray houses are barely distinguishable from the rock itself.

Although spoiled by overexposure, Gourdon is worth a visit for the majestic views from its terrace, and for its **château** (🖼 ✦ *open June-Sept 10am-noon, 2-7pm, Oct-May 2-6pm, closed Tues).* Built in the 13thC on the foundations of a Saracen fortress, it has an interesting collection of armor, as well as a collection of Naïve paintings, including one by Douanier Rousseau.

🍽 **Nid d'Aigle** *(☎93-42-50-04 ▥).*

PLACES NEAR GOURDON

Gorges du Loup (☆)   Gourdon is easily reached from N or S by the D3. To the N, the D3 winds down into the spectacular Gorges du Loup; you can then double back on the D6 along the green bed of the gorge, past the **Saut du Loup** (wolf's leap), and two waterfalls, to **Pont du Loup**, where a slim railway viaduct, ruined by the Germans in the war, can be seen.

Just S of Pont du Loup is the village of **Bar-sur-Loup**, notable for its 15thC Gothic church with a sumptuous Bréa retable. It also contains a fascinating and devilish 15thC painting known as a *Danse Macabre* or Dance of Death. One lady falls, struck in the breast by an arrow from Death, the archer: beside her a man lies slain, and from his mouth a demon is pulling out his soul, a tiny naked figure. Behind, lords and ladies dance gaily, but on the head of each is a little black devil, reminder of their doom soon to come. St Michael weighs the souls, and throws them into the jaws of hell. A commentary below warns sinners to repent. Probably the anonymous painting was done at the time of the plague.

For a really good view of the whole of this lovely region, drive on to ST-PAUL-DE-VENCE, then to VENCE, and back to the Gorges du Loup via TOURETTES-SUR-LOUP.

GRASSE

Maps 2D2 and 15F14 (Alpes-Mar.). 17km (10 miles) NW of Cannes. Postal code: 06130. Population: 41,400 ℹ pl. de la Foux ☎93-36-03-56.

"The balcony of the Côte d'Azur" sprawls along the southern slopes of a limestone plateau that protects it from the chilliest winds. Grasse faces seaward, across a wide vale of the flowers that have brought it wealth and fame as the world capital of the perfume industry. Outside its nucleus of ancient narrow streets, modern Grasse is built in terraces with long, looping boulevards, confusing at first for drivers. Everywhere are fine views, notably from just behind the cathedral and from the broad promenade of **Cours Honoré-Cresp**.

In the 12thC, Grasse was a tiny republic on the Italian model, and was closely linked with Pisa. At that time, its main industry was tanning. The perfume industry was introduced to Grasse from Italy at the instigation of Catherine de Medici. At first it was related to the local tanning industry because of the 16thC fashion for scented gloves. Then the cultivation of jasmin, roses and other flowers began in the valley, to provide the scent factories with their raw materials.

Today, some 30 factories in and around Grasse claim to treat nearly 90 percent of the world's flower essence for scents. Each year, they use thousands of tons of local flowers, as well as importing flowers from 20 other countries — patchouli from Java, for example, and eucalyptus from Australia. The total annual consumption is some 490 tons of roses, 250 tons each of jasmin and violets, 200 tons each of orange blossom and mimosa, and 130 tons of lavender. This may seem a great deal, but it takes 1,000 kilos/2,200lbs of rose petals, or 150 kilos/330lbs of lavender, to make one kilo/$2\frac{1}{4}$lbs of perfume essence.

The Grasse factories sell a little of their product direct to the public, and perfume counters exist for visitors to sample the goods after their guided tours of the premises. In the main, though, they are wholesalers, selling their essences in bulk to Dior, Chanel and the other great fashion houses in Paris, New York etc., which blend them into their own subtle varieties with fancy names. But much of the research is done in Grasse, where one leading firm, Fragonard, has a laboratory whose experts can distinguish 1,500 different scents (see MAISON FRAGONARD). This requires a nostril more finely tuned than any wine connoisseur's palate. The skill, always handed down from father to son, was in danger of dying out, so a School of Perfumers was established in Paris, and is doing well. Students must not smoke, drink — or catch cold.

To the N and W of the **cathédrale de Notre-Dame** is the **vieille ville**; it has steeply stepped old alleys, notably **rue de la Fontette**, and the fine arcaded **place aux Aires**. This quarter is now largely populated by Muslim immigrants and is full of Algerian bars and cheap restaurants. A colorful **market** *(place Jean-Jaurès)* takes place daily except Monday, and there is a daily food and flower market *(place aux Aires)*. Patrick Suskind's novel, *Perfume,* is set in 18thC Grasse.

In the 19thC, Grasse's sheltered position made it a fashionable winter resort; Queen Victoria wintered here several times, at the now defunct Grand Hotel or in the Rothschild villa. Today, although Grasse attracts many visitors (including businessmen using the conference center housed in the old *Belle Époque* casino), it has a less lively life of its own than many towns of the region, and is remarkably subdued at night.

Grasse is a nightmare for drivers. Parking is difficult, although there is a multistory garage on Cours Honoré-Cresp near the Fragonard factory, and other parking places in the boulevard Gambetta and near the Gare Routière. And the town itself, and the roads leading s from it, suffer serious traffic jams. If you have to get to or from the coast in a hurry, avoid lunchtime and the rush hour. Alternatively, if you don't mind a little careful map-reading, leave Grasse by the N85 (where congestion builds up as you go toward the coast) and then take the small D409 s to Cannes.

- **EVENTS**   In February, a **carnival**. • In May, a **rose festival**. • In June, a **music festival**. • In August, **beer and jasmine festivals**. • The **Centre International** *(av. Maximin-Isnard)* holds intermittent concerts, plays and other events throughout the year.

- **MARKETS**   There is a lively **market** in place Jean-Jaurès every day except Monday • There is also a **food and flower market** every day, in place aux Aires.

WHAT TO SEE IN GRASSE
Art et de l'Histoire de Provence, Musée d'
Rue Mirabeau ☎*93-36-01-61. Open June–Sept 10am–1pm, 2–7pm; Oct, Dec–June 10am–noon, 2–5pm. Closed Mon; Tues (Oct–June); Nov.*
Housed on three floors of this fine 18thC mansion is a collection of Provençal art and handicrafts, of various periods: faïence from Moustiers, tapestries, furniture and domestic utensils, as well as exhibits relating to the history of the town, and a room dealing mainly with local archeology.

There are also some paintings by the Provençal artist, Granet.

Fragonard, Villa-Musée
Blvd. Fragonard ☎*93-36-01-61. For admission details and opening times see* ART ET DE L'HISTOIRE DE PROVENCE, MUSÉE D'.
The painter Jean-Honoré Fragonard (1732–1806) was born in Grasse, but lived for most of his life in Paris, where he painted his sentimental and often sensuous canvases. During the Terror, however, he returned to the safety of Grasse and spent a year in this pleasant little villa.

Today, it is a museum dedicated to the artist, but contains little of his great works. There are good copies of the panels he painted for Louis XV's mistress Madame du Barry, which she oddly rejected, and which he brought to Grasse with him. The originals are in the Frick Collection in New York.

The staircase and landing may have been decorated by Fragonard or his son Évarist, and there are more pictures by both Fragonard and his son in the first-floor rooms.

Maison Fragonard ☆
Blvd. Fragonard ☎*93-36-44-65* 🔲 📷 𝄢 *of factory only. Factory open May–Oct Mon–Sat 8.30am–6.30pm, Sun 9am–noon, 2–6pm; Nov–Apr 9am–noon, 2–6pm.*
The factory mounts a skillful PR exercise, whereby expert, multilingual guides give a free conducted tour to thousands of tourists every day.

The three main processes of making scent from flowers — distillation, *éffleurage* and extraction — are shown and explained. The use of animal fluids as "fixatives" is also explained; these include civet from Ethiopian cats (not specially killed) and (believe it or not) whale vomit (from live whales, not dead, hunted ones) which provides the vital *ambergris* ingredient.

The final stage of the tour is a little shop full of tempting bottles and soaps — but you are not obliged to buy. The best days for a visit are Monday to Friday, when the factory staff are at work. The factory also houses a small museum, which you can wander around.

Other perfume manufacturers, including **Molinard** *(60 blvd. Victor Hugo* ☎ *93-36-01-62)* and **Gallimard** *(73 Route de Cannes* ☎ *93-09-20-00),* mount similar factory tours.

Marine, Musée de la

Hôtel de Pontèves, blvd. du Jeu-de-Ballon 🆔 *first and fourth Sun of month; otherwise* 🆔 ✍ *Open 10am–noon 2–6pm. Closed Sun; first two weeks of Nov.*
Admiral de Grasse (1722–88), born in nearby Bar-sur-Loup, was a famous French naval hero who helped America to win the War of Independence by blockading the British Army at Yorktown, Virginia. Later he was taken prisoner by Rodney and brought to London.

This little museum has some interesting souvenirs of his career, including maps, scenes of naval battles, and models of old warships.

Notre-Dame, Ancienne Cathédrale de ✝

Pl. du Petit Puy ✍
With its high, squat tower piercing the skyline, Notre-Dame stands grandly on a hilltop site on the edge of the Old Town. It is mostly 12thC (the facade shows Lombard influences) but was restored in the 17thC, with an 18thC curving double stairway in front.

Inside, the vaulted roof is supported by unusually broad and rough stone pillars, while walls and chapels hold various works of art. Above an altar in a side chapel hangs a Fragonard, *Washing of the Feet,* one of his rare religious works and with little feeling of piousness.

There are also three paintings by Rubens and, in a side-chapel off the right aisle, a fine 15thC triptych, said to be by Bréa, representing St-Honorat, patron saint of Grasse.

Parfumerie, Musée International de la

8 pl. du Cours ☎ *93-36-01-61* 🆔 *Open June–Sept, 10am–7pm; Oct, Dec–May Wed–Sun 10am–noon, 2–5pm. Closed Mon; Tues; Nov.*
After years of municipal planning, this museum finally opened in a 19thC building in 1989. It is about as comprehensive a museum of the history of perfume, soaps and cosmetics as you could hope for, with many attractive exhibits.

✥ **Panorama** *(2 pl. du Cours* ☎ *93-36-80-80* 🆔 *93-36-92-04* ▥ *36 rms* 🄰🄴 🆔 🆅🆂🄰 ☐ 🄲 ✍ *),* a hotel in modern style (opened 1984). The rooms facing the garden are best; others look onto the main street of Grasse. No ➜

✿ Other recommended hotels: **Bellevue** (*14 av. Riou-Blanquet* ☎ *93-36-01-96* ▥ *to* ▥), sedate, modernized. • **Les Palmiers** (🏠) (*17 blvd. Y.-E.-Baudoin* ☎ *93-36-07-24* ▥), with a drab front but lovely garden at the back, friendly owners and a homely atmosphere. • **Les Parfums** (*blvd. Charabot* ☎ *93-36-10-10* Ⓕⓧ *93-36-35-48* ▥ *to* ▥), Grasse's one smart hotel, with all comforts, but impersonal. • **Du Patti** (*pl. du Patti* ☎ *93-36-01-00* Ⓕⓧ *93-36-36-40* ▥ *to* ▥), comfortable, recently modernized, in the middle of the old town.

≡ Grasse is short on good restaurants, which is surprising, since taste and smell go hand in hand.

One reasonable place is **Maître Boscq** (*13 rue de la Fontette* ☎ *93-36-45-76* ▥). But **Amphitryon** (*16 blvd. Victor-Hugo* ☎ *93-36-58-73* ▥) is the best restaurant in town.

LOCAL DISHES Specialities of the area include: *Lou Fassam* (a rich dish of cabbage stuffed with liver, sausage and other ingredients); sweet dishes using marrow (squash) including *la tarte à la courge* and *beignets de fleur de courge;* and *la fougassette,* a *brioche* made with orange essence. Tripe is also a local favorite.

PLACES NEAR GRASSE

Auribeau (*9km/5 miles s of Grasse*). A picturesque old hill-village perched above the river Siagne, 3 kilometers (2 miles) NW of Pégomas off the D9. From the terrace beside the 18thC church (with a fine carved pulpit) on the summit, there are views of the Tuscany-like landscape around, with its knobbly, wooded hills, bright green vineyards and multicolored flower plantations. It's best to park in place de la Libération, just below the church, before strolling down the medieval alleys.

≡ ✿ LA VIGNETTE HAUTE

Auribeau-sur-Siagne ☎ *93-42-20-01* ▥ ▭ ▤ ➡ Ⓐ🄴 Ⓒ🄳 ▨ *Closed Tues lunch; Mon (except July, Aug); mid-Nov to mid-Dec. Last orders 9.30pm (10.30pm summer).*

In the village, an old farmhouse with rustic decor, where you dine pleasantly by the light of candles and oil-lamps, in the company of sheep and goats who are sleeping quietly in their pens and separated from the restaurant by no more than a pane of glass! The ambience may be touristic, but the cooking is honest and good. A simple formula: you choose your main dish, and the rest comes automatically. You can eat outside. The *auberge* also has ten fairly expensive rooms and a pool.

✿ ≡ **Auberge Nossi-Bé** (*pl. du Portail, 06810 Auribeau-sur-Siagne* ☎ *93-42-20-20* ▥ *closed Tues eve and Wed out of season, Mon and Wed lunch in season, early Jan to end Feb*), a pleasant and comfortable village inn, with sensible, reasonably priced food.

Mouans-Sartoux (*7km/4 miles SE of Grasse*). The village itself, on the main Grasse–Cannes road, has little to recommend it, save for one delightful restaurant, the PALAIS DES COQS, just outside.

≡ PALAIS DES COQS ✿

Chemin du Plan-Sarrain (on D409) ☎ *93-75-61-57* ▥ *to* ▥ ▬ 🍴 ➡ Ⓐ🄴 ▨ *Closed Wed eve Oct–June; Sat lunch July–Sept; Thurs; Jan; third week in June. Last orders 9.30pm.*

A restaurant that is surrounded by totally unspoiled countryside and with a lovely flower-filled garden. The food is very good and excellent value, especially on the dearer menu, where your five courses might include *pâté en croûte truffé, fricassée de queues d'écrevisses sur fondue de poireaux,* and, for dessert, *charlotte aux fruits rouges.*

Opio *(6km/4 miles E of Grasse)*. At the foot of this small village, by the D3/D7 intersection, is the Roger Michel olive-oil mill *(closed Sun)*. Two kilometers (1 mile) to the S, down a poorly signposted turn off the D3, the semi-ruined 11thC chapel of Notre-Dame-de-Brusc stands isolated amid farmland. It is closed and boarded up, but beside it you can make out the remains of a baptistry dating from the 6thC.

═🚗 ✍ MAS DES GERANIUMS

06650 Opio ☎93-77-23-23 ▥ ■ 🚗 ➡
Closed Sun eve; Oct–Feb. Last orders 7.30pm.

Although the prices at this charming restaurant have crept up over the years, a meal here is always a delight. M. Fradois and his wife are still, after a great many years, producing honest food — chicken with herbs or figs, red mullet, duck or *entrecôte au poivre vert* — and can rarely have encountered a dissatisfied customer. Lunch is the best meal, served in the agreeable garden, with the luxury of plenty of space between the few tables. An ideal place to escape from the hectic coast, especially if you have children who can amuse themselves on the swing in the garden while you eat.

There are also eight simple but congenial rooms (▥).

Pégomas *(10km/6 miles S of Grasse)*. A pleasant village on the river Siagne. All around this area are great sweeps of mimosa, both wild and cultivated, which blaze into golden blossoms in January and February.

✍ LE BOSQUET

06580 Pégomas ☎93-42-22-87 ▥ *18 rms* ➡ 🖼 📺 🎿 🍽 ≋ ♪ *Closed Nov. Location: On the N fringe of the village, just off the D209, amid wooded hills.* The exuberant personality of *patronne* Simone Bernardi, and the charms of the unusual country hotel she runs with her husband, draw a faithful clientele of foreigners, mainly English, many of whom return year after year. Two red-roofed villas, one a conversion, the other new, are set in spacious, leafy grounds. Seven of the rooms have kitchenettes.

St-Cézaire *(16km/10 miles W of Grasse)*. The village stands on a cliff above the deep **Siagne gorge** (☆). The terrace by the church offers excellent views of the gorge and of the mountains to the N. The village is fairly undisturbed, although many of the old houses have been restored as summer homes.

The Romanesque 12thC chapel on the SE outskirts has a Roman sarcophagus.

Grottes de St-Cézaire ☆

3km (2 miles) NE of St-Cézaire ☎93-60-22-35 ▦ *✗ available. Open 10am–noon, 2 or 2.30 to 6 or 6.30pm. Closed Nov–Feb.*
Formed by a glacier 4 million years ago, these remarkable caves plunge 60 meters (200 feet) into the limestone plateau. They were never inhabited by prehistoric man, and were discovered by chance in 1890 by a young peasant, father of the present owner.

The presence of iron oxide gives the caves a reddish hue, and they have been artfully lit to show off the bizarre shapes formed by the thousands of stalactites and stalagmites. Some of the shapes have been given names (the Vegetable Garden, the Fairy's Bed, the Skeleton, the Gulf of Hell), as the guide reveals in his half-facetious, half-scientific patter. These chalky stalactites also have musical properties, and the guide taps out tunes on them as if on a xylophone.

☜ CLAUX DE TALADOIRE

Route de Saint-Vallier-de-Thiey, St-Cézaire ☎ 93-60-20-09 ⓕ 93-38-72-18 ▢ 22 rms ══ ☐ ⌂

An auberge secluded amid trees, and ideal for a quiet vacation. Simple but comfortable, with a swimming pool and pleasant terrace.

St-Vallier-de-Thiey *(12km/7 miles NW of Grasse).* A summer vacation center on a verdant plateau, with deliciously clear air, and forests and mountains behind. A fine place for walking, riding, tennis and swimming.

☜ ══ LE PRÉJOLY ☙

06460 St-Vallier-de-Thiey ☎ 93-42-60-86 ⓕ 93-42-67-80 ▢ to ▥ 17 rms ➡ Ⓐ ▨ ☐ ☒ ♨ ⛄ *Closed Dec; Jan.* *Location: On the main road in the village, but facing open country at the back.* A traditional Provençal hostelry at its best: an *auberge* run with skill and warmth by a charming couple. Ask for a rear bedroom overlooking open parkland (it'll be quieter than one at the front).

A well-prepared and well-presented menu of good home cooking with some original touches, draws people from many miles around (▢ to ▥ ☐ ▣ ⛊ *closed Tues (Oct–May); last orders 10pm).* The only minor quibbles are these: the pressure of success has made the service sometimes slow, and the pleasure of eating on the elegant front terrace can be marred by the tooting of traffic.

Spéracèdes *(6km/4 miles SW of Grasse).* A quiet old village, less touristy than others in the area, and worth a visit.

══ LA SOLEILLADE ☙

Rue des Orangers ☎ 93-66-11-15 ▢ ☐ ▣ ⛊ *Closed Wed (except July, Aug, Oct). Last orders 9.30pm.* In his delightful little rustic dining room, the drily humorous M. Forest, a former circus artist, relies on fresh local pro-

duce to win over his guests. It's an excellent place, if you are exploring the delightful countryside around Grasse, to pause for a simple lunch. *Specialities: Pâté de grives avec salade aux croûtons, laperin aux herbes, caille à la romaine.*

• See also: ROUTE NAPOLÉON; ST-CASSIEN, LAC DE.

ISOLA 2000

Map **15***C15* (Alpes-Mar.). 94km (58 miles) N of Nice. Postal code: 06420. Population: 570 ⓘ in complex ☎ 93-23-15-15.

Negotiate several dozen wild hairpin bends on the D97, and high in the deserted mountains you will come across what looks like a giant space-age shopping center: Isola 2000. This popular, modern ski resort, built entirely by British enterprise, comprises one huge, snake-like complex of hotels, restaurants, apartments, shops and cafés. A central corridor connects one end with the other, with Paris Métro-style announcements telling you where you are and how many "stops" to go to your destination. It's all very far removed from the traditional alpine ski resort of one's imagination.

In summer, when the slopes are dry and strewn with rocks, and the stationary ski lifts give the air of a disused mine, the resort seems characterless; yet it does not lie fallow, but becomes a tennis center. In winter the harshness of the complex is somewhat mellowed by the snow and the frenetic activity all around. The skiing is varied, with elevators and cable cars right on your doorstep.

🐎 **Le Chastillon** (☎ 93-23-10-60 Ⓕ93-23-17-66 ▥), a very comfortable hotel by the ski runs, with many facilities; **Diva** (☎ 93-23-17-71 Ⓕ93-23-12-14 ▥ to ▥), luxurious and well appointed (two saunas): *demi-pension* only; **Druos** (☎ 93-23-12-20 Ⓕ 79-41-11-13 ▢ to ▥), a rather featureless establishment, but well run, with no proper restaurant, although grills, cooked on the open fire, are served in the small lobby.

JUAN-LES-PINS

Maps 2E3 and 15F14 (Alpes-Mar.). 9km (6 miles) E of Cannes. Postal code: 06160 i blvd. Charles-Guillaumont ☎93-61-04-98.

This suburb of Antibes owes its huge success as a resort to its sheltered position, facing SW across Golfe-Juan. Juan-les-Pins barely existed until the 1920s, when the American millionaire Frank Jay Gould set its trend as a major fashionable resort of the interwar years. Beside the casino, pine forests, from which Juan gets its name, stretch down to a long beach of fine sand. This was that "bright tan prayer rug of a beach" setting for *Tender is the Night.*

> Only the cupolas of a dozen old villas rotted like water-lilies among the massed pines between Gausse's Hôtel des Étrangers and Cannes, five miles away. The hotel and its bright tan prayer rug of a beach were one.
> In the early morning the distant image of Cannes, the pink and cream of old fortifications, the purple Alps that bounded Italy, were cast across the water and lay quavering in the ripples.
> (*Tender is the Night,* 1939, F. Scott Fitzgerald)

Traces of that fabled and sophisticated epoch still linger on in modern Juan, mainly in its two luxury hotels. But today this large resort is the most garish place on the whole coast. Par excellence it is a haunt of the young, who throng the place all summer. The nucleus of little streets off the casino is a maze of fast-food bars, pizzerias, second-rate boutiques and third-rate discos — all very lively, but certainly not chic. The local mayor, however, is doing his best to make Juan fashionable again, not least by opening the casino (in 1992) and planning to reopen the famous old Le Provençal hotel.

In winter, unlike most of the other resorts, Juan is pretty dead.

- **EVENT** Juan these days is best known for the important **international jazz festival**, founded in 1960, which takes place in the pine woods during the last two weeks of July *(details from Antibes tourist office)*. In the past, artists such as Ray Charles, Duke Ellington, Ella Fitzgerald and Miles Davis have all appeared.

🗝 WHERE TO STAY IN JUAN-LES-PINS

AMBASSADEUR 🏨
50-52 Chemin des Sables, 06160 Juan-les-Pins ☎93-67-82-15
📠93-67-79-85 🎗 to 🎗 246 rms 🍴
🖼 ⇌ AE 🅾 🔟 🎞 🖨 ♨ ☐ 🖵 🕭 ♣
《 🏋 🐎 🎿 ♈ ☂ ♉ 🖵

Location: Situated between the beach and the pine forest. This is a new luxury hotel with every modern facility including fitness center, indoor and outdoor swimming pools (as well as a private beach), nonsmoking rooms and satellite TV. There is a good restaurant and a poolside grill. All rooms have balconies. The only thing this hotel lacks is the period charm of the others in Juan.

BELLES-RIVES 🏨
Blvd. Baudoin, 06160 Juan-les-Pins ☎93-61-02-79 📠93-67-43-51 🎗 44 rms ⇌ AE 🔟 ♨ ☐ 🖵 《 🐎 🎿 Closed Oct–Easter.

Location: On the seafront, where Juan and Cap d'Antibes merge. Of Juan's two famous luxury hotels, this one has the merit of being right on the sea, with its own private jetty and private beach (mostly concrete, but a stretch of sand too). It's a glamorous hotel that has carefully kept its original Roaring Twenties cachet: most guests are young, smart and cosmopolitan. Beautiful outdoor dining terrace by the sea. Guests here have included Édith Piaf and the Duke and Duchess of Windsor.

JUANA 🏨
Av. Gallice, 06160 Juan-les-Pins ☎93-61-08-70 📠93-61-76-60 🎗 50 rms 🍴 🖼 No cards 🖨 ♨ ♣ ☐ 🖵 ♥
🐎 🎿 Closed Nov–Apr. For ⇌ see LA TERRASSE, below.

Location: In the quiet E part of Juan, facing a pine forest, 180 meters (200 yards) from the beach. The opulent leather upholstery in the bar-salon sets the style for this select and very sophisticated luxury hotel. Compared with its local rival the BELLES-RIVES, its handicap is that it lies away from the beach (although it has its own private one), with no sea views; its ambience, too, is less breezily youthful, more sedate. But comfort and service are of the highest order, in the classic prewar manner, with uniformed porters and waiters always on hand. The flowery garden beneath shady palm trees is most elegant.

PRÉ CATELAN
22 av. des Lauriers, 06160 Juan-les-Pins ☎93-61-05-11 📠93-67-83-11 🎗 18 rms ⇌ AE 🔟 🔟 🎞 🖨 🖵 ♣ ♥
🐎 Closed Mar to mid-Apr. Last orders in the restaurant 9.30pm.

Location: In a quiet residential street. This white-walled villa-style hotel is set in its own garden, and is well out of earshot of strident downtown Juan. Guests can lunch or dine out-of-doors in pleasant surroundings under creepers and gaily-colored parasols. The hotel has a private beach.

🗝 Other reasonable hotels include: **Astor** (*blvd. Raymond-Poincaré* ☎93-61-07-38 📠93-61-36-76 🎗); **Astoria** (*15 av. Maréchal-Joffre* ☎93-61-23-65 📠93-67-10-40 🎗); **Beauséjour** (*av. Saramatel* ☎93-61-07-82 📠93-61-86-78 🎗); **Garden Beach** (*15-17 blvd. Baudoin* ☎93-67-25-25 📠93-61-16-65 🎗 to 🎗); **Mimosa** (*rue Pauline* ☎93-61-04-16 🎗); **Sainte-Valérie** (*rue de l'Oratoire* ☎93-61-07-15 📠93-61-47-52 🎗 to 🎗).

⇌ WHERE TO EAT IN JUAN-LES-PINS

AUBERGE DE L'ESTEREL ♣
21 rue des Îles ☎93-61-86-55 🎗 🞐 🍱
🍴 AE 🔟 🎞 Closed Sun eve; Mon; Nov to mid-Dec. Last orders 9.15pm.
This ambitious restaurant is now under separate management from the hotel to which it is attached. The prices are moderate. You should choose a fine day and eat in the garden; the dining room is rather dull.

LA TERRASSE ⌂
Hôtel Juana, Av. Gallice ☎*93-61-08-70* ▥
▢▰▰▱▰▱ *No cards. Closed
Wed (except late June, July and Aug);
Nov–Apr. Dinner only, July–Aug. Last orders
10pm (10.30pm summer).*
Since the hotel is closed in winter, the
indoor dining room is little used, and is
severely formal and unenticing. But
there is a touch of magic about the
outdoor terrace by the garden, especially at night, when candles flicker and
soft music plays. It makes a worthy
setting for a cuisine that is among the
finest on the whole coast.

Christian Morisset took over from
the celebrated Alain Ducasse a few
years ago, but is now almost as accomplished and inventive as his predeces-
sor. Dishes vary with the season and the
market, but you can always rely on a
high standard. Prices are high. *Specialities: Poêlée de supions aux poiv-
rades, selle d'agneau de Pauillac cuite
en terre d'argile.*

(See 🗣 JUANA, above.)

◗ NIGHTLIFE IN JUAN-LES-PINS

Cafés   Most of the decibels in Juan are generated at the intersection
of the boulevards Baudoin and Wilson, near the casino, where two
huge, open-fronted cafés confront each other in frenetic rivalry: the
Festival and the **Pam-Pam Rhumeire**. Each has an ear-splitting Brazilian orchestra, lurid lighting and flamboyant "Brazilian" decor (especially the Pam-Pam). Each specializes in elaborate and expensive fruit
cocktails and alcoholic ice cream cups, and each nightly attracts a
goggling crowd of bystanders, amassed all the way down the street.
This is the center of Juan's nightlife, and no disco in town can compare
with this exuberant street theater. All summer the show goes on till 3 or
4am: if you're staying in a nearby hotel, best bring earplugs.

> On the back seat of the car Dick remained quiescent until the
> yellow monolith of Golfe-Juan was passed, and then the constant
> carnival at Juan-les-Pins, where the night was musical and strident
> in many languages.
>
> (*Tender is the Night,* 1939, F. Scott Fitzgerald)

Discos   Oddly, none of Juan's many discos is very exciting. But there
is a good disco at the **Maison des Pêcheurs** at Port-Gallice (see
BEACHES below).
Casinos   The **Eden Casino** *(blvd. E.-Baudoin* ☎*92-93-71-71)* opened
in 1992. It has a top-class restaurant, overseen by no less than Jacques
Maximin, formerly at the Negresco in Nice. Maximin is one of the finest
chefs in France, one of the original leaders of the *nouvelle cuisine*
movement. His cooking is light and very inventive; his art lies in his
ability to take classic local dishes and re-create them to suit modern
tastes and appetites.

🏖 BEACHES IN JUAN-LES-PINS
As in Cannes, the better beaches are private and paying, although free
beaches can be found away from the central area.

The **Maison des Pêcheurs**, at Port Gallice on the coast road to Cap
d'Antibes, is a lively complex that includes beach, lido, marina, snack-
bar/restaurant and nightclub.

PLACE NEAR JUAN-LES-PINS

Golfe-Juan   The name has nothing to do with a golf course, but refers to the deep Gulf of Juan, between Cannes and Cap d'Antibes, one of the finest anchorages on the coast and used by the US Navy before France left Nato. Golfe-Juan today is a flourishing swimming resort with a marina and long sandy beaches (most of them free), sheltered by the hills of Vallauris with their orange and mimosa trees.

Golfe-Juan has its place in history. It was here that Napoléon landed with some 800 men on March 1, 1815, on his return from exile in Elba, and started on the ROUTE NAPOLÉON to Paris. The famous proclamation was here nailed up for the first time: "The eagle, with the national colors, will fly from steeple to steeple as far as the towers of Notre-Dame." Today a memorial by the harbor marks the event.

🍴 In Golfe-Juan: **Beau Soleil** *(Imp. Beausoleil* ☎ *93-63-63-63* Ex *93-63-02-89* ▭ *to* ▤▥*); **De Crijansy** (av. J.-Adam* ☎ *93-63-84-44* ▥▥*); **Les Jasmins** *(on N7* ☎ *93-63-80-83* ▭*).

🍽 Good restaurants to try, in Golfe-Juan, include: **Nounou** *(on the beach* ☎ *93-63-71-73* ▭ *to* ▤▥*); and* **Tétou** *(av. des Frères-Roustan* ☎ *93-63-71-16* ▥▥*).

• See also: ANTIBES, CAP D'ANTIBES.

LUCÉRAM

*Maps **3**B4 and **15**D15 (Alpes-Mar.). 24km (17 miles) NE of Nice. Postal code: 06440. Population: 550 𝒊 at Mairie* ☎ *90-79-51-83.*

Not far from Nice, yet remarkably unspoiled, this high-perched fortified village is a jumble of stepped alleys and old houses staggered one above the other. Crowning all is the 15thC **church** with Italian Rococo decor; it is one of the most interesting in the Nice area, for Lucéram was a key center of 15thC religious painting. It has six retables of the prolific Bréa school (the finest, the **retable of Ste-Marguerite**, behind the high altar, shows a touching serenity), and a collection of old silver, including the unusual statuette of Ste-Marguerite (Lucéram's patron saint) standing on a dragon. If you require light, ask at the presbytery next door.

🍴🍽 **LA MÉDITERRANÉE**
Pl. Adrien-Barralis, 06440 Lucéram
☎ *93-91-54-54* ▥ *8 rms* ◁▷
Location: On a small square at the end of the village. This is the essence of rural Provence; a very simple old village inn, run by good-hearted country people. You may find villagers knocking back their morning drinks at the bar while you have your breakfast. In the restaurant *(* ▭ ◼◼ *last orders 9pm), la patronne,* grandmother Joséphine Gaetti and her family provide succulent home cooking at low prices — even the cheapest menu starts with a help-your-self trolley of enticing hors d'oeuvres including a delicious local smoked ham. *Specialities: Ravioli niçoise, lapin provençal, gigot des Alpes, sanglier (in season).*

PLACES NEAR LUCÉRAM

Peira Cava/Col de Turini *(10km/6 miles N of Lucéram).* The D21 from Lucéram winds up into wild alpine scenery, amid rock-strewn forests of giant pines. Of the two little skiing and summer resorts here, **Peira Cava** seems a little drab, while the **Col de Turini** has more style. From here you can drive through the lovely **Forêt de Turini**, with its towering pines and spruces, to the start of a 13-kilometer (8-mile) round-trip mountain drive, the *Circuit de l'Aution,* to the **Pointe-des-Trois-Communes**, where the views of the Alps are dazzling.

From Col de Turini in summer there are also guided rambles to the unique **Vallée des Merveilles** (see LA BRIGUE).

☜ TROIS VALLÉES

06440 Col de Turini ☎*93-91-57-21* ▢
26 rms ⇌ ≒ 🗎 ⌂ ⊄
Location: Beside the ski lifts at Col de Turini. A spacious alpine chalet for skiers and climbers. Bedrooms have dark wood decor, some with balconies facing the forests and snow peaks. Simple, copious food for hungry *sportifs* is served in the vast dining room.

• See also: COARAZE, SOSPEL.

MENTON ☆

*Maps 3C5 and 16E16 (Alpes-Mar.). 27km (17 miles) E of Nice. 2.5km (1½ miles) W of the Italian frontier. Postal code: 06500. Population: 29,150. **Railway station:** place de la Gare* ☎*93-87-50-50* **ℹ** *Palais de l'Europe, 8 av. Boyer* ☎*93-57-57-00.*

Menton is much the prettiest and least strident of the larger resorts on the Côte. It is also the warmest, with winters of balmy mildness, due to the sheltering mountains just behind it. Hence the semitropical fruits and plants that are here in profusion, and the acres of lemon groves, for which the town is famous.

Until the 19thC, Menton was a little-known fishing port, in liege to the Grimaldis. But in the 1850s, an English doctor, Henry Bennet, wrote a book in which he praised the town's beneficial climate, and the English gentry duly descended on Menton, to retire or to pass the winter. They were soon followed by other European aristocrats.

Today, all this has changed. The expatriate British population, once 5,000 and one of the largest in Continental Europe, has dwindled to a mere 120 or so. The palace hotels along the seafront, the Balmoral, the Bristol, the Majestic, have either been pulled down or converted into apartments. Yet there still exist echoes of the old days: the JARDIN DES COLOMBIÈRES, Katherine Mansfield's villa, the grandiose lobby of the old Imperial hotel, now apartments, and the air of faded nostalgia that envelops the town.

Menton stands along a wide bay. To the W of the port runs the elegant, palm-lined **Promenade du Soleil** (☆), and to the E are new beaches and marinas. Behind the port rises the picturesque **vieille ville** with its bustling alleys, and from here steps lead up to the 17thC **Église de St-Michel** and the nearby **Chapelle des Penitents Blancs**, both fine examples of Baroque architecture.

• **EVENTS** In the first half of August, a distinguished **festival of chamber music** is held in place de l'Église, superbly floodlit. • In February, the famous **lemon festival** takes place, with pretty girls and floats of fruit.

- **MARKETS**   There is a daily **indoor market** on Quai de Monléon, near the Musée Cocteau, and a **street market** near the Gare Routière. • Just across the border in Italy, 11 kilometers (7 miles) away, is the vast market at **Ventimiglia**, on Friday only, which attracts people from miles around with its wide choice and very cheap prices.

WHAT TO SEE IN MENTON

Cocteau, Musée

Quai Napoléon III ☎*93-57-72-30* ◙ ✖ *Open mid-Sept to mid-June 10am–noon, 2–6pm; mid-June to mid-Sept 10am–noon, 3–7pm. Closed Tues.*
Installed in the 17thC harbor bastion in 1957, this small museum contains tapestries, drawings and stage sets by the versatile painter and writer Jean Cocteau. Most eye-catching are the gaudy harlequin paintings.

Colombières, Jardin des ☆

Blvd. de Garavan (in NE suburbs, poorly signposted) ☎*93-35-71-90* ◙ ✖ ◀€
Open 10am–noon, 2–6pm.
This large Italianate garden on a steep hillside was laid out by Ferdinand Bac, humorist, writer and allegedly the illegitimate son of Napoléon III. It has tall cypresses, ornamental pools, urns and statues, and in its heyday must have been lovely, although it is now sadly unkempt. The present elderly owner can only afford one gardener, and fears the garden's days are nearly over.

In the grounds, the curious **Villa les Colombières** was exuberantly designed by Bac in Hellenic/Roman style, with frescos, arches and statues; an elegant, colonnaded atrium has a pool in the middle, now empty and dirty. The villa has bedrooms to let, with Roman-style baths, or you can simply take some lemon tea, gazing out over the glorious coast below.

Just below the garden is an old **olive grove**, and farther down the hill is the **Jardin Botanique Exotique**, full of unusual shrubs and trees. Near here is writer Katherine Mansfield's villa, Isola Bella. Farther w, beyond the road to Sospel, the **monastery of the Annonciade** stands high on its hilltop; it's worth going up for the views, but the monastery itself is not open to visitors.

Municipal, Musée

Palais Carnoles, Av. de la Madone ☎*93-35-49-71* ◙ *See COCTEAU, MUSÉE for opening times. Closed Tues.*
This 18thC former summer palace of the princes of Monaco, decorated with frescos, is set in fine citrus gardens. It houses Italian, Dutch, French and other paintings of the 14th–17thC, as well as minor works by such modern artists as Utrillo, Dufy, Vlaminck, Chagall, Modigliani and Picasso, and some contemporary paintings. In winter, chamber music concerts are held here. The gardens themselves (which contain contemporary sculpture) are at their best between December and March.

Palais de l'Europe

Av. Boyer ☎*93-57-57-00* ◙ *See COCTEAU, MUSÉE for opening times. Closed Sun; Mon.*

The former municipal casino has been used as a gallery since the 1950s, and now houses the town library as well as temporary art and photography exhibitions, some of international stature (contact the tourist office for details). It is also used for official ceremonies.

Préhistoire Régionale, Musée de la
Rue Loredan-Larchey ☎93-35-84-64 ▣ *See* COCTEAU, MUSÉE *for opening times. Closed Tues.*

The museum is known for its prehistory and archeology collection, including the skull of the famous *Menton Man* (c.30000BC), found in a cave on the shore nearby in the 19thC. Reconstructions and the latest audiovisual techniques are used to show the evolution of civilization. The museum is also devoted to local history and popular arts.

Salle des Mariages ☆
Hôtel de Ville, rue de la République ☎93-57-87-87 ▨ ✆ ✗ *available. Open 8.30am–12.30pm, 1.30–5pm. Closed Sat; Sun.*

This little room in the Town Hall, used for civil marriages, was decorated by Jean Cocteau in 1957 with a series of engagingly vivacious paintings in his characteristic style.

✎ L'AIGLON
7 av. de la Madone ☎93-57-55-55
🅵🆇93-57-40-20 ▥ *32 rms* 🍽 ⚓ 🆎 ◑ ◐ ■ 🔒 ⚘ ▢ 🅿 🛂 ⚓ 🐾
Location: On the main road, facing the beach, at the w end of the promenade. A former private house built around 1900, in a big garden with fruit trees; a pleasant hotel with a pool and shady terraces. Some rooms have balconies. No restaurant, but snacks are served by the pool at lunchtime, and in the bedrooms in the evening.

✎ Other recommended hotels include: • **Ambassadeurs** *(3 rue Partouneaux* ☎93-28-75-75 🅵🆇93-35-62-62 ▥ *to* ▥). • **Auberge Provençale** (🏠 ♣) *(11 rue Trenca* ☎93-55-77-29 ▥). • **Auberge des Santons** *(Colline de l'Annonciade* ☎93-35-94-10 ▥ *see also* ◼). • **Chambord** *(6 av. Boyer* ☎93-35-94-19 🅵🆇93-41-30-55 ▥).

• **Londres** *(15 av. Carnot* ☎93-35-74-62 🅵🆇93-41-77-78 ▥). • **Napoléon** *(29 Porte de France* ☎93-35-89-50 🅵🆇93-35-49-22 ▥). • **Orly** *(27 Porte de France* ☎93-35-60-81 🅵🆇93-35-40-13 ▥). • **Princess et Richmond** *(617 promenade du Soleil* ☎93-35-80-20 🅵🆇93-57-40-20 ▥). • **Viking** *(2 av. Général-de-Gaulle* ☎93-35-95-85 🅵🆇93-35-89-57 ▥).

◼ AUBERGE DES SANTONS
Colline de l'Annonciade ☎93-35-94-10 ▥ ▢ ◼ 🍴 ⚓ 🆎 ◑ *Closed Sun eve; Mon; mid-Nov to mid-Dec. Last orders 10pm (summer), 9.30pm (winter).*

The best food in Menton can be found at this modern white villa overlooking the sea. *Patron* and chef Bernard Simon continues to please his guests with *nouvelle cuisine* prepared with his customary tremendous finesse. *Specialities: Escalope de saumon cru mariné au basilic, feuilleté de ris de veau sauce porto.*

◼ In general, Menton has surprisingly few high-quality or interesting restaurants, but you might try one of the following for a satisfactory meal: **Chez Mireille-l'Ermitage** *(1080 promenade du Soleil* ☎93-35-77-23 ▥ *closed Mon),* in a fairly formal setting, with traditional food; **Le Merle Blanc** *(21 rue St-Michel* ☎93-35-77-53 ▥ *closed Fri)* offers straightforward cooking and good value;

L'Oursin (*3 rue Trenca* ☎*93-28-33-62* ▥ *closed Wed*) cooks good fish and other seafood; **La Trattoria** (*123 rue Longue* ☎*93-28-44-64* ▥ *to* ▥ *closed lunchtime, open late*) has a lively, youngish atmosphere and only a simple menu, mostly concentrating on pizza; **Viviers Bretons** (*6 pl. du Cap* ☎*93-35-24-24* ▥ *closed Tues*) is another restaurant where they serve mainly seafood.

◪ NIGHTLIFE IN MENTON

Casino   The **Casino Municipal** (*av. Félix-Faure* ☎*92-10-16-16* ◉ ❀ ♪) has gaming rooms open 4pm–3am. It is one of the Côte's most staid casinos. The dinner dance/cabaret is open in summer only. On Sunday afternoons there are *thés-dansants*.

Discos/piano bars   For disco dancing, go to **Le Queenie** (*1 rue Pasteur* ☎*93-57-58-46*). The hotel **Ambassadeurs** has a piano bar that stays open until 2am.

PLACES NEAR MENTON

Ste-Agnès (✩) (*11km/7 miles* NW *of Menton*).   Approached on a winding road, this is one of the highest and most striking of all the villages near the coast. It straddles the crest of a hill, and behind it a track leads up a cliff to the ruined Saracen castle. From Ste-Agnès it is possible to drive through the mountains to the attractive villages of **Peille** and PEILLON, and so on to Nice.

≕   **LOGIS SARRASIN** ☚ ♨
Ste-Agnès ☎*93-35-86-89* ▢ ▭ ▰ 🚗
◂ *Closed Fri; mid-Nov to mid-Dec.*
Thousands of other tourists have gotten here first — but don't be deterred by the crowds from eating at this well-known, old, family-run *auberge* in Ste-Agnès. Huge meals are provided for next to nothing, and there are marvelous views.

Gorbio (✩)   Reached by another road from Menton, the D23, Gorbio is another remarkable hilltop village.

- See also: ROQUEBRUNE-CAP-MARTIN.

≕☙ NEARBY

AUBERGE DU MOULIN ☚ ♨
Rue Garibaldi, Castellar (6km/3½ miles N *of Menton)* ☎*93-35-99-79* ▢ 🚗 *Closed eve out of season; Tues; Mar. Last orders 9pm.*
A remote, rough-and-ready inn in a hilltop village, where you can enjoy fresh and simple country cooking and a *pichet* of local wine under the olive trees or by an open fire in winter.

MONACO AND MONTE-CARLO
Maps 3C5 and 16E16, and see map on pages 264–65. Independent state, 18km (11 miles) E *of Nice. Area: 1.95sq.km (¾sq. mile). Postal code: 98000. Car identity letters: MC. Population: 30,000 inhabitants; 5,000 citizens* ⓘ *2a blvd. des Moulins* ☎*93-30-87-01* ⓘ *in English* ☎*93-50-07-51.* **Railway station:** *av. Prince-Pierre* ☎*93-50-92-27.*

Prince Rainier III rules like a Medici over his wealthy and dynamic little sovereign state, a 468-acre strip of land no bigger than Central Park, squeezed between sea and mountains, much of it now filled up with tiers of skyscrapers.

Monaco is the name of the principality, and also of the district on a prominent peninsula to the s of the Port de Monaco, where the Royal Palace stands. Across the harbor is the newer quarter, **Monte-Carlo**, on a rocky promontory to the N of the Port de Monaco. Gaudily glamorous, it still exerts a hypnotic appeal over the world's tourists.

MONACO'S HISTORY
The ruling family is the Grimaldi, who acquired Monaco from the Genoese in 1308, and in those days owned several lordships in the region, including ANTIBES and CAGNES. For centuries Monaco's history was a turbulent one; at various times it has been occupied by both the French and the Spanish, and been a protectorate of the French and of the kingdom of Sardinia.

Built in 1860, when the rest of the Nice area was ceded to France by the House of Savoy, Monaco managed to hold onto its independence. Bankruptcy threatened, however, for Prince Charles III was obliged to sell Menton and Roquebrune to Napoléon III, thus losing his revenues from the lemon and olive-oil trade. So he decided to build a casino; these were still banned in France, but were increasingly popular in Germany.

The casino was opened in 1865, on a low barren rock named Monte-Carlo in his honor; and, with the arrival of the railway, the aristocracy of Europe was soon crowding to Monte-Carlo to stay at the imposing new Hôtel de Paris and to indulge in the new pastime of gambling. Prince Charles had given the concession to an enterprising entrepreneur, François Blanc, who made a brilliant financial success of the new venture. Monaco grew rich, almost overnight.

> The resplendent names — Cannes, Nice, Monte-Carlo — began to glow through their torpid camouflage, whispering of old kings come here to dine or die, of rajahs tossing Buddhas' eyes to English ballerinas, of Russian princes turning the weeks into Baltic twilights in the lost caviare days.
>
> *(Tender is the Night,* 1939, F. Scott Fitzgerald)

POSTWAR MONACO
The principality has remained rich, but only by adapting to the times once again. Rainier III was only 25 when he came to the throne in 1949. Monaco was then gently on the wane, for high-society gambling was no longer a solid source of wealth. But in the 45 years since then, the astute prince and his associates have totally transformed and revitalized the place, turning it into one of the most modern, efficient and high-powered pleasure-cum-business centers in the world.

HIGH FINANCE AND REAL-ESTATE
Now only 5 percent of the principality's income is from gambling. Big banks have arrived, attracted by the tax advantages (Monaco holds more than $25 billion in deposits, 60 percent of which belong to non-residents); over 80 acres of land have been reclaimed from the sea, to make room for a new port and heliport (at Fontvieille to the W), two

more casinos, new beaches and nightclubs. Just below the main casino is a vast ultramodern convention center, Les Spélugues, built out over the sea, a showpiece of the prince's emphasis on "business tourism."

INTERNATIONAL STATUS

Just as Monte-Carlo in the late 19thC had an English flavor, so, until recently, it was very American — *"Las Vegas-plage"* as the French sometimes call it. Now it is reliant on Italians for much of its income and vitality. And business conventions are an essential part of its prosperity, particularly out of season. You will be told that the Monaco season lasts all year round, but this is belied by the fact that many hotels use the winter to effect refurbishments, and key facilities are often closed.

Yet it is a town of many facets, some of them vulgar, some chic and glamorous. It is still a magnet for the world's diamond-studded jetsetters (Stavros Niarchos's huge yacht is almost a landmark in the harbor), and its nightlife is the smartest on the coast. Here the Old World meets the New in high style: even the newly opened McDonald's in Fontvieille sports a salubrious green awning.

For 23 years, this union was symbolized by the marriage of Prince Rainier to Grace Kelly, Hollywood star and daughter of a Philadelphia industrialist. After her tragic death in 1982, in an automobile accident on the heights above the town, Monaco went into mourning and lost some of its panache. But it has mostly recovered. To cater to its rich inhabitants, security is tight. Monaco has more policemen per square yard than anywhere in the world, and even the public elevators and parking garages, with their marbled entrances, have elaborate video surveillance systems.

MONACO'S ATTRACTIONS

Monaco claims, perhaps fairly, that a greater diversity of activities and tourist attractions is crammed into this one small space than into any other comparable area of the globe: science (the famous MUSÉE OCÉANO-GRAPHIQUE), culture (the **Opéra** and a **leading orchestra**), sport (the **Grand Prix**, the **tennis championship** and the **Rally**) and international business. . . .

The company that keeps much of these activities running smoothly is still the same one created by Blanc in the 1860s, the **Société des Bains de Mer (SBM)**, in which the principality is a major shareholder. The SBM today owns or runs four of the leading hotels (with a new one planned), all the casinos, many of the office blocks, and most of the beaches, sports clubs and night spots.

THE MONARCHY AND THE PEOPLE

The principality of Monaco is a hereditary monarchy, as defined in the constitution of 1962. The Prince formally holds the reins of government, and delegates powers to the Minister of State.

Close links with France have evolved over a number of years, both in external and internal affairs. The principality is part of France for the purpose of Customs administration, so there are no border formalities. French currency is valid. Monaco has issued its own postage stamps since 1885, but these are needed only for destinations within Monaco.

Of Monaco's 30,000 population, most are French or Italian. Only 5,000 people have the privilege of being Monegasque citizens: they do no military service and pay no income tax.

- **EVENTS**   In January, **Monte-Carlo Rally** and **Festival of St-Devoté**, patron saint of the principality. • In February, **International Television Festival** and **International Circus Festival**. • In April, the **International Tennis Championships**. • In May, **Monaco Grand Prix**. • In June, the **International Swimming Meeting**. • In July, **theater performances**, the **Monte-Carlo Open Golf Championship**, and **Galas** at the Sporting Club • In July/August, the **International Fireworks Festival**, and **concerts** at the Prince's palace. • In August, the **Red Cross Gala** and **ballet performances**. • In November, the **Monegasque National Fête**. • The **national holiday** is on November 19.

TRANSPORT IN MONACO

Walking in Monaco (since much of it is likely to be uphill) can be a tiring business even though the distances are short. **Taxis** are very expensive compared with France, but the local **bus service** is excellent and cheap. The five public **elevators** running up and down from sea level are both safe and pleasant, and well worth using.

The relatively new **helicopter shuttle** services between Monaco and Nice airport, incidentally, are not only quick but cheap, at least when compared with the equivalent taxi ride. The trip takes 7 minutes, and a minibus transfers you free to your hotel or apartment. Monaco, unlike many resorts on the Côte d'Azur, has a **railway station**.

WHAT TO SEE IN MONACO/MONTE-CARLO

Automates et Poupées d'Autrefois, Musée National des (Museum of Automata and Dolls of Yesteryear)

Av. Princesse-Grace, Monte-Carlo ▉ 🍴 *available* ✸ *Open Oct–Mar 10am–12.15pm, 2.30–6.30pm; Apr–Sept 10am–6.30pm.*

This graceful little pink and white villa, built by Charles Garnier, architect of the Monte-Carlo Casino, contains one of the world's finest and largest collections of dolls, automata and mechanical toys. Sadly, they are set in motion only for groups, or when the museum is full. There are also some 2,000 miniature objects depicting life in the 18th and 19thC.

One striking exhibit is a huge 18thC Neapolitan crib with 300 figures.

Casino de Monte-Carlo ☆ ▥

Pl. du Casino ▉ ⚌ 🍴 *Public rooms open at noon, daily; private rooms at 3pm. Passports or identity papers must be shown by visitors.*

The world's most famous casino raises its four towers skyward between a formal garden full of tropical trees, and a terrace overlooking the sea. The building (illustrated on page 271) was designed by Charles Garnier, architect of several other Second Empire extravaganzas, including the Paris Opéra (now called the Opéra Garnier).

Even if you are not interested in gambling, it's worth going inside to see the sumptuous decor and recall the days of ostrich feathers and white tie and tails. In its heyday, in 1887, Charles Wells, an Englishman, became the "man who broke the bank at Monte-Carlo."

The Casino building also houses a small but highly ornate opera house, the **Salle Garnier**, where major productions are staged from time to time. Its grand outside entrance is reserved exclusively for the Prince, his family and their guests; the public enter through the casino lobby.

Centre d'Acclimatation Zoologique
Pl. du Canton, Monaco ■■ *Open Oct–Feb 10am–noon, 2–5pm; Mar–May 10am–noon, 2–6pm; June–Sept 9am–noon, 2–7pm.*
This is a rather cramped and crowded zoo, with elephants, lions, tigers, bright birds, gibbons, chimps, crocodiles and fish.

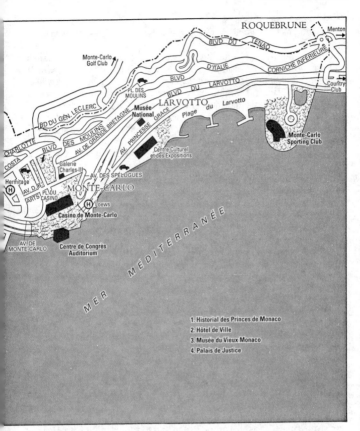

1. Historial des Princes de Monaco
2. Hôtel de Ville
3. Musée du Vieux Monaco
4. Palais de Justice

Jardin Exotique

Blvd. du Jardin Exotique, Moneghetti ☎ *Open 9am–6pm (7pm in summer).*

The garden, built on the cliffside at the w entry to Monaco, by the Middle Corniche, offers good views over the town, just below. The warm climate and damp conditions here are ideal for a wide variety of delicate tropical plants, and the garden contains some 1,000 different cacti, mostly from Africa and Latin America, many of them startlingly shaped; some are tall and triple-headed, like pagan totems; others resemble spiky soccer balls and are known as "mother-in-law's pillows."

The garden also contains the **Grottes de l'Observatoire**, which has caves full of stalactites and stalagmites, where Neolithic men once lived, and the **Musée d'Anthropologie Préhistorique**, which displays relics found in these caves and at the Red Rocks near Menton, as well as coins and other Roman remains.

Océanographique, Musée ☆

Av. St-Martin, Monaco ▨ ▨ ❋ *Open July–Aug 9am–9pm; Sept–June 9am or 9.30am–7pm.*

The finest museum of its kind in the world belongs to Monaco, thanks to Prince Albert I's passion for oceanography in the late 19thC, which he financed with the profits from the casino trade. He made 24 voyages in his luxury yachts, bringing back many rare species from the ocean beds. In 1910, the palatial museum was opened, built at the SE side of the headland. More recently it has been overseen by Commander Jacques Cousteau, the famous underwater explorer; his films are shown at regular intervals in the museum's cinema.

The aquarium is perhaps the best in Europe. Some 60 tanks contain a dazzling variety of fish, large and small, of every color imaginable, many with delicately patterned spots and stripes. The sea water is pumped up directly, through an elaborate system.

On the ground floor, a hall contains the skeletons of whales and other sea mammals. Upstairs is an elaborate display of marine technology, old and new, beautifully laid out: scientific instruments, and pictures and models of ocean beds.

The adjacent hall has a large array of seashells, some of them huge, and of objects made from the produce of the sea, from sharkskin bags and shoes to opera glasses encrusted with mother-of-pearl.

Palais du Prince and the Vieille Ville

Pl. du Palais, Monaco ▨ ✗ *available. Open June–Sept 9.30am–6.30pm; Oct 10am–5pm. Closed Nov–June.*

When the Prince is in residence (if he is, his flag will be flying), the palace is closed and visitors must content themselves with watching the changing of the guard *(daily at 11.55am),* in the paved square with views over the town and coast. Or they can visit the small **Musée Napoléon** in one wing of the palace, which contains souvenirs both of Napoléon's and of Monaco's history *(open until 6.30pm in summer, 5pm in winter, closed Mon).*

When the palace is open, visitors can see the fine 16thC arcaded courtyard; it leads to the Throne Room and to rooms hung with pictures by Brueghel, Holbein and others. Parts of the palace are 13th–16thC, but it was extensively rebuilt in the late 19thC, hence the mock-Moorish crenelated towers that were then in fashion.

Close by is the **cathedral**, also built using the casino profits, between 1875–1903, in ostentatious Neo-Romanesque style. The high altar and episcopal throne are of white marble, overlaid with mosaics. The building is on the site of a 13thC church, from which it has inherited two retables by Louis Bréa, and a *Pietà* over the sacristy door. The cathedral is also the burial place of the princes of Monaco, and the last resting place of Princess Grace.

The adjacent **Historial des Princes Wax Museum** *(27 rue Basse* ☎ *93-30-39-05)* offers panoramas of figures from Monaco's history. Move on to the **Monte-Carlo Story** *(Terrasse du Parking des Pêcheurs),* a newer multivision presentation. For something a little more old-fashioned, the **Musée du Vieux Monaco** *(rue Emile de Loth, open Wed 2.30-5.30pm)* is also near the Palace.

The Old Town *(Vieille Ville)* itself, with its narrow streets and pastel-colored houses, some of them very grand, certainly offers a contrast to Monte-Carlo's high-rises, even though the area is admittedly thronging with tourists, and full of tacky souvenir stores. It affords a pleasant walk, particularly in the evening, when a number of good and lively restaurants are in full swing.

For an idea of what Monte-Carlo must have been like before the high-rise buildings went up, visit the boulevard des Moulins, the main shopping street.

❧ WHERE TO STAY IN MONACO

ABELA

23 av. des Papalins, 98000 Monaco
☎92-05-90-00 📠92-05-91-67 ▥ to ▥
192 rooms ▦ ▣ ▣ ▣ ▣ ▣ ☎ ✚ ☐
▣ ♿ ☲ ▣ ▱ ▤

Location: In the Fontvieille area, near the Princess Grace rose garden. The Fontvieille district is rather like a high-rise Port-Grimaud — without the charm. But this hotel, under the same ownership as the Gray d'Albion in Cannes, is a good choice for families or for business trips, if you can see no clear reason to pay Monte-Carlo prices. You can be in the center of town in ten minutes by cab or using the free shuttle service. The hotel has comfortable, bright rooms, a nonsmoking floor, and special rooms and services for businesswomen traveling alone. There is a good brasserie, popular with locals, serving Lebanese specialities and typical French and Italian dishes. The swimming pool is shared with a neighboring apartment block.

BEACH PLAZA 🏨

22 av. Princesse-Grace, 98000 Monte-Carlo
☎93-30-98-80 📠93-50-23-14 ▥ *313 rms* ▦ ▣ ☲ ▣ ▣ ▣ ▣ ✚ ☐ ▱
☲ ◁ ☲ ☲ ☑ ☲ ▣ ☲ ▣ ♪

Location: On the beach of the Casino de Monte-Carlo, in the Larvotto district. This large, British-owned hotel (in the Forte group) is one of the two best for a beach vacation in the principality, and is particularly suitable for families. It lacks the *fin-de-siècle* majesty of the PARIS, or the HERMITAGE, but does have the advantage of a private beach, fine

sea views, and all the accompanying pleasures. But the imported sand is like gravel. The cheerful rooms have all been refurbished.

HERMITAGE 🏨 🏛

Sq. Beaumarchais, 98000 Monte-Carlo
☎93-50-67-31 📠93-50-82-06 ▥ *240 rms* ▦ ▣ ▣ ▣ ▣ ▣ ✚ ♿ ☐ ▱ ◁
☲ ☲ ☲ ☲ ☲ ☑ ▣ ☲ ☲ For ☲
see BELLE ÉPOQUE, overleaf.

Location: Near the Casino de Monte-Carlo, just above the harbor. A marvelous *Belle Époque* extravagance, this sumptuous palace was built in 1899 and has been stylishly renovated by its SBM owners. There are two entrances to the hotel, and its most famous feature is the winter garden lobby — designed by Gustave Eiffel — with its lofty domed ceiling of glass and its minty green decor. The bedrooms, alas, are no longer furnished in period, although they are undoubtedly very comfortable, with large marble bathrooms. *Fin-de-siècle* details can now only be seen in the restaurant and in one or two meeting rooms. This modernity is no doubt due to the demands of the conference trade. The most expensive rooms have views over the harbor. The piano bar was once Maria Callas' suite.

LOEWS 🏨

12 av. des Spélugues, 98000 Monte-Carlo
☎93-50-65-00 📠93-30-01-57 ▥ *650 rms* ▦ ▣ ☲ ▣ ▣ ▣ ▣ ✚ ☐ ♿ ▱
☲ ◁ ☲ ☲ ☲ ☲ ☲ ☲ ☑ ▣ ♪ ▣ ☲
Location: Built out over the sea on piles,

just below the Casino de Monte-Carlo and beside Les Spélugues, the conference center. Twice as large as any other hotel on the whole coast, Loews is a powerful symbol of the new Monte-Carlo. It is like an autarchic state-within-the-state, so wide is the range of its facilities and services: casino, six restaurants, five bars, shopping arcade, bank, congress hall, heated pool on the roof, sun terrace and health center. It's brash, efficient, airy and amusing. It provides a key vantage point during the Grand Prix (when prices soar), overlooking, as it does, an important hairpin bend. The hotel offers free excursions (with trilingual drivers) in its minibus.

MÉTROPOLE PALACE 🏨

4 av. de la Madone, 98000 Monte-Carlo
☎93-15-15-15 ⁑93-25-24-44 ▥ *170*
rms ▤ ▣ ▣ AE ▣ ▣ VISA ⁑ □ ▢ ⊄ ⌂
⌙ ▣

Location: Centrally located, near Blvd. des Moulins. This place, completely rebuilt on the site of an existing hotel, fulfills the dream of its Lebanese owner to own a grand hotel. It couldn't be much grander or more luxurious, from its huge, pastiche *Belle Époque* lobby, to its large, beautifully-appointed rooms, the best with sea views. Food, too, is given a high priority here, and the Métropole has two first-class restaurants, **Le Jardin** (only open for lunch) and **Les Ambassadeurs**. It is not a cheap hotel, but prices are somewhat lower than in most other top Monte-Carlo hotels. The Métropole has its own shopping arcade with 130 stores.

MIRABEAU 🏨

1 av. Princesse-Grace, 98000 Monte-Carlo
☎92-16-65-65 ⁑93-50-84-85 ▥ *103*
rms ▤ ▣ AE ▣ ▣ VISA ⁑ □ ▢ ⌂ ⌙
⊄ ▲ ⌀ ℘ ⁑/ ▽ ▣ ® *For* ⁑ *see* LA COUPOLE, *opposite.*

Location: Centrally located, near av. des Spélugues. A brightly-decorated modern hotel (part of a high-rise that includes apartments) with excellent amenities and a highly-regarded restaurant, LA COUPOLE, reputedly a favorite with Prince Rainier. The hotel is owned by the reclusive British Barclay brothers (who also own *The European* newspaper) but is run by the SBM.

MONTE-CARLO BEACH 🏨

St-Roman, 06190 Roquebrune-Cap-Martin
☎93-28-66-66 ⁑93-78-14-18 ▥ *46*
rms ▤ ▰ ⁑ AE ▣ ▣ VISA ⌂ ⁑ ⊄ □
▢ ⌙ ⊄ ⌀ ℘ ⁑ ▽ ⁑/ ▲ ▣ ▣
Closed mid-Oct to Mar.

Location: At the E end of Monte-Carlo, just inside France, by the beach. This hotel was built in 1928 as the Old Beach Hotel; the SBM gave it a complete facelift in 1993 — the second time in a decade — with bedrooms redecorated in cool pastel colors. Every room has a balcony just above the sea; try for the large circular one above the lobby, where Eva Perón stayed in 1947. This hotel has more charm than the vast complexes downtown, with the advantage of the **Monte-Carlo Beach** lido on its doorstep. It is a fashionable venue for a lunchtime buffet in summer, and the haunt of members of the royal family, and other local luminaries such as photographer Helmut Newton.

HÔTEL DE PARIS 🏨 🏛

Pl. du Casino, 98000 Monte-Carlo
☎92-16-30-00 ⁑93-15-90-30 ▥ *210*
rms ▤ ▰ AE ▣ ▣ VISA ⁑ □ ▢ ⌙
⊄ ⌀ ▲ ⁑/ ℘ ▽ ▣ ® *For* ⁑ *see*
LOUIS XV *and* LE GRILL DE L'HÔTEL DE PARIS,
opposite.

Location: Beside the Casino de Monte-Carlo, on the seafront. Opened in 1865 to house the kings, queens and grandees who flocked to the new Casino de Monte-Carlo, the Hôtel de Paris is still quite fashionable, although hardly as exclusive. Nowadays, flowery Bermuda shorts and track shoes clash merrily with the Neo-Baroque decor in the lobby. But the grand **American Bar**, open most of the night to accommodate celebrating winners (or losers drowning their sorrows) from the casino, is still a place to be seen, and the best suites are among the most glamorous anywhere. The now-famous Winston Churchill suite once housed the great statesman — as well as, later, Aristotle

Onassis and Frank Sinatra. The bronze equine statue in the lobby is traditionally touched for good luck before an evening at the tables — as you can tell by the fact that the horse's front leg is shinier than the rest of it. A garden fronts the sea, and a passageway leads direct to **Les Terrasses**, a bathing and health center that is free to residents.

Other recommended hotels: **Balmoral** *(13 av. de la Costa, 98000 Monte-Carlo* ☎*93-50-62-37* ▥▥ *to* ▥▥*),* traditional, family-run, with good views, is rather run-down but is being gradually restored; **Terminus** *(9 av. Prince-Pierre, 98000 Monaco* ☎*93-30-20-70* ▥▥*)* is modestly priced but comfortable.

☞ WHERE TO EAT IN MONACO

BELLE ÉPOQUE

Hôtel Hermitage, sq. Beaumarchais, Monte-Carlo ☎*93-50-67-31* ▥▥ ⃞ ▬ ☰ ⛽ ⟵ AE ⊡ ⊙ VISA *Last orders 10pm.*
Meals can be had on a spacious outdoor terrace, but for once in Provence it's more amusing to eat indoors, in the amazing Neo-Baroque banqueting room with its high frescoed ceiling and red-coated waiters. The restaurant serves ambitious and expensive *haute cuisine* with a delicate touch, and reasonably-priced set menus. *Specialities: Croustillant de saumon au poivre noir, filet d'agneau en éventail sauté a l'estragon.* (See ☜ HERMITAGE, above.)

CAFÉ DE PARIS

Pl. du Casino, Monte-Carlo ☎*93-50-57-75* ▥▥ ▦ ⃞ ▬ ⛽ ⟳ AE ⊡ ⊙ VISA *Last orders 3.30am.*
This totally rebuilt Monte-Carlo institution averages 1,000 meals a day (2,000 in summer, when the huge terrace is in use). Given the size of the task, service is surprisingly good, and the simple food is neither better nor worse than you might anticipate. Prices are fashionable although not unreasonable, given the location. Touristy it might be, but this café, with its green, *Belle Époque* decor, is still a people-watchers' paradise. It has its own small shopping arcade and, inevitably, a gaming room with slot machines.

LA COUPOLE

Hôtel Mirabeau, 1 av. Princesse-Grace, Monte-Carlo ☎*92-16-65-65* ▥▥ ▦ ⟵ ⃞ ▬ ⛽ AE ⊡ ⊙ VISA *Closed lunch July–Aug. Last orders 10pm.*

Although the hotel's star chef recently defected to the Métropole, his replacement still serves high-quality, if rather unexciting, food in a restful pink setting. *Specialities: Fricassée de cèpes et escalopine de foie gras chaud, poêlée de rougets aux tomates fraîches et basilic, poitrine de perdrix rôtie fumet au genièvre.* (See ☜ MIRABEAU, opposite.)

LE GRILL DE L'HÔTEL DE PARIS

Hôtel de Paris, pl. du Casino, Monte-Carlo ☎*92-16-30-02* ▥▥ *to* ▥▥ ⃞ ☰ ⛽ ⟵ AE ⊡ ⊙ VISA *Closed Mon; Dec. Last orders 10.30pm (summer 11pm).*
The main restaurant and banqueting hall, the fabulously ornate **Empire Room** with its great fresco across one wall, serves an unremarkable *haute cuisine.* Much more in vogue today — unless you feel like treating yourself to the Louis XV — is the smaller rooftop grill room with its sliding roof. *Specialities: Terrine de saumon au caviar, mille-feuille de moules et huîtres sauce poulette.* (See ☜ PARIS, opposite.)

LOUIS XV ☖ ⛫

Hôtel de Paris, pl. du Casino, Monte-Carlo ☎*92-16-30-01* ▥▥ ▦ ⟵ ⃞ ▬ ☰ AE ⊡ ⊙ VISA *Closed Wed (except dinner in summer); Tues; end Nov to Dec 21; mid-Feb to mid-Mar. Last orders 10.30pm.*
Alain Ducasse is one of the most celebrated chefs in France. His name, indeed, will evoke a smile of recognition among gastronomes world-wide. And, unsurprisingly, the prices and formality of his restaurant reflect the fact. But Ducasse, who trained with such names as Michel Guérard, Alain Chapel and

Roger Vergé, uses the very best fresh ingredients to produce a light, even simple, Mediterranean cuisine, with strong hints of both Provence and nearby Italy, which belies the gilded and chandeliered Neo-Baroque setting. *Specialities include: Petites tourtes de légumes, salade de fruits de mer tièdes, filet de rougets avec pommes nouvelles et courgettes à la purée d'olives, cannelloni au vert juste gratinés avec un sauté minute d'artichauts poivrade.* There are almost 300,000 bottles in the hotel's cellars. (See ✆ PARIS, on page 268.)

MAISON DU CAVIAR ♣
1 av. St-Charles, Monte-Carlo
☎93-30-80-06 ☐☐ ☐☐ ■■ ☐☐ *Closed Mon eve and Tues out of season; late June to late July.*

Don't be put off by the name. Yes, there is caviar on the menu (as there is in even the simplest of Monte-Carlo restaurants). This is a very good, family-run French restaurant that serves reasonably-priced food, and an extensive selection of openly-racked wines. The service is charming, and the atmosphere couldn't be friendlier. Many locals will tell you it's their favorite place.

SANTA LUCIA
11 av. des Spélugues, Monte-Carlo

☎93-50-96-77 ☐☐ ☐☐ ■■ ☐☐ ☐☐ ☐☐ *Last orders 1.30am.*

The relaxed and sociable ambience of an Italian inn makes this a popular dining place all year round. The wide-ranging menu includes some excellent fish dishes. There is a pianist most evenings.

➥ Some more moderately-priced restaurants: In Monaco: **Castelroc** *(pl. du Palais* ☎93-30-36-68 ☐☐*)*; not expensive, despite its superb location opposite the Palace. The menu includes Monegasque specialities. • **Le Texan** *(4 rue Suffren-Reymond* ☎93-30-34-54 ☐☐*)*; nobody really comes here for the food, which is average Tex-Mex/American, but it is known as a lively haunt of the *jeunesse d'orée* of Monaco. • **Pinocchio** *(30 rue Comte-Gastaldi* ☎93-30-96-20 ☐☐*)*.

In Monte-Carlo: **Polpetta** *(2 rue Paradis* ☎93-50-67-84 ☐☐*)*. • **Pulcinella** *(17 rue du Portier* ☎93-30-73-61 ☐☐*)*. • **Rampoldi** *(3 av. des Spélugues* ☎93-30-70-65 ☐☐ *to* ☐☐☐*)* is centrally located and one of the trendiest restaurants in town — although rather less fashionable than it was in the past.

In Fontvieille, on the port: **L'Offshore** *(22 quai des Sanbarbani* ☎92-05-90-99 ☐☐*)*.

⬛ NIGHTLIFE IN MONACO

Monte-Carlo at night is an incredible spectacle, with its floodlit gardens and squares, and its streets teeming with Rolls-Royces and Mercedes from which beautifully dressed women casually alight. Here, the nightlife industry is the most highly organized on the Côte d'Azur, with crowded gambling rooms, super-chic discos and lavish cabarets, as well as garish slot machines.

CASINO DE MONTE-CARLO
Pl. du Casino, Monte-Carlo ☎93-50-69-31 *(casino)* ☎93-50-80-80 *(cabaret)* ⬥ ☐ ⬛ ❀ ♫ ☘ *and revue. Public rooms open noon–2am. Private rooms open 3pm–4am. Cabaret open end Sept to end June; dinner-dance 9pm; floor show 10.30pm. Closed Tues.*

The *salles privées,* once reserved for high stakes and special players, are today no more private than the *salles publiques:* the entrance fee is the same,

but in the former, "proper dress" is required. People staying at SBM hotels are given a "gold card" allowing free access to the casino (as well as various other SBM facilities such as the **Monte-Carlo Golf and Country Clubs**). Some rooms have been turned over to gambling with American rules. Here the entrance is free, slot machines click and glitter, and most of the participants are dressed very casually. Security is tight everywhere, with video cameras and microphones artfully concealed at strategic points — "to avoid arguments," says the management.

The Casino de Monte-Carlo also contains an **Opera House**, the Salle Garnier, once one of the greatest in Europe; here Diaghilev created his *Ballets-Russes de Monte-Carlo*. Today the ballet company is no more, but there is still an opera company, which stages productions in winter and spring. More illustrious today is the **Monte-Carlo Philharmonic Orchestra**, and which gives concerts all year round in the Convention Center, and in summer in the Court of Honor at the Palace.

There are restaurants off both the private and public rooms (the very comfortable **Train Bleu**, off the public rooms, is open until 3am). And there is a large **nightclub** for dinner-dance and cabaret, a sumptuous room with red and black Naughty Nineties decor. It's enjoyable enough, if a little old-fashioned: the floor show tends to be better at LOEWS.

LOEWS HOTEL

Av. des Spélugues, Monte-Carlo
☎93-50-65-00 ⟵ ⋎ ⦿ 🞐 ⚘ ⋔ ⋎ *and revue. Casino open daily 5pm–4am. Folie-Russe dinner-dance 8.30pm; floor show 11pm; closed Mon. Jacket required.*
Just off the lobby of this enormous hotel is a **casino** with American gambling rules. Entrance is free and unrestricted, the ambience like that of Las Vegas. By contrast, the **dinner-dance/cabaret**, **La Folie-Russe**, is most sophisticated, with good acts and high-class dancing, set-design and lighting. The **Jockey Club** is a pleasant **bar** connected to the **Foie Gras** restaurant.

MONTE-CARLO SPORTING CLUB

Av. Princesse-Grace, Larvotto
☎93-30-71-71 ⋎ ⦿ 🞐 ⚘ ⋔ ⋎ *and revue. Sporting club open July to mid-Sept and on special occasions, e.g., the Grand Prix; Jimmy'z and Parady'z open from 11pm to dawn; Salle des Étoiles open from 9pm; casino open from 10pm.*
Monaco's temple to the night is misleadingly named, for there are no sports here. The luxurious complex is on a 14-acre stretch reclaimed from the sea, planted with trees and romantically lit. **Jimmy'z** is generally held to be the most fashionable discotheque on the Côte d'Azur; *le très beau monde* comes in force. Dress with chic if you want to be let in. **Parady'z**, the outdoor disco, which attracts younger people, and is open during the summer only, is due to move to a new site in 1994 or 1995.

La Salle des Étoiles, a huge hall with spectacular lighting and a roll-back roof, is used for nightly dinner-dance/cabarets. There are special galas on Friday, with evening dress much in evidence, and often an international star name on the bill. There's also a **casino** with nautical decor and both French and American gambling, an **outdoor movie house** and **Au Maona**, a venue for dinner-dances with tropical decor and cuisine.

🔊 Other popular nightspots are: **Le Café de Paris** (SEE RESTAURANTS). • **L'X Club** (*13 av. des Spélugues, open from*

11pm), for younger people. • **Tiffany's** (*3 av. des Spélugues, open from 11pm*). • **The Living Room** (*7 av. des Spélugues, from 11pm*), an enjoyable piano bar, with dancing. • **Tip-Top** (*11 av. des Spélugues*), a simple, inexpensive bar, serving snacks and open all night. • **Le Bistroquet** (*11 Galerie Charles-III*), a good bar/restaurant serving simple food until late.

SPORTS AND ACTIVITIES IN MONACO

The **Monte-Carlo Country Club** (☎93-78-20-45) has high-quality squash and tennis courts. Sailing lessons are given at the **Yacht Club de Monaco** (*quai Antoine-1ᵉʳ* ☎93-30-63-63) from July to August, and there are deep-sea fishing expeditions from July to October.

The **Monte-Carlo Golf Club** (☎93-41-09-11) has a fine 18-hole course high on the slopes of Mont Agel, over the border into France.

There are a number of companies offering boat trips or boats (of all sizes) for charter. Tourist flights by helicopter are also available, from **Héli Air Monaco** (☎93-30-80-88). The same helicopter company (there are also two others) can be used to get to and from Nice airport.

🏖 BEACHES/SWIMMING IN MONACO

Several new **beaches** have been created, by importing millions of tons of sand, and although the texture is still rather rough, it's better than gravel. There are no free beaches. The best-equipped beach complex is the **Monte-Carlo Beach** (*open Apr-Oct*), where jet-skiing, water-skiing, parasailing and windsurfing are possible. Also good: the **Beach Plaza Sea Club** (*open May-Sept*) and the **Plage du Larvotto** (*open May-Sept*).

The **Stade Nautique Rainier III** is an outdoor heated seawater swimming pool (*open May-Oct*). The **Prince Albert Nautical Center** in the Louis II Stadium, Fontvieille, has an indoor and an outdoor pool (*open Sept-July, closed Wed*).

Several large hotels, such as the MONTE-CARLO BEACH and the MIRABEAU, open their pools to the public for a fee. **The California Terrace** (a beauty center) has the best indoor seawater pool, with an open roof.

SHOPPING IN MONACO

Monte-Carlo is a shopper's paradise — at least if you are keen to spend a lot of money on high-ticket, big-name goods.

The area around the Casino is like a miniature Bond Street or Fifth Avenue. **Place du Casino**, **Avenue des Beaux-Arts** and **Avenue de Monte-Carlo** pack in most of the major luxury names for clothes, accessories and jewelry. There you will find YSL, Cartier, Bulgari, Dior, Vuitton, Chanel, Van Cleef and Arpels, Hermès, Valentino, and others.

The other main shopping areas are in and around the **Boulevard des Moulins** and **Rue Grimaldi**. Stores are generally open from 9am–noon and 3–7pm. Some stores close Saturday afternoon or Monday morning.

• See also: ÈZE, MENTON, ROQUEBRUNE-CAP-MARTIN, LA TURBIE.

MOUGINS

Maps 2D2 and 15F14 (Alpes-Mar.). 7km (4 miles) N of Cannes. Postal code: 06250. Population: 13,000 i av. Mallet ☎93-75-87-67.

This celebrated hill-village and surrounding countryside is today the fashionable garden-suburb of Cannes: the rich and famous have houses or villas here (the population has increased by more than one-third in the last decade), or come to play golf at the nearby Cannes Country Club, or to eat at one of Mougins' numerous quality restaurants. The village, with its narrow streets, is much restored and now very sophisticated, but it still keeps its charm. There is a 15thC fortified gate and the remains of ramparts; the tower of the Romanesque church affords the best panoramic view over this spectacular, if overbuilt, sector of the Côte d'Azur.

Just E of the village, up a narrow bumpy track E of the D3, the beautiful chapel of **Notre-Dame-de-Vie** stands alone on a hill beside an avenue of cypresses. The chapel, which was once a hermitage, has a 15thC stone cross, a 17thC porch, and Roman inscriptions. It is usually closed *(except for Mass at 11am on Sun),* but you can peep through the window at the fine Baroque altar and large 16thC gilded retable.

The nearby *mas* of Notre-Dame-de-Vie is the house where Picasso spent his final years and where he died. The town has a small but good **photographic museum** near the Porte Sarrasin *(☎93-75-85-67 ▨ open 1-7pm (2-11pm in July, Aug); closed Mon, Tues except July, Aug),* with a good permanent collection with works by Lartigue, Doisneau and Brassai, as well as temporary shows.

There is also a sleekly modern **automobile museum** off the A8 *(Aire des Bréguières ☎93-69-27-80 ▨ open Apr to end Sept daily 10am-7pm, Oct-Mar 10am-6pm).*

⌘ ≡ LE MAS CANDILLE ♦

Blvd. Rebuffel, 06250 Mougins
☎93-90-00-85 ▨92-92-85-56 ▥ to ▥
21 rms ▤ ⌨ AE ⊙ ⊚ VISA ⌂ ⌱ ✿
⟪ ≋ ⌁ ▣ *Closed Nov to early Dec.*
Location: On a wooded hillside, just w of the village. A 17thC white-walled farmhouse, lined by cypresses, is now an enchanting country hotel, offering civilized luxury at lower-than-average prices. The bedrooms are very pretty, many with 17thC beams, and there are wood fires in winter. This *auberge* remains refreshingly unpretentious. The dining room (♦) *(▥ to ▥ ⌱ ▦ ☗ ⌁ AE ⊙ VISA closed Thurs lunch; Wed; last orders 10pm)* is airy and elegant, but the hotel's best feature of all is the flower garden, where you can eat in fine weather overlooking the valley. Here there is a large, rustic candelabrum of red flickering candles, creating a romantic effect on summer evenings. The above-average food is good value.

≡ L'AMANDIER DE MOUGINS ♦

Pl. du Commandant-Lamy ☎93-90-00-91
▥ ▢ ▦ ≋ ☗ AE ⊙ VISA *Closed Wed; Sat lunch; early to mid-Feb. Last orders 10pm.*

Opened in 1977 by Roger Vergé, L'Amandier is a second outlet for the master-chef's style of cuisine, at prices less daunting than those of his mighty MOULIN DE MOUGINS. The restaurant is a converted 18thC mill, and the mill wheel still stands in the dim, low-ceilinged dining room. On fine days, make for the upstairs terrace with its far-reaching views. Service is cordial and unfussy but efficient, and chef Joel Manson's cooking deliciously light and varied. *Specialities: Terrine de filets de rougets de roche, papillote de langous-*

tines au foie gras, fricassée de poulet de Bresse et homard à l'estragon, suprême de loup de pays au beurre de basilic.

⊟ LE BISTROT DE MOUGINS ♣
Pl. du Village ☎ 93-75-78-34 ▯▢ ▮▬ ▣ ▨
Closed Tues; Wed (except dinner, July–Aug); Dec to late Jan. Last orders 10pm.

Alain Ballatoire and J.P. Giordano returned to their native Provence after working for ten years in New York. In their gaily decorated bistro, a 17thC vaulted cellar on the village square, they are proving that Mougins' gastronomic reputation does not have to equate with high prices; the set menu is excellent value. Service, always courteous, tends to become rather mechanical under pressure. *Specialities: Tourte aux blettes, timbale de morue, pieds et paquets, tarte aux figues.*

⊟ LA FERME DE MOUGINS
10 av. St-Basile ☎ 93-90-03-74 ▯▯ *to* ▯▯▯
▢ ▮▬ ⊟ 🖰 ▨ ⊙ ▣ ▨ *Closed Sun eve; Mon (except summer); Feb; mid-Nov to mid-Dec. Last orders 10pm (summer), 9.30pm (winter).*

It is most agreeable to eat on the wide, covered terrace overlooking a small swimming pool, and the cushioned chairs are delightfully comfortable. Service is thoughtful (shawls are provided when scantily-clad customers become chilly) and Jean-Louis Vosgien's food is imaginative, and very pleasantly light and tasty, with a slight Oriental influence. Good Provençal wines. *Specialities: Loup au sésame, rouleaux de boeuf aux épices, St-Pierre aux poireaux.*

⊟ ⊱ LE MOULIN DE MOUGINS ⌂
424 Chemin du Moulin (at Notre-Dame-de-Vie, 2½ km SE of Mougins, on the D3) ☎ 93-75-78-24 ▣ 93-90-18-55 ▯▯▯ ▢ ▮▬ ⊟ 🖰 ▥ ▬ 🖰 ⊙ ▣ ▨ *Closed Mon (except mid-July to end Aug); Thurs lunch; Feb to late Mar. Last orders 10.30pm.*

In France, a great chef is as celebrated and revered as a great actor or musician; Roger Vergé is among the elite, along with Paul Bocuse, Michel Guérard and a handful of others. He certainly looks the part: handsome, tall and silver-haired, he passes majestically at the end of the meal from table to table in his neat white robes, acknowledging the applause of his guests like an opera star taking a curtain call. A few disgruntled diners may whisper the heresy that possibly his is not the best restaurant in Provence, but such voices are still relatively rare, and his place in the firmament of star chefs remains secure.

In 1969, Vergé took over this 16thC olive-oil mill and, with his *cuisine du soleil*, has since built it up into the Côte's most fashionable eating place. Famous faces are often in evidence, as you eat from real Limoges porcelain, in the spacious and highly luxurious dining room, or under parasols in the garden. Vergé invents 50 new dishes each year and his menu changes frequently, but the sauces are always light and subtle, and the salads highly colored and unusually flavored. The cheeses, desserts and wines are all outstanding, with prices to match.

The friendly Vergé (his quite fluent English is the result of time spent in Kenya) also has a cookery school, a shop (see below) and a somewhat cheaper restaurant in town (see L'AMANDIER DE MOUGINS, on previous page). *Specialities: Poupeton de truffe noire de Valréas, fricassée de homard au sauternes, rougets de roche en croustillants de pommes, noisettes d'agneau à la fleur de thym.*

The restaurant has five sumptuous bedrooms (🛏) overlooking the gardens (▯▯▯ *to* ▯▯▯▯).

⊟ Another outstanding restaurant in Mougins is André Surmain's **Le Relais à Mougins** *(pl. de la Mairie* ☎ 93-90-03-47 ▯▯▯ *to* ▯▯▯▯*).*

SHOPPING IN MOUGINS
Roger Vergé's shop, the **Boutique du Moulin**, in the village square, sells many food and drink products bearing his name. Superb jams, liqueurs and sauces line the shelves.

• Mougins also has many small commercial art galleries.

PLACE NEAR MOUGINS

Castellaras *(5km/3 miles N of Mougins).* From afar this seems to be yet another old hill-village; in fact, it is a modern pastiche, the work of architect Jacques Couelle, who also designed Port-la-Galère at THÉOULE. He built the hill-crest "château" as a residence for a rich American in the 1920s. In the 1960s he added a group of unusual "sculpted houses," which blend harmoniously with the landscape.

Today, the complex is a luxury vacation village-cum-country club, and is strictly private. For information on renting a vacation villa, write to **Castellaras** *(06370 Mouans-Sartoux* ☎ *93-75-24-13).*

LA NAPOULE

Maps **2***E2 and* **15***G14 (Alpes-Mar.). 8km (5 miles) w of Cannes. Postal code: 06210 Mandelieu-La-Napoule. Population: 10,250* **i** *blvd. Henry-Clews* ☎*93-49-95-31.*

A thriving little seaside resort, close to the E foothills of the ESTEREL MASSIF. Long sandy beaches stretch around the Gulf of Napoule toward Cannes, and there is an excellent marina, golf course and casino.

Fondation Henry-Clews

▨ ✿ ✗ *available. For opening times* ☎*93-49-95-05.*

La Napoule's harbor is dominated by a great medieval castle, floodlit a lurid orange at night. It was purchased in 1917 by the eccentric American sculptor Henry Clews, heir of a banking family, who extensively restored it, lived and worked there, and was buried there on his death in 1937.

Today, part of the château is a museum of his work: his dullish paintings, and his sculptured grotesques of animals, birds and gnarled, naked human figures. They were inspired, so it is said, by pre-Columbian, African and medieval carvings. Even if you do not care for the sculptures, you will probably enjoy the gardens, with their views of sea and hills.

✍ Recommended hotels for a seaside vacation: **Ermitage de Riou** (▥) *(av. Henry-Cleus* ☎*93-49-95-56* [Fx]*92-97-69-05* ▦*);* **Parisiana** *(5 rue de l'Argentière* ☎*93-49-93-02* ▥*).*

➤ **L'OASIS** ⌂
Rue Jean-Honoré Carle ☎*93-49-95-52* ▦
▢ ▰ ⬛ ⬢ ▦ ▥ ⊙ ◉ ▨ *Closed Sun eve; Mon; lunch from mid-July to early Sept; mid-Nov to early Dec; early to mid-Mar. Last orders 9.30pm.*
By common consent for a couple of decades, this was one of the finest restaurants in Provence and indeed in France. Louis Outhier, *patron* and chef, was a disciple of the great Fernand Point of La Pyramide at Vienne; he followed in the master's steps with a repertoire that balanced classic dishes with his own inventions. Later, he flirted with *nouvelle cuisine,* while avoiding its sillier excesses. Outhier, much more diffident than most of the jet-setting top French chefs, built up his restaurant from a humble *pension.* Then, in the mid-1980s, he surprised everybody by announcing his retirement, and the closure of his restaurant caused consternation throughout France. But in 1991, to

the relief of gastronomes everywhere, he opened up again, no longer chef (that task falls to Stéphane Raimbault), but still *patron*. And today, the cooking at his low white villa (converted into a series of small, rather formal dining rooms with discreet pink–orange decor) is almost back to its previous adventurous standard. Nicest is the ravishing flower-filled patio with its tall palm tree (hence the restaurant's name). Service is as stylish as you would expect. *Specialities: Salade des pâtes fraîches safranées aux palourdes, langouste aux herbes, risotto de pageot aux fruits de mer.*

PLACES NEAR LA NAPOULE

La Napoule is the seaside suburb of the unlovely town of **Mandelieu**, just inland to the N, beside a sprawling modern road intersection. By contrast, the narrow D92, leading W out of town, climbs up through mimosa forests to the nearby heights of the wild **massif du Tanneron** and its wide views over the coast and the mountains behind Grasse.

- See also: MOUGINS, THÉOULE.

NICE ★

Maps 3C4 and 15E15 (Alpes-Mar.). 188km (117 miles) NE of Marseille. Postal code: 06000. Population: 342,500 **i** *av. Thiers* ☎93-87-07-07, *and 5 av. Gustave-V* ☎93-87-60-60. **Airport:** *Nice-Côte d'Azur, 7km (4 miles) W of central Nice* ☎93-21-30-30. **Railway station:** *av. Thiers* ☎93-87-50-50.

The Côte d'Azur's capital is more than simply the doyen of Europe's seaside resorts. It is also a large commercial city, excitingly diverse, at once earthy and sophisticated, whose own busy life throbs on throughout the year, irrespective of tourists.

The city extends along the silver shore of the Baie des Anges, sheltered by the curve of hills rising steeply behind. It is in two contrasting parts. To the E of the Paillon riverbed are the port and the shadowy twisting alleys of the Old Town, crowned by the rocky hill where the castle stood.

To the W of the Paillon area is the "new" post-17thC town, and the mighty Promenade des Anglais with its palace-hotels and palm trees. Here in modern Nice, all is chic and glitter, a blend of French elegance and Mediterranean sensuality. Life is lived late, and outdoors.

This is no place for a sea-swimming vacation, for the beach is gravel, but for those who are lured by the attractions of a big town, Nice is enormous fun. All year, it offers a lively parade of high-quality entertainments — opera, art exhibitions, sporting events, festivals and shows of every kind from books to dogs, culminating in the famous Lenten Carnival and the Battle of the Flowers.

Greeks from Marseille founded Nice in the 4thC BC, and gave it the name Nikêa (from *Niké*, their goddess of victory) to mark a defeat of local tribesmen. Later came the Romans, who built a major town on the hill at Cimiez (now part of the northern suburbs). Cimiez was then ruined by Saracen and Barbarian invasions. After the 10thC, Nice began to flourish, first under the counts of Provence, then (after 1388) under the Italian house of Savoy. Between about 1450 and 1550, it was the center of a notable school of religious painting, led by the Bréa family, much of whose work can still be seen in the region.

In 1631, Nice suffered a fearful plague, and in 1792–96 it was the scene of much toing-and-froing by the armies of Napoléon Bonaparte. The city remained under Savoy rule until 1860, when it was finally annexed to France.

By this time, Nice was a thriving seaside resort, thanks largely to the English, who had begun to winter here from the late 18thC, following the example set by the novelist Tobias Smollett in 1763. As a resort, Nice was established long before CANNES or MENTON. In 1822, the thriving English colony, frustrated by the difficult access to the shore, constructed a coastal path, which became the great promenade that still bears their name.

After the arrival of the railway in 1864, the tourist boom gathered pace: British, Russian and other aristocrats poured in for every winter season, led by Queen Victoria. The Russians built their splendid cathedral, while smart hotels sprang up all along the front, with names like Westminster and West End.

Today, echoes of that glory still linger: heads of state still come to stay at the Negresco. But some of the other great hotels, such as the Ruhl, have gone or have been turned into apartments. Nice has bowed to the need to broaden its tourist appeal since the days of the *Belle Époque:* it still has its luxury hotels, of course, but now they cater more to the conference trade and package tours than to duchesses and movie stars.

As in other big French cities, the mayor wields great power, and from 1928 until 1989, Nice was ruled by a kind of elective dynasty, the right-wing Médecin family. Jean Médecin had been mayor for 37 years on his death in 1965. His son Jacques took his place, and was re-elected for further 6-year terms in 1971, 1977 and 1983. His authoritarian style was much criticized; yet few would deny that he did much to modernize and revitalize the city.

Nice today has various light industries, a new university with 15,000 students, and France's busiest international airport outside Paris. M. Médecin was responsible for the building of numerous road tunnels and underground parking garages, to cope with the very dense traffic, and an elegant pedestrian zone was created in the heart of the modern town at rue de France, near the sea.

Médecin fled to Uruguay in 1990, accused of filtering off as much as 340 million francs in public funds from the Nice opera and other developments. By then, his tax affairs had already come under scrutiny.

But he left behind further monuments to his rule, including the MUSÉE D'ART MODERNE ET CONTEMPORAIN, a new theater, and the vast, ugly and controversial Acropolis conference center development. Médecin's links with organized crime were highlighted by Graham Greene in his 1982 pamphlet *J'Accuse.* Médecin was unashamedly right-wing, twinning Nice with Cape Town at a time when apartheid was at its height. It is not surprising, then, that Nice became a center of Front National activity; or that the city is known for corruption and crime gangs.

However, visitors have little to worry about, provided they act with the caution advisable in any big city, and keep an eye open for the biggest problem: pickpockets and bag-snatchers.

Nice is highly cosmopolitan: people come from all over the world, to visit or retire. But it is still dominated by its true inhabitants, the Niçois. Like most meridionals, they are at once easygoing and volatile — quick to pick a quarrel, just as quick to patch it up over a drink. Like Parisians, they can be brusque at first, but it's not hard, if you make the effort, to make them smile. Above all, though, unlike much of the rest of the Côte d'Azur, Nice is a great and bustling city, with a life and character all its own.

TRANSPORT IN NICE

There is a good and cheap **bus service** from the airport to Nice, going along Promenade des Anglais. The town's bus services are generally very good, with flat fares (you can either pay on the bus, or buy a book of tickets from a *tabac*), and well worth using, given the high **taxi fares** in the city.

The local **SNCF train service**, running between St-Raphael and Ventimiglia, is cheap, fast and efficient, and recommended unless you insist on driving. There is a non-SNCF train service, the **Chemin de Fer de Provence** *(4bis rue Alfred-Binet* ☎ *93-88-28-56 or 93-82-10-17)*, running the picturesque route northward to DIGNE.

Long-distance trains come into **Gare Nice-Ville** at av. Thiers *(☎ 93-87-50-50)*.

NICE'S CUISINE

Food in Nice has a strong Italian accent (pasta, for example, is found on most menus), and garlic, olives and olive oil are important ingredients, as well as basil and pine nuts (as found in *soupe au pistou*). Swiss chard is another common ingredient.

Typical dishes include *estoficada* (stockfish stew), *omelette à la poutine* (including small sardines and anchovies), *favouille* soup (made with tiny crabs), *trucha* (an omelet containing spinach), and *socca* (a flat cake made of chickpea flour, and fried in oil). *Boeuf à la niçoise* comes with tomatoes and olives. *Rouget à la niçoise* (red mullet) is cooked with tomato and garnished with anchovy, and lamb *à la niçoise* is cooked with zucchini (courgettes), tomatoes and small new potatoes.

The anchovy *(anchois)* is another much-used local ingredient, found, of course, in the famous *salade niçoise*. As with *bouillabaisse*, arguments rage about what a real *salade niçoise* should contain, but tomatoes, anchovy fillets (or tuna, or both), olives, onions, green beans and hard-boiled eggs are pretty well essential. Some chefs add artichokes. Others add green peppers, cucumber and lettuce. Potatoes, although often found in *salade niçoise*, and cooked vegetables of any sort, displease the purists.

Nice is a fine place for interesting snacks, including *pan-bagnat* (which is essentially a *salade niçoise* sandwich) and *fougassette* (a pastry made of *brioche* dough, and usually flavored with orange water, although sometimes it is found in savory versions). *Pissaladière* is a tart, not unlike pizza, baked with a topping of onions, olives and anchovies. It is usually coated with *pissalat*, an anchovy and herb purée, before being baked.

- **EVENTS** • In February, the **carnival**, an amazing spectacle of floats and flowers, occupies the two weeks preceding Lent, culminating in a **firework display** on Shrove Tuesday. • There is also a **festival of contemporary music**. • In March there is a **festival of film music**. • The main **Battle of the Flowers** is on the day after Ash Wednesday, on quai des États-Unis. (There are other flower battles during the summer.) • In April, there is a **tennis tournament** and a **marathon**. • In May, the **Fête des Maïs** is held every Sunday in the Cimiez Gardens. • There is also a **folklore festival** and an **automobile show**. • In June, there is a **music festival**. • In July, the **Grand Jazz Parade** takes place in Cimiez Gardens, one of Europe's foremost jazz festivals, attracting the biggest names. • There is also an international **folklore festival**. • In August, there is a **flower battle**. • In September, a **wine festival** takes place in Cimiez Gardens.
- The main newspaper is *Nice Matin*. The listings magazine *7 Jours 7 Nuits* is free, but for *La Semaine des Spectacles* you must pay.

WHAT TO SEE IN NICE
Anatole Jakovsky, Musée
Château Ste-Hélène, av. Val-Marie ☎ *93-71-78-33* ▣ *Open 10am–noon, 2–6pm (5pm winter). Closed Tues.*
Situated in the western suburb of Fabron, this museum of Naïve art is housed in a 19thC villa once belonging to François Blanc, founder of the Monte-Carlo casino. The museum opened in 1982, after the building was sold to the city by the heirs to the Coty perfume empire. Named after the art critic and Naïve painter Anatole Jakovsky, who donated his collection to it, the museum contains over 600 Naïve paintings from the 18thC to the present day.

Archéologie, Musée d'
160 av. des Arènes, Cimiez (access via av. Monte-Croce) ☎ *93-81-59-57* ▣ *Open 10am–noon, 2–6pm (5pm winter). Closed Sun am; Mon; Nov.*
A relatively new museum opened in 1989, on the western border of the Roman site at CIMIEZ *(times apply both to site and museum)*. It contains pottery, jewelry, statuary and sarcophagi found on the adjacent Roman site, and uses the latest audiovisual and display techniques.

Many of the exhibits were formerly housed in the Musée Matisse, nearby.

Art Moderne et d'Art Contemporain, Musée d' (MAMAC)
Promenade des Arts ☎ *93-62-61-62* ▣ *Open 11am–6pm (to 10pm Fri). Closed Tues.*
Opened in 1990, the museum (part of an arts complex that includes a new theater) is probably more interesting for its striking marble, steel and glass architecture than its collection. Designed by Yves Bayard and Henri Vidal, the museum, built as four towers connected by bridges, has a vast floor space. However, its opening was marred because of a boycott by culture minister Jack Lang and the French art establishment, in the wake of the scandal surrounding Jacques Médecin, whose pet project this was.

But the building is sparsely populated by works of art. The pop art collection is fairly interesting, and includes works by Warhol, Rauschenberg, Lichtenstein, Jim Dine and Claes Oldenburg. And there is work by modern Nice painters such as Yves Klein. But most of the contemporary work is less than first-rate. The museum also houses temporary exhibitions.

The roof terrace and its walkways give a good, if somewhat interrupted, view of Nice. There is also a lively café (see page 289), a stand selling classic items of modern design, and a decent bookstore.

Chagall, Marc, Musée National ★

Av. Docteur-Ménard ☎ *93-81-75-75* ▨ ✗ *available. Open July–Sept, 10am–7pm; Oct–June 10am–12.20pm, 2–5.20pm. Closed Tues.*

For Chagall-lovers, this museum is a sublime treat. Opened in 1973, it houses the world's fullest collection of the artist's work. It was built specially for his suite of 17 large canvases, the *Biblical Message*, painted over 13 years between 1954–67 when he was already an old man (he was born in Russia in 1887). In one large gallery, 12 of these paintings evoke the Creation, the Garden of Eden, the Ark, Abraham, Moses, and other biblical themes. In another, the Song of Songs is the inspiration for a five-part poetic series. Chagall uses bold, sensuous colors, combined with his visions of ingenuous fantasy, to convey the force of his spiritual and humanistic beliefs, based on his Jewish faith. The result is a stunning combination of lyricism and seriousness of subject.

The museum has much else, too, by Chagall. Outside, a large mosaic showing the prophet Elias rising to heaven in a chariot of fire; in the lobby, a multicolored tapestry; in other rooms, numerous drawings, gouaches and sculptures. The graceful music room (where concerts are held each month in summer) is bathed in a deep blue light from Chagall's vivid stained-glass windows depicting the Creation.

The grand old man lived at ST-PAUL-DE-VENCE until his death in 1985 at the age of 97.

Château

Approach from the far E end of quai des États-Unis. Ascend to the castle either by 400 steps or by elevator (ascenseur).

A rocky promontory, 93 meters (280 feet) high, forms a neat backdrop to Promenade des Anglais. Here, the early Greeks set their acropolis, and the dukes of Savoy later built their castle. This was destroyed in 1706, on the orders of Louis XIV, by Marshal de Berwick (the illegitimate son of James II of England), who became a naturalized Frenchman and commander in the French armies. Today the site is a public garden, planted with trees, but it is still known as the Château.

On the sw side of the hill *(use the same elevator)* is the **Musée Naval** in the Tour Bellanda (☎ *93-80-47-61* ▨ *open 10am-noon, 2-5pm Oct to May; 2-7pm June–Sept; closed Tues, mid-Nov to mid-Dec)*, where there are collections of historic weapons, models of old warships, and paintings of 19thC Nice. To the E of the Château is Nice's harbor, **Port Lympia**, built in 1750 and since extended. The harbor is crammed with fishing smacks and pleasure boats, and it is here that the ferries leave for Corsica.

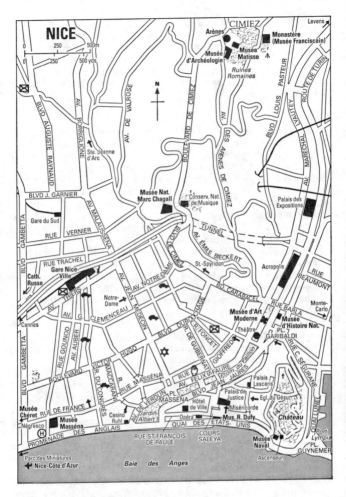

Chéret (des Beaux Arts), Musée ☆
33 av. des Baumettes ☎ 93-44-50-72 📷 🚫 *Open May–Sept 10am–noon, 3–6pm; Oct–Apr 10am–noon, 2–5pm. Closed Mon.*

This is Nice's main museum of art, built in 1876 as a private mansion. It houses works ranging from Italian and Flemish primitives through to paintings by Braque and ceramics by Picasso. The Van Loo family, who worked in the area, are very well represented, as is Carpeaux, who died in Nice. It has an interesting collection of the works of Ziem, whose paintings, in some ways, are reminiscent of Turner's. There are also works by Fragonard and by the Impressionists Monet, Sisley and Renoir, including Renoir's *Les Grandes Baigneuses,* and other 19thC paintings.

There are also examples of the St-Tropez school, notably by Signac, a couple of Dufys and pictures by Van Dongen. This varied collection also includes Orientalist art, and sculpture by Rodin among others. The works of Jules Chéret, after whom the museum is named, could be described as sugar-candy-sweet.

Cimiez

The hill of Cimiez in the N suburbs, with its big villas and gardens, was once the smart residential district of Nice. At the top of Boulevard de Cimiez there looms a titanic monstrosity in the rococo style of the late 19thC: the former hotel Regina where Queen Victoria used to winter. Today it is an apartment block, and shows few traces of its former glory.

Just to the E lies the **Roman settlement** of Cimiez (🕮 𝄃 *available),* which was excavated in the early 1980s. It includes a small amphitheater and the remains of 3rdC Roman baths; the 10-meter (33-foot) hunk of masonry is what is left of the Temple of Apollo. This area is now a public park, often used for festivals.

On its E side stands a **former monastic church,** 16thC with later additions: the *trompe l'oeil* is pure 19thC Gothic, but inside (in the first chapel on the right, the last chapel on the right up the nave and the chapel opposite) you will find three of the Bréa family's finest paintings on wood.

These sights are worth a visit, but Cimiez's foremost attraction is its MUSÉE MATISSE (see below).

Masséna, Musée (Musée d'Art et d'Histoire)
65 rue de France ☎ *93-88-11-34* 🔲 ✎ *Open 10am–noon, 2–5pm (winter); 10am–noon, 3–6pm (summer). Closed Mon; Nov.*

The imposing palace in which the museum is housed was built in the 1890s by the great-grandson of Marshal Masséna, Prince of Essling, son of an innkeeper at nearby Levens. Masséna, who was one of Napoléon's greatest marshals, is one of Nice's foremost sons — another, equally renowned, is Garibaldi — and there are memories of them both in the museum.

The palace now belongs to the Ville de Nice, and its fine Empire-style rooms on the ground floor are used for civic receptions. Upstairs are some Bréa and Durandi primitives, as well as collections of Oriental jewelry, pottery, armor, and artifacts illustrating local folklore and customs. Especially interesting are the rooms devoted to Nice's history: early pictures of the city, souvenirs of Napoléon, Masséna, Garibaldi, the 1860 plebiscite and the Carnival.

Matisse, Musée ☆
164 av. des Arènes-de-Cimiez ☎ *93-53-17-71* 🔲 ✎ 𝄃 *available. Open May–Sept 10am–noon, 2.30–6.30pm; Oct–Apr 10am–noon, 2–5pm. Closed Sun; Mon in Nov.*

Henri Matisse lived and worked for much of his life in Nice and Cimiez until his death there in 1954. He lies buried in the nearby cemetery.

The museum's collection spans his working life: 30 paintings, ranging from his sober early period, through the influence of the Impressionists, to the bright colors and simple shapes of his maturity, as in *Nature Morte aux Grenades* (1947). There are also many of his drawings, and engravings, sculptures and book illustrations. His sketches and models for the **Chapelle du Rosaire** at VENCE are contained in two rooms, and spread about the museum is a collection of his furniture and personal effects.

The museum also acts as a cultural center and mounts temporary thematic modern art exhibitions. It was extended, restored, and the exhibits rearranged in the early 1990s. The archeological collection that was once housed here has moved to the nearby MUSÉE D'ARCHÉOLOGIE.

Orthodoxe Russe, Cathédrale 血 ✝

Blvd. du Tzarevitch ▆▆ ✗ ✗ *available. Open 9.30am–noon, 2.30–6pm. Closed Sun morning.*

Nice's formerly large Russian colony may be dying out, but you can still hear plenty of Russian voices at its fine cathedral in the w suburbs, built in 1903. Its sumptuous exterior, with five bulbous green-gold cupolas, is matched by its interior, where rich ikons adorn the altar.

Parc des Miniatures ✽

Blvd. Impératrice Eugénie ☎ 93-44-67-74 ▆▆ ✽ *Open 9.30am–sunset.*

A sort of theme park, opened to the w of town in 1989; it celebrates the development of Nice and the Côte d'Azur, using scale models. Rather fun, for both adults and children.

Parc Phoenix

405 promenade des Anglais, opposite the airport ☎ 93-18-03-33 ▆▆ *Open 10am–sunset. Closed Mon.*

This large park on the w outskirts of Nice has a number of things to see, including aviaries and an artificial lake. Of special interest is a huge greenhouse (25m/82ft high); it houses seven zones containing a total of 2,500 different tropical and subtropical specimens.

Raoul-Dufy, Musée

77 quai des États-Unis ☎ 93-62-31-24 ▣ *Open 10.30am–noon, 2–6pm. Closed Sun am; Mon.*

The museum houses a superb collection of the works of Raoul Dufy, who captured the sparkle of the Riviera with his gay and witty paintings. The collection, donated by his widow and formerly housed in the Musée Chéret, includes 28 paintings, 87 drawings and much other work. Temporary exhibitions are also held here.

Vieille Ville (Old Town)

This triangle, bordered by the CHÂTEAU, the sea, and the open space of Jardin Albert 1er (the covered mouth of the Paillon River), makes a startling and delightful contrast to sophisticated modern Nice.

The Old Town can itself be divided into two parts: the 17thC quarter by the sea, with its orderly grid of streets; and, to the N, the older part, a maze of narrow alleys, full of little shops and bistros, teeming with its own noisy plebeian life. It is very Italian — you could well be in the back streets of Genoa — and bears witness to Nice's long past as part of Italy. Today it is being restored: its facades are being repainted in the traditional ocher colors, and artists and artisans are settling there.

A stroll through the Old Town could begin with the **Palais Lascaris** *(rue Droite* ☎ *93-62-05-54* ▣ ✗ *available, open 9.30am-noon, 2.30-6pm, closed Mon, Nov),* a sumptuous 17thC Genoese-style mansion, finely restored and decked out with period furniture, paintings and tapestries. To the NE of the Palace is a statue to Catherine Ségurane, the Niçoise folk-heroine who, dagger in hand, bravely repulsed the Turkish besiegers in 1543 — or so it is said. To the S of the Palace are some of the fine 17th and 18thC Italian Baroque churches, notably the **Chapelle de la Miséricorde** *(Cours Saleya)* and the **Église du Gésu** *(rue Droite).*

Visit, too, the **Opéra** *(rue St-François-de-Paule* ☎ *93-85-67-31);* the **Galerie de Malacologie** *(▣ 3 Cours Saleya* ☎ *93-85-18-44, open 10.30am-1pm, 2-6pm, until 6.30pm in summer, closed Sun, Mon, Nov),* with its remarkable collection of mollusks; and the markets in **Cours Saleya**, home of the world-famous flower market *(every day except Mon, although the wholesale market has moved).* Cours Saleya was once a meeting place for Nice's high society, and it is still lively, full of small restaurants and cafés. In his old age, Matisse lived in the yellow house in the tiny place Charles-Félix at its E end.

Just a little N of the Old Town is the ambitious **Musée d'Histoire Naturelle** *(60 blvd. de Risso* ☎ *93-55-15-24* ▣ *open 9am-noon, 2-6pm, closed Tues, mid-Aug to mid-Sept),* which includes aquariums full of exotic fish.

Ville Moderne

The *Ville Moderne* is modern only in a relative sense, as many of the buildings in this area date from the early 19thC.

Place Masséna is the hub of modern Nice: its imposing arcaded houses were built in the 1830s, in 17thC Genoese style. To the w, busy rue Masséna and a few adjoining streets have been pedestrianized, with the addition of fountains and flowerpots. With its many smart boutiques, open at night, and its sidewalk cafés and pizzerias, the area attracts the *beau monde*: shopping or window-shopping, meeting friends or just strolling by. To the sw, by the sea, is the elegant **Jardin Albert-1er**, where there is an open-air theater in summer.

Westward from there sweeps **Promenade des Anglais**, built by the expatriate English in 1822 to ease their passage to the sea. It is a major artery, as well as a place to stroll, and is nowadays strident with traffic, and has become upstaged by rue Masséna as the place for strollers to be seen. But the sea breezes and the palm trees still attract their crowds.

To the NE of place Masséna runs the line of boulevards that cover the enclosed River Paillon, the site of several recent developments. First the so-called "promenade des Arts," which contains the new MUSÉE D'ART MODERNE ET CONTEMPORAIN and the new theater, then the massive high-tech and fancifully-named **Acropolis** convention and arts center. Then, a mile to the NE up the Paillon valley, is the impressive but scarcely lovely exhibitions center (**Palais des Expositions**). All these are testaments to Jacques Médecin's grand plans for the city in the 1980s.

☞ WHERE TO STAY IN NICE

ALFA

30 rue Masséna, 06000 Nice ☎*93-87-88-63* ✉*93-88-17-30* ▯ to ▯ *42 rms* ▤ ▨◉◉◫ ♣▢▱

Location: Centrally positioned close to the sea, on the attractive and traffic-free rue Masséna. A small, modernized hotel, friendly and efficiently run. Although it's in the pedestrian zone, you can get the car to within 75 meters (80 yards) to unload baggage.

ASTON

12 av. Félix-Faure, 06000 Nice ☎*93-80-62-52* ✉*93-80-40-02* ▯ *156 rms* ▤ ▨⊒▨◉◉◫ ♣▱▢▱❦ ⟨⟨ ★▤

Location: Central, very near place Masséna and the Vieille Ville. The most pleasing feature of this large, modern hotel is the wide rooftop terrace, with deck chairs, parasols and panoramic views; buffet lunches are served in summer. Apart from this, it's not a hotel of any great character, although it has every comfort.

ÉLYSÉE PALACE

59 promenade des Anglais, 06000 Nice ☎*93-86-06-06* ✉*93-44-50-40* ▯ *150 rms* ▤▱⊒▨⟨⟨ ❦❦ ♈ ▨ ▱▱❦❧ ▣⊒▤

Location: Not far from the Jardin Albert 1ᵉʳ. You might consider this modern hotel, opened in 1988, rather vulgar and flashy; or you might consider that with its very good location, comfortable rooms with marble bathrooms, and rooftop swimming pool, it delivers high standards of comfort at competitive prices.

LE GOURMET LORRAIN ♣

7 av. Santa-Fior, 06100 Nice ☎*93-84-90-78* ✉*92-09-11-25* ▯ *11 rms* ▤ ▨ ◉◉◫ ▱▢▱❦ ❦ for children. For ⊒ see page 288.

Location: 2 kilometers (1 mile) N of the main railway station, in a side street in the N suburbs. Most unusual for Nice, this small hotel on the outskirts seems more like a rural inn. It is run in a personal style by the charming owners, the Leloups (he from Lorraine, she from Dunkerque). "We try to create a family party spirit, encouraging our guests to get to know one another," they say — and they succeed, without overdoing it.

MÉRIDIEN

1 promenade des Anglais, 06000 Nice ☎*93-82-25-25* ✉*93-16-08-90* ▯ to ▯ *314 rms* ▤⊒♣▱▢▱❦ ⟨⟨ ★▱ ❧ ❦ ❦ ▢▱❦

Location: Toward the w end of Promenade des Anglais. This modern hotel with a lively atmosphere is one of the best-located and equipped in Nice. The rooftop swimming pool and health club are special attractions. There is a piano bar, and outdoor dining in the summer.

NEGRESCO ♨ ▥

37 promenade des Anglais, 06000 Nice ☎*93-88-39-51* ✉*93-88-35-68* ▯ *150 rms* ▤▤ ▱▨▨◉◉◫▱♣▱▢▱ ⟨⟨ ❦ ★❦ ❧ ▣❦ For ⊒ see

CHANTECLER, page 288.

Location: Halfway along Promenade des Anglais. This vast white wedding-cake palace, a symbol of Nice and one of the world's most famous hotels, has been classified a *monument historique* by the French government: deservedly so, for its owners (who live in the hotel) have been careful to restore it to the 1912 style in which it was conceived. In this temple to *Belle Époque* grandeur, the bellboys still wear red breeches and white gloves. The huge circular **salon royal** is the setting for a Baccarat chandelier that was made for the Czar — and for 600 square meters (720 square yards) of Aubusson carpet.

The hotel actually halved its capacity in the 1930s (part of the building is now given over to apartments), but the lobby area remains that of the grandest of hotels. Works of art by Picasso, Léger and Cocteau (who once said: "The Negresco is to Nice what the Eiffel Tower is to Paris") adorn the walls; even the ground-floor rest-rooms, theatrical and witty, are worth a look. Upstairs, the sumptuous bedrooms are in varied styles: Chinese, Medieval, Louis XIV, Empire, and Napoléon III. It hardly needs saying that comfort and service are beyond reproach; but they are also, notably, friendly and helpful — a tribute to the hotel's dedicated and charming general manager, Michel Palmer. There is live music in the bar, which is a popular meeting place.

Across the years, practically anyone who was anyone has stayed at the Negresco, including countless movie stars and many reigning monarchs. Today the hotel still attracts many of the world's top names in the arts and politics. In 1980 the then President Giscard d'Estaing stayed here with 27 African heads of state. Andrew Lloyd-Webber composed part of *Cats* here, on a grand piano in one of the meeting rooms. The 1990s may be a far cry from 1912, but the Negresco could convince you that little has changed.

NOUVEL HÔTEL

19 blvd. Victor-Hugo, 06000 Nice
☎93-87-15-00 ⊠93-16-00-67 ▥ to ▥
60 rms ▤ ㏂ ▣ ▣ ▥ ‡ ▢ ▱
Location: Not far from place Masséna and Promenade des Anglais; entrance next door to the Banque de Rothschild. This is recommended among the many moderately-priced hotels in Nice. Situated in a tree-lined street, the hotel is in an old, typically French town block, where the rooms have high ceilings and tall, shuttered glass doors. The interior is not very modern, but it has character and is comfortable and friendly.

LA PÉROUSE

11 quai Rauba-Capeu, 06300 Nice
☎93-62-34-63 ⊠93-62-59-41 ▥ to ▥
65 rms ▤ ㏂ ▣ ▣ ▣ ▥ ⌂ ‡ ▢ ▱
▨ ㏃ ⟪ ⋙ ▨ ▾ ▱ ▣

Location: Halfway up the s side of the castle hill, facing the bay; ascend by elevator. One of the best-located hotels in Nice is also one of the most attractive and well run. It is built high into the side of the rock in the Château gardens, and many bedrooms have balconies with blissful views of the Baie des Anges below. Although there is no proper restaurant, light lunches are served in summer beside the pool, or in the idyllic garden full of lemon trees. Some bedrooms have kitchenettes. There's also a roomy bar with a log fire in winter, a discreet sunbathing terrace, and a sauna.

RELAIS DE RIMIEZ

128 av. de Rimiez, 06000 Nice
☎93-81-18-65 ⊠93-53-51-23 ▥ 24
rms ▤ ㏂ ▣ ▣ ⌂ ◌ ▢ ▱ ▾ ⟪ ▨
Closed Jan to mid-Feb.
Location: Perched on a hill in the suburbs behind Nice, only 10 minutes by car from the center. A small, simple, modern hotel in Provençal style, surrounded by countryside and absolute quiet. The ground-floor rooms give directly onto the garden; upper ones have balconies with a fine view. No restaurant, but a pleasant bar and tearoom.

SOFITEL SPLENDID

50 blvd. Victor-Hugo, 06000 Nice
☎93-16-41-00 ⊠93-87-02-46 ▥ 128
rms ▤ ▣ ▱ ㏜ ㏂ ▣ ▣ ▥ ◌ ‡ ▨ ▢
▱ ⟪ ㏃ ▨ ▨ ▾ ▣
Location: w-central, 350 meters (400 yards) from the promenade. A top-class hotel with great character. The Tschann family have owned it since 1905, when German and Russian princes were often among their guests. In 1964 they totally rebuilt it in a modern style, but they have managed to preserve in this new setting the classic tradition of personal service. All is elegance and discretion, even if the princes have long departed, to be replaced by a clientele varying from Japanese bankers to British rock bands. One delight is the swimming pool on the roof, eight floors up, with splendid views. Beside it are a bar, sauna, children's pool and walled-off sun-terrace.

WESTMINSTER CONCORDE

27 promenade des Anglais, 06000 Nice
☎*93-88-29-44* Fx*93-82-45-35* ▥ *110*
rms ▤ ➾ AE ● CB ▨ ⌂ ♣ □ ▱
☎ ⟪ ⛅ Y ▣

*Location: Situated to the E of the Musée
Masséna.* Built in 1880, the Westminster is one of the best-positioned hotels to be found in Nice. Quiet, old-fashioned and discreet, with fine views from most of the rooms, it has a slightly faded feel, even though the rooms were recently pleasantly redecorated. The public areas of the hotel look rather tired, although there is a splendid staircase and two fine, grand meeting rooms. More staff around the place might enliven things. But undoubtedly, the hotel has its devotees, a core of regular guests.

There is a small, serviceable restaurant, and a piano bar.

✆ Other hotels that can be recommended are: **Abela** (*223 promenade des Anglais* ☎*93-37-17-17* Fx*93-71-21-71* ▥). • **Altea Masséna** (*58 rue Gioffredo* ☎*93-85-49-25* Fx*93-62-43-27* ▥ *to* ▥). • **Beau Rivage** (*24 rue St-François-de-Paule* ☎*93-80-80-70* Fx*93-80-55-77* ▥). • **Cigognes** (*16 rue Maccarani* ☎*93-88-65-02* ▥). • **Gounod** (*3 rue Gounod* ☎*93-88-26-20* Fx*93-88-23-84* ▥).

• **Holiday Inn** (*20 blvd. Victor-Hugo* ☎*93-16-55-00* Fx*93-16-55-55* ▥). • **La Malmaison** (*48 blvd. Victor-Hugo* ☎*93-87-62-56* Fx*93-16-17-99* ▥). • **L'Oasis** (*23 rue Gounod* ☎*93-88-26-20* Fx*93-88-23-84* ▢). **Petit Palais** (*10 av. Emile-Bieckert* ☎*93-62-19-11* Fx*93-62-53-60* ▥). • **Plaza Concorde** (*12 av. Verdun* ☎*93-87-80-41* Fx*93-82-50-70* ▥). • **Pullman** (*28 av. Notre-Dame* ☎*93-13-36-36* Fx*93-62-61-69* ▥ *to* ▥). • **Sofitel Splendid** (*50 blvd. Victor-Hugo* ☎*93-16-41-00* Fx*93-87-02-46* ▥). • **Trianon** (*15 av. Auber* ☎*93-88-30-69* Fx*93-88-11-35* ▢). • **Victoria** (*33 blvd. Victor-Hugo* ☎*93-88-39-60* ▥).

➾ WHERE TO EAT IN NICE

• See also: NICE'S CUISINE, page 278.

AMPHITRYON

6 Cours Saleya ☎*93-85-73-06* ▢ *to* ▥
■ 🍴 AE ● ▨ *Last orders midnight.*
A lively, cheerfully-decorated place with a youngish, friendly atmosphere, which opened in 1991. The food is well presented and comes in large helpings. There is only one price: you choose a starter and a main course from a lengthy selection of dishes; the freshly prepared desserts are extra. The menu concentrates on Provençal and fish dishes, and the food offers good value, but wines (apart from house wine) are expensive. You can eat outside in summer.

BARALE ✿

39 rue Beaumont ☎*93-89-17-94* ▢ ■
Closed for lunch; Sun; Mon. Last orders midnight.
A visit to Nice's most eccentric restaurant is an instructive experience. Mme Barale, a volatile elderly widow, is a lady of iron caprice who may or may not deign to feed you: you must call first. You then eat what she chooses to give you, from a set menu scrawled on a blackboard in her large museum/dining room. The Barale family has owned this place for a hundred years and surrounds diners with its extraordinary collection of bygones, including two vintage Citroëns, a 19thC printing press and cash register, and a gigantic pair of ancient bellows. Later, the merry widow, hot from her stove, stages an impromptu cabaret act, taunting her guests and telling risqué stories. The cooking, needless to say, is archetypally Niçois, and very enjoyable. *Specialities: Socca, salade niçoise, estocaficada, ravioli, pissaladière.*

BOCCACCIO

7 rue Masséna ☎*93-87-71-76* ▥ *to* ▥
□ 🍴 AE ● *Last orders 11pm.*

The tables spill out across the traffic-free street, and the outdoor display of fresh shellfish looks enticing. For the weary shopper or sightseer in downtown Nice, this lively Italian-run restaurant, designed like a galleon inside, offers the solace of good *bouillabaisse* or *fruits de mer*. Or you can just take the pasta. The place attracts a lot of local people.

CHANTECLER △

Hôtel Negresco, 37 promenade des Anglais
☎93-88-39-51 ▦ ▢ �▮ ⚌ 🎴 ᴀᴇ ◙
🄌 ▩ *Closed mid-Nov to mid-Dec. Last orders 10.30pm.*

The very elegant Chantecler, the NEGRESCO's main restaurant, won high fame because of the dazzling success of its former chef, Jacques Maximin. He eventually branched out by himself in 1989, but the hotel found a worthy successor in Dominique Le Stanc, under whom the restaurant has regained its former eminence as the best restaurant in Nice. For such a grand hotel, the atmosphere is remarkably relaxed, and the service, in this room decorated with 18thC wood paneling, is amiable and much less fussy than you might expect. Le Stanc's cooking, light, simple and inventive, is beautifully presented, with a good choice of menus (the *Menu Plaisir* at lunchtime is a bargain) and much emphasis on fish and other local produce such as artichokes, lamb and pigeon. Desserts are a particular success. *Specialities: Ravioli ouvert aux asperges, artichauts et langoustines; langoustines et tête de veau en vinaigrette de févettes de tomates séchées; filet de loup rôti aux raviolis de pommes de terre et truffes; filet d'agneau rôti aux herbes, parmentier aux truffes; sorbets aux parfums de l'Arrière-Pays.*

The Negresco also has a much simpler restaurant, **La Rotonde** *(open till midnight; no cards or personal checks)*, which is cheerfully decorated as a fairground carousel. There, like many of the hotel's guests, you can eat simple, very reasonably-priced salads, pasta and grills — while still having the pleasure of being in the Negresco.

CHEZ LES PÊCHEURS

18 quai des Docks ☎93-89-59-61 ▦ ▢
▰▰ ⚌ ᴀᴇ ▩ *Closed Wed; Tues eve (winter); Thurs lunch (summer); Nov to mid-Dec. Last orders 10pm.*

Dedicated to Niçois fish, Roger Barbate's cheerful restaurant down by the port has roses on each table and a tank of live lobsters by one wall. *Specialities: Bouillabaisse, suprême de loup à l'estragon, filet de St-Pierre à l'oseille.*

L'ESTOCAFICADA 🍴

2 rue de l'Hôtel-de-Ville ☎93-80-21-64 ▢
▢ ▰▰ *Closed Fri eve; Sat. Last orders 9pm.*

A very simple family-run bistro. The name of the restaurant is that of a Provençal stockfish stew, and the cooking is authentic Niçois. *Specialities: Bouillabaisse, soupe de poisson au pistou, salade niçoise, squid, fresh sardines, and of course, estocaficada.*

LA FARIGOULA 🍴 ✿

6bis rue de France ☎93-87-11-21 ▢ to
▦ ▢ ▰▰ ◙ ▩ *Closed Sun. Last orders 10.30pm.*

Situated in the smart pedestrian zone w of place Masséna, this is one of the best places to eat at modest cost, in the newer part of town. It is neat and pretty, *auberge*-style, with red, checked tablecloths and a tank full of live trout. The cooking is partly Niçois, partly from Touraine.

LE GOURMET LORRAIN

7 av. Santa-Fior ☎93-84-90-78 ▦ to ▦
▢ ▰▰ ▬ 🎴 ᴀᴇ *Closed Sun eve; Mon. Last orders 9.30pm.*

Alain Leloup has justly won prizes for his cooking, served in the somewhat formal dining room decorated in *style Louis XIII.* The dishes complement the surroundings, for they are mainly classic — a welcome change from Niçois *cuisine.* Note the big silver duck press used for making *canard au sang.* There is, however, one notable oddity on the menu: *filet d'autruche aux cèpres* (the ostrich meat comes from Australia or, nowadays, from Europe). There is an outstanding list of 900 wines and *diges-*

tifs, some over 100 years old, and finely-kept cigars too. *Specialities: Filet de boeuf bordelaise, rognons de veau aux pétales de truffes, civet de langouste.*

(See ❧ on page 285.)

LE GRAND CAFÉ DES ARTS

Pl. Yves-Klein, at Musée d'Art Moderne ☎93-80-58-58 ▯▭♨◉◙▥ *Last orders midnight (sometimes later).*

The café attached to the modern art museum is a popular local meeting place. The ambience is youthful and arty, with wooden floors and tables, bright yellow benches, exotic plants, and rock music playing in the background. The light, simple food, from an extensive menu, is surprisingly good. You can sit on the terrace on fine days.

LE PALAIS JAMAÏ

3 quai des Deux-Emmanuel ☎93-89-53-92 ▯▯ ▤▤ ▨▥ *Closed Mon; Tues lunch; Mar. Last orders 10.45pm.*

Excellent Moroccan cuisine, served in a dream-like exotic setting down by the harbor.

QUEENIE

19 promenade des Anglais ☎93-88-52-50 ▯▯▭▧ ▨▥◉◙▥ *Last orders 2am (summer); midnight (winter).*

A popular and elegant bar/brasserie, where you can eat outdoors right on the promenade, beside the palm trees, and watch the people go by (and the noisy traffic too). Or you can opt for the large indoor *salle,* which is cool and fairly quiet. The clientele is cosmopolitan, both smart and not-so-smart. Service tends to be rather haphazard and off-hand, but the cooking is fresh and varied, taken seriously, and reasonably priced for this part of town. The *chef-patron,* who comes from Toulouse, specializes in southwestern French dishes such as *cassoulet* and *magret de canard,* as well as local fish. The menu changes daily.

LE SAFARI

1 Cours Saleya ☎93-80-18-44 ▯▯▭♨ ▨▥◉ *Closed Mon (except summer). Last orders 11pm.*

The locals themselves, especially young ones, flock to this very animated and informal bistro by the marketplace. With its loud pop music and rapid, take-it-or-leave-it service, there's more than a touch of Boulevard St-Germain about the place; yet the cooking is varied, good and truly Niçois, with the Piedmontese influence showing through clearly. An interesting feature is an open wood fire, used for grills and pizzas. *Specialities: Trouchiá, alouettes sans tête, bagna cauda.*

LA TACA D'OLI 🍴

35 rue Pairolière ☎93-80-44-15 ▯▯▭ ▧▥ *Last orders 11pm.*

Jokey posters cover the walls, and your elbow may be in your neighbor's plate at this student-filled bohemian little bistro in an Old Town alley. The exuberant *pied noir* owner greets all his guests with effusive familiarity whether he knows them or not. The food is good and plentiful: the *cuisses de grenouilles provençale* often seem to come from frogs the size of small chickens (the *patron* says they're from China). *Specialities: Pâtés au pistou, ris de veau aux coquilles St-Jacques.*

LA VILLA D'ESTE

6 rue Masséna ☎93-82-47-77 ▯▯▤▤▭ ▨▥◉◙▥ *Closed Sun (winter). Last orders (winter) 11.30pm (later in summer).*

Across the street from and owned by the same family as BOCCACCIO, this is a straightforward Italian restaurant serving good-quality pasta and pizza, as well as meat and fish dishes, at reasonable prices. The spaghetti with *fruits de mer* is unusually good. Service is swift, and there is a guitarist in summer.

Other restaurants worth trying in Nice are: **L'Âne Rouge** *(7 quai des Deux-Emmanuel* ☎93-89-49-63 ▥▥▥*),* high quality, specializing in seafood and regional dishes. • **Bông-Lai** *(14 rue Alsace-Lorraine* ☎93-88-75-36 ▥▥ *closed Mon, Tues),* Vietnamese. • **Café de l'Horloge** *(12 av. Félix-Faure* ☎93-80-62-52 ▯▯ *to* ▥▥*),* fish and local specialities. • **La Cambuse** *(5*

Cours Saleya ☎93-80-12-31 ▥ to ▥ *closed Sun)*, Niçois cuisine and fish. • **Les Dents de la Mer** *(2 rue St-François-de-Paule* ☎93-80-99-16 ▥ to ▥)*, seafood specialities. • **Flo** *(4 rue Sacha-Guitry* ☎93-80-70-10 ▥)*, traditional cuisine. • **Florian** *(22 rue Alphonse-Karr* ☎93-88-86-60 ▥ *closed Sat lunch, Sun)*, Claude Gillon's restaurant, one of the best in town. • Also at the same address, the cheaper **Bistrot du Florian** *(☎93-16-08-49 ▥)*. • **La Méranda** *(4 rue de la Terrasse* ▥ to ▥ *closed Sat, Sun, Mon)*, Niçois specialities. • **La Petite Maison** *(11 rue St-François-de-Paule* ☎93-92-59-59 ▥ *closed Sun)*, serving *nouvelle cuisine*. • **Le Regency** *(Abela Hotel, 223 promenade des Anglais* ☎93-37-17-17 ▥ to ▥)* offers Lebanese and Niçois specialities.

≈ NEARBY

JEAN-FRANÇOIS ISSAUTIER (Auberge de la Belle Route)
St-Martin-du-Var (27km/17 miles N of Nice)
☎93-08-10-65 ▥ to ▥ ▢ ▦ ▣ ▣
▢ ▥ *Closed Sun; Mon; early Nov; mid-Feb to mid-Mar. Last orders 9.30pm.*
An isolated restaurant, set beside the N202, just S of St-Martin. Inside, all is elegance, with silver candlesticks and Louis XIII chairs. Issautier is one of the best chefs in the area, and his wife a good hostess, making this a favorite place for out-of-town dining. He has been inventive, slowly raising his cuisine almost to the highest class, and experimenting with Oriental spicing. A short but intelligent menu. *Specialities: Fleurs de courgettes à la coque, marinière de poissons de roche aux aromates, rognon de veau rôti.*

🎵 NIGHTLIFE IN NICE

Those in search of exciting nightlife may find Nice a little staid and disappointing, for there are no really fashionable discos.

Clubs and discos **Blue Sea** *(24 quai Lunel* ☎93-55-23-34)*. • **Le Capitol** *(2 rue de la Tour* ☎93-13-44-33)*, a popular disco. • **Le Cinéma** *(29 av. Malausséna* ☎93-88-14-83)*. • **Le Offshore** *(29 rue Alphonse-Karr* ☎93-87-76-76)*, a large, high-tech disco. • **Le Quartz** *(18 rue du Congrès* ☎93-88-88-87)*, a club for gays, but not exclusively so.

Piano bars Try **Le Boa Night** *(3 rue Gabriel-Fauré* ☎93-88-37-77)*. • Or **Pam-Pam** *(pl. Masséna* ☎93-80-21-60 ♈ ♪)*. • Or **Le Valentino** *(3 prom. des Anglais* ☎93-87-09-27)*. • The hotels **Abela**, **NEGRESCO**, **ÉLYSÉE PALACE**, **WESTMINSTER CONCORDE** and **MÉRIDIEN** all have piano bars.

Casino The famous **Casino Ruhl** *(1 promenade des Anglais* ☎93-87-95-87 ▣ *open 5pm-5am)*, which closed its doors for a time, has reopened. It has a discotheque, **Jok Club**, and a floorshow. You will need to wear a tie (and produce your passport) for the gaming rooms.

Theater Nice's new **Théâtre** *(promenade des Arts* ☎93-80-52-60)*, near the Musée d'Art Moderne, presents a wide range of serious drama. There is an **open-air theater** in summer, in Jardin Albert-1er

SHOPPING IN NICE

The main shopping streets are **avenue Jean-Médecin** and the pedestrian **rue Masséna**, the latter being full of smart boutiques. **Galerie J. Soisson** *(4 rue Masséna)* sells beautiful jewelry and ivory goods, and **Actuel** *(28 rue Masséna, open every day until 10pm)* sells books and newspapers, many of them English or American.

Most traditional stores are in the Old Town.

Antiques   Try **Promenade des Antiquaires** *(7 promenade des Anglais),* which contains 22 shops. **Village Ségurane** *(28 rue Ségurane)* is a good antique market full of varied and tempting stalls. See also MARKETS, below.

Beauty   **Marotte** is a good chain of hairdressers, while on the tenth floor of the hotel MÉRIDIEN there is a health and beauty center.

Clothes   For locally-made clothes and fabrics, try **La Boutique Provençale** *(55 rue de France).* There are numerous fashionable boutiques to be found in rue Masséna.

Department stores   You can find a number of big-name stores around place Masséna. The best of them is **Galeries Lafayette**. The **Nice-Étoile** development on avenue Jean-Médecin contains a number of stores including a branch of the British **Marks & Spencer**.

Food   **Henri Auer** *(7 rue St-François-de-Paule)* sells its own delicious chocolates, pastries and crystallized fruits. Almost opposite, at #14, **Alziari** also sells its own produce: olives, olive oil and olive-oil-based products. At **La Confiserie du Vieux-Nice** *(quai Papacino),* you can watch the gaily-colored jams being cooked and prepared for sale.

Hypermarkets   The best are just W of town. **Géant Casino** is at Magnan in the W suburbs, while **Carrefour** is just N of the airport, W of the N202. Just W of the airport **Cap 3000**, a gigantic shopping complex, complete with parking, restaurants, cafés and a multilingual information desk *(open 11am-10pm, closed Sun).*

- **MARKETS**   Cours Saleya, in the Old Town, is the home of Nice's **flower market** and **fruit and vegetable market** *(closed Mon):* best to go in the morning. A good spot to shop for a picnic or just to gaze at the profusion of produce. • In nearby rue St-François is the **fish market** *(every morning),* where you can inspect the contents of your *bouillabaisse* in its natural state. • There is an **antique market** in rue Antoine-Gauthier from 10am–noon, 3–6.30pm, every day except Sunday. • The **flea market** is on place Guynemer/quai Amiral-Infernet in the port area *(closed Mon).*
  • Every Monday, there is a **bric-à-brac market** in Cours Saleya.

PLACES NEAR NICE

Several hilltops within close reach of Nice offer splendid coastal views: **Mont Alban**, **Mont Boron** (both one kilometer/½ mile E of Château) or **Mont Chauve d'Aspremont** (6 kilometers/4 miles N of Nice).

Close behind Nice are some pleasant hill-villages, notably **Falicon** (5 kilometers/3 miles) and **Aspremont** (8 kilometers/5 miles) and, farther away, **La Roquette** (20 kilometers/12½ miles N).

- See also: CAGNES-SUR-MER, ST-PAUL-DE-VENCE, VILLEFRANCHE-SUR-MER.

PEILLON ☆

*Maps 3C5 and 15E16 (Alpes-Mar). 19km (12 miles) NE of Nice. Postal code: 06440 L'Escarène. Population: 1,100 **i** at Mairie ☎93-79-91-04.*

Of the many hilltop villages behind Nice, this is one of those most worth a visit. Nearly all the residents are Niçois commuters or weekenders, and although this has killed Peillon's original peasant roots, the houses have at least been restored with care and taste — a common hill-village trend.

⌂ ═ AUBERGE DE LA MADONE ♣
Peillon, 06440 l'Escarène ☎93-79-91-173
▥ *18 rms* ▨ ▣ ▦ ⌂ ▢ ▤ ⊲
⌘ ☞ *Closed mid-Oct to mid-Dec.*
Location: On the edge of the village.
This rural *auberge* offers comfort and discreet elegance and attracts a discern-

ing clientele. It is one of the best hotels in the Nice hinterland, with the bonus of excellent food (▥ ▭ ▬ ▦ *closed Wed in winter, mid-Oct to mid-Dec, Jan, last orders 8.30pm*). Lunch outdoors under the olive trees, with views over the valley, is a particular delight.

PLACES NEAR PEILLON

Just to the N are the **Paillon gorges**, overlooked by a huge cement factory. Amid rugged scenery, 11 kilometers (7 miles) NE, is the equally fine hill-village of **Peille** (✰), with an interesting 13thC church. From here, two scenic routes lead via **Ste-Agnès** down to MENTON.

• See also: ÈZE, LA TURBIE.

PUGET-THÉNIERS

Maps **2**A2 *and* **14**D13 *(Alpes-Mar.). 65km (40 miles) NW of Nice; 6km (4 miles) E of Entrevaux. Postal code: 06260. Population: 1,700* **i** ☎93-05-05-05 *(summer only).*

A little town huddled at the confluence of the rivers Var and Roudoule. The old quarter is largely medieval, with overhanging roofs and houses tightly pressed together. The **church**, partly 18thC, is notable for the beautiful and moving retable above the altar, portraying St James wearing a scallop shell in his hat, the sign of a pilgrim to Santiago de Compostela in Spain. Equally fine are the Naïve and curious 15thC walnut wood carvings which represent, in detail, the Crucifixion, Burial and Resurrection of Christ.

═ Recommended hotel at Puget-Théniers: **Les Acacias** (♣) *(on N202* ☎93-05-05-25 ▢ *to* ▥ ▣ ▣ ▦ *closed eve, Mon, Jan).*

⌂ ═ At Touet-sur-Var (9km/6 miles E of Puget-Théniers), **Hôtel de la Poste** (☎93-05-71-03 ▢): good local cooking; comfortable beds.

PLACES NEAR PUGET-THÉNIERS

Gorges de la Roudoule The D16 leads N through the gorge, and past the **Pont St-Léger** suspension bridge with the old Roman bridge beneath, in a marvelous setting with good views.

Farther on to the right, the D416 leads to the tiny village of **La Croix-sur-Roudoule**, which can be seen perched against the rock from the road below.

ROQUEBRUNE-CAP-MARTIN

Maps **3**C5 *and* **16**E16 *(Alpes-Mar.). 5km (3 miles) SW of Menton. Postal code: 06190. Population: 12,350* **i** *at Mairie* ☎93-35-62-87, *and at Syndicat d'Initiative, 20 av. Paul-Doumer* ☎93-35-62-87.

This sprawling commune is in three main parts: **Cap-Martin** on the coast SW of MENTON; the modern resort; and the old village of **Roquebrune** high above the Grande Corniche.

Cap-Martin, with its pine and olive forests, has long been a preserve of the rich and famous, and is still largely given over to private villas with gardens. The Empresses Eugénie of France and Sissi of Austria used to stay here in the 19thC and first made the Cap fashionable. Later residents or regular visitors have included Winston Churchill, and Han van Meegeren, the forger of Vermeers; W.B. Yeats died here in 1939; and Le Corbusier, who spent many summers here, was drowned off the cape in 1965.

The medieval hill-village of **Roquebrune**, one of the finest in Provence, has been gracefully restored: brash souvenir stores are not too obtrusive. Steep alleys and stairways, neatly paved, wind up under Romanesque arches to the feudal castle on the summit. Rue Moncollet, lined by the medieval houses, is one of the most attractive.

Apart from strolling around the village, it is well worth taking the scenic footpath *(approx. 90mins walk)* that leads around Roquebrune Bay from avenue Winston Churchill on Cap-Martin to Monte-Carlo Beach. It's best to do the walk with the sun behind you.

- **EVENTS** A vow made by the villagers is said to have saved Roquebrune from the plague in 1467. In fulfillment, two remarkable **processions** have taken place annually in the old village, for the past 500 years. These are held on the afternoon of August 5 and the evening of Good Friday. With bold pageantry and a wealth of luminous emblems, the costumed villagers enact scenes from the Passion. • There is a **fête** in May, and **antique fairs** in both June and August.

Château 🏛 ☆

☎93-35-07-22 ▦ ✗ *available mid-July to Aug. Open May–Sept 10am–noon, 2–7pm; Oct, Dec–Apr 10am–noon, 2–5pm. Closed Fri; Nov.*

Roquebrune's castle is the oldest in France, and the only Carolingian castle left standing. It was first built in the 10thC as a defense against the Saracens, but the present structure is mostly 13thC. From 1350–1848 it was owned by the Grimaldi. In 1911 an English resident, Sir William Ingram, bought it, and gave it to the municipality.

It is an austere building of four stories, with walls up to 4 meters (13 feet) thick; yet the rooms are strikingly small for so lordly a residence. On the first floor is the ceremonial hall (now roofless); above this, the guardroom, with a comfortable prison beside; next, the seigneur's living quarters, with a primitive kitchen. From the roof terrace there are marvelous views. The castle is floodlit at night and is visible for miles around.

☞ **VISTA PALACE** 🏨

Grande Corniche, 06190 Roquebrune-Cap-Martin ☎92-10-40-00 ▣93-35-18-94 ▥ *68 rms* ▤ ▦ ▣ AE ⊙ ◉ ▨ ▢ ❄ ☐ ▨ ⅏ ✿ 《 ⇜ 👤 ❒ ☕ ♉ ⌘ ✧ ♈ ❐

Location: On a cliff beside the Grande Corniche, above Monte-Carlo. No ancient hill-village is sited as theatrically as this famous modern hotel built on 14 levels, giddily perched on its cliff, some 300 meters (1,000 feet) sheer above Monte-Carlo Beach. Formerly called the Vistaero, it has been much expanded. All the trappings of extreme luxury — comfort, swift service, glamorous decor, heated pool in a garden (some rooms have their own private pool) — match the spectacular setting and view. The food in the **Vistaero** restaurant is excellent, with a fabulous view to enjoy it by. This modern hotel is probably less expensive than you'd expect, given the quality of service and the facilities, which include a helicopter landing pad and a squash court. All rooms (some of them very spacious) have sea views.

✍ WESTMINSTER

14 av. Louis-Laurens, 06190 Roquebrune-Cap-Martin ☎93-35-00-68 ☒93-28-88-50
▥ *30 rms* ➦ ➾ *(dinner only, for residents only)* ▣ ▦ ▢ ▨ ❀ ❦ ❰
Closed Nov to mid-Feb.
Location: Near the Monaco border, just below the Lower Corniche, close to the beach. A modest, efficient hotel suitable for a simple beach vacation (if you don't mind gravel). The railway just below can be rather noisy in the daytime. But there is a very pretty terraced garden overlooking the sea.

• See also: ENTREVAUX.

➾ LES LUCIOLES ❀

12 av. R.-Poincaré ☎93-35-02-19 ▥ ▭
▰ ➾ ➾ *Closed Tues (winter); Nov to mid-Mar. Last orders 10pm.*
At the foot of the hill-village, a restaurant with a tropical touch to its decor, reflecting the fact that the owner once lived in the Seychelles. Lovely outdoor dining terrace, with views of castle and sea. The set menu presents a wide choice. *Specialities: Soupe seychelloise, tête de veau, lapin maison.*

➾ ROQUEBRUNE

100 Corniche inférieure ☎93-35-00-16
▥ ▭ ▰ ➾ ➾ ▣ ▣ ▣ ▦ *Closed Wed; Thurs lunch; lunch June–Aug (except weekends); early Nov to early Dec. Last orders 10pm.*
A sophisticated restaurant situated on the Lower Corniche, near the Monaco border, with pleasant sea views from its open terrace. The cuisine is serious and invariably excellent. *Specialities: Bouillabaisse; poissons du marché frits, grillés ou en papillote.*

ROUTE NAPOLÉON
Maps 2C1–E2 and 14D11–15F14.

The end of the road for Napoléon was the Battle of Waterloo, but he must have had little inkling of the fate in store for him when he marched triumphantly from Provence to Paris on his return from exile in Elba. The route that he and his men chose, over the mountains to avoid armed opposition, is still proudly commemorated and well marked.

After landing at Golfe-Juan (see JUAN-LES-PINS), Napoléon was rejected by the garrison at ANTIBES, so he marched to Cannes and camped by what is now the post office. He then followed roughly the present N85, via GRASSE, DIGNE and SISTERON, to Grenoble. It was a tough march in stormy weather, along tracks in many places impassable to carriages. But the ex-emperor's gamble paid off. The garrison at the citadel of Sisteron did not resist, and soon he was victoriously in Grenoble.

Today, plaques mark the exact spots where he halted. The finest scenery is on the Grasse–Digne stretch of the N85.

ST-CASSIEN, LAC DE
Map 14F13. 24km (15 miles) NW of Cannes.

Constructed after the 1959 Malpasset dam disaster (see FRÉJUS, page 181), this large, three-fingered artificial lake has become increasingly popular as a swimming and restricted sailing area, with windsurfing the main attraction: the placid, velvety water and fresh breezes make it an excellent place for both beginners and experts, and in summer the lake is peppered with brightly-colored sails. Sunbathing is not so easy, as the lake's thickly wooded shores are very rocky.

☰ AUBERGE DE PUITS JAUBERT

Route du Lac de Fondurance, Callian
☎94-76-44-48 ▨ ▭ ◼ ⊞ ⬟ *Closed Tues; mid-Jan to mid-Feb. Last orders 10pm (summer), 9pm (winter).*

An easily missed turnoff from the Draguignan–Grasse N562 and a very bumpy 3-kilometer (2-mile) lane are worth negotiating, to find this pleasant restaurant situated at the w tip of the Lac de St-Cassien. The food is served in the dining room under 15thC stone arches, or on a shady terrace. Chef and *patron* Alain Carro (who trained under Paul Haeberlin at the Auberge de l'Ill in Alsace) produces satisfying *nouvelle cuisine* dishes. This is a good place for lunch after an exhilarating morning's windsurfing on the lake. *Specialities: Feuilleté de cuisses de grenouilles, ragoût de rognons et de ris de veau, filet de veau aux morilles.*

- See also: GRASSE, MOUGINS.

ST-ÉTIENNE-DE-TINÉE

Just off map 15B14 (Alpes-Mar.). 91km (57 miles) N of Nice. Postal code: 06660. Population: 1,940 i̇ rue Commune de France ☎93-02-41-96.

The alpine air is sharp and clear in this superbly positioned village in the lovely **upper Tinée valley**. Once an important religious center, St-Étienne has a **church** with a fine Romanesque tower, and no fewer than three chapels with frescoes worth seeing: **Couvents des Trinitaires, St-Maur** and **St-Sébastien** *(all often locked; ask for keys at the tourist office).*

❧ ☰ LA PINATELLE ◼ ♣

Blvd. d'Auron, 06660 St-Étienne-de-Tinée
☎93-02-40-36 ▨93-02-47-90 ▭ 14 rms. Closed Oct–Nov.
Location: On the edge of the village. A modest family-run hotel much patronized by French couples seeking a quiet country vacation. There's a pretty orchard garden with a few tables. The dining room (▨ ▭ ◼ *last orders 8.15pm*) is not exactly a rowdy place; conversation takes place in gentle undertones, and most eyes are on M. Martinez's very fair *cuisine familiale.* The set *pension* menu will produce a four-course meal; the more expensive menu might include *crêpes gratinées au four* and *daube à la provençale.*

PLACES NEAR ST-ÉTIENNE-DE-TINÉE

Farther up the Tinée valley, a turning to the left leads to **St-Dalmas-le-Selvage**, a high and lonely mountain village amid wonderful scenery, with a **church** that contains an interesting 16thC retable of St-Pancrace.

The road along the valley finally climbs dizzily up to **Cime de la Bonnette**, at 2,802 meters (9,200 feet) one of the highest alpine passes and open only in summer. Here in August the aptly named oratory of **Notre-Dame-du-Très-Haut** attracts a pilgrimage accompanied by a car rally and shepherds' fête — something for all tastes.

- See also: AURON.

ST-JEAN-CAP-FERRAT

*Maps **3**C4 and **15**F15 (Alpes-Mar.). 10km (6 miles) SE of Nice. Postal code: 06290. Population: 2,250 **i** 87bis av. Denis-Séméria ☎93-76-08-90.*

Nearly every square yard of this lovely peninsula has long been bought up by the rich and famous for their stately villas and exotic private gardens. Two of the best-known are **Villa les Cèdres**, w of the port of St-Jean, which belonged to King Leopold II of Belgium and has a particularly fine garden, and Somerset Maugham's **Villa Mauresque** *(in av. Somerset-Maugham),* near the s cape, where the author spent his final years. Tourists would sometimes try to visit him as a local "sight" — to one who managed to gate-crash, he snarled, in his customary style, "What d'you think I am, a monkey in a cage?"

The profusion of flowers, palms and pines, and the many little rocky coves and headlands, are Cap-Ferrat's great assets, but the beaches are rock and gravel, and, as so much of the land is private, this is poor terrain for scenic walks. However, one coastal footpath does lead around the **Pointe St-Hospice**, starting from **Paloma beach** (allow 45 minutes). From the summit of the **lighthouse** by the s cape there are sweeping views over the whole coast from Italy to the Esterel *(165 steps up, open 9am–noon, 2-5 or 6pm).*

St-Jean itself is an animated fishing village, with little hotels, bars and bistros.

WHAT TO SEE IN ST-JEAN-CAP-FERRAT

Fondation Ephrussi de Rothschild (Musée Île-de-France) ☆
Blvd. Denis-Séméria ☎93-01-33-09 ■■ ✕ ✗ available. Open mid-Mar to Oct daily 10am–6pm (7pm July–Aug); Nov to mid-March weekends only 2–6pm. Last admission 30mins before closing time.

Baroness Ephrussi de Rothschild had this Italianate villa designed specially to accommodate her treasures: the ceilings, for example, were conceived as frames for her Tiepolos. On her death in 1934, she bequeathed the villa and its contents to the Académie des Beaux Arts.

The collection reveals the Rothschilds' catholic tastes, and ranges from the 14th to the 19thC. Here you will find Renaissance and Victorian furniture, Aubusson tapestries, Louis XVI costumes, Sèvres and Dresden china, chinoiserie, paintings by Fragonard, Monet, Sisley, Renoir. . . .

After the guided tour, visitors are free to wander through the villa's ornamental gardens, with their lily ponds, colonnades, exotic flowers and shrubs, and views over the sea. On summer evenings, concerts or theatrical events are often held in the villa. Part of the villa houses a small café with an excellent view.

Parc Zoologique (Zoo) ☆
Blvd. Général-de-Gaulle (NW of peninsula, near Villa les Cèdres) ☎93-76-04-98 ■■ ■ ✱ Open summer 9.30am–7pm; winter 9.30am–5.30pm.

A delightful, private zoo set in what was the lake (now drained) of King Leopold's former domain. There is a good variety of animals, reptiles and birds in spacious outdoor cages, and, six times daily, a chimps' tea party.

✆ WHERE TO STAY IN ST-JEAN-CAP-FERRAT

BEL-AIR CAP-FERRAT 🏨
Blvd. Général-de-Gaulle, 06290 St-Jean-Cap-Ferrat ☎93-76-50-50 ⊠93-76-13-02 🎟 59 rms 🖃 ➡ AE ⊙ ⊙ VISA ⌂ ‡ ☐ 🖃 💺 ⤕ ♨ 🕊 ⁓ ♉ ♈ ⊟ *For* ⊒ *see below.*

Location: On the southernmost point of Cap-Ferrat. One of the grandest of grand hotels (sister to the famous Bel-Air in Los Angeles), it competes with the Hôtel du Cap Eden-Roc at CAP D'ANTIBES as the smartest and most luxurious hotel on the coast — and about the most expensive. Built in 1908, and formerly called the Grand Hotel, it is now Japanese-owned and was totally refurbished in 1990. The location, on the s tip of the cape, is wonderful, as is the 14-acre garden, which provides a haven of calm and spaciousness in a crowded, land-scarce area. The facilities, too, are outstanding, from the stylishly-decorated lobby, with views of the sea from that first moment, to the bright, spacious and tastefully decorated rooms, and the excellent food. A funicular leads to the **Club Dauphin**, the hotel's private beach club, with its huge, heated sea-water pool and its own lunchtime terrace restaurant and bar.

BELLE AURORE
49 av. Denis-Séméria, 06230 St-Jean-Cap-Ferrat ☎93-76-04-59 ⊠93-76-15-10 🎟 19 rms ➡ ⊒ AE ⊙ ⊙ VISA ⌂ ☐ 🖃 💺 ⤕ ⁓ ♈ ♉ ⊟

Location: Centrally-located, near the Mairie and Post Office, yet in a quiet position. A well-situated hotel, suitable for families with young children (there is a small playground). The rooms, some recently modernized, are not particularly charming, but the hotel has good views, decent facilities, including a pool, a restaurant and outdoor dining, and is reasonably priced for the area.

CLAIR LOGIS
12 av. Centrale, 06290 St-Jean-Cap-Ferrat ☎93-76-04-57 ⊠93-76-11-85 🎟 16 rms ➡ AE ⊙ ⊙ VISA ⌂ 🖃 ⌗ 💺 *Closed mid-Dec to Jan.*

Location: On a quiet street in the center of the peninsula, near the port and sea. Enjoy the privileged elegance and calm of the Cap without paying prices to match, by staying at this villa-hotel set in its own large garden.

ROYAL RIVIERA 🏨
3 av. Jean-Monnet, 06230 St-Jean-Cap-Ferrat ☎93-01-20-20 ⊠93-01-23-07 🎟 77 rms 🖃 ➡ ⌂ AE ⊙ ⊙ VISA ⌂ ‡ ☐ 🖃 💺 ⤕ ♨ 🕊 ♉ ♈ ⊟

Location: At the entrance to the peninsula, just off the Basse Corniche. Built in 1904, and called the Bedford Hotel until 1988, the Royal Riviera has been thoroughly modernized to offer first-class comfort at slightly lower prices than the other luxury hotels on the cape. The large rooms are brightly but conventionally decorated. Many of them have sea views. Others have views over the colorful, flower-filled garden and large pool. Service is friendly and efficient. There are a number of terraces (one outside the bar), and a very good restaurant with a relaxing sea view. The hotel has a small, private (although rather rocky) beach and jetty, and buffet meals are served by the pool in summer. A gym and sauna have recently been added to the hotel's very good facilities.

LA VOILE D'OR 🏨
Av. Mermoz, 06290 St-Jean-Cap-Ferrat ☎93-01-13-13 ⊠93-76-11-17 🎟 50 rms 🖃 ➡ ⊒ ⌂ ‡ ♿ 🖃 💺 ⤕ ♨ ➤ ♉ ⁓ ♈ ⊟ *Closed Nov to mid-Mar. For* ⊒ *see below.*

Location: Directly beside the harbor and the open sea. All is *"luxe, calme et volupté"* at this hotel, one of the half-dozen best and prettiest on the Côte. The long ocher building blends perfectly with its setting, and the interior has been modernized with taste and rare harmony of color by owners Jean and Babette Lorenzi. Moreover, for all this sophistication, the ambience is far less affected than at some of the luxury palaces on the Côte d'Azur. Airy salons lead out to a glamorous terrace-garden, which gives onto two swimming pools with lidos, right beside the sea. The rooms have very large bathrooms. The only thing to spoil the otherwise fine view is the rather ugly concrete harbor wall running just below the hotel.

❧ Other hotels in Cap-Ferrat worth mentioning are: **Bagatelle** *(av. Honoré-Sauvan* ☎93-01-32-86 ⒺⓍ*93-01-41-00* ▭ *to* ▭*);* **Brise Marine** *(av. J.-Mermoz* ☎93-76-04-36 ⒺⓍ*93-76-11-49* ▭ *to* ▭*);* **La Frégate** *(av. Denis-Séméria* ☎93-76-04-51 ▭*).*

⊯ WHERE TO EAT IN ST-JEAN-CAP-FERRAT

BEL-AIR CAP-FERRAT ⌂
Blvd. Général-de-Gaulle ☎93-76-50-50 ▥
▤ ☎ ▭ ▩ ⊯ ♨ ⒶⒺ ⊙ ⒸⒹ ⒱⒮⒜ *Last orders 10pm (10.30pm in summer).*
Jean-Claude Guillon's light cooking is essentially simple, with occasional flourishes. Presentation is important here: beautifully-cooked dishes look the more appetizing for being served with extreme professionalism on Limoges plates, and the dining room itself, despite all the formality, is extremely pleasant, with its fine view, mural-painted walls, and marble and mosaic floors. You can also eat outside, looking out at the tip of Cap-Ferrat. Prices are lower than might be expected in a hotel of this class, and the set menus with themes like *Tout Poisson* or *Tout Foie Gras* are relatively good value. But beware of having a drink in the **Somerset Maugham bar** before or after dinner — unless you are prepared to pay through the nose for even the simplest of tipples. Dinner concerts are held here in March. *Specialities: Trois petites salades de langoustines, homard et scampi; gros ravioli ouvert de crustacés, fumet à la crème double; filet de St-Pierre rôti aux artichauts barigoule et aux girolles; carré d'agneau de Sisteron rôti arlésienne.*
(See ❧ above.)

LE CALABLU
Nouveau Port de St-Jean-Cap-Ferrat
☎93-76-01-66 ▭ ▭ ▩ ♨ ⒶⒺ ⒸⒹ ⒱⒮⒜
Closed Dec; Jan. Last orders midnight (summer), 9pm (winter).
The harbor is certainly not the prettiest on the Côte d'Azur, and parking is difficult, but this is as good a place as any to eat fresh fish and seafood. Both presentation and cuisine are simple, but the

quality is fine. Service is knowledgeable and friendly, and there are some interesting local wines on the list.

LA FRÉGATE ♥
Av. Denis-Séméria ☎93-76-04-51 ▭ ▭
▩ ♨ ☎ ⒶⒺ *Closed mid-Nov to mid-Dec. Last orders 9.30pm.*
Dine overlooking the port at this reasonably-priced restaurant, or in a small garden in back. Varied local cooking is served; try the *crudités provençale,* or *crêpes de moules St-Jeannoise.*

LES HIRONDELLES ⌂
36 av. J.-Mermoz ☎93-76-04-04 ▥ ▭
⊯ ♨ ☎ *Closed Sun; Mon mid-Nov to Jan. Last orders 10.30pm.*
Finely-prepared fish dishes in the classic Provençal style, in this elegant restaurant near the harbor. *Specialities: Bouillabaisse, sardines farcies.*

LA VOILE D'OR ⌂
Hôtel La Voile d'Or, av. J.-Mermoz
☎93-01-13-13 ▥ ▭ ▩ ♨ ▤ ☎
Closed Nov to mid-Mar. Last orders 10pm.
Food often disappoints at luxury hotels on the Côte d'Azur — but not at La Voile d'Or, where Jean Crépin's menu, particularly the fish, always delights. Meals are served in the warm, yellow dining room, on the canopied terrace or, for bathers, by the pool. *Specialities: Feuilleté d'asperges et d'écrevisses, millefeuille de saumon au beurre de cerfeuil, royale de loup St-Jeannoise, agneau de Sisteron, petits farcis Provençaux.*
(See ❧ above.)

⊯ Other restaurants: **Le Provençal** *(2 av. Denis-Séméria* ☎93-76-03-97 ▥ ⒸⒹ ⒱⒮⒜ *closed Mon, Sun eve in winter, mid-Nov to mid-Dec),* a smart place, one of the best in St-Jean; **Le Sloop** *(Nouveau Port* ☎*93-01-48-63* ▥ AE ⊙ ⊙ ▨ *closed Wed in winter,* *mid-Nov to mid-Dec),* offering very good, light cooking at reasonable prices for the area.

* See also: BEAULIEU, VILLEFRANCHE-SUR-MER.

ST-MARTIN-VÉSUBIE ☆
Map **15***C15 (Alpes-Mar.). 65km (40 miles)* N *of Nice. Postal code: 06760. Population: 1,050* **i** *pl. Félix-Faure* ☎*93-03-21-28.*

Equally popular with keen mountaineers and less hardy city-dwellers, St-Martin-Vésubie is a first-class alpine summer resort. It has an air of modern chic, yet preserves its charm, particularly in **rue du Docteur-Cagnoli**, a steep paved alley flanked by graceful old houses, with a rivulet rushing down its middle. The finely decorated 17thC **church** is notable for its 13thC wooden statue of The Virgin, richly dressed: on July 2 each year, this is taken in procession to the 14thC sanctuary of the **Madone de Fenestre**, aloft and isolated in the Alps *(the 12km/8-mile trip can also be made by car, along the D94).*

⚭ Small, family hotels in St-Martin-Vésubie: **La Bonne Auberge** *(*☎*93- 03-20-49* ▥ *);* **Edward's et Châtaigneraie** *(*☎*93-03-21-22* ▥ *).*

〓 **La Bonne Auberge** serves local dishes in its large *salle.*

PLACES NEAR ST-MARTIN-VÉSUBIE
Le Boréon *(8km/5 miles* N *of St-Martin).* Amid sensational scenery, Le Boréon marks the start of the **Réserve de Chasse du Mercantour**. If you wish to ramble (no cars, dogs or guns allowed) in this wildlife reserve, where you might spot chamois or marmots, leave the car by the hotel, close to the magnificent waterfall. This is excellent hiking country; it is also a center for mountaineering courses in high season *(contact the St-Martin tourist office for information).*

Valdeblore *(10km/6 miles* W *of St-Martin).* A handful of hamlets on a subalpine plateau: the air is invigorating and the scenery exhilarating, except that the place is filling up with chalets and apartments — tokens of its success as a new resort. Here at **La Colmiane** you can join courses in skiing in winter, and rock-climbing or hang-gliding in summer *(for details ask at the tourist office at Valdeblore* ☎*93-02-84-59).* The less athletic can take the funicular *(*▨ *open all year)* from Col St-Martin to the **Pic de Colmiane**, at 1,795 meters (5,889 feet).

Spare a thought too for Valdeblore's sad name, derived from *"val des pleurs"* (vale of tears), from the days when a local seigneur locked up his wives and starved them to death, ignoring their cries and tears.

Venanson *(5km/3 miles* S *of St-Martin).* A quaint village high above St-Martin, with glorious views. In a small square at the entrance to the village stands the minute **Chapelle de Ste-Claire** *(*☆*).* Don't fail to go inside, for the walls and ceilings are covered in vivid 15thC frescoes, the warm colors — rusts, greens, and golds — still excellently preserved, depicting the life and martyrdom of St-Sébastien *(keys from adjacent Bella Vista hotel).*

ST-PAUL-DE-VENCE

Maps 2C3 and 15E14 (Alpes-Mar.). 20km (12 miles) w of Nice. Postal code: 06570. Population: 2,900 i rue Grande ☎93-32-86-95.

One of the most sophisticated and cultured places in the region, the fortified hill-village of St-Paul has attracted many artists since 1918. It is among the most visited places in France and is always thronged with tourists. Mosaic-paved alleys lead through pretty piazzas with fountains, to the church on the hilltop and to the ramparts. These were built in the 16thC, when St-Paul was a French frontier post facing its rival Savoy across the river Var. They are still intact, and you can walk most of the way around them.

The landscape immediately around the village has always been enchanting — a succession of little hills and valleys covered with flowers, orchards and pine forests; but it is now grossly overbuilt with apartments and villas.

Parking is difficult, particularly in summer, and the village's one-way system might prove problematic for large cars. In summer, it is best to arrive very early or at the end of the day to find a space in one of the public parking lots near the entrance to the village.

WHAT TO SEE IN ST-PAUL-DE-VENCE
Fondation Maeght ★
☎93-32-81-63 ▧ *Open July–Sept 10am–7pm; Oct–June 10am–12.30pm, 2.30–6pm.*

One of the most distinguished modern art museums in France, the Maeght Foundation is remarkable for its setting, its contents and the building itself, the three elements fusing together to create an arresting and evocative display. It was built in 1964 by the Paris art dealer Aimé Maeght, an idealist with a zealous passion for spreading the love of modern art.

The architect was the Spaniard J.L. Sert, whose boldly original pink and white building is topped by two inverted domes, giving it a touch of fantasy. Inside are paintings by Bonnard, Braque, Miró, Soulages and many others. Chagall's *La Vie* is on display there: a huge colorful canvas on which the artist expressed his ingenuously radiant joy in all aspects of human life.

In the garden, sculptures and murals have been skillfully set amid lawns, patios and pine trees, to achieve maximum effect and yet blend harmoniously with the natural surroundings. The result is stunning. Sculptures by Arp and Hepworth, and mobiles by Calder, all stand in the front garden. Behind the museum, Miró holds sway with a witty array of fountains, mosaics and sculptures in fanciful shapes. A courtyard is peopled with Giacometti figures like giant emaciated chessmen, while the chapel has windows by Braque and Ubac.

The Foundation holds two special exhibitions a year, each usually devoted to a single artist. It has a library, a shop (selling reproductions), and a small cinema where films on art are shown daily *(from June-Sept)*. Access to the permanent collection is limited during the special exhibitions in summer.

St-Paul-de-Vence, Église ✝ ☆

The 12th–13thC church stands at the summit of the village. Its unexciting exterior belies what appears within, for it is rich in works of art: a painting of *Ste-Catherine,* thought to be by Tintoretto, at the end of the left aisle; a low relief of the *Martyrdom of St-Clément* on the last altar on the right; and, in the baptismal chapel, a 15thC alabaster *Madonna.*

Nearby, the **Musée d'Histoire de Saint-Paul** *(pl. de Castre* ☎ *93-32-53-09* 🖂 *open 10.30am-5.30pm, 10am-7pm in summer)* is a 16thC house, restored and refurbished in the style of that period, which evokes the history of the village, using modern techniques.

❧ LA COLOMBE D'OR 🏨

1 pl. du Général-de-Gaulle, 06570 St-Paul-de-Vence ☎*93-32-80-02* 🖭*93-32-77-78* ▥ *25 rms* ▤ ▨ ⇄ 🆎 ▣ ◎ ▥ ▱ ♿ ☐ ▱ ➳ 《 ≋ ♈ ▣
Location: At the entrance to the old village. The legendary Colombe d'Or is not only a luxury hotel, occupying an old building of character, but also contains a private collection of paintings and sculpture that would be the envy of many museums. It was built up by the hotel's founder, the late Paul Roux, art connoisseur and friend of many local painters. He accepted payment in kind for his hospitality and thus acquired his works of art. They include César and Miró in the snug little lounge, Braque and Calder by the lovely pool, Matisse, Picasso, Rouault and Utrillo in the dining room. Here, or under white parasols on the enchanting terrace with its superb Léger mural, the cooking is enjoyable.

❧ LE HAMEAU

528 Route de la Colle, 06570 St-Paul-de-Vence ☎*93-32-80-24* 🖭*93-32-55-75* ▥ *17 rms* ➳ 🆎 ◎ ▥ ▱ ▱ ➳ 《 ≋ ▣ *Closed mid-Nov to mid-Dec; Jan to mid-Feb.*
Location: On the road to La Colle, 2.5 kilometers (1½ miles) sw of St-Paul. An 18thC white-walled farmhouse with orange, lemon and apricot trees in the garden, vines overhanging the terrace, lovely views and a feeling of serenity. Inside, the furniture is sturdy and puritanical, the floors bare, with scattered rugs; the bedrooms are spacious, with wide, secluded terraces. The service is friendly, if sometimes vague.

❧ MAS D'ARTIGNY 🏨

Chemin des Salettes, 06570 St-Paul-de-Vence ☎*93-32-84-54* 🖭*93-32-95-36* ▥ *to* ▥ *82 rms* ▤ ▨ ⇄ 🆎 ◎ ▥ ▱ ✚ ♿ ☐ ▱ ➳ 《 ≋ ♒ 🏌 ♈ ▣
Location: 3 kilometers (2 miles) w of St-Paul (off the D7), secluded on a hilltop in its own 20-acre woodland park. Opened in 1973, here is one of the few recent bids by the Côte d'Azur to prove that its days of erecting luxury palace-hotels are not yet over. This building is a kind of Texan version of a Provençal mansion, grandiose and spacious. But the decor is modern, with lavish use of marble. There is a most elegant swimming pool and lido, and the bedrooms have wide balconies facing hills and sea. Best of all are 26 garden-level villa-suites, each with patio, lawn and pool, California-style. Much in demand for top-level business seminars and political conferences, this is where Giscard d'Estaing and Helmut Schmidt met in 1976. The cuisine is excellent, offering a range of regional and new dishes, as well as delicious outdoor barbecues. The set menus are competitively priced for a luxury hotel, as are local wines.

❧ LES ORANGERS

Chemin des Fumerates, 06570 St-Paul-de-Vence ☎*93-32-80-95* 🖭*93-32-00-32* ▥ *9 rms* ➳ ◎ ▥ ▱ ▱ ➳ 《 ▣
Location: A quiet, charming old farmhouse situated in orange groves just outside the village. The rooms are prettily decorated, with Provençal fabrics and furniture. This is about the best reasonably priced choice to be had in the vicinity of St-Paul. Most rooms have a good view.

☞ LE SAINT-PAUL 🏨

86 rue Grande, 06570 St-Paul-de-Vence
☎93-32-65-25 ⒻⒶ⒳93-32-52-94 ▥ *18
rms* ▦ ▭ AE ⊕ ⓄⒾ ▥ ⌂ ⌁ ☐ ▱ ⅏
♨ ⟪ ♨ ♈ ▣ *Closed Feb.*
Location: In the middle of St-Paul. This
hotel has overtaken the competition, to
become the best in the village. The 16thC
house was first converted into a hotel in
1989, but was let down by inappropri-
ately vulgar decor. It has been bought by
the general manager of the prestigious
Relais et Châteaux group, and redecorated with the accent on bright Provençal Souleiado fabrics; it now exudes
charm and cozy luxury, superbly run by
the husband-and-wife team of Yann and
English-born Joanna Zedde. There are
many thoughtful extras in the rooms,
and very good bathrooms. Rooms overlooking the village itself are cheaper
than those with the outstanding valley
views. The food, by a young chef, served
out on the pretty terrace or in the pleasant, vaulted dining room *(closed lunch
Wed and Thurs in summer; Wed-Thurs
in winter),* is exemplary.

⇒ LA BROUETTE

Vieille route de Vence ☎93-58-67-17 ▥
to ▥ ▭ ▦ ♨ ▰ *Open eve only.
Closed Tues; early Nov to mid-Dec. Last
orders 11pm.*
On the hills above St-Paul, and not easy
to get to, this is a convivial, intimate little
restaurant with pleasantly rustic decor.

It is run by two Danes, Olé and Birgitte
Bornemann, who serve good Nordic
food such as Lapland reindeer and
home-smoked trout, eel and pork. . .
well, it makes quite a change from *salade niçoise* and *lapin aux herbes.*

⇒ NEARBY

LA BELLE ÉPOQUE

*Route de Cagnes, La Colle-sur-Loup (5km/3
miles s of St-Paul)* ☎93-20-10-92 ▥ ▭
▦ ♨ ▰ AE ⊕ ▥ *Closed Tues; Wed;
early Jan to early Feb. Last orders 10pm.*
Flaming torches at the entrance, carriages artfully floodlit in the garden, a
telephone booth made out of an old
calash, kitsch *Belle Époque* decor: in-
auspicious touches, you may think, yet
it is hard not to be beguiled by this
sumptuous restaurant. The setting may
be contrived, but the warmth and charm
of the service is not; subtle and imaginative classic cuisine. *Specialities: Fricassée de lotte, canard de barberie aux
fruits, salade de caille aux pleurottes.*

⇒ **Le Diamant Rose** *(Route de St-
Paul* ☎93-32-82-20 ▥ *to* ▥*)* is
one of the best restaurants in the area,
with a view of St-Paul. At **Hostellerie
de l'Abbaye** *(Route de Grasse* ☎93-
32-66-77 ▥*),* Christian Plumail's
light and inventive cuisine is served, at
very reasonable prices, in a medieval
abbey with a shaded terrace.

◼ NIGHTLIFE IN ST-PAUL-DE-VENCE

St-Paul is pretty quiet in the evening, particularly out of season, but the
most popular meeting place is **Le Café de la Place** *(pl. du Général-de-
Gaulle* ☎93-32-80-03),* near the entrance to the village.

SHOPPING IN ST-PAUL-DE-VENCE

The village has many art, antique and handicraft stores, mostly expensive. Notable are: **H. and H. Dieken** *(64 rue Grande),* for paintings, and
unusual murals and frescoes; and **L'Herbier de Provence** *(Montée de
la Grande Fontaine),* selling local herbs, aromatic oils and soaps.

• See also: VENCE.

SAORGE ☆

*Map **16**D16 (Alpes-Mar.). 30km (18 miles) NE of Sospel. Postal code: 06540.
Population: 337 (including Fontan) i at Fontan Mairie* ☎93-04-50-01.

Approached from the N204, as it finally emerges from the impressive **Gorges de Saorge**, the village of Saorge suddenly appears, soaring high above, clinging to the mountainside — a crescent of old houses, yellow, pink and gray, balanced precariously one above the other. It looks unreachable, but there is a road from **Fontan**, 3 kilometers (2 miles) to the N. From there you must park, and climb on foot through the maze of steep stairways.

To the N of Saorge, the N204 continues to follow the Roya valley through the similar **Gorges de Bergue**, with their towering red rocks eroded into every kind of strange shape. Above the road are the numerous high viaducts of the Nice–Turin railway, a great feat of mountain engineering; the terrain is such that some tunnels make loops inside the mountain, and you can see a train entering the cliffside at one point, only to emerge minutes later directly above. The line, destroyed during World War II, was reopened in 1980.

- See also: LA BRIGUE.

SOSPEL

Maps 3B5 and 16D16 (Alpes-Mar.). Postal code: 06380. 22km (14 miles) N of Menton. Population: 2,600 ***i*** *at Mairie ☎93-04-00-26.*

A summer resort in a green valley on the Nice–Turin road, with attractive old streets and a fine medieval bridge with tollgate. The 17thC church, the Romanesque tower, houses a notable Bréa retable of *The Madonna.* Sospel is a good center for excursions and hill-walking.

☙ DES ÉTRANGERS ❧

7 blvd. de Verdun, 06380 Sospel
☎93-04-00-09 📠93-04-12-31 ▢ 35
rms ▤ ▬ ▣ ⇥ ▣ ▨ ✲ ▢ ▨ ⋙
🎿 ▣ *Closed Dec–Feb.*
Location: On the main Turin road, at the edge of town. The ebullient Jean-Pierre Domérégo, hotelier, cook, author and journalist, still finds time to introduce his beloved Sospel and its region to his flocks of satisfied Anglo-

American guests. After working in the US, he has returned to run this rather unattractively modernized but unpretentious little hotel, which has been in his family since 1862. M. Domérégo's cooking (▢ ▢ ▨ ☕ ▬ *closed Dec to mid-Jan, last orders 9pm)* is tasty and varied. Leave room for his *glaces,* which have won awards. *Specialities: Bouillabaisse de truites, cannelloni maison, soufflés, glaces.*

SHOPPING IN SOSPEL
Guy Pérus sculpts in local olive wood: objects ranging from furniture to baby chess sets *(av. Aristide-Briant).*

- **MARKET**   There is a market every Thursday.
- See also: SAORGE.

THÉOULE

Maps 2E2 and 15G14 (Alpes-Mar.). 10km (7 miles) SW of Cannes. Postal code: 06590. Population: 1,200 ***i*** *av. de Lérins ☎93-49-28-28.*

A lively little bathing resort at the N end of the Esterel massif, with reddish sandy beaches and wooded hills rising steeply behind. Between Théoule and **Le Trayas**, 10 kilometers (7 miles) to the s, the coast is rather built up, with hotels and villas along a succession of sandy coves. But s of Le Trayas there is no beach, and the coast becomes wild and empty. Here the waves dash against the bright red rocks, overlooked by the high russet crags of the Esterel massif, notably the **Pic du Cap Roux**.

Hotel nearby: **Miramar** (4km/2½ miles s of Théoule).

☙ LA TOUR DE L'ESQUILLON
Miramar, 06590 Théoule ☎93-75-41-51
Ⓕⓧ93-75-49-99 ▥ to ▥ 25 rms ▤ ▣
▦ ⒶⒺ ⓞ ⓞ ▨ ⅋ ▢ ▱ ✿ ❦ ⅏ ▰
▲ Closed Nov–Feb.
Location: Perched 90 meters (300 feet) above the sea, beside the N98 lower Corniche road. A select little vacation hotel with bright, modern decor and glorious views across the bay to Cannes. The hotel's own funicular plunges down to its private beach just below: this consists of a concrete platform with lido, so don't expect sand here. All the bedrooms have balconies facing the sea. The food is classic but unremarkable.

▰ **Chez Aristide** (46 av. de Lérins ☎93-49-96-13 ▥), which does a delicious bouillabaisse; **Lei Pescadou** (pl. Général-Bertrand ☎93-49-87-13 ▥), good for fish.

PLACE NEAR THÉOULE
Port la Galère (2.5km/1½ miles s of Théoule). Sculptured onto a hillside, this bizarre vacation village is certainly the most exciting postwar architectural development on the Côte, with the exception of PORT-GRIMAUD. It is the brainchild of Jacques Couelle, who also built Castellaras (see MOUGINS) and the Aga Khan's new vacation complex in Sardinia. Couelle has been called "the French Gaudí," and with reason: his "village" of 420 apartments and villas is a honeycomb of irregular facades, pink, white and yellow, some looking like cave dwellings or as if a clever child had molded them out of clay.

Some people find the result hideous; others think it merges harmoniously with the landscape. Couelle has imaginatively blended different Mediterranean ethnic styles, to create a lavish, sensuous fantasy. Some perspectives recall Greece, or Morocco, while Couelle has also acknowledged the inspiration of Le Corbusier: the central clubhouse bears a startling resemblance to the great architect's chapel at Ronchamps.

Port la Galère is an exclusive, private estate. It is not open to the public, unless you are interested in buying a villa or apartment, but a good view can be had by taking a boat offshore. The view from the road is disappointing.

• See also: MOUGINS, LA NAPOULE.

TOURETTES-SUR-LOUP ☆
Maps **2**C3 and **15**E14 (Alpes-Mar.). 6km (4 miles) w of Vence. Postal code: 06490. Population: 3,400 **i** 2 Route de Vence ☎93-24-18-93.

Three old towers give this fine fortified hill-village its name. From the main square, two gateways lead into the horseshoe-shaped **Grande Rue**, a steep medieval alley that was once the main artery. The 15thC

church has a triptych by Bréa and two retables in the form of gilded wooden sculptures.

Behind the high altar is the church's most curious feature: the remains of a Roman 1stC **pagan shrine** with the clear inscription to the god "Mercurio." The **town hall** is a 15thC castle, former home of the local lords, the Villeneuve-Tourettes family. Exhibitions and concerts are held there in summer.

- **EVENT** Tourettes is famous for growing violets, used in the local perfume industry. In March, there is a **fête** to celebrate the fact.

☙ ➡ Recommended hotels with restaurants in Tourettes-sur-Loup: **Auberge Belles Terrasses (�'·)** *(Route de Vence ☎ 93-59-30-03* ▢ *closed Mon);* **La Grive Dorée (➖ ♥)** *(11 Route Grasse ☎ 93-59-30-05* ▢*).*

SHOPPING IN TOURETTES

Many artists and craftsmen have settled in Tourettes, and you can stroll down the Grande Rue to see them at work, or visit their boutiques situated in ancient cellars.

Among the best are **Christian Massé**, for painting on silk, **A.M. and J. François**, for puppets, and **Paul Badié** *(on the Vence road),* for ceramics.

- See also: GOURDON, VENCE.

LA TURBIE

Maps 3C5 and 16E16 (Alpes-Mar.). 8km (5 miles) NW of Monaco. Postal code: 06320. Population: 2,600 **i** *at Mairie ☎ 93-41-10-10.*

An old town on the Upper Corniche, 450 meters (1,500 feet) above Monaco, with an attractive 18thC church. From the terrace by the celebrated TROPHÉE DES ALPES, there are spectacular views of the coast from Monte-Carlo to Italy, and, at night, of the glittering town below.

Trophée des Alpes ⛫ ☆

▩ ✗ *available mid-July to mid-Sept. Open May–Sept 9am–6pm; Oct–Apr 9am–noon, 2–4.30pm.*

In 6BC, the Roman Senate erected a mighty monument to celebrate Caesar Augustus' pacification of the local hill tribes who were disrupting links between Rome and Gaul. It stood 50 meters (164 feet) by 38 meters (125 feet) and was surmounted by a statue of Augustus, a salutary reminder of Rome's supreme power to all who beheld it.

Since that moment of glory it has served as a defensive position, a staging post on the Via Julia, has been neglected, dismantled and finally blown up by the French in 1705. In more recent times the generosity of an American, Edward Tuck, has enabled it to be partially restored, with a reconstruction of the huge inscription listing the names of the defeated tribes.

The adjacent **museum** has a model of the trophy in its original glory, as well as relics and information about Roman Provence.

✆ ⊨   **Césarée (● ♣)** *(16 av. Al-*   **léon** *(7 av. de la Victoire ☎ 93-41-00-*
bert 1ᵉʳ ☎ *93-41-16-08* ▢*);* **Napo-**   *54* [Fx] *93-41-28-93* ▢*).*

PLACES NEAR LA TURBIE
Laghet *(3km/2 miles NW of La Turbie).* Here is the 17thC sanctuary of
Notre-Dame, a popular place of pilgrimage, full of curious ex-votos.
The best are in the **museum** next to the church.
Mont Agel *(8km/5 miles NE of La Turbie).* Near the summit is one of
the best golf courses on the coast, and the most scenic.

* See also: ÈZE, MONACO, PEILLON.

UTELLE
Maps **3***B4 and* **15***D15 (Alpes-Mar.). 50km (31 miles) N of Nice. Postal code:*
06450. Population: 450 **i** *at Mairie* ☎*93-03-17-01.*

The D32 winds steeply up to this largely unchanged old village with
views over the Vésubie valley.

The **church (✰)**, situated on the main square, is large and handsome;
inside can be seen the Gothic vaulted roof standing on Romanesque
columns.

The most noticeable works of art are 16thC: a life-sized statue of the
church's patron St-Véran behind the altar, a sculpted wood altar front
representing the *Passion,* and a lovely painted *Annunciation* above the
N aisle altar.

✆ ⊨   **Bellevue** *(Route de la Ma-*   but serviceable hotel with air condition-
done ☎ *93-03-17-19* ▢*),* a modest   ing and a small pool.

PLACE NEAR UTELLE
Madone d'Utelle *(6km/4 miles W of Utelle).* The D132 zigzags up to a
lonely hilltop where stands this famous sanctuary, founded in 850 and
rebuilt in 1806. Today it is still the object of pilgrimage *(for keys to the
chapel, ask at any café in Utelle).*

From here, there are the most breathtaking views in the entire region
of the Alpes-Maritimes.

VALBERG
Map **15***C14 (Alpes-Mar.). 85km (53 miles) N of Nice. Postal code: 06470*
Guillaumes **i** *Centre Administratif* ☎*93-02-52-77.*

Amid the apartment blocks and chalet-style hotels of this winter-and-
summer-resort stand an old mountain church and a tumbledown stone
dwelling, reminders that Valberg was once no more than a sparsely
populated mountain pass.

In summer, the modern buildings rise messily from the slopes, but in
winter they manage to blend into the snowy landscape, and it is as a ski
resort that Valberg, together with neighboring ISOLA 2000 and AURON, can
best be enjoyed. As late into the spring as mid-April, it is possible to leave
the coast and go skiing here less than a two-hour drive away.

WHAT TO SEE IN VALBERG
La Croix du Valberg

An energetic walk or a chair lift takes you to the **Valberg (Sapet) Cross**, from where there are 360° views of the mountains.

Notre Dame des Neiges †
Apply to the tourist office for key.

This little mountain church has a simple and fresh interior, with its bright and lively decorations painted on a pale blue background between arches that rise directly from the floor. The exterior is quite plain, apart from the murals around the door depicting *Our Lady of the Snows.*

☞ ═ ADRECH DE LAGAS
06470 Valberg ☎ *93-02-51-64* ⒻⓍ *93-02-52-33* 🏨 *20 rms* 🅰 🅾 🅾 ⓌⒾ 🅰 ✻ ☐
🖭 🐾 ⛄ ▣ *Closed Oct; Nov; May; June.*
Valberg's best hotel is cheerful and bright, with comfortable bedrooms, each with a good-sized balcony. The *pension* terms are worth taking, as there

is no really good restaurant in Valberg and the food here is quite acceptable.

☞ Also worth trying in Valberg: **Le Chalet Suisse** (☎ *93-02-50-09* ⒻⓍ *93-02-61-92* 🏨 *to* 🏨 *);* **La Clé des Champs** *(20 av. de Valberg* ☎ *93-02-51-45* ⒻⓍ *93-02-62-52* 🏨*).*

SPORTS AND ACTIVITIES IN VALBERG

Valberg's skiing terrain stretches up to **Mont Raton** at 2,025 meters (6,650 feet) and across to **Beuil**, and includes 19 drag lifts, 2 chair lifts and 2 ski jumps. It has excellent skiing for beginners and will also keep intermediate skiers happy.

In summer, Valberg offers swimming, tennis, riding, walking, archery and shooting. Ask at the tourist office at the Centre Administratif for information.

PLACES NEAR VALBERG

Guillaumes *(14km/8 miles w of Valberg).* Take the D28 from Valberg via St-Brès for a spectacular drive to this sleepy village on the Var above the plunging **Gorges de Daluis**. Walk up to the ruined castle, if you have the energy, and then down for a simple lunch in one of the café/restaurants.

The road that connects the Daluis gorges with the **Tinée valley** affords magnificent views as it twists and turns. After Valberg it passes **Beuil**, a pleasing village with a richly decorated church, and **Roure**, clinging impossibly to the mountainside. Finally it reaches **St-Sauveur**, surrounded by magnificent chestnut trees.

Just before Beuil, the D28 drops s through the **Gorges du Cians** with their distinctive red rocks — among the finest gorges in the French Alps. For 20 kilometers (13 miles) the road follows the foot of this deep and narrow chasm: some sections of the wriggling road are one-way, carved out of the rock face. Elsewhere, there are majestic views of the jagged red rocks towering high above, their bold color contrasting with the lush green of the lichen and bushes that cling to them, while waterfalls cascade down.

Ten miles s of Beuil the gorge widens out, and a turnoff to the left zigzags up to **Lieuche**, a hamlet where the church contains an *Annunciation* by Louis Bréa.

More churches with remarkable retables and murals of this period (15th and 16thC) are to be found in the lonely hamlets of the upper Var valley, NW of Valberg: at **Entraunes, St-Martin-d'Entraunes** and (notably) at **Châteauneuf-d'Entraunes**.

VALBONNE

Maps 2D2 and 15F14 (Alpes-Mar.). 13km (8 miles) N of Cannes. Postal code: 06560. Population: 9,500 ℹ *av. Gambetta* ☎ *93-42-04-16.*

This is a seductive little town with a 17thC arcaded square and a fine 13thC church. The narrow streets are, unusually for old Provence, laid out in a crisscross grid pattern, and are gaily decorated with flowerpots.

Valbonne lies at the heart of Cannes' opulent hinterland — a lush, rolling country of pine and olive woods, vines and flower fields, with hundreds of smart, private villas and estates, and a fine golf course.

For ⌘ see **Sophia-Antipolis**, below and opposite.

⊨ CAVES SAINT-BERNARDIN ♣
8 rue des Arcades ☎ *93-42-03-88* ☐ ⊞ ■ AE VISA *Closed Sun; Mon; Jan to mid-Feb. Last orders 9pm or 10pm.*
Good value on the generous four-course menus makes this dark-paneled restaurant hugely popular, and it is always crowded. The tables are tightly packed, the chatter loud and the ventilation not ideal.

⊨ Also at Valbonne: **Le Bistro de Valbonne** *(11 rue Fontaine* ☎ *93-12-05-59* ☐ *closed Sun, Mon),* a popular restaurant with attractively-priced menus. Chef Louis Purgato used to be at the Caves St-Bernardin.

PLACE NEAR VALBONNE
Sophia-Antipolis *(5 kilometers/3 miles SE, to the left of the D103 to Antibes).* This ambitious new development zone may fascinate any student of modern architecture and planning. Here the international scientific park of **Sophia-Antipolis** marks a bid by the French government to promote this part of the Côte d'Azur as a center of advanced technology.

Various office and research buildings in bold, modern styles lie spread out over a wooded plateau (see ANTIBES, page 218). Just across the valley, to the NW, is a newly completed private boarding-school complex, imaginatively designed in bright colors. Adjacent is a new residential estate of ocher villas rising in tiers with alleys between, a pastiche of a local hill-village: the effect is a little austere.

⌘ NOVOTEL
290 rue Dostoievski, Sophia-Antipolis, 06560 Valbonne ☎ *93-65-40-00*
Fx *93-95-80-12* ☐ *97 rms* ⊞ ■ ⊨ AE ▣ ▣ VISA ▢ ✆ ➔ ⎔ 👁 ⬥ ✦ ✆ ♨
🛎 ♉ ▣
Location: In the Sophia-Antipolis business park, facing a pine forest. The Novotel chain is excellent, and this is one of the very best. It is used by business people, but could do equally well for a short vacation, since the location is quite idyllic. As in all Novotels, the bedrooms sleep three, and children

under 12 can stay free of charge.

🞱 Also at Sophia-Antipolis: **Mercure** *(rue Albert-Caquot, 06560 Valbonne* ☎*92-96-04-04* [Fx] *92-96-05-05*

• See also: GRASSE.

🕮*)* and **Pullman** *(Route Dolines, 06560 Valbonne* ☎*92-96-68-78* [Fx] *92-96-68-96* 🕮 *to* 🕮*).* Both have swimming pools; the Pullman also has tennis facilities.

VALLAURIS

Maps **2***D3 and* **15***F14 (Alpes-Mar.). 6km (4 miles)* NE *of Cannes. Postal code: 06220. Population: 21,200 (with Golfe-Juan)* **i** *av. de la Liberté* ☎*93-63-73-12.*

Students of Picasso will know that Vallauris owes its fame as a world center of ceramics to him alone. Potters had been active here for centuries, but their industry was in decline by 1947 when Picasso, then living at Golfe-Juan, came on a visit. Among the many indifferent potters he found one good one, Suzanne Ramie, who ran the Madoura pottery with her husband. His enthusiasm for her work then led to his own involvement in ceramics.

For the next six years he lived at Vallauris, and much of the time he spent decorating ceramics or twisting newly thrown pots into imaginative shapes (many of his Vallauris ceramics are in the Musée Picasso at ANTIBES: see page 219).

The master's presence gave the local industry a new lease on life: talented young potters came from Paris and elsewhere to work in his shadow, while local craftsmen turned their skills to making reproductions of his originals. Today, alas, Picasso's influence is wearing thin: the town has many potters, but few of them are really gifted.

Municipal, Musée

Pl. de la Libération ☎*93-64-16-05* 🎫 *(same ticket as* MUSÉE PICASSO*). Open 10am–noon, 2–5pm. Closed Tues.*

The 16thC castle (built on the foundations of a 12thC building), with its fine staircase, is devoted to the paintings of Alberto Magnelli, and to ceramics, including some work by Picasso.

There are also exhibitions of works of the winners of the ceramics biennale.

Picasso, Musée

Pl. de la Libération ☎*93-64-18-05* 🎫 *(same ticket as* MUSÉE MUNICIPAL*)* 🎟
Open Oct–Mar 10am–noon, 2–5pm; Apr–Sept 10am–noon, 2–6pm. Closed Tues.

The artist has left two major original works as permanent fixtures in Vallauris. One is the painting *War and Peace,* which entirely covers the walls and vaulted ceiling of this small 12thC chapel (long deconsecrated) at the top of the main street.

Invited by the town council to decorate the chapel, Picasso executed the work in his studio in Vallauris in 1952, when he was 70: he painted onto plywood panels, which were then fitted together. The result is one of the most haunting of all his works, reminiscent of *Guernica* in its expression of his horror of war.

To see his hands as he moulded the clay, small and feminine yet strong, gave a pleasure akin to watching a ballet, so complete was the coordination in their unhesitating movements. It seemed impossible for the clay not to obey.

(*Picasso,* 1958, a biography by Sir Roland Penrose)

Opposite the chapel, in a little square, is the second work: the curious bronze statue of a man holding a sheep, which Picasso made in Paris during the war, then donated to Vallauris. Bearded and naked, the man's stiff stance contrasts with that of the struggling sheep.

La Gousse d'Ail *(11bis av. Grasse* ☎ *93-64-10-71* ▢ *to* ▥*).*

SHOPPING IN VALLAURIS

By far the best ceramics gallery is still the **Madoura** *(open 9.30am-12.30pm, 2.30-6 or 7pm, closed Sat, Sun),* owned and run by Alain Ramie, son of Picasso's friends. This most elegant museum-store sells the original work of its pottery *(not itself open to visits),* and produces copies of Picasso's ceramics. The gallery also mounts special exhibitions.

The main street is lined with shops full of the work of local potters. Most are second-rate.

- See also: ANTIBES, BIOT, JUAN-LES-PINS.

VENCE ☆
Maps 2C3 and 15E14 (Alpes-Mar.). 22km (14 miles) w of Nice. Postal code: 06140. Population: 15,350 ℹ pl. du Grand-Jardin ☎ 93-58-06-38.

The history of this mild and sizeable resort stretches back to pre-Roman times, when it was an important tribal settlement. Vence held sway, too, under Roman rule (as Vintium), and as early as the 5thC it became a bishopric.

Nowadays, it attracts many foreign inhabitants, and is remembered as the place where D.H. Lawrence died in 1930.

Vence's Old Town, oval-shaped, is most attractive — a maze of bustling alleys, with shops selling antiques and local pottery. **Place du Peyra** has an urn-shaped fountain, while the Romanesque **cathedral** is worth a visit for its 15thC choir-stalls, with human figures carved by an unknown artist with a sharp sense of satirical humor.

The baptistry houses a 1979 mosaic, *Moses in the Bulrushes,* by Marc Chagall.

- **EVENTS** A **flower festival** at Easter. • **Concerts** during July. • A **fête** in August.

- **MARKETS** There is a **food market** every morning in place Surian, and a **flower market** in place Grand-Jardin. • An **antique market** takes place every Wednesday in place Clémenceau. • There are **flea markets** in place Godeau on Tuesday and Friday. • A **book market** happens on the first Thursday of the month.

WHAT TO SEE IN VENCE
Chapelle des Pénitents Blancs
Pl. Frédéric-Mistral. Open Apr–Dec 10am–noon, 3–7pm.
Dedicated to St-Bernadin, the patron saint of the White Penitents, the chapel dates back to the early 17thC, but it was built on the site of a much earlier chapel. It is the only surviving chapel of a number that once lined the road to Grasse.

Chapelle du Rosaire (Chapelle Matisse) ▥ ★
Route de St-Jeannet, 06140 Vence ☎93-58-03-26 ▣ ✄ Open Tues, Thurs 10–11.30am, 2.30–5.30pm; or by special arrangement. Closed Nov.
This exquisite little chapel was planned and decorated by Matisse when he was 80, in 1950. Although he was an agnostic, the chapel was his gift to the adjacent convent of Dominican nuns, who had nursed him during a long illness. Through stained-glass windows of patterned greens, blues and yellows, the light falls luminously onto white ceramic walls, decorated with line drawings of powerful simplicity.

Villeneuve, Château-Musée de (Fondation Emile-Hugues)
Pl. du Frêne ☎93-58-78-75. Open July–Oct 10am–7pm; Nov–June 10am–12.30pm, 2.30–6pm.
This castle, built by the Villeneuve family, lords of Vence, in the 15thC (and rebuilt in the 17thC), was donated to the city by Emile Hugues, a former mayor and Minister of Justice. It has been restored, and now houses the works of the painter Carzou. Temporary exhibitions are also held here.

☜ CHÂTEAU DU DOMAINE ST-MARTIN ▥
Route de Coursegoules, 06140 Vence ☎93-58-02-02 ▣93-24-08-91 ▥ 25 rms ▰ ᴁ ◉ ◍ ▨ ▱ ⛎ 🄰 ✆ ☙ ∿ ✇ ✦ ☞ ⛟ ☥ ✵ ☿ ▭ Closed mid-Nov to mid-Mar. For ⟾ see overleaf.
Location: On a hillside 3 kilometers (2 miles) NW of Vence, off the D2. Aubusson and Flemish tapestries, Renaissance and Louis XV furniture, a ruined fortress on its 6-acre grounds, a heart-shaped pool built at the request of Harry Truman: here is the old-fashioned opulence, refinement and aloofness, and the fabulous view, that only great wealth can buy. Even greater wealth can buy a stay in one of the miniature villas behind the hotel — luxury indeed, where the terraces are bigger than most hotel suites, and the bathrooms bigger than most bedrooms. Here is Relais et Châteaux at its imperious best: a hotel, owned by the same family since 1936, that has welcomed Merle Oberon, Gene Kelly, Faye Dunaway, Helmut Schmidt, Tina Turner and Robert de Niro, among many other equally luminous names.

☜ LA ROSERAIE
Av. Henri-Giraud ☎93-58-02-20 ▣93-58-99-31 ▭ to ▥ 12 rms ▰ ⟾ ᴁ ◉ ▨ ▱ ▭ ▱ ✆ ☙ ∿ ✇ ▭ Closed Jan.
Location: In the NW part of Vence, on the Route de Coursegoules. Maurice Ganier runs a simple, rather charming little hotel in a 19thC villa. Rooms are comfortable, pleasantly decorated, and contain Provençal furniture. There is a pool, and a garden with palms, cedars and magnolias. The cuisine is from southwest France. One of the best choices in Vence.

☜ Among other good hotels in Vence, two might be singled out: **Floréal** (*440 av. du Rhin-et-Daube*

☎93-58-64-40 ⓕ 93-58-79-69 ▥), bright and brisk, is a newish hotel on the Grasse road; **Relais Cantemerle** (258 Chemin Cantemerle ☎93-58-08-18 ⓕ93-58-32-89 ▥) has a pleasant garden, pool, split-level duplex rooms and vaguely 1930s decor (no ⇥).

≕ CHÂTEAU DU DOMAINE ST-MARTIN ⌂

Route de Coursegoules ☎93-58-02-02 ▥ ▢ ▰ ⌂ ▰ Ⓐ ⊙ ⊙ ▦ Closed Wed in winter. Last orders 9.30pm.

There's no doubt that the food here is as distinguished as the impressive setting and view. Chef Dominique Ferrières' cuisine is rich, flavorful and decently old-fashioned. Service is impeccable, as you would expect, and the local wines are fine. But watch out for the prices, which are some of the highest in the region. Specialities: Poularde en gelée de foie gras, salade de poissons et crustacés, cassoulette de langoustines au gingembre, filet de loup rôti et son ragout de pates aux champignons, canette de challans laquée au miel et au soja, tournedos poêlé au vin de Bellet, artichauts et morilles. (See ❧ above.)

≕ Other good restaurants in Vence: • **Auberge des Seigneurs** (pl. du Frêne ☎93-58-04-24 ▥ closed Sun eve, Mon), a friendly restaurant with good, straightforward Provençal cuisine, including spit-roasted meat. • **Auberge des Templiers** (39 av. Joffre ☎93-58-06-05 ▥ closed Sun eve, Mon), fish and lamb specialities cooked to a high standard, and which you can eat outside.

Le Vieux Couvent (68 av. Général-Leclerc ☎93-58-78-58 ▥ to ▥ closed Wed) is perhaps the best restaurant in Vence itself, building up quite a reputation for its elegant dining room and refined and inventive cuisine.

Worth considering for a simple, good-value meal is **La Farigoule** (15 rue Henri-Isnard ☎93-58-01-27 ▥ closed Fri and Sat lunch out of season).

PLACES NEAR VENCE

Château Notre-Dame-des-Fleurs/Musée du Parfum et de la Liqueur

2618 Route de Grasse, 2.5km (1½ miles) from Vence, between Vence and Tourettes-sur-Loup ☎93-58-06-00 ▨ ≕ Open 10am–12.30pm, 2–6pm. Closed Sun morning.

This castle was built in the 19thC, on the site of a Benedictine abbey dating from 1042, which had been the home of the bishops of Vence until the French Revolution.

Formerly called Our Lady of the Grotto, but renamed by the perfumer Bruno Court when the castle was built, it now houses a **perfume museum** run by the present owners, the Lavoillotte family.

≕ There is also a very recommendable restaurant, the **Château des Aromes** (☎93-58-70-24 ▥ closed Sun eve, Mon), on the ground floor of the castle, run by Gérard and Luby Mosiniak (she is English) in an impressive 11thC arched dining room. True to the spirit of the museum, the food, concentrating on fish and vegetable dishes, is deliciously aromatic, not least because Gérard Mosiniak uses a variety of essences in his cooking; there is also a vegetarian menu. You can eat outside in the garden.

Circuit of the "clues" ★

The entire route can be followed on maps **14** and **15**, and the eastern portion in greater detail on map **2**. Better still, obtain a serious, large-scale road map.

If you have a car, try hard to make this 160-kilometer (100-mile) round trip through this wild and constantly-changing mountain scenery, for it is among the finest in France. The narrow road passes close to several *clues* — rocky clefts filled by rushing torrents. The route described below is a round trip from Vence, but you could equally well start from another point, such as GRASSE (see page 246) or ENTREVAUX (page 177).

- Leaving crowded Vence heading N by the Coursegoules road (the D2), you climb, in a jiffy, into an utterly different world: desolate *garrigue* country, a rock-strewn plateau with breathtaking views.
- After the **Col de Vence** comes another sudden scene shift, as you enter a land of lush meadows, then wind down into the wooded valley of the Loup. Stop at **Gréolières**, a typical old hill-village, to admire the views. Stroll to the church, to see its 10thC *Virgin* in sculpted wood and its retables.
- From here, the road W twists up the side of a vertiginous gorge, onto a plateau with majestic open scenery of subalpine meadows and pine forests. A turnoff leads NE to the little ski resort of **Gréolières-les-Neiges**; and, farther on, another at **Thorenc**.
- At the "Chemins" crossroads, turn right along the D5, up and over the **Col de Bleine** with its views of towering rock peaks to the S and N.
- Soon comes the left turnoff to the deep **clue de St-Auban**, 6 kilometers (4 miles) to the W. It is worth the detour. To follow the circuit, take the narrow D10 that winds high along the side of the deep Estéron valley, with views of the stark **Cheiron massif**. It is hard to believe that Nice is a mere 32 kilometers (20 miles) away as the eagle flies, for there is hardly a house, save the odd hill-hamlet, hardly a soul (out of high season) but for the occasional tourist car, and only the silent uplands, rolling to distant horizons. Yet the sun beats hot, and the valley vegetation is lush, with even a sign of farming on the steep terraces.
- The **clue d'Aiglun** (to the E of the clue de St-Auban) is a rock cleft where the torrent has left pools that are suitable for swimming. Then, soon on the left, is the turnoff N to the **clue de Riolan** (another detour).
- The route loops to the SE, leading past the quaint village of **Roquestéron**. It then dives down into a thickly-wooded valley, only to climb yet again to the heights, with yet more breathtaking views. Remote, deserted hill-villages dot the vast landscape.
- Finally, at **Le Broc**, the 20thC returns with a shock, as suddenly you find yourself directly above the ugly urbanized plain of the lower Var. From here the road winds via **Carros**, an attractive village with castle and views of the Var, on to **Gattières** and **St-Jeannet** (see next page) and back to Vence. **Gattières** *(11km/7 miles NE of Vence)* is a quiet and pleasant hill-village.

✎ ☰ **Beau Site** *(Route de Vence, Gattières* ☎ *93-08-60-06* ▢▢*)*: there are good views from this simple hotel, which has a very pleasant restaurant *(closed Mon)* that offers reasonable food.

La Gaude *(10km/6 miles E of Vence)*. A small town in a region of flowers and orchards, now encumbered with rather too many modern villas. Just to the NE is the well-known **IBM Research Center**, a star-shaped building of striking design.

☙ ➥ **Alliance** (*Route de St-Laurent-du-Var* ☎ 93-24-47-77 [Fx] 93-24-85-84 ▥ *restaurant closed Sat lunch, Sun*), opposite the IBM building, is well thought of in this area; **Les Trois Mous-**quetaires (*Route de St-Laurent-du-Var* ☎ 93-24-40-60 ▢ to ▥ *restaurant closed Wed*), a pretty building, simple hotel and restaurant, is also quite well regarded.

St-Jeannet (*8km/5 miles NE of Vence*). The village lies at the foot of a giant rock, the **Baou**; the summit can be reached on foot by mule track.

➥ ☙ Local restaurant and hotel: **Auberge de St-Jeannet** (*pl. St-Barbe* ☎ 93-24-90-06 [Fx] 93-24-70-60 ▥ *restaurant open all year, with variable closure according to month*). This 300-year-old inn is run with brio by Jacques Plutino. He is proud of his Provençal country decor and ancient fireplaces. The regional cuisine is imaginatively enlivened by such inventions as *magret de canard au miel de lavande* and *rable de lapin farci façon grand-mère de St-Jeannet*. There is an interesting collection of contemporary paintings on the dining room walls. Nine cozy bedrooms with TV; bar and terrace.

Thorenc (*42km/26 miles NW of Vence*). A bracing summer resort in a peaceful upland valley. Good for mountain walks in summer and cross-country skiing in winter.

☙ ➥ Hotel/restaurant in Thorenc: **des Voyageurs** (▣) (*3 av. de Verdun* ☎ 93-60-00-18 [Fx] 93-60-03-51 ▥ *closed Nov-Feb, restaurant closed Thurs* out of season*) is a straightforward village *auberge* with attractive garden and orchard, serving good country cooking.

• See also: GOURDON, ST-PAUL-DE-VENCE, TOURETTES-SUR-LOUP.

VÉSUBIE, GORGES DE LA ☆
Maps 3B4 and 15D15. 32km (20 miles) N of Nice, Alpes-Mar.

Between St-Jean-la-Rivière and Plan-du-Var, the river Vésubie plunges through 10 kilometers (6 miles) of deep and winding gorges. One road follows the river bed; but to get the best views of this impressive chasm, take the upper road (the D19) from St-Jean to **Levens**. A noted beauty spot, with a 300-meter (1,000-foot) sheer drop below, is the point on this road that bears the sign **"Saut des Français"** (Frenchmen's Leap). The name is a grisly reminder that here, in 1793, Republican soldiers were hurled into the chasm by rebels from Nice.

Upstream, between St-Jean and the old village of Lantosque, the valley is less austere, broader and lined with steep terraces of vine and olive. Apart from Levens, other villages worth stopping at along the Vésubie are UTELLE and ST-MARTIN-VÉSUBIE.

☙ ➥ **Le Bon Puits** (*Route de St-Martin-Vésubie, Le Suquet* ☎ 93-03-17-65 ▥ to ▦ *closed Jan-Mar, restaurant closed Tues out of season*) for sound home cooking in the huge dining room; the friendly ambience of the *auberge* makes up for the bedrooms' pretentious decor.

VILLEFRANCHE ☆

Maps 3C4 and 15E15 (Alpes-Mar.). 6km (4 miles) E of Nice. Postal code: 06230 (Alpes-Mar.). Population: 8,100 i Jardin François-Binon ☎93-01-73-68.

Founded in the 14thC as a Customs-free port (hence its name), Villefranche today is still a lively fishing port. It lies in a deep, sheltered bay, one of the loveliest on the coast. The *vieille ville* is a maze of narrow stairways and alleys, some vaulted (rue Obscure, for example, which is dark indeed). The pretty harborfront is lined with red and ocher Italianate houses, tall and old, and with terrace-cafés and bistros where you can laze in the sun and watch the boats.

Before France left Nato, this was a US naval base; even today, it is visited by Allied warships.

Villefranche is relatively cheap compared with the rest of this part of the coast. Although it has no particularly special hotels or restaurants, or indeed many museum attractions, it might well provide a good base from which to visit BEAULIEU, ST-JEAN-CAP-FERRAT, NICE and other parts of the Côte d'Azur.

- **MARKET**   There is an **antique market** on Sundays.

Chapelle St-Pierre ☆

■ ⚡ ✗ *available. Open July–Sept 9.30am–noon, 2.30–7pm; Oct–Mar 9.30am–noon, 2–5pm; Apr–June 9.30am–noon, 2–6pm. Closed Mon; mid-Nov to mid-Dec.*

A 14thC chapel by the harbor was once a sanctuary for the village fishermen, who used to store their nets there. Jean Cocteau, charmed by the village, took up residence there in 1956, and decorated the walls and ceiling of this chapel with spiritual pastel frescoes, depicting both religious and lay. scenes in the life of St Peter, the patron saint of fishermen. The murals are very striking, but perhaps less so than at Cocteau's Salle des Mariages in MENTON (see page 259).

Admission fees go to the charity for ex-fishermen, which runs the place.

Citadelle Saint Elme

☎93-76-33-33 ▣ ✗ *by arrangement. Open June–Sept 10am–noon, 3–7pm; Oct–May 10am–noon, 2–5pm. Closed Sun am; Tues; Nov.*

The imposing 16thC fort, originally built by the Dukes of Savoy and later strengthened by Vauban, was restored in 1981 and now contains three minor collections: the **Volti museum**, consisting of the Villefranche-born sculptor's works; the **Goetz-Boumeester museum**, dedicated to the painter Henri Goetz and his wife, Christine Boumeester, with a collection of 100 pictures that includes works by Picasso and Miró; and the **Depot d'Archéologie Sous-marine** *(closed Sat, Sun)*, which contains the remains of a 16thC shipwreck found in Villefranche harbor. There are also memorabilia of a French Alpine regiment. The former **chapel** houses temporary exhibitions.

The citadel also contains the town hall, an auditorium, mostly used as a cinema, and an open-air theater.

☙ **WELCOME**
1 quai Courbet, 06230 Villefranche-sur-Mer
☎93-55-27-27 ⓕⓧ93-76-76-93 ⅢⅡ to ⅢⅡⅡ
32 rms ▦ ⃗ⱼ ⒶⒺ ⊙ ⒪Ⓓ ⓋⒾⓈⒶ ✱ ☐ ⌂ 🏊
♈ ▬ Closed end Nov to end Dec.
Restaurant closed Mon.
Location: Right on the harbor, opposite the Chapelle St-Pierre. This is a classic hotel of real character, with a fine view of the port from most of the rooms. The building, once the site of a convent, has been a hotel since the last century, with Jean Cocteau its most famous guest. The decorative style of the bedrooms (many with balconies) varies from floor to floor, but they are all furnished with flair. Rooms on the middle floors, for example, are quite formally decorated, others more casually. Rooms on the top floor are rather wittily designed as ship's cabins.

The **St-Pierre** restaurant on the ground floor has its own separate entrance for nonresidents and is one of the best in town, specializing in fish dishes. You can eat outside, by the harbor.

☙ ▬ᵾ **Bahia** *(Basse Corniche N98* ☎93-01-32-32 ⓕⓧ93-01-29-77 ⅢⅡ to ⅢⅡⅡ*),* a serviceable modern hotel with probably the best facilities in Villefranche, including pool, a very good view and competent cooking; **Provençal** *(4 av. Marêchal-Joffre* ☎93-01-71-42 ⓕⓧ93-76-96-00 ⅢⅡ to ⅢⅡⅡ*),* a straightforward family hotel; **Versailles** *(av. Princesse-Grace* ☎93-01-89-56 ⓕⓧ93-01-97-48 ⅢⅡ*),* a well-appointed if slightly charmless modern hotel, with a pool and good view and a reliable restaurant.

▬ᵾ Some restaurants: **Huitrière** *(Palais de la Marine, quai Ponchardier* ☎93-76-63-33 ⅢⅡ *closed Thurs),* seafood specialities, terrace dining; **Marinières** *(Plage des Marinières* ☎93-01-72-57 ⅢⅡ *closed Sun eve, Mon),* light meals and pizzas; **Mère-Germaine** *(quai Courbet* ☎93-01-71-39 ⅢⅡ to ⅢⅡⅡ *closed Wed in winter),* one of the best fish restaurants in town, where you can eat outside.

• See also: BEAULIEU, ST-JEAN-CAP-FERRAT, NICE.

VILLENEUVE-LOUBET
*Maps **2**D3 and **15**F14 (Alpes-Mar.). 16km (10 miles) sw of Nice. Postal code: 06270. Population: 11,500 **i** at Mairie* ☎93-20-20-09.

The coastal strip in front of the old village of Villeneuve-Loubet has caught the full force of modern development: tower blocks emerge at frequent intervals to mar the skyline. There are, however, two good reasons for pausing in Villeneuve-Loubet.

One is the very building development that has caused the most furore: **Marina Baie des Anges**. Seen looming up along the shore from miles away, these four long, strangely curling ziggurat blocks of apartments, designed in the 1970s by André Minangoy, exert a fascination, perhaps because of the sculptural grace of the twisting concrete pyramids. The complex contains many amenities including boutiques, restaurants and a thalassotherapy (saltwater cure) center. Apartments can be bought or rented.

The other reason for stopping is the **Fondation Auguste Escoffier** (★) *(3 rue Escoffier* ☎93-20-80-51 ▧ *open 2-6pm, closed Mon, Nov).* After a punishing Provençal lunch, a visit to a gastronomic museum may seem insufferable, but it's worth it to see the house where the great chef was born, and the rich array of memorabilia, such as icing-sugar models of a Japanese pagoda and Azay-le-Rideau château, and menus dating back to 1820. Devotees can even buy a set of 40 color transparencies about *bouillabaisse*. The *cuisine* of the "king of sauces" is today out of fashion, but *nouvelle cuisine* master Roger Vergé is also represented here by his menus.

There is also a **military museum** *(pl. de Verdun* ☎ *93-22-01-56* ✉ *open 10am-noon, 2-5pm, closed Mon),* founded in 1987, with a collection of uniforms, paintings, weapons, medals, and insignia relating to the two World Wars and the postwar French campaigns in Indo-China and North Africa.

SPORTS AND ACTIVITIES IN VILLENEUVE

The **Marina Baie des Anges** has moorings for 600 boats and a public swimming pool, as well as tennis, sailing, waterskiing, windsurfing and deep-sea fishing.

* See also: BIOT, CAGNES-SUR-MER, ST-PAUL-DE-VENCE.

Practical information

This chapter is organized into six sections:
- **BEFORE YOU GO**, below
- **GETTING THERE**, page 321
- **GETTING AROUND**, page 323
- **ON-THE-SPOT INFORMATION**, page 325
- **USEFUL NUMBERS AND ADDRESSES**, page 329
- **EMERGENCY INFORMATION**, page 331–32

Each section is organized thematically rather than alphabetically. Summaries of subject headings are printed in CAPITALS at the top of most pages. Words in SMALL CAPITALS indicate a **cross-reference** to an entry in the book.

Before you go

TOURIST INFORMATION OFFICES

Useful free information on visiting France can be obtained from the **French Government Tourist Office**:

- **London**   178 Piccadilly, London W1V OAL ☎(0891) 244123 *(48p per minute in peak time; 36p per minute after 6pm)*.
- **New York**   610 Fifth Ave., Suite 222, New York, NY 10020 ☎(212) 757-1125, or 1-900-990-0040 *(Mon–Fri 9am–7pm; 50¢ per minute)*.
- **Toronto**   30 St Patrick St., Suite 700, Toronto, Ontario M5T 3A3 ☎(416) 593-4723.
- **Montréal**   1981 Avenue McGill College, Suite 490, Montréal, Québec H3A 2W9 ☎(514) 288-4264.

DOCUMENTS REQUIRED

Visitors to France, if they are US or Canadian citizens or Japanese nationals, or are resident in the European Union (EU), do not need a visa: a **passport or identity card** is sufficient.

For stays of more than 3 months, you should apply for a **carte de séjour,** from the French Embassy in Washington, DC, or the nearest French consulate. There are eight consulates in the US: in Boston, Chicago, Detroit, Houston, Los Angeles, New Orleans, New York and San Francisco.

For British citizens the same applies: contact the visa section of the French Consulate *(6A Conway Place, South Kensington, London SW7 2EW ☎(071) 838-2000)*.

If you wish to drive while in France, you need a valid full **driver's license** and must be aged 18 or over. An international driver's license is not needed. If you are bringing a car into the country, you will also need the **vehicle registration certificate**, a **national identity plate** or sticker displayed at the rear of the vehicle, and a **certificate of insurance** or **international green card** proving that you have third-party insurance. Details of these and other requirements can be obtained from the AAA (in the US), or the AA or RAC (in the UK).

TRAVEL AND MEDICAL INSURANCE

It is advisable to travel with an insurance policy that covers loss of deposits paid to airlines, hotels, tour operators, etc., and the cost of dealing with emergency requirements, such as special tickets home and extra nights in a hotel, as well as cover against theft and a medical insurance policy. Be especially careful about medical insurance if you are going skiing.

The **IAMAT** (International Association for Medical Assistance to Travelers) is a nonprofit organization that has a list of English-speaking doctors who will call, for a fixed fee. There are member hospitals and clinics throughout Europe, including a number in this region of France. Membership is free, and benefits include information on health risks worldwide. For further information, and a directory of doctors and hospitals, write to IAMAT headquarters *(at 417 Center St., Lewiston, NY 14092, USA, or 57 Voirets, 1212 Grand-Lancy, Genève, Switzerland)*.

There is an **Anglo-American hospital** in Cannes *(133 av. de Petit Juas, Cannes 06400* ☎ *93-68-26-96)*, which accepts Blue Cross and Blue Shield medical insurance.

MONEY

The unit of currency is the franc (f), which consists of 100 centimes (c). There are coins for 5c, 10c, 20c, $\frac{1}{2}$f, 1f, 2f, 5f and 10f, and notes for 20f, 50f, 100f, 200f and 500f. There is no limit to the amount of currency you can bring into France, but you can take out no more than 50,000f when you leave, unless sums larger than that are declared on entry.

Travelers checks issued by American Express, Thomas Cook, Barclays and Citibank are widely recognized; make sure you read the instructions included with your travelers checks. **It is important to note separately the serial numbers of your checks and the telephone number to call in case of loss.** Specialist travelers check companies such as American Express provide extensive local refund facilities for lost checks through their own offices or agents.

Major international **charge/credit cards** such as American Express, Diners Club, Eurocard (MasterCard) and Carte Bleue (Visa) are widely accepted; indeed, in France, Eurocard and Carte Bleue are almost universal. However, do not assume that other cards will always be accepted.

American citizens who also bank in Europe can use the **Eurocheque Encashment** scheme whereby they can cash personal checks with a Eurocheque Encashment Card. American Express also has a **MoneyGram®** money transfer service, making it possible to wire money worldwide in just minutes from any American Express Travel Service Office. This service is available to all customers and is not limited to American Express Card members.

CUSTOMS ALLOWANCES

Since January 1, 1993 there has been no restriction on the quantities of duty-paid goods you can take **from one European Union country to another**, provided they are for your own use and not for resale. In practice, this means that quantities must be reasonable and not excessive.

- **For travel within the EU**, allowances considered to be "reasonable" for personal use are very generous indeed; any person over 17 may import 60 liters of champagne *or* 90 liters of table wine, *plus* 110 liters of beer, *plus* 10 liters of spirits *or* 20 liters of fortified wine, *plus* 800 cigarettes *or* one kilogram of tobacco.
- **Visitors traveling from countries outside the EU**, such as the US, will still have to declare any goods in excess of the French Customs allowances: these vary according to whether you are an EU or non-EU national. The duty-free limit for a non-EU national is lower: 2 liters of table wine *plus* one liter of spirits *or* two liters of sparkling wine, *plus* 200 cigarettes *or* 250 grams of tobacco, *plus* 50 grams of perfume.
- **For all travelers**, the import allowance for all other goods (such as perfume, electrical goods and gifts bought tax-free) brought into France is set for all EU countries at ECU 90 (about $100/£68/590f). This figure may increase in response to pressure from business.
- **Goods bought in duty-free shops within the EU** will continue to be subject to much stricter limits until June 30, 1999, so do not rely on being able to buy large supplies at the airport or on the boat.

Certain prohibited and restricted goods cannot be imported, such as narcotics, gold and weapons (except arms for sport and target shooting). Obtain a detailed list from the **French Government Tourist Office** before you leave home *(addresses on page 318)*.

VAT REFUNDS

Visitors from countries outside the EU are exempt from paying Value-Added Tax (*TVA* in French) on purchases above a certain value, on completion of a simple form and presentation of a passport at the time of purchase. However, to validate the refund, which will be made to you at your home address, or though a credit card refund, you must present the paperwork and goods at a Customs checkpoint before the passport control on leaving the country. Allow enough time to do this. A wise safeguard is to keep a photocopy of the Customs-certified VAT refund document.

TIME ZONES

France is 6 hours ahead of **Eastern Standard Time**, and 7–9 hours ahead of the other US time zones. It is 1 hour ahead of **Greenwich Mean Time** in the winter and 2 hours ahead in summer, i.e., 1 hour ahead of Great Britain most of the year.

CLIMATE

During the summer the average temperature on the coast is 24°C (75°F) and the average temperature of the sea is 19°C (66°F). There is very little rain, and the vegetation is arid. This is the time when fires can ravage the pine forests, so be particularly careful to obey the rules of fire prevention. However, when rain does come — as sometimes in late August or September — it can be torrential.

Even in late October it can still be bikini weather, although the hot spells are often punctuated by spectacular storms. The average temperature on the coast in January is a warm 9°C (48°F), but the inland hills are cold and snow-covered.

In spring, heavy but short showers encourage the flowers to burst into color, and the weather is warm and pleasant, except when the annoying Mistral begins to blow. Then, for days on end, powerful swirling gusts of wind prevail. Spring evenings can be chilly.

WHAT TO WEAR

The Côte d'Azur is informal but very fashion-conscious, and in all the main cities and towns you will find the classic French *chic* to live up to. In winter, be prepared for both warm and cold weather, and take both light shirts and skirts as well as jeans and sweaters.

It is well worth taking good walking shoes with you, whether to explore towns like Nice and Avignon, or to get closer to the magnificent scenery you will often encounter. You will need a tie to be able to enter some of the Côte d'Azur's smarter casinos.

POSTE RESTANTE (GENERAL DELIVERY)

You can have letters sent to the central post offices of most major towns. The envelope should be addressed as follows: name (the inclusion of words such as "Esq." can cause confusion)/Poste Restante/Poste Centrale/postal code (if possible) and town/France. You will need identification when you collect your mail, and a small fee may be charged. Travel companies such as American Express and Thomas Cook will also hold mail.

• Postal codes are given in this book under individual town entries.

Getting there

BY AIR

Nice-Côte d'Azur Airport and **Marseille-Provence Airport** are the busiest and most important French airports outside Paris. They are directly served **from the UK**, by **British Airways** and **Air France**.

There are a number of daily flights between London and Nice with **Air France** (☎ *(081) 742-6600*) and **British Airways** (☎ *(081) 897-4000*), and two flights a day with **British Midland** (☎ *(0345) 554554*).

From the US, there are daily **Air France** flights into Paris, as well as a number of flights by US airlines from many cities. From Paris, onward connections, usually by France's national internal airline **Air Inter**, can be made to Nice, Marseille or several other major towns (see page 323). Bear in mind that if making an onward transfer at Paris, you must take the shuttle bus between airports, from **Charles-de-Gaulle** to **Orly**, which takes half an hour. The **TGV** (see below) is a useful option if you are visiting northwestern Provence, as Paris to Avignon takes under 4 hours.

International car-rental companies offer efficient **fly–drive** services and can have your rented car waiting for you upon arrival. **Air France Holidays** (☎ *(081) 742-3377 in UK)* offer very competitive fly–drive and fly–rail packages, including accommodation if desired.

BY TRAIN
France's rail services are run by the **SNCF** (Société Nationale des Chemins de Fer). There is a frequent and excellent train service from Paris (Gare de Lyon) to Marseille (via Avignon) by the **TGV** *(Train à Grande Vitesse)* and thence along the coast and into Italy. One of the fastest trains in the world, the TGV takes under 5 hours from Paris to Marseille, under 4 hours to Avignon and around 7 hours to Nice. Or you can take one of the slower trains which stop at many of the resorts along the Côte d'Azur.

The most comfortable way to travel by train is overnight, in a couchette, which has six berths to a compartment if you are traveling second-class, four if traveling first-class; but be aware that there is no sex segregation. Or you can have a sleeping car with berths for one, two or three. Only some overnight trains have a buffet car or trolley service.

There is a **Motorail service** *(trains-autos-couchettes)* exclusively for passengers who wish to transport their cars to their destination by train. The **SNCF** office in New York (☎ *(212) 582-2110)* or London (☎ *(071) 409-1224)* will provide information and make arrangements for you.

BY BUS
If traveling from London, **National Express Eurolines** (☎ *(071) 730-0202)* have buses leaving three times a week and arriving the following evening. Seats have to be reserved in advance.

BY CAR
There is no more enjoyable a way to travel, if you are not in a hurry, than through the countryside along the minor roads. But if time is short, the region is well served by autoroutes. Tolls on these roads are expensive, but you can usually pay by credit card.

- By taking the A6 from Paris, which becomes the A7 after Lyon, **Marseille** can be reached in about 7 hours.
- **Nice** is within 9 hours of Paris via the A7, branching off onto the A8 just after Salon-de-Provence.
- For **Nîmes**, take the A9 off the A7 at Orange.
- For **Toulon** (avoiding Marseille), take the A52 off the A8 after Aix-en-Provence.

Remember that during the French vacation period from July 14 until the end of August, the traffic is very heavy, especially on weekends. The alternative direct route avoiding the autoroute, although much slower, is the N7, which passes through Orange, Avignon, Aix-en-Provence, Cannes, Nice and finally Monaco.

A third option is to follow the special alternative summer routes, which are marked with green arrows.

Getting around

Provence and the Côte d'Azur are adequately served by public transport, and local trains and buses are relatively cheap and dependable; but in the hinterland a car will prove a real bonus.

AIR SERVICES

There are international airports at **Nice** and **Marseille** and regional airports at **Avignon**, **Nîmes**, **St Raphael/Fréjus** (July and August only) and **Toulon**.

Within the region, it is only possible to fly between Nice and Marseille, with the regional airline, Air Littoral. The airports at Nice, Avignon and Cannes also cater to private planes, and there is a helicopter service from Nice to Monaco.

BUS SERVICES

Generally the bus services do not compete with the railway, but link villages with larger towns. Local buses, running from the coastal towns to the hinterland, are infrequent and crowded, so it is advisable to have a car if you are based inland. If you are based in one of the resort towns and want to see the hinterland in relative comfort, the **SNCF** runs bus excursions, which can be booked at railway stations. It is wise (and often obligatory) to reserve a seat in advance.

For more detailed information and for a complete set of timetables, contact the **SNCF**. In larger towns, the bus station *(gare routière)* is frequently located near the train station.

RAIL SERVICES

The coastal resorts are linked by a good train service. There is also a service from Nice to Tende, and a private service taking passengers through the charming mountain region between Nice and Digne. Although some lines have closed, a bus service, operated by the **SNCF**, now calls at the disused railway stations, thus continuing the service.

When traveling by train, you must validate your ticket by stamping it at a machine at the entrance to the platform. If you fail to do this, you may be treated as if you were intending to travel without a ticket and will have to pay a surcharge of 20 percent.

If you travel by TGV, you have to reserve your seat at the same time as buying your ticket: all seats are reserved, and trains are often very full. SNCF train services, especially the TGV, are efficient and the timings are generally dependable.

GETTING AROUND BY CAR

Driving in France is usually a pleasant experience; almost all roads have a good surface, and the mountain roads are extremely well engineered. The main drawback to driving in Provence, especially on and near the coast, is the presence of exceptionally heavy traffic in summer.

Autoroutes (superhighways/motorways) are designated by the letter **A**, national main roads by the letter **N** (or **RN**), and smaller local (or *départementale*) roads by the letter **D**. Other roads are likely to be narrow and are sometimes poorly maintained. Signposting on local roads is frequently perverse and misleading, so make sure you have a good, large-scale, up-to-date map. Provence's hinterland is not well served by gas stations: fill up before leaving the built-up areas.

You should be aware of the following **laws and practices**:

- **Speed limits** outside built-up areas are 130kph (80mph) on toll autoroutes, 110kph (69mph) on free autoroutes and major highways, and 90kph (56mph) on other roads. In wet weather, these speeds drop to 110kph (69mph), 100kph (62mph) and 80kph (50mph) respectively. Within built-up areas, the limit is 50kph (31mph).
- **On-the-spot speeding fines** are often imposed by the police. In the case of a more serious driving offense, they are entitled to confiscate your license and impound the vehicle.
- **Seat belts** must be worn by the driver and all passengers.
- **Children under ten** must not travel in the front seat.
- **Priority** sometimes belongs to cars coming from the right. Look for the signs *priorité à droite* (warning that cars coming from the right take priority over you) or *vous avez priorité* (you have right of way), or *passage protégé* (confirming that you have right of way). You will see signs saying simply *rappel* (reminder). This is a reminder that a previous command, such as priority, still applies.
- The use of **car telephones** while driving is prohibited.
- **Parking** is not easy in big towns, especially in summer. Beware of parking on a street marked *stationnement gênant* (parking is obstructive), where your car is liable to be towed away.
- **Car break-ins** are, alas, rife; never leave visible objects in the car, and try to park overnight on a well-lit main street. You are hardly less vulnerable if you drive a French rented car: most of them, and certainly those from large companies, carry Paris number plates, so you will instantly be recognized as a stranger to the region.

  In small towns and hill-villages, access to some roads is sometimes only allowed to local residents and hotel guests: look for signs with the words *sauf riverains* (residents only). But most hill-villages that are frequented by tourists have large parking lots near their entrance.

RENTING A CAR

Most international car rental companies have branches in the region, particularly at airports and major railway stations, and there are also many reliable and often cheaper local firms. **Payment** by credit card avoids the need for a large cash deposit, and it is often difficult (although not impossible) to pay in any other way.

A current **driver's license** is required, and the minimum age is usually 21, although some companies have raised it to 25. Make sure the car is **fully insured**, even if it means making separate arrangements for insurance against damage to other vehicles and injury to your passengers.

With some rental firms you can arrange to leave your car at your destination without having to return it, and fly–drive arrangements can also be made.

On-the-spot information

PUBLIC HOLIDAYS
On the following days, most museums close but many shops and restaurants remain open:

New Year's Day, **January 1**. **Easter Monday**. Labor Day, **May 1**. VE Day, **May 8**. Ascension Day (**sixth Thursday after Easter**). Whit Monday (**second Monday after Ascension**). Bastille Day, **July 14**. Assumption, **August 15**. All Saints' Day, **November 1**. Remembrance Day, **November 11**. **December 25**.

Some restaurants that would otherwise be closed specifically reopen for official holidays. The national holiday in Monaco is **November 19,** and there is another holiday there on **January 27**.

BANKS AND CURRENCY EXCHANGE
Normal banking hours are Monday to Friday 9am–noon, 2–4pm. However, in big towns, such as Nice and Marseille, some central banks have now reduced their midday closure to 12.30–1.30pm. In provincial towns, banks are often closed on Monday, and in small villages they may only be open one or two days a week.

Money can also be exchanged outside banking hours at *bureaux de change* found in hotels, travel agencies, railway stations and airports. But beware, for most hotels offer very poor exchange rates.

Remember that you will need your passport when changing money.
- See also MONEY on page 319.

SHOPPING AND BUSINESS HOURS
Siestas   This is a Mediterranean climate and culture, and from noon–3pm in some smaller villages and towns, only bars and restaurants will be open. To compensate, stores often open early in the morning (7 or 8am) and close late (7 or 8pm).

Food stores   Generally stores keep longer working hours, with shorter lunch breaks (closing at 1pm). In large towns they often stay open until 10pm. Food stores also open on Sunday morning.

Mondays/Saturdays   Many shops are closed on Monday (although some may open during Monday afternoon) and open on Saturday.

Department stores and supermarkets   They stay open through the day, and are open till late on certain evenings (varying from town to town).

Markets   Many towns have fruit- and vegetable-markets, usually once or twice a week, and some more frequently. Look in the separate entries in this book for the word **MARKETS**.

Museums   Many museums close for lunch. They are often also closed one day a week, and opening times frequently vary according to season and French school vacations. Fuller details, accurate at the time of writing, are given in our separate entries.

MAIL SERVICES

The local post office *(bureau de poste)* will be marked by a blue bird on a yellow background or by the words **PTT** or **Poste**.

Opening times   Larger post offices are open Monday to Friday 8am–7pm, Saturday 8am–noon; small branches may have shorter hours and close for lunch.

Stamps   Stamps *(timbres)* can be bought from cafés, *tabacs,* hotels and newsdealers (newsagents), and from yellow coin-operated vending machines.

Mail boxes   They too are yellow and are marked *boîte aux lettres.* Allow 7–10 days for a letter to travel, even by air mail, between France and the US or Canada, and 3–4 days between France and the UK.

Poste Restante   For details on Poste Restante/General Delivery, see page 321.

TELEPHONE SERVICES

Public telephones are found in post offices and cafés as well as on the streets. At airports and railway stations, it can sometimes be very difficult to find coin-operated pay phones. Those that accept cash (in cafés, bars and restaurants) will take $\frac{1}{2}$f, 1f, 2f and 5f pieces. It is well worth buying a phone card *(télécarte),* from any post office or tabac. Available in varying units (minimum 40f), it will enable you to make local or international calls from suitable phone booths.

Dialing   For **international calls**, look in the telephone directory for the direct dialing code for your country.

- **19** gives an international connection; then wait for another tone.
- Key a **1** for the United States or Canada, **44** for the United Kingdom, **353** for Ireland.
- Then the area code (leaving off any initial 0) and finally the number.

Ringing tone   This is a shrill, intermittent tone preceded by about a dozen fast pips. The busy or engaged tone is less shrill and more rapid.

Collect calls   Known in France as an *appel pcv,* a collect/reverse-charge call is made by keying **19**. Then wait for a tone, then key **33** for the international operator.

Home Direct   France Telecom also offers the Home Direct service if you wish to call abroad. Key the Home Direct number for your country and you will be connected (toll-free) with a local operator. Then you agree the method of payment (credit card, AT&T card, British Telecom charge card, collect call etc.), and the call is made for you.

- **AT&T USA Direct** ☎19-00-11
- **MCI US Direct** ☎19-00-19

- **Sprint US Direct** ☎19-00-87
- **Canada Direct** ☎19-00-16
- **UK Direct** ☎19-00-44
- **Ireland Direct** ☎19-00-353

International directory inquiries ☎19-33-12, then the dialing code for the country required. This type of inquiry works out rather expensive (7f).

Directory inquiries ☎12 for numbers within France.

Making calls within France Throughout France, telephone numbers consist of 8 digits (expressed in pairs). For Paris and the surrounding area, the number is preceded by **1**.

Operator ☎13

To call Provence from outside France Simply key in your international dialing code (**011** from the US, **010** from the UK), then **33** for France, then the 8-figure number. To call Paris and its surrounding area, prefix the 8-figure number by **1**.

Charges The cost of telephone calls within France is not terribly expensive. Nevertheless, if you want to call home, the cheapest time is after 10.30pm on Sundays and holidays. Remember that many hotels, certainly the smartest, charge large premiums for both local and international calls. Some hotels charge, occasionally heavily, for receiving faxes on your behalf.

Telegrams These can be sent from any post office or by telephone. To send a telegram abroad ☎05-33-44-11, a toll-free number.

ELECTRIC CURRENT

The electric current in France is 220V (50 cycles AC), although a few country areas are on 110V AC. Plugs *(prise de courant)* are usually standard European two-prong, but occasionally you will find three-prong sockets, so it is advisable to take an adaptor and a nonelectric razor with you. Adaptors *(transformateurs)* can be bought at any good electrical store or department store in larger towns and cities, or before you leave home, and, usually, in airport departure lounge stores.

CUSTOMS AND ETIQUETTE

The French are among the most manner-conscious of all nations and observe a rather rigid code of behavior in personal relationships, which is starting to be broken down by the younger generation. This consciousness is exemplified by the *vous* and *tu* forms of address; the former applies to everyone except relations, close friends and children.

Handshaking is common when greeting or saying goodbye among friends, as well as between acquaintances and strangers. When addressing someone, it is customary to say "Madame" or "Monsieur" without using a surname.

LAWS AND REGULATIONS

- There are no particularly surprising laws in France; but laws against **drug abuse** are as strongly enforced as elsewhere, with greater penalties for the buying and selling of drugs.

- **Nudity** is allowed on certain beaches, and **topless sunbathing** is common on others.
- **Hitchhiking** is forbidden on autoroutes, although it is tolerated on other roads.
- **Speed limits** and other driving regulations are given on page 324.
- **Smoking** is now banned in all public places, except in specially designated areas. The new law, introduced in late 1992, has met with some derision, for the French as a nation are still rather heavy smokers. In practice the law is frequently ignored — either overtly, or in the case of bars and cafés, with some imagination. There are a number of common ways of getting around it. One is by making the least attractive corner of the bar the designated nonsmoking area; the other is by placing cards reading *fumeurs* or *non fumeurs* on tables, depending on whether the customer wishes to smoke or not. Cafés and restaurants with outdoor tables almost always have their non-smoking area inside.

TIPPING

Tipping is less widely practiced in France today, as most bars, restaurants and hotels include 15-percent service and taxes in their prices *(service compris)*. If a meal or the service has been particularly good, show your appreciation by leaving a small extra tip for the waiter.

Small tips of only a few francs should be given to cloakroom attendants, tour guides, doormen and hairdressers. Airport and railway porters have a fixed charge per item, while taxi drivers expect about 12–15 percent.

DISABLED TRAVELERS

Special facilities for the disabled are becoming more commonplace in France, and the French Government Tourist Office has some useful leaflets describing them. They also indicate, in their regional lists, which hotels are accessible to wheelchairs. Recently-built hotels are required to have rooms and facilities suitable for handicapped people: some comply with this regulation more thoughtfully than others.

Disabled people might find hill-villages, with their steep, narrow, often cobbled and stepped streets, a chore to visit, particularly as very few of the hotels in these villages, except perhaps the smartest, have suitable facilities.

The **Comité National Français de Liaison pour la Réadaptation des Handicapés** *(38 blvd. Raspail, 75007 Paris ☎ 45-48-90-13)* will give general advice and guidance to the handicapped traveler in France.

For further information and details of tour operators specializing in tours for handicapped people, **US residents** should contact the **Travel Information Service** *(Moss Rehabilitation Hospital, 1200 W Tabor Rd., Philadelphia, Pa. 19141 ☎ (215) 456-9900)* or **Mobility International USA** *(P.O. Box 3551, Eugene, Or. 97403 ☎ (503) 353-1284)*.

UK visitors should contact **RADAR** *(12 City Forum, 250 City Rd., London EC1V 8AF ☎ (071) 637-5400)*.

- Throughout this guide, look for the ♿ symbol.

LOCAL PUBLICATIONS

As well as the FGTO publications that can be obtained before departure, you will find more specialized publications in local tourist or *Syndicat d'Initiative* offices.

In Aix, for example, the tourist office publishes *Le Mois à Aix,* covering Provence. Several local French newspapers such as *Nice-Matin* for the Côte d'Azur, *Le Provençal* and *Le Méridional* for Marseille, also include up-to-date information.

Useful numbers and addresses

TOURIST INFORMATION

An *Office de Tourisme* or *Syndicat d'Initiative* can be found in most towns and exists to help the visitor with travel and accommodation problems, and to supply local information including details of leisure activities, town maps, and lists of restaurants and museums.

These offices are open Monday to Friday 9am–noon, 2–6pm, and often on weekends in the summer. Some are combined with *Acceuil de France* offices and can make hotel reservations in other regions of France as well as in their own. In smaller or more remote towns and villages, tourist information offices sometimes only open in season. If there is no tourist office, the local *mairie* (town hall) will usually be able to provide a similar service.

- See individual town entries for addresses of tourist offices: look for the symbol *i* throughout this book and on our maps.

TOUR OPERATORS

Tourist offices have details of local tours. The following companies in Marseille, Monaco and Nice organize tours and provide information:

- **Allied Travel French Riviera**   455 Promenade des Anglais, Nice ☎93-18-81-11
- **American Express**   11 Promenade des Anglais, Nice ☎93-97-29-82
- **American Express**   35 blvd. Princesse Charlotte, Monte-Carlo ☎93-25-74-45
- **C.I.T.**   3 pl. Général-de-Gaulle, Marseille ☎91-33-66-00
- **Havas Voyages** (American Express representatives)   20 La Canebière, Marseille ☎91-22-70-00

AIRLINES
In Marseille
- **Air France**   Reservations: 14 La Canebière ☎91-54-92-92
- **Air France**   Terminal: Gare St-Charles, av. Pierre-Sémard ☎91-50-59-34
- **Air Inter**   2 rue Henri Barbusse ☎91-54-77-21
In Nice
- **Air France**   Reservations: 10 av. Felix Faure ☎93-80-66-11

- **Air Inter**   6 av. de Suède ☎93-31-55-55
- **Air Littoral**   ☎93-18-95-15
- **British Airways**   Reservations ☎05-12-51-25 (toll-free)
- **British Midland**   Reservations ☎05-05-01-42 (toll-free)

AUTOMOBILE CLUB
- **Touring Club de France**   11 Allée Léon-Gambetta, Marseille ☎91-64-73-11

MAIN POST OFFICES
- 1 rue Lapierre, Aix-en-Provence ☎42-27-68-00
- 13 rue Henri-Barbusse, Marseille ☎91-00-50-00
- Pl. Wilson, Nice ☎93-85-98-63
- Palais de la Scala, sq. Beaumarchais, Monte-Carlo ☎93-25-11-11

TELEPHONE SERVICES
Com'azur ☎92-96-06-06: a telephone number that will connect you with any of the tourist offices on the Côte d'Azur; service available in French and English

Weather:
- Côte d'Azur ☎36-65-02-06
- Marseille ☎36-65-01-01
- Alpes-Maritimes region (for snow report) ☎93-71-01-21 or 93-62-21-56

Speaking clock ☎36-99

Traffic report Marseille (personal reply, not a recorded message) ☎91-78-78-78

Traffic report for all of France (personal reply, not a recorded message) ☎48-94-33-33

CONSULATES
- **Australia**   4 rue Jean-Rey, 75015 Paris ☎40-59-33-00
- **Canada**   24 av. du Prado, 13006 Marseille ☎91-37-19-37
- **Ireland**   Villa les Chênes Verts, 152 blvd. Kennedy, 06600 Antibes ☎93-61-50-63
- **Japan**   352 av. du Prado, 13008 Marseille ☎91-71-61-67
- **New Zealand**   7ter rue Léonard-de-Vinci, 75016 Paris ☎45-00-24-11
- **UK**   24 av. du Prado, 13006 Marseille ☎91-53-43-32; Honorary Consul, 12 rue de France, 06000 Nice ☎93-82-32-04
- **USA**   13 blvd. Paul-Peytral, 13286 Marseille ☎91-54-92-00; 31 rue Maréchal Joffre, 06000 Nice ☎93-88-89-55

CHURCHES
There are, of course, many Catholic churches throughout Provence and the Côte d'Azur. There is also a reasonable selection of churches that hold services in English for the Anglo-American community. The major ones are:
- **All Saints**   Rue de Belloi, Marseille

Emergency information

EMERGENCY SERVICES
- **Police** ☎17
- **Fire** *(Sapeurs pompiers)* ☎18
- **Ambulance** ☎18

There is no unified ambulance service — the operator will offer you the numbers of several companies.

OTHER MEDICAL EMERGENCIES
- **Marseille** hospital emergency rooms operate in rotation — look in any local newspaper for details. But you can call ☎91-52-91-52 for a doctor.
- In **Nice**, go to **Centre Hospitalier St-Roch**, 5 rue Pierre-Dévoluy ☎93-03-33-33, or ☎93-85-01-01 for a 24-hour doctor service.
- **Elsewhere**, if you dial for an ambulance, the driver will know where to take you.

LATE-NIGHT PHARMACIES
Pharmacies in large towns stay open on a rotating basis: see the window of any pharmacy or a local newspaper for a list.

There are all-night pharmacies at:
- **Pharmacie du Chapître**, 10 sq. Stalingrad, Marseille ☎91-62-54-76
- **Pharmacie Principale**, 7 rue Massena, Nice ☎93-87-78-94, open 7.30pm–8.30am

AUTOMOBILE ACCIDENTS
- Do not admit liability or incriminate yourself.
- Ask any witness(es) to stay and give a statement.
- Contact the police.
- Exchange names, addresses, car details and insurance company details with any other drivers involved.
- In serious accidents, ask the police to contact the sheriff's clerk *(huissier)* to make out a legally acceptable account of the incident. You will have to pay for his services, but in any dispute his report will be accepted as authoritative.

- **Holy Trinity Anglo-American Church** 11 rue de la Buffa, Nice
- **St John** Av. Carnot, Menton
- **St John the Evangelist** Av. Paul-Doumer, St Raphael

SYNAGOGUES
- 117 rue Breteuil, Marseille
- 7 rue Gustave-Deloyé, Nice
- 1 rue Boissy-d'Anglas, Nice

CAR BREAKDOWNS

- Put on flashing hazard warning lights, and place a warning triangle 50 meters (55 yards) behind the car.
- Telephone police, who will arrange a breakdown van to collect you; call the **Touring Club de France** if you are a member of an automobile club affiliated to this association. Either the police or the Touring Club de France will advise you of the nearest appropriate garage.
- If in a rented car, call the number you have been given.

LOST PASSPORT/TRAVELERS CHECKS/CREDIT CARDS

Passport Contact the local police immediately, and your nearest consulate, who can give you emergency travel documents. (See CONSULATES on page 330.)

Travelers checks Notify the local police immediately, then follow the instructions provided with your travelers checks, or contact the issuing company's nearest office. Contact your consulate or **American Express** (see page 329) if you are stranded with no money.

Credit/charge cards If you lose your cards, contact the police immediately, then follow the instructions given to you by your credit card company or call the following numbers:

- **American Express** ☎19-1-914 683-0200 (US/collect) or 19-44-273-696933 (UK)
- **Carte Bleue/Visa** ☎1-44-21-35-12 (omit the initial 1 if calling from within Paris)
- **Diners Club** ☎1-47-62-75-00 (omit the initial 1 if calling from within Paris)
- **Eurocard/MasterCard** ☎1-43-23-41-52 (omit the initial 1 if calling from within Paris)

EMERGENCY PHRASES

Help! *Au secours!*
There has been an accident. *Il y a eu un accident.*
Where is the nearest telephone/hospital? *Où se trouve le téléphone/l'hôpital le plus proche?*
Call a doctor/ambulance! *Appelez un médecin/une ambulance!*
Call the police! *Appelez la police!*

Words and phrases

A guide to French

We cover here the basic language needs of the traveler: pronunciation, essential vocabulary and simple conversation, finding accommodation, visiting the bank, shopping, using public transport or a car. There is also a selection of Provençal words that may not be easily recognizable.

There are phrases connected with food — eating, choosing and ordering — and a 7-page French menu guide, plus a section on Provençal cuisine.

PRONUNCIATION

It is plainly impossible to give a summary of the subtlety and richness of the French language, but there are some general tips about pronunciation that it will be helpful to remember once you have decided to communicate with the French in their own language.

French tends to be pronounced in individual syllables rather than in rhythmic feet. For example, the word *institution* has four stresses in French but only two in English. In French the voice usually rises at the ends of words and sentences, whereas it drops in British (although not always in American) English. French vowels and consonants are shorter, softer and generally more rounded than their English counterparts.

The French language is full of characteristic sounds — the r, the u, the eau sound and the nasal sounds (e.g., an, en, ien, in, ain, on, un). These are not as difficult as they may seem: the key is to have confidence. The best way is to speak English while mimicking a strong French accent.

REFERENCE WORDS

Monday	*lundi*
Tuesday	*mardi*
Wednesday	*mercredi*
Thursday	*jeudi*
Friday	*vendredi*
Saturday	*samedi*
Sunday	*dimanche*
Public holiday	*jour férié* (m)

January	*janvier*
February	*février*
March	*mars*
April	*avril*
May	*mai*
June	*juin*
July	*juillet*
August	*août*
September	*septembre*
October	*octobre*
November	*novembre*
December	*décembre*

0	zéro	11	onze	22	vingt-deux
1	un	12	douze	30	trente
2	deux	13	treize	40	quarante
3	trois	14	quatorze	50	cinquante
4	quatre	15	quinze	60	soixante
5	cinq	16	seize	70	soixante-dix
6	six	17	dix-sept	80	quatre-vingts
7	sept	18	dix-huit	90	quatre-vingt-dix
8	huit	19	dix-neuf	100	cent
9	neuf	20	vingt	500	cinq cent
10	dix	21	vingt-et-un	1,000	mille

1994/95/96   *mil neuf cent quatre-vingt-quatorze/quinze/seize*

First	*premier, -ière*	Quarter-past . . .	*. . . et quart*
Second	*second, -e*	Half past . . .	*. . . et demie*
Third	*troisième*	Quarter to . . .	*. . . moins le quart*
Fourth	*quatrième*	Quarter to six	*six heures moins*
. . . o'clock	*. . . heures*		*le quart*

Mr	*monsieur/M.*	Ladies	*dames*
Mrs	*madame/Mme.*	Men	*hommes*
Miss	*mademoiselle/Mlle.*	Gentlemen	*messieurs*

BASIC COMMUNICATION

Yes   *oui* (*si*, for emphatic contradiction)
No   *non*
Please   *s'il vous plaît*
Thank you   *merci*
I'm very sorry   *je suis désolé/pardon, excusez-moi*
Excuse me   *pardon/excusez-moi*
Not at all/you're welcome   *de rien*
Hello   *bonjour, salut* (familiar), *allô* (on telephone)
Good morning/afternoon   *bonjour*
Good evening   *bonsoir*
Good night   *bonsoir/bonne nuit*
Goodbye   *au revoir*
Morning   *matin* (m)
Afternoon   *après-midi* (m/f)
Evening   *soir* (m)
Night   *nuit* (f)
Yesterday   *hier*
Today   *aujourd'hui*
Tomorrow   *demain*
Next week   *la semaine prochaine*
Last week   *la semaine dernière*
. . . days ago   *il y a . . . jours*
Month   *mois* (m)
Year   *an* (m) / *année* (f)

Here/there   *ici/là*
Over there   *là-bas*
Big   *grand, -e*
Small   *petit, -e*
Hot/cold   *chaud, -e/froid, -e*
Good   *bon, bonne*
Bad   *mauvais, -e*
Well   *bien*
Badly   *mal*
With   *avec*
And   *et*
But   *mais*
Very   *très*
All   *tout, -e*
Open   *ouvert, -e*
Closed   *fermé, -e*
Left   *gauche*
Right   *droite*
Straight ahead   *tout droit*
Near   *près/proche*
Far   *loin*
Up/down   *en haut/en bas*
Early/late   *tôt/tard*
Quickly   *vite*
Pleased to meet you.   *Enchanté.*
Agreed.   *D'accord.*
How are you?   *Comment ça va?*
(Formal: *comment allez vous?*)

Very well, thank you. *Très bien, merci.*

Do you speak English? *Parlez-vous anglais?*

I don't understand. *Je ne comprends pas.*

I don't know. *Je ne sais pas.*

Please explain. *Pourriez-vous me l'expliquer?*

Please speak more slowly. *Parlez plus lentement, s'il vous plaît.*

My name is . . . *Je m'appelle . . .*

I am American/English/Japanese *Je suis americain,-e,/anglais,-e/ japonais, -e.*

Where is/are? *Où est/ sont . . . ?*

Is there a . . . ? *Y a-t-il un . . . ?*

What? *Comment?*

How much? *Combien?*

How much does it cost? *Ça coute combien?*

That's too much. *C'est trop.*

Expensive *cher/chère*

Cheap *pas cher/bon marché*

Free *gratuit*

Paying *payant*

I would like . . . *Je voudrais . . .*

Do you have . . ? *Avez-vous . . ?*

You're right/wrong. *Vous avez raison/tort.*

You've made a mistake. *Vous vous trompez.*

Just a minute. *Attendez une minute.* (On telephone: *ne quittez pas!*)

That's fine/OK. *Ça va/OK/ça y est/d'accord.*

What time is it? *Quelle heure est-il?*

I don't feel well. *Je ne me sens pas bien/j'ai mal.*

ACCOMMODATION

Making a reservation by letter

Dear Sir or Madam, *Monsieur, Madame,*
I would like to reserve one double room *Je voudrais réserver une chambre pour deux personnes* (with bathroom), *(avec salle de bain),* one twin-bedded room *une chambre avec deux lits* and one single room (with shower) *et une chambre pour une personne (avec douche)* for 7 nights from 12th August. *pour 7 nuits à partir du 12 août.*

We would like bed and breakfast/half board/full board. *Nous désirons le petit déjeuner/la demi-pension/pension,* and would prefer a quiet room *et préférerions une chambre tranquille* overlooking the courtyard/sea. *qui donne sur la cour/mer.*

Please send me details of your terms with the confirmation. *Je vous serais obligé de m'envoyer vos conditions et tarifs avec la confirmation.*
Yours sincerely,
Veuillez agréer l'expression de mes sentiments distingués.

Arriving at the hotel

I have a reservation. My name is . . .
J'ai une réservation. Je m'appelle . . .
Do you have a room?
Avez-vous une chambre?
A quiet room with bath/shower/toilet/wash basin
Une chambre tranquille avec bain/douche/toilette/lavabo
. . . overlooking the park/street/back/sea.
. . . qui donne sur le parc/la rue/la cour/la mer.

Does the price include breakfast/service/tax?
Ce prix comprend-il le petit déjeuner/le service/les taxes?
That's too expensive. Have you anything cheaper?
C'est trop cher. Avez-vous quelquechose de moins cher?
This room is too large/small/cold/hot/noisy.
Cette chambre est trop grande/petite/froide/chaude/bruyante.
What time is breakfast?   *À quelle heure est le petit déjeuner?*
Can I drink the tap water?   *L'eau du robinet est-elle potable?*
What time does the hotel close?   *À quelle heure ferme l'hôtel?*
Will I need a key?   *Aurai-je besoin d'une clé?*
Is there a night porter?   *Y a-t-il un portier de nuit?*
Where can I park my car?
Où puis-je garer ma voiture?
Is it safe to leave the car on the street?
Est-ce qu'on peut laisser la voiture dans la rue?

Floor/story	*étage* (m)	Porter	*portier/concierge* (m),
Elevator/lift	*ascenseur* (m)		*porteur* (station)
Dining room/restaurant	*salle à*	Maid	*femme de chambre* (f)
manger (f)/*restaurant* (m)		Extension (telephone)	*poste* (f)
Lounge	*salon* (m)	Pillow/bolster	*oreiller/traversin*
Manager	*directeur* (m)		(m)

I am leaving tomorrow morning.   *Je vais partir demain matin.*
Please give me at call at . . .   *Voulez-vous m'appeler à . . .*
Come in!/Wait!   *Entrez!/Attendez!*

SHOPPING
Where is the nearest/a good . . . ?
Où est le . . . le plus proche?/Où y a-t-il un bon . . . ?
Can you help me/show me . . . ?
Pouvez-vous m'aider/voulez-vous me montrer . . . ?
I'm just looking.
Je regarde.
Do you accept credit cards/travelers' checks?
Est-ce que vous acceptez les cartes de crédit/chèques de voyage?
Can you deliver it to . . . ?
Pouvez-vous me le livrer à . . . ?
I'll take it/I'll leave it.
Je le prends/je ne le prends pas.
Can I have it tax-free for export?
Puis-je l'avoir hors taxe pour exportation?
This is faulty. Can I have a replacement/refund?
Celui-ci ne marche pas. Voulez-vous me l'échanger?
I don't want to spend more than . . .
Je ne veux pas mettre plus de . . .
I'll give . . . for it.
Je vous donne . . .

Shops

Antique store *antiquaire*
  (m/f)
Art gallery *galerie d'art* (f)
Bakery *boulangerie* (f)
Bank *banque* (f)
Beauty parlor *salon de beauté*
  (m)
Bookstore *librairie* (f)
Butcher *boucherie* (f)
Horse butcher *boucherie*
  chevaline (f)
Pork butcher *charcuterie* (f)
Tripe butcher *triperie* (f)
Cake shop *pâtisserie* (f)
Chocolate shop *confiserie* (f)
Clothes store *magasin de*
  vêtements/de mode (m)
Dairy *crèmerie* (f)
Delicatessen *épicerie fine* (f)/
  charcuterie (f)
Department store *grand*
  magasin (m)
Fishmonger *marchand de*
  poisson/poissonnier (m)
Florist *fleuriste* (m/f)
Greengrocer *marchand de*
  légumes (m)
Grocer's shop *épicerie* (m)
Haberdasher's *mercerie* (m)

Hairdresser *coiffeur* (m)
Hardware store *droguerie* (f)
Jeweler's *bijouterie/*
  joaillerie (f)
Market *marché* (m)
Newsdealer/newsagent
  marchand de journaux (m)
Optician *opticien* (m/f)
Perfumery *parfumerie* (f)
Pharmacy/chemist *pharmacie* (f)/
  drugstore (m)
Photographic store *magasin de*
  photographie (m)
Post office *bureau de poste* (m)
Shoe store *magasin de*
  chaussures (m)
Souvenir store *magasin de*
  cadeaux/souvenirs (m)
Stationer's *papeterie* (f)
Supermarket *supermarché* (m)
Tailor *tailleur* (m)
Tobacconist *bureau de*
  tabac (m)
Tourist office *syndicat*
  d'initiative (m)/*bureau/office de*
  tourisme (m)
Toy store *magasin de*
  jouets (m)
Travel agent *agence de voyage* (f)

At the bank

I would like to change some
  dollars/pounds/travelers' checks.
Je voudrais changer des
  dollars/livres/chèques de voyage.
What is the exchange rate?
Quel est le cours du change?
Can you cash a personal check?
Pouvez-vous encaisser un chèque?

Can I obtain cash with this
  credit card?
Puis-je obtenir de l'argent avec
  cette carte de crédit?
Do you need to see my
  passport?
Voulez-vous voir mon
  passeport?

In town

Banlieue suburb
Bois wood
Boulevard avenue
Caisse cash desk
Défense d'entrer no entry
Défense de fumer no smoking
Entrée entrance
Escalier stair
Étage floor
Gare station
Guichet des billets ticket
  office

Hôtel de ville town hall
Pont bridge
Porte city gate
Pousser push
Quai platform/quay
Rue street
Sortie exit
Sortie de secours emergency
  exit
Tirer pull
Voie track (at railway
  station)

From the pharmacy

Antiseptic cream   *crème antiseptique* (f)
Aspirin   *aspirine* (f)
Bandages   *pansements* (m) *bandes* (f)
Band-Aid/sticking-plaster   *sparadrap* (m)
Cotton (wool)   *coton hydrophile*
Diarrhea/upset stomach pills   *comprimés* (m) *pour la diarrhée/ l'estomac dérangé*
Indigestion tablets   *comprimés pour l'indigestion)*
Laxative   *laxatif* (m)

Sanitary napkins   *serviettes hygiéniques* (f)
Shampoo   *shampooing* (m)
Shaving cream   *crème à raser* (f)
Soap   *savon* (m)
String   *ficelle* (f)
Suntan cream/oil   *crème solaire* (f)/*huile bronzante* (f)
Tampons   *tampons* (m)
Tissues   *mouchoirs epapier* (m)
Toothbrush   *brosse à dents* (f)
Toothpaste   *(pâte) dentifrice* (f)
Travel sickness pills   *comprimés pour les maladies de transport*

Clothing

Bathing suit   *maillot de bain* (m)
Bra   *soutien-gorge* (m)
Coat   *manteau* (m)
Dress   *robe* (f)
Jacket   *veste/jaquette* (f)
Pullover   *pull* (m)
Shirt   *chemise* (f)

Shoes   *chaussures* (f)
Skirt   *jupe* (f)
Socks   *chaussettes* (f)
Stockings/pantihose (tights)   *bas/collants* (m)
Sunglasses   *lunettes de soleil* (f)
Trousers   *pantalon* (m)
Underpants   *slip* (m)

Miscellaneous

Film   *film* (m)/ *pellicule* (f)
Letter   *lettre* (f)
Money order   *mandat* (m)
Postcard   *carte postale* (f)

Stamp   *timbre* (m)
Telegram   *télégramme* (m)
Phonecard   *télécarte* (f)
Collect (reverse charge) call   *appel pcv* (m)

DRIVING

Gas/service station   *station-service* (f)
Fill it up.   *Le plein, s'il vous plaît.*
Give me . . . francs worth.   *Donnez m'en pour . . . francs.*
I would like . . . liters of gas/petrol.   *Je voudrais . . . litres d'essence.*
Can you check the working condition of. . . ?   *Voulez-vous vérifier l'état de marche de . . . ?*
There is something wrong with the . . .   *Il y a quelque chose qui ne va pas dans le . . .*
My car won't start.   *Ma voiture ne veut pas démarrer.*
My car has broken down/had a flat tire.   *Je suis tombé en panne/J'ai eu une crevaison.*
The engine is overheating.   *Le moteur chauffe.*
How long will it take to repair?   *Combien de temps pour la réparer?*

Battery	*batterie* (f)	Oil	*huile* (f)
Brakes	*freins* (m)	Tires	*pneus* (m)
Exhaust	*échappement* (m)	Water	*eau* (f)
Lights	*phares* (m)	Windshield	*pare-brise* (m)

Car rental

Where can I rent a car?	*Où est-ce que je peux louer une voiture?*
Is full insurance included?	*Est-ce que l'assurance tous-risques est comprise?*
Is it insured for two drivers?	*Est-elle assurée pour un autre conducteur?*
Unlimited mileage	*kilométrage illimité*
Deposit	*caution* (f)
By what time must I return it?	*À quelle heure devrais-je la ramener?*
Can I return it to another depot?	*Puis-je la ramener à une autre agence?*
Is the tank full?	*Est-ce que le réservoir est plein?*

Road signs

Aire (de repos) stopping place/layby
Autres directions other directions
Camion truck
Céder le passage yield/give way
Centre ville town center
Chaussée deformée irregular surface
Essence (sans plomb) (lead-free) gasoline
Garage garage/multistory car park
Ne pas se garer devant la porte keep exit clear
Parking interdit no parking
Parking ouvert parking lot
Passage à niveau level crossing
Passage protégé priority for vehicles on main road
Péage toll point

Piétons pedestrians
Priorité à droite priority for vehicles coming from the right
Ralentir slow down
Rappel remember that a previous sign still applies
Route barrée road blocked
Sens obligatoire through traffic
Sens unique one-way
Sortie exit
Sortie de secours emergency exit
Stationnement interdit no parking
Stationnement toléré literally, parking tolerated
Toutes directions all directions
Verglas (black) ice on road
Vitesse speed
Voie sans issue no through road

Other means of transport

Aircraft *avion* (m)
Airport *aéroport* (m)
Bus *autobus* (m)
Bus stop *arrêt d'autobus* (m)
Coach *car* (m)
Couchette/sleeper *wagon-lit* (m)
Ferry/boat *ferry/bateau/bac* (m)
Ferry port *port du ferry/bateau/bac* (m)

Hovercraft *hovercraft/aéroglisseur* (m)
Station *gare* (m)
Train *train* (m)
Ticket *billet* (m)
Ticket office *guichet* (m)
One-way/single *billet simple*
Round-trip/return *billet aller-retour*
Half fare *demi-tarif*

When is the next .. for .. ?	*À quelle heure est le prochain .. pour . . . ?*
What time does it arrive?	*À quelle heure arrive-t-il?*
What time does the last . . . for . . . leave?	*À quelle heure part le dernier . . . pour . . . ?*
Which track/platform/quay/gate?	*Quel quai/port?*
Is this the . . . for . . . ?	*Est-ce que c'est bien le . . . pour . . . ?*
Is it direct? Where does it stop?	*C'est direct? Où est-ce qu'il s'arrête?*
Do I need to change anywhere?	*Est-ce que je dois changer?*
Please tell me where to get off?	*Pourrez-vous me dire ou descendre?*
Is there a buffet car?	*Y a-t-il un wagon-restaurant?*

Food and drink

Have you a table for . . . ? *Avez-vous une table pour . . . ?*
I want to reserve a table. *Je voudrais réserver une table.*
A quiet table. *Une table bien tranquille.*
A table near the window. *Une table près de la fenêtre.*
Could we have another table? *Est-ce que nous pourrions avoir une autre table?*
Set menu *Menu prix-fixe*
I did not order this *Je n'ai pas commandé cela*
Bring me another . . . *Apportez-moi encore un . . .*
The bill, please *L'addition, s'il vous plaît*
Is service included? *Le service est compris?*

Some essential words

Breakfast *petit déjeuner* (m)
Lunch *déjeuner* (m)
Dinner *dîner* (m)
Hot *chaud*
Cold *froid*
Glass *verre* (m)
Bottle *bouteille* (f)
Half-bottle *demi-bouteille*
Beer/lager *bière* (f)/ *lager* (m)
Draft beer *bière (à la) pression*
Orangeade/lemonade *sirop d'orange/de citron* (m)
Mineral water *eau minérale* (f)
Fizzy/carbonated water *eau gazeuse* (f)
Still water *eau non-gazeuse*
Sparkling *pétillant*
Nonsparkling *plat*
Fruit juice *jus de fruit* (m)
Red wine *vin rouge* (m)
White/rosé *vin blanc/ rosé*
Vintage *année* (f)

Dry *sec*
Sweet *doux* (of wine)
  sucré (of food)
Plain *nature*
Salt *sel* (m)
Pepper *poivre* (m)
Mustard *moutarde* (f)
Oil *huile* (m)
Vinegar *vinaigre* (m)
Bread *pain* (m)
Butter *beurre* (m)
Cheese *fromage* (m)
Milk *lait* (m)
Coffee *café* (m)
Tea *thé* (m)
Decaffeinated *décaféiné*
Herbal tea *infusion* (f)
Chocolate *chocolat* (m)
Sugar *sucre* (m)
Steak *bifteck* (m)
  well done *bien cuit*
  medium *cuit à point*
  rare *saignant*
  very rare *bleu*
vegetarian *végétarien*

MENU GUIDE

à l'Alsacienne food cooked Alsace-style is served with *choucroute*, ham and frankfurter-style sausages
à l'Anglaise cooked in the English way — boiled or with boiled vegetables
à l'Armoricaine fish, especially lobster, cooked Breton-style with white wine, brandy, tomatoes, onions and herbs
à l'Arlésienne fish or meat cooked Arles-style, with tomatoes, onions, olives
Agneau lamb
Agneau de pré salé young lamb grazed in fields bordering the sea
Aiglefin haddock
Aigre-doux sweet and sour
Aiguillettes thin slices

Ail   garlic
Ailerons   chicken wings
Aïoli   garlic mayonnaise
Allumettes   puff pastry strips, garnished or filled
Alouette   lark
Alouette sans tête   thin slices of beef or veal around a savory filling
Amandes   almonds
Ananas   pineapple
Anchoïade   anchovy paste, usually served on crispy bread
Anchois   anchovies
Andouilles   cooked pork sausage with strips of chitterling
Andouillette   chitterling sausage
Anguille   eel
Arachides   peanuts
Artichaut   artichoke
Asperges   asparagus
Assiette anglaise   mixture of cold meats
Assiette assortie   mixture of cold *hors d'oeuvres*
Avocat   avocado
Baguette   long bread loaf
Banane   banana
Barbue   brill
Barquette   pastry boat
Basilic   basil
Baudroie   anglerfish, monkfish
Bavarois   cream and custard dessert, often with fruit
Béarnaise   sauce made mayonnaise-style, with tarragon
Bécasse   woodcock; roast with truffles *(à la Diane);* on fried bread with *foie gras (à la riche)*
Béchamel   white sauce flavored with onion or bay leaf
Beignet   sweet or savory fritter
Belle-Hélène   sauce (for pear) with ice cream and chocolate
Belons   flat-shelled oysters
Bergère, à la   chicken or meat cooked shepherd-style, with mushrooms, ham, onions and sliced potatoes
Betterave   beetroot
Beurre   butter
Bifteck   beefsteak
Bigorneaux   winkles

Bisque   thick creamy soup, usually of shellfish, made with white wine, cream and potatoes
Blanchailles   whitebait
Blanquette   white meat cooked in a white sauce, e.g., *blanquette de veau*
Blé   corn, wheat
Blé noir   buckwheat
Boeuf   beef
Bombe   elaborate dessert with ice cream
Bonne femme   poached in white wine with mushrooms
Bordelaise, à la   cooked Bordeaux-style, in a red wine sauce with shallots, tarragon and bone marrow
Bouchée   tiny *vol-au-vent*
Boudin (noir ou blanc)   (black or white) sausage pudding
Bouillabaisse   Mediterranean fish soup with fresh fish and saffron
Bouillon   stock or broth
Bourgeoise, à la   braised meat or chicken with bacon, onions and carrots
Bourride   Provençal soup of mixed fish with *aïoli*
Branche, à la   whole — as in vegetables like broccoli, spinach
Brandade de morue   purée of salt cod, milk and garlic
Bretonne, à la   cooked Breton-style in onion sauce with haricots
Brioche   soft bread
Broche, à la   spit-roasted
Brochet   pike
Brochette   meat or fish on a skewer
Brouillé   scrambled
oeufs brouillés   scrambled eggs
Brûlé   flamed
Cabillaud   fresh cod
Cachir   Kosher
Caille   quail
Cake   British-style fruit cake
Calamar   squid
Canard or *caneton*   duck
Carbonnade   braised or grilled meat
Carpaccio   thin slices of marinated raw beef
Carré (d'agneau)   loin (of lamb)

Carrelet   plaice
Carottes Vichy   carrots glazed with sugar and butter
Casse-croûte   snack
Cassis   blackcurrant
Cassoulet   casserole from Languedoc with beans, preserved goose and pork
Cèpes   wild, dark brown mushrooms
Cerise   cherry
Cervelles   brains
Champignon   mushroom
Chantilly   whipped cream with sugar
Chapon   capon
Chasseur   cooked hunter-style, with wine, mushrooms and shallots
Châtaigne   chestnut
Cheval   horse
Chèvre or *Chevreau*   goat
Chevreuil   venison
Chicorée or *frisée*   curly endive/chicory
Chips   potato chips (American)/potato crisps (British)
Chou   light puff pastry/cabbage
Chou-fleur   cauliflower
Choucroute   pickled white cabbage/sauerkraut
Choux de Bruxelles   Brussels sprouts
Citron   lemon
Citron vert   lime
Citrouille   pumpkin
Civet de lièvre   jugged hare
Clafoutis   baked batter pudding with cherries
Cochon de lait   sucking pig
Coeur   heart
Colin   hake
Concombre   cucumber
Confit   meat covered in its own fat, cooked and preserved
Confit d'oie   preserved goose
Confiture   jam
Contre-filet   sirloin steak
Coquillages   shellfish
Coquilles St-Jacques   scallops, usually cooked in wine
Corbeille de fruits   fruit basket
Cornichon   gherkin

Côte, côtelette   chop, cutlet
Coulis   thick purée, served as a sauce
Coupe   ice cream dessert
Court-bouillon   stock made with herbs, vegetables and white wine
Couscous   North African dish of cooked, rolled grains of semolina steamed over a stew of lamb, chicken and vegetables
Crabe   crab
Crème   cream
Crêpe   thin pancake
Cresson   watercress
Crevettes grises   shrimps
Crevettes roses   prawns
Croque-monsieur   toasted cheese-and-ham sandwich
Croquette   rissole
Croustade   small bread or pastry mould with savory filling
Croustille   snack of fried potato slices
Croûte, en   cooked in a pastry case
Cru   raw
Crudités, assiette de   selection of raw, sliced vegetables
Crustacé   shellfish
Cuisine du marché   dishes based on seasonal ingredients
Cuisine du terroir   local dishes
Cuisses (de grenouilles)   (frogs') legs
Cuit   cooked
Culotte de boeuf   rump of beef
Darne   thick slice, usually of fish
Daube   meat slowly braised in a rich wine stock
Dauphinoise, à la   (potatoes) sliced and baked in milk
Daurade   sea bream
Dijonnais   meat or poultry cooked with mustard sauce
Dinde   turkey
Dorade   sea bream
Échalote   shallot
Écrevisses   freshwater crayfish
Émincé   thinly sliced
Endive   chicory
Entrecôte   rib steak
Entremets   sweets
Épaule (d'agneau)   shoulder (of lamb)

Éperlans smelts
Épices spices
Épinards spinach
Escabèche various fish, fried, marinated and served cold
Escalope à la Viennoise veal dipped in egg and breadcrumbs, then sautéed
Escargots (à la Bourguignonne) snails stuffed with garlic butter and parsley
Espadon swordfish
Estouffade a stew marinated and fried, then slowly braised
Estragon tarragon
Faisan pheasant
Farci stuffed
Faséole kidney bean
Faux-filet sirloin steak
Fenouil fennel
Feuilleté light flaky pastry
Figue fig
Filet Américain raw minced steak
Filet mignon small fillet steak
Flageolets small French beans
Flambé flamed in spirit, especially brandy
Flétan halibut
Florentine food, often lightly poached eggs, cooked with spinach
Foie liver
Foie gras (d'oie) (goose) liver
(au) Four cooked in the oven
Fourré stuffed
Frais, fraîche fresh
Fraises strawberries
Framboises raspberries
Frappé served on crushed ice
Fricadelle a kind of meat ball
Fricassée chopped white meat, i.e., veal or chicken, cooked in thick white sauce
Frisée curly endive or chicory
Frit fried
Frites chips/French fries
Fritots fritters
Fromage cheese
Fromage de porc brawn
Fruits de mer seafood
Fumé smoked
Galantine cooked meat, fish or vegetables served cold in a jelly

Galette a pancake made with buckwheat flour
Gambas large prawns
Garbure very thick soup
Garni garnished
Gâteau cake
Gaufre wafer biscuit or waffle
Gelée, en in aspic
Gibier game
Gigot (d'agneau) leg (of lamb)
Gingembre ginger
Glace ice cream
Glacé iced, frozen, glazed
Goujons small strips of fish, coated in breadcrumbs and deep-fried
Gratin, au dish with a crust of browned breadcrumbs mixed with cheese
Grenouilles frogs
Grillé grilled
Grive thrush
Groseille redcurrant
Groseille à maquereau gooseberry
Hachis parmentier minced lamb, topped with mashed potato
Hachis minced
Harengs herrings
Haricot stew with vegetables/ beans
Haricots verts green beans
Hollandaise sauce made with butter, wine and lemon juice, thickened with egg yolks
Homard lobster
Homard à l'Armoricaine lobster served with a sauce of brandy, white wine, onions, tomatoes and herbs
Homard thermidor sautéed lobster cooked in a creamy white wine sauce
Huile (d'olive) (olive) oil
Huîtres oysters
Ile flottante favorite French dessert; an island of egg white poached in custard
Jambon d'Ardennes salty, smoked ham from the Belgian Ardennes
Jambon, jambonneau ham
Julienne thin vegetable strips poached in butter

Jus   juice, gravy
Lait   milk
Laitue   lettuce
Langouste   spiny lobster or crayfish
Langoustine   Dublin bay prawn
Langue (de boeuf)   (ox) tongue
Lapin   rabbit
Légumes   vegetables
Lièvre   hare
Limande   dab (fish)
Limon   lime
Lotte de mer   anglerfish, monkfish
Loup de mer   sea bass
Lyonnaise, à la   potatoes or liver, Lyons-style, cooked with onions
Magret (de canard)   breast (of duck) served pink and rare
Maïs   sweetcorn
Mange-tout   crisp, small pea pods, eaten whole
Maquereaux   mackerel
Marcassin   young wild boar
Marrons   chestnuts
Matelote   freshwater fish stew
Méchoui   barbecued lamb, North African-style, often with cumin
Médaillon   small round fillet steak
Menthe   mint
Merlan   whiting
Meunière, à la   flour-coated and grilled or fried with butter, lemon juice and parsley
Miel   honey
Mignonette   small round fillet of lamb
Mille-feuille   flaky pastry slices sandwiched with jam and cream
Mode, à la   marinated meat usually beef, braised in wine and vegetables
Morilles   edible dark-brown fungi
Mornay   with a cheese sauce
Morue   dried/salted cod
Moules   mussels
Moules parquées   raw mussels
Moules marinière   mussels cooked with white wine and shallots
Moutarde   mustard
Mouton   mutton
Mûre   mulberry
Mûre de ronce   blackberry

Museau de porc   pig's snout
Myrtille   bilberry
Navarin   stew of lamb and young root vegetables
Navet   turnip
Niçoise, à la   Nice-style, with tomatoes, garlic, anchovies and olives
Noix   nuts, usually walnuts
Noix de veau   a small round cut of veal
Nouilles   noodles
Oeuf/s   egg/s
Oeuf brouillé   scrambled egg
Oeuf à la coque   soft-boiled egg in its shell
Oeuf en cocotte   egg cooked in a small ramekin
Oeuf dur   hard-boiled egg
Oeuf frit or *à la poêle*   fried egg
Oeuf mollet   soft-boiled, shelled egg
Oeuf poché   poached egg
Oie   goose
Oignons   onions
Oiseaux sans tête   see *Alouette*
Oseille   sorrel
Oursins   sea urchins
Paillettes d'oignons frits   fried, crisp onion rings
Pain   bread
Palourdes   clams/cockles
Pamplemousse   grapefruit
(en) Papillote   cooked in oiled or buttered paper
Parmentier   a dish containing potatoes
Pâte   pasta or pastry
Pâte d'amandes   marzipan
Pâte brisée   shortcrust pastry
Pâte à chou   choux pastry
Pâte feuilleté   flaky/puff pastry
Pâte frollée   almond-flavored pastry
Pâte sablée   rich shortcrust with sugar
Pâté de campagne   coarse pâté
Pâté de foie gras   goose-liver *pâté*, sometimes with truffles
Pâté maison   smooth *pâté*, usually chicken or pig's liver
Paupiette   thin slices of meat or fish rolled up and filled

Pêche Melba   peach on ice cream with raspberry purée
Pêche   peach
Perdrix   partridge
Persil   parsley
Petit salé   salted pork
Petits fours   tiny cakes and sweets
Petits pois   peas
Pieds de porc   pigs' feet
Pigeonneau   young pigeon
Pignons   pine nuts
Piments doux/forts   sweet/chili peppers
Pintade   guinea fowl
Pissaladière   bread dough or pizza covered with tomatoes
Pissenlits   dandelion leaves, used in salads
Pistou   vegetable soup with a paste of garlic, basil and oil
Plat du jour   dish of the day
Poché   poached
Pochouse   fish stew
Poire   pear
Poireaux   leeks
Poires Belle-Hélène   cooked pears with ice cream and hot chocolate sauce
Poisson   fish
Poitrine de porc   belly of pork
Pomme   apple
Pomme de terre   potato
Porc   pork
Pot-au-feu   beef stew
Potage Crécy   carrot soup
Potage   soup
Potage parmentier   a potato-based soup, often with leeks
Poularde   capon
Poulet   young spring chicken
Poulet Marengo   chicken with garlic, mushrooms and tomatoes
Poulpe   octopus
Poussin   very small baby chicken
Praliné(e)   caramelized
Primeurs   young vegetables or wines
Provençale, à la   cooked the traditional Provençal way with oil, tomatoes, peppers, garlic, anchovies
Prune   plum
Pruneau   prune

Quenelle   boat-shaped mousse of puréed fish or white meat poached in liquid
Queue de boeuf   oxtail
Quiche   egg- and milk-based open pie
Radis   radishes
Ragoût   a stew prepared peasant-style
Raie   skate
Raifort   horseradish
Raisin sec   raisin
Raisins   grapes
Ratatouille   Provençal dish of eggplants, peppers, tomatoes, zucchini and garlic, cooked in olive oil
à la Reine   with chicken
Rémoulade   mayonnaise seasoned with mustard and herbs, capers or gherkins
Rillettes   potted minced or cubed pork, slow-cooked then shredded
Rillons   crisp pieces of pork or goose, browned and preserved in fat
Ris (de veau)   (calf's) sweetbreads
Riz   rice
Rognons   kidneys
Romarin   rosemary
Rosbif   roast beef
Rôti   roast
Rouget   red mullet
Rouille   garlic and chili sauce usually served with fish soups
Safran   saffron
St-Jacques   see *Coquilles*
St-Pierre   John Dory
Salade niçoise   salad including tomatoes, beans, potatoes, black olives and tuna
Salé   salted
Sanglier   wild boar
Saucisses   fresh wet sausage
Saucisson   dry sausage (salami-type)
Sauge   sage
Saumon, darne de   salmon steak
Saumon (fumé)   (smoked) salmon
Saumon   salmon
Saumon blanc   hake

Selle (d'agneau)   saddle (of lamb)
Selon grosseur   priced according to size, for example with lobster
Sole meunière   sole fried with lemon
Sole bonne femme   sole poached in white wine with mushrooms
Soubise   onion cream sauce
Soupe de poissons   fish soup
Steak tartare   raw minced steak
Sucre   sugar
Suprême de volaille   chicken breast and wing fillet
Tapenade   purée of black olives and olive oil
Terrine   coarse form of potted meat or *pâté*
Tête (de veau)   (calf's) head
Thon   tuna fish
Thym   thyme
Timbale   dome-shaped mould, or the pie cooked within it
Tournedos Rossini   steak with truffles, *foie gras* and Madeira sauce
Tournedos   small beef fillet
Tourte   covered tart
Tranche   slice/rasher

Tripe, oeufs à la   chopped hard-boiled eggs with onions
Tripes à la mode de Caen   tripe stewed with onions and herbs in cider
Truffes   truffles
Truite saumonée/de mer   salmon trout
Truite   trout
Vapeur, à la   steamed
Veau, blanquette de   breast of veal cooked in a white sauce
Veau   veal
Venaison   venison
Viande   meat
Vichyssoise   smooth and creamy leek and potato soup
Vinaigrette   oil-and-vinegar dressing
Vol-au-vent   puff pastry case filled with meat or fish
Volaille   poultry
Waldorf   salad of apple, walnut and celeriac
Washington   chicken served American-style with sweetcorn
Williams   type of pear
Yaourt   yogurt

Provençal words and phrases

There has recently been a revival, or at least an increasing consciousness, of the Provençal language, and a number of place signs are now given in both Provençal and French.

ON THE MENU

In country restaurants, and assertively Provençal restaurants elsewhere, you will find local words on the menu that you probably won't track down in a French dictionary. Below are listed just a few.

- See also: EATING AND DRINKING on pages 46–49 and a special section on *bouillabaisse* on page 115.

- Words that relate to Provençal specialities that are eaten throughout France will be found in the FOOD AND DRINK MENU GUIDE on pages 340–46.

Aïet   garlic
Aïgardin   eau de vie
Aïgo boulido   garlic soup
aïoli   garlic mayonnaise

bar   sea bass
blanqet   small white snail
brosse/brousso   sheep's milk cheese
cabro   goat

cacheille/cachéio a goat's milk cheese
cade/cado a chickpea pancake
calisson small almond cake
catigot Camarguaise eel soup
chambri crayfish
courgourdon zucchini/courgette
crèspèou a savory pancake or sardine omelet
estocaficada stockfish stew
ferigoulo thyme
fougasse/fougasso a savory or sweet bread
frucho fruit
lèbre hare
lesque/lesco slice
loup sea bass
maienque/maienco white truffle
mérinjane aubergine
merlusso salt cod
mèu honey
moutounesso mutton stew
musclo mussel
navette a small cake
oursinade a sea urchin dish
panisse chickpea-flour pasta
papaline chocolate sweet from Avignon

pèbre black pepper
pébron green pepper
pieds et paquets mutton tripe and trotters
pignate cooking pot
pitcholine/picholino a type of small olive
pompe/poumpo an olive-oil bread
pourpre octopus
quichié a piece of bread rubbed with garlic and oil
raïole/raiolo ravioli
rebasso truffle
rognonade/rougnounado beef or lamb steak
saran a reddish Mediterranean fish
socca ground-chickpea pancake
suce-miel/suco-meu a candy made of honey
supion small squid
tardon young lamb
tartifle potato
tian a large, baked flan
tourton small cake

OUT AND ABOUT

Below are some words that sometimes occur in place names, and some others that you might occasionally come across.

barri ramparts
bastidan someone who lives in a *bastide*
bastide rural house
baumo/beaume/baume cave
baux/baou cliff
biau canal
borie dry-stone-walled hut
cadière/cadiero chair
colo hill
ferrade/ferrado bullfight
grupi trough
jas shepherd's hut

marcat market
mourre literally snout, muzzle, usually meaning the end of a mountain range
olivades/ólivado olive harvest
oustau house
pastis confusion, muddle
pescadou fisherman
riou flood
ribo river bank
santon ornamental figure, especially used in Christmas cribs

CONVERSION FORMULAE

To convert	Multiply by
Inches to Centimeters	2.540
Centimeters to Inches	0.39370
Feet to Meters	0.3048
Meters to feet	3.2808
Yards to Meters	0.9144
Meters to Yards	1.09361
Miles to Kilometers	1.60934
Kilometers to Miles	0.621371
Sq Meters to Sq Feet	10.7638
Sq Feet to Sq Meters	0.092903
Sq Yards to Sq Meters	0.83612
Sq Meters to Sq Yards	1.19599
Sq Miles to Sq Kilometers	2.5899
Sq Kilometers to Sq Miles	0.386103
Acres to Hectares	0.40468
Hectares to Acres	2.47105
Gallons to Liters	4.545
Liters to Gallons	0.22
Ounces to Grams	28.3495
Grams to Ounces	0.03528
Pounds to Grams	453.592
Grams to Pounds	0.00220
Pounds to Kilograms	0.4536
Kilograms to Pounds	2.2046
Tons (UK) to Kilograms	1016.05
Kilograms to Tons (UK)	0.0009842
Tons (US) to Kilograms	746.483
Kilograms to Tons (US)	0.0013396

Quick conversions

Kilometers to Miles	Divide by 8, multiply by 5
Miles to Kilometers	Divide by 5, multiply by 8
1 meter =	Approximately 3 feet 3 inches
2 centimeters =	Approximately 1 inch
1 pound (weight) =	475 grams (nearly $\frac{1}{2}$ kilogram)
Celsius to Fahrenheit	Divide by 5, multiply by 9, add 32
Fahrenheit to Celsius	Subtract 32, divide by 9, multiply by 5

Clothing sizes chart

LADIES
Suits and dresses

Australia	8	10	12	14	16	18	
France	34	36	38	40	42	44	
Germany	32	34	36	38	40	42	
Italy	38	40	42	44	46		
Japan	7	9	11	13			
UK	6	8	10	12	14	16	18
USA	4	6	8	10	12	14	16

Shoes

USA	6	$6\frac{1}{2}$	7	$7\frac{1}{2}$	8	$8\frac{1}{2}$
UK	$4\frac{1}{2}$	5	$5\frac{1}{2}$	6	$6\frac{1}{2}$	7
Europe	38	38	39	39	40	41

MEN
Shirts

USA, UK	14	$14\frac{1}{2}$	15	$15\frac{1}{2}$	16	$16\frac{1}{2}$	17
Europe, Japan Australia	36	37	38	39.5	41	42	43

Sweaters/T-shirts

Australia, USA, Germany	S	M	L	XL
UK	34	36-38	40	42-44
Italy	44	46-48	50	52
France	1	2-3	4	5
Japan		S-M	L	XL

Suits/Coats

UK, USA	36	38	40	42	44
Australia, Italy, France, Germany	46	48	50	52	54
Japan	S	M	L	XL	

Shoes

UK	7	$7\frac{1}{2}$	$8\frac{1}{2}$	$9\frac{1}{2}$	$10\frac{1}{2}$	11
USA	8	$8\frac{1}{2}$	$9\frac{1}{2}$	$10\frac{1}{2}$	$11\frac{1}{2}$	12
Europe	41	42	43	44	45	46

CHILDREN
Clothing

UK						
Height (ins)	43	48	55	60	62	
Age	4-5	6-7	9-10	11	12	13
USA						
Age	4	6	8	10	12	14
Europe						
Height (cms)	125	135	150	155	160	165
Age	7	9	12	13	14	15

Index

- Page numbers in **bold** type indicate main entries.
- *Italic* page numbers indicate illustrations and town maps.
- Map references are also given to the color maps at the back of the book.

What readers from all over the world say:

- "We could never have had the wonderful time that we did without your guide to *Paris*. The compactness was very convenient, your maps were all we needed, but it was your restaurant guide that truly made our stay special . . . . We have learned first-hand: *American Express — don't leave home without it.*" (A. R., Virginia Beach, Va., USA)

- Of Sheila Hale's *Florence and Tuscany:* "I hope you don't mind my calling you by your first name, but during our recent trip to Florence and Siena [we] said on innumerable occasions, 'What does Sheila say about that?' " (H.G., Buckhurst Hill, Essex, England)

- "I have visited Mexico most years since 1979 . . . Of the many guides I have consulted during this time, by far the best has been James Tickell's *Mexico,* of which I've bought each edition." (J.H., Mexico City)

- "We have heartily recommended these books to all our friends who have plans to travel abroad." (A.S. and J.C., New York, USA)

- "Much of our enjoyment came from the way your book *(Venice)* sent us off scurrying around the interesting streets and off to the right places at the right times". (Lord H., London, England)

- "It *(Paris)* was my constant companion and totally dependable . . . . " (V. N., Johannesburg, South Africa)

- "We found *Amsterdam, Rotterdam & The Hague* invaluable . . . probably the best of its kind we have ever used. It transformed our stay from an ordinary one into something really memorable . . . . " (S.W., Canterbury, England)

- "Despite many previous visits to Italy, I wish I had had your guide *(Florence and Tuscany)* ages ago. I love the author's crisp, literate writing and her devotion to her subject." (M. B-K., Denver, Colorado, USA)

- "We became almost a club as we found people sitting at tables all around, consulting their little blue books!" (F.C., Glasgow, Scotland)

- "I have just concluded a tour . . . using your comprehensive *Cities of Australia* as my personal guide. Thank you for your magnificent, clear and precise book." (Dr. S.G., Singapore)

- "We never made a restaurant reservation without checking your book *(Venice).* The recommendations were excellent, and the historical and artistic text got us through the sights beautifully." (L.S., Boston, Ma., USA)

- "The book *(Hong Kong, Singapore & Bangkok)* was written in such a personal way that I feel as if you were actually writing this book for me." (L.Z., Orange, Conn., USA)

- "I feel as if you have been a silent friend shadowing my time in Tuscany." (T.G., Washington, DC, USA)

What the papers say:

- "The expertly edited American Express series has the knack of pin-pointing precisely the details you need to know, and doing it concisely and intelligently." **(*The Washington Post*)**

- "*(Venice)* . . . the best guide book I have ever used." **(*The Standard* — London)**

- "Amid the welter of guides to individual countries, American Express stands out . . . . " **(*Time*)**

- "Possibly the best . . . guides on the market, they come close to the oft-claimed 'all you need to know' comprehensiveness, with much original experience, research and opinions." **(*Sunday Telegraph* — London)**

- "The most useful general guide was *American Express New York* by Herbert Bailey Livesey. It also has the best street and subway maps." **(*Daily Telegraph* — London)**

- " . . . in the flood of travel guides, the *American Express* guides come closest to the needs of traveling managers with little time." **(*Die Zeit* — Germany)**

What the experts say:

- "We only used one guide book, Sheila Hale's *AmEx Venice*, for which she and the editors deserve a Nobel Prize." **(travel writer Eric Newby, London)**

- "Congratulations to you and your staff for putting out the best guide book of *any* size *(Barcelona & Madrid)*. I'm recommending it to everyone." **(travel writer Barnaby Conrad, Santa Barbara, California)**

- "If you're only buying one guide book, we recommend American Express . . . . " **(*Which?* — Britain's leading consumer magazine)**

- "The judges selected *American Express London* as the best guide book of the past decade — it won the competition in 1983. [The guide] was praised for being 'concise, well presented, up-to-date, with unusual information.' " **(News release from the London Tourist Board and Convention Bureau)**

American Express Travel Guides

spanning the globe....

EUROPE
Amsterdam, Rotterdam
& The Hague
Athens and the
Classical Sites
Barcelona, Madrid &
Seville
Berlin, Potsdam &
Dresden
Brussels
Dublin
Florence and Tuscany
London
Paris
Prague
Provence and the
Côte d'Azur
Rome
Venice
Vienna & Budapest

NORTH AMERICA
Boston and New
England
Los Angeles & San
Diego
Mexico
New York
San Francisco and
the Wine Regions
Toronto, Montréal &
Québec City
Washington, DC

THE PACIFIC
Australia's
Major Cities
Hong Kong & Taiwan
Singapore &
Bangkok
Tokyo

*Clarity and quality of information, combined
with outstanding maps — the ultimate in
travelers' guides*

KEY TO MAP PAGES

1

2–3 CÔTE D'AZUR

4–16 SOUTH OF FRANCE

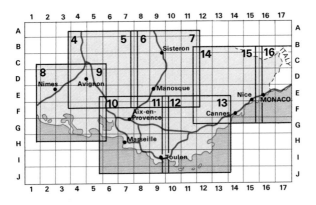

KEY TO MAP SYMBOLS

- ⊨O⊨ Autoroute (with access point)
- ═══ Main Road / Four-lane Highway
- ▬▬▬ Other Main Road
- ▬▬▬ Secondary Road
- ──── Minor Road
- ▭▭▭ Scenic Route
- N85 Road Number
- ─ ─ Ferry
- ═▬═ Railway
- ✈ Airport
- ✦ Airfield
- ▬▬▬ International Boundary
- ─ ─ ─ National Park Boundary
- ⛪ Church, Abbey
- ∴ Ancient Site, Ruin
- ♜ Château
- ▪ Other Place of Interest
- ⋈ Good Beach
- •1930 Height in Meters
- **10**▶ Adjoining Page No.

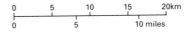

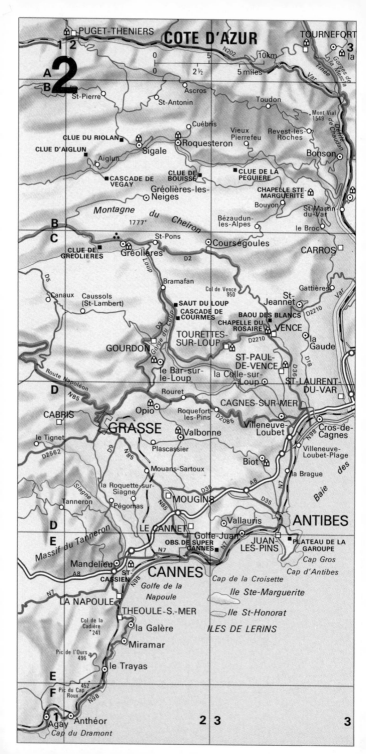

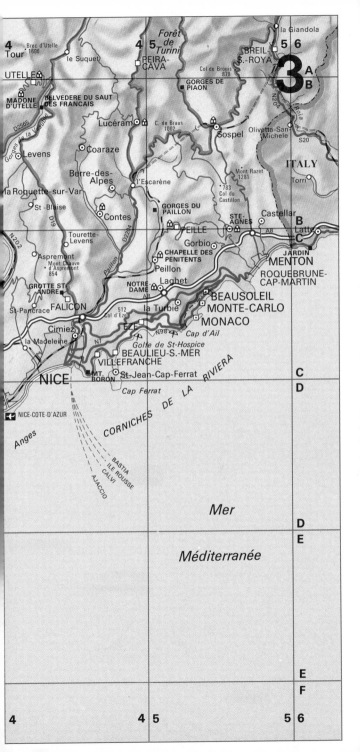

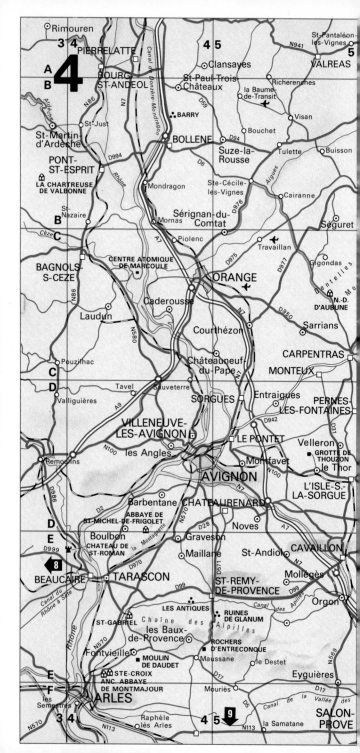

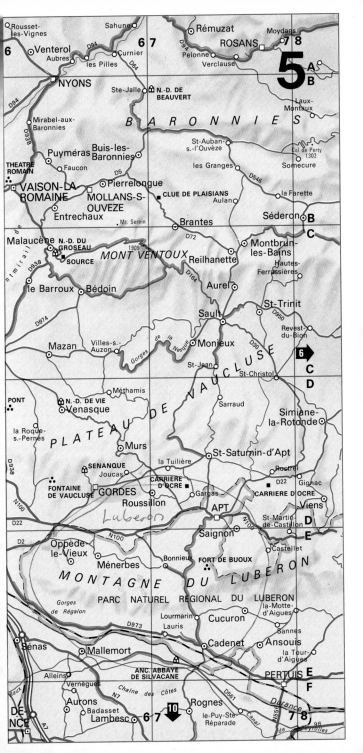

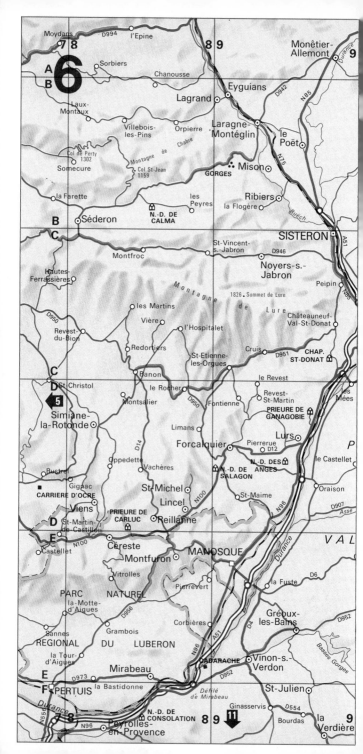

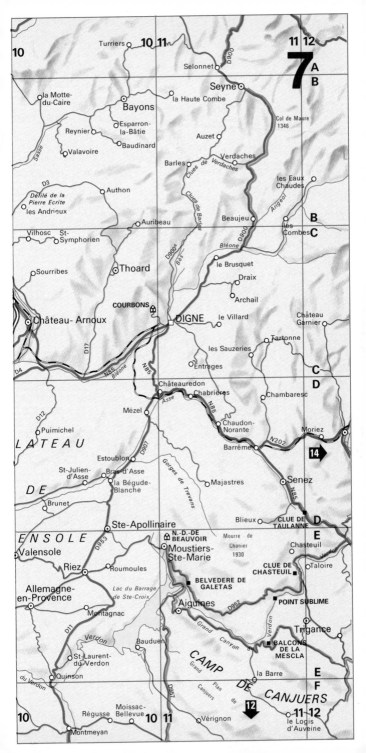

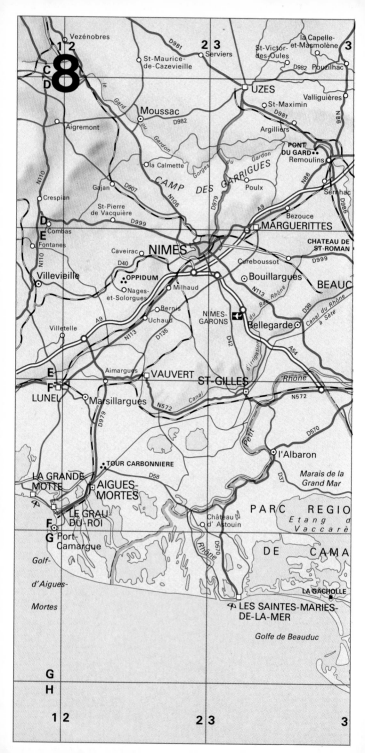

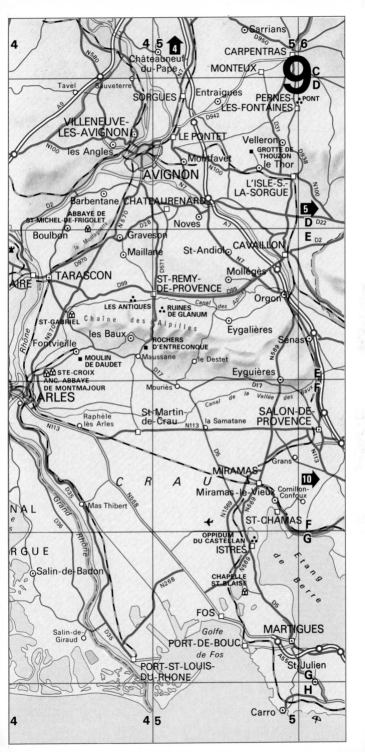

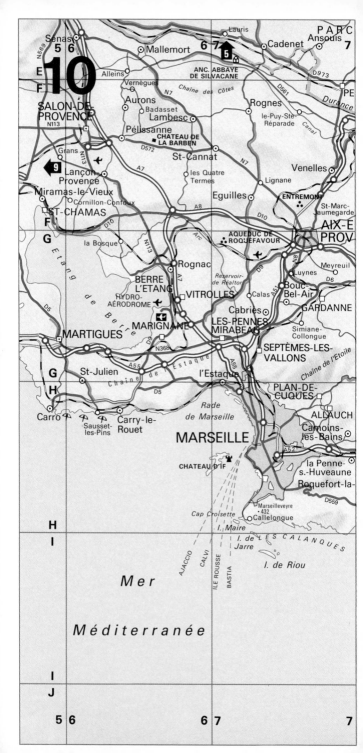

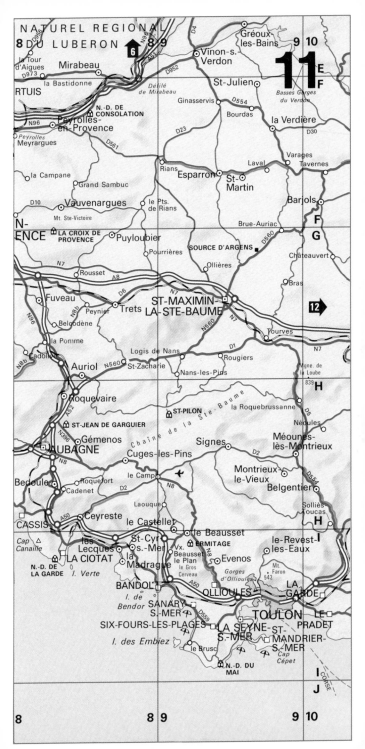

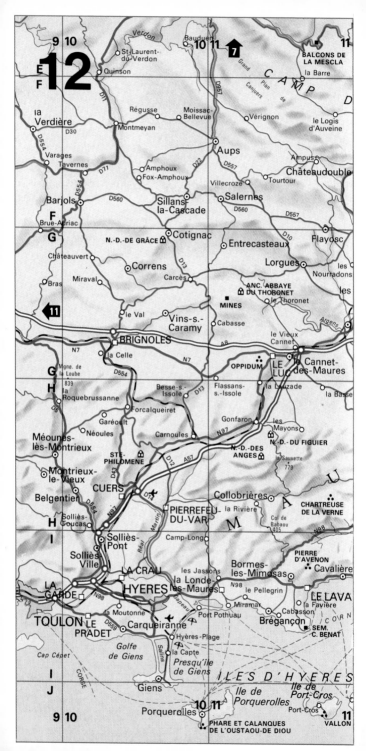

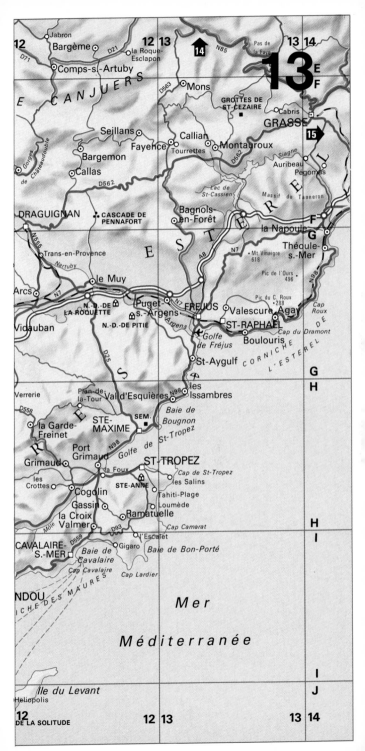

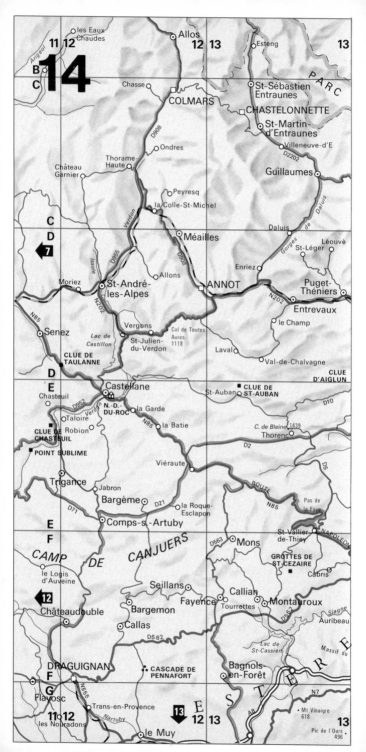

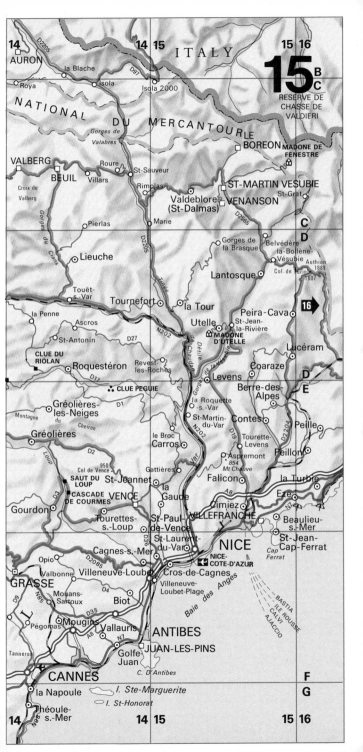

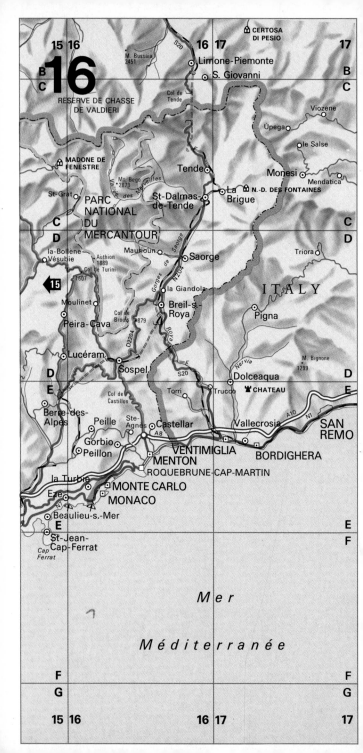